PUBLIC PROCUREMENT AND CONTRACT LAW

This open access anthology explores intersections and boundaries between public procurement and contract law, examining how these legal regimes diverge, influence, and occasionally overlap during the performance stage of public contracts.

While public procurement processes are largely harmonised across Europe through the EU Public Procurement Directives, the performance phase is only partially regulated. A sizeable part of public contract implementation remains subject to national laws, governed through a combination of administrative and contract law. This gives rise to a set of foundational questions: Does public procurement law fully occupy the legal space of public contract performance? In which instances – if any – does contract law retain relevance? Are classical contract law concepts transformed or distorted when applied to public contracts, and how does this affect mechanisms such as arbitration? To what extent do the answers to these questions vary depending on the regulatory model adopted by a given jurisdiction?

Part 1 introduces the topic, covering regulatory models for public contracts from procurement and contract law perspectives.

Part 2 examines general issues such as legal review asymmetries, tacit modifications, due diligence, loyalty obligations, and the doctrine of hardship under EU law.

Part 3 explores contemporary challenges, including digitalisation and sustainability.

Part 4 analyses arbitration in public contract disputes.

Public Procurement and Contract Law

Exploring Intersections, Defining Boundaries

Edited by
Marta Andhov
Michał Kania
and
Sylvie Cécile Cavaleri

•HART•
OXFORD • LONDON • NEW YORK • NEW DELHI • SYDNEY

HART PUBLISHING

Bloomsbury Publishing Plc

Kemp House, Chawley Park, Cumnor Hill, Oxford, OX2 9PH, UK

1385 Broadway, New York, NY 10018, USA

Bloomsbury Publishing Ireland Limited, 29 Earlsfort Terrace, Dublin 2, D02 AY28, Ireland

HART PUBLISHING, the Hart/Stag logo, BLOOMSBURY and the Diana logo are trademarks of Bloomsbury Publishing Plc

First published in Great Britain 2026

A catalogue record for this book is available from the British Library.

A catalogue record for this book is available from the Library of Congress.

ISBN: HB: 978-1-50998-945-4
ePDF: 978-1-50998-943-0
ePub: 978-1-50998-944-7

Typeset by Compuscript Ltd, Shannon

FOREWORD

Public contracts are a crucial vehicle by which public authorities across the Member States spend approximately two trillion euros annually. As expressly recognised in Article 70 of Directive 2014/24/EU, and in the case law of the Court of Justice, notably *Tim SpA* (C-395/18), public contracts often also serve broader policy objectives of sustainability, innovation, and social inclusion. The effective use of these funds depends not only on transparent and competitive procurement award procedures but also, crucially, on the sound performance of the contracts themselves.[1] Yet, these contracts generate persistent interpretative difficulties, often surfacing before the Court in relation to Articles 72 and 73 of the Directive concerning issues of modification and termination.

One of the Court's recent judgments, *Veolia Water Technologies* (C-82/24), once again drew attention to the delicate relationship between public procurement law and contract law, particularly when disputes arise in the performance phase.[2] This question has long occupied both national courts and scholars: where, precisely, do the boundaries of procurement regulation end, and where does ordinary contract law begin, if at all?

From the 1960s onwards, the European Community and later the Union have sought to regulate the award of public contracts through progressive directives. The 2004 reform represented a major effort to consolidate and modernise the Union's procurement regime, replacing a patchwork of sectoral directives with a more coherent legislative framework. The 2014 directives, in turn, furthered that process by embedding sustainability and innovation more deeply within public procurement. In relation to the performance phase of public contracts, the scope of EU harmonisation is fragmentary, addressed only in Articles 70–73 of Directive 2014/24/EU. Consequently, the post-award stage is governed largely by national law and shaped by domestic legal traditions and principles.

The coexistence of EU procurement directives with national contract law inevitably produces tensions. It requires jurists, legislators, and practitioners to reconcile two normative paradigms: one public, built on equality, transparency, and non-discrimination; the other private, rooted in freedom of contract and party autonomy. The precise balance between how far procurement law constrains contractual discretion, and when private law fills the residual space, remains unsettled. This volume situates itself within this area of uncertainty.

[1] Case C-395/18 *Tim SpA – Direzione e coordinamento Vivendi SA v Consip SpA, Ministero dell'Economia e delle Finanze* ECLI:EU:C:2020:58, [2020].

[2] Case C-82/24 *Veolia Water Technologies* EU:C:2025:396, Judgment of the Court (5 June 2025).

The relationship between public procurement law and contract law is not merely a technical issue. It goes to the heart of how we conceive the nature of the public contract itself. Is a public contract primarily an administrative act, an instrument of policy, or an agreement between parties exercising reciprocal obligations? The answer is not straightforward and varies across jurisdictions. Continental legal systems have historically oscillated between the *public-oriented* model, typified by the French approach, in which administrative law dominates, and the *private-oriented* hybrid exemplified by Germany, where civil law concepts exert greater influence even in public transactions. Between these poles lies a spectrum of mixed solutions, reflecting national constitutional traditions and market philosophies.

Edited by Marta Andhov, Michał Kania, and Sylvie Cécile Cavaleri, *Public Procurement and Contract Law: Exploring Intersections, Defining Boundaries* represents a significant contribution to European legal scholarship. It does not present a single, unified theory of the relationship between procurement and contract law, indeed, the editors and contributors expressly recognise that the field resists simple reconciliation. Rather, the book embraces controversy as a productive space for inquiry. Across its chapters, leading scholars and practitioners from multiple Member States explore how these two bodies of law overlap and collide.

What distinguishes the volume is its dialogical method: authors from both traditions – procurement specialists and contract lawyers – engage with one another's assumptions, vocabulary, and conceptual tools. Instead of attempting to harmonise, the book clarifies where disagreement persists, and why.

Several contributions examine how fundamental contract law notions of consent, modification, hardship, and risk allocation, operate when one party is a public authority constrained by EU procurement rules. Others address systemic challenges, such as the enforcement of sustainability clauses, digitalisation of procurement, and the implications of algorithmic or 'computational' contracting for public administration. The discussion of arbitration and dispute-settlement mechanisms, viewed through comparative lenses, raises important questions about ensuring the effectiveness of EU law when arbitral tribunals, rather than national courts, resolve disputes arising from public contracts. Across these diverse analyses, the authors collectively demonstrate that public procurement and contract law cannot be neatly separated. Their interaction reveals deep structural questions about the limits of regulation, the reach of administrative oversight, and the resilience of private law principles in the public sphere.

This book appears at a moment of renewed reflection on the future of EU public procurement law. The European Commission has initiated discussions on the possible revision of Directive 2014/24/EU, including its provisions on contract performance. That legislative process will inevitably confront many of the conceptual tensions addressed in this volume. The contributors' comparative insights, drawing on national experience, may therefore prove invaluable not only to scholars but also to policymakers and judges tasked with interpreting new norms.

The crises of recent years, the COVID-19 pandemic and the war in Ukraine, have highlighted the need for flexibility in public contracting without undermining the principles of transparency and equal treatment. As the Court has noted, extraordinary circumstances call for pragmatic yet legally sound responses.[3] The analytical frameworks developed in this book can enable the achievement of this equilibrium, showing how procurement objectives and contractual adaptability can coexist within the rule of law.

The significance of this collection lies in the depth of its individual studies. The editors have created a forum where differing national experiences inform a more coherent European understanding, without effacing legitimate diversity. This book invites its readers to rethink the traditional boundaries between public and private law and reconsider the doctrinal autonomy of contract law in a regulatory environment increasingly shaped by public values. It also encourages practitioners to view these instruments not merely as vehicles for expenditure but as expressions of legal principles that underpin the Union itself.

Public Procurement and Contract Law: Exploring Intersections, Defining Boundaries deserves to be read not as the final word on the subject but as the beginning of a sustained dialogue between two venerable branches of European legal thought. Its contribution lies precisely in revealing that the relationship between procurement and contract law is not one of subordination or replacement, but of continuous interaction. This interplay, between public purpose and private autonomy, between regulatory constraint and contractual freedom, will continue to define the law of public contracts in the years to come. The editors and contributors are to be commended for providing a rigorous and thought-provoking framework through which that evolution can be understood.

Maciej Szpunar
First Advocate General, Court of Justice of the European Union
Professor of Law, University of Silesia in Katowice

[3] Judgment of the Court (Fourth Chamber), *Advania Sverige AB, Kammarkollegiet v Dustin Sverige AB*, C-461/20, 3 February 2022, para 37.

ACKNOWLEDGEMENTS

This anthology is the result of work carried out under the Purchase Power – Sustainable Public Procurement through Private Law Enforcement (PurpLE) project, funded by the Carlsberg Foundation through the Semper Ardens: Accelerate Grant No CF21-0317, awarded to Associate Professor Marta Andhov at the University of Copenhagen in 2022.

From the outset, the anthology has been a collaborative effort in every sense. With this spirit of joint scholarship in mind, the editors wish to express their sincere gratitude to all who contributed to the development of this volume. Particular thanks go to the authors, who accepted the challenge of writing their individual chapters within a collaborative framework.

We are also grateful to the participants of the three scientific seminars held between September 2022 and September 2024. The first seminar, held at the University of Copenhagen, laid the foundation by shaping the overall outline of the anthology. The second, hosted by the University of Turin, focused on refining specific solutions and outlining the content of individual chapters. The third and final seminar, again held at the University of Copenhagen, was dedicated to providing feedback on draft chapters and shaping the final structure of the anthology.

Over the course of the last three years, the continuous exchange of feedback and ideas among authors during and after each seminar significantly enhanced the scholarly quality of the work. We are privileged to have worked with such a dedicated, thoughtful, and engaged group of scholars. We hope this anthology will be a valuable contribution to the existing scholarship and research, and if it is, it is thanks to this team's collective effort.

We also extend our deep appreciation to the PurpLE project team, particularly postdoctoral researcher Dr Ezgi Uysal and student assistant Pavol David, for their invaluable editorial assistance in preparing the final version of the anthology.

Special thanks are due to the many academics and practitioners who, while not authors of specific chapters, made crucial contributions to the anthology's development. Without their insights and expertise, many of the chapters would not have taken the form they did. We would especially like to thank:

Professor Roberto Caranta, Professor Mario Comba, and Professor Alberto Odenino (University of Turin)
Professor Jodi Gardner (University of Auckland)
Professor Elisabetta Manunza (Utrecht University)
Professor Tünde Tátrai (Corvinus University of Budapest)

Professor Arnaud Raynouard (Université Paris-Dauphine)
Associate Professor Marko Turudić (University of Zagreb)
Džeina Gaile, attorney-at-law and doctoral student (University of Latvia)
Jesper Fabricius, Partner and attorney-at-law (Accura)

We are grateful for their thoughtful comments, constructive critiques, and perspectives shared during seminars and discussions, many of which have shaped the content and direction of this anthology.

Finally, we thank Hart Publishing for their support throughout this project. Our special thanks go to Roberta Bassi, Verity Stuart, and Sasha Jawed for their professionalism, patience, and commitment in guiding this anthology to completion.

Without the contributions and support of all involved, this anthology would not have been possible.

The Editors
August 2025

CONTENTS

LIST OF CONTRIBUTORS

Alexandra Andhov, LLM, SJD, is the inaugural Chair in Law and Technology and Director of the Center for Advancing Law and Technology Responsibly (ALTeR) at the University of Auckland's Faculty of Law and Faculty of Business and Economics. She also serves as an Affiliated Associate Professor at the Centre for Private Governance (CEPRI) Faculty of Law, University of Copenhagen. Professor Andhov has received prestigious honours, including the world-renowned Fulbright and Inge Lehman scholarships, and has held visiting academic positions at Melbourne Law School, Arizona State University, the University of Western Australia, the University of Turin, and Cornell Law School. Her research focuses on corporate law, capital market law, and the regulation of emerging technologies such as blockchain and artificial intelligence. She has published extensively in leading European and US law journals and with esteemed publishers including Hart Publishing, Cambridge University Press, and Edward Elgar. Her notable works include *Start-up Law* (Cheltenham, Edward Elgar Publishing, 2020), *Computational Law: The Lawyer's Guide to Digital Technology* (Copenhagen, Karnov Group, 2022), which explores the intersection of computational and legal thinking, and the recent anthology *Hidden Fallacies in Corporate Law and Financial Regulation: Reframing the Mainstream Narratives* (Oxford, Hart Publishing, 2025), which examines long-standing but previously unexamined assumptions underlying corporate and financial law.

Marta Andhov, PhD, is an Associate Professor at the Law School and the Business School at the University of Auckland, New Zealand, and an affiliated Associate Professor at the Centre for Private Governance (CEPRI), Faculty of Law, University of Copenhagen. She led the *Purchase Power – Sustainable Public Procurement through Private Law Enforcement (PurpLE)* Project, under whose auspices this volume was produced. She has also served on the steering committee of the INT Marie Curie Horizon 2020 *SAPIENS Network* and is a member of the European Procurement Law Group. Her research focuses on public procurement law, governmental contracts, sustainability, and contract law. She has published widely in leading journals and with distinguished publishers, including Hart Publishing, Cambridge University Press, and Edward Elgar. Her work has been cited internationally, including by the First Advocate General of the Court of Justice of the European Union, reflecting her influence on legal interpretation and policy development. She has received numerous honours, among them a Fulbright Scholarship, the Semper Ardens: Accelerate Grant from the Carlsberg Foundation, the Elisabeth Haub School of Law (Pace University) Scholarship, and the TEDx

Ambassador Award. Marta has held visiting academic positions at leading institutions, including The Dickson Poon School of Law, King's College London; Arizona State University; and the University of Western Australia. She also co-hosts BESTEK – The Public Procurement Podcast.

Sylvie Cécile Cavaleri, PhD, is an Associate Professor at the Centre for Private Governance (CEPRI) at the Faculty of Law of Copenhagen University. She is a Swiss and Danish qualified attorney, specialising in international contract law and international commercial dispute resolution, with a special focus on construction law. Prior to starting her academic career in 2009, Sylvie worked as a practising attorney at two top-tier business law firms in Switzerland, as an in-house counsel with a bank in Denmark, and, after the completion of her PhD degree, as a senior legal counsel with a large Danish contractor active on international markets. Sylvie's research and teaching focus on her areas of practice, that is, international and comparative contract law and international dispute resolution, with a special emphasis on construction law. In parallel to her academic career, Sylvie regularly advises clients and authors legal opinions on various aspects of international contract law and dispute resolution.

Isabel Gallego Córcoles holds a PhD in Law from the University of Castilla-La Mancha (UCLM), where she is a Professor of Administrative Law and a researcher at the Centro de Estudios Europeos–Luis Ortega Álvarez. She is the author of six monographs and over 100 scholarly articles and book chapters. Her research primarily focuses on public procurement law, water law, and energy law. Professor Gallego Córcoles is also the co-editor of the second edition of *Tratado de Contratos del Sector Público* (Valencia, Tirant lo Blanch, 2024) and serves as co-director of the Master's Program in Public Procurement Law at UCLM.

Maria Edith Lindholm Gausdal, PhD, is an Assistant Professor of Private Law and Sustainability at the Centre for Private Governance (CEPRI), University of Copenhagen. Her research focuses on the development of commercial contract law in response to growing regulatory density, including related policies and norm shifts linked to sustainability and broader societal goals. Maria has worked extensively with the interface between contract law and the EU public procurement law, including as a legal adviser to the Danish government. She is a contributor to the European Commission's Working Group on Decarbonised Construction of Transport Infrastructure and a member of the Selection Committee for the Policy Fellow Programme on Climate Change Initiatives at Queen Mary Centre, University of Copenhagen.

Kirsi-Maria Halonen is a Professor of Public Economic Law at the University of Lapland, Finland. She is a co-lead of the European Procurement Law Group and a former member of the European Commission Stakeholder Expert Group on Public Procurement. Halonen leads research projects funded by the Academy of Finland and Finnish Ministries relating to effective public expenditure, public procurement, and security of supply. Professor Halonen has authored many articles and edited research books on public procurement and acts as an editor of the European Procurement Law Series (Elgar Publishing) and associate editor of the *Journal of Public Procurement*.

Ole Hansen is a Professor of Private Law and co-founder of the Centre for Private Governance (CEPRI) at the University of Copenhagen Faculty of Law. His research centres on contract law, with a particular focus on long-term contractual relationships, construction and energy contracts, and the interaction between private and public law. His latest research project focuses on Digital Construction Law, examining the legal implications of Building Information Modelling (BIM).

Pirkko Heikkinen is a university Lecturer in Property Law at the University of Lapland. She is also currently the Vice Dean for Education at the Faculty of Law. Her expertise is mainly in real estate transactions. Recently, she has been working on the efficiency of the remedies system in public procurement.

Willem A Janssen, PhD, is the Endowed Professor of Public Procurement Law, holding the chair of the Dutch Association for Public Procurement Law, and an Associate Professor of European and Dutch Public Procurement Law. He holds these positions respectively at the Faculty of Law, Groningen University and at the law department of Utrecht University. He is a researcher at the Centre for Public Procurement (UUCePP) and the Centre for Regulation and Enforcement in Europe (RENFORCE) and a co-host of BESTEK – The Public Procurement Podcast.

Michał Kania, PhD, is a Senior Researcher at the Centre for Private Governance at the Faculty of Law of Copenhagen University and an Associate Professor at the Faculty of Law and Administration of the University of Silesia in Katowice. He was a Visiting Fulbright Scholar at the George Washington Law School at GWU (2018–19) and a Visiting Fellow of Deutsche Akademische Austauschdienst (DAAD) at the Ludwig Maximilian University in Munich (2017). He is a Polish qualified attorney, specialising in public procurement law, public–private partnership, and concession agreements. Michał was previously an adviser to the Polish government on the creation of the Public Procurement Act of 11 September 2019 and a vice-president of the Silesian Arbitration Tribunal (2019–23). He has collaborated with the European Investment Bank and the World Bank on topics related to public–private partnerships. Michał's main research expertise and teaching focus on public procurement law, public–private partnerships, concession contracts, and administrative law. In parallel to his academic career, Michał regularly advises clients on various aspects of public procurement law and public–private partnerships.

Désirée Klingler is an Assistant Professor of Public Law at the University of St. Gallen, Switzerland. She brings a law and economics perspective to public procurement, developing frameworks for more efficient, sustainable and smarter government contracting. Désirée holds an LLM from Yale Law School, was a lecturer at the University of Hamburg and a visiting scholar at Yale, UC Berkeley

Haas School of Business and Copenhagen Business School. For her research, Désirée has won multiple scholarships and awards, including from the Swiss National Science Foundation, the International Public Procurement Award, the Walther Hug Prize, and the TED Ambassador Award from the European Commission. Désirée is an expert to and advising the UN Economic Commission for Europe (UNECE) on sustainability in public–private partnerships and is Managing Editor of the *European Procurement & Public Private Partnership Law* (*EPPPL*) Review. Before, Désirée was practising law at a New York law firm, advising clients on project finance of energy transition projects, and worked as a public sector consultant in Germany and at the Swiss Federal Administrative Court.

François Lichère is a Professor of Public Law at the University of Jean Moulin Lyon 3 (France), a public procurement expert, and Director of the Chair of public contracts law. He has published numerous books and articles, in French and in English, mainly concerning public law contracts and the economy and public law.

Mehdi Lahouazi is a Full Professor of Public Law at the University of Paris Nanterre. His research focuses on the development of arbitration and mediation in domestic and international public contracts. He has also been appointed as an arbitrator in domestic and international proceedings and acts as counsel in arbitrations involving public entities.

Sven Mikulic was a research assistant on the PurpLE project at the Faculty of Law, University of Copenhagen. He later completed a Blue Book Traineeship at the European Commission in the Unit for Public Procurement, contributing to the evaluation of the 2014 procurement directives. For over three years, his research has explored how legal and policy tools can promote more sustainable procurement practices. He is currently working in the pharmaceutical industry with a focus on supplier compliance.

Kateřina Mitkidis is an Associate Professor at the Department of Law, Aarhus University, Denmark. Kateřina is interested in the ways law and legal tools are designed and used to steer behaviour in a socially and environmentally sound and responsible direction. Her research particularly focuses on the practice of using typically private law tools, such as contracts, to advance public interests. She has published, contributed to, and co-edited books and academic articles on this topic, including *Sustainability Clauses in International Business Contracts* (The Hague, Eleven International Publishing, 2015) and *Law and Responsible Supply Chain Management: Contract and Tort Interplay and Overlap* (Abingdon, Routledge, 2019).

Matanja Pinto is an external PhD candidate at Maastricht University. His research focuses on the influence of the philosophical debate on free will on private law (and vice versa). Matanja obtained a master's degree in corporate law at Leiden University in 2004 and was admitted to the Dutch bar in 2005. He currently works as an attorney-at-law, specialising in public procurement law at the Dutch law firm //DVLP advocaten. In 2022, Matanja was appointed by the Dutch Minister of Economic Affairs as Vice Chair of the Committee of Procurement Experts – a Dispute Resolution Board for procurement procedures, established by the Ministry of Economic Affairs. He has published numerous articles and annotations on public procurement law and is a co-author of the leading commentaries on Dutch procurement law. Matanja also teaches public procurement law at the Radboud University of Nijmegen and Utrecht University and is a co-host of BESTEK – The Public Procurement Podcast.

Cristina Poncibò is a Full Professor of Comparative Private Law at the Law Department of the University of Turin, Italy and Fellow at the Collegio Carlo Alberto. In the academic year 2021–22, Cristina was a Faculty Member at the Georgetown Law Center for Transnational Legal Studies. She teaches Comparative Law, Contracts, and Digital Competition. Cristina is also a scientific coordinator of the Master's in International Trade Law organised by the University of Turin with ITC-ILO, UNCITRAL, and UNIDROIT. He has co-edited the book *Contracting and Contract Law in the Age of Artificial Intelligence* (Oxford, Hart Publishing, 2022, with Ebers and Zou). Cristina has been a Marie Skłodowska-Curie Fellow (Panthéon-Assas University) and studied at Cambridge University (MSt) and the European University Institute (Max Weber Fellow).

Aarne Puisto is a Doctoral Researcher at the University of Lapland, alongside his work as an attorney at Dittmar & Indrenius. His research focuses on the effectiveness of legal remedies under Finnish public procurement rules. He holds master's degrees from the University of Helsinki and Lund University.

Miguel Assis Raimundo is an Associate Professor of the University of Lisbon's School of Law, where he has taught since 2006, and a Research Fellow of LPL – Lisbon Public Law Research since 2013. He also maintains regular collaborations with other schools, namely the School of Law of the Portuguese Catholic University. He lectures and researches in different fields of public law, with a primary focus on the law of public procurement and public contracts, covering also other topics of administrative law and litigation, constitutional law, and fundamental rights. He also works as an attorney-at-law and legal adviser to public and private entities.

Michael Steinicke, PhD, is a Professor of EU Law and Public Procurement at the Department of Law, Aarhus University. Has written and edited a large number of articles and books related to public procurement in Danish and English. He has been head of the Department of Law at two different universities and has been a member of the Danish Complaint Board for Public Procurement.

Vibe Garf Ulfbeck is a Professor of Private Law and the Head of the Centre for Private Governance (CEPRI) at the University of Copenhagen Faculty of Law. Her primary research interests lie in contract law and tort law, with a particular focus on the intersection between private and public law and the role of private governance in regulating complex legal relationships. She is the author of numerous publications in both Danish and international law journals and has held visiting scholar positions in Europe and abroad.

Ezgi Uysal is a Post-Doctoral Researcher at CEPRI at the University of Copenhagen Faculty of Law. She is currently part of the PurpLE project, where her research focuses on the intersection of public procurement law, contract law, and corporate sustainability. She completed her PhD in 2024 as a Marie Curie Fellow at the University of Turin and holds a master's degree from Leiden University.

Steven Van Garsse is an Associate and Executive Professor at Hasselt University and Antwerp/Antwerp Management School. His expertise lies in public law, with a particular focus on public procurement, concessions, public–private partnerships, privatisation, and public administration. He heads the Research Unit on Administrative Law and Public Administration within the Faculty of Law, Centre for Government and Law at Hasselt University. In addition to his academic roles, Steven is an attorney-at-law, admitted to the Brussels Bar and a board member of the *European Public–Private Partnerships Law Review*.

Maciej Zachariasiewicz is an Associate Professor at the Kozminski University, Warsaw, Poland and a specialist in international legal transactions and commercial arbitration. Professor Zachariasiewicz is an author and co-author of books and articles concerning arbitration, EU law, and Polish civil law. An arbitrator at the Court of Arbitration at the Polish Chamber of Commerce, the Lewiatan Court of Arbitration, the Court of Arbitration at the General Prosecutor's Office, and in ad hoc proceedings. Author of opinions and expert reports for entrepreneurs and individuals, as well as state-owned companies and government administration. As an expert in foreign law (Anglo-American systems), Professor Zachariasiewcz prepared opinions for Polish courts, and as an expert in Polish law, for foreign courts and international arbitration tribunals.

Patrick Zimmermann is a Research Fellow and PhD Candidate at the Chair of Public Law, Business Administrative Law, Environmental and Social Security Law and the Research Center for Procurement Law and Administrative Cooperation under the direction of Professor Dr Martin Burgi at the Ludwig Maximilian University of Munich. Parallel to his scientific activities, he has been serving as a legal clerk at the Higher Regional Court of Munich since 2025.

LIST OF ABBREVIATIONS

2014 Public Procurement Directives	Directive 2014/23/EU; Directive 2014/24/EU; Directive 2014/25/EU
AG	Advocate General
CESL	Common European Sales Law
CISG	United Nations Convention on Contracts for the International Sale of Goods
CJEU	Court of Justice of the European Union
DCFR	C von Bar, E Clive and H Schulte-Nölke (eds), *Principles, Definitions and Model Rules of European Private Law Draft Common Frame of Reference (DCFR)* (Berlin, De Gruyter, 2008)
Directive 89/665/EEC	Council Directive 89/665 of 21 December 1989 on the coordination of the laws, regulations and administrative provisions relating to the application of review procedures to the award of public supply and public works contracts [1989] OJ L395/33, as amended by Directive 2007/66/EC of the European Parliament and of the Council of 11 December 2007 [2007] OJ L335/31
Directive 92/13/EEC	Council Directive 92/13/EEC of 25 February 1992 coordinating the laws, regulations and administrative provisions relating to the application of Community rules on the procurement procedures of entities operating in the water, energy, transport and telecommunications sectors [1992] OJ L76/14, as amended by Directive 2007/66/EC of the European Parliament and of the Council of 11 December 2007 [2007] OJ L335/31
Directive 2014/23/EU	Directive 2014/23/EU of the European Parliament and of the Council of 26 February 2014 on the award of concession contracts [2014] OJ L94/1

Directive 2014/24/EU	Directive 2014/24/EU of the European Parliament and of the Council of 26 February 2014 on public procurement and repealing Directive 2004/18/EC [2014] OJ L94/65
Directive 2014/25/EU	Directive 2014/25/EU of the European Parliament and of the Council of 26 February 2014 on procurement by entities operating in the water, energy, transport and postal services sectors and repealing Directive 2004/17/EC [2014] OJ L94/243
EC	European Community
ECHR	European Convention on Human Rights
EEA	European Economic Area
EEC	European Economic Community
MEAT	Most Economically Advantageous Tender
PECL	O Lando and H Beale (eds), *Principles of European Contract Law, Parts I and II* (The Hague, Kluwer Law International, 2000); O Lando, H Beale, A Prüm, E Clive and R Zimmerman (eds), *Principles of European Contract Law, Part III* (The Hague, Kluwer Law International, 2003)
PPP	Public–Private Partnership
Remedies Directives	Directive 89/665/EEC; Directive 92/13/EEC
SPP	Sustainable Public Procurement
TEU	Treaty on European Union
TFEU	Treaty on the Functioning of the European Union
UNCITRAL	United Nations Commission on International Trade Law
UNIDROIT	The International Institute for the Unification of Private Law

PART I

The Roadmap

1

Introduction

MARTA ANDHOV AND MICHAŁ KANIA

I. Introduction

Public Procurement and Contract Law: Exploring Interactions, Defining Boundaries is, in many ways, an experimental book. Unlike many legal academic collections, it does not aim to examine specific jurisdictions, apply a singular methodology, or advocate for a fixed normative standpoint. Instead, this anthology is both eclectic in scope and cohesive in focus. It brings together a diverse range of perspectives while maintaining a clear thematic coherence. Its central aim is to investigate the points of convergence, the underlying principles, and the often implicit assumptions that shape the relationship between two intertwined yet separate branches of law: public procurement law (including EU and national procurement systems) and contract law (encompassing both EU-level theoretical harmonisation efforts and national contract laws).[1]

The anthology is particularly concerned with the moments at which these domains intersect, interact, or even potentially overlap, most notably in the context of the execution of public contracts.

As academic disciplines, public procurement law and contract law have traditionally been treated as distinct and formally structured fields. Contract law has developed around dominant theoretical frameworks that are largely economic and market-driven. In contrast, public procurement law focuses on the delivery of public contracts with the public interest at its core. Established principles, doctrines, and legal classifications within these fields are often accepted, and the simplifications underpinning their interaction have rendered the intersection between them significantly underexplored.

[1] For the purposes of this anthology, any reference to 'contract law' is understood to mean the legal norms that govern contractual relationships between the parties to a private contract. The terms private contract law and commercial contract law are also used interchangeably. These norms are predominantly found in national civil codes, contract acts, or other sources of private law. Exceptions to this general understanding are discussed in ch 3 and ch 14. Accordingly, we distinguish between a 'public contract', which refers to a contract established through public procurement procedures involving at least one contracting authority, and a 'contract' or 'private contract', which refers to a commercial business-to-business (B2B) contract governed purely by private contractual rules.

The *Procurement and Contract Law* project seeks to unravel, or at the very least, illuminate, some of the key interactions between public procurement law and contract law. We see this project not only as a valuable intellectual undertaking but also as a long-overdue exercise in the scholarship that emerges at the intersection of these two fields. Many of the assumptions and distinctions examined in this anthology have been repeated or restated with such frequency that they have become de facto institutionalised truths. For example, the notion that a public contract, once procured, falls under a distinct legal regime, based on its public character, has often been treated as self-evident and has become widely accepted with little examination of the other side of the transaction: the 'private' dimension of the contractual relationship. Yet in many European jurisdictions, such public contracts are classified as similar to private commercial contracts at the national level, raising important questions: are the principles of contract law disregarded, subtly modified, or fundamentally distorted when applied to public contracts?

While the emphasis on the public nature of public contracts in continental Europe is undoubtedly valid, it has shaped a dominant perspective, one that reflects a particular normative orientation and is often treated as broadly the only applicable one.[2] As a result, scholarly legal analysis has largely centred on the public procurement law and position of the contracting authority, with comparatively little attention paid to the position of the private contractor as a contractual partner within public contracts. This imbalance has left aspects grounded in contract law interaction with public procurement law largely underexplored. Our project does not seek to undermine existing public doctrine; rather, it aims to supplement the conversation by offering additional insights and perspectives into how contractual relationships are shaped within publicly procured contracts.

This anthology encourages, invites, and celebrates deeper inquiry into the assumptions, perspectives, and claims that underpin so many of the interactions between these two fields. As editors, we intentionally rejected a uniform narrative approach. From the outset, we embraced a pluralistic editorial approach, allowing each author to articulate their insights in a manner that is authentic to their voice, so that the reader hears each contribution as distinct. We deliberately invited scholars from both public procurement and contract law, as well as those scholars with close ties to legal practice – recognising that many of the issues explored in this anthology arise in practical settings and are often resolved before ever reaching the courts. In addition to analytical quality, we prioritised diversity of viewpoints and strong representation from jurisdictions with a more 'private-oriented hybrid

[2] For lawyers in civil law countries, the term 'public contracts' refers to the distinction between contracts governed by public law and contracts governed by private law, whereas, for common law lawyers, the term has only a descriptive value. The application of contract law to procured contracts is well established in common law jurisdictions; however, these systems fall outside the scope of this anthology. See M Fromont, 'Changes in the Administration's Contract Law: Theoretical Differences and De Facto Convergences' in R Noguellou and U Stelkens (eds), *Comparative Law on Public Contracts* (Brussels, Bruylant, 2010) 264.

model', where the application of contract law plays a larger role.[3] This editorial approach has allowed for a richer and more nuanced exploration of the relationship between contract and procurement law.

While readers are to assess our success, we are extremely satisfied with the outcome. The chapters in this anthology combine theoretical and conceptual analysis with practical, country-specific solutions and considerations. By bringing together diverse ideas and perspectives, the anthology highlights the intricate interactions and shifting boundaries between contract and public procurement law, particularly in the context of public contract performance, while also considering these dynamics in the award phase, albeit to a more limited extent.[4] Our aspiration is to contribute to conceptual development and set the agenda for future research. To this end, each chapter delves into a specific, often underexplored topic related to public contracts, analysing it through both the public procurement law and contract law lenses. By shifting the analytical baseline across various dimensions, such as public and private, theoretical and practical, national and transnational, conceptual and comparative, the chapters collectively map the intersections of these two legal fields and illuminate both challenges and opportunities for legal interpretation and reform.

II. Interactions between Public Procurement Law and Contract Law

The term 'procurement' refers to the process of acquiring goods, services, or works from an external source. This applies both to commercial procurement undertaken by private companies and to public procurement carried out by central governments, departments, other public bodies, or local municipalities. While procurement typically takes place through contractual arrangements, the term is sometimes used more broadly to encompass acquisition mechanisms that are not strictly contractual in nature.[5] The concept of procurement can be understood in both broad and narrow terms. In its broadest sense, it refers to the entire contracting process – from planning, tender drafting, soliciting bids through public procurement procedures and specification to contract management, execution, and termination. More narrowly, it denotes the procedures leading up to the conclusion of a contract. This narrower understanding is closely aligned with the scope of public procurement law, which in the European context governs the award phase of public contracts through the public procurement process.[6] This EU public

[3] See ch 3.

[4] The relationship between public procurement law and contract law during the award phase is examined in ch 4 in the context of freedom of contract, and in ch 5 in relation to withdrawals, awards, and the allocation of risk.

[5] S Arrowsmith, *The Law of Public and Utilities Procurement*, vol 1, 3rd edn (London, Sweet & Maxwell, 2014) 1.

[6] ibid.

procurement process is followed by a standstill period unique to public contracts.[7] Once a contract is awarded, it enters the performance or execution stage, which is largely governed by the national laws of individual EU Member States.[8] It is this phase of the public contract lifecycle that forms the central focus of this anthology.

Due to its distinct public character, a public contract differs in several respects from a classic private commercial contract. One of the key sources of this difference lies in the way the contract is concluded, through a formal public procurement procedure that precedes its performance.

The formation of a public contract is governed by specific and highly formalised rules set out in EU public procurement law.[9] This anthology focuses in particular on the regulatory framework established by Directive 2014/24/EU. This procedural formalism stands in sharp contrast to the formation of private commercial contracts, which are generally not subject to the same level of regulation. In contract law, contract formation is largely left to the discretion of the parties, guided by the principles of parties' autonomy and freedom of contract.[10]

[7] The standstill period is governed by Art 2a Directive 89/665/EEC. This period refers to the mandatory interval between the selection of a contractor and the formal conclusion of the public contract. Its purpose is to ensure that unsuccessful tenderers are informed of the award decision in advance, thereby allowing them a meaningful opportunity to exercise their rights and, if necessary, initiate a review of the contracting authority's decision before the contract becomes legally binding. See C Bovis, 'Remedies' in M Trybus, R Caranta and G Edelstam (eds), *EU Public Contract Law Public Procurement and Beyond* (Brussels, Bruylant, 2013) 363.

[8] The separation between the award and performance phases of public contracts is an important aspect of EU public procurement law. One of its defining features is the absence of direct effect, meaning that the contract does not automatically come into force upon the selection of the winning bid. This marks a key distinction between public procurement law and commercial contract law. Comba has drawn attention to this issue, noting that under Directive 2004/18/EC (See Directive 2004/18/EC of the European Parliament and of the Council of 31 March 2004 on the coordination of procedures for the award of public works contracts, public supply contracts and public service contracts [2004] OJ L134/114), it became increasingly important to distinguish between the *award* of a contract and its *conclusion* or formalisation. While EU public procurement law consistently refers to the *award* of contracts, it does not provide an explicit definition of the term, nor does it clarify the precise relationship between the award and the conclusion of a contract. See M Comba, 'Effects of EU Law on Contract Management' in M Trybus, R Caranta and G Edelstam (eds), *EU Public Contract Law Public Procurement and Beyond* Brussels, Bruylant, 2013) 320.

[9] Directive 2009/81/EC of the European Parliament and of the Council of 13 July 2009 on the coordination of procedures for the award of certain works contracts, supply contracts and service contracts by contracting authorities or entities in the fields of defence and security, and amending Directives 2004/17/EC and 2004/18/EC [2009] OJ L216/76; Directive 2014/23/EU; Directive 2014/24/EU; Directive 2014/25/EU.

[10] See eg W Flume, *Allgemeiner Teil des Bürgerlichen Rechts: Das Rechtsgeschäft* (Berlin, Springer, 1979) 1, 2; F Bydliński, *System und Prinzipien des Privatrechts* (Vienna, Verlag Österreich, 1996) 147; D Medicus, *Allgemeiner Teil des BGB* (Heidelberg, CF Müller, 1997) 74; K Larenz and M Wolf, *Allgemeiner Teil des Bürgerlichen Rechts* (Munich, CH Beck, 1997) 1, 26; D Coester-Waljten, 'Constitutional Aspects of Party Autonomy and its Limits: The Prospective of Law' in S Grundmann, W Kerber and S Weatherill (eds), *Party Autonomy and the Role of Information in the Internal Market* (Berlin, De Gruyter, 2001) 41; K Riesenhuber, *Europäisches Vertragsrecht* (Berlin, Mohr Siebeck, 2006) § 4; T Mollers, 'Working with Legal Principles: Demonstrated Using Private Autonomy and Freedom of Contract as Examples' (2018) 14(2) *European Review of Contract Law* 113; E McKendrik, *Contract Law* (Oxford, Hart Publishing, 2023).

The purpose of Directive 2014/24/EU is to promote the free movement of goods, services, and establishment within the internal market by harmonising the rules governing the award of public contracts across Member States.[11] To this end, it requires contracting authorities to observe fundamental principles, namely, equal treatment, non-discrimination, transparency, and proportionality, alongside the increasingly recognised prohibition of distorting competition and the principle of sustainability.[12] Nonetheless, the effectiveness of EU public procurement law would be undermined if, after the conclusion of a public contract, the contracting parties were free to renegotiate all its terms, effectively disregarding the conditions and requirements set out in the previous procurement process. For this reason, EU public procurement law continues to exert influence beyond the award stage, albeit to a limited extent. This includes, for example, rules governing contract modification and termination, provisions requiring the annulment of contracts awarded unlawfully, and requirements that substantial amendments to existing contracts should be treated as new contracts subject to procurement procedures.

By contrast, private contracts are grounded in a different normative foundation, one that emphasises economic freedom of the contracting parties.[13] This foundation is reflected in the legal systems of the EU Member States, which recognise party autonomy as a core tenet of contract law.[14] Closely connected to this is the principle of freedom of contract, which allows legal subjects to shape their civil relationships through agreements of their own choosing.[15] Freedom of contract reflects the parties' ability to regulate their legal relationships through voluntary agreement, ensuring that businesses can freely choose their contracting partners and negotiate the terms of their transactions, forming the basis of an open, competitive, and market-oriented economy.[16] Restrictions on this principle

[11] M Trybus, 'Public Contracts in European Union Internal Market Law: Foundations and Requirements' in R Noguellou and U Stelkens (eds), *Comparative Law on Public Contracts* (Brussels, Bruylant, 2010) 97. See more in ch 2.

[12] See Art 18 Directive 2014/24/EU and Case C-395/18 *Tim SpA – Direzione e coordinamento Vivendi SA v Consip SpA, Ministero dell'Economia e delle Finanze* ECLI:EU:C:2020:58, [2020].

[13] See ch 4.

[14] Riesenhuber (n 10); Bydliński (n 10) 147 et seq; Flume (n 10); Medicus (n 10) 74; Larenz and Wolf (n 10) 1 et seq, 26.

[15] See for example, JB Auby, 'Comparative Approaches to the Rise of the Contract in Public Sphere' (2007) 1 *Public Law* 40; J Basedow, 'Freedom of Contract in the European Union' (2008) 16(6) *European Review of Private Law* 901.

[16] Freedom of contract is not explicitly recognised in EU primary law. It does not clearly or unambiguously articulate this principle. Art 3(3) Treaty on European Union (TEU) merely refers to a 'highly competitive social market economy', which cannot be readily interpreted as affirming the principle of party autonomy or, by extension, freedom of contract. However, in the evolving legal landscape, freedom of contract is increasingly acknowledged as a fundamental right. According to Advocate General (AG) Szpunar of the CJEU, Art 16 Charter of Fundamental Rights now serves as its legal foundation. This provision guarantees 'the freedom to conduct a business in accordance with Union law and national laws and practices', which includes the freedom of contract as an essential component of economic activity. M Szpunar, 'Basedow, Jürgen: EU Private Law. Anatomy of a Growing Legal Order. Cambridge, Antwerp, Chicago: Intersentia 2021. CXXVII, 788 pp' (2023) 87(2) *Rabels Zeitschrift für ausländisches und internationales Privatrecht* 353, 358. See Consolidated Version of the Treaty on European Union [2008] OJ C 115/13; Charter of Fundamental Rights of the European Union [2012] OJ C326/391.

are exceptions, typically arising from mandatory rules, for example, promoting overriding interests such as environmental protection.[17]

It thus quickly becomes apparent that public procurement law and contract law rest on different paradigms.[18] Yet, despite their seemingly distinct normative foundations, the two are closely linked in the context of public contract performance, where their principles converge and interact to varying degrees, depending on the national legal models governing the execution of public contracts.[19]

However, despite the distinct public nature of a public contract, it remains a legal instrument designed to regulate commercial relationships between the parties, namely, the contracting authority and the contractor. At its core, a public contract facilitates a typical exchange of considerations: the contractor undertakes to deliver goods, perform services, or execute construction works, while the contracting authority assumes the obligation to pay remuneration.[20] In this respect, public contracts give rise to a range of issues that are relevant from a contract law perspective. These include issues such as warranties, contractual penalties, joint and several liability, and the consequences of defective or non-performance of the contract, hardship clauses, withdrawals, modifications, and terminations. Furthermore, disputes may arise from the aforementioned issues, creating a potential interest in their prompt resolution through arbitration, an alternative dispute resolution mechanism rooted in contract law.

III. Approach and Analytical Framework for this Anthology

To date, the topic of public contracts has been examined predominantly through the lens of EU and national public procurement law. Much of this research has adopted a public law perspective, particularly focusing on the relationship between the award and performance phases of public contracts.[21] Within this framework, the performance phase has attracted some attention, especially regarding the modification of public contracts, a subject that has been explored in several scholarly works and addressed in judgments of the Court of Justice of the European

[17] Directive 2024/1760 of 13 June 2024 on corporate sustainability due diligence and amending Directive (EU) 2019/1937 and Regulation (EU) 2023/2859 (CSDDD).

[18] See ch 4.

[19] See ch 3.

[20] See Art 2(1)(5) Directive 2014/24/EU.

[21] See eg A Sanchez-Graells, 'Expanding the Scope of EU Public Procurement Law: Realigning the Procurement Directive with Its Internal Market Logic while Improving Its Fit with Strategic Procurement?' (2025) *Social Science Reasearch Network*, <papers.ssrn.com/sol3/papers.cfm?abstract_id=5213497>.

Union (CJEU).[22] Similarly, the termination of public contracts has been the focus of analysis in both scholarship and case law within the field of EU public procurement law.[23]

However, there remains a notable lack of legal scholarship that addresses the performance phase of public contracts from two key angles: (a) by juxtaposing the doctrines of contract law and public procurement law to examine their interaction, and (b) by adopting a broader, cross-cutting 'helicopter view' that considers trends and solutions from a broader perspective. The absence of such an approach can be attributed to several factors, including the complexity of the undertaking. Most notably, the existence of diverse national models governing public contract performance, the absence of harmonised European rules on contract law, and the scale of the task, which would require the collaboration of multiple experts from various jurisdictions, pose significant challenges. Despite these constraints, this anthology aims to take a step in that direction, while acknowledging the inherent limitations of such an endeavour, as discussed below. Given that, in practice, public procurement law interacts with contract law in several ways and to varying degrees, it is both timely and relevant to explore their intersections, the challenges that arise from them, and the ways in which those challenges are addressed across European countries.

One of the challenges in approaching this research from a broader perspective, specifically, in attempting to juxtapose EU public procurement law with contract law, is the absence of a harmonised European contract law. For this reason, we have chosen European contract law (defined below) as a conceptual point of departure. This allows us to offer a degree of generalisation in

[22] See for example, Case C-469/99 *Commission of the European Communities v CAS Succhi di Frutta SpA* ECLI:EU:C:2004:236, [2004] ECR I-03801; Case C-454/06 *pressetext Nachrichtenagentur GmbH v Republik Österreich (Bund), APA-OTS Originaltext-Service GmbH and APA Austria Presse Agentur registrierte Genossenschaft mit beschränkter Haftung* ECLI:EU:C:2008:351, [2008] ECR I-04401; Case C-91/08 *Wall AG v La ville de Francfort-sur-le-Main and Frankfurter Entsorgungs- und Service (FES) GmbH* ECLI:EU:C:2010:182, [2010] ECR I-02815; C-161/13 *Idrodinamica Spurgo Velox srl and Others v Acquedotto Pugliese SpA* EU:C:2014:307, [2014]; Case C-549/14 *Finn Frogne A/S v Rigspolitiet ved Center for Beredskabskommunikation* ECLI:EU:C:2016:634, [2016]; Case C-298/15 *UAB 'Borta' v VĮ Klaipėdos valstybinio jūrų uosto direkcija* ECLI:EU:C:2017:266, [2017]; C-223/16 *Casertana Costruzioni Srl v Ministero delle Infrastrutture e dei Trasporti* ECLI:EU:C:2017:685, [2017]; Case C-461/20 *Advania Sverige AB and Kammarkollegiet v Dustin Sverige AB* ECLI:EU:C:2022:72, [2022]; P Bogdanowicz, *Contract Modifications in EU Procurement Law* (Cheltenham, Edward Elgar Publishing, 2021); D Dragos, KM Halonen, B Neamtu and S Treumer (eds), *Contract Changes: The Dark Side of EU Procurement Law* (Cheltenham, Edward Elgar Publishing, 2023).

[23] See eg MA Simovart, 'Enforcement of Ineffectiveness of Unlawfully Modified Public Contracts' (2016) *Juridica International* 43; KM Halonen, 'Termination of a Public Contract – Lifting the Veil on Art. 73 of 2014/24 Directive' (2017) 5 *Public Procurement Law Review* 187; M Steinicke and PL Vesterdorf (eds), *Brussels Commentary on EU Public Procurement Law* (Oxford, Bloomsbury Publishing, 2018) 708–10; KM Halonen, 'Article 73 Termination of Contracts' in R Caranta and A Sanchez-Graells (eds), *Commentary on Directive 2014/24/EU* (Cheltenham, Edward Elgar Publishing, 2021); KM Halonen, 'Contractual Ineffectiveness as Seen from a Finnish Perspective' in CR Hamer, M Andhov, F Bertelsen and R Caranta (eds), *Into the Northern Light: In Memory of Steen Treumer* (Copenhagen, Ex Tuto, 2022).

our broader discussion by drawing on the general principles and foundational concepts embedded in the theoretical framework of European contract law, all of which are reflected across various national legal systems. Applying European contract law in this way allows us to establish a common benchmark for discussion before delving into specific jurisdictions. Moreover, since our research does not cover all 27 EU Member States, this approach enables jurisdictions not directly represented to reflect on how the issues discussed might be addressed within their own legal systems.

Accordingly, the majority of the chapters in this anthology engage with European contract law to some extent.[24] In chapters that present national perspectives, this engagement is complemented by reference to specific national sources of contract law. Adopting this approach has enabled us to address certain themes in a more conceptual and abstract manner, while still maintaining grounding in the doctrinal and practical realities of different jurisdictions.

A. What We Understand as European Contract Law in this Anthology*

While EU public procurement law has been substantially harmonised over the past 50 years,[25] efforts to harmonise European contract law, ongoing since the 1980s,[26] have unfortunately achieved much less success. Despite numerous directives,[27] extensive political discussions, and repeated attempts to establish a codified European Contract Code or European Sales Law,[28] both practitioners and

[24] The exception is the final two chapters, which focus on procedural aspects of arbitration rather than the substantive legal issues to which contract law would apply.

* This section draws on the historical background presented in Ezgi Uysal, Enforcing Sustainability in Contract Performance Under the Public Sector Directive (PhD thesis, University of Turin, 2024), ch 2.

[25] The harmonisation of EU public procurement law began already in the 1970s with the adoption of initial directives, Directive 71/305/EEC on public works and Directive 77/62/EEC on public supply contracts, which were designed to open up national public procurement markets to competition and to ensure transparency and fairness across the EU. See Council Directive 71/305/EEC of 26 July 1971 concerning the co-ordination of procedures for the award of public works contracts OJ [1971] L185/5; Council Directive 77/62/EEC of 21 December 1976 coordinating procedures for the award of public supply contracts [1977] OJ L13/1.

[26] The Commission on European Contract Law began work in 1982, based on a private initiative by Professor Ole Lando from Denmark.

[27] These directives were predominantly focusing on the area of consumer protection, however, there were some directives that addressed various standardised contractual clauses, such as Unfair Terms Directive or Digital Content Directive. Council Directive 93/13/EEC of 5 April 1993 on unfair terms in consumer contracts [1993] OJ L 95/29; Directive (EU) 2019/770 of the European Parliament and of the Council of 20 May 2019 on certain aspects concerning contracts for the supply of digital content and digital services [2019] OJ L 136/1.

[28] European Parliament legislative resolution of 26 February 2014 on the proposal for a regulation of the European Parliament and of the Council on a Common European Sales Law (COM(2011)0635 – C7-0329/2011 – 2011/0284(COD)) OJ C 285/638.

academics still face a fragmented landscape of European contract law.[29] As Kötz famously noted, there is no such thing as a European law of contract.[30] Instead, what exists within the EU is a complex patchwork of legal instruments and principles.[31] These include the *Acquis Communautaire*, which comprises Union-level legislation governing specific types of contracts, contractual issues, and transactions involving particular parties.[32] It also encompasses international conventions and a substantial body of comparative legal scholarship on the contract laws of the Member States.[33] These do not represent a unified or binding legal framework but rather various initiatives and efforts aimed at harmonising contract law across the Member States, driven by the need to facilitate the smooth operation of the internal market.

Although the European Commission has not yet succeeded in adopting a comprehensive 'European Contract Code', nearly 40 years of rigorous academic research on European contract law have provided valuable insights.[34] This anthology considers specifically two contributions: The Principles of European Contract Law (PECL), developed by the Commission on European Contract Law, and the Draft Common Frame of Reference (DCFR). These works represent advancements in the field and offer frameworks for understanding and analysing the complex landscape of European contract law. The Commission on European Contract Law, drawing inspiration from the United Nations Convention on Contracts for the International Sale of Goods (CISG), developed the PECL with the vision of articulating contract law principles common to all Member States, aiming to serve as a blueprint for potential future EU legislation.[35] Although the PECL never acquired the force of law, it does allow parties to stipulate that contractual disputes be

[29] On the history of European contract law, see L Miller, *The Emergence of EU Contract Law: Exploring Europeanization* (Oxford, Oxford University Press, 2011) 31–45; H Kötz, *European Contract Law*, 2nd edn (Oxford, Oxford University Press, 2017) 1–15.

[30] See Kötz (n 29) 1.

[31] See E Uysal, 'Sustainability Clauses in "Public" Contracts' (2024) 20(1) *European Review of Contract Law* 115.

[32] See HW Micklitz, 'European Private Law' in D Patterson and A Södersten (eds), *A Companion to European Union Law and International Law*, 1st edn (Hoboken, Wiley, 2016).

[33] See EA Farnsworth, 'Comparative Contract Law' in M Reimann and R Zimmermann (eds), *The Oxford Handbook of Comparative Law* (Oxford, Oxford University Press, 2006); HW Micklitz and F Cafaggi (eds), *European Private Law after the Common Frame of Reference* (Cheltenham, Edward Elgar Publishing, 2010); R Schulze and F Zoll, *European Contract Law* (Oxford, Bloomsbury Publishing, 2016) 6; MW Hesselink, *Justifying Contract in Europe* (Oxford, Oxford University Press, 2021) 17; S Grundmann and M Grochowski (eds), *European Contract Law and the Creation of Norms* (Cambridge, Intersentia, 2021) 13.

[34] This is also due to the fact that, within the principle of attributed competences (Art 5 TEU), the EU does not have general regulatory competence and nowhere in the Treaty can we find any explicit powers allowing the EU to operate in contract law, which is why we see the contract law principles coming through the 'consumer law'. For more on the constitutional limitations of contract law, see Miller (n 29) 44–50.

[35] C Castronovo, 'Contract and the Idea of Codification in The Principles of European Contract Law' in Lennart Lynge Andersen, Jens Fejø, and Ruth Nielsen (eds), *Festskrift til Ole Lando* (Copenhagen, Gadjura, 1997) 109.

resolved based on its principles.[36] Courts may also apply the PECL when parties have agreed that their contract should be governed by 'general principles of law' or by the *lex mercatoria* customary in commercial trade.[37] The most significant practical impact of the PECL, however, lies in its role as a guiding framework for legislatures,[38] courts and legal scholars on the direction that the development and interpretation of national contract laws should pursue to advance greater legal harmonisation in Europe.[39]

Building on the PECL, the Study Group on a European Civil Code expanded this foundation by drafting a broader set of model rules under the Principles of European Law (PEL). At the same time, recognising the need for greater consistency in European contract law, the European Commission issued an Action Plan advocating for a 'more coherent European contract law'.[40] This initiative led to the development of the Acquis Principles (ACQP) by the Research Group on Existing EC Private Law, which aimed to complement and refine the PECL. The Commission set itself the goal of focusing European contract law legislation not just on individual policies or industry-specific directives, but on overarching principles, definitions, and model rules that would function as a toolbox – the DCFR.[41]

The DCFR builds upon the principles of the PECL by extending its scope to a broader range of contractual and non-contractual obligations.[42] It integrates the PECL, ACQP, and PEL into a comprehensive framework, combining well-established principles of European Community law with insights derived from extensive comparative research. Book II DCFR is particularly significant, as it represents a robust blend of the ACQP and a comparative approach, leading to carefully drafted rules on the negotiation, conclusion, and content of contracts.[43] The sections on contract formation, interpretation, content, and effects are also predominantly grounded in detailed comparisons of national laws across the EU.[44]

[36] Art 1:101 (2) PECL. However, such a choice of law clause must only be observed by national courts where the applicable international private law allows the court to recognise reference to non-national law.

[37] Art 1:101 (3) PECL. See also Kötz (n 29) 4.

[38] See D Busch, E Hondius, H van Kooten, H Schelhaas, and W Schrama, *The PECL and Dutch Law: A Commentary*, vol 1 (The Hague, Kluwer Law International, 2002); L Antoniolli and A Veneziano, *Principles of European contract law and Italian law*, vol 2 (The Hague, Kluwer Law International, 2005); D Busch, 'The Principles of European Contract Law Before the Supreme Court of the Netherlands: On the Influence of the PECL in Dutch Legal Practice' (2008) 3 *Zeitschrift für Europäisches Privatrecht* 549–62.

[39] A practical example of this can be found in the reform of French contract law, which has been heavily influenced by the rules of the PECL. See the detailed account by F Ancel, B Fauvarque-Cosson, and J Gest, *Aux sources de la réforme du droit des contrats* (Courbevoie, Dalloz, 2017). See also J Basedow (ed), *Europäische Vertragsrechtsvereinheitlichung und deutsches Recht* (Berlin, Mohr Siebeck, 2000).

[40] Commission, 'Communication from the Commission to the European Parliament and the Council a More Coherent European Contract Law Action Plan' (2003).

[41] ibid 16.

[42] See DCFR.

[43] See Schulze and Zoll (n 33) 26.

[44] Book II DCFR, chs 4, 6, 9.

As a result, the DCFR, with its researched body of work, serves as a helpful source for European contract law in this publication.

Despite their non-binding nature, the PECL and the DCFR remain relevant in the context of European contract law. These frameworks offer a common set of principles and rules that provide valuable guidance for courts, legislators, and legal practitioners, assisting in interpreting and aligning national laws at the EU level.[45] Their influence is particularly notable in facilitating cross-border transactions and supporting ongoing efforts to harmonise contract law across the EU.

These frameworks contributed to shaping the discourse on European contract law, offering well-researched and coherent principles that transcend national boundaries. Their ability to provide a common language for the discourse makes them valuable for analytical and comparative research.[46] By integrating the PECL and the DCFR, this research capitalises on their success in harmonising legal thought, effectively addressing and overcoming the twentieth-century critiques centred on the risks of a '*Flucht in die Generalklauseln*' and the politics of harmonisation.[47]

B. Key Research Questions

The research questions at the heart of this anthology revolve around the fundamental issue of interaction between public procurement law and contract law, predominantly during the performance phase of public contracts, as well as during the resolution of disputes through arbitration that may arise from such contracts.

A particularly important question concerns the extent to which EU public procurement law influences, or potentially limits, the application of national contract law. For instance, when national contract law is applied to the performance of a public contract, is it applied directly but subject to modification in light of public procurement principles, or is it applied in parallel to public procurement law as a distinct normative framework or not at all? Closely related is the question

[45] See E Uysal, 'Enforcing Sustainability in Contract Performance Under the Public Sector Directive' (PhD Thesis, University of Turin, 2024) citing; Opinion of AG Trstenjak delivered on 6 July 2010 Case 137/08 *VB Pénzügyi Lízing Zrt. v Ferenc Schneider* ECLI:EU:C:2010:401, [2010]. For other cases where AGs have referred to DCFR in their opinions see Opinion of AG Trstenjak delivered on 11 September 2008 Case C-180/06 *Renate Ilsinger v Martin Dreschers (administrator in the insolvency of Schlank & Schick GmbH)* ECLI:EU:C:2008:483, [2008] para 49; Opinion of AG Trstenjak delivered on 7 May 2009 Case C-227/08 *Eva Martín Martín v EDP Editores SL* ECLI:EU:C:2009:295, [2009] para 51; Opinion of AG Sharpston delivered on 12 May 2016 Case C-555/14 *IOS Finance EFC SA v Servicio Murciano de Salud* ECLI:EU:C:2016:341, [2016] para 58.

[46] J Smits, 'A European Private Law as a Mixed Legal System' (1998) 5(4) *Maastricht Journal of European and Comparative Law* 328.

[47] See M Auer, 'Good Faith: A Semiotic Approach' (2002) *European Private Law* 279 et seq; M Hoch, 'Is Fair Dealing a Workable Concept for European Contract Law?' (2005) *Global Jurist* 5; S Grundmann and D Mazeaud (eds), *General Clauses and Standards in European Contract Law* (The Hague, Kluwer Law International, 2006).

of whether national contract law can constrain or shape the outcomes produced by public procurement law – and if so, how. This raises broader concerns about potential conflicts between the two legal regimes and how such conflicts are, or should be, resolved. Another dimension of this inquiry explores how the interplay between procurement and contract law affects the achievement of broader policy objectives, such as sustainability and digitalisation in public contracts. These questions underpin the structure of this anthology and inform the thematic focus of the individual sections and chapters that follow.

IV. Anthology Structure

Thematically, the chapters in this anthology are organised into four parts: Roadmap, General, Digitalisation and Sustainability, and Arbitration.

Part I, titled 'Roadmap', comprises four chapters and provides an introductory foundation for the further analyses developed in the subsequent chapters of the anthology.

Chapter two, 'Where Public Procurement Meets Contract Law: Mapping Entry Points' opens the analytical discussion of the anthology by establishing its conceptual foundations. It outlines the historical trajectory of extending EU public procurement law to public contracts and examines the notion of a public contract from both the perspective of EU public procurement law and European contract law. The chapter further maps the specific areas of public contract performance that have been overtaken or influenced by EU public procurement law, as well as those that remain within the regulatory discretion of the Member States.

Chapter three, 'National Models for Regulating Public Contracts', examines the consequences of the fact that Member States retain primary responsibility and control over regulating the performance phase of public contracts. It focuses on two overarching regulatory approaches, both of which are best described as arid. These models are neither purely public nor purely private. To reflect this, the authors adopt the terms 'public-oriented hybrid model', with the French system serving as its clearest example, and 'private-oriented hybrid model', more closely rooted in the German legal tradition.

Chapter four, 'Freedom of Contract: Contrasting Values and Principles in Contract Law and Public Procurement Law', delves into the conceptual and normative tensions between the two legal domains. It takes the principle of freedom of contract and its core elements as the primary lens through which to explore these contrasts, setting it against the values embedded in public procurement law. The chapter investigates key dimensions of contractual freedom, such as the choice of contracting partners, the determination of contractual form and content, and the ability to modify agreed terms. It also addresses related principles, such as good faith, fair dealing, and privity of contract, that subtly shape and constrain the exercise of contractual freedom.

Part II of this anthology, titled 'General', includes five chapters and addresses a range of recurring themes and issues occurring at the intersection of public procurement law and contract law. These chapters explore commonly encountered legal questions relevant to the anthology's central research inquiry.

Chapter five, 'Influencing Contractual Freedom through EU and Dutch Public Procurement Law: Legal Review Asymmetries in Cases on Withdrawals, Awards and Division of Risk', examines asymmetries in the judicial review of contracting authorities' decisions in EU and Dutch public procurement law, focusing on the principle of freedom of contract. It contrasts how courts exercise minimal review in withdrawal cases, while applying a more interventionist approach in risk allocation disputes. The chapter argues for a consistent judicial review standard, drawing on comparative insights.

Chapter six, 'The Diligent Contracting Authority: The Concept of Due Diligence in Public Procurement', explores the concept of 'due diligence' in EU and Danish public procurement law, investigating whether a general obligation to act diligently can be inferred despite limited explicit references. It contrasts how 'due diligence' is treated in private law, drawing on the DCFR, the PECL, and the Danish Sale of Goods Act, with its narrower application in public procurement contexts, particularly in relation to direct awards and contract modifications under Directive 2014/24/EU. The chapter highlights the tension between the flexibility of contract law and the formalism of procurement law, rooted in the imperative of maintaining fair competition.

Chapter seven, 'The Duty of Loyalty in the Contract Performance Stage: Contractual Adjustments Inside and Outside the Realm of Article 72 Directive 2014/24/EU', investigates the intersection of contract law and EU public procurement law in the Nordic context, focusing on the principles of loyalty and cooperation during contract performance. It highlights how growing demands for flexibility, driven by contemporary challenges, require greater adaptability in public contracts, challenging the traditional divide between public procurement rules and private law. The chapter unpacks how collaborative contract law principles can support or conflict with procurement regulations, offering insight into how these frameworks interact in practice.

Chapter eight, '"I Did Not Sign Anything": Can A Tacit Modification Constitute A Contract Amendment under EU Procurement Rules?', considers the legal treatment of tacit (ie implicit or unwritten) contract modifications within the EU public procurement law framework, particularly in contrast to contract law. It argues that while contract law may allow tacit amendments under certain conditions, the public procurement regime prioritises transparency and effectiveness, placing stricter limits on such modifications. Through case law and doctrinal analysis, the chapter questions whether a mutual intention to renegotiate, without formal documentation, can suffice to constitute a lawful amendment under EU rules.

Chapter nine, 'Applying the Doctrine of Hardship in Public Contracts', analyses how public procurement law impacts the interpretation and application of the contract law concept of hardship, also known as the *rebus sic stantibus* doctrine. The chapter considers challenges arising from recent crises such as the COVID-19 pandemic and the war in Ukraine, which have significantly impacted public contract performance. The analysis focuses on the interplay between Article 72(1)(c) Directive 2014/24/EU and the Polish and Danish legal frameworks governing hardship, examining how these systems respond to unforeseen and disruptive events.

Part III of this anthology, 'Digitalisation and Sustainability', comprises three chapters and considers the intersections between public procurement law and contract law in relation to two prominent contemporary themes: digitalisation and sustainability.

Chapter 10, 'Deconstructing Computational Contracts: A Critical Analysis of their Application in Private and Public Domain', provides a conceptual analysis of the integration and impact of computational contracts within European contract law and EU public procurement law. Taking a dual perspective that includes both private and public sector applications, it investigates the extent to which computational contracts meet the legal and practical requirements of traditional contracting. It offers a forward-looking reflection on how these evolving technologies may reshape established legal frameworks.

Chapter 11, 'Sustainability and Its Enforcement in Private and Public Contracts', explores the interpretation and enforcement of sustainability considerations in private and public contracts. It compares legal approaches in Germany, Switzerland, and Belgium, highlighting how different hybrid regulatory models influence the integration of environmental and social criteria. The chapter analyses a range of enforcement mechanisms, from traditional contract law tools to emerging soft law instruments, to assess how sustainability obligations are implemented in practice.

Chapter 12, 'Enforcing Sustainability Clauses in Public Contracts: Third-party Enforcement Caught Between the Privity of Contract and Conflicting Interests', investigates whether third-party enforcement can ensure compliance with sustainability clauses in public contracts, despite the constraints of the privity of contract doctrine. It examines the role of third-party beneficiaries, economic competitors, and public bodies and institutions in upholding sustainability obligations when contractual enforcement by the contracting authority is limited.

Part IV of this anthology, titled 'Arbitration', explores the potential for resolving disputes arising during the performance of public contracts through an alternative dispute resolution mechanism, namely arbitration. It includes two chapters.

Chapter 13, 'Can the Effectiveness of European Public Procurement Law Be Ensured If Disputes Related to the Performance of Public Contracts are Settled by Commercial Arbitration?', explores whether international commercial arbitration is compatible with the effectiveness of EU public procurement law when used to resolve disputes in the performance phase of public contracts. It assesses how the principles of EU public procurement can be upheld within the arbitration's more private and confidential framework. Using the 'private-oriented hybrid model' and drawing on examples from Denmark and Poland, the chapter critically reflects on arbitration's potential benefits and limitations in preserving public law objectives.

Chapter 14, 'Adjudicating Public Contracts: The Role of Arbitration in France, Portugal, and Spain', assesses how the legal traditions of the investigated jurisdictions, characterised by strong public law frameworks, influence the use of arbitration in public contract disputes. Despite longstanding resistance due to concerns about public interest and administrative control, these jurisdictions now allow arbitration under specific conditions tailored to safeguard the public dimension of such contracts. The analysis highlights how arbitration mechanisms are adapted, through limitations on arbitrability, authorisation requirements, and specialised procedural safeguards, to reflect the distinctive nature of public contracts in these systems.

The anthology concludes with chapter 15, 'Concluding Remarks'. Building on the rich material presented throughout the anthology, this final chapter offers a synthesis of the overarching insights emerging from the preceding contributions. It summarises the responses to the anthology's initial research questions, drawing on the diverse perspectives and analyses developed across the chapters.

2

Where Public Procurement Meets Contract Law: Mapping Entry Points*

MARTA ANDHOV AND MICHAŁ KANIA

I. Introduction

In its day-to-day operations, the public administration utilises a variety of legal forms, such as unilateral administrative decisions, material services (including the maintenance of public registers), and contracts concluded with private parties.[1] While the application of administrative acts tends to be relatively straightforward, the use of contracts by the public administration is more complex and often contentious, reflecting the intersection between private and public law within these agreements. The public administration relies on various types of contracts, from standard private law arrangements, such as employment contracts or contracts for the sale of real estate, to public contracts for the procurement of goods, works, or services.

The current extensive use of contracts by public administration results from the long evolution of this legal concept and its rich history.[2] The role of contracts

* This chapter has greatly benefited from the insights, comments, and contributions of the authors of the other chapters in this anthology, as well as from valuable input provided by professors Tünde Tátrai, Mario Comba, Elisabetta Manunza, and Marko Turudić, attorney-at-law Jesper Fabricius and Džeina Gaile (doctoral student). We are particularly grateful to Professor Roberto Caranta for his thoughtful ongoing feedback, which helped us improve and further develop the chapter. All errors and omissions remain the sole responsibility of the authors.

[1] The primary classification of public administration activities in EU countries differentiates between authoritative and non-authoritative (consensual) actions. Authoritative actions, historically central to public administration, primarily involve the unilateral issuance of administrative decisions and the jurisdiction of administrative courts. These actions often include administrative discretion, where administrative bodies interpret legal norms authoritatively. Through such interpretation, these bodies establish the rights and obligations of external subjects, which may be enforced through administrative enforcement measures. In contrast, non-authoritative or consensual actions pertain to mutual legal arrangements, primarily in the form of contracts. For further discussion, see M Fromont, 'L'évolution du droit des contrats de l'Administration – différences théoriques et convergences de fait' in R Noguellou and U Stelkens (eds), *Droit comparé des contrats publics* (Brussels, Bruylant, 2010).

[2] ibid 264; see also eg, U Steiner, *Öffentliche Verwaltung durch Private: allgemeine Lehren* (Hamburg, Hansischer Gildenverlag Heitmann, 1975).

in public administration has, however, significantly expanded over the decades, marking a pivotal transformation in the functioning of public administration.[3] This transformation is closely associated with neoliberal policies that advocate outsourcing and the development of the 'contracting administration' concept.[4] This represents a departure from traditional administrative actions, such as administrative acts, towards bilateral legal acts, like contracts.[5] These policy movements can be traced back to the 'Thatcher era', when New Public Management policies were introduced in response to perceived inefficiencies within the public sector, such as slow and ineffective decision-making processes, inadequate organisational and institutional frameworks, and a general lack of competition.[6] These challenges prompted a redefinition of the state's role and responsibilities,[7] transforming the relationship between the public and private sectors.[8] Neoliberal policies had a spillover effect across Europe, where similar approaches were increasingly adopted. The significance of various contracts, including concession contracts, public–private partnership (PPP) contracts, but also public contracts arising from public procurement procedures, has increased.[9] This chapter, as well as this anthology, focuses specifically on public contracts arising from public procurement procedures under Directive 2014/24/EU.[10]

[3] S Valaguzza, *Governing by Contract Procuring for Value: Creating Value Through Public Contracts* (Naples, Editoriale Scientifica, 2021).

[4] Z Giacometti, *Allgemeinez Lehren der rechtsstaatlichen Verwaltungsrecht* (Zurich, Polygraphischer Verlag, 1960) 95; E Forsthoff, *Lehrbuch des Verwaltungsrecht*, 1st edn (Munich, CH Beck, 1966) 477; LK Adamovich and BC Funk, *Allgemeines Verwaltungsrecht* (Vienna, Springer, 1980) 155; D Ehlers, *Verwaltung in Privatrechtsform* (Berlin, Duncker & Humblot, 1984) 607; H Bauer, 'Entwicklungslinien der Vertragsrechtslehre' in W Hoffmann-Riem, E Schmidt-Assmann and A Voßkuhle (eds), *Grundlagen des Verwaltungsrecht Band 2: Informationsordnung, Verwaltungsverfahren, Handlungsformen* (Munich, CH Beck, 2012) 1266; W Van der Valk, 'Public Sector Contracting' in J Grandia and L Volker (eds), *Public Procurement: Theory, Practices and Tools* (Cham, Palgrave Macmillan, 2023) 122–23.

[5] A Davies, *Accountability: A Public Law Analysis of Government by Contract* (Oxford, Oxford University Press, 2001); J Freeman and M Minov, *Government by Contract. Outsourcing and American Democracy* (Cambridge, Harvard University Press, 2009); F Lichère and L Richer, *Droit des contrats administratifs*, 13th edn (Paris, Librairie générale de droit et de jurisprudence, 2024).

[6] E Skietrys, A Raipa and EV Bartkus, 'Dimensions of the Efficiency of Public-Private Partnership' (2008) 58(3) *Engineering Economics* 45; see more on the privatisation movement in the 1980s in C Hood, 'A Public Management for All Seasons?' (1991) 69(1) *Public Administration* 3; DF Kettl, *Sharing Power, Public Governance and Private Markets* (Washington DC, Brookings, 1993); R Wettenhall, 'Public or Private? Public Corporations, Companies and the Decline of the Middle Ground' (2001) 1 *Public Organization Review* 41; SY Collin and E Smith, 'Democracy and Private Property: Governance of a Three-Party Public-Private Partnership' (2008) *8 Public Organization Review* 54.

[7] M Milosavljevic and S Benkovic, 'Institutions and Development: Modern Aspects of Public Private Partnership' (2009) 3 *Perspectives of Innovations, Economics & Business* 25.

[8] S Osborne, *Public-Private Partnerships: Theory and Practice in International Perspective* (London, Routledge, 2000) 29.

[9] S Domberger and P Jensen, 'Contracting Out by The Public Sector: Theory, Evidence and Prospects' (1997) 13(4) *Oxford Review of Economic Policy* 67; AM Bertelli and CR Smith, 'Relational Contracting and Network Management' (2010) 20(1) *Journal of Public Administration Research and Theory* 21; A Modrzejewski, 'Kontraktualizacja W Globalnym I Europejskim Prawie Administracyjnym' in A Doliwa and S Prutis (eds), *Wypieranie Prawa Administracyjnego Przez Prawo Cywilne* (Warsaw, Kluwer, 2012) 220.

[10] The term 'public contract', as defined in Art 2(1)(5) Directive 2014/24/EU, will be consistently used throughout this chapter. Similar terminology, such as 'public procurement contracts', is used in various

Legal doctrine has explored numerous issues concerning public contracts, including their classification as either 'public' or 'private' law concepts.[11] National legal systems adopt different approaches in this regard. In some European countries, such as France, Spain, Portugal, Croatia, Belgium, and Italy, judicial decisions play a crucial role in distinguishing public contracts from private law. Legislators in these countries have subjected public contracts to a specialised legal framework under public law.[12] This framework aligns with the origins of administrative law, emphasising the public sector's dominant position and the protection of the public interest.[13] Conversely, in other legal systems, such as those in the Nordic region (Denmark, Sweden, Norway,[14] and Finland), as well as Germany, the Netherlands, Poland, Latvia, and Switzerland (a non-EU, but still European country[15]), these agreements are still grounded in private contract law.[16] While private contract law applies to public contracts in these jurisdictions, it has been specifically adapted to

national regimes within the EU. In contrast, the American doctrine refers to these as 'governmental contracts'. See, for example, RC Nash Jr and J Cibinic Jr, *Formation of Government Contracts*, 5th edn (Deventer, Kluwer, 2023), for the definition of governmental contracts. In English 'public contracts', in German '*öffentliche Aufträge*', in Spanish and Portuguese '*contratos públicos*', in French '*marché public*', in Italian '*appalti pubblici*', in Danish '*offentlige kontrakter*', in Polish '*umowy w sprawie zamówienia publicznego*', in Dutch '*overheidsopdrachten*', in Finnish '*hankintasopimukset*', in Croatian '*ugovor o javnoj nabavi*', and in Latvian '*iepirkuma līgums*'.

[11] R Noguellou and U Stelkens, 'Propos introductifs' in R Noguellou and U Stelkens (eds), *Droit comparé des contrats publics* (Brussels, Bruylant, 2010) 11. On the typology of procurement contracts in the European continent see MA Flamme, *Traité Théorique et Pratique des Marchés Publics* (Brussels, Bruylant, 1969); JB Auby, 'Les problèmes posés par le développent du contrat en droit administratif comparé' in G Clamour and M Ubaud-Bergeron (eds), *Contrats Publics, Mélanges en l'honneur du Professeur Michel Guibal*, Vol 1 (Montpellier, Presses de la Faculté de Droit de Montpellier, 2006) 411; JB Auby, 'Comparative Approaches to the Rise of the Contract in Public Sphere' (2007) 1 *Public Law* 40; Fromont (n 1). Comba has suggested a classification of the existing legal traditions based on the 'legal location' of the rules that award public contractors special powers during the execution phase of contracts. See M Comba, 'Contract Execution in Europe: Different Legal Models with a Common Core' (2013) 3 *European Procurement & Public-Private Partnership Law Review* 302–08. Similarly, P Craig has attempted a typology based on the specific powers of public contractors. See P Craig, 'Specific Powers of Public Contractors' in R Noguellou and U Stelkens (eds), *Droit comparé des contrats publics* (Brussels, Bruylant, 2010). See also M Amilhat, *La notion du contrat administratif – L'influence du droit communautaire* (Brussels, Bruylant, 2014).

[12] See ch 3.

[13] C Guettier, *Droit des contrats administratifs* (Paris, Presses Universitaires de France, 2004) 424.

[14] EEA Agreement concluded between 27 EU Member States and three European Free Trade Association (EFTA) states, Iceland, Liechtenstein, and Norway, established a single market in public procurement. Under the EEA Agreement, EFTA countries have committed to adapting key provisions of Directive 2014/24/EU. Art 65 Agreement on the European Economic Area – Final Act [1994] OJ L 1/3 Annexe XVI 'Procurement'.

[15] Public procurement in Switzerland is governed by a multi-level framework comprising international agreements, as well as federal, cantonal, and communal legislation. Notably, Swiss public procurement law is influenced by international treaties, including the Bilateral Agreement between the European Community and Switzerland on Certain Aspects of Public Procurement, signed on 21 June 1999, which aligns certain Swiss rules with EU public procurement standards. See more ch 11.

[16] See ch 3. The relevant private contract law refers specifically to business-to-business (B2B), commercial contracts between professionals in trade or commerce as opposed to consumer or employment contract law.

account for their public nature.[17] These adaptations ensure the protection of public interest and alignment with fiscal law requirements. (eg the principles of efficiency and economy in preparing and executing the budget).[18]

The existence of 'public model' and 'private model', which refers to the application of public or private law to contractual matters in the performance stage of public contracts, is undisputed in legal doctrine.[19] Nevertheless, the demarcation lines and the complex, opaque interactions between the applications of public and private law remain fertile ground for new research. Numerous research questions, including those examined in this anthology, await exploration.

This chapter provides background for the research developed in the subsequent contributions. It begins with a brief historical overview of the Europeanisation of public procurement law in section II and then examines how the legal nature of the procurement award has been classified and interpreted in different Member States. Section III introduces the autonomous concept of the EU public contract and outlines its defining characteristics. Section IV explores whether the EU concept of a public contract shares features with contracts as understood in contract law. This structure is intentional: by analysing public contracts from both EU public procurement and contract law perspectives, the chapter identifies key points of entry into the broader debate. This dual lens highlights the chapter's central focus within this anthology – the public contract as, ultimately, a business transaction contract. Section V considers the spillover effect of EU public procurement law on the performance of public contracts, identifying areas regulated under Directive 2014/24/EU and, by contrast, those that remain within Member State competence. The chapter concludes by establishing a clear transition to chapter three.

II. Europeanisation of Public Procurement Law

The Europeanisation of public procurement law, understood as the extension of EU law to areas previously governed by national laws of Member States, has

[17] See ch 3.

[18] For example, in Germany, prior to the Europeanisation of public procurement law above the EU thresholds, there was a strong connection between public procurement and fiscal law. This link provided the state with particularly advantageous conditions, both materially and procedurally, when acting within private law. While the EU rules introduced additional principles above the thresholds, particularly emphasising competition not merely as a tool for achieving fiscal goals, the area below the thresholds retained the designation *Haushaltsvergaberecht* (Budgetary procurement law). For a detailed discussion, see U Stelkens and H Schröder, 'Allemagne' in R Noguellou and U Stelkens (eds), *Droit comparé des contrats publics* (Brussels, Bruylant, 2010) 314. In the Netherlands, so-called 'flanking policies' introduce additional requirements for contracting authorities. A notable example is the Proportionality Guide ensuring compliance with the EU and Dutch proportionality principle (Gids Proportionaliteit, *Staatsblad* (*Stb*) 2018, 1 and *Stb* 2016, 242). See also more in ch 5.

[19] Comba, 'Contract Execution in Europe' (n 11); Fromont (n 1). See Craig (n 11); Auby, 'Comparative Approaches to the Rise of the Contract in Public Sphere' (n 11).

significantly influenced the regulation of public contracts.[20] This has occurred not only across the EU but also more broadly in Europe, including European Economic Area (EEA) countries and Switzerland.[21] Driven by harmonisation efforts, this process continuously aims to create a cohesive legal framework that promotes transparency, competition, equal treatment, and non-discrimination in public procurement processes. As a result, national legal systems have had to adapt their regulatory approaches to align with EU public procurement law, transforming how public contracts are conceived and executed.

The Agreement establishing the European Economic Community (EEC), signed in Rome on 25 March 1957, did not directly address the procurement activities of governments, local authorities, and public institutions.[22] Nevertheless, the Treaty of Rome established fundamental principles that were both directly and indirectly applicable to public procurement matters, including the prohibition of discrimination based on nationality, the free movement of goods, services, and establishment, the safeguarding of open competition, as well as the prohibitions on abusing a dominant position and granting state aid. Together, these principles provided the basis for the subsequent development of specific legislation, jurisprudence, and policy in the field of EU public procurement law.[23]

[20] P Huber, 'The Europeanization of Public Procurement in Germany' (2001) 7(1) *European Public Law* 36.

[21] See EEA Agreement (n 14); on Swiss public procurement law (n 15). See more ch 10.

[22] Treaty establishing the European Economic Community, [1957] OJ Spec Ed 1.

[23] For example, the CJEU has consistently found national requirements favouring domestic products, services, or operators to be contrary to Treaty provisions. In Case C-45/87 *Commission of the European Communities v Ireland* ECLI:EU:C:1988:435, [1988], it struck down a requirement for materials to be certified by the contracting country's standards authority, rejecting equivalent certification from another Member State (Art 28 [30]). Similarly, in Case C-359/93 *Commission of the European Communities v Kingdom of the Netherlands* ECLI:EU:C:1995:14, [1995] ECR I-00157 and Case C-328/96 *Commission of the European Communities v Republic of Austria* ECLI:EU:C:1999:526, [1999] ECR I-07479 specifying a branded operating system without adding 'or equivalent' was deemed a breach of Art 28 [30]. In Case C-243/89 *Commission of the European Communities v Kingdom of Denmark* ECLI:EU:C:1993:257, [1993] ECR I-03353, a clause mandating maximum use of domestic products, equipment, and labour violated Arts 28 [30], 39 [48], and 49 [59]. In Case C-21/88 *Du Pont de Nemours Italiana SpA v Unità sanitaria locale N° 2 di Carrara* ECLI:EU:C:1990:121, [1990] ECR I-00889 and Case C-351/88 *Laboratori Bruneau Srl v Unità sanitaria locale RM/24 di Monterotondo* ECLI:EU:C:1991:304, [1991] ECR I-03641, reserving parts of contracts for firms from a particular country or region breached Art 28 [30]. Restrictions on participation – such as limiting tenders to companies majority-owned by the Italian State in Case C-3/88 *Commission of the European Communities v Italian Republic* ECLI:EU:C:1989:606, [1989] ECR 04035, Arts 43 [52] and 49 [59], requiring national operating authorisations in Case C-76/81 *SA Transporoute et travaux v Minister of Public Works* ECLI:EU:C:1982:49, [1982] ECR 00417, Art 49 [59], or mandating work permits or national employment channels for staff in Case C-113/89 *Rush Portuguesa Ldª v Office national d'immigration* ECLI:EU:C:1990:142, [1990] ECR I-01417, Arts 49 [59] and 50 [60] – were also struck down. In Case C-225/98 *Commission of the European Communities v French Republic* ECLI:EU:C:2000:494, [2000] ECR I-07445, using only national nomenclature to describe a contract was found to hinder cross-border access (Art 49 [59]), and in Case C-249/81 *Commission of the European Communities v Ireland* ECLI:EU:C:1982:402, [1982] ECR 04005, state-supported campaigns promoting domestic products breached Art 28 [30].

The EU legislator's interest in the adoption of the 2014 Public Procurement Directives was driven by the need to give concrete effect to the Treaty provisions on the free movement. Prior to harmonisation, divergent national rules and protectionist practices created de facto barriers to the internal market. EU public procurement law established binding, uniform procedural standards to ensure transparency, equal treatment, non-discrimination, proportionality, open competition, and sustainability compliance, thereby operationalising Treaty principles through secondary legislation.[24] They also provided legal certainty for cross-border economic operators and created enforceable rights, supplemented by the Remedies Directives, thus aligning Member States' procurement regimes with the jurisprudence of the CJEU.

The World Trade Organization (WTO) Government Procurement Agreement (GPA), to which all EU Member States have been parties since the EU's accession in 1996, has also influenced the evolution of EU public procurement law.[25] Combined with CJEU jurisprudence, the GPA has prompted successive directives to progressively broaden their scope.[26]

[24] Art 18 Directive 2014/24/EU.

[25] WTO Agreement On Government Procurement, as amended on 30 March 2012 (GPA 2012).

[26] EU public procurement law has been evolving since the early 1960s. In 1962, for the first time, the Member States of the European Communities adopted two General Programmes aimed at eliminating barriers that prevented or hindered the participation of foreign entities in local public procurement markets. The objective was to unify public procurement markets in each country, open them to foreign operators, and eliminate discrimination. See C Bovis, *EU Procurement Law* (Cheltenham, Edward Elgar Publishing, 2012) 17. The primary aim of these provisions was also to remove national barriers and preferences favouring domestic contractors. To this end, the European Commission enacted two directives requiring contracting authorities to accept foreign products, particularly by allowing equivalent solutions: Commission Directive 66/683/EEC of 7 November 1966 eliminating all differences between the treatment of national products and that of products which, under Articles 9 and 10 of the Treaty, must be admitted for free movement, as regards laws, regulations or administrative provisions prohibiting the use of the said products and prescribing the use of national products or making such use subject to profitability [1966] OJ 220/3748; Commission Directive 70/32/EEC of 17 December 1969 on provision of goods to the State, to local authorities and other official bodies [1970] OJ L 13/1. The next stage in the development of EU public procurement law began with the adoption of Council Directive 71/305/EEC of 26 July 1971 concerning the co-ordination of procedures for the award of public works contracts [1971] OJ L 185/5; Council Directive 77/62/EEC of 21 December 1976 coordinating procedures for the award of public supply contracts [1976] OJ L 13/1. In 1985, the European Commission published European Commission, 'Completing the Internal Market: White Paper from the Commission to the European Council' COM(85)0310 final, indicating that many countries had largely failed to implement the then-applicable directives. This critical assessment prompted the development of new legislation aimed at eliminating issues arising from past practices. Consequently, in 1988, the Council of the European Communities adopted Council Directive 88/295/EEC of 22 March 1988 amending Directive 77/62/EEC relating to the coordination of procedures on the award of public supply contracts and repealing certain provisions of Directive 80/767/EEC [1988] OJ L 127/1. The liberalisation of trade provided for in international agreements in the early 1990s primarily involved the free movement of goods, excluding regulations on the provision of cross-border services. As a result, access to contracts of this kind was significantly restricted. The EU legislator sought to address this problem, leading to the introduction of Council Directive 92/50/EEC of 18 June 1992 relating to the coordination of procedures for the award of public service contracts [1992] OJ L 209/1, which aimed to pave the way for the liberalisation of services in public markets. In the early 1990s, steps were taken to merge all previous EU public procurement legislation and provide a uniform regulatory framework. In 1993, a consolidated public procurement regime was introduced with three directives: Council Directive 92/50/EEC;

This expansion has led to the 'publicisation' of the award stage in public procurement, particularly in countries following the 'private-oriented hybrid model', as well as in the UK, which was an EU Member State at the time.[27] Here, 'publicisation' refers to the permeation of private contract law – and its inherent freedom of contract – by values characteristic of public law, marking a shift away from the assumptions of classical private contract law.[28]

It is reflected in the growing intervention of public bodies into spheres once reserved for the autonomous conduct of private undertakings, systematically replacing private law solutions with public law regulation. This process also signifies the increasing presence of the public interest in areas traditionally left to the exclusive determination of the contracting parties and the dispersion of institutions and mechanisms tailored to the narrowly defined objectives of specific regulations.[29] A key feature of the 'publicisation' of EU public

Council Directive 93/36/EEC of 14 June 1993 on the coordination of procedures for the award of public supply contracts [1993] OJ L 199/1; Council Directive 93/37/EEC of 14 June 1993 on the coordination of procedures for the award of public works contracts [1993] OJ L 199/54. Directives 93/37/EEC, 92/50/EEC, and 93/36/EEC, known as the 'classical directives', coordinated procedures for the award of works, supply, and service contracts by state and local authorities and bodies governed by public law. Procedures for the award of contracts by entities operating in the water, energy, transport, and telecommunications sectors were regulated separately by the 'sectoral directives': Council Directive 92/13/EEC of 25 February 1992 coordinating the laws, regulations and administrative provisions relating to the application of Community rules on the procurement procedures of entities operating in the water, energy, transport and telecommunications sectors [1992] OJ L 76; Directive 94/22/EC of the European Parliament and of the Council of 30 May 1994 on the conditions for granting and using authorizations for the prospection, exploration and production of hydrocarbons [1994] OJ L 164/3; Directive 98/4/EC of the European Parliament and of the Council of 16 February 1998 amending Directive 93/38/EEC coordinating the procurement procedures of entities operating in the water, energy, transport and telecommunications sectors [1998] OJ L 101/1, which provided states with protection for parts of the economy that were particularly important to them. A Green Paper on public procurement in the EU was published in 1998. Consequently, in 2004, the EU adopted two new directives: Directive 2004/17/EC of the European Parliament and of the Council of 31 March 2004 coordinating the procurement procedures of entities operating in the water, energy, transport and postal services sectors [2004] OJ L 134/1; Directive 2004/18/EC of the European Parliament and of the Council of 31 March 2004 on the coordination of procedures for the award of public works contracts, public supply contracts and public service contracts [2004] OJ L 134/114. In early 2011, the EU Commission published the European Commission, 'Green paper on the Modernisation of EU Public Procurement Policy – Towards a More Efficient European Procurement Market' COM (2011)15 final. Contemporary references concern Directive 2014/23/EU, Directive 2014/24/EU, Directive 2014/25/EU referred to as the 2014 Public Procurement Directives and Directive 89/665/EEC and Directive 92/13/EEC as amended with Directive 2007/66/EC, referred to as the Remedies Directives.

[27] See ch 3.

[28] K Hesse, *Verfassungsrecht und Privatrecht* (Heidelberg, Müller, 1988) 2; M Goettel and A Goettel, 'Prawo cywilne a prawo podatkowe' in M Goettel and M Lemonnier (eds), *Instytucje prawa cywilnego w konstrukcji prawnej podatków* (Warsaw, Kluwer, 2011) 14. See also E McKendrick, 'Judicial Control of Contractual Discretion' in JB Auby and M Freedland (eds), *The Public Law/Private Law Divide* (Paris, Editions Pantheon-Assas, 2004) 195 indicating the process of public law values entering private law. See also H Keren, 'Undermining Justice: The Two Rises of Freedom of Contract and the Fall of Equity' (2016) 2 *Canadian Journal of Comparative and Contemporary Law* 339, 353.

[29] PS Atiyah, *The Rise and Fall of Freedom of Contract* (Oxford, Oxford University Press, 1979); H Dagan, 'The Limited Autonomy of Private Law' (2008) 56(3) *The American Journal of Comparative Law* 809, 811–13.

procurement law's award stage is the recognition of third-party rights enforceable through legal remedies, a development made possible by the adoption of the Remedies Directive.[30]

As a consequence of the 'publicisation' of the award stage, the principles of EU public procurement law are now embedded in a complex framework of legal mechanisms – including exclusion grounds,[31] procedural rules,[32] award criteria,[33] and the protection of third-party rights (eg unsuccessful bidders) – applicable from the initiation of the procurement procedure through the conclusion of the public contract, and, to a limited extent, during its performance.

Beyond the Europeanisation and publicisation of public procurement, a further question concerns the legal nature of the award stage under national law, whether it differs from the performance phase, and the consequences of such a classification.[34]

A. Legal Nature of the Award Stage in Member States

Determining the legal nature of the award phase and the contract performance phase remains an open question in several Member States. In some states, the procedures for awarding contracts and overseeing contract performance are based on the so-called 'Two-stage theory' (*Zweistufentheorie*). The latter was established in Germany for the granting of subsidies (and later also the access to public facilities), noting that the award and the contract performance in Germany are generally based on private law.[35] According to *Zweistufentheorie*, when a public administration decides whether to enter into a legal relationship with a private company, that decision is typically classified as an administrative act – this constitutes the first

[30] See Huber (n 20); M Ruffert, 'Rights and Remedies in European Community Law: A Comparative View' (1997) 34(2) *Common Market Law Review* 307. See also more in ch 4 and ch 12.

[31] Art 57 Directive 2014/24/EU.

[32] ibid Arts 26–32.

[33] ibid Art 67. In Switzerland, Art 12 Swiss Federal Act on Public Procurement is the equivalent of Art 18 Directive 2014/24/EU and requires suppliers of federal public contracts to comply with health and safety regulations, labour conditions, equal pay for men and women and environmental law 'at the place of performance'. If suppliers do not comply, for example, with mandatory labour law, the procurement agency can exclude them from the tender. see *Bundesgesetz über das öffentliche Beschaffungswesen* of 21 June 2019 (Federal Law Gazette 172.056.1) (Swiss Federal Act on Public Procurement). See also Art 27 Swiss Federal Act on Public Procurement.

[34] On consequences, see ch 3.

[35] Bundesverwaltungsgericht (Federal Administrative Court), Decision of 2 May 2007 – BVerwG 6 B 10.07, BVerwGE 129, 9, 13 et seq; M Burgi, *Vergaberecht*, 3rd edn (Munich, CH Beck, 2021) s 2 paras 9–15. Since the legislature has in principle assigned public procurement law above the thresholds to private law the German Administrative Procedures Act (Verwaltungsverfahrensgesetz (*Verwaltungsverfahrensgesetz* (VwVfG), 1976, BGBl I 1253, as amended) is not applicable to the award procedure. See eg, W Kahl, 'Privatrechtliches Verwaltungshandeln und Verwaltungsverfahrensgesetz am Beispiel des Vergaberechts' in M Aschke and F von Zezschwitz (eds), *Selbstbestimmung und Gemeinwohl. Festschrift zum 70. Geburtstag von Professor Dr. Friedrich von Zezschwitz* (Baden-Baden, Nomos, 2005) 151 (154 et seq).

or 'if' stage.[36] However, how this legal relationship is executed ('how' stage), often involving the fulfilment of an obligation imposed on a public authority, can fall under either private or public law.[37]

Amongst others, Switzerland applies the *Zweistufentheorie*. Swiss law and doctrine distinguish between the internal decision-making process of public authorities, which leads to the public administrative decision to award a contract ('if'), and the subsequent conclusion of the contract itself, which is governed by private contract law ('how').[38] The same theory has also been adopted in Latvia.[39] In the case of public procurement in the first stage, the contracting authority takes an administrative decision, which indicates who will be granted the right to conclude a public contract. In the second stage, it implements the decision through private law. The implementation of private law begins with the conclusion of a public contract, which is recognised as a private law contract in most cases.[40]

In Croatia, the Croatian Public Procurement Act does not explicitly define an award decision as an administrative act.[41] However, following a recent Supreme Court judgment classifying public contracts as administrative contracts, award decisions are now regarded as administrative acts, since the conclusion of an administrative contract requires the implementation of obligations arising from a prior administrative act.[42]

[36] Developed for the granting of subsidies by HP Ipsen, 'Rechtsgutachten über das Verfahren und den Rechtsschutz bei der Gewährung und Verweigerung von Ausfallbürgschaften des Bundes für Filmproduktionskredite' (17 December 1951, unpublished) – first published in K Vogel and K Tipke (eds), *Festschrift für Gerhard Wacke* (Cologne, Verlag Dr Otto Schmidt, 1972) 139, 140 et seq; HP Ipsen, *Öffentliche Subventionierung Privater* (Cologne, Carl Heymanns Verlag, 1956) 59 et seq.

[37] Ipsen, 'Rechtsgutachten über das Verfahren und den Rechtsschutz bei der Gewährung und Verweigerung von Ausfallbürgschaften des Bundes für Filmproduktionskredite' (n 36); Ipsen, *Öffentliche Subventionierung Privater* (n 36).

[38] U Häfelin, G Müller, and F Uhlmann, *Allgemeines Verwaltungsrecht*, 8th edn (Zurich, Dike Verlag, 2020) 316 and 317.

[39] E Danovskis, *Publisko un privāto tiesību dalījuma nozīme un piemērošanas problēmas Latvijā* (Riga, Latvijas Vēstnesis, 2015) 198–99, 202. After the restoration of independence of the Republic of Latvia, the conceptual basis for the development of legal scholarship in the field of administrative law was provided by publications that set out the background of administrative law mostly in terms of the German administrative law system and basic concepts. See J Briede, E Danovskis, and A Kovaļevska, *Administratīvās tiesības. Mācību grāmata. Otrais izdevums* (Riga, Tiesu namu aģentūra, 2021) 21. Therefore, the two-stage theory has also been borrowed from the German legal system. However, it has also been noted that its application in Latvia is limited. It has been explained in the legal doctrine that in the case of the two-stage theory in Latvia, the fact that the decision is taken in the public law field stems not from the criteria used to distinguish between public and private law but from the reasons of expediency of the legislator that the legality of the decision should be verifiable under the administrative process. See ibid 21 and 27–28. Also see the Judgment of 4 April 2022 of the Senate of the Supreme Court of the Republic of Latvia, Department of Administrative Cases No A420159119, SKA-226/2022, ECLI:LV:AT:2022:0404.A420159119.7.S, para 13.

[40] Decision of 27 November 2009 of the Senate of the Supreme Court of the Republic of Latvia, Department of Administrative Cases in case no A8033609/25, SKA-853/2009, para 14 and ch 4.2.1. Regarding procurement in Latvia, see F Vaivods, 'Publiskā iepirkuma divējādā tiesiskā daba' (2004) *Likums un Tiesības* Nos 316, 317.

[41] Art 302 *Zakon o javnoj nabavi*, NN 120/2016 i 114/2022 (Croatian Public Procurement Act).

[42] Supreme court Judgment of 8 November 2023, Rev 139/2023-5. See eg M Turudić, 'Pravna priroda ugovora o javnoj nabavi u hrvatskom pravnom poretku' (2018) 9(34) *Sveske za javno pravo* 10.

In Czechia, the administrative character of decisions and actions taken in the award stage can be deduced from chapter three of the Czech Act on Public Procurement titled 'Administrative delicts' that outlines which decisions of contracting authorities can amount to an administrative delict, and from the possibility to challenge those within an administrative proceeding.[43] Such an approach can be supported in combination with legal practice and case law.[44]

In Belgium, the theory of the 'Detachable act' is applied. This legal concept, of French origin, was adopted in Belgian administrative law in the middle of the twentieth century.[45] It is based on the legal fiction that unilateral administrative acts issued by an administrative authority can be separated from the formation of a contract. This allows such acts to be challenged before the Council of State, which, as the highest administrative court in Belgium, exercises jurisdiction over administrative acts.[46]

In France, the theory of the 'detachable act' no longer plays a role when it comes to the award of a public contract since the Conseil d'Etat (Council of State, which is the highest administrative court in France) introduced a direct remedy for third parties called 'Recours Tarn-et-Garonne' in 2014.[47]

In Denmark, neither the Danish Public Procurement Act[48] nor the Danish Act on the Complaints Board for Public Procurement[49] explicitly defines an award decision as an administrative act. But these acts establish a type of *sui generis* administrative law for the award of contracts which are within the scope of EU public procurement law, and the Danish Complaints Board for Public Procurement applies principles of administrative law in its approach, for example when performing its judicial review of the contracting authority's exercise of its discretion in procurement decisions.[50] For contracts which are outside the scope of EU public procurement law and which do not have a certain cross-border interest, section 193(5) Danish Public Procurement Act states explicitly that a contracting

[43] Title II, Chs 1 and 2 *Zákon o zadávání veřejných zakázek* Act No. 134/2016 Coll (Czech Public Procurement Act).

[44] eg Supreme Administrative Court of the Czech Republic, 1 Afs 2/2013 – 46, para 23 (Thus, if the Supreme Administrative Court in the past considered certain actions taken during the tendering procedure in such a way that they exceeded the boundaries of private law and entered into public law, then the contracting authority's decision to exclude a bidder from the tender procedure undoubtedly falls within this category as well).

[45] The theory of the detachable act is generally traced back to the famous Conseil d'Etat ruling of 4 August 1905 'Martin' (D 1907, 3, 49, *concl. Romieu*), which ruled on an appeal against the deliberations of a general council relating to a tramway concession. This was a reaction towards the ban set by the Conseil d'Etat itself, to open judicial review to public contracts (CE 19 May 1899, Levrieux, Rec 401) see Richer and Lichère (n 5).

[46] See S Van Garsse, *Handboek Bestuursrecht* (Brussels, Academic & Scientific Publishers, 2023) 30.

[47] CE Ass 4 April 2014, *Département du Tarn-et-Garonne*, 358994.

[48] *Udbudsloven* no 2015/1564 (Danish Public Procurement Act), which transposes the 2014 Public Procurement Directives into Danish law.

[49] *Lov om Klagenævnet for Udbud* no 593/2016 (Danish Danish Act on the Complaints Board for Public Procurement), which transposes the Remedies Directives into Danish law.

[50] ibid. The Danish Complaints Board for Public Procurement is the Danish administrative body entrusted with the handling of complaints related to the 2014 Public Procurement Directives.

authority in its procurement procedures must act in accordance with general principles of Danish administrative law, including the principle of equal treatment and proportionality. When the public contract has been signed, the procurement rules are said to have exhausted their function, and the contract is subsequently governed by private contract law.

Under Polish public procurement law, the award phase is regarded in legal doctrine as an example of the 'publicisation' of private law.[51] However, this does not imply that administrative law, including the Polish Administrative Procedure Code, is directly applicable at this stage.[52] The provisions of the Polish Civil Code apply additionally to actions undertaken by contracting authorities and economic operators in procurement procedures, unless otherwise specified by the Polish Public Procurement Act.[53] Consequently, Polish legal doctrine characterises the award phase as having a distinct, hybrid legal nature and treats it as a form of cross-branch regulation.[54] The conclusion of the public contract and its performance phase are also subject to both public procurement law and the Polish Civil Code. However, the public contract itself is classified as a civil law contract.[55]

According to the Dutch legislator, the decisions that a contracting authority takes prior to and during a procurement procedure are preparatory acts leading to the conclusion of a private law contract.[56] The legal relation between the contracting authority and the participating economic operators is considered a pre-contractual legal relationship governed by private law principles, in particular the duty of good faith (*goede trouw*).[57]

Having briefly examined the Europeanisation of public procurement law and the legal nature of the award stage in Member States, attention now shifts to the formation of the contract itself. At this juncture, it is essential to distinguish between the EU's autonomous notion of a 'public contract', developed to define the scope of EU public procurement law and ensure its uniform application, and the concept of a contract in private contract law, which serves as the instrument for determining the mutual rights and obligations of the parties.

[51] K Horubski, 'Publicyzacja prawa prywatnego w obszarze prawa zamówień publicznych' (2018) 540 *Prace Naukowe Uniwersytetu Ekonomicznego we Wrocławiu* 79.

[52] *Ustawa z dnia 14 czerwca 1960 r – Kodeks postępowania administracyjnego* (Polish Administrative Procedure Code). See differently J Niczyporuk, 'Forma prawna wyboru najkorzystniejszej oferty' in M Stręciwilk and A Panasiuk (eds), *Funkcjonowanie systemu zamówień publicznych – aktualne problemy i propozycje rozwiązań* (Warsaw, Urząd Zamówień Publicznych, 2017) 81.

[53] *Ustawa z dnia 23 kwietnia 1964 r. – Kodeks cywilny* (Polish Civil Code); Art 8 *Ustawa z dnia 11 września 2019 r. – Prawo zamówień publicznych* (Polish Public Procurement Act).

[54] H Nowicki, P Nowicki, and M Wierzbowski, 'Nowe dyrektywy zamówieniowe a polskie prawo zamówień publicznych. Uwagi de lege ferenda' in H Nowicki and P Nowicki (eds), *Prawo zamówień publicznych. Stan obecny i kierunki zmian* (Wroclaw, Presscom, 2015) 1.

[55] H Nowak and M Winiarz (eds), *Prawo zamówień publicznych. Komentarz*, 2nd edn (Warsaw, Urząd Zamówień Publicznych, 2023) 1081.

[56] Art 8:3(2) *Algemene wet bestuursrecht* (Awb) (Dutch General Administrative Law Act).

[57] S Prent, *De redelijk handelende aanbesteder: Over de wisselwerking tussen het Europees aanbestedingsrecht en het Nederlands verbintenissenrecht bij een aanbestedingsprocedure* (Meppel, Boom juridisch, 2021) 84.

III. The Concept and Legal Nature of the EU Public Contract

A public contract is recognised as an autonomous concept under EU law, and as such, it forms a key element in defining what constitutes EU public procurement.[58] Furthermore, it plays a central role in determining the scope of the 2014 Public Procurement Directives.[59] Thus, the concept seems to operate more as a 'reference point' rather than a definition.[60] Importantly, the concept must be interpreted functionally, regardless of its classification under national legal systems.[61] This helps ensure that Directive 2014/24/EU captures all acquisitions involving risks of national preference and prevents significant divergence in coverage due to irrelevant criteria, such as how domestic law defines a contract.[62] Relying on national definitions would enable Member States to circumvent the rules by creating special non-contractual regimes for certain types of procurement. As Janssen notes, permitting alternative national interpretations would allow different forms of public contracts to emerge across Member States, undermining the consistent application of EU public procurement law.[63] However, as Arrowsmith argues, this inconsistency alone does not necessitate the introduction of an EU definition. As with other cases of bad faith, such issues could be addressed through a separate principle of applying EU public procurement law to the actual cases of abuse rather than through rigid rules that might unduly restrict the legitimate discretion of Member States.[64]

It should be emphasised that the label given to an agreement is not determinative. Even if a contracting authority does not formally refer to an agreement as a contract, it may still fall within the scope of a public contract definition under EU public procurement law if it meets the substantive criteria.[65]

[58] Art 1(2) Directive 2014/24/EU, 'Procurement within the meaning of this Directive is the acquisition by means of a *public contract* of works, supplies or services by one or more contracting authorities from economic operators chosen by those contracting authorities, whether or not the works, supplies or services are intended for a public purpose'. See Case C-220/05 *Jean Auroux and Others v Commune de Roanne* ECLI:EU:C:2007:31, [2007] ECR I-00385 para 40.

[59] See Case C-367/19 *Tax-Fin-Lex d.o.o. v Ministrstvo za notranje zadeve* ECLI:EU:C:2020:685, [2020] para 29.

[60] See A Sanchez-Graells, 'Article 2 Definitions' in R Caranta and A Sanchez-Graells (eds), *European Public Procurement: Commentary on Directive 2014/24/EU* (Cheltenham, Edward Elgar Publishing, 2021) 25.

[61] See Opinion of AG Kokott of 15 June 2006 in Case C-220/05 *Jean Auroux and Others v Commune de Roanne* ECLI:EU:C:2006:410, [2006] ECR I-00385 para 79. See also Case C-399/98 *Ordine degli Architetti delle province di Milano e Lodi, Piero De Amicis, Consiglio Nazionale degli Architetti and Leopoldo Freyrie v Comune di Milano, and Pirelli SpA, Milano Centrale Servizi SpA and Fondazione Teatro alla Scala* ECLI:EU:C:2001:401, [2001] ECR I-05409 para 65.

[62] S Arrowsmith, *The Law of Public and Utilities Procurement*, Vol 1, 3rd edn (London, Sweet & Maxwell, 2014) 388.

[63] WA Janssen, *EU Public Procurement Law & Self-organisation: A Nexus of Tensions & Reconciliations* (The Hague, Eleven Publishers, 2018) 55.

[64] See Arrowsmith (n 62) 388.

[65] Case C-382/05 *Commission of the European Communities v Italian Republic* ECLI:EU:C:2007:445, [2007] ECR I-06657.

A. Characteristics of a Public Contract under Directive 2014/24/EU

According to Article 2(1)(5) Directive 2014/24/EU, 'public contracts' are defined as:

> contracts for pecuniary interest[66] concluded in writing[67] between one or more economic operators[68] and one or more contracting authorities,[69] and having as their object the execution of works, the supply of products, or the provision of services.[70]

These characteristics distinguish public contracts from other forms of public sector activity and provide the legal foundation for determining whether EU public procurement law applies.[71]

i. In Writing

One of the characteristics of a public contract under the EU legal framework is that it must be concluded in writing. This requirement is generally uncontroversial, though it may give rise to legal questions at later stages, particularly in the context of contract modifications, for example, whether tacit modification of a public contract is permitted.[72] Article 2(18) Directive 2014/24/EU clarifies what is understood under the 'in writing' requirement:

> The written form encompasses any expression consisting of words or figures that can be read, reproduced, and subsequently communicated, including information transmitted and stored by electronic means.[73]

[66] The CJEU analysed the 'pecuniary interest' concept in Case C-606/17 *IBA Molecular Italy Srl v Azienda ULSS n. 3 and Others* ECLI:EU:C:2018:843, [2018]; Case C-796/18 *Informatikgesellschaft für Software-Entwicklung (ISE) mbH v Stadt Köln* ECLI:EU:C:2020:395, [2020]; C-367/19 *Tax-Fin-Lex* (n 59).

[67] Art 2(1)(18) Directive 2014/24/EU. See Joined cases C-441/22 and C-443/22 *Obshtina Razgrad and Obshtina Balchik* ECLI:EU:C:2023:970, [2023].

[68] Art 2(1)(10) Directive 2014/24/EU. See Case C-305/08 *Consorzio Nazionale Interuniversitario per le Scienze del Mare (CoNISMa) v Regione Marche* ECLI:EU:C:2009:807, [2009] ECR I-12129; Case C-568/13 *Azienda Ospedaliero Universitaria di Careggi-Firenze v Data Medical Service srl* ECLI:EU:C:2014:2466, [2014]; Case C-203/14 *Consorci Sanitari del Maresme v Corporació de Salut del Maresme i la Selva* ECLI:EU:C:2015:664, [2015]; Case C-396/14 *MT Højgaard A/S and Züblin A/S v Banedanmark* ECLI:EU:C:2016:347, [2016].

[69] Art 2(1)(1) Directive 2014/24/EU. See Case C-44/96 *Mannesmann Anlagenbau Austria AG and Others v Strohal Rotationsdruck GesmbH* ECLI:EU:C:1998:4, [1998] ECR I-00073; Case C-373/00 *Adolf Truley GmbH v Bestattung Wien GmbH* ECLI:EU:C:2002:207, [2002] ECR I-01931; Case C-606/17 *IBA Molecular Italy Srl* (n 66); Case C-567/15 *UAB „LitSpecMet" v UAB Vilniaus lokomotyvų remonto depas* ECLI:EU:C:2017:736, [2017].

[70] Footnotes added by authors. See eg Case C-367/19 *Tax-Fin-Lex* (n 59); Case C-51/15 *Remondis GmbH & Co. KG Region Nord v Region Hannover* ECLI:EU:C:2016:985, [2016].

[71] Art 2(5) Directive 2014/24/EU.

[72] See Joined Cases C-441/22 and C-443/22 *Obshtina Razgrad* (n 67) paras 57–59; and ch 8.

[73] See ch 10. See also M Andhov, CB Andersen and T Hebbard, 'A Roadmap to Simplify Procurement? The Potential of Visual Contracting in Australian and Danish Systems' (2025) 34(1) *Public Procurement Law Review* 47.

Concluding contracts in writing serves a dual function: it ensures transparency during the procurement process, allowing tenderers to understand and challenge decisions where appropriate, and facilitates subsequent verification that the applicable EU public procurement law has been observed.[74] Moreover, the written form contributes to legal certainty. This is particularly vital for complex and long-term infrastructure projects, where clear documentation of mutual obligations is essential.[75] Given these considerations, it is difficult to envisage a rational and transparent public administration entering into public contracts in any form other than writing.

ii. Involving Pecuniary Interest

Another feature of a public contract under the EU legal framework is that it must be concluded for pecuniary interest. While Directive 2014/24/EU refers to this requirement in Article 2(1)(5), it does not define the term, leaving its interpretation to the CJEU. Within the existing legal framework, the notion of pecuniary interest is closely linked to the concept of consideration. The CJEU adopts a broad interpretation of this requirement.[76] As Advocate General (AG) Bobek observed, a purely literal or systemic reading is insufficient to grasp the full meaning of 'contract for pecuniary interest', particularly given the nuanced notion of consideration embedded within the concept of contract itself.[77] Typically, the term implies that each party undertakes to provide something of value to the other, although this does not necessarily have to involve a direct monetary payment from the contracting authority.[78] This approach is supported by several key rulings. In *Spezzino*, the Court made clear that a contract does not fall outside the scope of the public contract under EU public procurement law merely because the remuneration is limited to the reimbursement of costs incurred in delivering the agreed service.[79] Similarly, in *Tax-Fin-Lex*, the Court addressed a scenario involving a zero-euro bid, concluding that pecuniary interest may be satisfied by a form of consideration other than monetary payment, as long as some value is exchanged.[80]

[74] M Steinicke, 'Commentary to Article 2§1(18)' in M Steinicke and PL Vesterdorf (eds), *Brussels Commentary on EU Public Procurement Law* (Oxford, Bloomsbury Publishing, 2018).

[75] P Bogdanowicz, *Contract Modifications in EU Procurement Law* (Cheltenham, Edward Elgar Publishing, 2021) 11.

[76] Opinion of AG Kokott (n 61) para 57. For more information on the inadequacy of regulations concerning pecuniary interest concerning current market needs, see A Sanchez-Graells, 'Expanding the Scope of EU Public Procurement Law Realigning the Classic Directive with Its Internal Market Logic while Improving Its Fit with Strategic Procurement?' (2025) *Social Science Research Network*, <dx.doi.org/10.2139/ssrn.5213497> 7–9.

[77] Opinion of AG Bobek delivered on 28 May 2020 in Case C-367/19 *Tax-Fin-Lex d.o.o. v Ministrstvo za notranje zadeve*, ECLI:EU:C:2020:400, [2020] para 40.

[78] ibid para 54; and Case C-606/17 *IBA Molecular Italy* (n 66) para 28.

[79] See Case C-113/13 *Azienda sanitaria locale n. 5 'Spezzino' and Others v San Lorenzo Soc. coop. Sociale and Croce Verde Cogema cooperativa sociale Onlus* ECLI:EU:C:2014:2440, [2014] para 37.

[80] Case C-367/19 *Tax-Fin-Lex* (n 59) para 25.

However, the CJEU has made clear that a contract under which the contracting authority is not legally obliged to provide any consideration in return for what the other party undertakes does not qualify as a public contract for pecuniary interest within the meaning of Directive 2014/24/EU.[81] In other words, mere benefit to the authority is insufficient – there must be a binding obligation to provide something in exchange. This point was reinforced in *NFŠ*, where the Court emphasised the synallagmatic nature of a public contract, that is, a structure of reciprocal and legally enforceable obligations. For a contract to meet the pecuniary interest requirement, both parties must benefit from the arrangement, and both must be bound by obligations that can be enforced under law.[82] Thus, the determining factor is whether the public contract creates a mutual exchange of legally binding consideration of economic value.[83]

iii. Parties to the Contract (Bilateralism)

EU public procurement law further stipulates that a public contract must be concluded between one or more economic operators and one or more contracting authorities. This requirement underlines the necessity of a bilateral legal relationship, where both parties voluntarily assume obligations under enforceable terms. Thus, a valid public contract presupposes the agreement of at least two parties on the subject matter, thereby binding themselves to the legal consequences of that agreement.[84] The formation of such a public contract requires that the terms be agreed upon with sufficient precision to define the mutual rights and obligations of each party, ensuring the public contract can be meaningfully performed.[85] This bilateral requirement was examined in *Tragsa*, where the Court clarified that if a contractor lacks the ability to negotiate, whether regarding acceptance of the tasks or the setting of remuneration, then the arrangement cannot be classified as a public contract.[86] The essential element of contractual autonomy would be absent.

Further emphasis on bilateralism appears in Recital 34 Directive 2014/24/EU, which explicitly excludes purely administrative relationships from the scope of EU public procurement law. For instance, when a legal entity acts merely as an internal instrument or technical service under national law, following binding orders from the contracting authority without any say in remuneration, it does not enter into a public contract. Such arrangements fall outside the public procurement procedures.

[81] ibid para 27; and also Opinion of AG Bobek (n 77) paras 63–65.

[82] Case C-28/23 *NFŠ a.s. v Slovenská republika konajúca prostredníctvom Ministerstva školstva, vedy, výskumu a športu Slovenskej republiky and Ministerstvo školstva, vedy, výskumu a športu Slovenskej republiky* ECLI:EU:C:2024:893, [2024] para 44.

[83] See Opinion of AG Bobek (n 77) para 57. See Janssen (n 63) 65.

[84] See Janssen (n 63) 57.

[85] See Opinion of AG Bobek (n 77) para 58.

[86] See Case C-295/05 *Asociación Nacional de Empresas Forestales (Asemfo) v Transformación Agraria SA (Tragsa) and Administración del Estado* ECLI:EU:C:2007:227, [2007] ECR I-02999 para 54.

iv. *Subject Matter of the Public Contract*

The subject matter of a public contract must concern the execution of works, the supply of products, or the provision of services. However, there is no requirement for the purchase in question to be made for a public purpose.[87]

Based on this classification, Directive 2014/24/EU establishes a taxonomy of public contracts, distinguishing between public works contracts, public supply contracts, and public service contracts.[88] This categorisation serves several important purposes. Notably, it determines the applicability thresholds of EU public procurement law, which are considerably higher for public works contracts due to their typically greater value and complexity.[89] It also informs the scope of derogations and exceptions, particularly in relation to certain types of services.[90] Directive 2014/24/EU introduces a lighter, more flexible regime for specific categories of social and other public service contracts, recognising their distinct nature and public interest dimensions.[91]

Discussion of the subject matter of public contracts inevitably connects with the broader concept of acquisition, which appears in the definition of public procurement. Acquisitions falling within the scope of EU public procurement law are not limited to outright purchases; they may also involve leasing or other contractual arrangements that deliver the relevant benefit to the contracting authority. Thus, the notion of acquisition must be interpreted broadly: it encompasses the act of obtaining the use or benefit of works, supplies, or services, even where no transfer of ownership to the contracting authorities occurs.[92]

B. Public Contract and Other Legal Arrangements

The specific legal characteristics of public contracts distinguish them from other forms of cooperation between the public sector and private entities. However, the boundary is not always clear-cut.[93] It is, nevertheless, essential to maintain this distinction, as EU public procurement law applies exclusively to public contracts, a defined legal category subject to specific procedural rules.

The CJEU has addressed the mentioned distinction in several rulings. In *Falk Pharma*, the Court introduced the notion of selectivity as a distinctive feature of public contracts. In the case concerned, the Court noted that a contractual scheme

[87] Art 1(2) Directive 2014/24/EU.
[88] ibid Arts 2(1)(6), 2(1)(8), 2(1)(9).
[89] ibid Art 4.
[90] ibid Art 10.
[91] ibid Arts 74–77.
[92] ibid Recital 4. See also Case C-126/03 *Commission of the European Communities v Federal Republic of Germany* ECLI:EU:C:2004:728, [2004] ECR I-11197 para 18.
[93] The literature highlights the lack of a clear definition of a public contract and its potential inappropriateness for current challenges. See, eg Sanchez-Graells (n 76).

does not constitute a public contract where a contracting authority intends to acquire goods on the market by allowing any economic operator, throughout the validity of the scheme, to commit to supplying those goods under predetermined conditions, without selecting among the interested operators, and permits them to join the scheme at any point during its duration.[94] This reasoning was further developed in *Tirkkonen*, where the Court held that a scheme does not constitute a public contract if a public entity simply accepts all economic operators who meet the eligibility criteria and pass the required assessment set out in the invitation to tender, without conducting any selection among them, even if no new operators can join the scheme during its limited period of validity.[95] Similarly, in *ASADE*, the Court distinguished public contracts from arrangements in which the contracting authority does not compare or evaluate competing offers, nor designates any specific operator to be awarded a contractual exclusivity. Such procedures fall outside the scope of the public contract definition and EU public procurement law.[96]

The need to distinguish public contracts from grants was considered in *Cambridge*.[97] The Court held that payments made merely to finance or support an organisation's general activities, without requiring specific services in return, qualify as public financing (ie grants). In contrast, where payments are made in exchange for defined deliverables, such as research tasks or the organisation of conferences, the arrangement constitutes a public contract.[98] What distinguishes the two is the requirement for consideration: a public contract exists only where the contracting authority receives something of substance in return.

Closely related to public contracts are concession contracts.[99] While this anthology does not address concession contracts in detail, they are discussed briefly here to clarify the legal and functional differences.[100]

Concession contracts have emerged over time as a separate category under EU law, originally grounded in the interplay between national administrative and civil law traditions.[101] Although they share certain formal characteristics with public

[94] Case C-410/14 *Dr. Falk Pharma GmbH v DAK-Gesundheit* ECLI:EU:C:2016:399, [2016] paras 38 and 42.

[95] Case C-9/17 *Proceedings brought by Maria Tirkkonen* ECLI:EU:C:2018:142, [2018] para 41.

[96] Case C-436/20 *Asociación Estatal de Entidades de Servicios de Atención a Domicilio (ASADE) v Consejería de Igualdad y Políticas Inclusivas* ECLI:EU:C:2022:559, [2022] para 68.

[97] Case C-380/98 *The Queen v H.M. Treasury, ex parte The University of Cambridge* ECLI:EU:C:2000:529, [2000] ECR I-08035 paras 21 and 22.

[98] ibid para 24.

[99] See more about the origins of concession contracts in R Caranta and P Patrito, 'An Intellectual History of Concessions and PPP Law' in P Bogdanowicz, R Caranta, and P Telles (eds), *Public-Private Partnerships and Concessions in the EU: An Unfinished Legislative Framework* (Cheltenham, Edward Elgar Publishing, 2020).

[100] See more, eg P Bogdanowicz, 'Regulation of PPP and Concessions in European Union Law – Different But Equal' in P Bogdanowicz, R Caranta, and P Telles (eds), *Public-Private Partnerships and Concessions in the EU: An Unfinished Legislative Framework* (Cheltenham, Edward Elgar Publishing, 2020) 1–3.

[101] Case C-134/05 *Commission of the European Communities v Italian Republic* ECLI:EU:C:2007:435, [2007] ECR I-06251 para 31. In France, concessions originated as royal privileges allowing private individuals to use public property for constructing infrastructure such as waterworks, municipal facilities, bridges, and ports, as well as exploiting natural resources. Over time, these concessions extended to

contracts, such as the requirement to be concluded in writing, for pecuniary interest, and between one or more economic operators and one or more contracting authorities or entities, they are governed by a separate legal instrument.[102]

The primary difference lies in the structure of remuneration and the transfer of operational risk in concession contracts. In contrast to public contracts, where the contractor is paid directly by the contracting authority, concession contracts typically involve a situation in which the concessionaire derives remuneration from the right to exploit the works or services, often by charging third-party users.

This distinction was clarified by the CJEU in *Parking Brixen*, where the Court ruled that when the concessionaire's remuneration is not paid by the public authority but rather by users of a service or facility, and when this method of remuneration entails that the concessionaire bears the risk of operating the service, the agreement qualifies as a public service concession rather than a public contract.[103] The same principle was affirmed in *Eurawasser*, where the Court confirmed that when the provider's compensation consists of the right to exploit the service, it also implies that the provider assumes the economic risk of performance.[104]

In practical terms, the concessionaire's revenue depends on market performance and user uptake, with no guarantee of payment from the public authority.[105] This transfer of operational and financial risk is the core element that distinguishes concession contracts from public contracts and accounts for their different legal treatment under EU law.

Thus, it follows from the above that there might be instances in which certain arrangements will not be classified as contractual in domestic law for the purpose

larger public domains, particularly in overseas territories, and often involved the delegation of limited public authority to concessionaires. See X Bézançon, 'Histoire du droit concessionnaire en France' (2005) 38(1) *Entreprises et Histoire* 24, 25. In Germany, the concession model initially mirrored the French approach but diverged in the late 18th century under Prussian and Austrian influence. A dual legal structure developed: a civil law contract granted property and exploitation rights, while administrative acts conferred public authority (eg expropriation for roads, railways, and water supply). See R Szostak, *Umowy o zamówienia publiczne w zarysie* (Warsaw, Urząd Zamówień Publicznych, 2018) 27. At the EU level, the notion of concession was originally linked to Treaty provisions on public contracts. It first appeared in secondary law in Art 3(1) Directive 71/305/EEC, solely to exclude it from the public works procurement regime. See FLH González, 'The Evolving Concept of Works and Service Concessions in European Union Law' (2016) 25 *Public Procurement Law Review* 51, 52. Concessions were formally regulated as a standalone instrument for the first time in Directive 2014/23/EU on the award of concession contracts. Directive 2014/23/EU was adopted mainly due to the risk of legal uncertainty related to divergent interpretations of EU law by national legislators and wide disparities among the legislations of various Member States. See Bogdanowicz (n 100) 5.

[102] Concession contracts are regulated in Directive 2014/23/EU on the award of concession contracts. Directive 2014/23/EU distinguishes between Art 5(1)(a) 'works concession' and Art 5(1)(b) 'services concession'.

[103] Case C-458/03 *Parking Brixen GmbH v Gemeinde Brixen and Stadtwerke Brixen* AG ECLI:EU:C:2005:605, [2005] ECR I-08585 para 40.

[104] Case C-206/08 *Wasser- und Abwasserzweckverband Gotha und Landkreisgemeinden (WAZV Gotha) v Eurawasser Aufbereitungs- und Entsorgungsgesellschaft mbH* ECLI:EU:C:2009:540, [2009] I-08377 para 59.

[105] Case C-324/98 *Telaustria Verlags GmbH and Telefonadress GmbH v Telekom Austria AG, joined party: Herold Business Data AG* ECLI:EU:C:2000:669, [2000] ECR I-10745 para 58.

of giving rise to contractual rights and obligations. This will not preclude them from being classified as contracts for the purpose of Directive 2014/24/EU.

IV. Public Contract and its Classification under Contract Law

Having considered the EU's autonomous concept of a public contract, the next step is to examine how this notion relates to the concept of a contract under private contract law as the instrument that determines the mutual obligations of the parties. The aim is to identify potential entry points for private contract law application into the regulation of public contracts and discuss it in a more general European context.[106] Thus, it is pertinent to ask instead whether the EU concept of a public contract shares characteristics with contracts as understood in private contract law. The answer to this question inevitably depends on the specific national contract law of the jurisdiction concerned, given the absence of harmonised European contract law. Nevertheless, as a general starting point for this – admittedly more intellectual than practical – discussion, reference can be made to European contract law, and in particular to the Draft Common Frame of Reference (DCFR), which will serve as the point of departure.[107]

A. Defining a Contract: Concepts and Characteristics

Contracts provide the basis for economic exchange and play a pivotal role in facilitating commercial transactions. However, there is no uniform definition of 'contract' across Member States. The term 'contract' itself does not have the same meaning everywhere.[108] Even when definitions of a 'contract' exist and seem similar, caution is advised, as reality could be very different from appearances. Instead, the concept of a contract often serves as a classic example for comparative lawyers, highlighting the incompatibility of legal terms among the diverse European legal systems.[109]

In the context of European contract law, it is noteworthy that the Principles of European Contract Law (PECL) do not explicitly define the concept of a contract.

[106] This concerns the gaps not governed by public procurement law or other specific legislation regulating contract performance, where, in the absence of explicit rules, private contract law may be applied to fill those gaps. The rationale is that, regardless of the contract's classification, it ultimately constitutes a commercial transaction – particularly from the perspective of the economic operator.

[107] For information on European contract law and the DCFR and how they are applied in this anthology, see ch 1.

[108] E Calzolaio, *Comparative Contract Law: An Introduction*, 1st edn (Oxfordshire, Routledge, 2022) 1.

[109] M Comba, 'Effects of EU Law on Contract Management' in M Trybus, R Caranta and G Edelstam (eds), *EU Public Contract Law: Public Procurement and Beyond* (Brussels, Bruylant, 2013) 320; R Austen-Baker and Q Zhou, *Contract in Context*, 1st edn (Oxfordshire, Routledge, 2014) 1–4.

Instead, they focus on outlining the conditions required for its conclusion, as well as other elements relating to its formation.[110] However, based on the framework of the DCFR, a general outline of the concept of a contract can be developed to determine whether a public contract satisfies the requirements of semantic correctness and can therefore be classified as a contract under private contract law.[111] According to the DCFR, a contract is an agreement intended to establish a binding legal relationship or produce another legal effect, functioning as a bilateral or multilateral juridical act.[112] Thus, the essence of every contract lies in the mutuality of consideration.[113]

A public contract clearly exhibits these essential features. It creates a binding legal relationship between the contracting authority and the economic operator (contractor), generating reciprocal obligations for both parties, which may be legally enforced.[114] As AG Bobek observes, despite differences in how national laws define and interpret the concept of a contract, the requirement for reciprocal consideration – mutually agreed upon – remains a fundamental characteristic of all contracts.[115]

The element of reciprocity is also what distinguishes public contracts from other forms of public sector activity – such as grants or administrative decisions – which are founded solely on the authoritative interpretation of one party.

The DCFR also recognises that the term 'contract' may refer to the document in which the agreement's terms are set out.[116] This requirement equally applies to public contracts, which must be concluded in written form (see section III).[117]

In light of these characteristics, contracts, including public contracts, operate within the broader framework of market exchange. In a market economy, the contractual model provides the most effective legal mechanism for ensuring that obligations are both reliable and enforceable. Accordingly, the obligatory

[110] Ch 2 PECL.

[111] C von Bar, E Clive, and H Schulte-Nölke (eds), *Principles, Definitions, and Model Rules of European Private Law: Draft Common Frame of Reference (DCFR) Articles and Comments* (Munich, Sellier, 2009) 58. The PECL do not define the contract. However, ch 2 PECL describes the formation of the contract. This process is regulated primarily through the exchange of two declarations of will: the offer and the acceptance. This approach is similar to the regulation in the Principles of International Commercial Contracts, where ch 2 outlines the grounds for forming a contract. On the conceptual deficits in the understanding that underpins the notion of contract in the DCFR/CFR/CESL, see HW Micklitz, 'European Private Law' in D Patterson and A Södersten (eds), *A Companion to European Union Law and International Law*, 1st edn (Hoboken, John Wiley & Sons, 2016) 268.

[112] Art II–1:101(1) DCFR. See also AG Chloros, 'The Doctrine of Consideration and the Reform of the Law of Contract: A Comparative Analysis' (1968) 17(1) *International and Comparative Law Quarterly* 137.

[113] Chloros (n 112).

[114] Case C-28/23 *NFŠ* (n 82) para 44.

[115] Opinion of AG Bobek (n 77) para 58. See Case C-367/19 *Tax-Fin-Lex* (n 59) para 25 and judgments indicated there, including: Case C-51/15 *Remondis* (n 70) para 43; Case C-796/18 *Informatikgesellschaft für Software-Entwicklung* (n 66) para 40; Case C-328/19 *Proceedings brought by Porin kaupunki* ECLI:EU:C:2020:483, [2020] para 47.

[116] See also C-220/05 *Jean Auroux* (n 58) para 45; Case C-606/17 *IBA Molecular Italy* (n 66) para 28.

[117] See ch 10.

relationships arising from public contracts should be recognised as commercial obligations.

Challenges arising in the performance phase of public contracts often parallel those in private contracting, encompassing the place, time, method, and quality of delivery; the transfer of rights and obligations; and potential grounds for invalidity, including error or fraud. They also cover claims for contract modification, remedies for non-performance – such as termination, restitution, damages, and liquidated damages – together with methods of dispute resolution and approaches to contract interpretation.

In the European context, such issues in private commercial business are addressed through contractual clauses and governed by contract law as a form of statutory regulation. The contract itself holds primacy in this relationship, while contract law serves two roles. First, it restricts contractual interference through mandatory provisions, preventing, for example, the exploitation of the weaker party. Second, it offers default rules under *ius dispotivium* provisions when the contract lacks specific regulations set by the parties.

The same approach applies to public contracts, which serve as a source of obligations for the parties to the contract. These obligations are constrained by public procurement law, contract law, and administrative law – including financial and budgetary restrictions – through the application of mandatory provisions.[118] One such constraint is found in EU public procurement law, which, in recent decades, has extended, albeit to a limited extent, beyond the award phase also to regulate aspects of public contract performance.

V. Spillover Effect of EU Public Procurement Law on Public Contracts Performance

The effectiveness of EU public procurement law could be at risk if its scope is confined solely to the award phase. Even with the safeguards provided by Directive 89/665/EEC, excluding the performance stage from regulatory oversight would risk undermining the integrity of the entire framework.[119] For instance, while a change of contractual partner may be permissible under private contract

[118] The prevalence and relative importance of contract law versus administrative law will depend on the model applied in the Member State. See ch 3. The content of public contracts will also be influenced by the provisions of substantive law related to the contract's subject matter, which falls outside the scope of this chapter. See more on this M Andhov, R Caranta, WA Janssen and O Martin-Ortega, 'Shaping Sustainable Public Procurement Laws in The European Union: An Analysis of the Legislative Development from "How to Buy" to "What to Buy" in Current and Future EU Legislative Initiatives' (2022) The Greens/EFA in the European Parliament https://share.google/zlFPnrWz8y5wxEkyc; W Janssen and R Caranta, *Mandatory Sustainability Requirements in EU Public Procurement Law. Reflections on a Paradigm Shift* (Oxford, Hart Publishing, 2023).

[119] For example, the conclusion of a public contract that disregards procedural provisions entirely undermines the implementation of the principles governing the procedure.

law with the consent of the contracting authority, such a modification is generally prohibited under EU public procurement law.[120] Likewise, the obligation to re-tender in cases of substantial contract changes may conflict with traditional interpretations of the right to amend public contracts in certain countries, such as France and Belgium, as well as with established practices on modifying works contracts, as observed in Denmark.[121] If the parties to a contract were free to make amendments permitted under contract law – particularly those affecting core elements of the winning bid, such as price renegotiations or changes to the contract's scope – these changes could easily circumvent the award procedure. Such circumvention would, in turn, violate the principles of non-discrimination and equal treatment.[122] This relatively simple action illustrates the potential fragility of relying solely on the award phase regulations to implement public procurement principles.[123] Due to these risks, and based primarily on CJEU case law, the EU legislator has increasingly moved to regulate key aspects of public contract performance such as contract modifications, invalidity, and termination.[124] With respect to modifications, CJEU jurisprudence developed a formula determining which amendments to public contracts are permissible – later codified in Article 72 Directive 2014/24/EU – which now provides a detailed set of conditions under which a public contract may be altered.[125]

[120] There are exceptions where substitution of a contractual partner is justifiable in Art 72(1)(d) Directive 2014/24/EU. See Case C-456/06 pressetext *Nachrichtenagentur GmbH v Republik Österreich (Bund), APA-OTS Originaltext-Service GmbH and APA Austria Presse Agentur* ECLI:EU:C:2008:351, [2008] ECR I-04401.

[121] S Treumer, 'Regulation of Contract Changes Leading to a Duty to Retender the Contract: The European Commission's Proposals of December 2011' (2012) 21(5) *Public Procurement Law Review* 153.

[122] V Auricchio, 'The Problem of Discrimination and Anti-competitive Behaviour in the Execution Phase of Public Contracts' (1998) 7(5) *Public Procurement Law Review* 113.

[123] M Bowsher, 'EC Procurement Law and Change During the Tender or the Contract' (2003) 20 *International Construction Law Review* 154; A Brown, 'When Do Changes to an Existing Public Contract Amount to the Award of a New Contract for the Purposes of the EU Procurement Rules? Guidance at Last in Case C454/06' (2008) 6 *Public Procurement Law Review* 253; S Poulsen, 'The Possibilities of Amending a Public Contract Without a New Competitive Tendering Procedure Under EU Law' (2012) 21(5) *Public Procurement Law Review* 167.

[124] S Treumer, 'Contract Changes and the Duty to Retender Under the New EU Public Procurement Directive' (2014) 3 *Public Procurement Law Review* 148; MA Simovart, 'Old Remedies for New Violations? The Deficit of Remedies for Enforcing Public Contract Modification Rules' (2015) 1 *Upphandlingsrättslig Tidskrift* 33l; P Bogdanowicz, *Contract Modifications in EU Procurement Law* (Cheltenham, Edward Elgar Publishing, 2021); KM Halonen, 'Contractual Ineffectiveness as Seen from a Finnish Perspective' in CR Hamer, M Andhov, E Bertelsen, and R Caranta (eds), *Into the Northern Light: In Memory of Steen Treumer*, 1st edn (Copenhagen, Ex Tuto, 2022); D Dragos, KM Halonen, B Neamtu, and S Treumer (eds), *Contract Changes: The Dark Side of EU Procurement Law* (Cheltenham, Edward Elgar Publishing, 2023).

[125] Case C-496/99 *Commission of the European Communities v CAS Succhi di Frutta SpA* ECLI:EU:C:2004:236, [2004] ECR I-03801; Case C-456/06 pressetext *Nachrichtenagentur* (n 120); C-91/08 *Wall AG v La ville de Francfort-sur-le-Main and Frankfurter Entsorgungs- und Service (FES)* GmbH ECLI:EU:C:2010:182, [2010] ECR I-02815; Case C-549/14 Finn Frogne A/S v Rigspolitiet ved Center for Beredskabskommunikation ECLI:EU:C:2016:634, [2016]; C-461/20 *Advania Sverige AB and Kammarkollegiet v Dustin Sverige AB* ECLI:EU:C:2022:72, [2022].

Regarding the invalidity of public contracts, the CJEU in *Commission v Germany* confirmed an infringement of EU law as a continuous, rather than momentary, breach.[126] The Court held that such an infringement persists for the entire duration of the contract. EU public procurement law also lays down rules on the ineffectiveness of contracts and on circumstances in which contracting authorities must be able to terminate a contract during its term.[127] These include situations involving unlawful modifications, the failure to exclude an ineligible contractor, or cases where the contract should not have been awarded at all due to a serious breach of Article 258 Treaty on the Functioning of the European Union (TFEU) or Directive 2014/24/EU obligations – a breach subsequently confirmed by a CJEU ruling.[128]

Directive 2014/24/EU also regulates two aspects of the performance phase through non-mandatory provisions. First, Article 70 permits the inclusion of economic, innovation-related, environmental, and social or employment-related considerations in public contracts.[129] This article is more declarative and encourages contracting authorities to include clauses that enable the implementation of sustainable development, which the CJEU has recognised as a principle of EU public procurement law.[130]

Second, Directive 2014/24/EU addresses subcontracting, traditionally governed by private contract law. The EU legislator recognised that inadequate oversight in this area may lead to the circumvention of Directive 2014/24/EU, allowing public contracts to be awarded to economic operators whose capabilities were not properly assessed by the contracting authority.[131] To counter this risk, Article 71 not only ensures compliance with EU public procurement law but also

[126] Case C-503/04 Commission of the European Communities v Federal Republic of Germany ECLI:EU:C:2007:432, [2007] ECR I-06153 para 36. See also R Caranta, 'Are the Principles of European Contract Law Relevant for Public Contracts' in S De La Rosa and PV Fernandez (eds), *Les principes des contrats publics en Europe (Principles of Public Contracts in Europe)* (Brussels, Bruylant, 2022) 86.

[127] S Treumer, 'Towards an Obligation to Terminate Contracts Concluded in Breach of the EC Public Procurement Rules: The End of the Status of Concluded Public Contracts as Sacred Cows' (2007) 6 *Public Procurement Law Review* 371. By contrast, Art 43(1)(f) Swiss Federal Act on Public Procurement only requires the procurement agency to cancel the tender in case of substantial modifications of the good/service but does not regulate the contract performance stage or stipulate the agency's obligation to terminate the contract. Nonetheless, Swiss jurisprudence found that even though the termination of a public contract constitutes a private law declaration of intent, public contracts are preceded by a public decision, which can be appealed under public administrative law. See Obergericht des Kantons Schaffhausen, Decision No 60/2007/32 of 9 November 2011, E.2.b; and the decision from the Swiss Supreme Court, 2C_314/2013 of 19 March 2014, E.1.1. See also Häfelin, Müller, and Uhlmann (n 38) 317.

[128] Consolidated Version of the Treaty on the Functioning of the European Union [2012] OJ C 326/47; Art 73 Directive 2014/24/EU. See also KM Halonen, 'Termination of a Public Contract: Lifting the Veil on Art 73 of 2014/24 Directive' (2017) 5 *Public Procurement Law Review* 187, 194–95.

[129] M Andhov, 'Article 70 Contract Performance Conditions' in R Caranta and A Sanchez-Graells (eds), *European Public Procurement: Commentary on Directive 2014/24/EU* (Cheltenham, Edward Elgar Publishing, 2021).

[130] Case C-395/18 *Tim SpA – Direzione e coordinamento Vivendi SA v Consip SpA and Ministero dell'Economia e delle Finanze* ECLI:EU:C:2020:58, [2020].

[131] J Stalzer, 'Article 71 Subcontracting' in R Caranta and A Sanchez-Graells (eds), *European Public Procurement: Commentary on Directive 2014/24/EU* (Cheltenham, Edward Elgar Publishing, 2021) 759.

seeks to protect subcontractors and uphold procurement principles throughout the supply chain.[132]

Beyond the provisions in Articles 70–73, the regulation of all other matters remains within the autonomous competence of the Member States. EU public procurement framework does not prescribe general regulatory models for the performance of public contracts.

As AG Sánchez-Bordona noted in his opinion in *Veolia Water Technologies*, this autonomy is not without limits. Even where matters fall outside the scope of EU public procurement provisions, Member States must exercise their regulatory competence in a manner consistent with the fundamental principles of EU public procurement law.[133]

A wide range of operational matters thus remain beyond the scope of EU public procurement law. These include, for example, the determination of price, time, and place of performance; rules on payment delays; joint and several liabilities; errors in the declaration of will; and liquidated damages. Such issues are governed by national legal frameworks.[134]

It is therefore for each Member State to determine the applicable rules – whether mandatory provisions or *ius dispositivum* norms – governing the performance of public contracts. The selection and application of these rules reflect the specific national models of public contract regulation, which are examined in greater detail in chapter three of this anthology.

VI. Conclusion

Public contracts are the legal outcome of procurement procedures and the framework through which contracting authorities and private parties exchange goods, services, or works. Their dual character, combining the enforceable obligations of contract law with the regulatory constraints of EU public procurement law, creates two key intersections with contract law. First, they share the essential features of commercial contracts: as bilateral legal acts, they establish reciprocal obligations supported by consideration, enforceable under law. Second, they govern ongoing contractual relations, raising issues typical of other commercial arrangements,

[132] Case C-314/01 *Siemens AG Österreich and ARGE Telekom & Partner v Hauptverband der österreichischen Sozialversicherungsträger* ECLI:EU:C:2004:159, [2004] ECR I-02549 para 47. See M Andhov, 'Regulating for a Sustainable and Resilient Single Market: Challenges and Reforms in the Area of Public Procurement' (2023) European Trade Union Institute <www.etui.org/publications/regulating-sustainable-and-resilient-single-market> 26.

[133] Opinion of AG Campos Sánchez-Bordona delivered on 6 February 2025 in Case C-82/24 *Miejskie Przedsiębiorstwo Wodociągów i Kanalizacji w m.st. Warszawie S.A v Veolia Water Technologies sp. z o.o* ECLI:EU:C:2025:66, [2025] para 80.

[134] The issue of late payment in the context of commercial transactions has been partially covered by the regulation contained in Directive 2011/7/EU of the European Parliament and of the Council of 16 February 2011 on combating late payment in commercial transactions [2011] OJ L 48/1.

particularly in the performance phase. These features make regulation through contract law indispensable.

In practice, contractual clauses provide only part of the regulatory framework for public contractual relations. The remainder stems from EU public procurement law and supplementary legislative measures at the national level, which vary across Member States. While Europeanisation has progressively shaped this area, harmonisation remains partial: the performance phase is addressed only in limited respects under Articles 70–73 Directive 2014/24/EU, which focus on matters such as contract modifications and termination. Many aspects of contract performance continue to fall within the exclusive competence of Member States. Nonetheless, the interpretative role of the CJEU may gradually expand the EU influence into additional aspects of contract performance in the future.

The limited regulation of the performance phase under EU public procurement law means that this stage continues to be governed primarily by national frameworks. Chapter three will examine the regulatory models adopted by Member States for governing public contracts under both public and private contract law.

3

National Models for Regulating Public Contracts*

MARTA ANDHOV AND MICHAŁ KANIA

I. Introduction

EU public procurement law does not end its relevance once a public contract has been awarded. Although its primary focus lies in regulating the award stage, it also extends, albeit to a limited extent, into the performance phase of public contracts.[1] This is reflected in Articles 70–73 Directive 2014/24/EU, which aim to safeguard the effectiveness of EU public procurement law. Beyond these provisions, however, a field of contractual issues remains outside the scope of EU public procurement law. These matters are governed by national legal systems, each shaped by its own traditions and approaches to managing relationships between the public and private sectors. As a result, there is no uniform model across Member States, but rather a variety of regulatory frameworks reflecting domestic legal characteristics.

This diversity prompts important questions: Which models have emerged among Member States, and what distinctive features do they display? The present chapter seeks to explore these questions. It is structured as follows: section II sets out a taxonomy of public contract models based on the division between public law and private law, while recognising the intricate interplay between the two. Section III examines the 'public-oriented hybrid model'. Section IV turns to the 'private-oriented hybrid model'. Finally, section V draws together the conclusions of the chapter.

* This chapter has greatly benefited from the insights, comments, and contributions of the authors of the other chapters in this anthology, as well as from valuable input provided by professors Tünde Tátrai, Mario Comba, Elisabetta Manunza, Marko Turudić, attorney-at-law Jesper Fabricius, and Džeina Gaile (doctoral student). We are particularly grateful to Professor Roberto Caranta for his thoughtful ongoing feedback, which helped us improve and further develop the chapter. All errors and omissions remain the sole responsibility of the authors.

[1] See ch 2.

II. Taxonomy of National Models of Public Contract Regulation

The development of the models currently governing public contracts in Member States is closely tied to the frameworks that existed before the Europeanisation of public procurement law.[2] The fundamental distinction, rooted in traditional assumptions and European legal theory, lies between the 'public model' and the 'private model'.[3] While not challenging the accepted division, it is important to acknowledge that the split between 'public' and 'private' law is among the most fundamental yet contested legal concepts.[4] At the EU level, the importance of distinguishing between public and private sectors is a contentious issue since the Union does not consider this distinction to hold fundamental significance.[5] An analysis of various theories relating to this division often reveals contradictions, allowing the assumptions of one theory to be challenged based on the findings of another.[6]

Additionally, the boundary between 'public' and 'private' law varies between Member States, influenced by the chosen criterion of division, traditions, and legal culture.[7] For some authors, this division is of cardinal importance, determining the manner and limits of the regulation of legal relations.[8] Some scholars,

[2] See ch 2.

[3] The public–private law distinction reflects long-standing national traditions and legal theories. In continental Europe, it has served as a basic organising principle, while the Anglo-Saxon tradition largely disregards it. On these trends, see B Binder and L Fröhler, *Die Haftung der Gemeinden für ausgegliederte Unternehmungen* (Munich, Volk Verlag, 1982); M Ruffert, 'Rights and Remedies in European Community Law: A Comparative View' (1997) 34(2) *Common Market Law Review* 307; D Budäus, 'Privatisierung öffentlich wahrgenommener Aufgaben' in C Gusy (ed), *Privatisierung von Staatsaufgaben: Kriterien – Grenzen – Folgen* (Baden-Baden, Nomos, 1998); U Di Fabio, 'Privatisierung und Staatsvorbehalt: zum dogmatischen Schlüsselbegriff der öffentlichen Aufgabe' (1999) *Juristenzeitung* 585.

[4] M Rosenfeld, 'Rethinking the Boundaries Between Public Law and Private Law for the Twenty First Century: An Introduction' (2013) 11(1) *International Journal of Constitutional Law* 125; A Jakab, *European Constitutional Language* (Cambridge, Cambridge University Press, 2016); J Varuhas, 'Transcending the Public Law-Private Law Divide' in C Harlow (ed), *A Research Agenda for Administrative Law* (Cheltenham, Edward Elgar Publishing, 2023) 163 ff.

[5] N Reich, 'The Public/Private Divide in European Law' in HW Micklitz and F Cafaggi (eds), *European Private Law after the Common Frame of Reference* (Cheltenham, Edward Elgar Publishing, 2010) 56 ff. The statement should, however, be subject to contextualisation. For example, in relation to the Right of establishment referred to in ch 2 Treaty on the Functioning of the European Union, Art 51 indicates that the provisions of the chapter do not apply to activities which in that State are connected, even occasionally, with the exercise of official authority. See Treaty on the Functioning of the European Union [2012] OJ C326/47.

[6] M Usami, 'Law as Public Policy: Combining Justice with Interest' in T Biernat and M Zirk-Sadowski (eds), *Politics of Law and Legal Policy. Between Modern and Post-modern Jurisprudence* (Warsaw, Wolters Kluwer, 2008) 294–95; Rosenfeld (n 4) 125–26.

[7] M Szpunar, *Odpowiedzialność podmiotu prywatnego z tytułu naruszenia prawa wspólnotowego* (Warsaw, Kluwer, 2008) 194–95.

[8] These authors include O Gierke, *Deutsches Privatrech: Bd. Allgemeine Teil und Personenrecht*, Vol 1 (Leipzig, Duncker & Humblot, 1895) 26–33; A Ross, *On Law and Justice* (London, Stevens and Sons, 1958) 203.

particularly experts in administrative law, even rejected the possibility of applying private law to public administration, whether directly, as guiding principles of the law, or by analogy.[9] Nevertheless, clear division lines are increasingly blurred, with the two categories intermingling.[10] As a result, some authors do not view the division between 'public' and 'private' law as strictly dichotomous,[11] while others criticise its practical relevance in managing public contracts.[12]

This non-dichotomous nature is manifested in its multi-functionality and context dependence.[13] Consequently, applying public law to an institution or a legal relationship does not necessarily exclude the application of private law to the same institution or legal relationship.[14] The intermingling of both categories is a dynamic process influenced by economic and social changes and the rapid development of new technologies. This results in a cardinal division into 'public' and 'private' law, becoming more a matter of conventional distinctions rather than clear-cut demarcation lines.

For this anthology, the authors will utilise two terms. The first is the 'public-oriented hybrid model', which is traditionally aligned with France and other Member States sharing similar legal traditions. The second is the 'private-oriented hybrid model', which is exemplified by Germany and countries with similar legal traditions. These models illustrate general themes in the approaches of Member States which cannot be classified as purely 'public' or purely 'private'.

Both models discussed below are hybrids in which various aspects of public contracts are governed by both public and private law. The primary difference lies in the degree of emphasis. The 'private-oriented hybrid model' Member States predominantly favour contract law and Civil Codes when dealing with the performance of public contracts but still apply some scope of special public rules. By contrast, in the 'public-oriented hybrid model' Member States, public law will be predominantly applied, and exactly opposed, private contract law will have limited application. The situation is further complicated by variations within the same model, even among Member States classified in the same group. Using an analogy, a spectrum can be imagined where the westernmost point represents 100 per cent private law application, and the easternmost point represents 100 per cent public

[9] O Mayer, 'Zur Lehre vom öffentlichrechtliche Vertrage' (1888) 3(1) *Archiv des öffentlichen Rechts* 3, 42; R Szczepaniak, 'The Nature of the Division into Public and Private Law, with Particular Emphasis on Polish Experiences' (2015) 20(2) *Comparative Law Review* 33, 41.

[10] JM McLean, 'For a Law of Public Contract Per Se: An Intervention from Liberal Contract Theory' (2019) 39(4) *Oxford Journal of Legal Studies* 856.

[11] W Hoffmann-Riem and E Schmidt-Aßmann (eds), *Öffentliches Recht und Privatrecht als wechselseitige Auffangordnungen* (Baden-Baden, Nomos, 1996); M Burgi, 'Rechtsregime' in A Voßkuhle, M Eifert and C Möllers (eds), *Grundlagen des Verwaltungsrechts*, Vol 1, 3rd edn (Munich, CH Beck, 2022) 18.

[12] ME Comba, 'Contract Execution in Europe: Different Legal Models with a Common Core' (2013) 8 *European Procurement & Public Private Partnership Law Review* 302.

[13] JF Van Ommeren, 'The Public-Private Divide in English and Dutch Law: A Multifunctional and Context – Dependant Divide' (2012) 71(1) *Cambridge Law Journal* 172.

[14] Szczepaniak (n 9) 39.

law application to public contracts. No Member State would be positioned at either extreme. Instead, all Member States would be situated along the spectrum. Thus, differences are inevitable. This understanding should be considered as a disclaimer before we proceed to illustrate the two models.

Furthermore, it is worth noting that the authors' classification differs from Auby's, which distinguishes between the French 'public' model, the British 'private' model, and the German 'hybrid' model.[15] Since common law countries fall outside the scope of this anthology, the authors are instead inspired by Fromont's division of public and private models, while highlighting the hybrid aspects present in both.[16]

Two countries pose a particular challenge for classification: Belgium and Italy. Depending on the sources consulted, they are grouped into different models. In Auby's classification, Italy is grouped with the Netherlands and Germany, aligning with what we define as the 'private-oriented hybrid model'.[17] In contrast, Fromont places Italy and Belgium within the French model, emphasising that in these countries the French model is modified and adapted, where some private law rules are applied, despite the fact that the background rules stem from public law.[18] Acknowledging these differing perspectives, the authors classify Italy and Belgium as the most private representations of the 'public-oriented hybrid model' for the purposes of this anthology.

III. 'Public-Oriented Hybrid Model'

The 'public-oriented hybrid model' of regulating public contract performance has a strong emphasis on public elements. These include the distinction of a separate category of contracts, referred to as 'administrative contracts', which are subject to a specific legislative framework not applicable to private law contracts.[19] Additionally, the model features a predominant focus on the public interest, the dominant position of the public contracting party with special powers, and, as a general rule, the jurisdiction of administrative courts over disputes arising from public contracts. Consequently, the application of private contract law in the public contract performance phase is largely limited, with elements of contract law rarely present directly, although private law can be an indirect source of law, but outside the scope of the award. For instance, the question of timing for action is drawn upon the Civil Code by principle, unless there is a reason of general interest not to follow civil law.

[15] JB Auby, 'Comparative Approaches to the Rise of the Contract in the Public Sphere' (2007) 1 *Public Law* 40.

[16] M Fromont, *Droit administratif des Etats européens* (Paris, Presses Universitaires de France, 2006) 297–324.

[17] Auby (n 15).

[18] Fromont, *Droit administratif des Etats européens* (n 16).

[19] Auby (n 15).

France, as an archetype of the 'public-oriented hybrid model', follows a legal tradition that maintains a clear division between public and private law in the context of public contracts. Most contracts entered into by the administration – including public contracts – are classified as public law contracts (*Contrats administratifs*). These contracts are subject to specific rules, many of which have been established through the case law of the Conseil d'État. Their adjudication falls under the jurisdiction of administrative courts. A further consequence is the availability of specific legal remedies, such as actions of third parties against administrative contracts, which can result in the contract being terminated or even annulled for serious unlawfulness[20] or the possibility for third parties to ask for the annulment of the refusal to terminate a contract.[21] The contracting activities of the public administration are regulated by rules based on jurisprudence and legal doctrine created to prioritise the public interest.[22]

A. Administrative Contract

Administrative rules in the 'public-oriented hybrid model' not only govern the award of the contract but also influence their performance, distinguishing them from private law counterparts.[23] These rules reflect the unique role of the state, leading to the development of administrative contracts as a distinct legal category in several jurisdictions. Besides France, where a *sui generis* legal classification of 'administrative contracts' has been established,[24] similar legal frameworks exist in other 'public-oriented hybrid model' countries, including Spain, Portugal, Croatia, and Belgium, where contracts involving public authorities have been treated as legally distinct from private contracts.

In Portugal, courts, administrative bodies, legislators, and legal scholars began differentiating contracts of public authorities as early as the nineteenth century, eventually recognising the autonomous concept of 'administrative contracts'.[25] Similarly, in Spain, the distinction between contracts concluded by public authorities and private contracts first emerged in the regulatory sphere in the middle of the nineteenth century. Initially, this distinction was procedural, but under French influence, disputes involving public contracts were assigned to administrative jurisdiction as early as 1845.[26]

[20] CE Ass, 4 April 2014, *Département du Tarn-et-Garonne*, no 358994, Lebon 70.

[21] CE Sect, 30 June 2017, *SMPAT*, no 398445.

[22] R Le Mestre, *Termes du droit administratif* (Paris, Gualino, 2006) 58; J Bell and F Lichère, *Contemporary French Administrative Law* (Cambridge, Cambridge University Press, 2022) 270, 271.

[23] Bell and Lichère (n 22) 271.

[24] G Vedel, *Droit administratif* (Paris, Presses Universitaires de France, 1973) 230.

[25] For an appraisal of how administrative contracts were acknowledged and regulated in Portuguese law, going back to the 19th century, see MA Raimundo, *A formação dos contratos públicos. Uma concorrência ajustada ao interesse público* (Lisbon, Associação Académica da Faculdade de Direito de Lisboa, 2013) 249 ff and 292 ff.

[26] EG de Enterría, 'La figura del contrato administrativo' (1963) 41 *Revista de Administración Pública* 99, 101.

In Croatia, the opinions on the legal classification of public procurement contracts vary, with interpretations ranging from (1) administrative contracts,[27] (2) contracts of mixed administrative and civil law nature,[28] (3) contracts *sui generis*,[29] and (4) civil contracts.[30] After extensive legal analysis, Turudić concluded that public contracts in Croatia most closely resemble administrative contracts, aligning them with the legal traditions of France, Portugal, and Spain.[31] This approach has been confirmed recently by the Croatian Supreme Court.[32]

In Belgium, public contracts have traditionally been regarded as the archetype of administrative contracts.[33] More recently, scholars have questioned the validity of this distinction, arguing that the notion of 'administrative contracts' is largely a legal fiction.[34] According to this view, all contracts are essentially civil in nature, though contracts entered into by public authorities are subject to public law rules, many of which are rooted in the French concept of administrative contracts, which confer distinctive legal characteristics.[35]

France, Portugal, Spain, Italy, and Croatia have enacted specific statutes governing public contracts. In France, Portugal, and Italy, these are codified as 'Codes', explicitly addressing public contracts covered by public procurement rules.[36] These 'Codes' (and even acts not identified as Codes, as is the case of the Spanish Law on Contracts of the Public Sector[37] or in the Croatian Public

[27] B Ljubanović and BB Vetma, 'Hrvatsko pravo javne nabave – usklađenost s pravom EU' (2011) 48(2) *Zbornik Pravnog fakulteta Sveučilišta u Splitu* 412; D Aviani, 'Posebnosti upravnih ugovora i njihove sudske kontrole u hrvatskom pravu' (2013) 50(2) *Zbornik Pravnog fakulteta Sveučilišta u Splitu* 351.

[28] G Matešić, 'Odnos obveznog prava i prava javne nabave kroz ugovor o nabavi' (2006) *Pravo u gospodarstvu* 230.

[29] W Van Gerven, *Hoe blauw is het bloed van de prins* (Deventer, Kluwer, 1984) 61; I Koprić and S Nikić, 'Upravni ugovori – područje primjene i primjena prava' (2010) *Zbornik Susreta pravnika Opatija* 271, 298.

[30] R Andersen, 'Autorité et contrat dans l'administration moderne en Belgique' (1997) 20 *Annuaire Européen d'Administration Publique* 35, 37; A Drmić, 'Pravna priroda ugovora o javnoj nabavi' (2014) 14(2) *Hrvatska i komparativna javna uprava: časopis za teoriju i praksu javne uprave* 493, 500.

[31] M Turudić, 'Pravna priroda ugovora o javnoj nabavi u hrvatskom pravnom poretku' (2018) 9(34) *Sveske za javno pravo* 10.

[32] Croatian Supreme Court decision of 8 November 2023, Rev 139/2023-5.

[33] MA Flamme, *Droit administratif* (Brussels, Bruylant, 1989) 822.

[34] K Wauters, 'Zin of onzin van een leer van het administratief contract in België?' in D D'Hooghe, K Deketelaere and AM Draye (eds), *Liber amicorum Marc Boes* (Brugge, Die Keure, 2011) 589–606.

[35] ibid.

[36] See *Code de la commande publique* adopted by the 'Ordonnance' no 2018-1074 of 26 November 2018 (amended). Official consolidated version (in French) <www.legifrance.gouv.fr/codes/texte_lc/LEGITEXT000037701019/> (French Public Procurement Code; *Código dos Contratos Públicos Decreto-Lei no 18/2008, de 29 de janeiro* (Portuguese Public Contracts Code); *Codice dei contratti pubblici* adopted with *Decreto Legislativo 31 marzo 2023, no 36* (Italian Public Contracts Code). More about the reform of the Italian Public Contracts Code, see eg, M Macchia, 'The New Public Procurement Code: A Way to Simplify?' (2024) 16(1) *Italian Journal of Public Law* 69; L Pardi, 'A Tool to Improve Public Contracting Efficiency: Digitalisation in the New Italian Public Procurement and Concession Code' (2024) 19(1) *European Procurement & Public Private Partnership Law Review* 77.

[37] *Ley 9/2017, de 8 de noviembre, de Contratos del Sector Público* (Spanish Law on Contracts of the Public Sector).

Procurement Act[38] and the Croatian General Administrative Procedure Act[39]) extend beyond EU public procurement law, incorporating provisions that regulate not just the award of contracts but also their performance, thereby reinforcing the distinct legal status of administrative contracts in these jurisdictions. The situation in Belgium is somewhat similar, albeit nowadays it is accepted that these specific rules do not alter the legal nature of the contracts.[40] However, in France, despite the existence of the 'Code', most rules that differ from the French Civil Code[41] in relation to public contracts remain uncodified and continue to be shaped by the case law of the Conseil d'État.

These 'Codes' cover (with different degrees of detail according to the jurisdiction) general matters such as: regime of entering into force and unlawfulness/ineffectiveness of the contract,[42] conditions for conclusion of the contract,[43] non-compliance and contractual penalties,[44] a specific regime of *exceptio non adimpleti contractus*, with more demanding conditions for the contractor to invoke it than the ones that would result from civil law,[45] performance bonds,[46] maximum deadlines for compliance, duty to pay interest in case of delay and other issues related to payments,[47] termination for fault or reasons of public interest.[48] Considering rules for specific contracts, and taking the example of public works contracts, specific rules relate to issues such as the obligations of the parties,[49] measurement of the works and respective payments,[50] suspension of the works,[51] *force majeure*,[52] verification of compliance and remedy of defects by the contractor, including warranty against defects,[53] and penalties for delays in compliance by the contractor.[54] Similar rules exist for services[55]

[38] *Zakon o javnoj nabavi*, NN 120/2016 i 114/2022 (Croatian Public Procurement Act).

[39] *Zakon o Općem Upravnom Postupku*, NN 47/2009, 110/2021 (Croatian General Administrative Procedure Act).

[40] S Van Garsse (ed), *Handboek Bestuursrecht* (Brussels, Politeia, 2020) 104.

[41] *Code civil* <www.legifrance.gouv.fr/codes/texte_lc/LEGITEXT000006070721/> (French Civil Code).

[42] Arts 283–287 Portuguese Public Contracts Code; Art 151 Croatian General Administrative Procedure Act.

[43] Art 150 Croatian General Administrative Procedure Act.

[44] Arts 325–329 Portuguese Public Contracts Code; Arts 192–194 Spanish Law on Contracts of the Public Sector; Art 126 Italian Public Contracts Code.

[45] Art 327 Portuguese Public Contracts Code.

[46] ibid Art 88 and 89.

[47] ibid Arts 299, 299-A, 326; Arts 198–199 Spanish Law on Contracts of the Public Sector.

[48] Arts 332–335 Portuguese Public Contracts Code; Arts 211–213 Spanish Law on Contracts of the Public Sector; Art 153 Croatian General Administrative Procedure Act.

[49] Arts 346–354 Portuguese Public Contracts Code; Arts 238–241 Spanish Law on Contracts of the Public Sector.

[50] Arts 387–393 Portuguese Public Contracts Code.

[51] ibid Arts 365–369; Art 121 Italian Public Contracts Code.

[52] Art 239 Spanish Law on Contracts of the Public Sector.

[53] Arts 394–398 Portuguese Public Contracts Code; Arts 243–244 Spanish Law on Contracts of the Public Sector.

[54] Arts 403–404 Portuguese Public Contracts Code.

[55] ibid Arts 450–454; Arts 308–315 Spanish Law on Contracts of the Public Sector.

and supply contracts.[56] These provisions cover aspects otherwise regulated by private contract law. In fact, these contracts have their equivalents in private law, but are qualified by law as administrative contracts as long as they include an administrative authority acting in that capacity and/or are subject to public law provisions.[57]

B. Specific Powers and Special Rights of Contracting Authorities

In the 'public-oriented hybrid model', the public authority is granted a dominant position, as it is considered to exercise public functions and protect the public interest while awarding and overseeing the contract's performance.[58] As Craig stated, the French model established 'specific powers' (existence of 'exorbitant clauses' – '*Clauses exorbitantes du droit commun*') of the public sector during the performance stage of the contract.[59] The existence of some unilateral power and special rights, for instance, to modify or terminate the contract, is one of the most significant indicators of the 'public-oriented hybrid model' of the contract.[60] The general rationale for such a power is that the public body has to serve public interests, which means that it will, on some occasions, have to be able to modify or terminate the contractual relationship without the consent of the contractor.[61]

In earlier stages of legal evolution, these prerogatives in countries like Spain and Portugal were shaped primarily through case law, heavily influenced by French law. However, both jurisdictions now include general statutory provisions that explicitly confer these special powers on the public party in administrative contracts.[62] The same general rules exist in Croatia.[63]

The concept of specific powers and special rights introduces a significant distinction to typical contract law.[64] The source of these powers is of relevance. Specific powers and special rights in the 'public-oriented hybrid model' are derived

[56] Arts 431–436 and 437–449 Portuguese Public Contracts Code; Arts 298–307 Spanish Law on Contracts of the Public Sector.

[57] For the legal conditions that a contract must have to qualify as an administrative contract, in Portuguese law, see Art 280(1) Portuguese Public Contracts Code.

[58] M Laazouzi, *Les contrats administratifs a character international* (Paris, Economica, 2008) 17.

[59] P Craig, 'Specific Powers of Public Contractors' in R Noguellou and U Stelkens (eds), *Comparative Law on Public Contracts* (Brussels, Bruylant, 2010) 174. See also P Folliard, *Droit administratif* (Paris, 2008) 241–42.

[60] Folliard (n 59) 241–42.

[61] ibid.

[62] Art 190 Spanish Law on Contracts of the Public Sector enumerates a series of special rights ('*Prerrogativas de la Administración Pública en los contratos administrativos*'). In the same vein Art 302 Portuguese Public Contracts Code foresees a series of 'conforming powers' ('*poderes de conformação da relação contratual*').

[63] Arts 150–154 Croatian General Administrative Procedure Act.

[64] C Guettier, *Droit des contrats administratifs* (Paris, Presses Universitaires de France, 2004) 424.

from mandatory provisions and conferred upon public entities, thereby disrupting the equilibrium between the parties.[65] Such powers are rarely attributed to one party within a contractual relationship under private contract law.[66] However, even under contract law, similar clauses may mostly result from an agreement between the parties acting within the freedom of contract. The agreement of the parties may also include the incorporation and modification of standard form contracts into the contract's content, granting specific powers to the public body.

Specific powers and special rights present in the 'public-oriented hybrid model' include, (i) the power of direction and control, (ii) the power to impose sanctions, (iii) the power of unilateral modification of the contract, (iv) the power to suspend contract's performance, and (v) the power to unilaterally terminate the contract.[67]

i. *The Power of Direction and Control*

In France and Belgium, the power of direction and control enables public administration to verify at any time during the public contract performance whether the project is being executed appropriately, assess the state of progress, and evaluate the degree of financial resource utilisation.[68] These powers encompass various types of administrative actions, depending on the specific nature of the task being carried

[65] The granting of specific powers on the side of the public entity does not imply a deprivation of the rights of contractors. Specific rights of the contractors are related to such concepts as: imprévision, force majeure administrative, sujétions imprévues, travaux indispensables, fait du prince. See more, Bell and Lichère (n 22) 277–79. The *Imprévision* theory was introduced in 1916 by the famous case of Gaz de Bordeaux (CE 30 March 1916, *Compagnie générale d'éclairage de Bordeaux*, no 59928, Lebon 143), which regards concession contracts but has been extended to public procurement contracts. When an external event entails an increase in the costs to an extent which exceeds the extreme limits of the increases which could have been envisaged by the parties at the time of the conclusion of the concession contract and the economic substance of the contract has been completely upset, the contractor can be partially compensated, from 75 per cent to 95 per cent of the extra costs. (See CE *Avis*, 15 September 2022). The *fait du prince* theory in administrative law allows for full compensation of the extra costs which are attributable to the public contractor acting in its capacity of a public authority, ie in its public interest role and not as a contractor. For instance, the State must pay damages for the land of which a company was deprived despite the contractual expectations, due to a modification of the urban planning regulation made by the State. (See CE, 29 December 1997, *Société civile des Néo-Polders*, no 146753.) Finally, the unforeseen situations (*sujétions imprévues*) are material difficulties encountered in the performance of the contract, of an exceptional nature, unforeseeable at the time of conclusion of the contract and whose cause is external to the parties. They permit private contractors in case of public procurement, dealing with works or services (but not supplies) to claim full compensation of the extra costs.

[66] Guettier (n 64) 426. eg Art 1661 Italian Civil Code foresees that also private companies have the right to unilaterally modify the contract up to 1/6 of the contract value. *Codice Civile* adopted with *Regio Decreto 16 marzo 1942, no* 262 (Italian Civil Code).

[67] Art L6 French Public Procurement Code; Art 190 Spanish Law on Contracts of the Public Sector; Art 302 Portuguese Public Contracts Code list all of the abovementioned powers or rights, or the vast majority of them. See G Dupuis, MJ Guedon, and P Chretien, *Droit administrative* (Paris, Sirey, 2004) 433.

[68] See Guettier (n 64) 428. See for Belgium s 6 (Direction and control) Royal Decree of 14 January 2013 establishing the general rules for the execution of public procurement contracts, Official Gazette 14 February 2013 (Belgian Executive Decree on the Performance of Public Contract).

out.[69] Public entities also have the right to issue binding instructions to rectify irregularities and defects in the work performed, or even to order the execution of work not initially stipulated in the contract, which can lead to contract suspension or modification. In such situations, the contractor is obliged to comply with the instructions of the administration.[70]

A similar approach is adopted in Croatia, where an administrative contract must be concluded to implement the rights and obligations established by a decision (administrative act) resolving an administrative matter.[71] Such a contract must not contradict the operative part of the decision, mandatory legal provisions, or the public interest, nor may it be concluded to the detriment of third parties. This requirement firmly links the execution of these contracts to the procedure that precedes the award decision, placing them within an administrative, rather than private contract law, framework.

In Portugal, the law grants the contracting authority general powers of direction and control, explicitly regulated in the law.[72] These are considered 'instrumental' or ancillary powers, meaning they enable the authority to steer contract performance toward fulfilling the public interest objectives.[73] The scope of these powers is understood in a manner similar to French law. However, certain matters, such as modifying the contract to include additional work, are generally not considered to fall under these powers.[74] Instead, such modifications are seen as part of a separate, autonomous authority to unilaterally alter the contract for reasons of public interest.

Spanish law likewise recognises a power of control ('*Inspección*') along with other provisions for specific contracts.[75] This includes the power to interpret the contract and resolve disputes regarding its compliance. While the interpretive criteria are generally drawn from the Spanish Civil Code,[76] the distinctive feature of the administrative regime lies in the legal nature of the contracting authority's interpretations. They are treated as binding unilateral administrative decisions. If a contractor disagrees with such a determination, they must challenge it in court, just as they would any other administrative act.[77]

[69] See D De Laubaudere and P Delvolve, *Traite des contrats administratifs* (Paris, Librairie générale de droit et de jurisprudence, 1984) 1166.

[70] See X Philippe, *Droit administrative general* (Marseille, Presses universitaires d'Aix-Marseille, 1993) 164.

[71] Art 150 Croatian General Administrative Procedure Act.

[72] Art 302, paras a) and b) and Arts 303–305 Portuguese Public Contracts Code. See PC Gonçalves, *Direito dos Contratos Públicos*, 1st edn (Coimbra, Almedina, 2015) 525 ff.

[73] Explicitly, Art 303(1) Portuguese Public Contracts Code.

[74] MA Raimundo, *Direito dos Contratos Públicos*, Vol 2 (Lisbon, Associação Académica da Faculdade de Direito de Lisboa, 2022) 289.

[75] Art 190 Spanish Law on Contracts of the Public Sector and Art 303 for supply contracts.

[76] *Código Civil* approved by *Real Decreto de 24 de julio de 1889* (Spanish Civil Code).

[77] SM Machado, *Tratado de Derecho administrativo y Derecho público general, Contratos del Sector Público*, Vol 13 (Madrid, Agencia Estatal Boletín Oficial del Estado, 2018) 173–74; SGV Ibáñez, *Tratado de Derecho Administrativo*, Vol 3, 4th edn (Cizur Menor, Civitas/Thomson Reuters, 2020) 772–73.

In Italy, the contracting authority exercises control and supervisory powers over the execution of public contracts, particularly in relation to the quality and performance of the works or services.[78] These powers include oversight of compliance with technical, economic, and qualitative standards, as well as verification that contractual objectives and timelines are met. Public contracts are generally subject to acceptance procedures and conformity checks to ensure alignment with agreed terms and conditions.

Although some differences exist between legal systems, they often appear more formal than substantive. For instance, Spanish law does not explicitly refer to a 'power of direction', unlike Portuguese law, where it is expressly mentioned. Nonetheless, the practical scope of this power in Portugal, which includes issuing orders on matters 'insufficiently regulated by the contract',[79] seems to correspond to what, in Spain, is encompassed within the power of interpretation under Article 190 Spanish Law on Contracts of the Public Sector.

ii. The Power to Impose Sanctions

The power to impose sanctions in France and Belgium allows the administration to penalise the contractor for delays or improper performance of the contract. Sanctions range from fines to other measures,[80] with legal doctrine identifying three types of sanctions.[81] First, monetary penalties can be applied for contractor delay. Second, the sanction of forced execution is employed when the continuity of contract performance is jeopardised by the private contractor's improper conduct. In such instances, the public party has the right to substitute the private contractor or entrust the task's performance to another party at the contractor's expense and risk.[82] Third, the sanction of termination of the contract by the public entity is justified for gross misconduct of the private contractor.[83] The sanctions imposed by the contracting authority are unilateral actions categorised as enforcement orders. However, if an administrative court finds the penalty to be irregular, the administration is obliged to compensate the contracting party.[84]

The power to impose sanctions on contractors is also recognised in both Portugal and Spain.[85] These sanctions typically include the imposition of

[78] Arts 114–116 Italian Public Contracts Code.

[79] Art 304(1) Portuguese Public Contracts Code.

[80] See s 7 (Means of action) Belgian Executive Decree on the Performance of Public Contracts. Flamme (n 33) 838.

[81] Guettier (n 64) 432.

[82] ibid 433.

[83] J Morand-Deviller, *Cours de droit administratif* (Paris, Librairie générale de droit et de jurisprudence, 2003) 411.

[84] Guettier (n 64) 433.

[85] Art 302(d) Portugese Public Contracts Code; Arts 190 and 194(2) Spanish Law on Contracts of the Public Sector.

contractual penalties, most commonly fines, and the termination of contracts. In both legal systems, such measures are treated as unilateral and binding administrative acts.[86] This means that the contractor is legally required to comply with them, and they are directly enforceable unless formally challenged in court.[87]

Because these decisions are directly enforceable, the public authority does not need to obtain a court order to implement them. For example, if a contract is terminated for non-compliance and the contractor refuses to vacate the premises where the contract is being executed, the contracting authority may request assistance from law enforcement to take 'administrative possession' of the site. This stands in sharp contrast to private contract law, where a party must usually obtain a judicial order to achieve the same effect.[88]

The regime governing non-compliance and its consequences highlights several important distinctions, similarities, and areas of overlap between public and private contract law in Portugal. One noteworthy example – sometimes also regarded as a 'sanction' – is the public authority's ability to replace a non-compliant contractor with another party at the expense of the original contractor. In private contract law, such a substitution generally requires prior judicial authorisation.[89]

However, the existence of a comprehensive set of general overriding rules in the Portuguese Public Contracts Code does not mean that private contract law is entirely excluded from application. As established by Article 280(4) Portuguese Public Contracts Code, private contract law is to be applied to public contracts in all matters not specifically governed by public law rules or principles. For instance, the Portuguese Public Contracts Code does not include an express provision on the presumption of fault for contractual breaches – a principle whereby the breaching party must prove that non-performance was not their responsibility and resulted from an exonerating circumstance. In such cases, it is common practice to apply Article 799 Portuguese Civil Code, which enshrines this presumption, even within the context of public contracts.[90]

In Italy, contracting authorities have the right to impose sanctions for delays in the performance of contractual obligations.[91] Penalties are mandatory and calculated based on the duration of the delay and the value of the contract or affected services. In public works contracts, the legal framework includes

[86] Also, in Spain this is understood to be the nature of the application of penalties – cf Machado (n 77) 211.

[87] Arts 307, 309 Portuguese Public Contracts Code.

[88] MA Raimundo, 'Execução coerciva das decisões do contraente público sobre incumprimento e extinção do contrato' in MA Raimundo (ed), *Contratos Públicos: Presente e Futuro – Actas das III Jornadas de Direito dos Contratos Públicos (29 de Setembro a 1 de Outubro de 2021, FDUL)* (Lisbon, Associação Académica da Faculdade de Direito de Lisboa, 2022) 249–69.

[89] Art 325 Portuguese Public Contracts Code; Raimundo, *Direito dos Contratos Públicos* (n 74) 247.

[90] See Raimundo, *Direito dos Contratos Públicos* (n 74) 247. *Código Civil Decreto-Lei no 47344, de 25 de novembro de 1966* (Portuguese Civil Code).

[91] Art 126 Italian Public Contracts Code.

mandatory rewards for early completion.[92] Sanctions may also take the form of early termination of the contract in cases of serious breach of obligations by the contractor.[93]

iii. The Power to Unilaterally Amend a Contract

The power to unilaterally amend a contract allows the public entity to modify the original contractual provisions. This power derives from the general rules applicable to administrative contracts and has been confirmed in court decisions in France. For example, in a judgment of 2 February 1983, the Conseil d'État emphasised that:

> Based on the general rules applicable to administrative contracts, a public law entity may unilaterally amend its contracts in the public interest. Following the refusal by the counterparty to perform the contract modification, the public body is entitled to terminate the contract.[94]

Amendments by the public entity are typically made for reasons of public interest. A contractor is protected in case the public entity uses this power and is entitled to financial compensation if obliged to bear new burdens resulting from the exercise of this power.[95]

A significant change in the approach to contract variation, through a unilateral decision by the contracting authority, emerged as a consequence of implementing the grounds for public contract modification set forth in Article 72 Directive 2014/24/EU. The Europeanisation of public procurement law introduced 'contractualisation' into the French national tradition of administrative contracts. It could be speculated that 'contractualisation' of administrative contracts, while preserving the public interest elements inherent to these contracts, places the contractor in a more advantageous, or at least a less unequal, position. This is achieved as modifications are now subject to EU public procurement law stemming from, among others, the CJEU case law.[96] The law mandates that modifications must be mutually agreed upon. Consequently, the French public contract has subtly shifted to lean more towards a civil contract, evolving into a 'lighter' administrative version compared to its original administrative form prior to the Europeanisation of public procurement law.[97] However, recent case law has introduced specific new powers for contracting authorities. They may now unilaterally terminate a contract on the grounds of illegality,[98] set

[92] ibid.
[93] ibid Art 126 (3).
[94] Union des transports publics urbains et régionaux, 34027, Rec 33.
[95] See Guettier (n 64) 441.
[96] Case C-456/06 *Peek & Cloppenburg KG v Cassina SpA* ECLI:EU:C:2008:232, [2008] ECR I-02731.
[97] On the transition to a public contract see eg, M Guibal, 'Droit public des contrats et concurrence: le style européen' (1993) 15 *La semaine juridique. Cahiers de droit de l'entreprise* 161.
[98] CE 10 July 2010, *Société Comptoir Négoce Équipements*, no 430864.

aside an unlawful clause if it is severable from the rest of the contract,[99] or even modify such a clause.[100]

In Belgium, the power to make changes was historically very broad, comparable to France.[101] Nowadays, changes are regulated by section five of the Belgian Executive Decree on the Performance of Public Contract, which is fully aligned with Article 72 Directive 2014/24/EU.

In Italy, private contract law applies by default to the performance phase, and the contracting authorities have overriding unilateral powers to modify the contract.[102]

In Portugal and Spain, there are general provisions allowing the contracting authority to unilaterally modify administrative contracts.[103] In addition, the rules may provide for other changes, which can be imposed by the contracting authority. For example, in works contracts, the contracting authority may impose additional work which the contractor is obligated to carry out, unless the contractor demonstrates that it lacks the staff or technical means to undertake those additional tasks.[104] As the modifications imposed by the contracting authority are based on public interest, they must not lead to breaching the economic balance of the contract against the contractor.[105] The underlying assumption is that the contractor only undertakes to perform a public contract for the consideration or revenue received. Therefore, a change in the contract conditions for reasons of public interest that demands more (or different) work must lead to full compensation of the contractor's costs. Similarly, in Portugal where if the modification breaches the economic balance of the contract (worsening the position of the contractor compared to the initial version of the contract), compensation is due.[106] Otherwise, the contracting authority would be unfairly benefited.[107] The full compensation is explicitly foreseen in general provisions and in provisions included in the legal regimes of each contract.

In Spain, according to general rules, modifications may only be unilaterally imposed on the contractor up to a threshold of a 20 per cent increase in the initial price. Above that increase, the modification must be agreed by the contractor. If

[99] CE 13 June 2022, *Centre hospitalier d'Ajaccio*, nos 453769 and 453770.

[100] CE 8 March 2023, *SIPPEREC*, no 464619.

[101] Flamme (n 33) 825. See Belgian Executive Decree on the Performance of Public Contracts.

[102] ME Comba, *L'esecuzione delle opere pubbliche: con cenne di diritto comparator* (Turin, Giappichelli, 2011).

[103] Arts 302(c) and 311(1)(c) Portuguese Public Contracts Code; Arts 203 and 206 Spanish Law on Contracts of the Public Sector.

[104] Subject to the conditions of Art 370 Portuguese Public Contracts Code which transposes Art 72(1)(b) Directive 2014/24; and Art 371(2) Portuguese Public Contracts Code.

[105] LL Martins, *Empreitada de obras públicas. O modelo normativo do regime do contrato administrativo e do contrato público (em especial, o equilíbrio económico-financeiro)* (Coimbra, Almedina, 2014) 531 ff.

[106] Regarding the power to modify administrative contracts in Spanish law, see Machado (n 77) 174 ff; Ibáñez (n 77) 837 ff.

[107] MA de Almeida, 'Apontamento sobre o problema da repartição do risco e do reequilíbrio financeiro nos contratos de concessão' in P Otero, CA Gomes, T Serrão (eds), *Estudos em Homenagem a Rui Machete* (Coimbra, Almedina, 2015) 679–92.

this agreement is not possible and the modifications are necessary, the contract is terminated.[108]

iv. Power to Suspend a Contract

French case law also grants the public administration the power to suspend contract performance if the other party fails to fulfil its contractual obligations, applying the *exceptio non adimpleti contractus* (ENAC). This right is not extended to the contractor, as maintaining the continuity of public service takes precedence.[109] In Belgium, ENAC cannot be used by the contractor with one exception; it is entitled to delay the works in case of non-payment.[110]

In Portugal, the contracting authority may suspend the performance of the contract in cases where compliance is made (temporarily) impossible, or by the application of ENAC.[111] ENAC can be invoked by the contracting authority in general terms, but conversely, there are important limitations for the contractor to invoke it against the contracting authority. Since 2008, Portuguese law has provided for a balanced approach, under which this right is not excluded, but has specific conditions, which attempt to ensure the continuity of public missions.[112] Thus, the contractor must give at least a 15-day notice before suspending the performance of the contract if the contracting authority is not complying with the contract.

In such cases, the contracting authority may respond by invoking an overriding public interest, a decision which may be subject to judicial review. If the authority relies on public interest grounds, the contractor is generally required to continue performing the contract, unless doing so would 'manifestly jeopardise' the contractor's solvency or render performance 'excessively onerous'.[113] In the equivalent situation in private contract law, no similar conditions exist.[114]

Similarly, in Italy, contracting authorities have the power to suspend the performance of a public contract in cases of exceptional circumstances or for reasons of overriding public interest.[115] Such suspension, however, must be limited to the period strictly necessary to address the situation. By contrast, the Croatian legal framework does not grant contracting authorities a comparable power to suspend contracts.

[108] Arts 206 and 211(1)(g) Spanish Law on Contracts of the Public Sector.

[109] CE 27 March 1957, *Carsalade*, no 21919, Lebon 216.

[110] See Art 70 Belgian Executive Decree on the Performance of Public Contracts; and see VRD en Demetsenare, 'Art. 70' in S Van Garsse (ed), *Artikelsgewijze commentaar op de (nieuwe) wetgeving overheidsopdrachten* (Brussels, Politeia, 2017) 584.

[111] Art 297 Portuguese Public Contracts Code.

[112] ibid Art 327.

[113] Raimundo, *Direito dos Contratos Públicos* (n 74) 255–56.

[114] Art 428 Portuguese Civil Code.

[115] Art 121(1) and (2) Italian Public Contracts Code.

v. Power to Unilaterally Terminate the Contract

The last specific power is the ability of the contracting authority to unilaterally terminate the contract in the event of a serious breach by the contractor. The power can be invoked as a form of sanction or for the general interest.[116] Moreover, a contract may also be terminated unilaterally when its continued execution no longer serves the public interest.[117] The power to unilaterally terminate a contract due to public interest is a contracting authority's prerogative that largely falls outside private contract law. The exercise of this power must be accompanied by appropriate compensation: full compensation in case of termination for general interest, which includes damages and lost profits suffered by the contractor and no compensation in case of serious fault.[118] These principles can be found in French and Belgian administrative law.[119]

Spain distinguishes between contract types for compensation. For example, in concession contracts, the contractor is entitled to compensation for both damages and lost profits.[120] In the case of supply and service contracts, termination is permitted at any time – although 'reasons of public interest' are not explicitly mentioned – with compensation for lost profits payable if the provision of goods or services has begun.[121]

In Croatia the contracting authority can unilaterally terminate an administrative contract for several reasons: (i) if the parties cannot agree on amendments, (ii) if the contractor is not fulfilling its obligations, (iii) if it is necessary to eliminate a serious and immediate threat to human life, health and public safety, and (iv) if this situation could not be eliminated by other means that would be less detrimental to acquired rights.[122] Furthermore, the contracting authority can terminate the contract if the contractor fails to comply with the provisions of the Croatian Public Procurement Act, as established by a final judgment of the competent administrative court.

Italian law provides for both mandatory and discretionary termination of public contracts by the contracting authority.[123] Mandatory termination applies in specific cases, such as those set out in Article 73 Directive 2014/24/EU, and in national provisions addressing anti-mafia legislation and related preventive

[116] L Richer and F Lichère, *Droit des contrats administratifs*, 13th edn (Paris, Librairie générale de droit et de jurisprudence, 2024); Art 334 Portuguese Public Contract Code.

[117] Guettier (n 64) 437.

[118] ibid 440; Art 334 Portuguese Public Contract Code.

[119] For Belgium see Flamme (n 33) 827; see also very critical S Van Garsse, *De concessive in het raam van de publiek-private samenwerking* (Bruges, die Keure, 2007) 492.

[120] Arts 279 and 280 Spanish Law on Contracts of the Public Sector for works concessions and Arts 294 and 295 for services concessions.

[121] ibid Arts 306 and 307 for supplies, and Art 313 for services.

[122] Art 153(2) Croatian General Administrative Procedure Act. Additionally, Art 322 Croatian Public Procurement Act outlines situations where the contracting authority must terminate the contract implementing EU public procurement law.

[123] Art 122 Italian Public Contracts Code.

measures.[124] Public contracts may also be terminated in cases of serious breach of contractual obligations, where such breach compromises the successful execution of the contract. In all forms of termination under Italian law, compensation to the contractor is limited to payment for services, works, or supplies that have been duly performed.[125] This approach appears more restrictive than the compensation regimes in some of the jurisdictions discussed above. Italian law also recognises the contracting authority's right to withdraw from a public contract at any time.[126] In such cases, the authority is required to provide compensation to the contractor.

C. Jurisdiction of Administrative Courts or Dual System

Reflecting the emphasis on public interest and the public character of outsourcing through procurement, the 'public-oriented hybrid model' generally assigns jurisdiction over disputes concerning the performance of public contracts to administrative courts. This approach has been adopted in countries such as France and Portugal. In contrast, a dual system, where jurisdiction is shared between administrative and civil courts, operates in Spain, Italy, and Belgium. In Croatia, jurisdiction over public contract disputes lies exclusively with the civil courts.

French law has developed the control exercised by administrative courts and the Conseil d'Etat based on the concept of 'public service'.[127] According to Rivero, the essence of the 1903 ruling by the Conseil d'Etat in *Terrier* was that all matters related to the organisation and functioning of public services – whether general or local – constitute administrative acts subject to administrative courts, regardless of whether the administration employs contracts or authoritative acts.[128] Exceptions to this general rule exist, particularly when it is evident that a public entity operates under conditions identical to those of a private entity and is subject to the same legal regulations and judicial forums, including civil courts. This typically occurs when the contract is signed by a private law body (in the French sense), even though it may qualify as a contracting authority under EU public procurement law definitions. Nevertheless, there are exceptions established by legislation and case law where such contracts are deemed administrative in nature.[129]

[124] Italian Code of Anti-Mafia Laws and Prevention Measures <www.gazzettaufficiale.it/atto/serie_generale/caricaDettaglioAtto/originario?atto.dataPubblicazioneGazzetta=2011-09-28&atto.codiceRedazionale=011G0201>.

[125] Art 122 (5) Italian Public Contracts Code.

[126] ibid Art 123.

[127] See Bell and Lichère (n 22) 272 with the reference to *Therond*, CE 4 March 1910, no 29373, Lebon 193.

[128] See J Rivero, *Existe-t-il un critère du droit administrative* (Paris, Librairie générale de droit et de jurisprudence, 1953); Franco-Polish seminar on administrative law organised in 1998 by the Institute of Law and Administrative Science in Krakow, reproduced in F Mélin-Soucramanien and F Mellary, *Le professeur Jean Rivero: ou la liberté en action* (Paris, Dalloz, 2012) 67 (1).

[129] F Licherie, *Les contrats administratifs entre personnes privées* (Thesis, Université Montpellier, 1998).

In Portugal, administrative courts have jurisdiction over any litigation arising from the formation, interpretation, lawfulness, and performance of any contracts covered by public procurement law, regardless of the nature of the contracting authority.[130] This includes all disputes regarding the procurement procedure (such as challenges to the award decisions but also tender documents) and all disputes regarding contract performance, including non-compliance or damages resulting from breach of contract.[131] Some contracts bound to public procurement rules are private law contracts; for example, some contracts of private entities acting in the utilities sector will not qualify as administrative contracts. Administrative courts may end up applying private contract law,[132] a solution justified by reasons of legal certainty.[133]

In Spain, not all matters related to the performance of public contracts are attributed to the administrative jurisdiction ('*Orden jurisdiccional contencioso-administrativo*'). Administrative courts are competent for all matters (formation and performance) regarding administrative contracts, and also for 'the acts of preparation and award of other contracts subject to the legislation on public procurement'.[134] This means that, unlike Portugal, Spain does not submit matters regarding the performance of public contracts which are not qualified as administrative contracts to the administrative courts. The litigation arising from the breach of private contract law, which was subject to public procurement rules, but is not qualified as an administrative contract, will fall to the civil courts in Spain.

While Croatia is classified as a 'public-oriented hybrid model' historically, disputes arising from public contracts have been adjudicated by civil courts, applying both the Croatian Public Procurement Act and the Croatian Law of Obligations.[135] This approach is based on the understanding that, alongside the specific provisions of the procurement legislation, the Croatian Law of Obligations applies appropriately to regulate the responsibilities of the contracting parties.[136] Notably, the subsidiary application of the Croatian Law of Obligations is also a characteristic of administrative contracts.[137] Although the Croatian Supreme Court has recently classified public contracts as administrative contracts, jurisdiction over such disputes has not yet been shifted to administrative courts. This is largely due to the legislature's reluctance to incorporate the Supreme Court's

[130] Art 4(1)(e) *Lei no 13/2002, de 19 de fevereiro Estatuto dos Tribunais Administrativos e Fiscais* (Portuguese Law on Administrative and Tax Courts).

[131] See decisions of the Court of Conflicts ('Tribunal dos Conflitos') of 27 November 2024, case 0679/20.7BELSB-S1-CP, and of 30 October 2024, case 0173/23.4T8VNC-A.S1.

[132] Explicitly acknowledging this, JCV de Andrade, *A Justiça Administrativa (Lições)*, 19th edn (Coimbra, Almedina, 2021) 109.

[133] ibid 109–10.

[134] Art 2(b) of *Ley 29/1998, de 13 de julio, reguladora de la Jurisdicción Contencioso-Administrativa* (Spanish Law on Contentious-Administrative Jurisdiction).

[135] *Zakon o obveznim odnosima* Official Gazzette Nos 35/05, 41/08, 125/11, 78/15, 29/18, 126/21, 114/22, 156/22, 155/23 (Croatian Law of Obligations).

[136] Art 313(3) Croatian Public Procurement Act.

[137] Art 151 Croatian General Administrative Procedure Act.

interpretation into the Croatian Public Procurement Act. This makes Croatia, to some extent, an outlier in the 'public-oriented hybrid model' in terms of jurisdiction.

In Italy and Belgium, jurisdiction over public contracts is also divided between administrative and civil courts, creating a dual system. In Italy, the nature of the legal relationship between the parties to a contract determines which court holds jurisdiction, with particular emphasis on the type of entitlement asserted by the opposing party.[138] Where the public administration exercises authoritative powers, the entitlement of the other party is typically characterised as a 'legitimate interest', placing the dispute under the jurisdiction of administrative courts.[139] By contrast, where the dispute involves a 'subjective right', jurisdiction lies with the civil courts.[140] A 'legitimate interest' arises whenever a public authority exercises – or fails to exercise – a public power that affects an individual's legal sphere.[141] It is generally understood as 'something less than a full right', insofar as the individual's entitlement is constrained by a conflicting public interest pursued through the exercise of public authority.[142] In the context of public contracts, the distinction between 'legitimate interest' and 'subjective right' often mirrors the divide between the phases of contract award and contract performance. Even during the performance phase, if the administration continues to exercise public power, the contractor's entitlement may still be classified as a 'legitimate interest', thereby maintaining the jurisdiction of administrative courts.[143]

In Belgium, disputes concerning the performance of public contracts are adjudicated by civil courts.[144] This approach aligns the country more closely with the 'private-oriented hybrid model', under which such disputes are treated primarily as private contractual in nature. In resolving these cases, judges generally apply private contract law, unless specific public law rules take precedence. Notably, the conduct of public authorities – including during the performance of contracts – is subject to unwritten principles of good administration, such as proportionality, impartiality, and due care. Failure to observe these principles is considered unlawful. However, in many instances, courts resolve disputes without expressly invoking public law principles, instead relying on private contract law doctrines such as good faith and the prohibition of abuse of rights, which reflect similar underlying values. Public contracts in Belgium are understood to operate within a dual framework: they are governed by specific public law rules and principles,

[138] M Comba, 'Enforcement of EU Procurement Rules. The Italian System of Remedies' in S Treumer and F Lichère (eds), *Enforcement of the EU Public Procurement Rules* (Copenhagen, DJØF Publishing, 2011) 236.

[139] E Silvestri, 'Administrative Justice in Italy' (2016) 2 *BRICS Law Journal* 67, 68; Comba, 'Contract Execution in Europe: Different Legal Models with a Common Core' (n 12) 304.

[140] Silvestri (n 139) 73.

[141] ibid.

[142] See Comba (n 138) 235.

[143] See for instance Cons Stato Sez V, 27 January 2022, no 590.

[144] Van Garsse, *Handboek Bestuursrecht* (n 40) 104.

supplemented by private law where appropriate. In practice, the tender documents – which form part of the contractual arrangement – often incorporate or are interpreted in light of private law. While some scholars consider public contracts to constitute a distinct legal category, private law remains the default regime, applied unless expressly displaced by public law provisions.

IV. 'Private-Oriented Hybrid Model'

The 'private-oriented hybrid model' is based on the principle that public administration operates on an equal footing with private parties in contractual relationships. This means that, as a contracting party, the public administration does not possess special privileges beyond those typically granted to private entities. There are numerous exceptions within this framework, as various public law provisions continue to apply to such contracts. As Comba observes, in certain instances, these exceptions blur the distinction between private and public law, potentially making the private law classification more of an exception than the norm.[145]

A. Equivalent Private Law Contract?

Germany is often regarded as the quintessential 'private-oriented hybrid model'. However, several other countries, including the Nordic nations (Denmark, Sweden, Finland, Norway, and Iceland), as well as the Netherlands, Poland, Czechia, Latvia, and non-EU Switzerland, can also be classified within the 'private-oriented hybrid model'.

In Germany, an explanatory memorandum to a former version of the German Competition Act (GWB) classified all public contracts as private law contracts.[146] Similarly, the Federal Administrative Court has stated that 'Works and services contracts concluded by the public sector are exclusively subject to private law'.[147] Section 103(1) GWB defines public contracts as agreements for pecuniary interest between contracting authorities and contractors for the procurement of goods, works, or services. This definition suggests that public contracts share key characteristics of private law contracts, including voluntariness, binding obligations, and pecuniary interest.[148]

In the Netherlands, decisions made within public procurement procedures are regarded as preparatory steps for private law acts, as public contracts are classified

[145] Comba, 'Contract Execution in Europe: Different Legal Models with a Common Core' (n 12) 304.

[146] *Gesetz gegen Wettbewerbsbeschränkungen* (GWB), BGBl I 1957, 1081 (German Competition Act); BT-Drs 13/1940, 12, 15.

[147] Federal Administrative Court Decision of 2 May 2007, BVerwG 6 B 10.07, BVerwGE 129, 9, 13 para 6, with further evidence (our own translation).

[148] K Bitterich, *Vergabeverfahren und Bürgerliches Recht* (Baden-Baden, Nomos, 2013) 265–72.

as civil law agreements.[149] Similarly, in Finland, the preparatory works of the Finnish Public Procurement Act explicitly state that a public contract is a private law agreement between two distinct legal entities.[150] In Poland, a public contract is judicially defined as a fundamentally civil law agreement.[151] This is confirmed by legal doctrine stating that a public contract is a civil law contract evidenced by its bilateral binding nature and the reference to the application of the provisions of the Polish Civil Code in matters not regulated by the Polish Public Procurement Act.[152]

A similar approach is taken in Czechia, where the relationship between the supplier and the contracting authority is primarily considered a private contract law relationship: 'After the contract is concluded, the rights and obligations of the contracting authority and the selected bidder, as contracting parties, are governed by private law regulations' (own translation).[153] This is further reflected in a Czech Supreme Administrative Court judgment, which states:

> The relationship between the supplier and the contracting authority has a private-law character, albeit with the reservation that certain obligations of the contracting authority arise from public law, and their (non-) fulfilment affects the public subjective rights of the bidders.[154]

In Latvia, both legal doctrine and case law recognise that public contracts are private law contracts.[155] For public entities, the Latvian State Administration Structure Law[156] sets out specific conditions for entering into such contracts. Contracts must be concluded without discrimination, and the contracting parties must be treated as equals.[157] However, it should be noted that in certain cases, public contracts may be classified as administrative law contracts, depending on the contract's purpose and subject matter.[158]

[149] AJ Van Heeswijck, 'The Dutch System of Legal Protection in Public Procurement Procedures' (2015) 6 *Public Procurement Law Review* NA 192–201. See A De Moor-Van Vugt and W Konijnenbelt, 'Le contentieux des contrats publics en Europe, Pays Bas' (2011) *Revue Francaise de Droit Administratif* 62.

[150] Finnish Public Procurement Act (1397/2016). GP 108/2016 ls, Government Proposal to the Parliament for Legislation of Procurement Procedure 74. Only in the exceptional situation where the contract involves the exercise of public authority and concerns the performance of a public administrative duty, it can be considered an administrative contract under s 3 Finnish Administrative Procedure Act (434/2003).

[151] Judgment of the Polish Supreme Court of 13 September 2001 (IV CKN 381/00).

[152] H Nowak and M Winiarz (eds), *Prawo zamówień publicznych. Komentarz*, 2nd edn (Warsaw, Urząd Zamówień Publicznych, 2023) 1081. See *Ustawa z dnia 23 kwietnia 1964 r. – Kodeks cywilny* (Polish Civil Code); *Ustawa z dnia 11 września 2019 r. – Prawo zamówień publicznych* (Polish Public Procurement Act).

[153] Regional Court in *Brno* judgment No 62 Af 64/2011 – 41 of 3 January 2013.

[154] Supreme Administrative Court of the Czech Republic, 1 Afs 2/2013 – 46, para 23.

[155] Judgment of 8 February 2007 of the Senate of the Supreme Court of the Republic of Latvia, Department of Administrative Cases in case No SKA-30/2007, para 11.2.

[156] *Valsts pārvaldes iekārtas likums* of 21 June 2002 <likumi.lv/ta/id/63545-valsts-parvaldes-iekartas-likums> (Latvian State Administration Structure Law).

[157] ibid Art 89.

[158] Judgment of 3 March 2020 of the Senate of the Supreme Court of the Republic of Latvia, Department of Administrative in case No A420689310, SKA-235/2020, ECLI:LV:AT:2020:0303.A420689310.8.S para 35.

In Denmark, the Danish Public Administration Act, which sets out the basic regulation and principles of administrative law for Danish public authorities, generally does not apply to 'contractual relationships' of public authorities or similar dispositions by a public authority of a 'private law nature'.[159] Danish public authorities, therefore, do not enjoy special privileges in their contractual relationships, but will be subject to the same general principles of Danish contract law as private entities. Upon closer examination, the picture may, however, become blurred. Depending on the nature of the public contract, it may not be possible to categorise all issues related to public contracts as merely of a 'contractual' or 'private law' nature, but a mix of contractual law and administrative law principles may apply. This applies particularly for types of public contracts, which relate to the exercise of public authority or are otherwise closely related to core public interests.[160]

In non-EU Switzerland, the government, when procuring goods, services, and works in the private market, is considered a 'private law subject', operating on the same level as private parties.[161]

B. Civil Code or General Reference to Contract Law Through Doctrine and Case Law

In countries with the 'private-oriented hybrid model', private contract law applies to areas not explicitly covered by public procurement law. This integration occurs in two ways. The first approach explicitly incorporates private contract law rules by referencing broader legal frameworks, such as the Civil Code. An example of this can be found in the Polish Public Procurement Act, which directly refers to the application of the Polish Civil Code in matters not regulated by public procurement law.[162]

The second approach relies on doctrine, legal tradition, and case law to determine the applicability of contract law regulations. In Germany, this has been confirmed by a ruling of the German Federal Administrative Court, which stated:

> The public sector generally operates on the basis of private law when awarding public contracts, so that disputes concerning the selection of the contractual partner to be

[159] *Forvaltningsloven* no 433/2014 (Danish Public Administration Act); N Fenger, *Forvaltningsloven med kommentarer*, 2nd edn (Copenhagen, DJØF Publishing, 2020) 83, with reference to the preparatory works of the Danish Public Administration Act.

[160] A Abkenar, *Delegation af myndighedsudøvelse til private aktører* (Copenhagen, DJØF Publishing, 2017) 207. More generally see, RG Nielsen, *Forvaltningskontrakter* (Stockholm, Karnov Group, 2021) with a summary in English on page 763ff.

[161] U Häfelin, G Müller, and F Uhlmann, *Allgemeines Verwaltungsrecht*, 8th edn (Zurich, Dike, 2020) 314.

[162] According to Art 8(1) Polish Public Procurement Act, 'Provisions of [the Polish Civil Code] shall apply to actions undertaken by contracting bodies, economic operators, and design contest participants in the procurement procedure and a design contest and to public contracts unless provisions of this Act provide otherwise'. However, Polish public procurement law regulates a number of issues that go beyond the scope of Arts 70–73 Directive 2014/24/EU, which is similar to the solutions provided for in the 'public-oriented hybrid model'.

> made in this context are not subject to administrative law, but to the ordinary courts' (own translation).[163]

In Finland, the Finnish Public Procurement Act does not regulate conduct during the contract period, except for the prohibition of substantial contract modifications. Since Finland does not have a single unified Civil Code, the Finnish Public Procurement Act also does not contain a reference to such a Code. Conduct during the contract period is governed by general principles of contract law. Consequently, contractual relationships are governed by general doctrines of contract law, as well as the provisions of the Finnish Contracts Act[164] and, where applicable, the Finnish Sale of Goods Act,[165] particularly concerning issues such as the fulfilment of contractual obligations, interpretation of contract bindingness, notifications of defects, and the termination and cancellation of contracts.[166]

In Czechia:

> While in this first phase (contractual) the relationship is fundamentally governed by the Act on Public Procurement and the Civil Code is applied subsidiarily to certain situations that are not expressly regulated by the Act on Public Procurement (eg, calculation of deadlines, etc.), in the second phase – after the conclusion of the implementation contract it is opposite; the legal relationship continues to be fundamentally governed by the concluded contract and the Civil Code, with the fact that the Act on Public Procurement applies additionally and only if the case provided for by this law occurs (withdrawal from the contract, the need to assign additional work, contract changes, etc.) (automated translation).[167]

Thus, while in Czechia there is no express reference to the Czech Civil Code[168] in the Czech Act on Public Procurement,[169] application of the Czech Civil Code comes from case law and doctrine.[170]

In Denmark, public contracts are generally governed by the same provisions and principles of law as private contracts. The Danish Contracts Act,[171] which sets out the basic rules and principles of the formation and validity of contracts of property law, also applies to public contracts. The Danish Sale of Goods Act[172] also applies to public contracts related to the sale or purchase of goods, unless the parties have agreed otherwise. Transactions concerning the sale and purchase of services and real

[163] See Federal Administrative Court Decision of 2 May 2007 (n 147); M Burgi, *Vergaberecht*, 3rd edn (Munich, CH Beck, 2021) s 2 paras 9–15.
[164] Finnish Contracts Act (228/1929).
[165] Finnish Sale of Goods Act (355/1987).
[166] E Pekkala, M Pohjonen, K Huikko, and M Ukkola, *Hankintojen kilpailuttaminen ja sopimusehdot* (Helsinki, Tietosanoma, 2019) 589.
[167] K Zuska, 'Veřejné zakázky z pohledu odpovědnosti dodavatele projektových a stavebních prací' *Holec Advokáti* <www.holec-advokati.cz/cs/verejne-zakazky-z-pohledu-odpovednosti-dodavatele-projektovych-a-stavebnich-praci/>. See also Regional Court in *Brno* judgment No 62 (n 153).
[168] *Občanský zákoník* Act No 89/2012 Coll (Czech Civil Code).
[169] *Zákon o zadávání veřejných zakázek Act* No 134/2016 Coll (Czech Act on Public Procurement).
[170] Supreme Administrative Court of the Czech Republic (n 154).
[171] *Aftaleloven* no 193/2016 (Danish Contracts Act).
[172] *Købeloven* no 1853/2021 (Danish Sale of Goods Act).

estate are not explicitly regulated in Denmark in the same way as transactions related to goods, but the principles governing private law contracts will also apply to public contracts. A public authority is liable for breach of contract in exactly the same way as a private party.[173] However, where specific regulations apply – such as those governing public procurement – these specialised rules take precedence. Thus, statutory provisions of public procurement law and, to some extent, the *lex specialis* principle, ensure that procurement rules override general contract law where applicable.[174]

In the Netherlands, decisions made by contracting authorities before or during a procurement procedure are not subject to appeal before the administrative court, as they concern preparatory acts leading up to a private law agreement.[175] This is why the Dutch General Administrative Law Act (AwB) explicitly excludes the procurement phase from its scope.[176] Disputes arising from procurement procedures and the contracts subsequently awarded are adjudicated by the civil courts, with private law governing their performance and interpretation.[177]

In Latvia, the Latvian Public Procurement Law[178] includes a chapter on the 'Conclusion and Performance of the Procurement Contract', which sets out requirements such as the minimum content, maximum duration, and other contractual aspects.[179] The law does not explicitly address the application of the Latvian Civil Law[180] during the contract performance phase. This is confirmed through legal doctrine and case law. Additionally, a Cabinet of Ministers instruction – applicable to contracts financed by foreign financial instruments and concluded by the central public administration – expressly requires that such contracts comply with the Latvian State Administration Structure Law, the Latvian Civil Law, and other external regulatory acts governing the legal relationships arising under the contract.[181] The Latvian Civil Law itself contains a few references to public

[173] S Bønsing, *Almindelig Forvaltningsret* (Copenhagen, DJØF Publishing, 2023) 501.

[174] On the impact of public procurement law on public contracts, see J Fabricius, *Offentlige indkøb i praksis*, 5th edn (Stockholm, Karnov Group, 2024) 887. See more, ch 6.

[175] Art 8:3(2) *Algemene wet bestuursrecht* (Awb) (Dutch General Administrative Law Act).

[176] The general principles of good administration (*algemene beginselen van behoorlijk bestuur*) appear to have limited influence on the Dutch contracting context. AJ Van Heeswijck, *Rechtsbescherming van ondernemers in aanbestedingsprocedures* (Groningen, University of Groningen, 2014).

[177] E Manunza and RGT Bleeker, 'De invloed van het Europees recht op het Nederlandse aanbestedingsrecht' in AS Hartkamp, CH Sieburgh and LAD Keus (eds), *De invloed van het Europese recht op het Nederlandse privaatrecht* (Deventer, Kluwer, 2007). The primary exception to this rule concerns reviews of public transport concessions, which are handled by the administrative courts (*Wet Personenvervoer* 2000 (Dutch Act on Public Transport 2000) as these fall under the scope of the ambit of Regulation 1370/2007/EC of the European Parliament and of the Council on public passenger transport services by rail and by road and repealing Council Regulations (EEC) Nos 1191/69 and 1107/70 [2007] OJ L315/1).

[178] *Publisko iepirkumu likums* of 29 December 2016 <likumi.lv/ta/id/287760-publisko-iepirkumu-likums> (Latvian Public Procurement Law).

[179] ibid ch 7. It also incorporates provisions from Directive 2014/24/EUs (contract modifications).

[180] *Civillikums* of 20 February 1937 <likumi.lv/ta/id/225418-civillikums> (Latvian Civil Law).

[181] Para 4 Instructions for the preparation and conclusion of civil law contracts financed by foreign financial instruments in direct public administration of 20 September 2016, <likumi.lv/ta/id/285534-arvalstu-finansu-instrumentu-finansetu-civiltiesisku-ligumu-izstrades-un-slegsanas-instrukcija-valsts-tiesas-parvaldes-iestades>.

procurement rules. For instance, in the context of supply contracts, it affirms that both the Latvian Civil Law's provisions on supply and the relevant laws on public works and procurement apply.[182]

The Swiss Federal Act on Public Procurement does not regulate the performance phase.[183] It does not even regulate the modification of the public contract during its term, meaning it is more limited than EU public procurement law. It only regulates the cancellation of the award procedure and not the termination of the contract. Topics such as contract modification, contract termination and contract performance are regulated in the Swiss Code of Obligations,[184] which is applicable after the contract has been awarded.[185] In this context, public procurement law is understood to 'specify, supplement, and supersede' private contract law.[186]

C. Equality of Parties: A Utopian Idea?

Rather than emphasising hierarchical subordination, the 'private-oriented hybrid model' prioritises contractual equality between the parties. Unlike the 'public-oriented hybrid model', there is no presumption of special powers for the contracting authority over the private party through mandatory provisions. The principle of party equality is exemplified, for instance, in the Czech context by a Regional Court in the *Brno* judgment, which stated 'Although the contracting authority may, in other cases, be a public authority that operates in a superior, sovereign capacity, it does not hold such a position within the procurement procedure'.[187] Similarly, Polish legal doctrine emphasises the equality of public contract parties.[188] Also, the German Federal Constitutional Court decided:

> The state acts as a buyer on the market in order to meet its need for certain goods or services. In this role as a buyer, it is not fundamentally different from other market participants. It does not rely on its superior public legal power when awarding a contract.[189]

[182] Arts 2111 and 2212 Latvian Civil Law.

[183] *Bundesgesetz über das öffentliche Beschaffungswesen* of 21 June 2019 (Federal Law Gazette 172.056.1) (Swiss Federal Act on Public Procurement).

[184] Federal Act on the Amendment of the Swiss Civil Code (Part Five: The Code of Obligations) of 30 March 1911 (Federal Law Gazette SR 220).

[185] P Galli, A Moser, E Lang, and M Steiner, *Praxis des öffentlichen Beschaffungsrechts*, 3rd edn (Zurich, Schulthess, 2013), 504; See also Supreme Court Decision BGE 125 I 214, E 6b.

[186] A Leuthold, *Offertverhandlungen in öffentlichen Vergabeverfahren: Privatrechliche und vergaberechtliche Aspekte* (Zurich, Schulthess, 2009) 41–42.

[187] Regional Court in *Brno* judgment No 62 (n 153).

[188] Nowak and Winiarz (n 152) 1081; A Fermus-Bobowiec, 'Wybrane zagadnienia dotyczące wykorzystania umowy cywilnoprawnej jako instrumentu działania administracji, Zeszyty Naukowe' (2018) 61(4) *Zeszyty Naukowe Katolickiego Uniwersytetu Lubelskiego Jana Pawła II* 126.

[189] German Federal Constitutional Court, Decision of 13 June 2006 – 1 BvR 1160/03, BVerfGE 116, 135, 149–150 (own translation).

Also, with regard to the performance, the state has 'basically no superior position' when using private law instruments – the usual case for public contracts.[190] The state and the private contractor are on a 'level of equality'.[191]

Similarly, in the Netherlands, private contract law is grounded in the principle of formal equality between contracting parties. Once a contract is concluded, both parties are regarded as legal equals, as they are, in principle, entitled to access the same legal remedies. Dutch law does not consider the identity of a party, whether or not it is a contracting authority, as legally relevant. However, this formal equality does not necessarily reflect the practical realities of the contractual relationship, where significant disparities in bargaining power, resources, or institutional position may lead to de facto inequality between the parties.

Thus, even within the 'private-oriented hybrid model', the contracting authority retains certain advantages resembling special powers, raising questions about the emphasis on party equality. These special powers often stem from public laws, particularly procurement laws or contractual clauses. For example, in Germany, Procurement and Contract Standards for Construction Works regulate the requirement for private contractors to provide contract performance security, which serves as a deposit for the contracting authority.[192] Similarly, the German Ordinance on Prices for Public Contracts contains a regulation on maximum prices for public contracts except for works contracts.[193] The purpose of the latter regulation is to curb consumer price inflation, which could be triggered by overpriced public contracts. To achieve this expression of public interest, public contracts are void insofar as they exceed the respective maximum price of the German Ordinance on Prices for Public Contracts.[194] The contractor is then obliged to repay the difference between the contract price and the maximum price.[195] If there is only one tender, cost-plus prices come into play because one tender price cannot guarantee the market price, according to the German Ordinance on Prices for Public Contracts. Due to the weaker competition for legal, political, economic, and technological reasons, the prime example for this is defence procurement.[196] However, if the procurement procedure results in competitive market prices, that is, at least

[190] German Federal Court of Justice, Judgment of 6 June 1967 – VI ZR 214/65, NJW 1967, 1911 (our own translation).

[191] German Federal Constitutional Court, Decision of 13 June 2006 (n 189).

[192] s 9c EU of Part A Vergabe- und Vertragsordnung für Bauleistungen, BAnz AT 19.01.2016 B3; <www.vob-online.de/de/vob-gesamtausgaben>.

[193] s 2(5) *Verordnung PR No 30/53 über die Preise bei öffentlichen Aufträgen* of 21 November 1953, BAnz 1953 No 244 as last amended by Art 1 *Verordnung* of 25 November 2021, BGBl I S 4968 (German Ordinance on Prices for Public Contracts).

[194] s 134 *Bürgerliches Gesetzbuch* of 18 August 1896, RGBl. S. 195, as last amended (most recently by Art 1 *Gesetz* of 21 December 2022, BGBl. I Nr. 51, p 2805) (BGB) (German Civil Code) and s 1(3) German Ordinance on Prices for Public Contracts.

[195] In detail P Zimmermann, in M Burgi, M Dreher, and M Opitz (eds), *Beck'scher Vergaberechtskommentar*, Vol 2, 4th edn (Munich, CH Beck, 2025); s 1 German Ordinance on Prices for Public Contracts paras 20, 25–28.

[196] ibid; Eingangsformel German Ordinance on Prices for Public Contracts para 3.

two tenders are eligible for the award, the German Ordinance on Prices for Public Contracts does not play a major role (as market price equals maximum price).[197]

A third example under German public procurement law is contract performance conditions, which the public contracting authority is mandated to prescribe for the private contractor. These may only be specified based on a federal or land statute.[198] For instance, the Thuringian Act on the Award of Public Contracts requires the inclusion of contractual clauses on penalties for breaches related to tax payment, social security regulations, and the avoidance of controls guaranteed to the contracting authority.[199] Additionally, the Brandenburg Act on Minimum Requirements for the Award of Public Contracts mandates the introduction of a contractual provision allowing the contracting authority to inspect the contractor's compliance with minimum wage conditions.[200] Furthermore, section 10(2) Brandenburg Act requires public contracts to include provisions allowing the contracting authority to terminate the contract in the event of the contractor's breach of social considerations.

The general terms and conditions (GTC) of the Swiss Confederation for the procurement of goods and services also form a mandatory part of all public contracts.[201] These foresee a unilateral right of the contracting authority to impose contractual penalties for (1) the contractor's violation of employment conditions and environmental law and (2) the contractor's delays.[202]

In light of the above, it is worth pointing out the validity of the view presented by Comba, who observes:

> A well-hidden paradox, according to which, despite the proclaimed equality of parties in the countries that follow a private law regime, the inclusion of these 'superpowers' as

[197] s 1(1), (2) and (4) of the German Ordinance on Prices for Public Contracts.

[198] s 129 GWB. GWB applies to public procurement procedures that exceed the threshold for a European-wide tender. (S 106 GWB). Regulations above the EU thresholds are supplemented by German Ordinance on the Award of Public Contracts (*Verordnung über die Vergabe öffentlicher Aufträge – VgV*), German Ordinance on the Award of Public Contracts in the Field of Transport, Drinking Water Supply, and Energy Supply (*Verordnung über die Vergabe von öffentlichen Aufträgen im Bereich des Verkehrs, der Trinkwasserversorgung und der Energieversorgung – SektVO*), German Ordinance on the Award of Concession Contracts (*Verordnung über die Vergabe von Konzessionen (Konzessionsvergabeverordnung) – KonzVgV*) and the German Construction Contract Procedures Part A/EU (*Vergabe- und Vertragsordnung für Bauleistungen Teil A – VOB/A*). Below the threshold for European-wide tenders, public procurement is regulated under budget law ('Haushaltsvergaberecht'). The federal and state's budget codes and the respective administrative regulations refer primarily to the Rules of Procedure Governing Supply and Service Contracts Below the EU Thresholds – (*Unterschwellenvergabeordnung – UVgO*) and the VOB/A (basic sections).

[199] S 13 *Thüringer Gesetz über die Vergabe öffentlicher Aufträge* of 23 January 2020 (GVBl, 29), as last revised by Act of 16 November 2023 (GVBl, 331) (Thuringian Act on the Award of Public Contracts).

[200] S 9 *Brandenburgisches Gesetz über Mindestanforderungen für die Vergabe von öffentlichen Aufträgen* of 29 September 2016 (GVBl.I/16, no 21) (Brandenburg Act on Minimum Requirements for the Award of Public Contracts).

[201] Art 11(2) *Verordnung über das öffentliche Beschaffungswesen Verordnung über das öffentliche Beschaffungswesen* of 12 August 2020, SR 172.056.1 (Swiss Public Procurement Ordinance of 2020).

[202] Swiss GTC <backend.bkb.admin.ch/fileservice/sdweb-docs-prod-bkbadminch-files/files/2024/06/19/9c525dce-d080-4769-b55c-2e19148e8065.pdf>.

contractual clauses provides less protection to the private contracting party compared to the exercise of a discretionary power enabled by administrative legislation.[203]

D. Civil Courts Jurisdiction

The 'private-oriented hybrid model' of public contracts influences court jurisdiction, directing disputes arising under such contracts to civil courts. This is achieved through a variety of mechanisms. In some jurisdictions, specialised procurement complaint bodies are established as the first stage of recourse, with subsequent appeals directed to civil courts. In others, parties are permitted to bring disputes directly before civil courts. Notably, in certain legal systems, administrative courts retain specific competencies during the contract performance phase of public contracts, adding a layer of complexity to the division of jurisdiction.

For example, in Czechia, the Office for the Protection of Competition oversees compliance with the Czech Act on Public Procurement, including rules on contract modifications.[204] Decisions of the Office can be appealed to an administrative court. However, disputes concerning public contracts outside the scope of the Czech Act on Public Procurement fall under the jurisdiction of civil courts.

In Denmark, the Danish Complaints Board for Public Procurement[205] is a special administrative body entrusted with deciding complaints related to the Danish Public Procurement Act[206] and EU public procurement law, including breach of the public procurement rules on contract modifications.[207] Complaints which are filed during the standstill period must be brought before the Complaints Board and cannot be brought before the civil courts, but outside the standstill period, the plaintiff may decide to bring the case directly to the courts rather than to the Complaints Board, which rarely happens. Decisions by the Complaints

[203] Comba, 'Contract Execution in Europe: Different Legal Models with a Common Core' (n 12) 302–08; As M Fromont observes, public authorities universally asserted intervention powers that exceeded those recognised under private contract law. To achieve this, several legal techniques were employed. The first involved establishing the principle that the performance of such contracts should be governed by rules that deviated from private or ordinary law. These rules, initially developed through case law in France, were later codified by statute or regulation in many countries. The second technique involved systematically incorporating clauses into the most significant contracts, which granted the administration a superior position. In some instances, these clauses were so broadly interpreted by the courts that they effectively became as binding as statutory or regulatory provisions. M Fromont, 'L'évolution du droit des contrats de l'administration – différences théoriques et convergences de fait' in R Noguellou and U Stelkens (eds), *Comparative Law on Public Contracts* (Brussels, Bruylant, 2010) 263–80.

[204] s 248 Czech Act on Public Procurement.

[205] Klagenævnet for Udbud, established by *Lov om Klagenævnet for Udbud* no 593/2016 (Danish Act on the Complaints Board for Public Procurement).

[206] *Udbudsloven* no 2015/1564 (Danish Public Procurement Act).

[207] Denmark does not have administrative courts. The Complaints Board has, however, been recognised by the European Court of Justice (ECJ) as a 'court' in the sense of Art 267 Consolidated version of the Treaty on the Functioning of the European Union [2012] OJ C326/47. See C-396/14 *MT Højgaard A/S and Züblin A/S v Banedanmark* ECLI:EU:C:2016:347, [2016].

Board can be appealed to a civil court, although this occurs rarely. The Complaints Board has on several occasions stated that it does not have the competence to decide on disputes relating to the parties' compliance with contractual obligations of public contracts or the interpretation of contractual rights and obligations for the parties to a public contract.[208] Such disputes will then be subject to the jurisdiction of the Danish civil courts.

In Switzerland, administrative courts have jurisdiction over cases involving a contracting authority's right to terminate a public contract due to substantial contract modifications. In such cases, disputes are handled by administrative courts rather than civil courts.[209] Contracts awarded to winning bidders fall under private law. Their form, modification, and termination are governed by Swiss private law, with civil courts handling related disputes.[210] However, the jurisdiction and extent to which courts can interpret the content (and modifications of the content) of a concluded public contract is less certain in Switzerland. The Zürich Administrative Court made clear that only the award, but not the contract, can be challenged in the administrative court, but left it open how to proceed if the content of a concluded contract was modified.[211] Under Article 58(2) Swiss Federal Act on Public Procurement, after a contract is concluded, the Swiss Federal Administrative Court may only assess whether the award decision violated the applicable law. Once finalised, the contract cannot be terminated, and the court can only determine damages for the unsuccessful bidder.[212]

In Finland, public procurement law matters can be appealed to the Market Court, including tender calls.[213] Market Court rulings may be appealed to the Supreme Administrative Court with leave.[214] However, disputes concerning public contracts, such as interpretation of the contract and damages claims, are contractual matters handled in district courts, the court of first instance for civil matters, unless the parties have agreed otherwise.[215]

In Latvia, disputes arising during the performance of a public contract may follow different resolution paths, depending on both the type of contract and the nature of the dispute. If the dispute concerns ineffectiveness, as addressed in Directive 89/665/EEC, it falls within the jurisdiction of the administrative court, regardless of the type of procurement contract.[216] While administrative courts do not have inherent jurisdiction to annul procurement contracts or their terms – since such contracts typically result in private law agreements – the legislator has

[208] Fabricius (n 174) 887, with references to decisions of the Danish Complaints Board.
[209] Decision of the Swiss Federal Supreme Court, 2C_314/2013 of 19 March 2014, E 1.1; and High Court of the Canton of Schaffhausen Decision No 60/2007/32 of 9 November 2011, E 2b.
[210] Galli, Moser, Lang, and Steiner (n 185) 504.
[211] FN, VG Zürich, VB.2000.00183, E 3a.
[212] Art 58(3) Swiss Federal Act on Public Procurement.
[213] Ss 145–146 Finnish Public Procurement Act (1397/2016). See KHO 2014:129.
[214] Finnish Public Procurement Act (n 213) s 165.
[215] Ch 2, s 1 Finnish Courts Act (673/2016).
[216] Art 73(2) Latvian Public Procurement Law.

provided for exceptional cases in which the administrative court is granted this competence.[217]

As previously noted, contracts awarded through public procurement are generally considered private law contracts. Accordingly, disputes concerning their execution (eg contractual penalties or delays) are adjudicated by civil courts.[218] However, some public contracts are classified as administrative law contracts. Disputes involving such contracts fall under the jurisdiction of the administrative court, which adjudicates matters governed by public law.[219]

In the Netherlands, disputes concerning public procurement procedures and the resulting contracts are adjudicated by the civil courts, with private law governing the performance and interpretation of the contract.[220] Additionally, complaints may be submitted to the Public Procurement Experts Committee, which can issue non-binding advisory opinions aimed at resolving conflicts. These opinions hold significant authority within Dutch legal culture and are often taken into account by the courts.

In Germany, the Public Procurement Tribunals exercise jurisdiction over disputes regarding the award of a public contract.[221] The second and third instances for consideration of appeals related to these disputes are the civil courts.[222] For disputes regarding the contract performance, civil courts have jurisdiction over public contracts that are classified as private law contracts.[223]

Under Polish law, disputes concerning public contracts fall into two main categories. The first involves disputes that arise during the public procurement procedure, while the second concerns disputes stemming from the performance of public contracts. In both instances, civil courts play a central role. Public contract disputes in Poland are treated as civil law cases and fall within the jurisdiction of the relevant civil courts.[224] These disputes may involve claims based on the provisions of the Polish Civil Code – such as actions for payment, the mitigation of contractual penalties, or the liability of an investor towards subcontractors – as well as cases that require the court to rule on the application of the Polish Public Procurement Act.[225]

[217] Decision of the Department of Administrative Cases of the Supreme Court of 27 April 2017 in case No A670004317, SKA-1046/2017, para 4.

[218] Art 23 *Civilprocesa likums* of 3 November 1998 <likumi.lv/ta/id/50500-civilprocesa-likums> accessed 15 September 2024 (Latvian Civil Procedure Law).

[219] Art 103(1) *Administratīvā procesa likums* of 14 November 2001 <likumi.lv/ta/id/55567-administrativa-procesa-likums> accessed 15 September 2024 (Latvian Administrative Procedure Law).

[220] See Manunza and Bleeker (n 177).

[221] Ss 155–170 GWB.

[222] ibid ss 171–184.

[223] s 13 *Gerichtsverfassungsgesetz* in the version promulgated on 9 May 1975 (BGBl I 1077), as last amended by Art 14 *Gesetz* of 27 December 2024 (BGBl 2024 I Nr. 438) (GVG) (German Courts Constitution Act).

[224] Art 1 Polish Civil Code.

[225] See W Dzierżanowski, *Prawo do sądu w zamówieniach publicznych* (Warsaw, Kluwer, 2018) 183.

V. Conclusion

The absence of comprehensive regulation of the performance of public contracts under EU public procurement law results in this phase being primarily governed by national models. The approaches adopted by the Member States can be broadly divided into the 'public-oriented hybrid model' and the 'private-oriented hybrid model'. Both models differ in the positions of the parties and the legislative techniques used to regulate issues not covered under EU public procurement law.

The 'public-oriented hybrid model' traditionally relies on the dominant position of contracting authorities, acting as custodians of the public interest. In contrast, the 'private-oriented hybrid model' theoretically grants both parties to a public contract an equal position, typical and inherent in private contract law. The 'public-oriented hybrid model' is characterised by the comprehensive regulation of the contract performance phase under public law, with peripheral application of private contract law provisions. Conversely, the 'private-oriented hybrid model' applies private contract law to matters not regulated by public procurement law.

The findings in this chapter open new avenues for research, encompassing at least two areas of analysis. First, since some Member States apply private contract law more extensively to the performance phase of public contracts, there is scope to examine the key private law principle of freedom of contract within the framework of public procurement law. The central question is the extent to which this principle may conflict with the inherent nature of public contracts. This issue will be addressed in the next chapter of this anthology.

Second, the absence of harmonised rules on the performance of public contracts offers an opportunity to explore the relationship between public procurement and national laws, whether public or private, that govern contractual obligations between the parties to a public contract in relation to specific matters. Selected individual issues will be addressed in the rest of this anthology.

4

Freedom of Contract: Contrasting Values and Principles in Contract Law and Public Procurement Law

VIBE GARF ULFBECK, MARTA ANDHOV, CRISTINA PONCIBÒ AND MICHAŁ KANIA

I. Introduction

Public contracts – particularly within the context of EU law – occupy a distinctive position at the intersection of several legal domains, each contributing different normative frameworks to the public procurement process. Chief among these are public procurement law, administrative law, and contract law that regulate public contracts.[1]

During the award phase of public contracts, public procurement law assumes a central role. EU public procurement law imposes rigorous standards designed to uphold transparency, foster competition, and ensure non-discrimination and fairness in the selection of contractors.[2] Directive 2014/24/EU serves to harmonise public procurement practices across Member States, thereby securing equal access to public tenders for economic operators throughout the EU.[3] In this initial phase, the influence of general contract law remains relatively limited.[4]

[1] See on differentiation in the usage of terminology of values, principles and rules in the context of contract law: KP Purnhagen, 'Principles of European Private or Civil Law? A Reminder of The Symbiotic Relationship Between the ECJ and the DCFR in a Pluralistic European Private Law' (2012) 18(6) *European Law Journal* 844; MW Hesselink, 'The General Principles of Civil Law: Their Nature, Roles and Legitimacy' in D Leczykiewicz and S Weatheril (eds), *The Involvement of EU Law in Private Law Relationships* (Oxford, Hart Publishing, 2013) 131–80; Y Adar and P Sirena, 'Principles versus Rules in the Emerging European Contract Law' in J Rutgers and P Sirena (eds), *Rules and Principles in European Contract Law* (Antwerp, Intersentia, 2015) 7–32. See also ch 2.

[2] Art 18 Directive 2014/24/EU.

[3] S Arrowsmith, *The Law of Public and Utilities Procurement: Regulation in the EU and UK*, Vol 1, 3rd edn (London, Sweet & Maxwell, 2014). See Directive 2014/23/EU; Directive 2014/24/EU; Directive 2014/25/EU.

[4] On the possible application of the contract law doctrine of pre-contractual liability, see M Andhov, M Kania, A Saljic, and T Schrøder-Hansen, 'Culpa in Contrahendo: A Solar Eclipse between Contract and Public Procurement Law?' (2025) *Uphandlingsrätslig Tidskrift* 47–77.

However, once the contract has been awarded, the legal landscape shifts. Contract law and administrative law become more prominent, governing some aspects of the execution, interpretation, and potential disputes arising from the contract. The extent and manner in which these legal frameworks apply vary across jurisdictions, depending on the legal traditions and regulatory models adopted by Member States.[5]

A. 'Public-Oriented Hybrid Model'

In countries that follow the 'public-oriented hybrid model', public contracts are predominantly treated as public law contracts.[6] This model reflects a distinction between public and private legal regimes, where public contracts are governed by specific rules that emphasise the public interest, administrative oversight, and the unique responsibilities of public authorities. Under this model, public law heavily influences the formation, execution, variation, and termination of contracts, often imposing stricter terms than would be found in private commercial contracts.[7] The emphasis is on safeguarding public resources and ensuring that public authorities maintain control over the execution of contracts in line with public interest objectives. In this context, the public interest is often regarded as a foundational element of national public procurement law which, in turn, is partially embedded within the broader concept of the administrative contract.[8]

B. 'Private-Oriented Hybrid Model'

Conversely, in countries that adhere to the 'private-oriented hybrid model', public contracts are largely treated as private commercial contracts.[9] In this model, contract law assumes a much greater role in governing the relationship between public authorities and contractors. Public contracts are formed and executed under general private law principles, meaning that public authorities enter into contractual relationships much like private commercial entities. This approach prioritises flexibility, commercial efficiency, and legal certainty, with fewer administrative constraints than the 'public-oriented hybrid model'.

The distinction between the 'public-oriented hybrid model' and the 'private-oriented hybrid model' highlights a divergence in how Member States handle

[5] See ch 3.
[6] ibid.
[7] ibid.
[8] ibid.
[9] ibid.

the interplay between EU public procurement law, administrative law, and contract law.[10]

In the 'public-oriented hybrid model' jurisdictions, administrative law rules may impose additional requirements on contract execution, such as unilateral modification rights for the public authority or heightened standards for contract termination to protect the public interest.[11] The integration of public law reasoning in the administrative contract and the emphasis on the public purpose of the contracts may indeed push the application of contract law to the periphery, thereby limiting its application.[12] Nevertheless, even in these jurisdictions, a margin for the application of contract law to public contracts persists, as public law has not comprehensively regulated all aspects of public contracts.

In contrast, the 'private-oriented hybrid model' jurisdictions rely more heavily on the mutual obligations defined by the contract itself, with fewer opportunities for administrative intervention once the contract is signed.

The divergence also extends to the legal remedies available in the event of contract disputes. In the 'public-oriented hybrid model', disputes may be resolved through administrative courts, which have specialised jurisdiction over public contracts, whereas in the 'private-oriented hybrid model', disputes related to contract issues are more likely to be settled in ordinary civil courts or in arbitration under standard contract law procedures.[13]

This chapter sets the stage for the analysis in subsequent chapters of the interplay between public procurement law (inclusive of both EU public procurement law and national public procurement acts) and contract law by exploring the foundational rationales underpinning public procurement law and contract law, respectively. It contrasts the core values and guiding principles of each regime, with particular attention to their divergent objectives. To highlight these differences in their most distinct form, the focus is placed on comparing public procurement law with classical commercial contract law, rather than with the contract law governing administrative contracts in the 'public-oriented hybrid model'.[14]

To achieve its objectives, this chapter is structured as follows: it begins by examining the foundational principle of freedom of contract, analysed with particular attention to its adoption in public contracts (section II). It then considers its key subcategories in the same context, namely freedom in selecting the contractual counterparty (section III), freedom regarding contract form (section IV), freedom in determining contract content (section V), and freedom to modify the contract (section VI). Section VII provides introductory reflections on the related principles of good faith and fair dealing, and privity of contract, respectively.

[10] ibid.
[11] ibid.
[12] ibid.
[13] ibid.
[14] The differences between basic principles in administrative contract law and procurement will be less stark since public law thinking is embedded in the administrative contract.

The chapter concludes in section VIII. The interaction between contract law and public procurement law – particularly in relation to the principle of freedom of contract – is explored in greater depth in several of the subsequent chapters of this anthology.[15]

II. The General Principle of Freedom of Contract

The origins of the principle of contractual freedom can be traced back to Roman law, but it was first explicitly codified in Article 1134 French Civil Code of 1804.[16] This provision stated that 'Contracts legally entered into become law for those who enter into them' (author's translation). A similar concept was later adopted in the Austrian Civil Code (ABGB) of 1811.[17]

The principle of freedom of contract later became a cornerstone of various national contract law frameworks, including the German Civil Code (BGB),[18] and the Polish Code of Obligations of 1933.[19] Likewise, Nordic contract law is grounded in the principle of freedom of contract, although this principle is not expressly stated in the Nordic Contracts Acts.[20] In Denmark, as in other Nordic jurisdictions, the notion of contractual freedom derives from a broader context of Nordic legal pragmatism, legal culture, and tradition.[21] As Basedow observes, 'the principle of contractual freedom has, since the nineteenth century, developed into a foundational tenet in the regulation of economic activity within all European states'.[22]

A. Freedom of Contract in EU Law

The principle of freedom of contract is also embedded in EU primary law.[23] According to Professor Szpunar, First Advocate General (AG) of the Court of

[15] See on the freedom of contract ch 5; on the principle of good faith and fair dealing ch 7; on the principle of *pacta sunt servanda* ch 9; on the principle of privity of contract, ch 12.

[16] The French Civil Code was adopted in 1804 and has, of course, been profoundly amended since. A consolidated version (in French) prepared by the French official legal service (Legifrance): *Code civil* <www.legifrance.gouv.fr/codes/texte_lc/LEGITEXT000006070721/> (French Civil Code).

[17] *Allgemeines bürgerliches Gesetzbuch* (ABGB), JGS Nr 946/1811 (Austrian Civil Code).

[18] *Bürgerliches Gesetzbuch* (BGB), 1896, RGBl. S. 195, as amended (German Civil Code).

[19] *Rozporządzenie Prezydenta Rzeczypospolitej z dnia 27 października 1933 r. – Kodeks zobowiązań.* See M Szpunar, 'Zasada swobody umów w prawie wspólnotowym' in C Mik (ed), *Zasady ogólne prawa wspólnotowego* (Torun, Towarzystwo Naukowe Organizacji i Kierownictwa 'Dom Organizatora', 2007) 307.

[20] For Danish law: *Aftaleloven* no 193/2016 (Danish Contracts Act).

[21] See P Letto-Vanamo, D Tamm, M Gram Mortensen and O Bent (eds), *Nordic Legal Mind (in) Nordic Law in European Context* (Berlin, Springer, 2019) 1–19. See also ch 7.

[22] See J Basedow, 'Freedom of Contract in the European Union' (2008) 16(6) *European Review of Private Law* 901, 902.

[23] In its early development, European primary law did not explicitly or unambiguously articulate the principle of freedom of contract. For instance, Art 3(3) TFEU refers only to the objective of establishing

Justice of the European Union (CJEU), freedom of contract is currently protected under Article 16 Charter of Fundamental Rights of the European Union.[24] This provision affirms that: 'The freedom to conduct a business in accordance with Union law and national laws and practices is recognised'.[25]

Szpunar contends that the ongoing constitutionalisation of EU law requires fundamental rights to be taken into account, and that freedom of contract forms an inherent element of the broader freedom to conduct a business, as preserved in Article 16.[26]

The CJEU has invoked the principle of contractual freedom in several of its judgments, including in the field of labour law – an area generally considered part of civil law in most Member States.[27] In *Werhof v Freeway Traffic Systems*, the Court emphasised that the essence of a contract lies in the freedom of the parties to mutually determine their rights and obligations, including the voluntary choice to enter into a contractual relationship.[28]

Furthermore, the principle has been analysed in rulings based on Member States' laws, such as in *Commission v SNUA Srl*, where the Court interpreted Article 1322 Italian Civil Code[29] regarding the principle of freedom of contract in the context of parties' ability to define grounds justifying contract termination.[30]

a 'highly competitive social market economy', which does not amount to a definitive affirmation of contractual freedom. Nevertheless, the EU's broader commitment to economic freedom, property rights, and the internal market implies individual autonomy, including the freedom to contract – whether as professionals or consumers. Accordingly, freedom of contract may be understood as an implicit foundational principle underpinning the functioning of the Union's fundamental freedoms, despite the absence of direct textual articulation in the treaties. See Basedow (n 22). See Consolidated version of the Treaty on the Functioning of the European Union [2012] OJ C326/47.

[24] Charter of Fundamental Rights of the European Union [2012] OJ C326/391.

[25] See M Szpunar, 'Private Law within the Process of Europeanization' in R Szczepaniak (ed), *The Constitutionalization of Private Law Versus the Europeanization of Private Law: A Legal Study Based on the Example of Selected Countries of Central and Eastern Europe Belonging to the European Union*, Vol 8 (Leiden, Koninklijke Brill, 2025) 55–70. Fundamental rights play a crucial role in ensuring the coherence of the legal system. According to the second sentence of Art 52(5) Charter of Fundamental Rights of the European Union, such rights may be invoked in judicial proceedings for the interpretation of legal acts and the assessment of their legality – an essential function for safeguarding the values these rights embody. However, these principles typically cannot serve as direct grounds for legal claims. Rather, they operate to fill normative gaps, as such gap-filling is a natural element of legal interpretation that draws upon fundamental rights principles. See AC Ciacchi, 'Party Autonomy as a Fundamental Right in the European Union' (2010) 6(3) *European Review of Contract Law* 303.

[26] See M Szpunar, 'Basedow, Jürgen: EU Private Law. Anatomy of a Growing Legal Order. – Cambridge, Antwerp, Chicago: Intersentia 2021. CXXVII, 788 pp' (2023) 87(2) *Rabels Zeitschrift für ausländisches und internationales Privatrecht* 353, 358.

[27] See Case C-33/89 *Maria Kowalska v Freie und Hansestadt Hamburg* ECLI:EU:C:1990:265, [1990] ECR I-02591; Case C-15/96 *Kalliope Schoning-Kougebetou v Freie und Hansestadt Hamburg* ECLI:EU:C:1998:3, [1998] ECR I-00047; Case C-499/04 *Hans Werhof v Freeway Traffic Systems GmbH & Co. KG.* ECLI:EU:C:2006:168, [2006] ECR I-02397. See J Adams-Prassl, 'Freedom of Contract as a General Principle of EU Law? Transfers of Undertakings and the Protection of Employer Rights in EU Labour Law: Case C-426/11 Alemo-Herron and others v. Parkwood Leisure Ltd.' (2013) 42(2) *Industrial Law Journal* 434.

[28] See Case C-499/04 *Hans Werhof* (n 27) para 23.

[29] *Codice Civile* adopted with *Regio Decreto 16 marzo 1942, no 262* (Italian Civil Code).

[30] See Case C-67/97 *Commission v SNUA Srl* ECLI:EU:C:1999:204, [1999] ECR I-02363 para 23.

In *Automec Srl v Commission*, the Court of First Instance rejected the claimant's request for the Commission to order a company to conclude a contract with the complainant as part of measures to eliminate the infringement of competition, as this would contravene the principle of freedom of contract. The Court noted that the Commission has other means to address competition law infringements without violating this principle.[31]

B. Freedom of Contract in European Contract Law

Freedom of contract is likewise recognised as a foundational principle and a cornerstone of European contract law and thus is reflected in both the Draft Common Frame of Reference (DCFR) and the Principles of European Contract Law (PECL).[32] According to Article 1:101 DCFR: 'Parties are free to make a contract or other juridical act and to determine its contents, subject to any applicable mandatory rules'.[33]

Similarly, Article II–1:102(1) DCFR states: 'Parties are free to make a contract or other juridical act and to determine its contents, subject to any applicable mandatory rules'.

It is also articulated in Article 1:102 PECL: 'The parties are free to enter into contracts and to determine their contents subject to the requirements of good faith and fair dealing, and the mandatory rules established by these Principles'.

These provisions highlight that contractual freedom grants legal subjects the competence to shape their legal relations through contracts. In other words, parties have the autonomy to define their legal relationships as they see fit, provided there are no conflicting legal provisions.[34]

C. Freedom of Contract and EU Public Procurement Law

Freedom of contract is notably curtailed within the context of EU public procurement law, where the guiding principles of transparency, fairness, and non-discrimination are paramount. In this domain, mandatory legal provisions are primarily designed to give effect to the values and objectives articulated in Directive 2014/24/EU. Directive 2014/24/EU mandates, under Article 18(1), that contracting authorities must treat economic operators equally and without

[31] See Case T-24/90 *Automec Srl v Commission* ECLI:EU:T:1992:97, [1992] ECR II-02223 paras 51–52.

[32] See ch 1 for an explanation of the rationale behind the inclusion of European contract law and the scope within which it is understood in this anthology.

[33] See JW Rutgers, 'The European Economic Constitution, Freedom of Contract and the DCFR' (2009) 5(2) *European Review of Contract Law* 95.

[34] TM Möllers, 'Working with Legal Principles – Demonstrated Using Private Autonomy and Freedom of Contract as Examples' (2018) 14(2) *European Review of Contract Law* 101, 113.

discrimination, while also acting in a transparent and proportionate manner.[35] Additionally, paragraph (2) of the same article obliges Member States to ensure that, in the execution of public contracts, economic operators comply with relevant obligations in the areas of environmental, social, and labour law. These obligations arise under Union law, domestic legislation, collective agreements, and the international instruments listed in Annex X.[36] Collectively, these principles of EU public procurement law establish a paradigm that results in a comprehensive regulatory framework.[37]

In particular, public procurement procedures, various aspects of contract awards, and remedies are regulated to ensure the equitable and non-discriminatory treatment of all bidders. As contracting authorities must adhere to the principles of transparency and non-discrimination, they are limited in the flexibility typically associated with other types of contracts. This ensures that all potential suppliers have an equal opportunity to compete, which is crucial for maintaining public trust and integrity.[38] Public contracts are executed in the public interest, prioritising the public's needs and welfare over purely commercial considerations.[39] In this context, contemporary issues such as environmental concerns, particularly climate change, and the use of innovative developments like Artificial Intelligence (AI) in the public procurement process are of particular importance.[40] These considera-

[35] Case 45/87 *Commission of the European Communities v Ireland* ECLI:EU:C:1988:435, [1988] ECR I-04929; Case C-243/89 *Commission of the European Communities v Kingdom of Denmark* ECLI:EU:C:1993:257, [1993] ECR I-03353; Case C-324/98 *Telaustria Verlags GmbH* ECLI:EU:C:2000:669, [2000] ECR I-10745; M Steinicke, 'Article 18 Principles for the Conclusion of the Contract' in M Steinicke and PL Vesterdorf (eds), *Brussels Commentary on EU Public Procurement Law* (London, Bloomsbury Publishing, 2018) 290.

[36] Art 18(2) Directive 2014/24/EU was elevated to the status of a public procurement principle in the CJEU ruling in Case C-395/18 *Tim SpA – Direzione e coordinamento Vivendi SA v Consip SpA and Ministero dell'Economia e delle Finanze* ECLI:EU:C:2020:58, [2020] para 38.

[37] M Andhov, 'Contracting Authorities and Strategic Goals of Public Procurement – a Relationship Defined by Discretion?' in S Bogojevic, X Groussot and J Hettne (eds), *Discretion in EU Procurement Law* (Oxford, Hart Publishing, 2019).

[38] I Rizzo, 'Efficiency and Integrity Issues in Public Procurement Performance' (2013) 31 *Journal of Public Finance and Public Choice* 111; S Joković, *Competition and Integrity in Public Procurement*, 2nd edn (Chennai, Notion Press, 2022).

[39] Public interest is a broad concept that evolves according to changing conditions and demands of public authorities over time. The EU has defined its priorities eg through the EU Green Deal and the EU Industrial Policy. These documents introduced the concept of a Twin Transformation, which encompasses both environmental aspects and digitalisation. See European Commission, 'Communication from the Commission to the European Parliament, the European Council, the Council, the European Economic and Social Committee and the Committee of the Regions, the European Green Deal' COM(2019) 640 final; European Commission, 'Communication from the Commission to the European Parliament, the European Council, the Council, the European Economic and Social Committee and the Committee of the Regions a New Industrial Strategy for Europe' COM(2020) 102 final.

[40] M Andhov and F Muscaritoli, 'Climate Change and Public Procurement: Are We Shifting the Legal Discourse?' in W Janssen and R Caranta (eds), *EU Public Procurement Law: Reflections on a Paradigm Shift* (Oxford, Hart Publishing, 2023) 21; M Kania, 'Current Challenges and Prospects for the Development of the Polish Public Procurement' (2023) 85(1) *Ruch Prawniczy, Ekonomiczny i Socjologiczny* 55; M Andhov, N Darnall and A Andhov, 'Leveraging AI for Sustainable Public Procurement: Opportunities and Challenges' (2025) 6 *Frontiers in Sustainability* 1603214.

tions necessitate additional safeguards and oversight that may not be as prominent in private sector contracts.[41]

The following sections undertake a closer examination of key subcategories of the principle of freedom of contract, drawing a comparative analysis between its treatment in contract law and its application within the context of public procurement law.

III. Freedom in Selecting the Contractual Counterparty

The decision to enter into a contract constitutes an initial expression of the principle of freedom of contract. In general, contract law does not impose any obligation to form a contractual relationship, thereby enabling parties to determine not only whether to contract but also with whom.[42] This discretion in contractor selection is typically guided by considerations of economic advantage, though the criteria remain discretionary and may vary and evolve in line with the contracting party's particular needs or objectives.

There are only limited exceptions to the freedom to choose one's contracting partner. In certain sectors providing universal services – such as energy, water, or specific modes of transport – providers may be under a legal obligation to contract.[43] Further constraints may stem from mandatory legal provisions, notably those arising from economic sanctions imposed by the EU or domestic authorities, which may prohibit contractual dealings with companies or individuals from designated jurisdictions.[44]

[41] On the risks of artificial intelligence, technology in public procurement see Deloitte, 'Study on up-take of emerging technologies in public procurement' DG GROW G.4, Req No 146 Framework Contract DI/07624 – ABC IV Lot 3 D01.06: Final Report February 2020 <ec.europa.eu/docsroom/documents/40102>; NA Sava, 'Artificial Procurement Intelligence and Public – Deciphering the Interdisciplinary Perspectives of the Literature' (2023) 4(2) *European Review of Digital Administration & Law* 79; A Sanchez-Graells, *Digital Technologies and Public Procurement Gatekeeping and Experimentation in Digital Public Governance* (Oxford, Oxford University Press, 2024).

[42] Art 0:101 DCFR and Art 1:102 PECL. C Von Bar, E Clive and H Schulte-Nölke (eds), *Principles, Definitions, and Model Rules of European Private Law: Draft Common Frame of Reference (DCFR)* (Munich, Sellier European Law Publishers, 2009) 62.

[43] Centralist-planned economies are models seen in countries such as those of the former Soviet Union, North Korea, and Russia, where central and local authorities had the power to impose contracts on private companies, compelling them to produce a specified quantity of goods or provide certain services. Within such systems, the obligation to contract arises from public sector policies that dictate both the contracting party and the content of the contract. In these cases, the contractor is compelled to conclude a contract as determined by another legal entity, causing the contract to bear a closer resemblance to an administrative decision than to a mutual agreement.

[44] C Abely, *The Russia Sanctions. The Economic Response to Russia's Invasion of Ukraine* (Cambridge, Cambridge University Press, 2023). See Also M Andhov and M Kania, 'Ever-growing Restrictions on Whom Public Buyers Can Contract with – Contemporary Developments in the EU Public Procurement' (15 June 2023) *Bestek Blog*, <bestek-procurement.com/ever-growing-restrictions-on-whom-public-buyers-can-contract-with-contemporary-developments-in-the-eu-public-procurement/>.

Public law intervention may also restrict freedom of contract, particularly in cases involving breaches of competition law, such as the abuse or risk of abuse of a dominant or monopolistic market position.[45] In such circumstances, regulatory authorities may prohibit agreements with certain entities or, conversely, impose an obligation to contract with others in order to facilitate specific technical or market-based outcomes.[46]

In contrast to the contract law paradigm, where limitations on counterparty choice are exceptional, such restrictions are inherent to public contracts. Here, freedom of choice is curtailed not only by financial considerations but also by overarching public interest objectives arising from the EU primary law.[47] Restrictions on counterparty selection are rooted in the need to uphold the principles that underpin EU public procurement law, themselves derived from the foundational values of the internal market.[48]

Public procurement procedures are marked by a high degree of formalisation in their pre-contractual phase. The initiation of, or participation in, such procedures triggers specific legal implications. These include the obligation to apply the predetermined award criteria for identifying the most economically advantageous tender (MEAT), as well as compliance with non-negotiable minimum requirements in more flexible procedures.

A key legal construct concerning the selection of a contractual counterparty is found in the exclusion grounds set out in Article 57 Directive 2014/24/EU.[49] This provision, which enumerates both mandatory and discretionary grounds for exclusion, offers contracting authorities a structured framework for determining whom not to contract with.[50] Beyond the situations expressly covered by Article 57, further limitations on the freedom to select contractors may arise under other legal instruments. For instance, the Deforestation Regulation introduces additional

[45] M Steiner, *Economics in Antitrust Policy: Freedom to Compete vs. Freedom to Contract* (Boca Raton, Universal-Publishers, 2007).

[46] M Andhov and M Kania, 'Restricting Freedom of Contract – the EU Foreign Subsidies Regulation and its Consequences for Public Procurement' (2023) 24(1) *Journal of Public Procurement* 21.

[47] R Caranta, 'Are the Principles of European Contract Law Relevant for Public Contracts?' in SDL Rosa and PV Fernández (eds), *Principles of Public Contracts in Europe* (Brussels, Bruylant, 2022) 86.

[48] See ch 2.

[49] Case C-124/17 *Vossloh Laeis GmbH v Stadtwerke München GmbH* ECLI:EU:C:2018:855, [2018]; Case C-101/18 *Idi Srl v Arcadis – Agenzia Regionale Campana Difesa Suolo* ECLI:EU:C:2019:267, [2019]; Case C-41/18 *Meca Srl v Comune di Napoli* ECLI:EU:C:2019:507, [2019]; Case C-267/18 *Delta Antrepriză de Construcţii şi Montaj 93 SA v Compania Naţională de Administrare a Infrastructurii Rutiere SA* ECLI:EU:C:2019:826, [2019]; Case C-395/18 *Tim SpA* (n 36); Case C-387/19 *RTS infra BVBA and Aannemingsbedrijf Norré-Behaegel v Vlaams Gewest* ECLI:EU:C:2021:13, [2021]; Case C-210/20 *Rad Service Srl Unipersonale and Others v Del Debbio SpA and Others* ECLI:EU:C:2021:445 [2021]; Case C-416/21 *Landkreis Aichach-Friedberg v J. Sch. Omnibusunternehmen and K. Reisen GmbH* ECLI:EU:C:2022:689, [2022]. See also P Friton and J Zöll, 'Article 57 Exclusion Grounds' in R Caranta and A Sanchez-Graells (eds), *European Public Procurement: Commentary on Directive 2014/24/EU* (Cheltenham, Edward Elgar Publishing, 2021) 588–635.

[50] Andhov and Kania (n 46) 21.

sustainability-oriented constraints.[51] Under Article 25 Deforestation Regulation, Member States are required to establish penalties for non-compliance by operators and traders, which may include temporary exclusion from public procurement procedures for up to 12 months. In doing so, the Deforestation Regulation sets new mandatory minimum exclusion criteria, thereby further limiting discretion in contractor selection within public procurement.[52]

The divergent foundations of private contract law and public procurement law are also evident in their respective approaches to the withdrawal from negotiations. In contract law, the general presumption is that parties may withdraw from negotiations at any time without incurring liability for doing so. Compensation may only be claimed in exceptional cases, typically where the withdrawing party has breached a duty of good faith during the pre-contractual phase.[53] Such claims are occasionally grounded in the doctrine of *culpa in contrahendo*, though the rules on pre-contractual liability vary across jurisdictions.[54]

By contrast, public procurement law imposes stricter requirements. The right to terminate a procurement procedure without awarding a contract is not absolute and must be justified.[55] This ability – to terminate the procedure without concluding a contract – can be conceptualised as 'freedom from contract'.[56] According to established jurisprudence of the CJEU, a contracting authority may withdraw from the conclusion of a contract, even after initiating a call for competition, only where significant reasons or exceptional circumstances can be demonstrated.[57]

IV. Contract Form

The principle of freedom of contract is also evident in the rules applying to contract form. In the context of private contracts, the general rule is the absence of formal requirements. This principle is clearly affirmed in both the DCFR and the PECL.

[51] Regulation (EU) 2023/1115 of the European Parliament and of the Council of 31 May 2023 on the making available on the Union market and the export from the Union of certain commodities and products associated with deforestation and forest degradation [2023] OJ L 150/206.

[52] C Falvo and F Muscaritoli, 'Towards Deforestation-Free Public Procurement?' (2024) 19(2) *European Procurement & Public Private Partnership Law Review* 91.

[53] These principles are expressed in Art 2:301 PECL: negotiating contrary to good faith, s 3, II–3:301 DCFR: negotiating contrary to good faith and fair dealing. See F Kessler and E Fine, 'Culpa in Contrahendo, Bargaining in Good Faith and Freedom of Contract: a Comparative Study' (1964) 77 (3) *Harvard Law Review* 402; J Cartwright and M Hesselink (eds), *Precontractual Liability in European Private* Law (Cambridge, Cambridge University Press, 2009).

[54] Andhov, Kania, Saljic and Schrøder-Hansen (n 4).

[55] ibid. See also Case C-92/00 *Hospital Ingenieure Krankenhaustechnik Planungs-Gesellschaft mbH (HI) v Stadt Wien* ECLI:EU:C:2002:379, [2002] para 63; Case C-440/13 *Croce Amica One Italia Srl v Azienda Regionale Emergenza Urgenza (AREU)* ECLI:EU:C:2014:2430, [2014] para 36. See ch 5.

[56] See ch 5.

[57] See Case C-440/13 *Croce Amica* (n 55).

According to DCFR Article–II. 1:106: 'A contract or other juridical act need not be concluded, made or evidenced in writing nor is it subject to any other formal requirements as to form'.

Similarly, the PECL, Article 2:101(2) provides: 'A contract need not be concluded or evidenced in writing nor is it subject to any other requirement as to form. The contract may be proved by any means, including witnesses'.

Thus, contracts may be concluded verbally or through tacit consent.[58] This flexibility facilitates the conclusion of contracts in day-to-day interactions, especially in low-value or routine transactions – such as the purchase of food or other minor purchases – where no particular formalities are expected. Only a limited number of exceptions depart from this general rule, typically in cases where formality serves a protective or evidentiary function.[59]

In contrast, EU public procurement law places a clear limitation on the freedom to determine the form in which contracts are concluded. Pursuant to Article 2(1)(5) Directive 2014/24/EU, public contracts must be concluded in writing.[60] Directive 2014/24/EU further defines 'written form' as any expression in words or figures that can be read, reproduced, and subsequently communicated, including information transmitted and stored electronically.[61]

The principal rationale for this formal requirement lies in the principle of transparency.[62] A written contract ensures that the terms are accessible to interested parties, including unsuccessful tenderers who, under national laws implementing Article 72(1) Directive 2014/24/EU, may seek access to the contents of a modified public contract. This is particularly pertinent when modifications are made under points (b) and (c) of Article 72(1) Directive 2014/24/EU and a corresponding notice is published in the Official Journal of the European Union.[63] In addition, civil society actors such as non-governmental organisations (NGOs) may invoke access to information laws to scrutinise the content of public contracts.[64]

[58] MPP Viscasillas, 'The Formation of Contracts & (and) the Principles of European Contract Law' (2001) 13(2) *Pace International Law Review* 371, 386; H Kötz, *European Contract Law* (Oxford, Oxford University Press, 2017) 25–32.

[59] As an example, can be mentioned the requirement of writing with regard to consumer credit contracts, see eg s 8 *Kreditaftaleloven* no 817/2019 s 8(1) Danish Consumer Credit Act).

[60] Exceptional challenges to this requirement arose in the context of the COVID-19 pandemic. See European Commission, 'Guidance from the European Commission on Using the Public Procurement Framework in the Emergency Situation Related to the COVID-19 Crisis' [2020] OJ C 108I/1.

[61] Art 2(1)(18) Directive 2014/24/EU. On the requirement of 'form' and 'in writing' see ch 10. See also M Andhov, CB Andersen and T Hebbard, 'Visual Contracting – A Roadmap to Simplify Procurement Law?' (2025) 34(1) *Public Procurement Law Review* 47.

[62] M Steinicke, 'Article 2(1)(18)' in M Steinicke and PL Vesterdorf (eds), *Brussels Commentary on EU Public Procurement Law* (London, Bloomsbury Publishing, 2018).

[63] In Spain, Poland, and Romania (though less effectively in the latter), all contracts and contract amendments must be published in a public online register. See D Dragos, KM Halonen, B Neamtu and SP Treumer (eds), *Contract Changes: The Dark Side of EU Public Procurement Law* (Cheltenham, Edward Elgar Publishing, 2023).

[64] M McDonagh, 'Disclosure of Information Relating to Public Procurement: The Role of Freedom of Information Law' (2002) *Public Procurement Law Review* 172. On NGOs' interest in public contracts, see ch 12.

Beyond transparency, the written form also serves to protect the interests of the contracting authority in the event of a dispute. It provides a verifiable record of the parties' rights and obligations. Moreover, the written form requirement reflects a broader accountability framework, ensuring compliance with control and audit mechanisms imposed by national oversight bodies within public procurement systems.[65]

V. The Content of the Contract

Contract law proceeds from the clear premise that parties are generally free to determine the content of their contract. This discretion is a core element of the principle of freedom of contract. However, exceptions exist, largely driven by the need to protect the weaker party in a contractual relationship.[66] Consumer law offers a clear illustration: the Unfair Contract Terms Directive prohibits the inclusion of certain terms deemed inherently unfair in consumer contracts.[67] Labour law presents another example, where statutory protections address the structural imbalance between employer and employee and prevent exploitation arising from subordination or dependency.[68]

Over time, the scope of these protective content-related constraints has expanded. Initially centred on safeguarding weaker parties, regulation has increasingly come to reflect broader external interests, including requirements related to product safety and, more recently, overarching objectives such as sustainability and digital transformation.[69] Nonetheless, in private contracting, such restrictions remain exceptions to the overarching rule of contractual freedom.

[65] Directive 2014/24/EU specifies the form in which a public contract must be concluded but does not explicitly address the form required for its modification. This particular issue was recently examined in the CJEU ruling in Joined cases C-441/22 and C-443/22 *Obshtina Razgrad and Obshtina Balchik* ECLI:EU:C:2023:970, [2023] as discussed in ch 8.

[66] ME Storme, 'Freedom of Contract: Mandatory and Non-Mandatory Rules in European Contract Law' (2007) 2 *European Review of Private Law* 233; OO Cherednychenko, 'Fundamental Rights, Contract Law and Transactional Justice' (2021) 17(2) *European Review of Contract Law* 138; M Andhov M and B Bergsson, 'Equal Pay and EU Public Procurement Law – Case Study of Mandatory Icelandic ÍST85 Standard' (2021) 4(1) *Nordic Journal of European Law* 1.

[67] Council Directive 93/13/EEC of 5 April 1993 on unfair terms in consumer contracts [1993] OJ 95/29.

[68] H Rösler, 'Protection of the Weaker Party in European Contract Law: Standardized and Individual Inferiority in Multi-level Private Law' (2010) 4 *European Review of Private Law* 729, 731.

[69] See eg Directive 2009/48/EC of the European Parliament and of the Council of 18 June 2009 on the safety of toys [2009] OJ L170/1; Directive 2013/29/EU of the European Parliament and of the Council of 12 June 2013 on the harmonisation of the laws of the Member States relating to the making available on the market of pyrotechnic articles [2013] OJ L178/27; Directive 2013/53/EU of the European Parliament and of the Council of 20 November 2013 on recreational craft and personal watercraft [2013] OJ L354/90; Directive 2014/28/EU of the European Parliament and of the Council of 26 February 2014 on the harmonisation of the laws of the Member States relating to the making available on the market and supervision of explosives for civil uses [2014] OJ L96/1; Directive (EU) 2024/1760 of the European Parliament and of the Council of 13 June 2024 on corporate sustainability due diligence and amending Directive (EU) 2019/1937 and Regulation (EU) 2023/2859 [2024] OJ L2024/1760. See also Regulation (EU) 2018/848 of the European Parliament and of the Council of 30 May 2018 on organic production and labelling of organic products [2018] OJ L150/1.

By contrast, in public procurement, the freedom to determine the content of a contract is more restricted. First, the definition of a public contract under Article 2(1)(5) Directive 2014/24/EU expressly limits permissible content by requiring that the contract concerns a matter of pecuniary interest.[70] Second, in practice, the contractor's ability to influence the content of a public contract is notably constrained, particularly in open and restricted procedures.[71] In these settings, contractors typically accept the terms as prescribed by the contracting authority, with any influence generally limited to seeking clarifications.[72] Greater flexibility may exist in negotiated procedures, where the interaction between the parties more closely resembles that found in contract law.[73] Third, Article 67(2) Directive 2014/24/EU requires that all award criteria used in tenders be linked to the subject matter of the contract.[74] This principle itself limits the freedom to shape contractual content.

In addition, there is a growing body of substantive provisions in EU law that define or influence the subject matter of public contracts. These provisions derive primarily from legislative or soft law acts promoting specific policy goals, particularly in relation to sustainability and digitalisation. Examples of voluntary solutions include EU Green Public Procurement (GPP) criteria for computers, monitors, tablets and smartphones,[75] EU GPP criteria for data centres, server rooms and cloud services,[76] or EU GPP criteria for food, catering services, and vending machines.[77] The mandatory requirements for public contracts are outlined in normative acts such as the Energy Efficiency Directive[78] and the Clean Vehicles Directive.[79] As a result, contracting authorities increasingly face restrictions not only in how they purchase, but also in

[70] Case C-367/19 *Tax-Fin-Lex d.o.o. v Ministrstvo za notranje zadeve* ECLI:EU:C:2020:685, [2020].

[71] See for the award procedures R Caranta, 'The Changes to the Public Contract Directives and the Story They Tell About How EU Law Works' (2015) 52 *Common Market Law Review* 391, 451; C Krönke, 'Article 27 Open Procedure' in R Caranta and A Sanchez-Graells (eds), *European Public Procurement: Commentary on Directive 2014/24/EU* (Cheltenham, Edward Elgar Publishing, 2021); C Krönke, 'Article 28 Restricted Procedure' in R Caranta and A Sanchez-Graells (eds), *European Public Procurement: Commentary on Directive 2014/24/EU* (Cheltenham, Edward Elgar Publishing, 2021).

[72] Arrowsmith (n 3) 606.

[73] P Bogdanowicz, 'Article 29 Competitive Procedure with Negotiation' in R Caranta and A Sanchez-Graells (eds), *European Public Procurement: Commentary on Directive 2014/24/EU* (Cheltenham, Edward Elgar Publishing, 2021) 323; P Telles, 'Article 30 Competitive Dialogue' in R Caranta and A Sanchez-Graells (eds), *European Public Procurement: Commentary on Directive 2014/24/EU* (Cheltenham, Edward Elgar Publishing, 2021) 330.

[74] A Semple, 'The Link to the Subject-Matter: A Glass Ceiling for Sustainable Public Contracts?' in B Sjåfjell and A Wiesbrock (eds), *Sustainable Public Procurement Under EU Law – New Perspectives on the State as Stakeholder* (Cambridge, Cambridge University Press, 2016); Andhov (n 37) 117–37.

[75] See European Commission, 'Commission Staff Working Document EU green public procurement criteria for computers, monitors, tablets and smartphones' SWD(2021) 57 final.

[76] See European Commission, 'Commission Staff Working Document EU green public procurement criteria for data centres, server rooms and cloud services' SWD(2020) 55 final.

[77] See European Commission, 'Commission Staff Working Document EU green public procurement criteria for food, catering services and vending machines' SWD(2019) 366 final.

[78] Directive 2023/1791 of the European Parliament and of the Council of 13 September 2023 on energy efficiency and amending Regulation (EU) 2023/955 [2023] OJ L231/1.

[79] Directive 2009/33/EC of the European Parliament and of the Council of 23 April 2009 on the promotion of clean and energy-efficient road transport vehicles [2009] OJ L120/5.

what they purchase – reflecting a notable shift in the orientation of public procurement from procedural compliance to substantive outcome.[80] Restrictions on the formation of a public contract's content may also stem from national legislation, as exemplified by Dutch law. Under the Proportionality Guide (*Gids Proportionaliteit*), Dutch law imposes specific restrictions on the allocation of risks within public contracts, further limiting the freedom of contractors in shaping the contract's content.[81]

VI. Contract Modifications

The need to modify contracts is particularly pronounced in the context of long-term contractual relationships, where it is often difficult to define all obligations with precision at the time of formation. As circumstances evolve, adjustments to the original agreement may become necessary. In contract law, the ability to modify a contract offers flexibility to the parties and is generally facilitated through mutual and consensual declarations of intent.[82]

In public procurement law, however, the modification of concluded public contracts is distinctly limited.[83] Restrictions on a contracting authority's ability to agree to modifications of public contracts are primarily rooted in the overarching principles of equal treatment and non-discrimination.[84] Post-award alterations – particularly those affecting the subject matter or essential terms – risk

[80] For instance, see also M Andhov, R Caranta, W Janssen and O Martin-Ortega, 'Shaping Sustainable Public Procurement Laws In The European Union – An analysis of the legislative development from "how to buy" to "what to buy" in current and future EU legislative initiatives' <www.greens-efa.eu/files/assets/docs/shaping_sustainable_public_procurement_laws_in_the_european_union.pdf>.

[81] See ch 5.

[82] In some situations, a party may also have a unilateral right to modify a contract. This often applies in insurance law, construction contracts and other 'mass contracts'. On modification rights in long-term contracts in general, see O Hansen (ed), *Ændringsregler i længerevarende kontrakter* (Copenhagen, Djøf Publishing, 2014). Unilateral variations rights constitute an exception in commercial contract law. In legal systems which apply the concept of the administrative contract, the public entity has more far-reaching variation rights.

[83] See O Hansen, S Treumer, and M Andhov, 'Social Services and Contract Changes: The Legality of Social Service Outsourcing Practices in EU Procurement Law' (2018) *Public Procurement Law Review* 217; P Bogdanowicz, *Contract Modifications in EU Procurement Law* (Cheltenham, Edward Elgar Publishing, 2021); O Hansen, M Andhov, and TT Jacobsen, 'Bygherrens opgivelse af rettigheder i udbudspligtige kontrakter: – Hvilke regler gælder for ændringer under bagatelgrænsen i udbudslovens § 180?' in HC Risvig Hammer, M Andhov, E Bertelsen, and R Caranta (eds), *Into the Northern Light – In memory of Steen Treumer* (Copenhagen, Ex Tuto Publishing, 2022); D Dragos, KM Halonen, B Neamtu, and S Treumer (eds), *Contract Changes – The Dark Side of EU Procurement Law* (Cheltenham, Edward Elgar Publishing, 2023).

[84] Case C-454/06 *pressetext Nachrichtenagentur GmbH v Republik Österreich (Bund), APA-OTS Originaltext-Service GmbH and APA Austria Presse Agentur registrierte Genossenschaft mit beschränkter Haftung* ECLI:EU:C:2008:351, [2008] ECR I-04401; Case C-91/08 *Wall AG v La ville de Francfort-sur-le-Main and Frankfurter Entsorgungs- und Service (FES) GmbH* ECLI:EU:C:2010:182, [2010] ECR I-02815; Case C-549/14 *Finn Frogne A/S v Rigspolitiet ved Center for Beredskabskommunikation* ECLI:EU:C:2016:634, [2016]; Case C-461/20 *Advania Sverige AB and Kammarkollegiet v Dustin Sverige AB* ECLI:EU:C:2022:72, [2022].

undermining these principles and may infringe upon the legitimate expectations of third parties, especially unsuccessful bidders.[85] At the same time, a blanket prohibition on modifications would be impractical, potentially preventing the effective performance of public contracts in response to unforeseen developments.[86]

To reconcile these competing interests, the CJEU has developed a framework – through its jurisprudence – that can be argued to aim at balancing the freedom to modify public contracts and the limitations imposed by EU public procurement law.[87] This balance was later codified in Article 72 Directive 2014/24/EU and has been further elaborated in the subsequent case law.[88] Article 72 delineates the circumstances under which public contracts may be lawfully modified without triggering the requirement of a new public procurement procedure.[89]

This regulatory framework inevitably raises questions about the implications of EU public procurement law on the contractual relationship between the parties. The answers to such questions may vary across jurisdictions, depending on the interaction between procurement regulation and domestic contract law.[90]

VII. Related Principles

While the previous sections focused on the core dimensions of the principle of freedom of contract, this section turns to two adjacent principles that, although not always explicitly associated with contractual freedom, play a crucial role in shaping its contours: the principle of good faith and fair dealing and the principle of privity of contract.[91] Principles of good faith, fair dealing, and privity of the

[85] See S Treumer, 'Contract Changes and the Duty to Retender Under the New EU Public Procurement Directive' (2014) 3 *Public Procurement Law Review* 148.

[86] MA Simovart, 'Unforeseen Circumstances That Justify Changes to Public Contracts' in D Dragos, KM Halonen, B Neamtu, and S Treumer (eds), *Contract Changes – The Dark Side of EU Procurement Law* (Cheltenham, Edward Elgar Publishing, 2023).

[87] See Case C-454/06 *Pressetext Nachrichtenagentur* (n 84).

[88] See Case C-461/20 *Advania Sverige AB* (n 84); Joined cases C-441/22 and C-443/22 *Obshtina Razgrad* (n 65). See on this case ch 8.

[89] See also relevant judgments of the CJEU in Case C-454/06 *Pressetext Nachrichtenagentur* (n 84); Case C-91/08 *Wall AG* (n 84); Case C-549/14 *Finn Frogne* (n 84); Case C-298/15 *UAB 'Borta' v VĮ Klaipėdos valstybinio jūrų uosto direkcija* ECLI:EU:C:2017:266, [2017].

[90] See ch 7.

[91] On other foundational principles of contract law – amongst others party autonomy, *pacta sunt servanda*, and the equality of the parties see S Grundmann, 'Information, Party Autonomy and Economic Agents in European Contract Law' (2002) 39 *Common Market Law Review* 269; AS Hartkamp, 'Principles of Contract Law' in AS Hartkamp, M Hesselink, EH Hondius, C Mak, and ED Perron (eds), *Towards a European Civil Code*, vol 4 (Nijmegen, Ars Aequi Libri, 2011) 239–59; MA Eisenberg, *Foundational Principles of Contract Law* (Oxford, Oxford University Press, 2018); KM Belikova, 'Evolution of Basic Doctrines and Principles of Contract Law in Europe' (2019) 8(22) *Amazonia Investiga* 173; SC Symeonides, 'The Story of Party Autonomy' in D Girsberger (ed), *The Choices of Law in International Commercial Contracts* (Oxford, Oxford University Press, 2021) 129–31; O Lando, *The Principles of European Contract Law* (Leiden, Martinus Nijhoff Publishers, 2023).

contract are particularly significant because they operate either as inherent limits on, or structural assumptions underpinning, the exercise of contractual freedom. The principle of good faith and fair dealing introduces substantive constraints on how parties may exercise their rights, while privity of contract sets boundaries on who may be affected by the agreement and who can interfere with its content. Examining these two principles in parallel allows for a deeper understanding of how freedom of contract functions in both private and public contexts, and how it interacts with broader legal and institutional concerns.

A. Principle of Good Faith and Fair Dealing

Contract law recognises – albeit to varying degrees across jurisdictions – the principle of good faith and fair dealing, which plays a role both in the formation and performance of contracts.[92] These principles introduce a normative expectation that a contracting party must, to some extent, consider the legitimate interests of the other party and act with integrity in fulfilling contractual obligations and exercising contractual rights.[93]

It is widely accepted that the duty of good faith cannot be contractually excluded.[94] This is reflected in the DCFR, which expressly states that 'the duty may not be excluded or limited by contract'.[95] This reinforces the notion that parties are expected to refrain from conduct that is contrary to, or undermines, the interests of the other party. The obligation of good faith is complex and multifaceted.[96] In some legal systems, it also serves as a mechanism for promoting social justice within the framework of contract law.[97] In this sense, the principle of good faith and fair dealing operates as a limitation on the general principle of freedom of contract.

In contrast, public procurement law does not make explicit reference to the principle of good faith and fair dealing. Nonetheless, it incorporates analogous requirements. A foundational expectation in public procurement is that contracting authorities must conduct procedures in a fair, transparent, and non-discriminatory

[92] See RE Speidel, 'The "Duty" of Good Faith in Contract Performance and Enforcement' (1996) 46(4) *Journal of Legal Education* 537.

[93] III–1:103 DCFR: Good faith and fair dealing, see Von Bar, Clive and Schulte-Nölke (n 42) 303.

[94] JP Schmidt, 'Art 1:201: Good Faith and Fair Dealing' in N Jansen and R Zimmermann (eds), *Commentaries on European Contract Laws* (Oxford, Oxford University Press, 2018) 154.

[95] III–1:103 (2) DCFR. See also M Mekki and M Kloepfer-Pelèse, 'Good Faith and Fair Dealing in the DCFR' (2008) 3 *European Review of Contract Law* 338.

[96] Eisenberg (n 91) 304. On the principle in general, see also E Navarretta, 'Good Faith and Reasonableness in European Contract Law' in J Rutgers and P Sirena (eds), *Rules and Principles in European Contract Law. European Contract Law and Theory* (Cambridge, Intersentia, 2015) 135–50.

[97] See H Collins, 'Social Market and the Law of Contract' (1992) 49 *Archiv für Rechts-und Sozialphilosophie, Beiheft* 85; See MW Hesselink, 'CFR & Social Justice. A short study for the European Parliament on the values of underlying the Draft Common Frame of Reference for European private law: what role for fairness and social justice?' (Centre for the Study of European Contract Law Working Paper Series) No. 2008/08 <ssrn.com/abstract=1270575> 15 et seq.

manner, avoiding any form of manipulation or preferential treatment.[98] For example, during bid evaluation, authorities are obliged to assess tenders honestly and consistently with the pre-defined criteria, thereby excluding arbitrary or biased decision-making.

Furthermore, Article 72 Directive 2014/24/EU imposes strict limitations on contract modifications in order to prevent abuse. Permissible changes must be both transparent and justified by legitimate grounds, such as changes in market conditions or unexpected obstacles in the execution of the contract. These principles are primarily aimed at securing the functioning of the internal market and safeguarding the interests of all potential tenderers. However, unlike the principle of good faith and fair dealing in contract law, these public procurement law principles are not designed specifically to protect the contracting party's counterparty. Any such protection is incidental rather than purposive.

This divergence raises a broader question: to what extent does public procurement law allow for the contractual principle of good faith and fair dealing to function as a supplementary or 'gap-filling' norm in public contracts?[99]

B. Principle of Privity of Contract

In contract law, it is a well-established principle that contracts operate solely between the parties to the agreement and do not confer rights or impose obligations on third parties.[100] This doctrine, known as the principle of privity of contract, is closely tied to the broader notion of freedom of contract.[101] It reflects the idea that contracting is a private matter: parties are free to choose their counterparts and to define their mutual obligations without interference from or implications for others. As a result, contractual rights and duties are generally limited to those who have consented to the agreement, and breaches of contract typically concern only the signatory parties of the contract.[102]

Permitting third-party duties would run counter to this foundational premise, as it would impose legal consequences on individuals who have not freely elected to enter into a contractual relationship. Nevertheless, contract law recognises limited exceptions to the principle of privity of contract.[103] The most prominent of these

[98] Art 18 Directive 2014/24/EU.

[99] This question is dealt with in ch 7.

[100] S Vogenauer, 'Art 6:110: Stipulation in Favour of a Third Party' in N Jansen and R Zimmermann (eds), *Commentaries on European Contract Laws* (Oxford, Oxford University Press, 2018) 876–78. See also ch 12.

[101] The principle is expressly pronounced in Art 1199 French Code Civil. In German law it can be deduced from articles in BGB including Art 241. Also, the DCFR establishes in II–1:103 that the contract is binding upon the parties. See in general V Ulfbeck, *Kontrakters relativitet* (Copenhagen, GadJura, 2000).

[102] Kötz (n 58) 319.

[103] S Vogenauer, 'The Effects of Contracts on Third Parties: The Avant-projet de reforme in a Comparative Perspective' in J Cartwright et al (eds), *Reforming the French Law of Obligations:*

is the concept of the third-party beneficiary contract, which allows a non-party to enforce contractual rights where it can be demonstrated that such rights were intentionally conferred by the contracting parties.[104] This exception is reflected in several civil codes, as well as in Article 6:110 PECL and Article II.–9:301 DCFR.

In public procurement law, the position is almost diametrically opposed. Here, third-party interests are not only recognised but form a central concern of the legal framework.[105] A core objective of EU public procurement law is to ensure that the interests of competing bidders – who are by definition third parties to any eventual public contract – are protected in order to maintain the integrity and functionality of the market.[106] Moreover, public contracts involve the expenditure of public funds and serve public interest, meaning that their content and execution implicate broader societal interests. While the concept of the contractual law concept of third-party beneficiary may also apply to public contracts, the notion of third-party interests is much broader in public procurement law.[107]

VIII. Conclusion

Public and private contracts share a number of structural similarities. Public contracts are often driven by the same commercial imperatives as private contracts, including the pursuit of value for money, the assurance of quality, and the fulfilment of specific needs. At their core, public contracts involve a financial exchange similar to private-sector commercial transactions. Contracting authorities procure construction works, goods, and services from private entities, thereby creating a buyer–seller relationship governed by the dynamics of supply and demand. Like private contracts, public contracts are established through mutual consent, with the terms and conditions agreed upon by both parties.

Nonetheless, contract law and public procurement law are founded on different principles and values. While similarities exist, these are frequently framed as exceptions within each system. The general principle of freedom of contract – along with its associated subcategories and related principles – is central to contract law but is significantly curtailed in public procurement, where principles

Comparative Reflections on the Avant-Projet de Réforme Du Droit Des Obligations et de La Prescription ('the Avant-Projet Catala') (Oxford, Bloomsbury Publishing, 2009) 239.

[104] J Hellebeek, 'Contracts for a Third Party Beneficiary: A Brief Sketch from the Corpus Iuris to Present-Day Civil Law' (2007) 13(2) *Fundamina: A Journal of Legal History* 11; Vogenauer (n 100) 870; Kötz (n 58) 323. The concept of the third-party beneficiary concept is explained in ch 12.

[105] GM Racca, 'The Role of Third Parties in the Execution of Public Contracts' in L Folliot-Lalliot and S Torricelli (eds), *Contrôles et Contentieux des Contrats Publics – Oversight and Challenges of Public Contracts* (Brussels, Bruylant, 2018) 416.

[106] Most recently on the private enforcement of EU public procurement law, see R Caranta and V Fričová, 'EU Procurement and Concessions Law' in M Scholten (ed), *Research Handbook on the Enforcement of EU Law* (Cheltenham, Edward Elgar Publishing, 2023) 416–19.

[107] For an analysis of these aspects, see ch 12.

such as equality, non-discrimination, and transparency take precedence. Yet, the two regimes necessarily converge at the moment a public contract is formed.

In jurisdictions adopting the 'public-oriented hybrid model', the concept of the administrative contract partly bridges this divide by incorporating public law values into the contractual framework.[108] In such systems, the administrative contract serves to internalise public law requirements, thereby reducing (though not eliminating) the questions of interplay between procurement law and contract law. In contrast, under the 'private-oriented hybrid model', questions regarding the interaction between the two regimes remain more prevalent, and the questions are numerous.

A notable issue concerns whether the public procurement law should be viewed as a *lex specialis* which prescribes mandatory contract law principles binding both the contracting authority and the private contractor, and thus limiting the principle of freedom of contract between the parties. This approach largely reduces the role of contract law, relegating it to a gap-filling role in areas not exhaustively regulated by public procurement law. Even when contract law is applied, there remains the issue of its modification to reflect the principles governing public procurement law.[109] In some legal systems, the approach, which is based on the *lex specialis derogat lex generalis* rule, appears to have more support than in others.

However, an alternative understanding exists in other jurisdictions, where public procurement law is viewed as primarily addressing the contracting authority. According to this view, public procurement law establishes obligations solely on the contracting authority, while the legal position of the parties under the contract – as the starting point – is unaffected by public procurement law and governed by the contract between the parties. According to this view, an infringement of public procurement law by the contracting authority does not, in itself, invalidate the resulting contract with the private party. Instead, such breaches may give rise to public law sanctions and civil liability of the contracting authority.[110]

The following chapters explore the interaction between public procurement law and contract law through various thematic lenses, drawing on examples from different national legal systems. They reveal the diversity of approaches to the integration – or separation – of these two regulatory regimes.

[108] See ch 3.
[109] Case C-82/24 *Miejskie Przedsiębiorstwo Wodociągów i Kanalizacji w m.st. Warszawie S.A. v Veolia Water Technologies sp. z o.o. and Others* ECLI:EU:C:2025:396, [2025] para 36.
[110] An example of this approach is reflected in ch 7.

PART II

General

5

Influencing Contractual Freedom Through EU and Dutch Public Procurement Law: Legal Review Asymmetries in Cases on Withdrawals, Awards, and Division of Risk

MATANJA PINTO AND WILLEM A JANSSEN

I. Introduction

The review of alleged violations of EU and Dutch public procurement law before the courts is of vital importance, particularly given the absence of a fully fleshed-out supervisory authority with enforcement powers in the Netherlands.[1] Accordingly, this system of law and review mechanisms that is also found in many other Member States heavily relies on the willingness of economic operators to engage in litigation to ensure the law's effectiveness. If the rules are not enforced in the courts, it is unlikely that the law's objectives will be achieved. Access to the courts is, thus, of great importance, and any barrier must stand the test of scrutiny.

In light of its objective to achieve an internal market, EU public procurement law is regulated by the 2014 Public Procurement Directives, which are vested on principles of equality, transparency, and proportionality.[2] This legal framework provides the boundaries of the discretion given to contracting authorities, enabling them to engage in contractual relations, fulfil their own needs and increasingly fulfil other public policy objectives in light of sustainability, innovation, and social

[1] The Dutch Competition Authority for Consumers and Markets (Autoriteit Consument en Markt) does have power to intervene in matters of competition law within the context of public procurement law, as implied by Art 2, para 5 *Instellingswet ACM* (ACM Establishment Act). For further reference, see MJJM Essers and CAM Lombert, *Aanbestedingsrecht voor overheden: naar een maatschappelijk verantwoord aanbestedingsbeleid* (Alphen Aan den Rijn,Vakmedianet, 2017) 815 et seq.

[2] Directive 2014/23/EU; Directive 2014/24/EU; Directive 2014/25/EU.

considerations. In the Netherlands, the mentioned public procurement rules find their implementation in a civil law setting, and the main body of law is found in the Dutch Public Procurement Act (Awet 2012).[3] Accordingly, legal review by aggrieved bidders takes place before the Dutch civil courts.[4]

In this chapter, it is asserted that allowing a less-than-full review of a decision made by a contracting authority is functionally equivalent to imposing a barrier to the judicial review of a decision. In the Dutch private law context, courts fall back – often tacitly – on principles like freedom of contract wherever a gap in legislation exists. Judicial review based on principles tends to be less fine-grained than judicial review based on detailed sets of rules. The influence of EU and Dutch public procurement law on private law is, therefore, a significant factor in Dutch case law, as it provides a detailed set of rules for decisions by contracting authorities and opens the possibility for in-depth review.[5] Nevertheless, examples of asymmetries in judicial review of decisions by contracting authorities in various phases of procurement and contracting are abundant. The most prominent asymmetry is perhaps the difference in review between withdrawal decisions and other decisions in the procurement phase. The existence of this asymmetry is problematic because it makes contesting withdrawal decisions virtually impossible. In this contribution, it is shown that Dutch courts are more than willing to intervene in other decisions than withdrawal decisions. The willingness to intervene reached a peak in two cases regarding the division of risk. In this context, these cases are compared with the case law on withdrawal decisions and the conclusion is drawn that, in the Dutch public procurement setting, the asymmetry between the judicial review of withdrawal decisions and other decisions is the result of an overly broad application of the principle of freedom of contract.

This chapter is structured as follows. First, the principle of freedom of contract is examined, aiming to highlight some implicit assumptions about this principle (section II). Next, the Dutch civil law context is discussed in public procurement that implements EU public procurement law (section III). This analysis considers how the principle is interpreted in two specific settings: withdrawal decisions by a contracting authority (section IV) – containing comparative work into Dutch, Finnish, and Danish case law, which are three Member States with comparable civil law cultures and systems, but with different implementations of freedom of contract – and the allocation of risk between a contracting authority and an economic operator that has been awarded a public contract (section V). The comparison between withdrawal decisions and division of risk aims to offer

[3] *Aanbestedingswet* (Awet) 2012 (Dutch Public Procurement Act).

[4] One noted exception is public transport concessions pursuant to the *Wet Personenvervoer 2000* (Dutch Act on Public Transport 2000), but these generally fall under the ambit of Regulation 1370/2007/EC of the European Parliament and of the Council on public passenger transport services by rail and by road [2007] OJ L 315/1.

[5] E Manunza and RGT Bleeker, 'De invloed van het Europees recht op het Nederlandse aanbestedingsrecht' in AS Hartkamp, CH Sieburgh, and LAD Keus (eds), *De invloed van het Europese recht op het Nederlandse privaatrecht* (Alphen aan den Rijn, Kluwer Law International, 2007).

insights into how the Court of Justice of the European Union (CJEU) in the EU public procurement law setting and Dutch courts in a civil law setting can take a different interpretative stance. More importantly, it aims to shed light on the freedom of contract and how it is interpreted inconsistently between the procurement and contractual phases. Given that the influence of EU public procurement law appears to differ between these phases, the chapter concludes with a way forward to overcome these asymmetries and to ensure that review options before the courts are the same irrespective of the nature of the phase in which an economic operator finds itself (section VI).

II. Freedom of Contract: Essence and Functions

Withdrawal decisions and freedom of contract are closely related. In this section, it is argued that a withdrawal decision is akin to a refusal to contract. The essence of the freedom of contract is this right to refuse. To shed light on the relationship between withdrawal decisions and the freedom of contract, a brief overview is offered of the essence and function of freedom of contract and then our attention is turned to withdrawal decisions.[6]

A clear definition of the freedom of contract in the EU setting is absent. There is no single codification of the principle of freedom of contract within the EU, as each Member State has its own history with the principle. Like many other principles, for instance, the principle has also not been codified in the Netherlands.

However, freedom of contract does come to the fore in the Principles of European Contract Law (PECL)[7] and the Draft Common Frame of Reference (DCFR).[8] Freedom of contract under those frameworks can roughly be understood as the freedom to decide upon (i) whether or not to enter into a contract, (ii) which economic operator to enter into a contract with, and (iii) the contents of the contract.[9] Importantly, though, all three elements of the freedom of contract can be derived from the first element, namely the freedom to decide whether or not to contract (the refusal to contract). After all, contracting authorities that wish to enter into a certain contract with a certain economic operator can simply refuse all other offers until they are able to conclude a contract on acceptable terms with an acceptable economic operator. The true essence of freedom of contract,

[6] See also on the principle of freedom of contract ch 4.

[7] Art 1:102(1) PECL: 'Parties are free to enter into a contract and to determine its contents, subject to the requirements of good faith and fair dealing, and the mandatory rules established by these Principles.'

[8] Art II–1:102(1) DCFR: 'Parties are free to make a contract or other juridical act and to determine its contents, subject to any applicable mandatory rules.'

[9] MJ Pettit, 'Freedom, Freedom of Contract, and the Rise and Fall' (1999) 79 *Boston University Law Review* 263; DCFR, para 24, 7: 'As a rule, natural and legal persons are free both to decide whether or not to contract and to agree on the terms of their contract.'

therefore, lies in the 'freedom from contract', that is, the liberty to refuse any proposal.[10] In the remainder of this chapter, freedom from contract is regularly addressed, noting that this term ultimately also includes the freedom of contract.[11]

It has been argued that the freedom of contract can be derived from Article 8 European Convention on Human Rights (ECHR) (Right to respect for private and family life).[12] As Snijders clearly expressed:

> Indeed, starting from the observation that Article 8(1) serves personal autonomy too, there is no jumping to another conclusion when we state that this provision includes the right to freedom of contract itself. … However, in the modern interpretation of Article 8, implying that it not only allows people to be left alone but also gives them personal autonomy, Article 8 is undoubtedly a very comfortable basis for the right to freedom of contract.[13]

Note that if the principle of freedom of contract is indeed derived from Article 8 ECHR, then personal autonomy lies at the heart of that principle. More recently, Mak argued that while autonomy and freedom of contract are not explicitly addressed in the Charter of Fundamental Rights of the European Union, they are implicitly conditional on several fundamental rights in that charter.[14] Moreover, Mak views freedom of contract as the expression of autonomy in contract law.[15]

The question remains though: why is the principle there at all? Why do all private law systems incorporate some form of freedom of contract? What would be the problem if it were not entirely up to the contracting authority to decide whether it wishes to contract? These questions address the function of freedom of contract. In the following paragraphs, a closer look is given to this function. The functionalist approach that holds sway in studies in the field of comparative law has inspired our analysis in this respect.[16]

For an analysis of the function of freedom of contract, the dichotomy of predominant functions of this freedom is taken from Kim.[17] The first function

[10] H Snijders, 'Privacy of Contract' in K Ziegler (ed), *Human Rights and Private Law: Privacy as Autonomy* (Oxford, Bloomsbury Publishing, 2007) 105; H Dagan and M Heller, 'Freedom of Contracts' (2013) Columbia Law and Economics Working Paper 458.

[11] Our description of the function of freedom from contract does not necessarily overlap with the 'classic doctrine' of freedom from contract. It might very well be that what is generally deemed to be part of the doctrine, *does not* lie within the scope of its function and what is generally deemed not to be part of the doctrine, *is* part of the function.

[12] AC Ciacchi, 'Party Autonomy as a Fundamental Right in the European Union' (2010) 6(3) *European Review of Contract Law* 303; Snijders (n 10).

[13] Snijders (n 10).

[14] V Mak, 'A Tale of Two Systems. Europa en het Nederlandse vermogensrecht in tijden van (r) evolutie' in BJ Drijber and V Mak (eds), *Het spanningsveld tussen nationaal en Europees privaatrecht* (Zutphen, Uitgeverij Paris, 2024) 71.

[15] ibid 104.

[16] M van Hoecke, 'Methodology of Comparative Legal Research' (2013) *Pravovedenie* 121; B van Roermund, 'Law and Functionalism: The Limited Function of Law' (2015) 4 *Law and Method*; R Michaels, 'The Functional Method of Comparative Law' in M Reimann and R Zimmermann (eds), *The Oxford Handbook of Comparative Law* (Oxford, Oxford University Press, 2019) 345.

[17] N Kim, 'Mistakes, Changed Circumstances and Intent' (2007) *University of Kansas Law Review* 473.

of freedom of contract is to promote 'autonomy'.[18] Freedom of contract can, in this view, be described as one of the fundamental liberties in modern society.[19] Freedom of contract is a liberty in the same vein as freedom of speech and freedom of religion. Typically, liberties like freedom of speech and freedom of religion are thought to apply to natural persons (willing actors). The idea would be that for freedom of contract, the state ought to guarantee the free exercise of individual will regarding contracting – just as it ought to guarantee the free exercise of individual will regarding speech acts – subject to the constraint that willing actors should respect the rights of other willing actors.[20] A distinction can be made between the private and public spheres, whereas personal autonomy certainly belongs to the private sphere, as Mak points out:

> In scholarly writings, the legal concept of 'private autonomy' is usually defined in a sense that comes close to Kennedy's understanding of 'individualism'. It emphasises the freedom of the individual in the private sphere, as opposed to the public sphere within which the citizens have to respect the decisions of the democratically legitimised State. Freedom of contract forms an expression of this autonomy, since it gives individuals the space to arrange their relationships in the private sphere as they see fit, in principle concluding contracts on the terms they wish.[21]

For the remainder of this chapter, this aspect of the function of freedom of contract – the function to promote autonomy – the 'autonomy aspect' of freedom of contract is referred to.

The second predominant function of freedom of contract is that it encourages market transactions and is beneficial to a market economy.[22] In that sense, freedom of contract is merely a means to ensure that a transaction renders the optimal result. The underlying assumption is that the economic operators involved in a particular transaction have the best knowledge of the circumstances and goals relevant to the transaction they wish to conclude. Parties are best left free, because this freedom renders optimal results for society. Freedom of contract, in this sense, serves both a particular and a general purpose: both

[18] C Mak, *Fundamental Rights in European Contract Law: A Comparison of the Impact of Fundamental Rights on Contractual Relationships in Germany, the Netherlands, Italy, and England* (Alphen aan den Rijn, Kluwer Law International, 2008).

[19] NS Wilson, 'Freedom of Contract and Adhesion Contracts' (1965) 14(1) *International & Comparative Law Quarterly* 172; C Fried, 'Contract as Promise: Lessons Learned' (2019) 20 *Theoretical Inquiries in Law* 367.

[20] R Pound, 'The End of Law as Developed in Juristic Thought' (1914) 27(7) *Harvard Law Review* 605; D Kennedy, 'From the Will Theory to the Principle of Private Autonomy: Lon Fullers' Consideration and Form' (2000) 100 *Columbia Law Review* 94.

[21] Mak 'Fundamental Rights in European Contract Law' (n 18).

[22] See references by N Kim to LA Kornhauser, 'An Introduction to the Economic Analysis of Contract Remedies' (1985) 57 *University of Colorado Law Review* 683; RA Posner, *The Problems of Jurisprudence* (Cambridge, Harvard University Press, 1993); R Craswell, 'Two Economic Theories of Enforcing Promises' in P Benson (ed), *Readings in the Theory of Contract Law* (Cambridge, Cambridge University Press, 2001); AM Polinsky, *An Introduction to Law and Economics* (Burlington, Aspen Publishing, 2018).

the parties to a contract and society benefit from the optimal distribution facilitated by the freedom of contract.[23] Because, in many instances, contracting authorities do not merely aim at 'market' goals but also broader societal goals (sustainability, social welfare, etc), this second aspect of freedom from contract is referred to as the 'societal interest' aspect.[24] For the sake of brevity, all interests of the contracting authority are treated as societal interests. Note that even if the counterpart of the contracting authority has a more limited interest in, say, shareholder value, freedom of contract can still be said to function as a means to ensure optimal results. The parties to the contract are the best-informed parties regarding the transaction at hand and should, therefore, be given a certain discretion regarding the details of that transaction.

Further, a distinction could be made between the direct interests of a contracting authority itself (eg office supplies) and the broader public interest served by the contracting authority. For this chapter, the assumption was made that all interests of the contracting authority directly or indirectly relate to the public interest, so that contracting authorities ultimately always serve societal interests.

The distinction between these two functions of freedom from contract, serving (i) individual autonomy and (ii) societal interest, might not seem to bear relevance for the judicial practice in the Member States at first glance. At least, it is legitimate to ask what difference it makes for judicial practice if different assumptions are made about the function of freedom from contract. A first observation can be made that the personal autonomy of contracting authorities can hardly be compared to the personal autonomy of individuals. There is no reason why that difference should not be reflected in case law. Concerning the 'societal interest' aspect, the difference between individuals and contracting authorities is more subtle: the freedom of contract can in all cases, be said to function as a means to ensure optimal results, regardless of the contents of those results. Because the two aspects of the function of freedom of contract are typically not distinguished, courts can assign a 'personal autonomy' right of refusal to a contracting authority in a case regarding a withdrawal decision. However, such personal autonomy considerations should be left out of the equation when reviewing a withdrawal decision.

A second observation can be made that freedom from contract is often assigned to contracting authorities under the guise of their 'discretion'. In the context of entering into contracts, discretion and freedom from contract are two sides of the same coin. In this chapter, discretion is used in a practical sense as brought forward by Caranta: 'the law is not exhaustive in the sense that it leaves margins of choice to the rule-makers or decision-makers. Discretion is the name given to

[23] U Mattei, *Social Justice in European Contract Law: a Manifesto Study Group on Social Justice in European Private Law* (2004) <www.semanticscholar.org/paper/Social-Justice-in-European-Contract-Law-%3A-a-StudyMattei/693e0533e202d7fed64f2be2ba93780a6348e83b>.

[24] WA Janssen, *Sustainable Public Procurement Law: Reassessing the Internal Market for Public Contracts, Inaugural Lecture* (Groningen, Groningen University Press, 2025) 5.

these margins'.[25] As he points out, in practice, discretion is what margins of choice the courts are ready to leave undisturbed.

It is argued below that tacit assumptions regarding the function of freedom of contract dictate the outcome of court cases. The asymmetry in Dutch case law regarding withdrawal decisions and other decisions can be explained by this distinction in function. Similarly, this is visible when it comes to decisions on the division of risk, whereby Dutch courts are willing to significantly impede the freedom of contract.

An important difference between the perspective in which freedom of contract serves individual autonomy and the perspective in which it serves societal interest lies in the ability to contest decisions based on freedom from contract. From an individual autonomy perspective, which typically has natural persons in mind, contract coercion is just as impossible as forced conversion to a state religion. Contract coercion would violate the core of freedom from contract: the autonomy of the individual. From this perspective, it is entirely up to the individual to decide whether or not to contract, even if refusing to enter into a contract would be contrary to the manifest interests of the individual. The grounds on which a refusal is based are irrelevant, just as it would be irrelevant to investigate why an individual adheres to a certain religion. In short, according to the individual autonomy perspective, wide discretion applies to decisions based on freedom from contract and, as a consequence, judicial review should be limited.

The autonomy aspect of freedom of contract cannot be invoked by contracting authorities (cf Article 8 ECHR). Thus, if a contracting authority refuses to enter into a contract and freedom of contract only serves societal interest, then a plaintiff should be able to contest the refusal by taking the position that the relevant societal goals are better served if the contracting authority does enter into the contract. If it is established that entering into a contract would yield better results than refusing to enter into that contract, there should be no fundamental hindrance to a court order with the effect of forcing the contracting authority to enter into the contract. From this perspective, it is legitimate for a court to investigate why a contracting authority refuses to enter into a contract. In other words, according to the societal interest perspective, the grounds on which a refusal is based should be open to judicial review and contract coercion is possible. Moreover, discretion regarding a decision will fade into the background, as the grounds for the decision can be subjected to full judicial review. If contracting authorities can base a refusal on autonomy alone, then the grounds for refusal are irrelevant. Contracting authorities that can ground a refusal on autonomy, therefore, have maximum discretion. That discretion will greatly diminish if a contracting authority is obliged to offer grounds for a refusal to enter into a contract. The contracting authority does have some leeway as to how it can optimally serve the societal interest it is supposed to

[25] R Caranta, 'Book Review: Discretion in EU Public Procurement Law, edited by Sanja Bogojevic, Xavier Groussot & Jörgen Hettne. Oxford: Hart, 2019.)' (2020) 57(4) *Common Market Law Review* 1328.

serve, but economic operators can challenge every aspect of a decision, thereby minimising the contracting authority's discretion (see also section IV of this chapter).

III. The Dutch Civil Law Context of Public Procurement

The abovementioned essence and functions of the freedom from contract also play a role in Dutch public procurement law, and this context is relevant for the subsequent discussion about the freedom of contract in relation to withdrawal decision and division of risk.

In the Netherlands, public procurement law consists of the mentioned Awet 2012, which was last reformed on 1 July 2016 by implementing the 2014 Public Procurement Directives, and the *Gids Proportionaliteit* (Proportionality Guide).[26] The latter is an extensive explicitation of the principle of proportionality in each phase of a public procurement procedure. This binding legal act works on a 'comply or explain' basis. In addition, there are various supporting policy documents, including the Procurement Regulations for Works 2016.[27] The Remedies Directive was implemented in the Awet 2012 and contains the possibilities for appeal before the courts.[28]

The Dutch legislator has clarified in the legislative history of predecessors of the Awet 2012 that compliance with public procurement rules should be enforced under civil law. According to the legislator, the decisions that a contracting authority takes prior to and during a procurement procedure are not decisions subject to appeal to the administrative court under Dutch law, because these always concern preparatory acts that precede the conclusion of a private law agreement.[29] This is why the Dutch Administrative Law Act (Awb) explicitly coins the procurement phase of contracting authorities to fall outside of its scope.[30] Accordingly, disputes related to public procurement procedures and the subsequently awarded contract are settled before the civil courts, and private law, in principle, applies to the functioning and interpretation of the contract.[31] In addition, complaints can also be filed before the Commissie van Aanbestedingsexperts (Public Procurement Experts Committee, CvAE). The CvAE can issue a non-binding advice to resolve

[26] Respectively and most recently, *Staatsblad (Stb)* 2018, 1 and *Stb* 2016, 242.

[27] *Aanbestedingsreglement Werken* 2016 (ARW 2016) (Dutch Procurement Regulations for Works). Both the Proportionality Guide and the Dutch Procurement Regulations for Works 2016 were last amended on 1 July 2020.

[28] See ch 4 Awet 2012.

[29] Art 8:3(2) *Algemene Wet Bestuursrecht* (Awb) (Dutch General Administrative Law Act).

[30] The general principles of good administration (*algemene beginselen van behoorlijk bestuur)* appear to have limited influence on the Dutch contracting context. See AJ van Heeswijck, *Rechtsbescherming van ondernemers in aanbestedingsprocedures* (Groningen, University of Groningen, 2014).

[31] See the exemption is Dutch Act on Public Transport 2000.

a conflict. Its advisory work has a high status in Dutch legal culture, and is often followed up by the courts as well.[32] The CvAE was established to handle complaints about procurement procedures in an accessible manner, in order to improve legal remedies and tendering practices in the Netherlands.

IV. Freedom from Contract and Withdrawal Decisions

Drawing on the sketched discussion in section II, withdrawal decisions are readily recognisable as 'the freedom from contract of the contracting authority'. Functionally, there is little difference between refusing to continue a procurement procedure, as a result of which no contract will be concluded, or refusing to enter into a contract. Withdrawal decisions are governed by Article 55 Directive 2014/24/EU. The article states that contracting authorities shall inform each candidate of decisions reached concerning the award of the contract, including the grounds for any decision not to award a contract for which there has been a call for competition. To be clear, the text of this article implies no asymmetry between withdrawal decisions and other award decisions. That means that the judicial review of withdrawal decisions would appear to be as thorough as the judicial review of other decisions.

In Dutch, Finnish, and Danish practice, however, contracting authorities have wide discretion regarding withdrawal decisions and limited discretion regarding most other decisions, such as decisions on the type of procurement procedure to follow for the award of a particular contract. Consequently, judicial review of withdrawal decisions is limited, whereas other decisions are subject to full judicial review. It is asserted that Dutch, Finnish, and Danish courts, knowingly or unknowingly, assume that contracting authorities can invoke the autonomy aspect of their freedom of contract to withdraw a tender, as will be elaborated below. The wide discretion regarding withdrawal decisions and limited judicial review as a result is, thus, based on the autonomy aspect of the principle of freedom of contract.

A. Freedom of Contract in EU and Dutch Public Procurement Law

When it comes to public procurement law, the principle of freedom of contract remains unmentioned in the law or case law. The principle is not noted in the 2014 Public Procurement Directives or the CJEU's case law on public procurement. In

[32] See also on this topic Manunza and Bleeker (n 5).

Dutch public procurement law, the principle is also not noted, except in a handful of cases regarding withdrawal decisions discussed below.

However, the CJEU has referred to this principle in its judgments outside of the public procurement area. This has been the case, inter alia, in judgments of the Court concerning labour law cases which are treated as part of civil law in most Member States. In *Hans Werhof*, the Court pointed out that the essence of a contract is the freedom of the parties to mutually determine their rights and obligations, in particular, the parties may voluntarily bind themselves to a contractual relationship.[33] Furthermore, the principle of freedom of contract has been analysed when ruling based on the law of one of the Member States. Such a situation arose in *Commission v SNUA* in which the Court interpreted Article 1322 Italian Civil Code, which stipulates the principle of freedom of contract in the context of the possibility for the parties to define the grounds justifying the termination of a contract.[34] In *Automec*, the Court of First Instance dealt with the applicant's request that the Commission should order the company to conclude a contract with the complainant as part of measures to eliminate the infringement of competition law.[35] The Court pointed out that taking such a position remains contrary to the principle of freedom of contract. It also pointed out that the Commission has other means at its disposal, like the imposition of fines, to eliminate infringements of competition law that do not breach the principle of freedom of contract.

B. Dutch Withdrawal Cases

Due to an incomplete implementation of Directive 2014/24/EU, withdrawal decisions are not governed by the Awet 2012. The part of Article 55 regarding withdrawal decisions is not implemented, whereas the rest of this law follows Directive 2014/24/EU quite closely. As the legislator has not provided an explanation for the incomplete implementation, it simply appears to be an omission. According to Dutch scholarship, this gap is filled by the principle of freedom of contract.[36] However, this argument is not expanded on any further. Stating that the principle of freedom of contract fills the gap seems, erroneously, a sufficient argument. This illustrates that Dutch legal practitioners consider invoking the principle of freedom of contract for withdrawal decisions self-evident. Dutch courts also seem to think along these lines.

The first example is found in an archetypical Dutch withdrawal case. It concerned an IT platform, where one of the parties involved in the winning consortium was also

[33] Case C-499/04 *Hans Werhof v Freeway Traffic Systems GmbH & Co. KG.* ECLI:EU:C:2006:168, [2006] ECR I-02397 para 23.

[34] Case C-69/97 *Commission of the European Communities v SNUA Srl* ECLI:EU:C:1999:204, [1999] ECR I-02363 para 23. *Codice Civile* adopted with *Regio Decreto 16 marzo 1942, no 262* (Italian Civil Code).

[35] Case T-24/90 *Automec Srl v Commission of the European Communities* ECLI:EU:T:1992:97, [1992] ECR II-02223 paras 51–52.

[36] Essers and Lombert (n 1) 512.

involved in preparing the assignment. The court ruled that the principles of public procurement law limit freedom of contract in the pre-contractual phase. The court reminded the contracting authority that it had stated in the hearing that it preferred awarding the contract over restarting a procurement procedure, which would limit its freedom of contract. Subsequently, the court considered that 'The [contracting authority]'s freedom of contract is therefore limited in this case, although it always has the option to withdraw the procedure'.[37] In other words, although the freedom of contract of a contracting authority is limited once a procurement procedure has commenced, contracting authorities always have the option to withdraw a procedure. Thus, the court apparently operated under the assumption that, whatever limitation the principles of public procurement law imposed on the contracting authority, it could always still invoke its freedom from contract and withdraw the tender. By stating that the freedom of contract is limited in the pre-contractual phase, but the option to withdraw a procedure is never limited, the court granted the contracting authority wide discretion regarding withdrawal decisions.

At this point, it is important to recall that unconditional freedom from contract is linked to the 'autonomy' aspect of freedom of contract. If a contracting authority can only invoke the 'societal interest' aspect of freedom of contract, contracting authorities should not have wider discretion regarding withdrawal decisions, and judicial review of those decisions should not be limited (note the last two paragraphs of section II of this chapter above). Moreover, contract coercion should be one of the available remedies for situations in which a contracting authority has failed to offer objective grounds for its withdrawal decision.

In a second case, a Dutch court considered a situation in which the autonomy and societal interest perspectives are presented as opposites. The case concerned a dispute with the incumbent supplier of catering services at a school. The incumbent supplier had terminated the current contract and stated that the school was obliged to put a new catering contract out to tender, particularly so that its staff could be taken over by the successor contractor. The court ruled that no such obligation existed because of the freedom of contract. The COVID-19 crisis may have played a role in this decision. The court considered that it was evident that the needs of the school had changed and that a successor contractor would not be able to offer work to the 84 employees of the incumbent supplier. Nonetheless, the court's decision was clear: where the individual autonomy of the school and the societal interests (put forward by the incumbent supplier) collide, the individual autonomy of the contracting authority prevails. As noted by the court:

> The preliminary relief judge firstly stipulates that [contracting authority] rightly invokes the principle of freedom of contract as it applies in the Netherlands. That principle means that [contracting authority] is free to determine whether it wants to conclude an agreement with a new contractor.[38]

[37] District Court of Amsterdam, Judgment of 8 April 2010, ECLI:NL:RBAMS:2010:BM1229 para 4.7.
[38] District Court of Den Bosch, Judgment of 11 September 2020, ECLI:NL:RBOBR:2020:4374 para 4.5.

Several Dutch courts do not explicitly refer to the freedom of contract, they rather generally point to the wide discretion contracting authorities have regarding withdrawal decisions without offering a clear explanation why.[39] If courts do not explain why they grant this wide discretion, one can only guess the legal reasoning behind it. Similar to Dutch legal practitioners who consider invoking the principle of freedom of contract for withdrawal decisions not even questioned (which was seen regarding the incomplete implementation of Article 55 Directive 2014/24/EU), it is argued that courts also do not feel the need to explicitly refer to the principle of freedom of contract. That means that, also, in cases where the principle of freedom of contract is not explicitly referred to, wide discretion regarding withdrawal decisions is based on a tacitly assumed freedom from contract.[40]

C. Finnish and Danish Withdrawal Cases Similar to Dutch Case Law, Poland Differs

It appears that the principle of freedom from contract is explicitly connected to withdrawal decisions in none of the Member States. Yet, contracting authorities are typically granted wide discretion to withdraw a public procurement procedure based on public procurement law. As mentioned earlier, without reference to the autonomy aspect of freedom of contract, it is unclear why contracting authorities should have this wide discretion.

The asymmetry between withdrawal decisions and other decisions is also noted in Finnish literature on the matter:

> Discretion is at its widest when the prerogative leaves the outcome of the decision largely or even entirely to the discretion of the official. … Although the Court of Justice [of the EU] has … taken a position on the possibility to suspend the procurement procedure and the general conditions for suspension, the legal basis for suspension is national. According to the Public Procurement Act, the Special Procurement Act and the Act on Public Defence and Security Procurement, the procurement procedure can only be suspended for a real and justified reason. … In view of the content of the law in force and the main points made in the preamble and the case-law on the conditions for suspension, it can already be considered that, as an administrative decision, a suspension decision is one of those decisions in which the authority has a wide

[39] District Court of Haarlem, Judgment of 23 November 2007, ECLI:NL:RBHAA:2007:BB9853 para 4.1; District Court of Den Bosch, Judgment of 5 November 2008, ECLI:NL:RBSHE:2008:BW2949 paras 4.1.1–4.3.3; District Court of the Hague, Judgment of 15 March 2016, ECLI:NL:RBDHA:2016:6394 para 4.3.

[40] Noteworthy in this respect is the recent shift towards a stricter approach of withdrawal decisions by the District Court of Utrecht: District Court of Utrecht, Judgment of 19 September 2024, ECLI:NL:RBMNE:2024:5561 paras 3.18 and 3.20; District Court of Utrecht, Judgment of 14 February 2025, ECLI:NL:RBMNE:2025:390 paras 3.2, 3.9, 3.13, 3.14, 3.16.2, and 3.18. In these cases, the court did not order the contracting authority to enter into a contract, but did deem the withdrawal decisions unlawful. The approach of the District Court of Utrecht can thus be compared to the Polish approach.

> margin of discretion. … The procurement procedure is regulated in detail in the public procurement directives and in national law. In this respect, the rules on the suspension of the award procedure constitute an exception to the extent of the discretion left to the contracting authority.[41]

The Finnish Public Procurement Act contains a general obligation to make a reasoned decision.[42] More specifically, a public procurement procedure may only be withdrawn due to a 'real and legitimate reason'.[43] Withdrawal of the procedure does not, however, require the existence of serious or exceptional circumstances, and in Finnish case law, the withdrawal of the procurement procedure has been treated 'relatively permissively'.[44] Even actions of the contracting authority itself can be grounds for withdrawal. A Finnish court concluded that withdrawal was permissible due to the ambiguity of the tender documents, even though the contracting authority had not invoked this fact as a reason for the withdrawal.[45] Another acceptable reason for withdrawal was that the object of procurement or the need for procurement had been changed during the procurement procedure.[46] It seems that courts grant a wide discretionary power to contracting authorities, based on some assumed personal autonomy of contracting authorities. Once the personal autonomy of contracting authorities is assumed, granting a wide discretion concerning withdrawal decisions is only a small step. It is argued that contracting authorities should not enjoy the same protection of personal autonomy as individuals; regarding contracts, however, they are treated quite similarly to individuals. This similar treatment seems to be the result of the conflation of the two aspects of the function of freedom of contract, both in Finnish and Dutch case law.

As a general rule, Danish public procurement law does not obligate the contracting authority to enter into a contract with any bidder. The contracting authority retains the right to cancel the procurement process before contract conclusion, provided the withdrawal is justified. This justification must be based on objective reasons, and the decision must not contravene the fundamental EU law principles or otherwise be deemed unjustified.[47] The question of justifiable cancellations of public procurement procedures has been heard by the Danish Complaints Board for Public Procurement as well as before the civil courts. Non-exhaustive examples where the cancellation of a procurement process has been recognised as justifiable encompass, for example, the following situations: there is only one suitable

[41] V Parkkari, 'Hankintamenettelyn keskeyttäminen ja valitus markkinaoikeuteen' (2024) 3 *Defensor Legis* 392 (translation by Perplexity December 2024).

[42] Finnish Public Procurement Act (1397/2016).

[43] ibid s 125(1).

[44] Government Proposal on the Finnish Procurement Act 182/2010, 22.

[45] MAO 684/15.

[46] MAO H315/2021 and MAO 501/20.

[47] See UfR 2011.3129 H – *ISS Facility Services and Danish Confederation of Industries v Municipality of Silkeborg*; Complaints Board for Public Procurement case of 7 April 2021 *Urbaser A/S v Silkeborg Genbrug og Affald A/S*; Complaints Board for Public Procurement case of 10 November 2021 *A/S Bladkompagniet v HOFOR A/S*; Complaints Board for Public Procurement case of 26 September 2024 *Silkeborg Jordemoderhus ApS v Region Syddanmark*.

bidder (lack of competition),[48] errors have occurred in the tendering procedure or the tender material,[49] changed budgetary and structural conditions mandates it, the contracting authority assesses that the task is best handled by the contracting authority itself,[50] or the bids are significantly higher priced than what the contracting authority has budgeted for.[51] In case the amount is only a negligible amount, it may not be considered a valid reason to cancel the tender. It is up to the complainant to prove that the cancellation is contrary to the principle of equal treatment or is otherwise considered unreasonable.

In Poland, however, discretion is contrarily severely limited, which is an indication that freedom from contract is seen as less self-evident.[52] The Polish Public Procurement Act indicates explicitly and exhaustively in which situations the contracting authority may terminate the procedure without selecting the most advantageous offer. The contracting body shall cancel the procurement procedure if:

1. No request to participate has been submitted, or no tender has been received;
2. All submitted requests to participate or tenders are subject to rejection;
3. The price or cost of the most advantageous tender, or the lowest-priced tender exceeds the allocated budget for the contract, unless the contracting body can increase the budget to match the most advantageous tender;
4. Additional offers with the same price or cost have been submitted, as referenced in Article 248(3), Article 249, and Article 250(2);[53]
5. Unforeseen significant changes in circumstances have occurred, making the continuation of the procedure or contract execution no longer in the public interest;
6. The procedure contains an irreparable defect that prevents the conclusion of a valid public procurement contract;
7. The economic operator has either failed to provide the required security for contract performance or has refused to conclude the contract, in accordance with Article 263;

[48] See eg *Silkeborg Jordemoderhus ApS v Region Syddanmark* (n 47).

[49] See eg Complaints Board for Public Procurement case of 25 November 2009 *A/S Jens Jensen og sønner m.fl. v Viborg Kommune*; Complaints Board for Public Procurement case of 6 August 2010 *HedeDanmark A/S v Greve Spildevand A/S*; Complaints Board for Public Procurement case of 23 September 2010 *Getinge Danmark A/S v Region Midtjylland*; and of 4 April 2017 *P. Olesen & Sønner A/S v Hørsholm Kommune*.

[50] See eg *ISS v Silkeborg* (n 47).

[51] See eg Complaints Board for Public Procurement case of 28 November 2023 *ABB A/S v Udviklingsselskabet By og Havn I/S*.

[52] The authors are grateful to M Kania for his guidance on the Polish context. Art 255 *Ustawa z dnia 11 września 2019 r. – Prawo zamówień publicznych* (Polish Public Procurement Act). See H Nowak and M Winiarz (eds), *Prawo zamówień publicznych. Komentarz* (Warszawa, Urząd Zamówień Publicznych, 2021) 762–79; M Taraszkiewicz, 'Wada postępowania jako przesłanka unieważnienia postępowania o udzielenie zamówienia publicznego' (2023) 11 *Prawo Budżetowe Państwa i Samorządu* 55.

[53] The articles referred to concern situations where, due to the initial impossibility of selecting an offer, the contracting authority requested additional offers, which also did not result in the selection of the most advantageous one.

8. In the case of single-source procurement, negotiations did not result in the conclusion of a contract.[54]

In accordance with Article 256, the contracting authority may cancel the contract award procedure either before the deadline for submitting requests to participate or before the deadline for receiving tenders, if circumstances arise that render the continuation of the procedure to be unfounded.

In accordance with Article 257, the contracting authority may cancel the procurement procedure if the public funds intended to finance all or part of the contract have not been granted, provided that the possibility of cancellation on this ground was stipulated in:

1. The contract notice – applicable in procedures conducted under open and restricted procedure, negotiated procedure with competition, competitive dialogue, or innovation partnership, or
2. The invitation to negotiations – in the procedure conducted under negotiated procedure without publication or single-source procurement.

The Polish approach appears to be more aligned with the 'societal interest' perspective, which should prevail in the public procurement setting. Examples of Polish cases in which a withdrawal decision was refuted by the court are relatively abundant.[55] Nevertheless, none of those cases resulted in a court order to enter into a contract, indicating that in all Member States examined, contract coercion is clearly 'a bridge too far'.

D. CJEU: From *HI* with Full Review to *Croce Amica One* with Limited Review

One might object that the wide discretion and consequent limited judicial review have nothing to do with freedom of contract, but rather stem from the case law of the CJEU. The Court, after all, based the wide discretion regarding withdrawal decisions on the fact that Directive 2014/24/EU does not contain any provision concerning the substantive or formal conditions for a withdrawal decision. In the following paragraphs, it is argued that the Court appears to grant a wider discretion or limit its review if there is no provision in the 2014 Public Procurement Directives on the subject. That means there must be another reason why the Court grants contracting authorities wide discretion regarding withdrawal decisions. The conclusion is, again, that the reason might

[54] Art 255 Polish Public Procurement Act.

[55] See eg Judgment of the National Appeals Chamber of September 23, 2011 (KIO 1948/11); Judgment of the National Appeals Chamber of November 19, 2021 (KIO 3133/21); Judgment of the National Appeals Chamber of February 16, 2024, (KIO 185/24); Judgment of the National Board of Appeals of March 7, 2022 (KIO 442/22).

be the tacit assumption that contracting authorities can invoke their freedom from contract.

Whatever the case may be, the CJEU seems to embrace the view that withdrawal decisions are indeed of a different nature than other award decisions. As a result, award decisions are subject to full judicial review. In contrast, withdrawal decisions are subject to a somewhat more restricted review because of the 'wide discretion [of contracting authorities] to withdraw a tendering procedure'.[56]

Originally, the CJEU held that wide discretion did not imply a restricted review per se. It considered in *HI* that:

> neither the letter nor the spirit of [the Remedies Directive] permits the conclusion that it is lawful for Member States to limit review of the legality of a decision to withdraw an invitation to tender to mere examination of whether it was arbitrary.[57]

Accordingly, it is argued that wide discretion automatically implies limited judicial review. If a contracting authority has wide discretion regarding a decision, but the court fully reviews that decision, little is left of the wide discretion. And vice versa, if a contracting authority should strictly comply with a set of criteria, little is left of that obligation if only limited judicial review occurs.

Later, in *Croce Amica One*, the CJEU ruled that a contracting authority cannot be required to carry to its conclusion an award procedure that has been initiated and to award the contract in question, provided the principles of transparency and equal treatment are complied with.[58] This might not seem like a big step away from *HI*, but materially, this consideration *does* imply a break with it, because the wide discretion and limited review are linked together by the CJEU. Consequently, since *Croce Amica One*, an asymmetry exists between withdrawal decisions and other decisions.

E. Explicit Asymmetry between Withdrawal and Award Decisions: *Croce Amica One* versus *CAS Succhi di Frutta*

The asymmetry comes to the fore when comparing the key consideration of the famous *Succhi di Frutta* case to the key consideration of *Croce Amica One*.[59] In *Succhi di Frutta*, it falls to the contracting authority to strictly comply with the

[56] Opinion of AG Tizzano delivered on 8 November 2001 in case C-92/00 *Hospital Ingenieure Krankenhaustechnik Planungs-Gesellschaft mbH (HI) v Stadt Wien* ECLI:EU:C:2002:367, [2001] paras 28 and 37.

[57] Case C-92/00 *Hospital Ingenieure Krankenhaustechnik Planungs-Gesellschaft mbH (HI) v Stadt Wien* ECLI:EU:C:2002:379, [2002] para 63.

[58] Case C-440/13 *Croce Amica One Italia Srl v Azienda Regionale Emergenza Urgenza (AREU)* ECLI:EU:C:2014:2430, [2014] para 36.

[59] Case C-92/00 *HI* (n 57); Case 440/13 *Croce Amica One* (n 58).

criteria which it has laid down, not only in the public procurement procedure per se, but also up to the end stage during which the contract is performed:

> Against that background, it consequently falls to the Commission, in its capacity as contracting authority, strictly to comply with the criteria which it has itself laid down on that basis not only in the tendering procedure per se, which is concerned with assessing the tenders submitted and selecting the successful tenderer, but also, more generally, up to the end of the stage during which the relevant contract is performed.[60]

In *Croce Amica One*, a withdrawal decision will stand, provided the principles of transparency and equal treatment are complied with. That leaves plenty of discretion to the contracting authority:

> As a consequence, provided the principles of transparency and equal treatment are complied with, a contracting authority cannot be required to carry to its conclusion an award procedure that has been initiated and to award the contract in question, including where there remains only one tenderer in contention.[61]

Accordingly, there is a clear asymmetry between the discretion left to the contracting authority regarding award decisions and withdrawal decisions in these cases. Contracting authorities are free to decide which criteria they set to determine the most economically advantageous tender (MEAT). However, once those criteria are set, they 'must comply strictly' with the established criteria.[62] This compliance is also required during the performance phase.[63] Likewise, contracting authorities are free to decide whether they wish to organise a procurement procedure and award a contract in conclusion of that procedure. Once that decision has been made, why are contracting authorities not obliged to 'comply strictly' with that decision?

Of course, pivotal in creating this asymmetry was the consideration of the CJEU in *Croce Amica One* that Directive 2014/24/EU does not contain any provision concerning the substantive or formal conditions for a withdrawal decision.[64] However, the strict standard of *Succhi di Frutta* is not the result of a provision in Directive 2014/24/EU either. The strict *Succhi di Frutta* standard is the final part of an argument based solely on the principle of equality. The lack of a provision concerning the conditions for a withdrawal decision is an insufficient explanation for the existence of the asymmetry. Our view is that the Court has tacitly assumed, much like the courts of the Member States, that full review of a withdrawal decision would restrict the autonomy of the contracting authority.

[60] Case C-496/99 *Commission of the European Communities v CAS Succhi di Frutta SpA* ECLI:EU:C:2004:236, [2004] ECR I-03801 para 115.

[61] Case C-440/13 *Croce Amica One* (n 58) para 36.

[62] E Uysal, 'Contract Compliance for Sustainable Public Procurement: To Monitor or Not to Monitor' *SAPIENS Working Paper* (2024) 2.

[63] ibid 5, 19 where reference is made to Case C-337/98 *Commission of the European Communities v French Republic* ECLI:EU:C:2000:543, [2000] ECR I-08377 para 115.

[64] Case C-440/13 *Croce Amica One* (n 58) para 30.

V. Freedom from Contract and Division of Risk

As with withdrawal decisions, Directive 2014/24/EU does not contain any provision concerning the substantive or formal conditions for the division of risk. However, Dutch courts are more than willing to intervene in decisions regarding risk division. Dutch courts infringe on the autonomy of contracting authorities in these cases, perhaps because there is less obvious association with freedom of contract when dealing with decisions related to the division of risk.

Two cases – *Youth Care* and *Damen* – illustrate how the Dutch courts perceive freedom from contract.[65] In both cases, the courts ruled on the division of risk from a proportionality perspective, thereby influencing the contractual conditions of the agreement by taking a societal interest perspective. This is contrary to the discussed withdrawal decisions, in which the autonomy perspective took precedence.

A. Asymmetry between Withdrawal and Division of Risk Decisions

To support the argument that an asymmetry exists between different decisions in a public procurement context, it is relevant to consider *Youth Care*, which concerns a procurement procedure for youth care services. This resulted from the decentralisation of care services, which made municipalities responsible for providing these services in the Netherlands. In 2017, the Court of Appeal's ruling on this case considered, similar to the District Court, that municipalities, in their role as contracting authorities, are free to design the relevant procedure and its modalities, which are limited by the Awet 2012. Similarly, economic operators are free to submit a bid but need to comply with the relevant rules once they decide to participate in the procedure.[66] Accordingly, it seems that the Court of Appeal in the Hague implicitly referred to elements of the freedom from contract.

In this case, the most prominent legal boundary is the proportionality principle, as outlined in Article 1.10 Awet 2012. According to the court, the background of this principle is to prevent certain operators from being unable to participate in a procedure due to (too) high demands and conditions and thus aims to increase competition. The most prevalent legal question was if the appellant had received sufficient information about the contract and if the way in which the division of risk had taken place was proportionate. The proportionality principle is further explained in the mentioned Dutch Proportionality Guide. In light of the 'comply

[65] Court of Appeals, The Hague, Judgment of 14 February 2017, ECLI:NL:GHDHA:2017:260 (*Youth Care*); District Court of Haarlem, 14 February 2022, ECLI:NL:RBNHO:2022:3274 (*Damen*) paras 5.22 et seq.

[66] ECLI:NL:GHDHA:2017:260 *(Youth Care)* (n 65) paras 6–7.

or explain' approach to this binding act, rule 3.9A stipulates that 'the contracting authority shall allocate the risk to the party which can best manage effects of the risk'. When deciding on who can best manage risks, the contracting authority must include the following aspects in weighing up the risk. First, it should be considered that a risk may be realised, along with the potential consequences of such an event. Accordingly, as noted by the Guide, placing a risk on an economic operator that is not or barely foreseeable, arises only in exceptional cases, or has potential effects that could undermine the continuity of the supplier, is more likely to be disproportionate compared to a reasonably foreseeable risk with minor or manageable effects.[67] Second, it must be considered if the risk for one of the two parties is insurable on reasonable/realistic conditions, noting that not everything is insurable. Furthermore, rule 3.9D considers that 'The contracting authority does not want liability which is not limited in any way'. In considering proportionality of liability, the contracting authority takes note of (1) the risks which the contracting authority actually runs and (2) the usual liability requirement in the relevant industry or for the relevant contract by nature and size. Accordingly, unlimited liability is always disproportional, whereas the two requirements must inform decisions about other types of liability.

Within this legal context of rule 3.9A, the court determined that the proportionality principle had been violated in this case.[68] First, the maximum budgets were likely to be insufficient for the required services, meaning that it was a realistic assumption that the economic operator would likely need to go over budget to perform the services in line with the set requirements. Second, the court concluded that insufficient information was given to the economic operator to carefully estimate what was required to perform the contract (ie the size of the youth population, current care services, length of services, cost of current care, length of waiting lists, etc). This combination of insufficient information with insufficient budgets meant that the court concluded that 'fully placing all risks on the economic operator … is disproportionate under these circumstances'.[69] Hence, the Dutch Court of Appeal was willing to intervene in the procurement procedure extensively by declaring the contractual conditions relating to the budget and the resulting allocation of risk illegitimate. Given that Dutch public procurement law has regulated the allocation of risk, courts can provide judicial review in light of a societal perspective on freedom from contract in the procurement phase. Accordingly, it is quite contrasting to the approach taken with withdrawal decisions, in which such a review remains insufficient.

Similarly in 2022, the District Court of Amsterdam intervened in *Damen*. This case concerned the procurement of a research vessel by NIOZ, the Dutch Oceanographic Institute. Damen, a shipbuilder, challenged the contractual conditions of the related public contract before the court based on Article 10 Awet 2012

[67] Explanation of Rule 3.9A Proportionality Guide (see n 26).
[68] ECLI:NL:GHDHA:2017:260 *(Youth Care)* (n 65) paras 19–26.
[69] ibid para 27.

and rules 3.9A (division of risk) and 3.9D (liability). The court concluded that various aspects of the contract did not meet the proportionality test. Interestingly, the payment scheme with high upfront investments for a long-term project with a value of 62 million euros was not deemed disproportionate. One condition related to underwater noise was deemed disproportionate. In addition, the court ruled that the condition related to *force majeure* was also disproportionate. The *force majeure* clause did not include strikes, lack of personnel, issues with delayed materials from abroad or reliance on third parties. Damen challenged this based on the war in Ukraine, COVID-19, and the raw material crisis leading to shortages. Furthermore, it noted specifically that security reasons had led one of the largest steel manufacturers in Ukraine to stop production altogether and that supply from China was severely limited by COVID-19 measures. The court concluded that the risk of delays in this context cannot be put entirely on the shoulders of the economic operator. It particularly addressed the fact that the current ship was still in operation, as a consequence of which the award lacked urgency. Moreover, the risks that the contracting authority allocated to the economic operator were not insurable. Similar to *Youth Care*, the court was willing to intervene in the division of risk based on the provisions of Dutch public procurement law, thereby limiting the freedom of contract and allowing judicial review in light of proportionality.

Finally, the court also deemed the liability condition to be disproportional.[70] A strictly linguistic interpretation of the clause would lead to unlimited liability for the contractor for all damage, including indirect, caused by any of its suppliers. NIOZ was unable to convince the court why this was necessary. Thus, NIOZ did not meet the 'comply or explain' requirement related to rule 3.9D.[71]

The court went beyond conclusions on proportionality and proposed a new contractual condition with a different set of fines and timelines in case of delay, including an extended description of *force majeure* situations. Accordingly, the court drafted specific contractual conditions in its ruling, thereby going far beyond a mere test of the current condition.[72] One could question if such an approach is suitable for a summary proceeding, but nonetheless, it re-emphasised the link between the societal perspective on the freedom from contract and the possibility of review.

VI. Conclusion

In this chapter, two prominent interpretations of freedom from contract were interpreted: individual autonomy and societal interest. Both interpretations are clearly present in the Dutch context and appear to be present in the Finnish, Danish,

[70] ECLI:NL:RBNHO:2022:3274 *(Damen)* (n 65) paras 5.44 et seq.
[71] ibid paras 5.43 et seq.
[72] ibid para 5.30.

Polish, and European context as well. Accordingly, it has been argued that there is no substantive reason to support this difference, particularly when comparing withdrawal decisions and decisions on the division of risk.

From a societal interest perspective, restricting the autonomy of contracting authorities seems more prudent. Subsequently, it is considered that the autonomy perspective on the principle of freedom from contract needs scrutiny, particularly when there is an asymmetry between the judicial review of a withdrawal decision and the judicial review of an award decision or the judicial review of the contents of a contract, considering the division of risk. In this light, and more broadly, it is concluded that protecting the 'individual autonomy' of contracting authorities should not take centre stage to ensure a level playing field between the contracting parties of an agreement. Relevant here, though, is the regulatory crevice filled by the Dutch Proportionality Guide when it comes to the division of risk, in which the influence of public procurement law comes to the fore as a limit to the freedom from contract. It appears that because there are legal rules, judicial review can take place, meaning that the law forces a specific perspective on the freedom from contract. Should the freedom from contract be regulated extensively to avoid discussions about the intensity of review? As such, it would seem useful to further explore this starting point for other decisions in the public procurement context.

6

The Diligent Contracting Authority: The Concept of Due Diligence in Public Procurement

MICHAEL STEINICKE

I. Introduction

Although the concept of 'due diligence' is only mentioned a few times in the 2014 Public Procurement Directives, it has a strong but varied history in many Member States' legal traditions.[1] In some areas of law, it has evolved into an important legal standard.[2]

Even though the concept of due diligence is a part of various legal areas, there is only a limited role of such term in EU public procurement law. The public procurement rules are primarily based on behavioural norms, suggesting that a term like due diligence should fit well within the framework of the procurement regime.[3] However, an examination of the rules in the 2014 Public Procurement Directives reveals that due diligence does not play a prominent role, with only a few direct references found.[4] Furthermore, the literature has not devoted much attention to the issue. According to the author's knowledge, only one comprehensive effort to address the concept of due diligence in a public procurement context has been published.[5]

[1] Directive 2014/23/EU; Directive 2014/24/EU; Directive 2014/25/EU.

[2] See s II.A below.

[3] In this context, behavioural norms mean a very detailed and comprehensive regulation of the explicit requirements of the behaviour of public entities in a purchasing situation.

[4] For more on these, see s II.A.i below.

[5] This contribution is Kadri Härginen's PhD thesis: K Härginen, *Due Diligence Obligations of a Contracting Authority Under the EU Public Procurement Law* (Tartu, University of Tartu Press, 2023). The thesis was defended in August 2023. For another recent contribution, see L Treviño-Lozano, 'Due diligence a standard of conduct for contracting authorities and business contractors' (SAPIENS Network Working Paper, 2024) <sapiensnetwork.eu/wp-content/uploads/2024/07/ESR8_WorkingPaper-Duediligence-1.pdf> 2. This contribution aims to cover the existing legal loopholes in the theory and practice of contracting authorities' due diligence.

The focus of this chapter is partly whether the due diligence concept is a general part of public procurement (and if this is answered in the affirmative, to lay down the basic content of this phenomenon) and partly how this concept in a public procurement context relates to similar private law instruments. This analysis is relevant in determining whether examples of due diligence in private law can aid in understanding the specific provisions that establish a due diligence obligation within EU public procurement law. Additionally, it examines the extent to which private law instruments or sources could serve as a foundation for such an obligation in the context of public procurement. The second section of this chapter begins by exploring the general concept of due diligence from a broad perspective, drawing on various sources. This serves to highlight the concept's extensive scope from both linguistic and legal standpoints. Section III then examines specific private law provisions through the lens of due diligence with a focus on provisions that apply in circumstances similar to those outlined in Article 72(1)(c) Directive 2014/24/EU, which permits contract modifications. Section IV shifts the focus to due diligence within public procurement, analysing in greater detail the role of a 'diligent contracting authority'. This analysis is based on Directive 2014/24/EU, relevant case law from the Court of Justice of the EU (CJEU), and the limited contributions in legal literature. Section V contains a comparison between the relevant private law and EU public procurement law, and this includes an analysis of the differences in the importance of due diligence in the two regimes. Finally, section VI provides conclusions.

A. The Relationship between Contract Law and Public Procurement: The Danish System

The relationship between contract law and public procurement law in Denmark can be described in the following way: current Danish contract law is based on a century-long legislation and an even longer tradition from early Danish principles.[6] Contract law in this specific situation consists of pre-contractual provisions, principles, and rules, which regulate the concluded contract.[7] The general regime for the former category is settled in the Danish Contracts Act, which is of general application in most circumstances.[8] The latter category (the concluded contracts) is primarily

[6] There have been private law rules dating back to the late 1600s, see the Danish Code from 1683, including 5-1-1 establishing the freedom of contract, and that both oral and written contracts are binding. The original version of the Danish Contract Act was from 8 May 1917 (Act no 242/1917) and the original version of the Danish Sale of Goods Act was from 6 April 1906 (Act no 102/1906). For more on the early development of contract law in Denmark, see S Jørgensen, *Kontraktsret*, vol 1 (Aarhus, Juristforbundets Forlag, 1972).

[7] Both these phases are relevant since the public procurement law regulates both the pre-contractual phase and the contractual phase (the latter to a lesser degree).

[8] *Aftaleloven* no 193/2016 (Danish Contracts Act).

subject to the Danish Sale of Goods Act,[9] which is also of general application.[10] This law will give way in situations where there is a more specific regulation in place for specific contracts (consumer contracts, work contracts, etc). The relation between the Danish Contracts Act and the Danish Sale of Goods Act on the one side and EU public procurement law on the other side is that the former will subside for the latter, based on specific provisions,[11] the *lex specialis* principle, and the basic EU principle that dictates that EU law will be pre-empting national law in case of conflict.[12] Since the introduction of EU public procurement law more than 50 years ago, the Danish Contracts Act has had a decreasing importance in a public procurement context, which is also the case (but to a lesser degree) for the Danish Sale of Goods Act. Besides the specific provisions in the two acts and the *lex specialis* principle, the EU principle that the EU rules pre-empt national rules also leads to the same conclusion. A practical expression of this balance is that the Danish Complaints Board for Public Procurement has expressly stated that it cannot apply contract law – or other branches such as administrative or competition law – namely, as its competence is strictly limited to public procurement law. As a result, while the Danish Complaints Board for Public Procurement does not engage with contract law in its proceedings, this does not prevent bidders from bringing such matters before the civil courts. However, this possibility does not alter the outcome: various legal principles consistently indicate that rules on contract formation are generally not applicable in the context of public procurement procedures governed by procurement law. It is, therefore, worth emphasising that contract law cannot be engaged in proceedings before Denmark's primary enforcement body for public procurement – the Danish Complaints Board for Public Procurement. In the pre-contractual phase of public procurement, which lies at the heart of procurement regulation, private law pre-contractual rules play only a limited role.

In the contract phase of public procurement, Article 72 Directive 2014/24/EU plays a crucial role.[13] This provision applies in all relevant circumstances, taking precedence over general contract law without reservation. However, beyond the specific requirements of Article 72, the interpretation of a contract's content generally falls under contract law, as it would for any other contract.[14]

[9] *Købeloven* no 1853/2021 (Danish Sale of Goods Act).

[10] The general application of the Danish Sale of Goods Act is more limited than the Danish Contracts Act, since there are, however, certain specific rules for different types of contracts, and the Danish Sale of Goods Act only covers the sale of goods. An example is the area of construction contracts. Such contracts are to a large degree regulated by different agreed documents.

[11] For both acts, see their s 1.

[12] These results are mentioned in GS Ølykke, M Ohm, and CF Petersen, *EU's udbudsregler – i dansk kontekst* (Copenhagen, DJØF Publishing, 2022) 82–85.

[13] Implemented in ss 178–184 *Udbudsloven* no 2015/1564 (Danish Public Procurement Act).

[14] For more on the relationship between contract law and public procurement in Denmark, see M Steinicke, 'Aftaleretten og offentlige udbud: samspil og konflikter' (2000) *Juristen* 302; M Steinicke, 'Aftalelovens ugyldighedsregler anvendt på aftaler indgået gennem offentlige udbud' in B Iversen (ed), *Juridiske emner ved Syddansk Universitet 2001* (Copenhagen, DJØF Publishing, 2001) 167–80; M Steinicke 'Kontraktfrihed – retten til at undlade at indgå kontrakt' in KN Olesen and M Steinicke (eds), *Udførelse af offentlig opgave via kontrakt* (Copenhagen, DJØF Publishing, 2004) 117.

II. The Concept of a 'Diligent Contracting Authority'

The notion of due diligence is widely known but is rarely precisely defined. The base of the term will have a starting point in the linguistic understanding. Due diligence can be defined with the following words: 'the care that a reasonable person exercises to avoid harm to other persons or their property'.[15] Another version is: 'action that is considered reasonable for people to be expected to take in order to keep themselves or others and their property safe'.[16] Yet a variation covers behaviour such as 'an assessing, evaluating, etc conducted with prudent or necessary care'.[17] The core of the concept is therefore derived from the thoroughness of an effort in a certain context. Diligence (and the due diligence) is present when a person exerts a sufficient level of effort in order to attain a certain goal.

The combination of 'due' and 'diligence' leaves us with the expectation that the diligent behaviour must be qualified and elevated to a specific level. The linguistic opposition to 'diligent' will be 'negligent', which covers an effort that is not enough.[18] Even though diligence in itself pictures a certain level of effort, it is further qualified when combined with 'due'. As pointed out, 'Due diligence is no free-standing obligation, but a modality attached to a duty of care for someone or something else (including the duty to prevent and mitigate harm)'.[19] There is a contextual element in using the concept, and in public procurement, the context is that the due diligence will have to be in regard to the question of whether a competitive tendering procedure must be initiated or not.[20]

The concept of due diligence has been introduced into different areas of law. The fact that there is a requirement of due diligence in many corners of the legal system does not mean that such a behavioural standard will be identical in various contexts. Some prominent examples of due diligence are: for example in regard to the purchase of a company, there will often be a 'due diligence investigation',[21] and the new corporate sustainability due diligence as seen in the Corporate Sustainability Due Diligence Directive (CSDDD).[22] In the former situation the due diligence obligation requires a thorough investigation of a target company's

[15] Merriam-Webster Dictionary <www.merriam-webster.com>.

[16] Cambridge Dictionary <www.dictionary.cambridge.org>.

[17] Collins Dictionary see <www.collinsdictionary.com>.

[18] According to the Cambridge Dictionary, negligence covers 'the fact of not giving enough care or attention to someone or something'. Cambridge Dictionary <www.dictionary.cambridge.org>.

[19] See Härginen (n 5).

[20] See s IV.A below.

[21] This is basically a practical phenomenon, but is a well-known and essential part of the buying process, even though there is no explicitly or uniform content of such a process.

[22] Directive (EU) 2024/1760 of the European Parliament and of the Council of 13 June 2024 on corporate sustainability due diligence and amending Directive (EU) 2019/1937 and Regulation (EU) 2023/2859 [2024] OJ L2024/1760 (CSDDD). For more on the CSDDD and the link to public procurement, see L Treviño-Lozano and E Uysal, 'Bridging the Gap Between Corporate Sustainability Due Diligence and EU Public Procurement' (2023) 30(5) *Maastricht Journal of European and Comparative Law* 554.

entire situation including taxes, accounts, intellectual property rights (IPR), and so on, whereas due diligence in the latter situation covers obligations like integrating due diligence into companies' policies and risk management systems, identifying and assessing actual or potential adverse impacts (to human rights and the environment), preventing and mitigating potential adverse impacts (again – to human rights and the environment), and bringing such actual adverse impacts to an end (non-exhaustive list).[23] In both situations, the concept covers a comprehensive investigation with the purpose of thoroughly shedding light on and examining a certain situation. Both situations show that due diligence as a concept is very broad, even though it contains the same characteristics. It also shows that when used legally, the concept is still founded in its linguistic meaning, whereas the legal content may differ substantially between different areas of law.

III. Due Diligence between Private and Public Law

The concept of due diligence is not confined to either public or private law. Especially in the broad sense of due diligence, the idea seems universal across the legal system. In private law, the concept may be most prominent in relation to the buying of companies, but similar phenomena – that a party is subject to a qualified behavioural standard – are acknowledged throughout many areas of private law.[24] In public law, the situation is quite similar, and a very actual example of due diligence in a public law remedy is seen in the CSDDD. However, a qualified behavioural standard may be found using different terminology in many areas. In traditional administrative law, the public sector is frequently subject to a requirement of a high level of diligence in relation to ensuring that citizens are given the proper rights in administrative cases.[25]

A slightly different question would be which public or private law instruments or sources could construct the basis for a due diligence obligation within public procurement. There is an obvious link to administrative law since this area of regulation sets the tone for the behaviour of the public entities in basically all situations. Even though public procurement in some cases falls outside the traditional administrative law due to not covering public authority, but rather public

[23] Art 5 CSDDD.

[24] In contract law – both regarding traditional business contracts but especially regarding consumer contracts – there are requirements of prudent and diligent behaviour.

[25] In Danish public administration law such examples could be an obligation to diligently provide the facts of a case in order to enlighten the case sufficiently (this is a principle and it is not consolidated in the Danish Public Administration Act, in Danish: *officialprincippet*. For more on the principle, see S Bønsing, *Almindelig forvaltningsret* (Copenhagen, DJØF Publishing, 2023) at 152–57), an obligation to ensure that the parties are heard throughout a process of preparing a case with the purpose of making a decision directed at a specific citizen or company (Act Ch 5 Ss 19–21 Danish Public Administration) and the obligation to provide guidance when needed S 7 *Forvaltningsloven* no 433/2014 (Danish Public Administration Act).

contracting. Regardless, the focus on the good faith public entity seems to extend from public authority to any other public business.[26]

Even though the connection between different sources of administrative law and public procurement law is not entirely convincing, it is safe to say that there seems to be a link between public purchasing and other public behaviour standards. Among the most important principles in Danish administrative law, we see standards of behaviour that mirror the major principles of public procurement law: the principle requiring equal treatment, the principle of proportionality, and the requirement to ensure transparency in the public sector.

A. Focus on Private Law: Pre-Contractual Rules and Amending Contracts

The two areas of public procurement law where we detect rules on due diligence are (1) when assessing whether it is possible to conduct a direct award without competitive tendering and (2) when assessing whether it is possible to adapt an existing contract without initiating a competitive tendering. The private law regulation of these two situations and whether or not there is a due diligence obligation for the parties will be shown to be fundamentally different from procurement law.

i. The Basic Rules and Principles for Pre-Contractual Activities

There does not seem to be any rules in private law that have the same scope as Article 32 (2)(c) Directive 2014/24/EU. The major difference between private law (formation of contract rules) and EU public procurement law is that the former is characterised by a large component of freedom to contract, including *with whom* you would like to contract and also freedom to choose the *procedure of formation of a contract* that suits you.

In Danish law, the freedom of contract is based on the Danish Code of 1683 in Sections 5-1-1 and 5-1-2 and the principle of *pacta sunt servanda*.[27] The principle has been in place since then, and there is still widespread freedom of contract in Denmark. The level of freedom of contract varies due to the specific rules within different areas (consumer law, insurance law etc) and due to whether the subject matter is regulated by EU law or not. The Danish Contracts Act contains a few rules primarily concerned with the main concepts of entering into an agreement, for example, the concept of an offer, an acceptance, and modifications.[28] There are

[26] Härginen also sees a web of public rules to support due diligence in the public procurement regime, see Härginen (n 5) 51 and more.

[27] See more general information about the principle of freedom of contract and its relation to public procurement law in ch 4.

[28] See the Danish Contracts Act, Part I: Conclusions of Contracts ss 1–9.

no provisions on procedural issues, such as who must initiate the process or which documents to exchange.

Public procurement law, however, represents a more strict process with limitations to the freedom to choose with whom you would like to contract.[29] Examining the different international sources on the formation of contracts, there are no provisions where due diligence seems to be required in this specific situation (described in Article 32 (2)(c) Directive 2014/24/EU).[30] The rules in these sources are all related to the instrumental part of the formation of contracts, for example, issues like what is an offer, what is an acceptance, what if a declaration is delivered late, and so on. There are a few requirements related to how to behave, such as good faith and fair dealing.[31] These requirements related to behaviour are not dealing with *when to* prescribe an expectation that all contract negotiations are pursued with the legitimate intent of concluding a contract. The good faith requirement has a different role than the due diligence as the latter is seen in EU public procurement law. Whereas the principles of good faith and fair dealing are establishing a requirement that the parties to a contract should deal with each other honestly and fairly, with the purpose of enabling (or at least not destroying) the right of the other party to receive the benefits of the contract.[32] In the context of EU public procurement law, due diligence refers to the assessment of whether a specific procedure – outlined in Directive 2014/24/EU – should be applied. The due diligence in public procurement does not have an *inter partes* element, which is different from the good faith and fair dealing standard.

It can be concluded that the preparatory standard in public procurement – requiring due diligence and potentially leading to the application of procurement rules under Directive 2014/24/EU – is not present in traditional contract formation instruments.

ii. Private Law Provisions Allowing for Contractual Changes

Unlike the absence of pre-contractual provisions containing a due diligence obligation, there are a few provisions on due diligence in relation to changes of contracts. In the following, the focus will be on a few elements that separate these private law instruments from the public procurement instruments. The focus will be on (1) the equality between the parties, (2) the consequences of changes due to unforeseen circumstances, and (3) the importance of competition.

[29] See ch 4 examining whether there is a certain level of freedom of contract in public procurement. This author is of the opinion that there are substantial limitations to freedom of contract when applying the public procurement rules.

[30] See eg PECL ch 2: Formation; CISG, Part II: Formation of the Contract; DCFR Book II, ch 4: Formation; see also ss 1–9 Danish Contracts Act.

[31] See PECL ch 1, s 2: General Duties; Book I: General provisions DCFR; and Ch 2, Art 7 CISG.

[32] See more about principles of good faith and fair dealing and their relation to public procurement law in ch 4.

a. Rules Allowing for Amendments in Selected Private Law Instruments

In the following section, the focus will be on the Principles of European Contract Law (PECL), the Draft Common Frame for References (DCFR), and the Danish Sale of Goods Act.[33] All provisions have the starting point that the parties must fulfil their obligations unless the conditions change, and that this change comes around due to circumstances that could not be foreseen by the parties in advance.[34]

Article 6.111 PECL initially states that a party is bound to fulfil its obligations even if performance has become more onerous. However, in the second sentence, it is established that if the performance becomes excessively onerous because of a change of circumstances, the parties will be obligated either to adapt the contract or terminate it. Such negotiations should be conducted provided three conditions are met:

(a) the change of circumstances occurred after the time of conclusion of the contract,
(b) the possibility of a change of circumstances was not one which could reasonably have been taken into account at the time of conclusion of the contract, and
(c) the risk of the change of circumstances is not one which, according to the contract, the party affected should be required to bear.[35]

Especially conditions (a) and (b) are of interest when compared with the public procurement rules.

A similar provision is found in the DCFR Book III–3:104: Excuse due to an impediment. The rule provides that:

> a debtor's non-performance of an obligation is excused if it is due to an impediment beyond the debtor's control and if the debtor could not reasonably be expected to have avoided or overcome the impediment or its consequences.

According to 3:104(2), non-performance is not excused if the debtor could reasonably be expected to have taken the impediment into account at the time when the obligation was incurred. This applies where the obligation arose out of a contract or other juridical act. Furthermore, the provision makes a distinction between temporary and permanent impediments: when a temporary impediment is present, the excuse has effect for the duration of the impediment (3), whereas the obligation is extinguished when the impediment is permanent (4).

[33] More specifically, Art 6.111 PECL; book III–3:104 DCFR; s 24 Danish Sale of Goods Act; see also Art 25 CISG.

[34] The principle of *rebus sic stantibus* ('things standing thus') is basically stating that if the conditions in a contract change, the parties will have a chance to escape the obligations or even terminate the contract. The chosen provisions are to different degrees expressions of the principle.

[35] If the parties fail to reach an agreement as a result of the negotiations, the courts may either terminate or adapt the contract, see Art 6.111(3) PECL.

Under the Danish contract law, the situation is more complex. The Danish Contracts Act contains several provisions addressing invalid declarations of intent, but none closely resemble the examples discussed above.[36] Most of these provisions establish invalidity based on circumstances existing at the time of contract formation. Only a few address changes in circumstances after the contract's conclusion, and none explicitly focus on changes in the contract's underlying basis.[37]

The most suitable of all the provisions in the Danish Contracts Act is probably Section 36, despite the shortcomings of this rule. In this provision, it is explicitly mentioned in Section 36(2) that 'regard shall be had to the circumstances existing at the time the contract was concluded, the terms of the contract and subsequent circumstances'. Therefore, the time spectrum relevant to the due diligence provisions – the change of circumstances from the time of conclusion of the contract to when the unforeseen circumstances are presented – is therefore relevant in Section 36. However, the focus in Section 36 is on unfair relations between the parties, and the due diligence assessment does not seem to be part of the provision.

The closest pre-contractual source compared to the due diligence provisions, which can be found in the PECL and the DCFR in the Danish pre-contractual regime, might be the principle of presumptions.[38] This principle is outside the Danish Contracts Act and purely based on case law.[39] The principle covers the following: that a specific issue is determining/decisive for one of the parties in relation to the conclusion of the contract, and this issue later turns out to be changed, false, and so on, and thereby allowing the said party to escape the contract. The conditions for a successful claim to this approach are the following:

1) the specific issue/element has been decisive for one contracting party in order to conclude the contract,
2) was known to the other contracting party that the element would be essential to the first contracting party, and
3) that it would be reasonable to place the risk of the element on the contracting party.

The basic premise for all the rules on invalid declarations is that the result of specific conditions to be present is that the agreement will be void and/or that the party's obligations will be annulled. There are no explicit provisions on renegotiations and modifications of contracts. The core assumption is that changes will be up to the parties and that any change will be acceptable as long as the parties agree

[36] See ss 28–38 Danish Contracts Act, Part III.

[37] ibid ss 33 and 36. Both these provisions are general clauses with a very broad scope of application.

[38] There does not seem to be an official translation of the Danish concept – *forudsætningslæren/bristende forudsætninger*. A presentation in English of the doctrine can be found in B Iversen and LL Petersen, *Danish Business Law* (Copenhagen, DJØF Publishing, 2015) 172–73.

[39] It has been noted that the importance of this principle has decreased since the introduction of s 36 Danish Contracts Act in 1974, see Iversen and Petersen (n 38) 173; LL Andersen, *Aftalelovens § 36 – fra kontraktfrihed til urimelighedskontrol* (Copenhagen, Ex Tuto, 2018) 421.

to it. There is no competition element and only very few third-party considerations to be found in Danish contract law. The most comparable source to the due diligence provisions, which can be found in the PECL and the DCFR, is probably the principle of *force majeure*, requiring that a substantial change in the external circumstances of a contract would lead to the absence of responsibility of the parties. This principle has been incorporated into the Danish Sale of Goods Act and states:

> In a sale of generic goods, the seller shall pay damages even if the delay is no fault of his unless he has reserved the right to be exempted from paying damages or the performance of the contract must be deemed impossible by reason of circumstances that are not of such a nature that the seller should have had them in contemplation at the time of the conclusion of the contract, including accidental loss of all goods of the type or the bulk to which they relate, war, import restrictions etc.[40]

The restriction on this is that the Danish Sale of Goods Act only directly applies to the sale of goods and, therefore, in principle, not to contracts regarding services or construction. The provision is considered to be a specific expression of the general *force majeure* principle that is widely known and especially plays a role in common law countries.

Circumstances like bad weather conditions in general, for example frozen waters, long-lasting periods of rain or drought, extreme snow, and so on, will not be enough for the seller to escape the damages due to delay.[41] Other elements that might be considered impossible conditions are riots, export bans, boycotts, public seizure, fires, and natural catastrophes.[42]

IV. The Role and Importance of Due Diligence within Public Procurement

This section enquires whether the notion of due diligence, as presented above, has a place in EU public procurement law. The basis of due diligence requiring a party to an agreement to be thorough in preparation for all parts of the contract is very much in line with the core of EU public procurement law, where the responsibility of the pre-contractual process is on the contracting authority. The question is, however, if the concept of due diligence can be detected within the regulatory regime of EU public procurement law and furthermore, if there is a need for this concept or the intentions followed by the due diligence doctrine are already met through other regulatory instruments in EU public procurement law.

[40] S 24 (from the chapter in the act that concerns delay on the seller's side) Danish Sale of Goods Act.

[41] See the Joined Cases C-441/22 and C-443/22 *Obshtina Razgrad* ECLI:EU:C:2023:970, [2023] where unusual weather conditions were not sufficient to use the provision in Art 72(1)(c) Directive 2014/24/EU.

[42] H Ussing, *Køb*, 4th edn (Copenhagen, A Vinding-Kruse, 1967) 76.

A. Does Due Diligence have a Place in Public Procurement?

Directive 2014/24/EU contains a large number of provisions, and the first sign of a relation between the concept of due diligence and public procurement would be expected to show. However, there are only a very few explicit references to due diligence. Recital 109 and Article 72(1)(c) Directive 2014/24/EU mention the 'diligent contracting authority'. The case law on the latter provision is limited due to the recent date of Directive 2014/24/EU.[43] A few provisions contain similar obligations, however, without the use of the specific terms. The most prominent is Article 32(2)(c).[44]

It has been submitted that the procurement provisions and the related literature contain a larger number of sources to support the existence of a more widespread due diligence obligation.[45] It has furthermore been submitted that a number of different additional sources would contribute to reaching the conclusion that due diligence is a part of the public procurement regime. In short, legal sources like the Financial Regulation (directed towards the EU institutions), and the Charter of Fundamental Rights of the EU, Article 41, would be essential for the inclusion of due diligence in public procurement.[46]

Even though the concept of due diligence is not given a significant general role in public procurement, it is obvious that the core of the concept sits well with public procurement. The basis of public procurement is that the contracting authority will have to be diligent throughout the entire process, and especially in the early stages, since the basic premise of the two generally available procedures (restricted procedure and open procedure) is that everything relating to the procurement procedure must be prepared and settled before commencing the procurement procedure. Even for negotiated procedures, the largest part of the content of the contract will be established in advance and cannot be amended. This requires prudent preparation. Also, the concept of due diligence would fit well with the (heightened) requirements that go with the spending of public money, provisions that are fighting corruption and increasing transparency.[47]

[43] Basically, at this point the CJEU has only decided Joined Cases C-441/22 and C-443/22 *Obshtina Razgrad* (n 41); and Case C-683/22 *Adusbef* ECLI:EU:C:2024:936, [2014]; C-452/23 *Fastned Deutschland GmbH & Co KG* ECLI:EU:C:2025:28; Case 549/14 *Finn Frogne A/S v Rigspolitiet ved Center for Beredskabskommunikation* ECLI:EU:C:2016:634, [2016] is not dealing with this specific provision but will also contribute to the assessment of role played by due diligence in public procurement, see s IV.C.iv.b below.

[44] The CJEU also established a link of similarity between the issue of unexpected circumstances and this specific provision, see C-549/14 *Finn Frogne* (n 43).

[45] See Härginen (n 5) 38 and more.

[46] Art 41 Regulation (EU, Euratom) 2018/1046 of the European Parliament and of the Council of 18 July 2018 on the financial rules applicable to the general budget of the Union [2018] OJ L 193; Charter of Fundamental Rights of the European Union [2012] OJ C326/391. See also Härginen (n 5) 46–47. As a contrast to this, it has also been submitted that since national administrative law does not have an EU nature, it will not be authoritative for the development of a European standard, such as due diligence.

[47] See Art 18 Directive 2014/24/EU which requires transparency in every step of the process, see also recital 1. According to Art 57(1) the contracting authority is obligated to exclude economic operators that have been engaged in certain and been convicted for criminal activities (such as participation in a criminal organisation or laundering of money).

Even though such an obligation should be respected throughout the entire procurement process, there are stages where it will be more obvious to apply the obligation to act diligently. The two most important stages would be the preparation phase (up until the publication of the contract notice) and the contract phase (after the award and signing of the contract).[48]

The reason for this categorisation is twofold. First, these stages of the procurement procedure are less regulated than the specific procurement procedures. The phase of the preparation of the procurement procedure is barely regulated, and only in relation to the contracting authority's access to seeking advice are there explicit provisions.[49] Therefore, the process of preparing, producing the procurement documents, and making important decisions regarding the potential tender procedure is scarcely regulated.

The stage after the contract has been signed has historically been seen as outside the scope of the public procurement rules, but rather covered by traditional contract rules.[50] Hence, there was no explicit regulation on that part of the procurement process before Article 72 was introduced in Directive 2014/24/EU.

Second, the other reason why the obligation of due diligence is limited to the stages before the procurement procedure is started and the stage after the contract has been signed is that these stages relate to key competitive questions (eg whether the contracting authority should conduct a procurement procedure or whether it may settle with a different and often less straining and more pragmatic solution). The obvious reference is Article 72(1)(c),[51] but other examples could be the general expectations of prudent examination of any situation when the contracting authority estimates the economic value of the contract with the purpose of finding out whether the economic thresholds are exceeded, and a procurement procedure should be initiated.[52]

It could be considered if due diligence covers other issues than those relating to whether or not there is an obligation to tender a new contract (the scope of both Articles 32 and 72).[53] As an example, it may be considered whether other choices could be subject to the issue, for example if the contracting authority took some choices as regards to for example the use of award criteria, selection criteria, framework agreements, subcontracts, and so on. It is not obvious that these situations would include a due diligence obligation; rather, they would 'just' be subject to the general principles (equal treatment, transparency, and proportionality).

[48] See for a different approach, Härginen (n 5) 67–75. Härginen lists a number of specific due diligence obligation within the three phases: preparation, the conduct phase of the procurement process, and the contractual phase.

[49] See Arts 40–41 Directive 2014/24/EU.

[50] This author is basing the view on the Danish approach, see furthermore ch 3 'private-oriented hybrid model'.

[51] Where the contracting authority may amend a contract if the need for amending is based on issues that were unforeseeable by the contracting authority, see more in s IV.C.iv.

[52] See Art 5 Directive 2014/24/EU on calculating the contract value.

[53] Härginen is proposing a wider scope, see Härginen (n 5) 67 and forward.

If due diligence is accepted as an (integrated) part of the public procurement regime, the question will be what the relation between the general principles in Article 18(1) and the due diligence obligation is. Due diligence will primarily have significance if the core of the concept differs from what we already have – the principles. The difference between the two types of behavioural standards may be that the general principles assess the 'explicit expressions of contact' between the contracting authority and the economic operators – regardless of the shape in which this contact may be manifested: as conditions in the procurement documents, as communication throughout the procedure or in the decisions made (eg exclusion of economic operators). In contrast to this role, the due diligence obligation may be more focused on whether the contracting authority has been thorough in specific parts of the process. In the latter case, it is not (only) the specific decision made in the process that is under scrutiny, but rather the effort made in order to reach the conclusion the contracting authority has made.

B. A Critical Approach: The Role of Due Diligence in Public Procurement

From a basic understanding of the concept of due diligence, the term fits very well into the context of public procurement. Therefore, there might be an inclination to include the concept because it is seemingly well-suited – public procurement is fundamentally a set of rules and principles with a uniform core of a certain standard of behaviour. However, as it is shown above, the legal basis for a general due diligence in public procurement may not be entirely convincing. This means that there is no strong legal background enabling to introduce a due diligence at a general level in public procurement. Furthermore, and this supports the critical approach, the role that due diligence would have is already filled by other provisions and obligations – primarily the principles. However, it has been submitted in the previous section that there might be a difference between a due diligence obligation and the application of the principles. This leaves some room for a due diligence obligation, even though only to a limited degree.

From a formal, restrictive approach, due diligence is only to a very limited degree found within the public procurement regime, whereas a broader approach would include due diligence (and similar obligations) and would accept due diligence as an integrated (and even important) part of public procurement.[54]

Therefore, even though it may be questioned whether the Directive 2014/24/EU contains general rules on due diligence, the following will be from the point of view that there indeed is something like a due diligence obligation in EU public procurement law.

[54] The latter approach is consistent with Härginen (n 5) 14.

C. Provisions Relating to the Due Diligent Contracting Authority

The few provisions in Directive 2014/24/EU that explicitly or implicitly contain an obligation to act diligently are Articles 72 (1)(c) and 32 (2)(c). Since they both relate to diligent behaviour from the contracting authority, and even though it has been suggested that Article 72(1)(c) is inspired by Article 32(2)(c), the two provisions are examined separately in the following.[55]

i. The Possibility of Changes in Existing Public Contracts

In the following, first a short introduction to the primary provision related to due diligence will be given, namely Article 72(1)(c), and afterwards to the case law relating to this provision.[56] All the provisions allowing for modifications in existing public contracts are new in Directive 2014/24/EU. The majority of the provisions in Article 72 are based on the case law of especially *Pressetext*, but the provision in Article 72(1)(c) is not (directly) derived from this case.[57] Therefore, it is of particular importance to lay out the key points of this provision and subsequently focus on the case law, which is essential considering the lack of background for Article 72(1)(c).

a. Circumstances Unforeseeable to the Diligent Contracting Authority

As mentioned previously, Article 72 (1)(c) is the only provision with explicit reference to the diligent contracting authority. This article contends that contracts may be modified without a new procurement procedure in accordance with Directive 2014/24/EU when 'the need for modification has been brought about by circumstances which a diligent contracting authority could not foresee'.[58] This wording is not further elaborated in the text of the provisions. However, Recital 109 Directive 2014/24/EU contains a contribution to the explanation of the phrase in

[55] And rightfully so, see T Indén, 'Article 72 Modification of Contracts During Their Term' in M Steinicke and PL Vesterdorf (eds), *Brussels Commentary on EU Public Procurement Law* (Oxford, CH Beck Hart Nomos, 2018) 768.

[56] See more about Art 72(1)(c) Directive 2014/24/EU in the context of hardship and its relation to contract law in ch 9.

[57] Case C-454/06 *pressetext Nachrichtenagentur GmbH v Republik Österreich (Bund) APA-OTS Originaltext-Service GmbH and APA Austria Presse Agentur registrierte Genossenschaft mit beschränkter Haftung* ECLI:EU:C:2008:351, [2008] ECR I-04401.

[58] Further conditions for applying this provision are: 1) the modification does not alter the overall nature of the contract and 2) any increase in price is not higher than 50 per cent of the value of the original contract or framework agreement. Additionally, where several successive modifications are made, the 50 per cent limitation shall apply to the value of each modification. Finally, any consecutive modifications may not be aimed at circumventing Directive 2014/24/EU.

Article 72(1)(c). It is stated in the Recital that the term 'unforeseeable circumstances' refers to:

> circumstances that could not have been predicted despite reasonably diligent preparation of the initial award by the contracting authority, taking into account its available means, the nature and characteristics of the specific project, good practice in the field in question and the need to ensure an appropriate relationship between the resources spent in preparing the award and its foreseeable value.

Besides Recital 109 Directive 2014/24/EU, there are no suitable sources for delineating the concept of due diligence in the context of Article 72(1)(c). The CJEU will once again make a major contribution to understanding the concept.[59]

b. Case Law from the CJEU on Amending Existing Contracts

The CJEU only in a few cases had the chance to address the expected level of diligence in Article 72(1)(c), specifically in *Obshtina Razgrad* and *Obshtina Balchik*[60] and in *Adusbef*.[61] The cases concerned two different public contracts entered into by two different contracting authorities. Common to the cases, however, was that the contracting authorities had made a change to the existing contract.[62]

In the first case, finishing the construction of a fitness building was postponed from the end of November to the end of February, and in the second case, the time of estimated completion for the development of a coastal promenade was postponed (from 45 days to 250 days). In both cases, the primary reason for the postponements was poor weather conditions. Both cases were brought forward in the Bulgarian administrative and legal system and ended up at the CJEU with the question relevant to this context of whether weather conditions in relation to the two contracts constituted unforeseeable conditions that could lead to a legal change (without the requirement for a subsequent tender).[63]

The submitted question was reformulated by the Court and concerned whether Article 72(1)(c)(i) Directive 2014/24/EU (combined with Recital 109) must be interpreted as meaning that the care that the contracting authority must have shown requires that the contracting authority, in connection with the preparation of the contract, has taken into account the risks that the usual weather conditions

[59] Similar provisions are found in Art 43(1)(c) and Recital 76 Directive 2014/23/EU; Art 89(1)(c) and Recital 115 Directive 2015/25/EU.

[60] Joined Cases C-441/22 and C-443/22 *Obshtina Razgrad* (n 41). For more on these cases, see A Brown, 'Clarification of Article 72 of Directive 2014/24 on modifications to an existing contract: Joined Cases C-441/22 and C-443/22 Obshtina Razgrad' (2024) *Public Procurement Law Review* NA 28.

[61] Case C-683/22 *Adusbef* (n 43).

[62] These joined cases are also analysed in ch 8 but from the perspective of the admissible contract modifications.

[63] Another question posed was whether there is only a change to a contract if the change has resulted in a written addendum describing the changes. This was answered in the negative.

(and the relevant statutory prohibitions on the execution of works) pose to the compliance with the deadline for the execution of the contract.

The Court stated that according to Recital 109 Directive 2014/24/EU, unforeseeable circumstances are external circumstances that could not be foreseen at the time of contract award even after reasonably careful preparations at the initial award by the contracting authority, taking into account the available funds, the specific project's nature and characteristics, good practice in the area in question and the need to ensure a relevant relationship between the resources used to prepare the award and its foreseeable value.[64]

Specifically, it follows from Article 72(1)(c)(i) that the usual weather conditions cannot be considered circumstances that a prudent contracting authority could not foresee as referred to in these provisions. The Court was of the opinion that these conditions were foreseeable and pointed out that in such cases, the contracting authority could have foreseen the need for changes and established a change clause for adjustments in those situations.[65] It must be noted that it is usual weather conditions that do not justify changes to the contract, whereas unusual weather conditions seem to be able to legitimise a change to the contract. It is not clear from the case what the weather conditions were specifically (apart from the fact that it was bad weather). Since the category 'usual weather conditions' normally would cover a wide spectrum of weather types depending on the season (rain, sun, a certain range of temperatures, etc), it must require quite a bit more before the conditions are considered 'unusual weather' and therefore conditions that could not be foreseen by the contracting authority.

The referring Bulgarian court had also submitted a question regarding whether conditions that have occurred after the conclusion of the contract can be unforeseeable according to the wording of the provision. Based on the answers already given, the Court did not consider it necessary to answer this question.

A similar provision to Article 72(1)(c) from Directive 2014/23/EU has been subject to interpretation from the CJEU in *Adusbef*, decided on 7 November 2024. The case concerned a concession agreement concluded on 12 October 2007 between the Autostrade per l'Italia SpA (ASPI) and the Azienda Nazionale Autonoma delle Strade (Autonomous National Motorways Agency, Italy).[66] The agreement concerned the management of a collection of sections of motorways, covering over 2,800 km of sections. There was a shift of contracting authority in 2012, and the responsible authority was the Ministry of Infrastructure and Sustainable Mobility. On 14 August 2018, the Morandi Bridge in Genoa collapsed, causing the death of 43 people. That bridge was part of a section of a motorway, which was awarded to ASPI. Days after the collapse, the Ministry of Infrastructure and Transport initiated proceedings against ASPI for serious failure to fulfil the

[64] See C-441/22 and C-443/22 *Obshtina Razgrad* (n 41) para 68.
[65] ibid para 69.
[66] Case C-683/22 *Adusbef – Associazione difesa utenti servizi bancari e finanziari v Presidenza del Consiglio dei Ministri and Others* EU:C:2024:936 (CJEU, 7 November 2024).

obligations to maintain and preserve the motorway network. Based on a proposal from ASPI, the parties concluded a settlement agreement (including ASPI compensation to the contracting authority and promises to strengthen the safety standards of the motorway network). This agreement concluded the proceedings initiated against ASPI. The question afterwards was whether this agreement would be an infringement of Directive 2014/23/EU and the provisions on modifications of an existing contract.

The Court considered several provisions in order to assess whether the modifications were lawful, one of which was point (c) of the first subparagraph of Article 43(1) Directive 2014/23/EU, which is similar to Article 72(1)(c) Directive 2014/24/EU.[67] The CJEU mentioned that the referring court was uncertain as to whether that provision would be applicable where the need for the modification made to the concession during its term has been brought about by the concessionaire's failure to fulfil contractual obligations. The CJEU stressed that it was for the national court alone to assess whether the concessionaire has committed such a failure to fulfil its contractual obligations in the circumstances of the dispute in the main proceedings and, as the case may be, whether there is a causal relationship between that failure to fulfil obligations and the modification made to the concession during its term.[68]

With reference to Recital 75 Directive 2014/23/EU, the CJEU stated that concession contracts typically involve long-term and complex technical and financial arrangements which are often subject to changing circumstances, with the result that the EU legislature considered it necessary to clarify the conditions under which modifications of a concession during its performance require a new concession award procedure to be organised, taking into account the relevant case law of the Court. This is supplemented by Recital 76, where it is emphasised that:

> the directive is intended to confer on contracting authorities and contracting entities a certain discretion to adapt the concession to external circumstances that they could not foresee when they awarded the concession.[69]

In paragraph 64, the CJEU concludes that:

> a concessionaire's failure to fulfil contractual obligations cannot, per se, be regarded as a circumstance which a diligent contracting authority could not foresee for the purposes of point (c) of the first subparagraph of Article 43(1) of Directive 2014/23. As a result, having regard to the purpose of that provision as follows from Recital 76 of

[67] C-683/22 *Adusbef* (n 43) para 59.

[68] ibid para 61.

[69] Similar is written in Recital 109 Directive 2014/24/EU. Despite the similarities between the recitals and the specific provisions in the two directives the fact remains that the length and complexity of concessions contracts may be different in relation to concession contracts, and this could support that the room for allowable changes within Directive 2014/23/EU would be larger than within the scope of Directive 2014/24/EU.

> that directive, a concessionaire's failure to fulfil its contractual obligations is not liable to justify modification of a concession during its term without opening up to competition.

It is stated by the CJEU that the concessionaire's failure per se cannot be regarded as something that the 'diligent contracting authority' should foresee.[70] The wording slightly opens the possibility that there might be supporting circumstances that could allow contract failure to be something that could not be foreseen. It is not obvious what circumstances might lead to this different conclusion. It is unclear whether an unforeseen contract failure could stem from aspects unrelated to the contract's main activity or if additional factors – other than a direct breach of contract – could influence the assessment of whether a failure becomes unforeseeable.

In his opinion, the Advocate-General (AG) Campos Sánchez-Bordona mentioned that, according to the referring court, the modifications to the agreement were not the result of 'circumstances which a diligent contracting authority or contracting entity could not foresee'.[71] The AG pointed out that 'the focus should be not so much on whether the event was unforeseeable as on the "need" for the contractual modification to have been brought about by that event'.[72] Regardless of the clear requirement in Article 43(1)(c)(i) Directive 2014/23/EU referring to the modifications that have been brought about by circumstances that a diligent contracting authority could not foresee, the AG continues:

> Whatever the cause of the modifications agreed, what matters in this dispute is whether they are to be classified as substantial, in which case it will fall to be decided whether, irrespective of their origin, a tendering procedure should have been organised because those modifications altered the subject matter or the overall nature of the concession.

The AG has a different focus than the CJEU and seems to diminish the importance of the wording in Article 43(1)(c) and the requirement that the provision can only be used when the contracting authority cannot foresee the need for changes. It is difficult to align the opinion of the AG and the decisions by the Court in the first two cases. The AG seems to have reached the conclusion that the modifications were not in breach of Article 43.[73]

In *Finn Frogne*, the CJEU addressed changes in a public contract. The circumstances of the case pre-dated Directive 2014/24/EU, and the Court's decision was based on the general principles. As opposed to Article 72(1)(c), the CJEU had a very different approach to the question of the importance of the 'diligence of

[70] This seems to be supported by other language versions. In the Danish version it is written that a contract failure '*ikke i sig selv*' (not in itself) will be unforeseeable.
[71] Opinion of AG Campos Sánchez-Bordona delivered on 30 April 2024 in Case C-683/22 *Adusbef* ECLI:EU:C:2024:376, [2024].
[72] ibid para 67.
[73] ibid para 71.

the contractor's authority'. The case concerned a contract that was reduced significantly. The CJEU stated that:

> neither (i) the fact that a material amendment of the terms of a contract results not from the deliberate intention of the contracting authority and the successful tenderer to renegotiate the terms of that contract, but from their intention to reach a settlement in order to resolve objective difficulties encountered in the performance of the contract nor (ii) the objectively unpredictable nature of the performance of certain aspects of the contract can provide justification for the decision to carry out that amendment without respecting the principle of equal treatment from which all operators potentially interested in a public contract must benefit.[74]

The statement could very well be seen as a sign that the circumstances leading up to the changes – including the scrutiny shown in any preparation of the contract – will be without importance when assessing whether there is a scope for making amendments without triggering an obligation to tender. In other words, due diligence is not decisive regarding whether a contract change may be legitimate. It may be difficult to assess the importance of *Finn Frogne* after adopting Directive 2014/24/EU. The jurisprudence may still have value when the amendment of a contract is outside the scope of Directive 2014/24/EU. The significance in the context of this chapter is, however, whether the statement of the CJEU is an expression of some fundamental characteristic of EU public procurement law. If this were so, it would be very difficult to unite with the content of Article 72(1)(c).

ii. Possible Direct Award

Another of the very few provisions containing obligations to due diligence is Article 32(2)(c) Directive 2014/24/EU, which establishes that when strictly necessary for reasons of extreme urgency brought about by events *unforeseeable by the contracting authority*, the contracting authority may conduct a direct award.[75] Additional conditions are that the time limits for the open or restricted procedures or competitive procedures with negotiation cannot be complied with, and that the circumstances justifying extreme urgency cannot be attributable to the contracting authority. Although there is no explicit reference to a due diligence obligation, the requirement that urgency must be unforeseen – combined with the condition that the circumstances justifying extreme urgency cannot, under any circumstances, be attributable to the contracting authority – effectively imposes a similar 'duty of diligence'.

[74] Case C-549/14 *Finn Frogne* (n 43) para 32.

[75] For more on this provision, see S Arrowsmith, *The Law of Public and Utilities Procurement*, vol I (London, Sweet and Maxwell, 2014) 1072 and more, and R Caranta, 'Article 31 Innovation Partnership' in M Steinicke and PL Vesterdorf (eds), *Brussels Commentary on EU Public Procurement Law* (Oxford, CH Beck Hart Nomos, 2018) 436 and more.

Article 32(2)(c) requires that the situation enabling the use of this procedure was not to be foreseen by the contracting authority. This is a very familiar assessment compared to the assessment connected to Article 72(1)(c). Any occurrence that could be foreseen by a 'diligent' contracting authority will not enable the application of Article 32(2)(c).[76] Even though the wording is not identical, there is a level of similarity between the two provisions.

The Danish Complaint Board for Public Procurement decision from 10 April 2024, *DiaLab, Dansk Diagnostika- og Laboratorieforening*, deals with the application of Article 32(2)(c) in relation to COVID-19 – probably the largest single international circumstance used to invoke the access to direct award in all Member States.[77] The Danish Complaint Board for Public Procurement concluded that the emergence of COVID-19 was considered a situation not foreseeable by contracting authorities.[78] The more difficult question in this context is when the circumstances are no longer so unforeseeable that the provision may be invoked.[79] After a period of time, the pandemic cannot be seen as 'urgent' as in the early days of COVID-19. The Danish Complaint Board for Public Procurement did not find that this was the case and therefore allowed the application of the exception.

The CJEU has touched upon the issue of foreseeability in several cases.[80] In *Commission v Germany*, which concerned construction works on the Ems river, the relevant public authority declined to give approval of the construction project, and the CJEU stated that the risk of a lack of approval from the relevant authority is a foreseeable incident.[81] Furthermore, when a contracting authority is not showing due diligence in relation to the timing of a project, the availability of a direct award will not be present.[82]

In *Commission v Italy*, the CJEU stated that the award of contracts for the completion of the construction of overflow basins to retain certain flood waters did not fulfil the requirements of the provision. The CJEU pointed out that the

[76] The requirements in Art 32(2)(c) also include an 'urgency' obligation which is connected to the issue of 'unforeseeability'. The former will not be analysed further in this context.

[77] The specific provision in the Danish Procurement Act is s 80(5) which is the implementation of Art 32(2)(c) 2014/24/EU.

[78] This was also implicitly the conclusion drawn by the Commission in Communication from the Commission, 'Guidance from the European Commission on Using the Public Procurement Framework in the Emergency Situation Related to the COVID-19 Crisis' [2020] OJ C 108I/1.

[79] This element was not subject to the case before the Danish Complaints Board for Public Procurement.

[80] Besides the cases mentioned below, see also C-525/03 *Commission of the European Communities v Italian Republic* ECLI:EU:C:2005:648, [2005] ECR I-09405, where the AG had some interesting views (the CJEU did not rule in the case) and the comments to this by Caranta (n 74) 437.

[81] Case C-318/94 *Commission of the European Communities v Federal Republic of Germany* ECLI:EU:C:1996:149, [1996] ECR I-01949 para 18.

[82] Case C-107/92 *Commission of the European Communities v Italian Republic* ECLI:EU:C:1993:344, [1993] ECR I-04655. In this case, the Italian Government received a geological report regarding the unforeseeable and imminent risk of avalanches. They waited for more than three months to act upon this situation, and the Commission found that the conditions for using the provision were therefore not met. The CJEU agreed with the Commission.

original contracts relating to the flood protection works had been awarded in the 1980s and that it had been anticipated from the start that the works would be carried out in lots as and when funding became available. Therefore, the situation was not unforeseeable.[83]

V. Analysis of the Similarities and Differences between Private Law and Public Procurement Law

In the following, there will be an analysis of the public procurement and private law provisions on due diligence with the purpose of illustrating similarities and differences in the rules. The focus of the analysis will be on three essential issues that will illustrate the differences between private law and public procurement law: the private law assumption of equality of the parties, the different consequences of modifications in contracts and the importance of competition for the content of the private law instruments, respectively, the public procurement law.[84]

A. Equality of the Parties: Balance in the Contract

A general assumption in most private law instruments is that the parties to an agreement may be construed as equal. This principle includes all aspects of a contract's existence, including modification of the contract. Professional parties as the model or typical participants in the market are the norm in relation to the chosen private law provisions, and hence, the rules are based on the principle of equality of parties (professional entities).

It could be argued on the grounds of Directive 2014/24/EU that this balance between the parties of a contract may be crooked in a public procurement context, and also specifically in the context of Article 72(1)(c)(i). Furthermore, if there is such an imbalance, this would introduce a breach of the classic private (contract) law principle of equality of parties.[85] A situation might be suggested in which the

[83] Case C-24/91 *Commission of the European Communities v Kingdom of Spain* ECLI:EU:C:1992:134, [1992] ECR I-01989; and Case C-394/02 *Commission of the European Communities v Hellenic Republic* ECLI:EU:C:2005:336, [2005] ECR I-1777; Arrowsmith contends that if there indeed is an urgency, but this should have been foreseen by the contracting authority, the contracting authority making a direct award may not be met by suspension, particularly if there is a threat to life or health, see Arrowsmith (n 74) 1076.

[84] On relationship between contract law principles and public procurement law see also ch 4.

[85] The equality of parties is the starting point, but it seems also clear that an imbalance between parties can also be present, eg where a large business (in any sector) has smaller business partners or sub-contractors. This reservation towards the starting point may also apply specifically in relation to the contracting authority-private seller balance. However, there are fundamental differences between the two parties that validate the argument at a general level.

economic operator's request for a modification of the content of the public contract is rejected by the contracting authority based on the assumption that unforeseen circumstances do not fall within the contracting authority's area of unawareness, although they were certainly unforeseeable by the economic operator and can cause damage to him. Since the relevant entity in relation to Article 72(1)(c) is the contracting authority, such an imbalance may occur. However, in many cases, it must be assumed that both parties may be equally unable to foresee the impending circumstances. The ability to foresee such circumstances may depend on the sector's specificity and especially the contracting authority's experience and knowledge of external factors influencing the contract.

Another approach to the assessment of whether Article 72(1)(c) conflicts with the basic idea that the parties of a contract are equal in relation to the contract is to focus on whether the provision contains any imbalance in relation to who might initiate or approve the amendments.

As a structural premise in the procurement rules, it is the contracting authority that is responsible for the procedure. The wording of Article 72(1)(c) does not seem to indicate that, even though the burden of controlling the procedure is on the contracting authority, only the contracting authority can initiate the contract's modification process. Therefore, the economic operator may start the discussions of potential amendments, just like nothing suggests that the contracting authority has the last word concerning which changes may be included in the contract. It is correct that the contracting authority is aware of the limits of the changes and aware that if these changes exceed the boundaries set forth in Article 72(1)(c), this will directly lead to terminating the contract and to a prospect of a new procurement procedure. This conclusion relating to the result of the negotiation of changes applies to both parties. Therefore, it might be argued that both parties should have equal access to agreeing to the potential changes of the contract – and therefore, both parties may veto the negotiations at any point. It might even be submitted that the economic operator has a greater interest in landing the modifications within the limits of Article 72(1)(c) since failing to do so will lead to the situation where the contract (after a procurement procedure) may end up in the hands of another company. In line with this, the situation might occur where the economic operator applies for a change due to its weakened situation and where the contracting authority submits that the reason for the deterioration was not foreseen. In this situation, the solution seems to be that the amendment cannot be made since the primary condition is not met (the contracting authority's ability to foresee the circumstances).

The basic premise of equality of parties, which seems to be the foundation of private contract law, has never been part of the public procurement system. It might be argued that the balance between the two parties of a public purchasing contract will be different from what we see between two entirely professional parties.

The imbalance between the parties will be in the context of the public procurement provisions. When the contract has been signed, the public procurement rules will only be used in relation to amendments subject to Article 72 Directive 2014/24/EU. In other relations, the contract will be subject to a traditional application of contract law, and in those circumstances, the balance between the parties will be seen in accordance with these rules. In Denmark, there are no (explicit) rules or provisions dictating that the contracting authority should be seen in any other light than other contracting parties when applying the traditional contract rules.

Even though it seems fair to say that there is an imbalance, it is not entirely clear, however, in which direction the balance has shifted. It might be argued that the contracting authority could be seen as either the 'stronger party' or the 'weaker party'. The result may be very different depending on the premise on which one views the contracting authority. There may be two specific elements influencing the balance: the 'process power' and the 'knowledge power'.

The 'process power' is the power of leading the process of the formation of a contract. In the public procurement context, the contracting authority will be the bearer of substantial process power. The contracting authority has initiated and will be controlling the process; the contracting authority has decided the framework of the procurement process as well as the outline of the contract in question. The process is characterised by a strong competitive component between the economic operators, all in favour of the contracting authority. In this regard, one might argue that the contracting authority has the upper hand in relation to the process.

The 'knowledge power' may be seen in favour of the economic operators. The contracting authority is obligated to purchase all kinds of goods and services within very different sectors. The contracting authority will clearly be at a disadvantage concerning the choice of solutions and technology since they rarely have the necessary (professional) knowledge of the products or services in question.[86] Through this perspective, the contracting authority may be seen as a 'consumer' – a purchaser that is not knowledgeable of the subject matter of the contract to the same degree as the selling party. Regardless of the label (consumer or not), the contracting authority will be at a disadvantage knowledge-wise and may therefore be considered the weaker party in this context. In relation to some specific procurement contracts, the process element may be dominant, giving the contracting authority some additional weight, whereas the knowledge element may be dominant in relation to other purchasing contracts, often providing leverage to the economic operators.

Therefore, it may be argued that the equal relationship between the buyer and the seller in a public procurement context was never a reality. This should lead to the conclusion that the potential imbalance introduced by the procurement rules is natural due to the specific characteristics of such contracts.

[86] This imbalance in favour of the economic operators is also quite clearly seen in the legal set-up of the contracting authority's access to seeking advice in order to prepare the procedure and the contract, see Arts 40–41 Directive 2014/24/EU.

B. The Importance of the Consequences of the Changes in an Existing Contract

There is a big difference in the consequences of the changes to the contract in Directive 2014/24/EU, the PECL, the DCFR, and the Danish Sales of Goods Act.[87] The PECL requires that there will be negotiations with the purpose of solving the contractual issue, and the DCFR establishes that when a debtor is nonperforming in situations where an impediment has occurred, which was not due to the debtor's lack of diligence, this non-performance will be excused.[88]

According to Section 24 Danish Sale of Goods Act, the consequence will be that the seller will be exempt from the obligation to pay damages due to the delay of delivery when this could not be foreseen. The consequence of unforeseeable changes in a public contract is that the parties are allowed to modify the contract to adjust to the new circumstances. In this way, there are large similarities between Directive 2014/24/EU and the PECL (both allowing negotiations to overcome unforeseen changes). However, due to the stringent approach in public procurement, unlike the provision in the PECL, the frame for negotiations within EU public procurement law is limited by additional conditions all established due to the competitive focus, which is at the core of public procurement. These limitations to the negotiations within the public procurement system will discipline the parties in relation to potential strategic approaches to the negotiations. A presumed common interest in maintaining the contract may restrict the potential outcome of the negotiations to stay within the additional conditions set forth in Article 72(1)(c).

In contrast, the negotiations according to the PECL are not restricted in a similar fashion, which may lead to more intense and comprehensive (frameless) negotiation scenarios.[89] The competitive element requires the contracting authority not just to focus on the parties of the contract, but instead, the contracting authority must also direct attention to how any negotiations impact third parties – companies that might have participated in the original procurement procedure when the contract was formed.[90] This is a major difference between the public procurement regime and the private law instruments.

C. The Importance of the Competitive Element: A Public Procurement Basic Characteristic

One of the major differences between the private law instruments and the public procurement rules is that the latter is fundamentally influenced by the element of

[87] There are a number of different potential consequences of such occurring changes: re-negotiation, adaption/termination, or discharge of an obligation.

[88] Art 6.111(2) PECL; Book III–3:104 DCFR.

[89] M Kovac, 'Duty to Renegotiate in International Commercial Law and Uncontemplated Behavioural Effects' (2020) 27(4) *Maastricht Journal of European and Comparative Law* 445.

[90] See more about 'Interested parties' in ch 12.

competition. This element basically brings in a third-party issue that disturbs the balance of and approach to handling changes in the contract.

The private law sources allowing for amendments in existing contracts exclusively have their focus on the *inter partes* relation and the balance between the contracting parties in the specific circumstances. The major difference between public procurement and other (private law) pre-contractual situations is that the competition element (and thereby the consideration to third parties – other offerors/participants) will set the stage differently for the access to amending the contract.[91] Whereas the parties' potential acceptance of the changes in a traditional contractual setting depends only on the shared will of the two (or more) parties to the contract, this is not the case for a public procurement contract. The mere definition of changes resulting in an obligation to conduct a new competitive tender procedure is based on whether other participants could have participated in the tender procedure or have even won the competition had the amendments been a part of the contract originally.

VI. Conclusion

The term due diligence has a broad application in different areas of the legal system, including in private law. In EU public procurement law, the concept of due diligence is only mentioned a few times and is visible in a couple of provisions, see Articles 72(1)(c) and 32(2)(c) Directive 2014/24/EU.

The chapter introduces the concept of due diligence in a broad perspective as well as in the context of EU public procurement law, with an analysis of the mentioned provision in Directive 2014/24/EU. As part of the analysis, several private law instruments are chosen to compare the role of due diligence within contract law and public procurement law, such as the PECL, the DCFR, and the Danish Sale of Goods Act. These offer a range of similar and yet different approaches to incorporating due diligence in contract law.

The final analysis is based on three different essential issues with the purpose of illustrating the differences between private law and public procurement law when it comes to the specific provisions promoting due diligence. These issues are the balance of the parties in the agreement, the consequences of amending an existing contract and the importance of the element of competition. The analysis shows that there are some significant differences between the contract/private law approach and the public procurement regime, especially the issue of competition and subsequently, the interest of third parties is a major difference between contract law and public procurement law in this specific context.

[91] See also ch 12. The authors deal with the doctrine of privity, according to which contracts impose obligations on and render rights only to the contractual parties. Their analysis shows the inclusion of third parties in regard to the enforcement of sustainability elements in contracts.

7

The Duty of Loyalty in the Contract Performance Stage: Contractual Adjustments Inside and Outside the Realm of Article 72 Directive 2014/24/EU

MARIA EDITH LINDHOLM GAUSDAL, OLE HANSEN
AND VIBE GARF ULFBECK

I. Introduction

Nearly two decades have passed since *Pressetext*[1] overturned the belief that EU public procurement law had fully served its purpose after contract award, introducing the substantial modifications regime that was later codified in Article 72 Directive 2014/24/EU. While the performance stage is still, overall, considered less intensively regulated, the legal standing of substantial modifications is continuously being refined, and the interface between contract law and EU public procurement law is intensifying.[2]

Recent economic, legal, and global developments have made the growing need for contracts to accommodate variation and cooperation during performance increasingly apparent. Flexibility in contracting is essential and will become more so in the years ahead. For instance, the realisation of highly prioritised climate-reduction projects inherently calls for a rethinking of entrenched roles, incentives, and risk allocation within otherwise firmly established contracting practices across different sectors.[3] Notably, the European Commission has expressed a wish

[1] Case C-454/06 *pressetext Nachrichtenagentur GmbH v Republik Österreich (Bund), APA-OTS Originaltext-Service GmbH and APA Austria Presse Agentur registrierte Genossenschaft mit beschränkter Haftung* ECLI:EU:C:2008:351, [2008] ECR I-04401.

[2] See ch 2. See also CR Hamer, *Udbudsret*, 3rd edn (Copenhagen, Djøf Forlag, 2025) 743.

[3] On risk allocation, see further ch 5. On the control of third parties in the enforcement of contractual clauses relating to sustainability issues, including in particular the role of organisations representing general public interests, see ch 12.

for contracting parties to include continuous technical innovation *during* the performance of long-term infrastructure projects.[4] The basis for the forthcoming revision of EU public procurement law includes, among other things, an increased focus on innovation, green solutions, the continuous development of technology, and collaboration – factors that, by their very nature, intensify contractual complexity and the need for flexibility.[5]

Although Directive 2014/24/EU aimed to introduce greater flexibility, and although EU public procurement law has, perhaps, to some extent, shifted towards less rigidity, it remains uncertain whether the current rules and legal interpretations on contract modifications can adequately accommodate the necessary developments.[6] Ongoing innovation, for example, by the introduction of new technological solutions during the performance of long-term projects, can fairly easily alter the nature of the original contract. Subsequent developments may render an offered (eg green or digital) technology outdated or otherwise give rise to challenges that are not *unforeseeable* within the meaning of the EU public procurement law modification regime.[7] In recent years, the vulnerability of global supply chains to crisis-driven disruptions – and the emergence of regulation as a significant commercial risk in an increasingly regulation-dense society – has become increasingly evident.[8] These dynamics all point to a general need for

[4] For instance, accommodating green solutions – now increasingly used as competitive parameters and contractual conditions in public contracts – requires greater flexibility. In this context, a recent working group highlighted the need to better integrate collaborative elements and to enhance consistency between the tender documents, the contract, and underlying contract law throughout the project. The group also emphasised the barriers that EU public procurement law currently poses to these necessary developments (The Industry WG on Construction Decarbonisation and the Academic WG on Construction Decarbonisation, 2024). See P Cox and K Bergmeister (eds), *Decarbonisation of the Transport Infrastructure Construction: Joint Final Report from the Industry and Scientific Experts Working Groups* (Brussels, European Commission DG MOVE, April 2024) <transport.ec.europa.eu/news/decarbonisation-transport-infrastructure-construction-final-report-2024-04-16_en>.

[5] See M Draghi, 'Report on the Future of the Single Market – Part B' (Independent High-Level Report, January 2024) <commission.europa.eu/topics/eu-competitiveness/draghi-report_en>; E Letta, *Much More than a Market: Speed, Security, Solidarity* (Report for the European Commission, April 2024) <single-market-economy.ec.europa.eu/news/enrico-lettas-report-future-single-market-2024-04-10_en>. The reports underlie the Commission's work with preparing the coming reform of the procurement rules which includes considerations on how to provide more flexibility to amend tender documents and contracts, see JO Gonzalez (DG GROW, European Commission), *Revision of the EU Public Procurement Framework* (presentation, EU Public Procurement anno 2025 – Are the Rules Fit for Purpose?, University of Copenhagen, 23–24 April 2025) <jura.ku.dk/english/research/safeguarding-competition-and-equal-access-to-central-purchasing-bodies-agreements/> 11, 18.

[6] In 2023 the European Court of Auditors released a report with the findings that Directive 2014/24/EU had not led to increased flexibility. European Court of Auditors, *Public procurement in the EU: Less competition for contracts awarded for works, goods and services in the 10 years up to 2021* (Special Report 28/2023) <www.eca.europa.eu/en/publications?id=103211> 8, 26, 44.

[7] Art 72(1)(c) Directive 2014/24/EU.

[8] For example, the global pandemic, rising cyberattacks, climate change-related disruptions, and Russia's invasion of Ukraine – along with the resulting introduction of comprehensive trade sanctions – have all contributed to increased uncertainty. On trade sanctions, see M Andhov and M Kania, 'Ever-Growing Restrictions on Whom Public Buyers Can Contract With: Contemporary Developments in the EU Public Procurement' (Bestek Blog, 3 April 2023) <bestek-procurement.com/ever-growing-restrictions-on-whom-public-buyers-can-contract-with-contemporary-developments-in-the-eu-public-procurement/>.

contractual flexibility and cooperation during contract performance: extensions of deadlines, price adjustments, reallocation of risks, and flexibility in the application of remedies. Accordingly, contract law practices are changing, reflecting the likely occurrences of problems affecting performance. The need for flexibility is reflected in shifting drafting practices with broad modification clauses, duties of renegotiation,[9] risk-sharing provisions,[10] and open-ended suspension rights.[11] A common feature is that these clauses require cooperation and a degree of openness around the core of the contract to accommodate the unpredictable.[12] However, while contract law may offer what is needed (albeit still under development), an extensive need for ongoing adaptations contradicts the essence of EU public procurement law on contract modification. The latter clearly stipulates that a substantial contract modification of the initial contract requires a new public procurement procedure according to Article 72 Directive 2014/24/EU. In this case, the contracting authority may end the contract under Article 73.

At least in civil law jurisdictions and in Nordic law, contracting parties are considered to operate under a general obligation of good faith (loyalty) in the contract performance period.[13] This fundamental principle is also reflected elsewhere in instruments such as Article 1:102 Principles of European Contract Law (PECL), Article III-1:103 Draft Common Frame of Reference (DCFR), and Sections 1-6 Restatement of Nordic Contract Law. Its importance is growing as contracts are concluded at early stages, often with performance requirements deliberately left unclear, and in long-term contractual settings where changes in performance conditions are to be expected. Nordic law recognises that public contracts entered into by contracting authorities for goods, services, or construction works are governed by the general rules and principles of private contract law.[14] The Nordic countries can thus be said to

[9] For example, the International Chamber of Commerce revised its *force majeure* and hardship clauses in the wake of COVID-19 to meet the need for expanded options for contract adaptation, see ICC Force Majeure and Hardship Clauses <iccwbo.org/news-publications/icc-rules-guidelines/icc-force-majeure-and-hardship-clauses/#top>. On hardship in public contracts see ch 9. See also Art 6:111 PECL; Art III–1:110 DCFR; Art 6.2.3 Unidroit Principles.

[10] For example: Iris' Clause Climate Contract Risk Sharing (ex Force Majeure) <chancerylaneproject.org/clauses/climate-contract-risk-sharing-ex-force-majeure/>; Sanctions Clause for Voyage Charter Parties 2020 <www.bimco.org/contractual-affairs/bimco-clauses/current-clauses/sanctions_clause_for_voyage_charter_parties_2020/>.

[11] For example: Yara General Terms and Conditions <www.yara.com/siteassets/this-is-yara/suppliers/supplier-requirements/yara-general-terms-and-conditions-of-purchase.pdf>.

[12] Modifications foreseen in contractual clauses may under EU public procurement law regime lead to the modification not being deemed substantial. However, it is doubtful whether the developing contractual practices will meet the criteria of the clear, precise, and unequivocal review clauses as required under Art 72(1)(a) Directive 2014/24/EU for the modification not being substantial. The question is further dealt with in s 4.

[13] M Hesselink, 'The Concept of Good Faith' in A Hartkamp and others (eds), *Towards a European Civil Code* (Alphen aan den Rijn, Wolters Kluwer, 2011) 619–80; and below in s II. For the foundation of the standard of good faith in civil law, see further: S 242 BGB; Arts 6:20 and 6:248 French Code Civil; Arts 1337, 1366, and 1375 Italian Civil Code.

[14] TE Madell, *Det allmänna som avtalspart: särskilt avseende kommuns kompetens att ingå avtal samt avtalens rättsverkningar* (Stockholm, Norstedts Juridik, 1998) 59, 75; KN Olesen, *Samfundsloddet: obligationsretten og kontrakter af samfundsmæssig interesse* (Copenhagen, Karnov Group, 2004) 86; MB Andersen, *Grundlæggende aftaleret*, 5th edn (Copenhagen, Gjellerup, 2021) 129.

reflect a 'private-oriented hybrid model'.[15] This means that not only the private party but also contracting authorities, during contract performance, are equally under a general obligation to act in good faith and – to some extent – to loyally cooperate with the private supplier during the contract performance period. This contractual obligation may, however, overstep the boundaries for admissible contract amendments established in Article 72 Directive 2014/24/EU.

In this chapter, the authors examine the potential role of the duty of loyal cooperation *within* the framework of Article 72, as well as instances where these boundaries *have been breached*. Section II outlines the relationship between national contract law and EU public procurement law as distinct yet mutually influential normative systems. Section III examines the legal foundation of the contractual duty of loyal cooperation in Nordic law. Building on this foundation, section IV considers the extent to which EU public procurement law can accommodate contract law thinking and the duty of loyal cooperation when assessing the boundaries set by Article 72 Directive 2014/24/EU. Section V then evaluates how contract law, through the duty of loyal cooperation, can accommodate principles EU public procurement law in cases where a contract has been substantially modified and, as a consequence, ended by the contracting authority under Article 73 Directive 2014/24/EU. The chapter concludes in section VI. Throughout, the term 'duty of loyal cooperation' refers to an aspect of the general, contractual duty of loyalty (the good faith principle). The analysis centres on Nordic law to illustrate a model for understanding the complex interaction between procurement law and contract law in legal systems that treat them as distinct legal regimes.[16]

II. The Relationship between EU Public Procurement Law and Contract Law in the Context of the Contract Modification Regime

If substantial modifications arise during contract performance, EU public procurement law and contract law inevitably cross paths. The former acknowledges the possible necessity of certain amendments to public contracts after they have been awarded and concluded with the supplier. For the contracting authority, the scope for such flexibility is governed by what is permissible under Article 72 Directive 2014/24/EU. However, Directive 2014/24/EU does not require the provision to be understood as also regulating the legal position of the private party. In contrast, as Stelkens points out, EU law does not distinguish between public and

[15] See ch 3.

[16] See further s II. Though Norway a Nordic Law country is not an EU Member State, pursuant to Annexe XVI Agreement on the European Economic Area [1994] OJ L1/3 it is under the obligation to transpose EU public procurement law, including Directive 89/665.

private law.[17] This implies that each Member State is free to treat the provisions of Directive 2014/24/EU as the direct bearer of contract law solutions, but is notobliged to do so. Member States can also choose to see Directive 2014/24/EU as purely public law regulation of the position of the contracting authority.

Nordic law is generally based on the understanding that EU public procurement law remains conceptually distinct from domestic contract law.[18] This means that the two systems apply in parallel and that procurement law is not regarded as a *lex specialis* that dictates the legal outcome of contractual questions in public contracts.[19] The Swedish *Nordens Välfärdscenter* may be mentioned as an example.[20]

Nordens Välfärdscenter concerned the question of exclusivity under a framework agreement. In the case, it was argued – as had also been put forth in legal theory – that the answer to the conflict between the parties could be found in EU public procurement law on framework agreements. The court expressly rejected the view:

> It should be emphasised in this context that the purpose of the procurement rules is, as a starting point, to regulate the procedures applied by contracting authorities and entities when procuring goods, services and construction works. The aim is therefore not to govern civil law relationships, but primarily to establish rules on how contracting authorities and entities must proceed to subject their purchases to competition …. The Court of Appeal, therefore, does not share the view expressed in certain legal doctrine that such framework agreements may be interpreted as granting the supplier exclusivity regarding the authority's procurement of the services covered by the agreement. … The fact that the parties' agreement was concluded following a procurement procedure under the LOU (Swedish Public Procurement Act) is thus not, in the Court's opinion, of independent significance for the assessment of the parties' contractual obligations.[21]

[17] U Stelkens, 'Substantive Law Applicable to EU Public Contracts' in M Trybus, R Caranta and G Edelstam (eds), *EU Public Contract Law: Public Procurement and Beyond* (Brussels, Bruylant, 2014) 409.

[18] This distinction between contract law and procurement law is widely reflected in the literature. See for example, K Krüger, 'Tolkning av kontrakter som er tildelt ved anbudskonkurranse' in JE Barbo and L Simonsen (eds), *På rett grunn: Festskrift til Norsk forening for bygge- og entrepriserett* (Oslo, Gyldendal Akademisk, 2010) 111–29; S Arrowsmith, *Law of Public and Utilities Procurement*, Vol 1, 3rd edn (London, Sweet & Maxwell, 2014) 388–90, 394–95; T Høg, AE Riberholt-Rischel and TL Larsen, 'Håndhævelse af udbudsreglerne' in S Treumer (ed), *Udbudsretten* (Copenhagen, Ex Tuto Publishing, 2019) 486; GS Ølykke, M Ohm and CF Petersen, *EU's udbudsregler: i dansk kontekst*, 3rd edn (Copenhagen, Djøf Forlag, 2022) 1006, 1028–31; MEL Gausdal, 'Scener fra et (tvangs)ægteskab: om grænsefladen mellem udbudsret og kontraktret' in CR Hamer, M Andhov, E Bertelsen and R Caranta (eds), *Into the Northern Light: In Memory of Steen Treumer* (Copenhagen, Ex Tuto Publishing, 2022) 545–50; MEL Gausdal and CR Hamer, 'Den offentlige kontrakt i et complianceperspektiv' in CR Hamer and HM Motzfeldt (eds), *Compliance i den offentlige sektor* (Copenhagen, Djøf Forlag, 2022) 291–93; CR Hamer, *Udbudsret*, 3rd edn, (Copenhagen, Djøf Forlag, 2025) 831.

[19] For an interpretation that may offer a different perspective, see ch 6.

[20] Svea hovrätt T 8524-19.

[21] ibid.

A similar approach can be seen in the Norwegian Supreme Court's decision in Rt. 2001 s. 1288 (HR-2000-1279), where the Court noted:

> The parties have, during the proceedings, to a considerable extent addressed the question of what significance the procurement rules have for the issue of whether a contract has been concluded. The starting point is clear. An agreement is valid under contract law between the parties even if it involves a breach of procurement rules intended to ensure equal competitive opportunities.[22]

In addition, numerous decisions from across the Nordic jurisdictions affirm this distinction.[23] For instance, in *PDC A/S v Region Hovedstaden*, the Danish Complaints Board for Public Procurement clearly drew a distinction between contract law and procurement law:

> Procurement law does not govern the legal relationship between the parties with respect to matters of contract law. This also applies to questions concerning remedies for breach, including the right to terminate the contract and any associated settlement. Such matters are instead governed partly by the general rules of the law of obligations – that is, contract formation and performance – and partly by the terms of the concluded contract itself.[24]

In short, the distinction between public procurement law and contract law as separate legal regimes is well established in Nordic law.[25]

III. The Duty of Loyalty in Nordic Contract Law

A general duty of good faith and fair dealing is deeply rooted in Nordic contract law. Inspired by the German Civil Code (BGB),[26] the Common Nordic Contracts

[22] Norwegian Supreme Court in Rt. 2001 s. 1288 (HR-2000-1279). The case has been confirmed in a later decision from the Supreme Court, Rt. 2005 s. 1481 (HR-2005-1781-A).

[23] The Norwegian Complaints Board for Public Procurement only addresses cases 'regulated by procurement law' and accordingly does not consider contract law questions; see, for example, Complaints Board for Public Procurement case 2005/21 of 14 March 2005 *Vestnorsk Engineering AS v Avinor*; Complaints Board for Public Procurement case 2006/148 of 16 April 2007 *AFS-Krüger Consortium v Oslo Municipality*; Complaints Board for Public Procurement case 2007/19 of 13 August 2007 *Tele Trading AS v Norwegian Public Roads Administration*. From the Danish Supreme Court, see UfR 2011.3129 H: 'as Silkeborg Municipality has also not acted in a manner that, from the perspective of the duty of loyalty, could incur liability towards ISS, the Supreme Court upholds the judgment'. See also UfR 2013.2551 H. From the Danish Complaints Board, which also does not consider contract law questions, see Complaints Board for Public Procurement case of 13 February 2006 *Haubjerg Interior A/S v Vejle Amt*; Complaints Board for Public Procurement case of 22 June 2011 *Ecolab ApS v Region Sjælland*; Complaints Board for Public Procurement case of 16 March 2017 *Holbech Lys v DSB*; Complaints Board for Public Procurement case of 10 April 2018 *Sea Environment v Ministry of Defence*.

[24] Complaints Board for Public Procurement case of 23 June 2020 *PDC A/S v Region Hovedstaden*.

[25] This is generally also the perspective under common law. Since Brexit, Ireland, Malta, and Cyprus remain as common law or common law-founded European jurisdictions.

[26] *Bürgerliches Gesetzbuch* (BGB), *1896, RGBl. S. 195*, as amended (German Civil Code).

Act, adopted in Denmark in 1917,[27] emphasises the notion of a promise made 'in good faith' as a fundamental criterion for its validity in cases involving duress, fraud, or mistake[28] – thereby protecting the reasonable expectations of both the promisor and the promisee. The Common Nordic Contracts Act does not apply as such, but is transposed into a specific statute in each of the Nordic countries.

Though it apparently takes the parties' subjective conception of the promise as the point of departure for determining its legal content, Nordic law, like contract law in general, has veered towards a more objective approach.[29] However, this more objective approach entails more than an increased focus on the letter of the contract. Rather, it is the understanding of subjective criteria through the lens of general standards of good faith. In 1946, the Danish legal scholar Henry Ussing stated that 'the parties to the contract have a certain obligation to take each other's reasonable interests into account'.[30] With some variations, similar conceptions were expressed in Finnish, Swedish, and Norwegian literature in the second half of the twentieth century.[31] Accordingly, contextual analysis will usually not be determined against what the parties specifically thought and did, but against general behavioural norms, for example, as they may be derived from default law.[32] This normative approach[33] is driven by the Nordic courts' tradition of rejecting formalism in private law in favour of balanced outcomes grounded in fundamental conceptions of justice and common sense – often described as 'legal pragmatism'.[34]

The duty of loyalty is closely linked to the general standard of good faith and the rule on unfair contract terms in Section 36 Common Nordic Contracts Act. It can be understood as both a limitation on – and a prerequisite for – the principle of freedom of contract.[35] The parties to the contract may concretise and adjust the standard loyalty in their agreement· However, they cannot erase its core elements.[36] Though a

[27] The Act was a result of the legal collaboration between Denmark, Sweden, and Norway in that period. With minor variations, it was adopted in Sweden in 1915 and in Norway in 1918.

[28] Ch 3 Common Nordic Contracts Act.

[29] V Ulfbeck, *Kontrakters relativitet: det direkte ansvar i formueretten* (Copenhagen, Thomson, 2000) 426.

[30] H Ussing, *Dansk obligationsret: almindelig del*, 3rd edn (Copenhagen, GEC Gad, 1946) 25.

[31] For a general account of this development, see A Holm, 'Den avtalsgrundade lojalitetsplikten: en allmän rättsprincip' (Doctoral Thesis, Linköpings universitet, 2004) 64–85; J Munukka, *Kontraktuell lojalitetsplikt* (Stockholm, Jure Förlag, 2007) 52–70 (with references to, eg, F Stang, K Andersen, LE Taxell and J Hellner); and H Nazarian, *Lojalitetsplikt i kontraktsforhold* (Oslo, Cappelen, 2007) 141–56.

[32] LL Andersen and PB Madsen, *Aftaler og mellemmænd*, 8th edn (Copenhagen, Karnov Group, 2022) 356.

[33] This can be referred to as normative contract interpretation; cf O Hansen and V Ulfbeck, *Lærebog i aftaleret*, 2nd edn (Copenhagen, Djøf Forlag, 2023) 86–91.

[34] See, for example, MEL Gausdal, 'Soft Law Business as Usual? Fundamental Labour Standards in Private and Public Commercial Contracts' (PhD thesis, University of Copenhagen, 2021) 11–13 with further references.

[35] Munukka (n 32) 71–73. On the principle of freedom of contract in the context of public procurement see ch 4.

[36] Munukka (n 31) 489; Nazarian (n 31) 134–39; and O Hansen, *Det entrepriseretlige hjemmelsproblem: modsætningsforhold eller fællesskab?* (Copenhagen, Jurist-og Økonomforbundets Forlag, 2008) 182.

general standard of good faith is assumed to exist as an implied term in all contractual relations, it is clear that the role and impact of this general principle of contract law vary significantly, depending upon, for example, the nature and type of the commitments. Typically, discrete one-time agreements on the exchanges of well-defined goods or services leave little room for normative interpretation or the adjustment or supplementation of the parties' obligations under standards of good faith. In contrast, Nordic scholarship and court practice display considerable room for applying the standard of loyalty in complex – and often 'incomplete' – long-term contracts.[37] To a large extent, this state of the law reflects commercial realities in which the parties are unable to specify performance requirements in detail and must instead rely on a shared understanding of the overall objective of the transaction. Due to the values at stake – rather than the binding force of the agreement's exact wording – the realisation of the contract becomes paramount.[38] Often, commercial interests are pursued within business models supported by framework agreements, contractual clusters, networks, or supply chains. Thus, in such settings, the legal effect of a bilateral contract must be understood under consideration of the contractual context in which it occurs. In Nordic contract law, it is generally acknowledged that under such circumstances, a general standard of loyalty – even without explicit support in the contract terms – may evolve from a principle of interpretation into a binding contractual duty of cooperation, requiring performances from the parties that are not expressly stated in their agreement.[39] Obligations deduced from the general principle of loyalty will often include acts or performances which are deemed to be a prerequisite for the other party's own performances (or that party's execution of its own rights) and, as such, the completion of the contract as a whole.

The developed agreed documents for construction, which, to a large extent, can be assumed to reflect gap-filling principles of (construction) contract law, are illustrative in this respect. The Danish AB 18, which is a standard contract form for building and construction works, contains in Clause 33 a rule on the 'duty of cooperation and good faith', according to which 'the parties have a duty to work together in good faith so that errors, delays and cost increases are avoided'.[40] This is in line with arbitration practice, where the duty of loyal cooperation has been implied in the often complex situations where works are disrupted by external factors or situations not anticipated by either or both parties.[41]

[37] Andersen and Madsen (n 32) 427–35; V Hagstrøm, *Obligasjonsrett*, 3rd edn (Oslo, Universitetsforlaget; 2021) 125, both with the mentioned cases. See also S Nystén-Haarala, *The Long Term Contract: Contract Law and Contracting* (Helsinki, Finnish Lawyers' Publishing, 1998) 129; Munukka (n 31) 491; Nazarian (n 31) 305–27.

[38] K Grønfors, *Avtal och omförhandling* (Stockholm, Nerenius & Santérus, 1995) 23.

[39] Holm (n 31) 110; Munukka (n 31) 74; Hansen (n 36) 181.

[40] See, for example, the Norwegian standard form for construction, NS 8405, clause 5, which states: 'The parties are obliged to collaborate and to display loyalty during the completion of the contract'. The Finnish standard form contract for construction works, YSE 1998, includes in s 7 and 8 detailed provisions on duties of cooperation and collaboration. See also the preface to the Swedish standard form AB 04, which emphasises similar principles.

[41] On arbitration and public procurement and public contracts see ch 13 and ch 14.

In an early case, KfE 1982 280 VBA,[42] concerning the construction of a harbour on the coast of the North Sea, the contractor encountered difficulties anchoring concrete elements to the seabed. The arbitral tribunal found that the primary cause of the issue was the contractor's own miscalculations, rather than any design failures attributable to the employer (ie employer risk), and stated that 'it is the contractor's duty to complete the works in time'.[43] However, because the employer had failed to cooperate with the contractor in resolving the problems, it was not awarded full liquidated damages. The arbitral tribunal concluded:

> However, in the present situation, the (timely completion) could only take place by way of the employer's positive participation. One or both parties' passivity will frustrate the progression. In this case, both parties have sinned in this respect on different occasions.[44]

A similar reasoning was applied in the arbitration case TBB 2024 81 VBA, which involved significant delays in the construction of a runway at the airbase in Thule, Greenland.[45] The delay was primarily due to issues with a wear layer failing to adhere to the runway. Although the arbitral tribunal found that the delay stemmed from the contractor's fault or risks allocated to the contractor, it also noted that the employer failed to assist when the contractor requested help. Owing to the employer's 'somewhat dismissive approach', its claim for damages was reduced. Thus, the case law illustrates how the duty to collaborate emerges from the general duty of loyalty and, in specific situations, evolves into an independent duty to allocate resources in support of the other party's efforts to fulfil the contract. These resources typically cannot, or only with difficulty, be calculated in advance.

As noted, public contracts are, as a clear point of departure, governed by the general principles of commercial contract law in Nordic jurisdictions.[46] Accordingly, the described notion of fairness and the duty of loyal cooperation apply to public contracts regardless of whether these are governed by the public procurement regime or not. In fact, many public contracts – such as construction contracts – exhibit precisely the features of complexity and long-term performance that give rise to a duty of loyal cooperation.[47] This means that, according to

[42] Decision from Voldgiftsnævnet for bygge- og anlægsvirksomheds of August 18, 1981, in the Case C-757 published in Kendelser om fast ejendom, DJØF forlag.

[43] ibid.

[44] ibid.

[45] Decision from Voldgiftsnævnet for bygge- og anlægsvirksomheds of October 15, 2003, in the Case C-6558 published in Tidsskrift for Bolig- og Byggeret.

[46] See above in s I.

[47] Private contract law – including duties of cooperation and loyalty – also apply to concession contracts and Public-Private Partnership (PPP) contracts. For example, the Danish PPP standard contracts issued by the Danish Competition Authority explicitly emphasise the duty of loyalty (see <kfst.dk/udbud/offentlig-privat-samarbejde/offentlig-private-partnerskaber/opp-standardmodel-for-nyanlaeg/fase-3-udbud-og-kontrakt/opp-standardkontrakt/>). Similarly, in the context of concession contracts, para 12.1 Danish Road Authority's contract paradigm reflects this duty, see <vejregler.dk/h/7e0fba84-06dd-483b-898a-c7b3e3affaa1/48d5795d0ccd44aa9ad4d689104247bd?showExact=true#i5e0abb241>.

general principles of Nordic contract law, a contracting authority may be obligated to invest unanticipated resources into the contract to enable the private supplier to fulfil its obligations, or to refrain from enforcing remedies for breach. Depending on their nature, the monetary value of such obligations or the loss of a remedial right, this may amount to a substantial modification.

IV. The Potential of EU Public Procurement Law to Accommodate the Duty of Loyalty and Cooperation when Assessing Contract Modifications under Article 72 Directive 2014/24/EU

As previously noted, the forthcoming revision of EU public procurement law is driven in part by a growing emphasis on innovation, ongoing technological advancement, and enhanced collaboration – factors that, by their very nature, intensify contractual complexity and the need for greater flexibility.[48] These issues are closely linked to the possibility of adapting the contract accordingly while remaining within the boundaries of EU public procurement law. In light of this development, it is natural to ask whether the current framework may already be interpreted in a manner that reduces the conflict between contractual obligations of loyalty and cooperation and the realm of admissible modifications. In other words, the question is whether and to what extent the circumstances relevant to the duty of loyalty and cooperation – and the related contract law position of the parties – can play a part in EU public procurement law assessment of modifications under Article 72 Directive 2014/24/EU.

A. The Current Approach of the Court of Justice of the European Union (CJEU) to Circumstances Relevant to the Duty of Loyalty and Cooperation

EU public procurement law assessments are not determined by national contract law,[49] and the CJEU has often avoided venturing into contract law reasoning.[50] Hence, no case law directly addresses the question of the contradiction between

[48] European Commission, DG GROW C2. Call for evidence for an evaluation. Public procurement directives – evaluation. Ares (2024)8928678, Brussels, 13.12.2024.

[49] For example Opinion of AG Leger delivered on 7 December 2000 on Case C-399/98 *Ordine degli Architetti and Others* ECLI:EU:C:2000:671, [2000] para 71; Case C-399/98, *Ordine degli Architetti and Others* ECLI:EU:C:2001:401, [2001] 2001 ECR I-05409 paras 52–55, 65, and 75. See also Arrowsmith (n 18) 388f; CR Hamer, 'The Concept of a "Public Contract" Within the Meaning of the Public Procurement Directive' (2016) 3 *Upphandlingsrättslig Tidskrift* 179, 182–83.

[50] For example Gausdal, 'Scener fra et (tvangs)ægteskab' (n 18) with references 551–52.

contractual duties to cooperate in good faith and the EU public procurement law modification regime. Still, the Court is not precluded from taking contractual considerations into account, within the framework of EU public procurement law. Two judgments from the CJEU, the well-known *Finn Frogne*[51] and the recent *Simonsen & Weel*,[52] illustrate the extent to which loyalty and cooperation, grounded in the contractual relationship, may be relevant to the assessment of a modification under Article 72 Directive 2014/24/EU.

The contractual duty of loyalty and cooperation is imperative when the parties encounter difficulties during contract performance in complex contracts. In this situation, the parties will be contractually obligated to find reasonable solutions, even if this requires adjustments to the contract. In *Finn Frogne*, the possible substantial modification consisted of a settlement between the parties as an alternative to premature termination of the contract under circumstances where the performance of the contract 'appeared impossible'.[53] The Court stated that 'objective difficulties encountered in the performance of the contract' and the contract having an 'objectively unpredictable nature of performance of certain aspects of the contract'[54] could not provide justification for a substantial modification under EU public procurement law. Instead, the assessment of substantial modifications was to be analysed from 'an objective point of view, based on the *Pressetext* case criteria'.[55]

Finn Frogne exposes the potential conflict between the contractual obligations to resolve the difficulties and EU public procurement law. When a contracting authority faces 'objective difficulties encountered in the performance of the contract' or difficulties due to the 'objectively unpredictable nature' of a contract, its duty of loyal cooperation will surely be triggered. This, in turn, raises the issue of the extent to which the contracting authority can lawfully adapt or renegotiate the contract to fulfil this duty – all while staying within the confines of Article 72 Directive 2014/24/EU. While the Court accepted that the parties in *Finn Frogne* had no intention of circumventing EU public procurement law, the extent of its legal effect may be understood on the basis that, in the end, it was relatively clear that the contract modification was difficult to reconcile with Article 72 Directive 2014/24/EU. Nevertheless, the Court articulated its reasoning in general terms and has referred to the judgment in its subsequent case law.[56] Still, there must be scope to consider whether the CJEU might, in the future, take into

[51] Case C-549/14 *Finn Frogne A/S v Rigspolitiet ved Center for Beredskabskommunikation* ECLI:EU:C:2016:634, [2016].

[52] Case C-23/20 *Simonsen & Weel* ECLI:EU:C:2021:490, [2021].

[53] Case C-549/14 *Finn Frogne* (n 51) para 18.

[54] ibid para 32.

[55] ibid para 33. The criteria are derived from Case C-454/06 *pressetext* (n 1). A modification constitutes a new award if it: 1) constitutes a material change to the essential terms of the initial contract; 2) alters the economic balance of the contract; 3) extends the scope of the contract considerably.

[56] Case C-461/20 *Advania Sverige and Kammarkollegiet* ECLI:EU:C:2022:72, [2022] para 19; and Joined Cases C-441/22 and C-443/22 *Obshtina Razgrad* ECLI:EU:C:2023:970, [2023] para 71.

account factors such as a contract's inherent complexity and particular characteristics – as well as the nature of performance-related difficulties – when assessing whether a modification is substantial under Article 72 Directive 2014/24/EU. This consideration becomes particularly pertinent in cases where a modification cannot be justified under the unforeseeability exception in Article 72(1)(c) Directive 2014/24/EU, yet is less clear-cut than in *Finn Frogne*. While the CJEU in *Finn Frogne* appeared reluctant to allow fundamental contract law principles – such as the duty of loyal cooperation – to influence its interpretation of Article 72 Directive 2014/24/EU, subsequent case law may indicate a gradual shift toward a more flexible, contract-aware approach.

Simonsen & Weel concerned a framework agreement.[57] As discussed in section III, the duty of loyal cooperation becomes particularly relevant in fully or partially open-ended settings, such as framework agreements. Indeed, under Nordic contract jurisprudence, this duty has served as a basis for interpreting contractual supply and purchase obligations involving open-ended quantities in long-term commercial framework agreements effectively acting as the guiding principle for balanced contract performance.[58] From EU public procurement law perspective, framework agreements are generally considered more flexible and, to some extent, more open-ended than the public contract.[59]

In *Simonsen & Weel*, the Court considered whether placing orders exceeding the estimated value of a framework agreement would constitute a substantial modification.[60] The key question was whether, much like exceeding a credit-card limit, the framework is deemed 'maxed out' once the total value of individual orders reaches the amount specified in the tender. The Court considered this issue by examining its potential effects on the supplier's legal position under contract law – particularly concerning the content and scope of their contractual supply obligations. The Court stated that:

[57] On framework agreements see for example: M Andrecka, 'Framework Agreements, EU Procurement Law and the Practice' (2015) 2 *Upphandlingsrättslig Tidskrifts* 127; M Andhov and D Soloveičik, 'The Relationship Between Initial Tender and Mini-Competition: EU and Lithuanian Perspectives on Framework Agreements' (2021) 121 *Teisė* 45.

[58] eg SH 2009.H 73/06, concerning a potential purchase obligation for A under a long-term contract, at a time when issues had arisen due to new regulation. The court found that A had 'loyally sought to enter into dialogue' to resolve the issue, without any luck. On the basis of 'general principles of contract law concerning loyal conduct and consideration for the counterparty' the court held that, under these circumstances, A was under no obligation to purchase additional quantities. See also *Nordens Välfärdscenter* case T 8524-19; and O Hansen, S Treumer and M Andhov, 'Social Services and Contract Changes: The Legality of Social Service Outsourcing Practices in EU Procurement Law' (2018) 5 *Public Procurement Law Review* 217.

[59] The case concerned a framework agreement, 'the purpose of which is to establish the terms governing contracts to be awarded during a given period, in particular with regard to price and, where appropriate, the quantity envisaged' under Art 33(1) Directive 2014/24/EU. See further M Andhov, 'Article 33 Framework Agreements' in R Caranta and A Sanchez-Graells (eds), *European Public Procurement: Commentary on Directive 2014/24/EU* (Cheltenham, Edward Elgar Publishing, 2021) 363–76.

[60] See Case C-23/20 *Simonsen & Weel* (n 52) para 44.

> if the required initial maximum estimated value or quantity were not indicated or if that indication were not legally binding, the contracting authority could flout that maximum quantity. As a result, the successful tenderer could be held contractually liable for non-performance of the framework agreement if he or she were to fail to supply the quantities requested by the contracting authority, even though those quantities exceed the maximum quantity in the contract notice. Such a situation would be contrary to the principle of transparency as laid down in Article 18(1) Directive 2014/24/EU.[61]

As will be seen, the Court departed from its usual reluctance towards the use of contract law reasoning in defining the content of EU public procurement law principles. Thus, when choosing which way to lean on substantial modifications, it directly attached weight to the contractual implications of the EU public procurement law outcome. Moreover, in doing so, the Court drew on precisely the same considerations that underlie the contractual duty of loyal cooperation. In sum, the interpretation of EU public procurement law that would result in a contractually imbalanced outcome to the one-sided detriment of one party would, in this case, be incompatible with the principle of transparency, given the prospect of a potentially unlimited, open-ended demand for quantities under the framework agreement that would otherwise flow from the requirement to indicate a maximum value.[62] However, one swallow does not make a summer. It remains to be seen whether this judgment marks a genuine softening towards the inclusion of contract-law reasoning in support of EU public procurement law arguments. If so, the Court would, on the one hand, have to consider its findings carefully to avoid dissolving the normative delineations between the two legal disciplines within the overall framework of EU law. On the other hand, some contract law-principles are so pervasive that parties to public contracts across many Member States will inevitably find themselves in the same contradictory predicament: being contractually bound to adapt to challenges during performance of a contract in a manner that Article 72 cannot accommodate.

At present, the legal landscape remains dominated by *Finn Frogne*, with its generalised dismissal of aligning EU public procurement law assessments with contractual realities. *Simonsen and Weel*, by contrast, dealt with the interpretation of EU public procurement law obligation – the requirement to indicate an estimated value – and showed how contract law- implications supported a more tightly woven interpretation of EU public procurement law, thereby limiting the scope of admissible modifications under Article 72. However, given the growing need for flexibility, the crucial question is whether those same contractual considerations could be successfully invoked before the CJEU in favour of a more flexible modification regime. There are sound indications that the current EU public procurement law regime already contains sufficient interpretative leeway

[61] ibid para 64.
[62] ibid paras 10–18.

to accommodate greater alignment with contractual realities – by interpretation alone.[63]

B. Procurement Law Assessments from Nordic Review Bodies: A Potential Path Towards Alignment?

In Denmark and Norway, the award criterion 'best price–quality ratio' is applied more frequently than in many other EU Member States,[64] and collaboration during contract performance is generally recognised as a legitimate award criterion in tender evaluations.[65] Despite these recognised practices, the contractual duty of loyalty and cooperation is not directly reflected in the reasoning of the Danish and Norwegian review boards in the assessment of possible infringements.[66] On the contrary, a principle of loyalty towards procurement law has been established.[67] Nevertheless, in some cases, the Nordic review boards have taken into account the typical characteristics and complexity of the contract, as well as the nature of the performance difficulties, when assessing whether a modification is substantial, in a manner that aligns well with both the contractual duty of loyal cooperation and procurement law. This practice is particularly interesting in view of the somewhat dismissive approach in *Finn Frogne*.

Joint Venture Salini-Impregilo-Samsung-Bunte v Femern A/S (*Femern*) is noteworthy.[68] In 2016, the Danish Public Procurement Complaints Board assessed

[63] The interpretation of 'unforeseeable circumstances' under Art 72(1)(c) Directive 2014/24/EU – which, according to recital 109, should factor in 'the nature and characteristics of the specific project' and 'good practice in the field in question' – also presents a similar tension. Yet, this provision has been interpreted likewise strictly. See and Joined Cases C-441/22 and C-443/22 *Obshtina Razgrad* (n 56) para 68.

[64] The Danish Competition Authority concludes that the percentage of awards based on 'price only' is 32–35 per cent in Denmark and 25 per cent in Norway, compared to a Member State average of 58 per cent. In 2020, 'best price–quality ratio' was, for example, applied in two-thirds of EU tenders in Denmark, with a higher weight on quality over price. Sweden stands out, with a high use of 'price only' in 79 per cent of EU tenders. See Konkurrence-og Forbrugerstyrelsen, *Status for offentlig konkurrence 2021* (KFST 2022) 39.

[65] Tenderers, for example, compete on the proposed organisation, methods, and specific plans for collaboration. For an example, see Complaints Board for Public Procurement case of 8 May 2019 *Vraa Dampvaskeri A/S v Aalborg Kommune*. On large and complex IT projects, see AN Westergaard and E Bisgaard, 'Indsigt og fleksibilitet ved udbud af it-anskaffelser efter udbudsloven' in K Hagel-Sørensen (ed), *Aktuel Udbudsret II* (Copenhagen, Djøf Forlag, 2016) 385.

[66] Norway is fully subject to Directive 2014/24/EU due to its membership of the EEA Agreement (n 16).

[67] Complaints Board for Public Procurement case 2009/55 of 5 November 2009 *TT Maskin og Transport AS v Hadsel Kommune*.

[68] Complaints Board for Public Procurement case of 12 April 2016 *Joint Venture Salini-Impregilo-Samsung-Bunte v Femern A/S*. The modification was made during the competitive dialogue, as it turned out that regulatory approvals in Germany could be a problem. As such, the change did not formally concern Art 72, as the contract was not yet concluded. However, KLFU expressly accepted the contracting authority's argumentation that changes in the specifications of the contract period during the competitive dialogue would certainly be compliant with public procurement law if the changes could lawfully have been made after the conclusion of the contract. The assessment was, therefore, based on the rules of contract modification.

whether substantial modifications had occurred in the main contracts related to the mega-project of constructing the Fehmarn Belt fixed link tunnel. Due to a much longer-than-anticipated environmental-planning approval process, two of the contracts were extended from 68 to 87 months, while a third contract was prolonged from 78 to 105 months. Despite the considerable extensions – at the heart of substantial modifications – the Danish Public Procurement Complaints Board found that the contracts had not been substantially modified.[69]

It is common that issues concerning regulation, such as permits, arise in the performance of complex contracts. While this will often be *generally* foreseeable, outlining all possible scenarios and their implications in a regulation-dense society, and exhaustively allocating risk while maintaining contractual 'equilibrium', all in advance, is quite another matter.[70] It is in precisely these types of situations that the duty of loyalty proves its value, binding the parties to seek a contractually meaningful resolution. Nevertheless, the realisation of regulatory risks – and their possible solutions – will often have a significant impact, cause delays, and affect the financial framework of the project.

In *Femern*, the Danish Public Procurement Complaints Board stated that:

> according to the information provided, this is Northern Europe's largest construction project to date, that the list of applicants, as expected, included all known players in the market for such very large construction projects, that the extensions are due to circumstances related to known conditions for regulatory approval, and that an extension of the contract period is effectively quite common in infrastructure projects and other major construction projects.[71]

Had the Danish Public Procurement Complaints Board taken an interpretation in line with *Finn Frogne*, disregarding the typical characteristics of the contract, the complexity, and the nature of the difficulties in performance, the outcome could have been very different. Since the question was never referred to the CJEU, it remains uncertain whether the Court would have applied the same stringent interpretation it used in *Finn Frogne*. However, such a finding would almost certainly have appeared overly formalistic and disconnected from the contractual realities at play. By taking into account the contract's inherent characteristics and complexity, as well as the nature of the performance-related difficulties – as seen, for example, in the evaluation of the pool of potential tenderers – *Femern* does more than align with the parties' contractual obligations; it also grounds the validity and credibility of the outcome under EU public procurement law. The case rings true because including these factors – mirrored in the duty of loyalty and cooperation – leads to a more accurate and informed EU public procurement law assessment. As such, there does

[69] The same argumentation is applied by the Norwegian Complaints Board for Public Procurement, eg Complaints Board for Public Procurement case 2012/19 of 4 February 2014 *Gunnar Johnsen v Lenvik Kommune*; Complaints Board for Public Procurement case 2012/222 of 11 March 2014 *Demokratene Askøy v Askøy Kommune*.

[70] On risk allocation, see further ch 5.

[71] *Klagenævnet for Udbud, Joint Venture Salini-Impregilo-Samsung-Bunte v Femern A/S* (12 April 2016) 2016-2237, p 11.

seem to be a path towards increased alignment that could, at least to some extent, accommodate the need for increased flexibility and the use of the principle of loyal cooperation as an element in the interpretation of EU public procurement law on contract modifications under Article 72 Directive 2014/24/EU.

V. Potential for Contract Law and the Duty of Loyalty to Accommodate EU Public Procurement Law in the Context of Ending Public Contract under Article 73 Directive 2014/24/EU

In this section, the perspective is reversed: instead of examining how the interpretation of EU public procurement law can be influenced by contract law, it explores whether some effects of EU public procurement law can influence the understanding of the contractual obligations between the parties. The section starts by clarifying what 'ending a contract' under Article 73 entails and the relationship between Articles 72 and 73 Directive 2014/24/EU.[72] Next, the authors examine the legal relationship between the contracting authority and the private party upon ending a public contract, including how the duty of loyal cooperation brings the implications of EU public procurement law into the contractual relationship. Finally, the section considers specific contract clauses that aim to regulate the role of the duty of loyal cooperation when a contract is ended under Article 73.

A. Ending a Public Contract under Article 73 Directive 2014/24/EU

There can be several reasons to modify a contract. Article 72 Directive 2014/24/EU defines the extent to which the contracting authority can make such modifications without being obliged to retender.[73] However, as described in section II,

[72] The English version of Directive 2014/24/EU uses the unspecified term 'termination'. It is unclear what this means under contract law as this may be by notice or by breach under common law. The Danish version uses the term *opsigelse* (cancellation) which implies that the situation has nothing to do with recission of the contract. The French version uses the term *resiliation* which can mean both termination in case of breach (*Résiliation pur faute*) and cancellation (*Résiliation unilatérale/avec préavis*). Because of this lack of clarity, we use in this section the neutral term 'to end a contract' that have been employed in the s 185 *Udbudsloven* no 2015/1564 (Danish Public Procurement Act).

[73] See S Treumer, 'Contract Changes and the Duty to Retender Under the New EU Public Procurement Directive' (2014) 3 *Public Procurement Law Review* 148; MA Simovart, 'Old Remedies for New Violations? The Deficit of Remedies for Enforcing Public Contract Modification Rules' (2015) 1 *Upphandlingsrättslig Tidskrift* 33; P Bogdanowicz, *Contract Modifications in EU Procurement Law* (Cheltenham, Edward Elgar Publishing, 2021); D Dragos and others (eds), *Contract Changes: The Dark Side of EU Procurement Law* (Cheltenham, Edward Elgar Publishing, 2023).

Article 72 does not in itself render inadmissible modifications contractually invalid.[74] In Nordic law, the prevailing view is that the provision merely delineates the permissible scope of contractual modifications by the contracting authority – beyond which a retendering obligation and potential liability to third parties would arise.[75] Thus, if a contracting authority subsequently finds that a modification made by the parties to the contract must be considered 'substantial', the contracting authority may want to end the public contract with the private party to comply with EU public procurement law, be able to retender and avoid liability towards third parties.[76] An example of the situation could be this: A contracting authority (for instance its management) discovers that its employee (for example a contract manager) has repeatedly accepted that the supplier missed milestones during project meetings. The contracting authority assesses whether the contract has been modified under contract law. It finds this to be the case. It then assesses whether this constitutes a substantial modification under Directive 2014/24/EU and finds this to be the case. For such situations, Article 73(1) Directive 2014/24/EU provides that Member States shall ensure that contracting authorities can end a public contract during its term if the contract has been subject to a substantial modification which, in the contracting authority's assessment, would have required a new procurement procedure pursuant to Article 72.[77]

Article 73 broke new ground when it was introduced, since it concerns the ongoing contractual relationship between the contracting authority vis-à-vis the private party in the performance phase. As stated in the legal literature: 'For the first time in history, Directive 2014/24/EU now regulates the issue of contract termination'.[78] The question is what this means in the context of the relationship between contract law and public procurement law, as described in section II.

The provision has been implemented in diverse ways across Member States. Under the Swedish Public Procurement Act, contracting authorities are required to include termination clauses in their contracts.[79] Hereby, the Swedish legislator has sent the clear message that it is up to the contracting parties to determine the consequences of termination. According to the preparatory works, this approach is justified by the inherent difficulties in establishing the 'contractual and liability-related consequences'.[80]

[74] See also F Wilman, *Private Enforcement of EU Law Before National Courts: The EU Legislative Framework* (Cheltenham, Edward Elgar Publishing, 2015) 306.

[75] See further s II.

[76] The Complaints Board for Public Procurement has competence to assess whether the decision to consider the modification substantial is justified.

[77] See Wilman (n 74).

[78] Bogdanowicz (n 73) 20.

[79] Ch 17, s 17 *Lag* (2016:1145) *om offentlig upphandling* (Swedish Act on Public Procurement).

[80] See Lagrådsremiss, *Kompletterende bestämmelser om upphandling*, 28 April 2016, 56–57 and SOU 2014:41, *nya regler om Upphandling*, 3 July 2014, 885. A similar solution has been chosen in English law, see the Public Contracts Regulations 2015 No 102, pt 2, ch 2, s 6, reg 73.

Denmark has adopted a different model.[81] Under the Danish Public Procurement Act, the contracting authority holds the right to end a contract under the circumstances specified in Directive 2014/24/EU.[82] The right to end the contract is unilateral and does not depend on any breach by the private party.[83] However, neither Directive 2014/24/EU nor the Danish Public Procurement Act specifies the contractual consequences of exercising this unilateral right. The preparatory works for Section 185(1) state:

> This provision has no implications for any possible liability as a consequence of the termination of the contract pursuant to this provision. The question concerning liability must be decided on the basis of the ordinary rules in Danish law.[84]

The statement makes it clear that the consequences of invoking Article 73 by the contracting authority to end the public contract are governed by general contract law. In accordance with fundamental contractual principles, the general rule under Nordic contract law is that contracts cannot be unilaterally ended unless such a right is expressly provided for in the contract. If a contract is nevertheless ended without contractual grounds, it constitutes a breach, and damages may be claimed. As an exception to this rule, it is accepted that contracts, which would otherwise run indefinitely, can be ended without giving rise to liability, provided sufficient notice has been given.[85] In practice, public contracts usually run for a specified time period, and consequently, this exception rarely applies.[86] This means that, unless specifically allowed for in the contract, a unilateral ending of the contract by the contracting authority will normally constitute a breach of contract and entitle the private party to damages. The question is how these general contractual rules apply in the context of Article 73 Directive 2014/24/EU.

If a public contract has been subject to a substantial modification and the contracting authority chooses to end the contract based on Article 73 Directive 2014/24/EU, the legal position of the private party will depend on the details of the public contract.[87] Three different situations can be identified:

A. The contract aligns with Article 73 Directive 2014/24/EU by including a termination clause that grants the contracting authority the right to end the contract, while also entitling the private party to compensation, the amount of which is contractually defined. In this situation, the case is straightforward: the private party has the right to claim the compensation as stipulated in the contract.[88]

[81] A similar model has been chosen in Norwegian law, see Gausdal, 'Scener fra et (tvangs)ægteskab: om grænsefladen mellem udbudsret og kontraktret' (n 18) 463.

[82] s 185(1) Danish Public Procurement Act.

[83] Gausdal, 'Scener fra et (tvangs)ægteskab: om grænsefladen mellem udbudsret og kontraktret' (n 18) 465–66.

[84] Proposal for Act no 19 of 7 October 2015, on the Danish Public Procurement Act, 203.

[85] T Iversen, *Obligationsret*, vol 1, 6th edn (Copenhagen, Djøf Forlag, 2019) 40.

[86] Gausdal, 'Scener fra et (tvangs)ægteskab: om grænsefladen mellem udbudsret og kontraktret' (n 18) 467.

[87] s 185(1) Danish Public Procurement Act.

[88] Issues of interpretation may arise if the contract contains a termination clause independently of s 185(1) Danish Public Procurement Act, and without making reference to this provision.

B. The contract runs contrary to Article 73 Directive 2014/24/EU by stating that the contract cannot be ended by the contracting authority.
C. The contract is silent about the issue.

In the latter two cases, Article 73 Directive 2014/24/EU entails a right for the contracting authority to end the contract irrespective of the contractual regulation. In these situations, it follows from the Danish preparatory works related to Section 185(1) that the extent to which the private party can claim damages depends on the 'ordinary rules of Danish law'. The question is what this entails. One line of reasoning holds that, since ending the contract was lawful under Article 73 Directive 2014/24/EU, there is no basis for liability of the contracting authority vis-à-vis the contracting party. This interpretation clashes with the Danish preparatory works, which explicitly state that Article 73 Directive 2014/24/EU has 'no implications for any possible liability following the ending of the contract pursuant to this provision'. Instead, it could be argued that ending a contract unilaterally is generally impermissible under contract law. Consequently, if the contracting authority wilfully ends the agreement without a contractual basis, the private party has the right to claim damages for breach of contract. The right to end the contract granted under Article 73 Directive 2014/24/EU only means that the private party cannot claim specific performance of the contract.[89] Hereby, retendering becomes possible for the contracting authority, but it must still pay damages to the private party. This understanding would be in line with the Danish preparatory works that presume that damages can come into play in case the public contract is unilaterally ended by the contracting authority. However, even if it is assumed that the private party can, as a starting point, claim damages, that right may be modified if it consciously agreed to a substantial modification of the public contract knowing that the modification would place the contracting authority in breach of EU public procurement law. Taking the example from above, the situation could be as follows: An employee (eg a contract manager) of a contracting authority has repeatedly accepted that the supplier missed milestones at project meetings. The acceptance constitutes a substantial modification under EU public procurement law, but the employee is unaware of this. At the same time, it follows from the circumstances that the supplier, who is a professional party, has been fully aware of EU public procurement law problem. However, the supplier has not raised this issue during negotiations with the employee of the contracting authority. Under these circumstances, it might be argued that although it is not a primary duty of the private party to ensure that the contracting authority does not breach EU public procurement law, the private party has breached its duty of loyalty towards its contractual partner (acted contrary to good faith) by not drawing attention to the problem with the procurement rules and for this reason, the amount of damages that the private party can claim should be reduced. In this way, the

[89] More precisely: The private party loses its right to deliver specific performance of the contract against payment.

duty of loyalty may bring in some effects of EU public procurement law to the contractual relationship *through the back door*. There are sometimes attempts to regulate this interplay directly through specific contract clauses.

B. Contractual Variations of the Duty of Loyalty

As explained, despite the right of the contracting authority to end the contract under Article 73 Directive 2014/24/EU, Nordic contract law will still protect the private supplier and form the basis for a claim for damages against the contracting authority. Since the contract – irrespective of EU public procurement law – forms the basis for the claim, the same contract may limit or narrow the private supplier's access to compensation in case the contracting authority has invoked Article 73 Directive 2014/24/EU.

In fact, the drafting of public contracts shows a tendency for contracting authorities to anticipate their legal position in cases where the contract is discontinued due to EU public procurement law infringements. These contractual practices can, in themselves, be understood as an acknowledgement or awareness of the persistent role of contract law when the contract is ended under Article 73 Directive 2014/24/EU.

However, it is not evident that contract clauses aiming to allocate the risk in these situations will lead to the desired result. Apart from depending upon the content of the specific clauses, these clauses must be interpreted in accordance with general principles of national contract law. Even in a commercial contract setting, fundamental principles of contract law may restrict the parties' autonomy.[90] As mentioned in section III above, the duty of loyalty and good faith represent deep layers of Nordic contract law, defining the core legal nature of the contract. Accordingly, they cannot be entirely overridden by the parties without challenging the validity of the agreement.[91] In radical cases, clauses may be set aside as unfair or unconscionable, for example, with reference to Section 36 Nordic Contracts Act.[92] However, Nordic courts generally interpret clauses adjusting the duty of loyalty narrowly, operating under the presumption that the parties did not intend to establish an invalid agreement. As a result, clauses that attempt to allocate the entire risk or liability for EU public procurement law infringements onto the private supplier will rarely have a significant legal effect. Illustratively, the central purchasing body for the Danish state and municipalities (SKI) has developed the following standard clause, which clearly aims at barring a contractual claim from the private supplier in case of termination:

> If the Supplier at the time of conclusion of the Framework Agreement knew or should have known of the factual and/or legal circumstances causing the Framework

[90] On public procurement and contract law autonomy, see also ch 4.
[91] Munukka (n 31) 489; Nazarian (n 31) 134–39; Hansen (n 36) 182.
[92] For example, with reference to s 36 *Aftaleloven* no 193/2016 (Danish Contracts Act). See above in s 3 on the relation between the general standard of loyalty and s 36 Danish Contracts Act.

> Agreement to be terminated, the Supplier shall have no claim for damages or any other form of compensation for losses, including, for example, costs in relation to the terms and conditions or requirements passed on by SKI in the termination notice. In the assessment of whether the Supplier 'should have known' as mentioned above, it shall be taken into account that the Supplier acts as a professional operator and has been assisted by professional experts within procurement law in connection with the tendering procedure.[93]

As established in the above section, the private supplier may, fully or partially, lose a contractual claim against the contracting authority if the private supplier has itself contributed negligently to the infringement. The cited clause clearly underlines that the supplier's 'own actions' related to events constituting a breach of public procurement law are relevant to the assessment of the supplier's private law claim. However, the clause will hardly exempt the contracting authority from contractual liability merely based upon the supplier's knowledge of the 'circumstances causing the (contract) to be terminated'. Essentially, the private supplier has no authority to prevent the contracting authority from acting in breach of its legal obligations and will not be held liable for the contracting authority's unlawful conduct.

What the clause anticipates is the fact that a substantial (unlawful) variation will often require the consent and the participation of the private supplier. Consequently, one could argue that, in principle, the supplier may freely deny accepting an unlawful amendment. However, commercial standard terms for long-term and complex contracts, for example construction contracts, will often clearly authorise the contracting authority to demand variations. In general, such variation clauses are not aligned with the contract amendment regime under EU public procurement law, but will give the contracting authority, in some ways, broader contractual rights to order variations than those accepted under Article 72 Directive 2014/24/EU.[94] Consequently, the private supplier will often be in breach of contract if it refuses a variation order within the scope of the contractual variation right.[95]

The decisive criterion when determining whether the private supplier is entitled to a claim upon termination will likely be whether the supplier *contributed in bad faith* to the contracting authority's breach of EU public procurement law, other than simply complying with the contract terms. One example of such a

[93] SKI, Framework Agreement 16.08 Air Journeys (2023), s 13.1.4.

[94] Variation rights defined in standard terms for construction are not defined in accordance with the criteria known from Art 72 Directive 2014/24/EU. For instance, according to the Danish standard form contract for construction works AB 18, s 23 the employer 'may order variations to the works when such variations are naturally linked to the services agreed upon'. Accordingly, Ch 2 s 2 Swedish AB 04 places a duty upon the contractor to perform variations ordered by the employer during the contract period. Variations must be in 'immediate connection' (*umedelbart samband*) with the works defined in the contract and must not be of a 'significant other nature' than these. According to the Norwegian NS 8405 clause 22.1 a variation 'must have a connection to' and not be 'of a significant different nature' than the works under the contract.

[95] It is the fundamental characteristic of the employer's variation right that the contractor is under an obligation to perform the variation as long as the variation order falls within the boundaries set in the contract for the employer's variation right, cf. eg AB 18 s 23; AB 04 Ch 2 s 2; and NS 8405 clause 22.1.

contribution could be situations where a private supplier actively seeks to encourage the contracting authority to take actions that will constitute a breach of EU public procurement law. Though difficult to describe in general terms, the contract may regulate specific types of actions, from which the supplier must refrain. By concretising the standard of loyal cooperation, the contracting authority can reinforce the legal effect by clarifying that certain types of conduct constitute a breach of contract.

Indeed, even framework agreements awarded in full compliance with EU public procurement law may give rise to a purchasing environment in which private suppliers can exploit a more limited understanding of procurement law among the public employees responsible for day-to-day ordering. This imbalance in awareness of the legal implications of routine purchases under the agreement may be taken advantage of in a disloyal manner by the private supplier. Whereas attempts to generally tighten the private supplier's duty of loyal cooperation – thereby lowering the bar for admissible conduct for the contracting authority itself – may, for the reasons mentioned, not have considerable effect, the contracting authority may be able to pre-empt claims from the private supplier by concretising what will be conceived as loyal conduct or, conversely, disloyal contribution to a breach of the procurement rules.

An example of a more effective agreement can be found in SKI's standard framework agreements, which contain the following clause on the 'Obligation to act in good faith and provide guidance':

> The Supplier shall not encourage the Customers to make any purchases outside the Framework Agreement if the Customers' needs can be covered by the range of products/services under the Framework Agreement. The Supplier shall not encourage or induce the Customers to make any purchases in breach of applicable procurement rules or to use the Framework Agreement in breach of its provisions.[96]

Though it admittedly may still be difficult to assess how the term 'encourage' shall be interpreted, the context and the criterion for disloyal behaviour are here more narrowly described. Further, the duty to refrain from 'encouraging unlawful purchases' is not unlike omission duties known from, for example, marketing agreements.

VI. Conclusion

Due to the complexity of services, the uncertainty of circumstances related to performance and tight public regulation, there is an increasing need for flexibility in contracts entered into by contracting authorities as well as in purely commercial settings. For the contracting authority, the need for public contract amendment is accommodated within the boundaries set by Article 72 Directive 2014/24/EU.

[96] Framework Agreement 16.08 Air Journeys (n 92) s 5.4.

However, in Nordic law, this provision does not function as a civil law *lex specialis* that invalidates contract amendments that go further.

In contrast, public contracts entered into by contracting authorities and private service providers in Danish and Nordic law are governed by general principles of contract law. This means that a public authority may be under a contractual obligation to loyally cooperate with the private supplier during the contract performance period. Hereby, the contracting authority may overstep the boundaries for public contract modification in Article 72 Directive 2014/24/EU. Consequently, the relation between the contract modification regime under EU public procurement law and the general duty of loyal cooperation becomes relevant.

Practice from the CJEU may be evolving and, in particular, domestic courts and review boards illustrate that although EU public procurement law is a separate legal regime, the interpretation of the procurement rules may be affected by contractual realities and contract law thinking and transaction-based considerations when assessing whether contractual modifications comply with EU public procurement law. In this way, contract law principles, including the duty of loyal cooperation, may influence the interpretation of EU public procurement law.

Conversely, in situations where a public contract is ended under Article 73 Directive 2014/24/EU, the contractual principle of loyal duty to cooperate may import EU public procurement law thinking into the contractual relationship between the parties. Article 73 Directive 2014/24/EU, as implemented in domestic Nordic law, does not exclude a contractual claim for damages by the private supplier if the contracting authority ends the contract. However, the private supplier's involvement in the events leading to the end of the tendered-out public contract may affect the claim and, to some extent, import EU public procurement law considerations into the contractual relationship via the principle of good faith.

This is also illustrated by contractual practices among contracting authorities, which aim to place the commercial risk of ending a contract under Article 73 Directive 2014/24/EU on the supplier, or at least to push back against such potential claims by emphasising and specifying the standard of loyalty for the private service provider. It is submitted that the contracting authority cannot by way of an agreement transfer the full risk and/or liability for the contracting authority's compliance with EU public procurement law to the supplier, but that a duty for the private supplier to refrain from specific types of disloyal conduct leading to the contracting authority's breach of EU public procurement law may be given effect. Such clauses may then limit the possibility of a private law-based claim for damages where the contract has been ended in accordance with Article 73 Directive 2014/24/EU.

These observations suggest that in Nordic law, procurement law and private contract law are two distinct legal regimes, operating individually, yet without mutual immunity in the sense that core principles of contract law may influence the interpretation of procurement law rules and vice versa. This chapter has demonstrated that the contractual principle of the duty to cooperate loyally plays a crucial role in the interplay between the two legal regimes.

8

'I Did Not Sign Anything': Can a Tacit Modification Constitute a Contract Amendment under EU Procurement Rules?

AARNE PUISTO, KIRSI-MARIA HALONEN AND PIRKKO HEIKKINEN

I. Introduction

Since *Succhi di Frutta* and *Pressetext* from the Court of Justice of the EU (CJEU)[1] and especially since the adoption of the 2014 Public Procurement Directives,[2] contract modifications have probably been one of the most discussed topics in public procurement literature and practice.[3] This focus is understandable given that the majority of public contracts encounter the necessity for modifications during their lifecycle. The interpretation of contract modifications' nature – whether a modification is considered significant or not – is crucial, as false interpretation risks the existence of the contract since a significant contract modification is considered equivalent to a direct award. Regardless of the academic

[1] Case C-496/99 P *Commission of the European Communities v CAS Succhi di Frutta SpA* ECLI:EU:C:2004:236, [2004] ECR I-03801; Case C-454/06 *pressetext Nachrichtenagentur GmbH v Republik Österreich (Bund), APA-OTS Originaltext-Service GmbH and APA Austria Presse Agentur registrierte Genossenschaft mit beschränkter Haftung* ECLI:EU:C:2008:351, [2008] ECR I-04401.

[2] Directive 2014/23/EU; Directive 2014/24/EU; Directive 2014/25/EU. In this chapter, we solely refer to Directive 2014/24/EU. Nonetheless, the conclusions and analyses are relevant to public contracts or concession contracts governed by any of the 2014 Public Procurement Directives, as the approach to contract modifications remains consistent.

[3] See eg MA Simovart, 'Enforcement of Ineffectiveness of Unlawfully Modified Public Contracts' (2016) 24 *Juridica International* 43; V Wangelow, 'EU Public Procurement Law: Amendments of Public Works Contracts After the Award Due to Additional Works and Unforeseeable Circumstances' (2020) 15(2) *European Procurement & Public Private Partnership Law Review* 107; AL Jaramillo Villacís and AI Peiró Baquedano, 'Contract Modifications and the CJEU: The Evolution of Public Procurement Case Law' (2021) 16(1) *European Procurement & Public Private Partnership Law Review* 78; D Dragos et al (eds), *Contract Changes: The Dark Side of EU Procurement Law* (Cheltenham, Edward Elgar Publishing, 2023).

interest towards contract modifications, the impact of private contract law on their interpretation has received limited attention.

One of the overlooked topics regarding contract modifications in the public procurement context is whether a tacit modification constitutes a contract amendment under EU public procurement law. This chapter aims to build a framework for evaluating different forms of contract modifications. It covers principles of European contract law and national contract law rules, and analyses their relationship to EU public procurement law.[4]

Public contracts are subject to written form, but there are no specific rules on the formal requirements of contract modifications. Instead, under contract law principles, one could argue that by default, the same formal requirements that apply to the conclusion of the contract also apply to its modifications unless agreed otherwise by the parties.[5] National public or contract law rules apply to public contracts, and in most of the northern Member States, the contracts are governed by private law rules ('the private-oriented hybrid model').[6] These private law rules are similar to European contract law rules and principles, such as the Principles of European Contract Law (PECL) and the Draft Common Frame of Reference (DCFR), which often serve as examples for national rules and are sometimes also referred to in national case law. This chapter discusses these principles and European contract law to analyse the question of what tacit modifications of public contracts are.

Under the PECL and the DCFR, as well as Finnish contract law, a contract can be concluded not only in written form but also in the form of a verbal or tacit contract.[7] The latter two should not be confused with each other, as they differ fundamentally. An oral contract is formed when the contracting parties express their intention to enter into or modify a contract through verbal statements. The formation of a tacit contract, instead, is not based on the explicit expressions of intent by the parties, but the existence of the contract is inferred from other actions of the parties, such as the long-term acceptance of a certain state of affairs or established practices followed by the parties.[8] These different methods of expressing intent and forming a contract can be illustrated by means of Figure 1 below.

[4] In this chapter, the term 'rules' is used in a general sense, and in the case of specific written legislation, such as a Directive or an Act, these are referenced specifically. When explicitly referring to principles, the term 'principles' is used.

[5] M Hemmo, *Sopimusoikeus II*, 2nd edn (Helsinki, Talentum, 2003) 36–37 and 133–34.

[6] See ch 3.

[7] Unlike many other countries, Finland does not have a single unified civil code that contains all the regulations concerning contracts. Contracts are governed by numerous laws, the most central of which is the Finnish Contract Act (228/1929). Moreover, general doctrines and principles of contract law established, particularly in case law form an essential part of Finnish contract law. See A Saarnilehto and V Annola, *Sopimusoikeuden perusteet*, 8th edn (Helsinki, Alma Talent, 2018) 16.

[8] KKO 2012:86 (Finnish Supreme Court). The term 'tacit modification' here refers to a form of contract or contract modification that has not been agreed upon with explicit written or oral expressions. In private contract law, it has traditionally been considered clear that explicit expressions of will are not absolute requirements for a contract to be binding. The contract can also be formed based on the actual activity or conduct of the parties. The consideration of the existence of an implicit agreement

Figure 1 Different methods of expressing intention and forming a contract

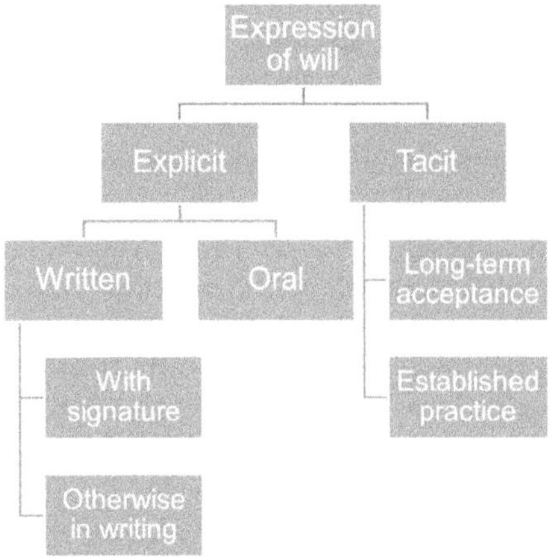

Correspondingly, a tacit modification refers to an implied change to a contract, deduced from the conduct and practices of the parties rather than from explicit verbal or written agreements. For the purposes of this chapter, tacit modification is also understood as a modification where one contractual party's intent is based on an implied action, and the other party has explicitly expressed its will in writing. The questions relating to the formal requirements concern not only the contract's conclusion, but also the contract execution stage, where there can be significant changes, deviations, or delays without the parties specifically agreeing on amendments thereto. If a contracting authority does not react to such events, under contract law, it may be regarded as an acceptance of the amendment or, alternatively, a breach of contract. Luckily, for the purposes of writing this chapter, the CJEU has recently addressed this question on formal requirements of contract modifications in its case law.[9]

Public contracts and other types of commercial contracts share common grounds but also deviate from each other. Public contracts in the 'private-oriented hybrid model' are based on the foundations of private commercial contracts, but due to the priority of EU law and its requirements of effective legal remedies, openness, and equal treatment, the public contract needs to be interpreted with an additional set of objectives providing rights also to third parties. In private contract settings, the law protects the privity of contract and contractual freedom, and does not allow third parties to challenge the contract's existence.[10] In the public procurement context, private contract law rules are applied to the contracts,

is usually based on an overall assessment that requires strong and consistent arguments in favour of its existence, see M Hemmo, 'Sopimuksen hiljainen jatkuminen sen muodollisen päättymisen jälkeen' in V Vahtera (ed), *Yhtiö, Velka, Velvoite Juhlajulkaisu Seppo Villa* (Helsinki, Alma Talent, 2021) 175.

[9] Joined cases C-441/22 and C-443/22 *Obshtina Razgrad and Obshtina Balchik* ECLI:EU:C:2023:970, [2023].

[10] See more ch 12.

but with limitations. Private national contract rules apply in the 'private-oriented hybrid model' only when they do not endanger the effectiveness and interests of EU public procurement law. Such interests, as outlined in Article 18 Directive 2014/24/EU, include principles of non-discrimination, equal treatment, proportionality, and open competition, which limit the contracting authority's and its contractor's rights to agree on changes to the original procurement procedure and public contract. Moreover, Directive 89/665/EEC[11] also requires that an economic operator – a potential tenderer or contractor – has the possibility to effectively challenge infringements and to seek legal remedies.[12] Consequently, public contracts cannot be freely amended, and they are not protected from 'external attacks' by procurement monitoring authorities or their competitors.

The research aims to answer whether a tacit modification can constitute a contract amendment under EU public procurement law and what the impact of contract law rules is in that analysis. To answer the research question, it is necessary to examine the following sub-questions: What are the formal requirements for modifying a public contract? What is the nature of an amendment if the possible formal requirement is not met? Does EU public procurement law and/or the requirement of its effectiveness somehow limit the applicability of contract law rules? Moreover, if a contracting authority does not monitor the contract, changes may occur without its knowledge. In such a case, is the deviation even a contract modification or rather a breach of contract?

This chapter is structured as follows: It begins with an examination of the formal requirements for contracts and their modifications under private contract law, focusing on European contract law, as well as Finnish contract law. The discussion then shifts to procurement rules governing the formal requirements for public contracts and their amendments. Section IV explores the topic primarily through the lens of Finnish legislation and case law, supplemented with examples from Estonia, the Netherlands, Norway, and the United Kingdom. Section V addresses the legal interpretation of formal requirements and the role of tacit modifications in the procurement context.

II. Formal Requirements and Tacit Modifications in Private Contract Law

This section examines how formal requirements and tacit modifications are understood and applied in private contract law. It begins by exploring European contract law before turning to national contract law in Finland. This analysis provides an essential foundation for understanding how these concepts may translate into the public procurement context.

[11] See also Directive 92/13/EEC.
[12] For this purpose, Directive 89/665/EEC was amended by Directive 2007/66/EC.

A. PECL and DCFR

The aim of the PECL is to strengthen the internal market by facilitating cross-border trade and providing 'model rules' for national courts and legislators to transpose both within and outside the EU. In particular, the PECL is intended to bridge the gap between civil law and common law.[13] The DCFR has very similar objectives. It aims to promote knowledge of private law in the jurisdictions of the EU by demonstrating the common characteristics of national private laws.[14]

A contract can be concluded in various ways. Freedom of form is a strong principle under European contract law (the PECL and the DCFR) and national contract law in Finland.[15] Thus, an agreement can also be concluded implicitly. However, certain contracts may have formal requirements. The various formal requirements are based, inter alia, on the need to ensure clarity of ownership, publicity, evidence, or effective exercise of remedies. A formal requirement may also be justified by commercial practice, particularly in large commercial contracts.[16] An example of such a practice is a private equity contract, where long duration, complexity, and high asset values impose form requirements even during negotiations, prior to contract conclusion. In contrast, despite similarly high asset values, construction contracts typically do not follow this practice.[17] Despite the benefits of form regulations, at times, they may slow down the process of concluding a contract, increase costs, and even prevent desired legal actions.

The DCFR's general approach to formal requirements is informality, according to DCFR II–1:106: 'A contract or other juridical act need not be concluded, made or evidenced in writing nor is it subject to any other formal requirements as to form'.

Where a contract must be in writing, DCFR I–1.106 defines what is meant by 'in writing' and similar expressions such as 'textual form' or 'durable medium'. As stated above, the contract can also be concluded implicitly due to II–9.101 'The terms of a contract may be derived from the express or tacit agreement of the parties, from rules of law or practices established between the parties of usages'.

What the parties have tacitly agreed on depends, for example, on the interpretation of the contract, such as the conduct and the nature of the parties.[18] As to the

[13] H Beale, 'The Role for European Contract law: Uniformity of Diversity' in Francisco de Elizalde (ed), *Uniform Rules for European Contract Law?: A Critical Assessment* (Oxford, Bloomsbury, 2018) 9.

[14] C von Bar et al (eds), *Principles, Definitions and Model Rules of European Private Law: Draft Common Frame of Reference (DCFR)*, Interim Outline edn (Munich, Sellier-European Law Publishers, 2008) 2–3.

[15] Saarnilehto and Annola (n 7).

[16] See M Hemmo, 'Tavat ja käytännöt kansainvälisessä välimiesmenettelyssä' (2017) 3(1) *Liikejuridiikka* 75, 75–76; The United Nations Convention on Contracts for the International Sale of Goods (CISG), Art 9(2).

[17] E Pälä, 'Osakassopimus pääomasijoittajan välineenä sijoituskohteen omistusrakenteen muutoksessa' (2006) 39 *Oikeustiede – Jurisprudentia* 221, 241.

[18] See II–8.102 DCFR Relevant matters.

tacit prolongation of a contract, the DCFR has general and some specific terms. According to the general provision (III–1.111):

> Where a contract provides for continuous or repeated performance of obligations or a definite period and the obligations continue to be performed by both parties after that period has expired, the contract becomes a contract for an indefinite period, unless the circumstances are inconsistent with the tacit consent of the parties to such prolongation.[19]

In the PECL, freedom of form is stated in Article 2:101:

> Conditions for the Conclusion of a Contract (1) A contract is concluded if: (a) the parties intend to be legally bound, and (b) they reach a sufficient agreement without any further requirement. (2) A contract need not be concluded or evidenced in writing nor is it subject to any other requirement as to form. The contract may be proved by any means, including witnesses.

According to the PECL Article 2:106:

> Written Modification Only (1) A clause in a written contract requiring any modification or ending by agreement to be made in writing establishes only a presumption that an agreement to modify or end the contract is not intended to be legally binding unless it is in writing. (2) A party may by its statements or conduct be precluded from asserting such a clause to the extent that the other party has reasonably relied on them.

In other words, the PECL does not have a form requirement but rather allows other forms of amendments provided that the other party had an intent to amend the contract and had relied on the changes.[20] How do formal requirements relate to the exception mentioned above? The underlying idea is to allow flexibility between the parties and reduce bureaucratic hurdles in contract amendments. However, when a contract includes a form requirement, it limits the ability to rely on other forms of evidence, as the requirement raises the evidentiary threshold for proving that a modification took place.[21]

The role of the DCFR and the PECL as sources of law has been a topic of debate in Finland in recent years. While they are sometimes used to interpret Finnish law, they are regarded as merely complementary sources.[22] Their use is typically justified by their international relevance and practical orientation. However, the DCFR has not attained the level of influence that some Finnish legal scholars suggested in the early 2000s. In contrast to academic literature, Finnish case law

[19] The tacit prolongation of the contract is also provided for in the DCFR in relation to the lease period of goods. The DCFR provides that either party may prevent the tacit prolongation of the contract by giving notice to the other party before the tacit prolongation takes place, see IV.B–2:103.

[20] A similar clause can be found in UNIDROIT Principles (Art 2.1.18). See Unidroit Principles of International Commercial Contracts (2016) 65–66 <www.unidroit.org/english/principles/contracts/principles2016/principles2016-e.pdf>.

[21] Hemmo, *Sopimusoikeus II* (n 5) 40–42.

[22] O Norros, 'Sopimusoikeudellisten periaatekokoelmien oikeuslähdearvo' (2007) 105(1) *Lakimies* 25–42; T Wilhelmsson, 'Siviilioikeuden hiipivä eurooppalaistuminen ja Suomen oikeuslähdeoppi' (2020) 118 *Lakimies* 1172–96.

rarely refers to these instruments. As Norros notes, this is unsurprising, given that neither the DCFR nor the PECL is binding in any jurisdiction but represent scholarly proposals for potential transnational rules.[23] Overall, their influence on Finnish contract law has been limited – for instance, the Finnish Supreme Court has cited them only twice in over two decades, despite their conceptual similarity to Finnish contract law.[24] While they provide useful principles, national contract law remains the primary framework for most contractual relationships.

B. Finnish Contract Law

Finnish contract law embraces the principle of freedom of form, which serves as a foundational starting point for contracts. However, freedom of form may be restricted by various formal requirements. Formalities are traditionally divided into i) actual, ii) informal, and iii) instructional form requirements.[25] The question of the actual form requirement arises, for example, in chapter two, section one Finnish Real Estate Act (540/1995),[26] which regulates the form requirement for the sale of real estate. Failure to comply with it renders the contract null and void.[27] Failure to comply with an informal requirement has an immediate legal effect other than the invalidity of the act. Pursuant to section three Finnish Food Market Act (1121/2018), a contract concerning the supply of agricultural products from a producer to a medium-sized or large food industry or wholesale or retail enterprise shall be concluded in writing. Failure to comply with this informal requirement does not result in the nullity of the contract but in a reprimand or public warning by the Finnish Food Authority. The provision requiring the lease of a commercial apartment to be in writing is an example of an instructional form requirement. If the lease agreement is not in writing, it is considered valid for an indefinite period (Finnish Act on Commercial

[23] O Norros, 'Keskustelua ratkaisusta KKO 2019:13' (2020) 118 *Lakimies* 123, 129.

[24] Norros 'Sopimusoikeudellisten periaatekokoelmien oikeuslähdearvo' (n 22); Wilhelmsson (n 22); KKO 2015:26, ECLI:FI:KKO:2015:26; KKO 2018:37, ECLI:FI:KKO:2018:37.

[25] PJ Muukkonen, *Muotosäännökset: Varallisuusoikeudellisia sopimuksia koskeva tutkimus* (Helsinki, Suomalainen lakimiesyhdistys, 1958) 79–80.

[26] The Finnish statutes (acts and decrees) are published in the Statute Book of Finland. Each statute is assigned a unique number, which consists of the statute's number and the year it was issued. When referring to Finnish statutes, this number is used to identify the statute, since the Statute Book of Finland does not have similar series and issue numbers like the Official Journal of the European Union. Both the original and consolidated versions of the statutes are available for review in Finnish and Swedish on Finlex, the electronic database of Finnish legislation <www.finlex.fi/en/>. Finlex also contains unofficial translations of statutes into various languages, mainly English.

[27] For the contract to be binding it shall be concluded in writing, the seller and the buyer or their attorneys shall sign the deed of sale, a notary shall attest the sale in the presence of all the signatories of the deed of sale and the deed of sale shall indicate: (1) the intent to convey; (2) the real estate to be conveyed; (3) the seller and the buyer; and (4) the price or other consideration. The actual form requirements are also quite common in family and inheritance law, see J Kaisto, *Oikeustoimiopin perusteet* (Helsinki, Kauppakamari, 2015) 230–31.

Leases 482/1995).[28] Non-compliance with instructional requirements does not, in itself, carry substantive legal consequences, but it may serve as evidence of a contractual breach or the parties' intent.[29]

The most common form requirement in Finnish contract law is that the contract must be in writing. Unlike the DCFR (DCFR 1–1:106), Finnish law does not contain a provision defining in general terms what the requirement of 'in writing' means.[30] The Finnish Act on Public Procurement and Concession Contracts (1397/2016) also requires contracts to be in writing.[31] The requirement of a written form usually also means that the contract is not binding unless the contract document is signed. From a systematic perspective, it is important to distinguish between the written form requirement and the signature requirement, even though they often appear together in practice. In contractual contexts, when the law requires a written form, the signature is generally considered an integral part of fulfilling that requirement.[32] However, a written form requirement does not necessarily mean the contract must be physically signed.[33] According to Section 181 Finnish Act on Electronic Communications Services (917/2014):

> If a contract must be concluded in writing according to the law, this requirement is also met by an electronic contract with contents that cannot be unilaterally altered, and which remain accessible to the parties. If a contract must be signed according to the law, separate provisions on electronic signatures shall be applied. The provisions of this subsection shall correspondingly apply to notifications and other measures by the parties relating to the contractual relation, which must be in writing or signed.[34]

The separation of the written form and the signature requirement can be justified by the fact that in certain form requirements, the signature is explicitly mentioned

[28] However, written form does not require a signature according to the government proposal of the law, see Hallituksen esitys Eduskunnalle uusiksi huoneenvuokralaeiksi ja niihin liittyvien lakien muuttamisesta HE 304/1994 vp, 102.

[29] K Mäenpää, *Sopimuksen syntyminen ja vahingonkorvausvastuu sopimusneuvotteluissa* (Helsinki, Alma Talent, 2022) 235.

[30] Kaisto (n 27) 244. According to s 3(2) Finnish Arbitration Act (967/1992) an arbitration agreement is deemed to be in writing if it is contained in a document signed by the parties or in an exchange of letters between the parties. An arbitration agreement is also deemed to be in writing when the parties, by exchanging telegrams or telex messages or documents produced in another such manner, have agreed that a dispute shall be decided by one or more arbitrators.

[31] Art 2(1)(1) Directive 2014/24/EU and s 4(1)(1) Finnish Act on Public Procurement and Concession Contracts.

[32] Kaisto (n 27) 246.

[33] Unlike the DCFR (DCFR I–1:107), Finnish law does not provide a comprehensive definition of what constitutes a signature.

[34] The provision corresponds to Art 9 Directive 2000/31/EC of the European Parliament and of the Council of 8 June 2000 on certain legal aspects of information society services, in particular electronic commerce, in the Internal Market [2000] OJ L 178/1. See also s 4 Finnish Act on Public Procurement and Concession Contracts where is defined what is meant by 'written' or 'writing': 'Written or in writing shall denote any expression consisting of words or figures which can be read, reproduced and subsequently communicated, including information transmitted and stored by electronic means'.

as a condition of validity.[35] If a written contract always required a signature, there would be no need to specify this separately in cases where the form requirement explicitly includes a signature.[36]

It has traditionally been accepted that an explicit expression of will is not strictly necessary for a contract to be binding; a contract may also arise from the parties' conduct. However, for the contract to be enforceable, the parties must mutually agree to be bound by it and accept its terms.[37] The assessment of whether an implicit agreement exists typically involves a comprehensive evaluation, requiring strong and consistent evidence to support its existence. In contrast, even modest counter-arguments may be sufficient to conclude that no such agreement was formed.[38]

When a contract is not subject to formal requirements, it can be amended in any form. However, when formal requirements exist, modifications should generally follow the same form as the original contract, unless both parties demonstrably intended to modify the contract regardless of initial form requirements.[39]

Issues concerning the tacit prolongation of contracts should be distinguished from those involving the original formation of a tacit contract, even though both rely on interpreting the parties' conduct and other externally observable facts. In cases of tacit continuation, the key question is whether the original contract is being silently extended or whether a completely new contract is being tacitly concluded.[40]

III. Formal Requirements and Contract Modifications under Directive 2014/24/EU

Pursuant to Article 2(1)(1) Directive 2014/24/EU, public contracts are defined as:

> contracts for pecuniary interest concluded in writing between one or more economic operators and one or more contracting authorities and having as their object the execution of works, the supply of products or the provision of services.

[35] See ch 2 s 1(1): Finnish Code of Real Estate: A sale of real estate shall be concluded in writing. The seller and the buyer or their attorneys shall sign the deed of sale. A notary shall attest the sale in the presence of all the signatories of the deed of sale.

[36] Kaisto (n 27) 244–46; Mäenpää (n 29) 238.

[37] Hemmo, *Sopimusoikeus II* (n 5) 175.

[38] M Hemmo, *Sopimusoikeus I* (Helsinki, Talentum, 2003) 136.

[39] Some contracts may have terms and conditions that are often subject to change. In such special situations, it may be appropriate to compromise on the form requirements, Hemmo, *Sopimusoikeus II* (n 5) 40–41. In general, the formal requirement for concluding a contract also determines the manner in which material changes to the contract must be made. However, scholarship suggests that a formal contract may be amended or supplemented, eg orally, if the amendment is insignificant in relation to the overall agreement. It is also possible that a single term agreed upon in breach of formal requirements may be unenforceable, but this will not affect the validity of the remainder of the transaction. See Hemmo, *Sopimusoikeus I* (n 38) 190–91.

[40] Hemmo, *Sopimusoikeus II* (n 5) 177.

Article 2(1)(18) stipulates that 'written' or 'in writing' means:

> any expression consisting of words or figures which can be read, reproduced and subsequently communicated, including information transmitted and stored by electronic means.

Although the definition of public contract has remained the same since Directive 71/305/EEC,[41] the requirement that the public contract cannot be concluded by informing the winning tenderer of the acceptance of its bid is based on the case law of the CJEU. In practice, this often means the conclusion of a separate contract document at a later stage. The CJEU found in *Alcatel* that there must be a sufficient period between the decision awarding a public contract and the conclusion of the public contract, so that the tenderers have a real chance of an effective review procedure.[42] For this reason, the public contract is not concluded at the moment when the winning tenderer receives notification of the acceptance of its offer, as is usually the case in contract law. In other words, the private law is applied to public contracts but is precluded by the requirement of effective remedies under Directive 89/665/EEC. Thus, a public contract cannot become binding before the standstill period has expired, in accordance with the effectiveness requirements set out in *lex specialis*, that is, EU public procurement law. However, in some jurisdictions, the acceptance of an offer may still give rise to certain obligations under general contract law – provided that the acceptance does not include a reservation that the contract will only be concluded upon the signing of a separate written agreement. This was the case in Finland prior to specific rules on the contract's conclusion. In the past, the simultaneous application of public procurement law and contract law led to paradoxical outcomes for contracting authorities – for example, a procurement decision could be annulled by a procurement court, while damages were still awarded in civil proceedings for loss of contract. Consequently, a provision was added to the Finnish Act on Public Procurement and Concession Contracts stating that a binding contract is concluded only by signing a separate written agreement.[43]

Correspondingly, there were no provisions on material contract changes before the CJEU had taken a position on the matter. The CJEU ruled in *Pressetext* that amendments to the provisions of a public contract during the contract term constitute a new award of a contract when they are materially different in character from the original contract and, therefore, such as to demonstrate the intention of the parties to renegotiate the essential terms of that contract.[44] Like the requirement of the written form, this interpretation was also

[41] Council Directive 71/305/EEC of 26 July 1971 concerning the co-ordination of procedures for the award of public works contracts [1971] OJ L 185/5.

[42] Case C-81/98 *Alcatel Austria AG and Others, Siemens AG Österreich and Sag-Schrack Anlagentechnik AG v Bundesministerium für Wissenschaft und Verkehr* ECLI:EU:C:1999:534, [1999] ECR I-07671.

[43] S 128 Finnish Act on Public Procurement and Concession Contracts.

[44] Case C-454/06 *pressetext* (n 1) para 34. See also Case C-496/99 P *Suchhi di Frutta* (n 1) para 125; Case C-161/13 *Idrodinamica Spurgo Velox and Others* ECLI:EU:C:2014:307, [2014] paras 39 and 47.

intended to protect other economic operators by ensuring their equal treatment and transparency of procedures. The prohibition of substantial modifications applies not only to the contract period but also to changes made to the tender documents during the procurement procedure.[45] For this reason, it is equally forbidden to sign a substantially different contract than what was mentioned in the call for tenders.[46]

Directive 2014/24/EU sought to clarify the conditions under which modifications to a public contract during its performance necessitate a new procurement procedure.[47] The list of material changes largely reflects the criteria previously established by the CJEU in *Pressetext*.[48] Pursuant to Article 72(4) Directive 2014/24/EU, a change is always considered substantial if it renders the public contract materially different in character from the one initially concluded, the public contract is significantly different from before, the change expands the scope of the contract, the public contract becomes more economically advantageous for the contractor, the contract partner changes, or if the change introduces conditions that could have had an influence on the outcome of the procurement procedure or which tenderers participated in the procedure.

Since contracting authorities may encounter unforeseen circumstances that justify modifying the original contract without launching a new procurement procedure.[49] Articles 72(1) and 72(2) Directive 2014/24/EU outline the permitted modifications, including minor (*de minimis*) changes, along with the specific conditions under which they are allowed.[50] Primarily, these conditions aim to prevent situations where changing the supplier would lead to incompatibility or disproportionate technical difficulties in operation and maintenance.[51] In addition, the provisions were designed to offer contracting authorities a degree of flexibility and to enhance legal certainty – not only for the authorities themselves but also for their contracting partners.[52]

[45] See KM Halonen, 'Fundamentals of Contract Modifications in EU Procurement Rules' in D Dragos et al (eds), *Contract Changes: The Dark Side of EU Procurement Law* (Cheltenham, Edward Elgar Publishing, 2023) 17, 24–25; Case C-298/15 *UAB 'Borta' v VĮ Klaipėdos valstybinio jūrų uosto direkcija* ECLI:EU:2017:266, [2017] paras 68–70.

[46] In Finnish case law, the Market Court was to assess in case MAO 11/17 whether a substantial modification had been made to the content of the procurement specified in the tender documents, and whether it was a question of such a significant reduction of the scope of the procurement that other than the original bidders would also have been able to participate in the procurement. The Market Court referred to the case law of the CJEU in this regard: Case C-454/06 *pressetext* (n 1) and Case C-549/14 *Finn Frogne A/S v Rigspolitiet ved Center for Beredskabskommunikation* ECLI:EU:C:2016:634, [2016]. The Market Court found that the scope of the procurement had only slightly reduced and dismissed the appeal.

[47] Recital 107 Directive 2014/24/EU.

[48] Case C-454/06 *pressetext* (n 1) paras 35–37 and 47.

[49] See more ch 9.

[50] Recitals 108 and 109 Directive 2014/24/EU.

[51] ibid Recital 108.

[52] ibid Recital 107.

A. *Obshtina Razgrad* and its Implications

Although Directive 2014/24/EU sets the previously described form requirement for a public contract, it does not take an explicit position on whether modifications to the public contract must also be made in writing. Fortunately, the question has recently been addressed in the case law of the CJEU.[53] Joined cases *Obshtina Razgrad and Obshtina Balchik*, concerned the works of two Bulgarian municipalities, Razgrad and Balchik.[54] The works contracts included provisions setting a maximum duration and a deadline for completion. However, due to weather conditions and other factors, the projects were delayed. The cases differ in that, in Razgrad, the parties agreed to an addendum extending the completion date, but the document was never signed. In contrast, in Balchik, the deadline was extended through the parties' implied conduct.[55] In both cases, the municipalities chose not to exercise their contractual rights to claim liquidated damages or other compensation for the delay.[56]

In both cases, the Bulgarian court's first two questions asked whether Article 72(1)(e) and (4) Directive 2014/24/EU should be interpreted to mean that, for a modification to a public contract to qualify as 'significant' under Directive 2014/24/EU,[57] the parties must have signed a written amendment, or whether it is sufficient for there to be other written evidence from the parties demonstrating a mutual intention to modify the contract.[58]

In its judgment, the CJEU reiterated the written form requirements for contracts and other procurement documents under Directive 2014/24/EU while also noting that Article 72 does not impose specific formal requirements for public contract amendments. Pursuant to Recital 58 Directive 2014/24/EU:

> [w]hile essential elements of a procurement procedure such as the procurement documents, requests for participation, confirmation of interest and tenders should always be made in writing, oral communication with economic operators should otherwise continue to be possible, provided that its content is documented to a sufficient degree.

The Court also emphasised that requiring a specific signed amendment for a modification to be deemed significant would risk undermining Directive 2014/24/EU and its effectiveness *(effet utile)*, potentially enabling its circumvention.[59] Referring to Recital 107 Directive 2014/24/EU and its prior case law, the CJEU explained

[53] See more ch 6.

[54] Joined cases C-441/22 and C-443/22 *Obsthina Razgrad* (n 9).

[55] ibid para 32.

[56] ibid paras 16–20 and 28–30. In the case of the municipality of Razgrad, the contract was delayed by approximately eight months, while in Balchik, the original 45-day completion period was extended to 250 days.

[57] If the modification is not substantial, the contract may be amended without the need to initiate a new procurement procedure.

[58] Joined cases C-441/22 and C-443/22 *Obsthina Razgrad* (n 9) paras 26, 35, and 55.

[59] ibid paras 58 and 62.

that a modification qualifies as significant if it demonstrates the parties' intent to renegotiate essential terms or conditions of the public contract.[60] Importantly, the Court clarified that this intent does not need to be demonstrated through a formal written amendment explicitly referencing the change. Instead, it may be inferred from other written exchanges or communications between the parties.[61] On that basis, the Court concluded that a contract modification can be deemed material even without a signed amendment, provided there is evidence – written or otherwise – of a shared intention to alter the contractual terms.[62] Although the CJEU did not directly address formal requirements for contract modifications, its reasoning suggests that what matters is the demonstrable intent to renegotiate. While written evidence may serve this purpose, other forms of proof are not categorically excluded.

It is worth noting that the Bulgarian court had naturally framed its preliminary questions in a way that ensured the CJEU's responses would be relevant to resolving the specific cases at hand, given their factual context. In both instances, the parties' intentions to modify the contracts were evident from written communications. As a result, the CJEU did not need to consider situations where no written elements were present. Consequently, its judgment does not address all possible scenarios involving tacit contract modifications.

It is, nevertheless, unfortunate that the CJEU did not take the opportunity to explicitly address all the questions referred to it. In both cases, the Bulgarian court had asked whether extending the contractual deadline could be regarded as a form of incomplete performance, to which Article 72 Directive 2014/24/EU would not apply – even though such a modification might otherwise qualify as a substantial change under paragraph 4 of that article. The CJEU considered it unnecessary to respond to these questions in light of the answers it had already provided.[63] Still, it would have been helpful if the Court had offered an obiter dictum clarifying whether, in certain circumstances, deviations from the original terms might constitute mere improper performance rather than a formal contract modification.

B. Distinguishing between Public Contract Modification and Non-compliance

The nuanced distinction between unlawful public contract modification and non-compliance has received limited attention in legal literature. Klingler and Telles explore this issue from a comparative perspective, noting that in some jurisdictions – such as the Netherlands, Finland, and Denmark – non-compliance

[60] ibid para 63.
[61] ibid para 64.
[62] ibid para 65.
[63] ibid paras 49 and 74.

may itself be treated as a contract modification.[64] Dutch case law, in particular, has established that non-compliance amounts to an illegal modification when the contracting authority fails to act against a non-compliant contractor and the contractor supplies non-conforming goods.[65]

Based on *Obshtina Razgrad*, it appears that a 'pure tacit change' – that is, a modification lacking any written or even oral evidence from which the parties' intent to renegotiate can be inferred – does not qualify as a material modification under Directive 2014/24/EU. If a tacit change to a public contract does not qualify as a modification within the meaning of Directive 2014/24/EU, it is likely that the rules governing permissible modifications would not apply. Instead, such changes may be treated as entirely new contracts – effectively independent direct awards. In that case, their legality would presumably be assessed against the criteria established for direct awards. By contrast, a negotiated procedure without prior publication involves explicit negotiations between the parties and typically reflects a shared intention to enter into a public contract.

In conclusion, two key requirements appear to govern the form of contract modifications. First, there must be a mutual intention by both parties to amend the contract. Second, this intention must be evidenced – either in writing or through other forms of communication between the parties. However, it is submitted that a substantial modification under Article 72 Directive 2014/24/EU may also arise through oral agreement or implied conduct, provided that the shared intent to modify the contract can be otherwise established, for example, through the conduct of the parties.[66]

Although contract modifications generally require mutual agreement between the contracting parties, the possibility of a unilateral act resulting in a substantial change cannot be entirely excluded. In *Simonsen & Weel*, which the CJEU referenced in *Obshtina Razgrad*, the Court did not adopt an absolute position but stated that by *definition*, such a modification is consensual and, therefore, requires the agreement of the successful tenderer.[67] Similarly, in *Succhi di Frutta* – widely regarded as the starting point of the CJEU's case law on contract modifications – the Court held that a contracting authority may not unilaterally alter the general scheme of the invitation to tender by subsequently amending an essential condition of the award.[68]

[64] D Klingler and P Telles, 'Non-compliance with Government Contract Terms: A Comparative View on Procurement Regulation and Contractual Remedies' in D Dragos et al (eds), *Contract Changes: The Dark Side of EU Procurement Law* (Cheltenham, Edward Elgar Publishing, 2023) 52–53.

[65] E Plas and WA Janssen, 'Contract Modifications in the Netherlands' in D Dragos et al (eds), *Contract Changes: The Dark Side of EU Procurement Law* (Cheltenham, Edward Elgar Publishing, 2023) 239.

[66] A Brown, 'Clarification of Article 72 of Directive 2014/24 on modifications to an existing contract: Joined cases C-441/22 and C-443/22' (2024) 2 *Public Procurement Law Review* 2, 6.

[67] Case C-23/20 *Simonsen & Weel A/S v Region Nordjylland og Region Syddanmark* ECLI:EU:C:2021:490, [2021] para 70.

[68] Case C-496/99 P *Succhi di Frutta* (n 1) para 116. It is noteworthy that the third scenario described above in s V.B, where the contracting authority is aware of the breach or deviation but (unilaterally)

This line of reasoning was further clarified in *Finn Frogne*, where the CJEU stated that the deliberate intention of the parties to renegotiate is not, in itself, a decisive factor. Rather, the determination of whether a material amendment has occurred must be assessed objectively.[69]

Accordingly, the legal nature of a modification remains somewhat ambiguous and is subject to a case-by-case analysis of all relevant circumstances. While an explicit and deliberate agreement by both parties is not always required, there must nevertheless be some evidence of mutual intent. Notably, where the contract includes specific provisions governing the form of amendments, the threshold for satisfying these requirements is likely to be higher.

IV. National Rules and Case Law on the Formal Requirements of Public Contract Modifications

In this section, specific issues and aspects that have been addressed in national case law will be covered. Due to the authors' background, the focus is particularly on Finnish case law, but the section also includes examples from Estonia, the Netherlands, Norway, and the UK. From a national procurement rules point of view, there are no formal requirements for contract modifications under the Finnish Act on Public Procurement and Concession Contracts. Similarly to Directive 2014/24/EU, the public contract itself is defined as a written document (section four). Pursuant to Section 128, a public contract must be concluded after an award decision.

A. Tacit Modification and the Distinction between Modification and Breach in Finnish Case Law

Formal requirements have received limited attention in Finnish case law. While the issue of tacit contract modification had already been brought before the

decides not to react to it, can result in a significant advantage for the supplier in future tender procedures as well. This is because such inaction prevents the grounds for exclusion under Art 57(4)(g) Directive 2014/24/EU from arising, as no sanctions are applied. Nevertheless, malperformance may still constitute grave professional misconduct under Art 57(4)(c).

[69] C-549/14 *Finn Frogne* (n 46) para 33. Although from the perspective of tacit contract modifications, the issue may not be as relevant, we submit it cannot be ruled out that the contracting authority could unilaterally make a substantial change to a public contract as referred to in the procurement rules. An example of this is a situation where the original contract covers multiple services (without a minimum purchase obligation, as is customary in public contracts), and the supplier uses equipment owned by the contracting authority to provide one of these services. However, the contracting authority decides to retender only this service and demands the return of the equipment it owns. The supplier may have priced their offer in such a way that the best margin comes precisely from this service. Therefore, returning the equipment would substantially alter the agreement to the supplier's disadvantage, and this cannot occur by mutual consent of the parties.

Market Court prior to the CJEU's *Obshtina Razgrad* in December 2023, the court has not yet addressed such cases with reference to that judgment. Nevertheless, several rulings by the Market Court have addressed factual scenarios that raise the question of whether deviations from the original public contract amount to tacit modifications or should instead be understood as breaches of contract.[70] The decisive factor in these cases has often been how the contracting authority responded to the deviation – particularly whether it accepted the altered performance or acted to enforce the original terms.

A clear example of tacit modification can be found in MAO 469/18. In this matter, the contracting authority and its contractor neither drafted a specific document concerning the additional purchases nor amended the original public contract in writing, as required by the contract terms. Nevertheless, products not covered by the original agreement were regularly purchased.[71] The contracting authority acknowledged ordering additional products but argued that these were covered by the original contract and thus there was no modification. Consequently, unlike in *Obshtina Razgrad*, the Market Court proceedings did not focus on evaluating what type of evidence would have been necessary to prove that a modification took place. The Market Court did not explicitly address the issue of formal modification requirements; instead, it found that the purchases were not included in the original contract, that they amounted to a material modification, and that the public contract had been de facto amended. As a result, the Market Court declared the contract ineffective. In reaching this conclusion, the court relied on written evidence of the parties' conduct, following a similar logic to that later was adopted by the CJEU in *Obshtina Razgrad*.

In contrast, a line of Finnish cases demonstrates the Market Court's reluctance to treat deviations as tacit modifications where the contracting authority actively worked to uphold the original terms of the public contract. In MAO 603/18, the contracting authority entered into a public contract with a supplier despite the supplier's failure to submit a required list of buses prior to signing, as stipulated in the call for tenders. During the public contract period, the contracting authority was alerted – via an email from a competitor – that the supplier's buses did not comply with the original technical requirements. In response, the contracting authority took steps to bring the buses into compliance. The Market Court held that the contracting authority had not, at any point, waived the technical requirements or otherwise accepted non-compliance. Accordingly, the court concluded that the contracting authority's conduct did not constitute an unlawful direct award, nor did it amount to unequal treatment of bidders.[72]

[70] MAO 854/17; MAO 603/18; MAO H275/2022; and MAO 44/2023.

[71] MAO 469/18. In Finland, the well-established identification details of decisions from the highest courts (the Supreme Court and the Supreme Administrative Court) and special courts (such as the Market Court) consist of the court's abbreviation, the case number, and the year. This case law is available in Finnish on Finlex (n 26).

[72] For some reason, the case was not assessed from the perspective of contract modifications at all.

A similar outcome was reached in MAO H275/2022, where the supplier proposed changes to the minimum bus requirements specified in the call for tenders via email to the contracting authority.[73] This proposal was submitted after the public contract had been signed but before its execution began. The contracting authority responded by stating that it accepted the proposed changes. However, the supplier ultimately acquired a bus that met the original requirements, which was put into service two months after the public contract commenced. The contracting authority imposed a contractual penalty for the two-month period during which the bus did not comply with the initial specifications. The Market Court reached a conclusion similar to that in the previously discussed case, holding that the contracting authority had not *definitively* waived the original requirements. Although the contracting authority acknowledged that it had initially approved the proposed change in error, the court found that the contract had not been substantially modified.

In MAO 44/2023, the buses supplied did not meet the technical specifications outlined in the procurement documents.[74] The contracting authority responded by repeatedly notifying the contractor of the deficiencies, issuing complaints, and imposing contractual sanctions as provided for in the public contract. It also warned the contractor of the potential termination of the public contract. The Market Court held that these actions demonstrated the contracting authority had not de facto[75] accepted the deviations, and thus, the situation constituted a breach rather than a modification of the contract.

In MAO 854/17, the appellant claimed that the contracting authority had waived several contractual requirements after the construction project had commenced, thereby altering the content of the procurement.[76] However, based on the evidence presented, the Market Court found that the authority had de facto objected to the use of incorrect machinery, prompting its replacement with compliant equipment. As a result, the court concluded that the parties had not renegotiated the terms of the contract.

In each of these cases, the Market Court focused on whether there was a mutual intention to alter the public contract. Where the contracting authority actively resisted the deviation and sought to enforce the original terms, the court consistently found that no modification had occurred. Instead, the circumstances were treated as breaches of contract, not tacit amendments.

The Finnish Market Court's approach to determining whether a contracting authority has definitively waived a requirement appears to align with the position in Finnish private law literature. According to Hemmo, such situations may involve a tacit waiver of a right – considered a unilateral legal act – rather than a

[73] MAO H275/2022.

[74] MAO 44/2023.

[75] The Market Court again chose this wording, even though the appellant and the contracting authority had used the expression tacit modification of the contract in their arguments.

[76] MAO 854/17.

tacit contract modification.[77] He emphasises that a contract should not be deemed modified solely due to continuous non-compliant behaviour. While a party may lose the right to invoke past breaches, it can still require future compliance with the contract. In such cases, the other party cannot reasonably claim that the contract has been altered to permit previously non-compliant conduct.

B. Comparative Perspective: Dutch Case Law

Similar reasoning can be observed in Dutch jurisprudence.[78] In a case involving translation services, the supplier failed to meet key performance indicators during the contract period, prompting the contracting authority to intervene.[79] Although the deficiencies were not fully corrected, and the contract was not terminated, the authority engaged in discussions to bring the service in line with contractual obligations. Ultimately, the public contract was not deemed to have been substantially modified. A similar conclusion was reached in another Dutch case, where a supplier used second-hand materials instead of new ones for a period of several months.[80] Given the long duration of the contract – a 15-year concession – this deviation was not considered substantial. In a third Dutch case concerning an IT procurement, the court examined whether extending a fixed completion deadline constituted a material modification.[81] The Dutch court held that the mere expiration of a contractually agreed deadline – even a so-called 'hard deadline' – did not alter the nature or scope of the contract. Rather, the supplier's delay amounted to a breach of contractual performance, not a modification. However, the CJEU's ruling in *Obshtina Razgrad* might suggest a different interpretation. In that case, the actual duration of works nearly doubled compared to the original public contract, whereas the Dutch IT project had a five-month deadline and was expected to be delayed by approximately six months.

C. Meeting of Minds: Estonian and Norwegian Perspectives

Simovart and Sõrm have described Estonian case law as emphasising that non-compliant performance of a public contract alone does not amount to a contract modification; rather, a mutual intention of the contracting parties – whether

[77] Hemmo, *Sopimusoikeus II* (n 5) 36–37 and 133–34.

[78] Dutch case law has also addressed the question of when a breach of contract amounts to a substantial modification. For the analysis of the so-called de-icing salt tetralogy (ECLI:NL:RBDHA:2017:15465; ECLI:NL:RBDHA:2018:4940; ECLI:NL:RBDHA:2018:10933 and ECLI:NL:RBDHA:2019:54), see Plas and Janssen (n 65) 239–40.

[79] ECLI:NL:RBDHA:2024:6426. As a procedural side note, the Dutch court stated that a mere threat that a substantial modification could occur was not considered an annullable matter.

[80] ECLI:NL:RBLIM:2021:8493.

[81] ECLI:NL:RBMNE:2024:457.

explicit or implicit – is required.[82] This conclusion is based on two cases decided prior to the CJEU's ruling in *Obshtina Razgrad*.

In the first case, the contracting authority and the supplier had agreed to expand the scope of a concession contract within the 10 per cent *de minimis* threshold.[83] However, the supplier went beyond the agreed terms by providing services across a wider area and offering services not included in the public contract – services that had been part of the successful bid by the complainant in the original procurement. The court found that the contracting authority had not accepted these deviations but had instead requested that they be corrected. As a result, even implicit consent was deemed absent, and the contract was not considered to have been modified.[84]

In the second case, the contracting authority failed to require a guarantee (ex post) from the contractor – an obligation clearly stipulated in the tender documents.[85] While the court of first instance viewed this omission as a substantial modification of the public contract, the decision was overturned on appeal. The appellate court found no evidence of an intention by the parties to modify the contract. It emphasised that, under Estonian private contract law, an expression of intent cannot result from mere negligence; even silence or inaction must reflect a deliberate and conscious decision.

Although the discussion above clearly supports the notion that a mutual intent is required for a contract modification to occur, national case law has also produced contrary interpretations. Notably, the Norwegian Public Procurement Complaints Board has held that a contracting authority's failure to enforce a contract may constitute a substantial modification.[86] In a case concerning waste collection and transportation services, there was no indication that the parties had agreed to waive the Euro-standard requirement. On the contrary, the contracting authority had expressly required compliance. Nonetheless, the supplier was allowed to continue non-compliant operations for a significant portion of the contract period without consequence. The Norwegian Public Procurement Complaints Board considered this situation tantamount to an unlawful direct award.[87]

In its reasoning, the Norwegian Public Procurement Complaints Board cited Arrowsmith's view that failure to enforce contractual terms may amount to a substantial contract modification.[88] Arrowsmith, in turn, had referred to an English case where the judge acknowledged that deliberate condoning of non-compliance

[82] M Simovart and M Sõrm, '10 Years of Changing Contracts: For Better or For Worse?' (2024) 3 *Upphandlingsrättslig Tidskrift* 215, 218–21.

[83] Tln HK o 3-19-304.

[84] ibid paras 23–27.

[85] Tln RK o 3-21-1711 paras 14–15.

[86] Complaints Board for Public Procurement case 2015/27 of 30 June 2015.

[87] ibid paras 25–43.

[88] S Arrowsmith, *The Law of Public and Utilities Procurement: Regulation in the EU and UK*, Volume 1, 3rd edn (London, Sweet & Maxwell, 2014) 591. The Norwegian Public Procurement Complaints Board also referenced Treumer's commentary on a Danish case. See S Treumer, 'Regulation of Contract Changes Leading to a Duty to Retender the Contract: The European Commission's proposals of December 2011' (2012) 5 *Public Procurement Law Review* 153.

could constitute a contract modification – though this was not ultimately found to be the case in that instance.[89]

D. Contractual Sanctions: Contracting Authority's Right or Supplier's Obligation?

In MAO 184/2023, the procurement documents granted the contracting authority the right to either refrain from signing the contract if the winning bidder failed to do so or to terminate the contract if the contractor did not commence operations at the agreed start date.[90] The termination clause included a provision obligating the supplier to pay damages to the contracting authority. According to the Finnish Market Court, this clause specifically conferred a *right* on the contracting authority. Since the contracting authority neither refrained from signing the contract nor terminated it, it was not deemed to have amended the contract – as claimed by the appellant – by choosing not to claim damages from the winning bidder.

Had the clause instead imposed a direct obligation on the supplier to pay damages, rather than granting the contracting authority a discretionary right to demand them, the outcome might have differed. In practice, however, even under such a formulation, it would still have been up to the contracting authority to pursue payment from the supplier. Contractually, a distinction may also arise regarding whether the contracting authority has the right to withhold compensation directly from the amount payable to the supplier. Furthermore, it could be argued that failing to claim damages for contractual breaches might constitute unlawful state aid.[91]

V. The Legal Nature of Modifications in the Public Procurement Context

Having examined both private contract law principles and public procurement rules, we can now assess how these legal frameworks interact when it comes to tacit modifications of public contracts. Private contract law generally allows flexibility regarding formal requirements, with both the PECL and the DCFR permitting modifications in forms other than writing when mutually agreed upon

[89] *J Varney & Sons Waste Management Ltd v Hertfordshire County Council* [2010] EWHC 1404 (QB) 210.

[90] MAO 184/2023.

[91] The possibility of State Aid in the context of contract modification was assessed by the European Commission in the London Underground case. However, the Commission concluded that the contracts had not been economically modified in a way that would make them inconsistent with market conditions. See Commission Decision State Aid No N 264/2002 – United Kingdom, *London Underground Public Private Partnership*, Brussels, 2 October 2002 3578 final, especially paras 121–25. See also Arrowsmith (n 88) 303 and 313.

by the contractual parties. This approach reflects the principle that contractual relationships should be governed primarily by the parties' intentions rather than strict formalities.

In the context of public procurement, the CJEU seemed to establish in *Obshtina Razgrad* that in order for an amendment to be considered as a contract modification under Directive 2014/24/EU, there needs to be an intention by both of the contracting parties to renegotiate the terms of the public contract and this intention can be determined through written communication by the parties. Thus, it appears that a tacit modification from which there is no communication between the parties at all appears not to constitute a modification under EU public procurement law. However, in the digital age, most modifications leave some kind of written track and evidence behind, and the discussion on 'pure tacit modifications' may be of a rather theoretical nature.

A. Scenarios of Deviations from the Original Public Contract and their Legal Interpretations

Different deviations from the original public contract may appear. As the wording of individual contracts plays a crucial role, assessing these situations requires a case-by-case approach. However, some general scenarios can be identified, such as those where 1) a contracting authority is not aware of the deviation; 2) a contracting authority is aware of it, has notified the contractor, and possibly applied some contractual sanctions;[92] and 3) a contracting authority is aware of, but decides for one reason or another, not to notify the contractor or to apply contractual sanctions.[93] Based on the rules set out by the CJEU in *Obshtina Razgrad*, the first two situations appear rather clear, as there is no intention from the side of the contracting authority to renegotiate the contract, but rather, the deviation constitutes a breach of contract.

The third situation – where the contracting authority is aware of a breach or deviation but chooses not to respond – is the most ambiguous. Under general contract law principles, the default rule is that contract modifications must follow the same form as the original contract.[94] However, in certain circumstances, a party may reasonably assume that the contract has been tacitly modified if the other party fails to respond to a deviation within a reasonable time.[95]

In the context of public procurement, however, this assumption is less likely to hold. The CJEU's case law suggests that an intention to modify the public contract must be supported by some form of evidence. That said, such evidence may exist

[92] As in the Finnish case law concerning bus service procurements, which was discussed in s IV.A.

[93] In some countries, such as in Poland, contracting authorities are obliged to apply contractual sanctions. See Klingler and Telles (n 64) 50–51.

[94] Hemmo, *Sopimusoikeus II* (n 5) 40–41.

[95] Hemmo, *Sopimusoikeus I* (n 38) 135–37.

in cases where the supplier formally notifies the contracting authority of its intention to deviate from the agreed terms – for example, due to a substantial delay or a necessary operational change – and even seeks the authority's consent but receives no response. In such cases, there is at least a written indication of one party's intent, which may carry evidentiary weight.

It is, therefore, important to distinguish between two types of scenarios: (1) where the contracting authority independently becomes aware of the supplier's non-compliance, and (2) where the supplier proactively informs the authority. In the former, it is at least theoretically possible that the breach results from the supplier's negligence and that the supplier is unaware of the non-compliance. Such unawareness is more plausible in cases involving non-compliance with technical or quality specifications rather than substantial delays, which are typically more apparent to both parties. This distinction might be crucial for determining whether a given situation constitutes a contract modification under EU public procurement law or merely a breach of the original contract terms.

B. The Role of Written Communication in Determining Intent

The interpretation that written evidence is typically required to establish mutual intent seems logical and straightforward. However, it raises important questions regarding situations in which the parties have, in practice, amended the public contract without any corresponding written documentation. Such circumstances may arise, for instance, when a contractor no longer meets the financial or technical criteria specified in the original tender or award documents, and the contracting authority takes no action – perhaps due to a reluctance to terminate the contract or replace the supplier.

In such a scenario, the economic balance of the contract has de facto shifted from its original terms, yet there may be no written evidence indicating an intention to amend the public contract. If this kind of amendment does not satisfy the formal requirements for contract modification under EU public procurement law, could it then be viewed as a new, direct award – one not subject to the same formalities? This poses a fundamental challenge: whether de facto changes without formal acknowledgement might escape proper regulatory scrutiny under the guise of inaction.

Given the broad interpretation of 'written' or 'in writing' under Directive 2014/24/EU, it is reasonable – especially in today's digital age – to question whether parties ever agree on anything significant (such as changes to price, scope, or delivery dates) without leaving some form of written trace.[96] In many instances, the parties' mutual intention can be inferred from such written elements, even if no formal

[96] Art 2(1)(18) Directive 2014/24/EU.

amendment is signed. For example, if a contracting authority places an order with the supplier that falls outside the scope of the original public contract – or after the contract has expired – the presence of mutual intent may still be inferred from written communications. This can be the case even if the supplier does not explicitly confirm the order but instead proceeds to perform the requested service, carry out construction work, or deliver goods. The supplier's conduct, in this context, strongly suggests tacit acceptance of the contracting authority's proposal to modify or extend the contract. Moreover, particularly in construction projects, the parties typically hold regular site meetings during which key agreements and decisions are recorded in meeting minutes. These records often serve as written evidence in the event of a dispute and can, therefore, be relied upon to demonstrate mutual intent regarding any modifications to the public contract. Given their evidentiary function, such documentation can play a crucial role in verifying the existence and content of agreed-upon changes.

An interesting question arises when a supplier unilaterally increases prices – possibly without explicitly notifying the contracting authority – even though the public contract stipulates that prices shall remain fixed throughout its duration. This might occur, for example, at the turn of the year, when businesses commonly adjust their pricing. If the contracting authority proceeds to pay the higher invoices without objection, such conduct may constitute written evidence suggesting that the parties have, by mutual understanding, effectively renegotiated the contract prices.

Based on the case law discussed in this chapter, it appears that written elements evidencing contractual modifications are more readily found in the context of works and goods contracts than in service contracts. One key reason is that deliveries of goods and construction works often have clearly defined deadlines set by the contracting authority. As a result, delays are more easily noticed. These deadlines typically reflect the contracting authority's operational needs – such as requiring a building or goods to be ready by a specific date. For instance, if a school building is not completed by the start of the academic year but only becomes available in the spring term, the contracting authority is unlikely to overlook the delay. In such cases, the authority is also likely to incur additional costs, making it more probable that it will take action in response to the breach rather than remaining passive.

While delays can also occur in service contracts, monitoring compliance is generally more complex. As the bus cases referenced in section IV illustrate, issues often arise not from delays but from a supplier failing to meet non-temporal minimum requirements. Services are frequently provided on a daily basis, making it more difficult for the contracting authority to consistently monitor whether the terms are being fully met. In contrast, in construction projects, the contracting authority typically conducts a handover procedure, during which any non-compliance should be identified. Similarly, defects in delivered goods tend to be noticed upon receipt and use.

By comparison, in the bus case, the primary harm caused by the use of higher-emission vehicles was to the environment, not directly to the contracting authority. This made the breach both less visible and less likely to trigger a contractual response.

C. Obstacles to Judicial Review of Contract Modifications: Insufficient Transparency

One particularly noteworthy aspect of *Obshtina Razgrad* is that the contract modifications were not challenged by the contractors' competitors in the national court. Instead, the case reached the judiciary after a national authority imposed financial corrections of 25 per cent due to delays in contract implementation, and the municipalities involved appealed those decisions.[97] Similar cases have also arisen in Estonia, where court proceedings were triggered by financial corrections imposed by national authorities.[98] This illustrates a broader issue: Competitors often face significant challenges in obtaining sufficient evidence to contest contract modifications. These difficulties stem from several factors, including the absence of open contract registers in many countries, limited transparency, and the protection of trade secrets. It is, therefore, possible that a case such as *Obshtina Razgrad* might never have reached a national court – let alone the CJEU – had an external authority not conducted an audit of the municipalities' activities.[99] This is especially true in situations where the contract in question has already been fully executed, leaving competitors with little to gain – if anything – from pursuing an appeal.

VI. Conclusion

The relationship between private contract law and public procurement rules is often ambiguous – particularly when it comes to how contract law influences the interpretation, form, and modification of public contracts.[100] In the context of public procurement, however, private contract law is subordinate to the

[97] Joined cases C-441/22 and C-443/22 *Obshtina Razgrad* (n 9) paras 21–22 and 31–32.

[98] Simovart and Sõrm (n 82) 220–21.

[99] In Finland, the Finnish Competition and Consumer Authority (FCCA), which oversees particularly illegal direct awards and unlawful contract modifications, had its deadline to bring a case to the Market Court significantly extended in 2024. Previously, the FCCA had to detect a contract modification within six months (which is the competitors' deadline to file an appeal in such situations), and then it had another six months to submit a sanction proposal to the Market Court. Now the deadlines are 12 months and 12 months. It remains to be seen whether tacit contract modifications will be taken to the Market Court in the future by the FCCA, which, in addition to having a longer period, also has the advantage that trade secrets do not limit its operations. Especially in a situation like the *Obshtina Razgrad* case, where the contract has already been executed, ie the contract has already ended, the contractors' competitors have much less to gain from an appeal, if anything. Correspondingly, in Denmark and Sweden, the competition authorities have a similar monitoring task.

[100] See more ch 4.

lex specialis of public procurement law. Where the application of national private law would undermine the effective enforcement of procurement rules, it is precluded.

Directive 2014/24/EU defines public contracts as written agreements but contains no specific provisions regarding the form of contract modifications. According to general contract law principles and European contract law, such as the PECL and the DCFR, the default rule is that any modifications must meet the same formal requirements as the original contract. Exceptions may be made where it is clearly established that both parties intended to amend the contract by other means. However, when the contract itself sets out specific formal requirements for modifications, the burden of proving mutual intent becomes significantly higher.

In the recent *Obshtina Razgrad* case, the CJEU examined whether a contract modification can be deemed to have occurred in the absence of a formal amendment document. The Court concluded that two key conditions must be met for a change to qualify as a contract modification under public procurement rules. First, there must be a mutual intention by both contracting parties to renegotiate the terms of the contract. Second, this intention can be demonstrated, among other means, through written communication between the parties. Consequently, tacit modifications – those lacking clear or substantial evidence – do not typically amount to a valid contract modification under EU public procurement law. However, in the digital age, most changes generate some form of written trace or documentation, rendering the notion of 'pure' tacit modifications largely theoretical. It is, therefore, more probable that a modification under EU public procurement law will not be recognised either due to the absence of demonstrable mutual intent or because the original contract has not been significantly altered in a way that contravenes Article 72 Directive 2014/24/EU.

The nature of contract modification remains somewhat ambiguous and is typically assessed on a case-by-case basis, taking into account all relevant factors and circumstances. While an explicit expression of intent from both parties may not be strictly required, there must be some evidence indicating mutual agreement. The burden of proof in this regard may be significantly higher if the contract contains specific provisions stipulating that amendments must be made in writing.

Nonetheless, tacit modifications have been accepted in the public procurement context in certain jurisdictions, such as Denmark and Finland.[101] Additionally, national legal frameworks differ in their classification of specific situations – for instance, whether a delay in delivery constitutes non-compliance or a contract modification. A key factor in such assessments is whether the contracting authority's intent – such as the acceptance of late delivery – can be established based on the available evidence. Where mutual intent is lacking, the scenario is

[101] Klingler and Telles (n 64) 52–53.

more accurately characterised as a breach of contract rather than a contractual modification.

These jurisdictional differences, along with the ongoing uncertainties surrounding the influence of private contract law on the interpretation of public contracts, ensure that this topic will remain a subject of academic interest in the years to come. Furthermore, it is reasonable to assume that the CJEU has not yet delivered its final word on the matter. It is likely that the Court will continue to interpret Directive 2014/24/EU in a way that preserves its effectiveness (*effet utile*), ensuring that instances of non-compliance do not undermine Directive 2014/24/EU's objectives.[102] Finally, the ongoing revision of Directive 2014/24/EU may address whether contracting authorities are obliged to impose contractual sanctions – as already required in some Member States – and whether the failure to do so could amount to a substantial modification of the contract.[103]

[102] Joined cases C-441/22 and C-443/22 *Obshtina Razgrad* (n 9) paras 58 and 62.
[103] Klingler and Telles (n 64) 50–51.

9

Applying the Doctrine of Hardship in Public Contracts

MICHAŁ KANIA AND MARTA ANDHOV

I. Introduction: An Old Problem in a New Guise?

In the early twentieth century, the city of Bordeaux, France, entered into a 30-year concession agreement with a private company to supply gas and electricity to a substantial portion of the city.[1] Initially, the contract proceeded smoothly, but this stability was soon disrupted by unforeseen historical events. The assassination of Archduke Franz Ferdinand of Austria on 28 June 1914 triggered World War I, resulting in four years of severe economic turmoil. This upheaval was further intensified by the Spanish flu pandemic, which lasted from 1918 to 1920 and led to significant human and economic losses, with up to 100 million fatalities worldwide. In that era, the combined impact of war and pandemic was almost impossible to foresee, leaving both contractual parties unprepared for the ensuing financial challenges. The crisis led to severe hyperinflation, sharply increasing the cost of essential resources. For example, the price of coal – a critical resource for energy production – rose from around 35 francs to 117 francs per tonne, marking a 250 per cent increase. Facing substantial financial losses, the private company sought to revise the fixed gas prices stipulated in the contract. However, the city of Bordeaux refused, insisting on adherence to the contract's original terms. The case eventually went to court, where the initial ruling was against the company, upholding the principle of *pacta sunt servanda* – 'agreements must be kept'. In the French legal system, this principle requires contracts to be maintained as agreed, irrespective of external changes affecting the parties.[2] Consequently, unless both parties consent to modifications, the

[1] J Bell, S Boyron, and S Whittaker, *Principles of French Law* (Oxford, Oxford University Press, 1998) 199. *Gaz de Bordeaux* is presented solely to illustrate the context in which public contracts may be modified due to unforeseen circumstances such as pandemics and war. This presentation does not aim to analyse the development of French legal solutions concerning hardship under civil law or public procurement law.

[2] KP Berger and D Behn, 'Force Majeure and Hardship in the Age of Corona: A Historical and Comparative Study' (2019) 6(4) *McGill Journal of Dispute Resolution* 76, 117.

original contract terms remain binding, even if it leads to financial hardship or bankruptcy for one party. The company appealed, bringing the case before the French administrative court of last resort, the Conseil d'État. Here, the court faced a dilemma: whether to strictly enforce the *pacta sunt servanda* principle, risking the failure of the concession, or to allow for modifications in light of unforeseen circumstances to safeguard the public interest.[3]

This historical case highlights a tension that remains highly relevant today. Recent economic crises caused by the COVID-19 pandemic and the war in Ukraine have posed similar challenges, significantly impacting public procurement markets across the EU. The pandemic disrupted global supply chains, resulting, for example in sharp price increases for essential medical supplies. Lockdowns and quarantine measures further exacerbated the situation, leading to labour shortages that complicated both procurement processes and contract performance. The war in Ukraine has similarly destabilised markets, particularly in the energy sector, where price fluctuations and supply chain disruptions have affected access to critical resources. In countries like Poland, Hungary, Germany, and Slovakia, the situation was further strained by the outflow of Ukrainian workers called to military service, creating labour shortages that proved especially challenging in labour-intensive sectors like construction and transportation.

The often-conflicting interests of contracting parties, as illustrated by *Gaz de Bordeaux*, have led to a search for solutions, including the doctrine of hardship. This solution seems to be particularly complex in public contracts. Public contracts are concluded in the public interest and funded with taxpayer money, making adherence to agreed terms a matter of public accountability and legal integrity. The *pacta sunt servanda* principle in this context also serves as a safeguard for the equal treatment of bidders, ensuring that procurement processes remain fair and transparent. Allowing modifications based on hardship could, in theory, disrupt the equal footing of bidders, particularly those who were unsuccessful in their bids. However, the unprecedented nature of recent crises has led to calls for flexibility, challenging the notion that the grounds for contract modification outlined in Article 72 Directive 2014/24/EU are exhaustive.[4]

This chapter analyses how EU public procurement law influences the interpretation of contract law in the context of hardship. To achieve this objective, the chapter is structured as follows: Section II introduces the principle of *pacta sunt servanda* in relation to hardship. Section III explores the origins of hardship in national regulations and within European contract law. Section IV examines the

[3] Conseil d'État, *Compagnie générale d'éclairage de Bordeaux*, Rec 125, concl Chardenet, 30 March 1916, quoted in M Long and P Weil, *Les Grands Arrêts de la Jurisprudence Administrative* (2003) 188–89.

[4] On modifications to public contracts during COVID-19, see MA Simovart, 'Unforeseen Circumstances That Justify Changes to Public Contracts' in DC Dragos, KM Halonen, B Neamtu, and S Treumer (eds), *Contract Changes: The Dark Side of EU Public Procurement Law* (Cheltenham, Edward Elgar Publishing, 2023).

conditions under which a public contract may be modified under Article 72(1)(a) and (c) Directive 2014/24/EU. Section V focuses on the application of hardship in public contracts under Danish law, while section VI discusses the Polish approach to this concept. Finally, the concluding section summarises the key findings of the chapter.

Methodologically, this chapter begins by tracing the origins of the doctrine of hardship and its interaction with the principle of *pacta sunt servanda*. The analysis then progresses to an examination of national legal regimes, concluding with a discussion of the regulation of the hardship doctrine within non-binding academic frameworks, specifically, the Principles of European Contract Law (PECL) and the Draft Common Frame of Reference (DCFR). The focus then shifts to EU public procurement law, particularly its approach to contract modifications. For the national-level analysis, the chapter examines Danish and Polish law, drawing upon court cases and legal doctrine in the areas of public procurement and contract law.

II. *Pacta Sunt Servanda*: Stability in the Face of Hardship

Parties seek to protect their economic interests by concluding a written contract, which sets out the terms of their cooperation and establishes a foundation of stability and reliability. This aim is underpinned by one of the fundamental principles of most national contract laws: *pacta sunt servanda*.[5] According to this principle, parties are bound to their commitments, and the courts will uphold their intentions in the event of a dispute.[6] However, questions arise as to whether the *pacta sunt servanda* principle can always be strictly enforced. This issue is particularly pertinent in long-term contracts, which are common in public works or service agreements. Applying the *pacta sunt servanda* principle in these contracts can present practical challenges. Unforeseen circumstances – such as unexpected increases in raw material prices, embargoes, export bans, or sudden currency depreciation – may alter the economic balance to the extent that continued performance of the contract is no longer in the best interests of the economic operator or contracting authority or may even result in undue hardship.

The *pacta sunt servanda* principle in public contracts holds the same meaning as in contract law. However, it takes on particular significance within the public procurement context for several reasons. First, public contracts are established in the public interest, which has two main aspects. The first is fulfilling public needs,

[5] In Anglo-Saxon doctrine, this principle is referred to as the 'principle of sanctity of contract'. G Block, 'Semantics and the Sanctity of Contracts' (1981) 38(3) *A Review of General Semantics* 290, 293.

[6] H Wehberg, 'Pacta Sunt Servanda' (1959) 53(4) *The American Journal of International Law* 775.

such as building infrastructure – bridges, schools, roads, hospitals – delivering essential services, or procuring critical assets like aircrafts or medical equipment. The second relates to the responsible expenditure of limited public funds by the contracting authority. Second, the *pacta sunt servanda* principle serves as a safeguard for the equal treatment and non-discrimination of bidders, a cornerstone of EU public procurement law.[7] Adhering to the terms and conditions specified during the procurement process helps to protect the rights of unsuccessful bidders, ensuring that the awarded contract respects the principles of fairness and transparency. Thus, public contracts must be honoured not only for the benefit of the contracting parties but also to maintain trust and equity in the broader public procurement system. Nevertheless, questions arise regarding the rigidity of the *pacta sunt servanda* principle, especially when rapid and unpredictable changes in economic and social conditions affect the contracting parties. Until recently, events such as pandemics or wars in Europe were considered scenarios that had largely faded into history.

A. Hardship and the *Pacta Sunt Servanda* Principle

Contract law has developed doctrines to protect parties' rights in extraordinary circumstances. These legal mechanisms vary in name across jurisdictions but are most commonly known as the 'hardship doctrine'.[8] Generally, the concept of hardship arises when the performance of a contract, while still feasible, has become excessively burdensome.[9] Hardship may be addressed in a clause agreed upon by the parties within the contract[10] or, in the absence of such a clause, may be invoked under statutory provisions or doctrines designed to address unforeseen events.[11] These concepts are reserved for cases of genuine difficulty arising from

[7] Art 18(1) Directive 2014/24/EU.

[8] The doctrine of hardship appears under different names in national legal orders. For example, in Italy, the doctrine of hardship occurs as *eccessiva onerosità sopravvenuta*, in Denmark as doctrine of failed assumptions, in Germany as *Wegfall der geschaftsgrundlage*, in France, as *imprévision*. J Perillo, 'Force Majeure and Hardship Under the UNIDROIT Principles of International Commercial Contracts' (1997) 5 *Tulane Journal of International and Comparative* 5, 8–9; KP Berger and D Behn (n 2) 115–25.

[9] D Maskow, 'Hardship and Force Majeure' (1992) 40(3) *The American Journal of Comparative Law* 657, 662. The doctrine also highlights the differences between the meaning of a hardship clause and the doctrines of *imprévision* or frustration. Hardship clauses are contractual provisions that define what constitutes hardship within the specific agreement and provide a procedure for adapting the contract should the defined hardship arise. In contrast, hardship doctrines address situations where a fundamental disruption occurs in the economic balance of a contract due to unforeseeable or unforeseen supervening events at the time the contract was concluded. For a comprehensive discussion, see J Gold, *Hardship, Impracticability, Unconscionability, Unforeseeability in Legal Effects of Fluctuating Exchange Rates* (USA, International Monetary Fund, 1990) 226–27.

[10] See Art III–1:110 DCFR and Art 6.111 PECL, as well as s 36 *Aftaleloven* no 193/2016 (Danish Contracts Act) or Art 357(1) *Ustawa z dnia 23 kwietnia 1964 r. – Kodeks cywilny* (Polish Civil Code).

[11] Berger and Behn (n 2) 79, 115.

circumstances that the parties generally could not have anticipated. While hardship may resemble *force majeure*, key distinctions exist. *Force majeure* refers to an unexpected, irreversible event beyond the affected party's control, rendering performance impossible and potentially resulting in the discharge of liability or even termination of the contract.[12] In contrast, hardship is intended to preserve the contractual relationship despite unforeseen challenges. In such cases, the parties are expected to adapt by renegotiating the terms of the contract. Alternatively, if renegotiation fails or has not been undertaken at all, a court may intervene to modify the contract.

Hardship can be interpreted in two ways in relation to the principle of *pacta sunt servanda*. On the one hand, hardship can function as a mechanism for modifying or terminating an obligation between parties, serving as a narrow exception to the principle of *pacta sunt servanda*. On the other hand, hardship can also be applied to preserve the contractual relationship, allowing obligations to continue despite circumstances that might otherwise lead to termination. In most cases, it is in both parties' interests to take this broader approach and maintain the contract, even when unforeseen events disrupt the economic balance. Renegotiating a new agreement can be both lengthy and costly, particularly in contracts involving specialised resources where a replacement partner would be difficult to find. Long-term collaborations also foster cordial, trust-based relationships and valuable knowledge exchanges, which can be challenging to re-establish with a new contractor.[13] Maintaining a contract can, therefore, be achieved through various adaptive measures that prevent premature termination, preserving the investment of time and resources by both parties.[14] The doctrine of hardship, in this regard, offers an appealing solution, especially in the context of public contracts.

The application of hardship in public contracts raises significant questions. The main issue is whether hardship concepts, known in contract law, can serve as an independent basis for modifying public contracts beyond the grounds specified in Article 72 Directive 2014/24/EU or if these concepts are subject to modification based on the regulation contained in Directive 2014/24/EU.

These differing perspectives on the potential role of hardship within public contracts highlight the complexity of balancing contract stability with the need for flexibility in times of crisis. Understanding the origins and treatment of the hardship doctrine across various national legal systems and under European contract law provides valuable insight into its potential application in public contracts. The following section delves into these origins, setting the stage for a deeper exploration of hardship's regulation and adaptability.

[12] ibid 90.

[13] A Frignani, 'Le clausole di hardship' in U Draetta and C Vaccà (eds), *Inadempimento, Adattamento, Arbitrato. Patologie dei Contratti e Rimedi* (Milano, Egea, 1992) 327.

[14] EC Zaccaria, 'The Effects of Changed Circumstances in International Commercial Trade' (2004) 9 *International Trade and Business Law Review* 135, 137.

III. Historical Development of Hardship and its Regulation under National Legislations and European Contract Law

The concept of hardship appears to have evolved in response to various crises.[15] It has played a role in contractual relations for centuries, although its development was largely halted by the great codifications of the nineteenth century, which emphasised the *pacta sunt servanda* principle. Notably, the concept of hardship was absent from major codifications such as the Napoleonic Code of 1804, the Austrian Civil Code of 1811, and the German Civil Code of 1896. However, it persisted in older frameworks like the Bavarian Code of 1756 and the Prussian National Law of 1794.[16] The importance of hardship saw a resurgence during World War I and the subsequent period of hyperinflation, leading to its reintroduction in various legal systems through legislative intervention, judicial decisions – particularly in Austria and Germany – and new codifications.[17] Interest in hardship concepts revived again after World War II, driven by similar post-war economic pressures, and expanded further during the oil crisis of the 1970s.[18] Different countries have developed various approaches to addressing hardship, typically influenced by the origin and impact of extraordinary circumstances on contract performance. While these approaches differ, a common feature across legal systems is the allowance for judicial intervention in cases of severe changes in circumstances, although this is often seen as an exception to the general rule of non-interference in contracts.

A. 'Open' and 'Closed' Legal Systems: Judicial Intervention in Contractual Hardship

A key distinction in national approaches to hardship lies in whether a legal system provides a mechanism for adapting contracts to changed circumstances. Hondius and Grigoleit indicate that, broadly, legal systems can be divided into 'open' and 'closed' categories.[19]

In 'open' systems, with some modifications, there is generally a provision for altering contractual terms in response to hardship. This approach is seen in Germany, Italy, Austria, Greece, Lithuania, Spain, the Netherlands, Portugal,

[15] Maskow (n 9) 659.

[16] A Dragan, 'European Conceptions on Hardship: A Comparative Study on German, English and French Law on Hardship' (2016) 1 *Romanian Journal of Comparative Law* 75, 77–78.

[17] ibid.

[18] M Fontaine and F De Ly, *Drafting International Contracts: An Analysis of Contract Clauses* (Leiden, Brill, 2009) 458.

[19] E Hondius and H Grigoleit, 'Change of Circumstances in European Contract Law – An Approach to the Relevant Issues and Doctrines' in E Hondius and H Grigoleit (eds), *Unexpected Circumstances in European Contract Law* (Cambridge, Cambridge University Press, 2011) 10–12.

Sweden, Poland, Switzerland, Bulgaria, Romania, and the Czech Republic.[20] For example, in Germany, the doctrine of hardship is known as *Wegfall der Geschäftsgrundlage* (disappearance of the basis of the transaction) or *Störung* (disruption). Under this doctrine, when circumstances change fundamentally, undermining the foundation of the contract, parties are no longer bound by their initial commitments.[21]

Similarly, the Italian contract law addresses the concept of excessive onerousness, either direct or indirect, in contractual obligations.[22] Italian case law typically applies a strict interpretation of onerousness, broadly excluding many instances of supervening hardship. However, this strict approach is somewhat relaxed in specific contracts, such as leases, mortgages, and insurance.[23] Despite this, the Italian Supreme Court of Cassation remains reluctant to address 'contractual' contingencies such as those cited above, which are often viewed as part of normal market fluctuations.[24] Remedies in Italian contract law tend to be abrogative or extinguishing, meaning they do not preserve the contract, and when applied broadly, as highlighted during the COVID-19 pandemic, these remedies can harm the overall economic system by causing simultaneous shocks to both supply and demand. In other words, Italian contract law does not clearly support the continuation of contracts through fair modifications to their terms and conditions unless the creditor – the stronger party in the relationship – chooses to explore this option. This lack of provision limits opportunities to prevent the parties from engaging in self-serving behaviour under adverse circumstances.

Belgium is an interesting example of a country that migrated from a closed system to an open one. Belgium's recent reform in Book 5 Belgian Civil Code, effective from 1 January 2023, introduced a formal hardship provision. This reform aims to increase contract law accessibility by incorporating case law and scholarly insights. Prior to this, Belgian law did not formally recognise hardship, except in public procurement.[25] As a general rule, parties were required to fulfil the contract, even if an extraordinary change in circumstances altered the contract's balance beyond their control. Under the new Belgian Civil Code

[20] ibid 11.

[21] Art 313 *Bürgerliches Gesetzbuch* (BGB), RGBl 1896, 195 (German Civil Code) which regulates the doctrine of hardship under German law.

[22] Art 1467 *Codice Civile* adopted with *Regio Decreto 16 marzo 1942*, no 262 (Italian Civil Code) for general provisions on excessive onerousness. R Sacco, 'I rimedi per le sopravvenienze' in R Sacco and G De Nova, *Il contratto*, 3rd edn (Torino, UTET, 2004) 722 ff.

[23] Arts 1623, 1635, 1636, 1664, 1818, 1897, and 1898 Italian Civil Code. E Rimini, 'La protezione del programma negoziale dalle vicende soggettive sofferte dalle parti: tracce di un valore nell'ordinamento' (2021) 4 *Rivista di diritto bancario* 627. The author provides references to the main Italian scholarship about the institute of the *eccessiva onerosità sopravvenuta*.

[24] A Dolmetta, 'Obbligazioni e contratti. Il problema della rinegoziazione (ai tempi del coronavirus)' (2020) *Giustizia Civile* para 9, who, with particular regard to the specific topic of contractual contingencies, indicates the judgment of the Italian Supreme Court and, precisely, Cass. Sez. Un., 19 October 2017, no 24675, in the case of supervening usury in the context of a mortgage contract.

[25] S Van Lock, 'The Introduction of Change of Circumstances (Hardship) in the Belgian Civil Code and Arbitration' (2024) 1 *Belgian Review of Arbitration* 16.

provision, a party can request renegotiation to adapt or terminate a contract if certain conditions are met: (1) the performance of the contract has become excessively onerous due to a change in circumstances; (2) the change results from natural, economic, legal, political, or health-related factors; (3) the change was unforeseeable at the time the contract was made; (4) the change is not attributable to the debtor; (5) the debtor has not assumed the risk, and (6) neither the law nor the contract excludes this possibility.[26] The reform requires parties to continue fulfilling obligations during renegotiations. If renegotiation fails, either party can seek court intervention to modify or terminate the contract. The court has the authority to modify the contract to reflect what the parties would reasonably have agreed upon if they had anticipated the changed circumstances. Alternatively, the court may decide to terminate the contract, in whole or in part, effective from a date not earlier than the change in circumstances, with terms determined by the court.

In contrast, 'closed' systems exclude or strictly limit the possibility of modifying a contract due to hardship. Examples include France, Denmark, Ireland, Slovenia, and Luxembourg.[27] For example, the French Civil Code does not provide specific rules or guidance for situations where the performance of a contract becomes more burdensome due to changed circumstances; French courts are well-known for their strict adherence to the *pacta sunt servanda* principle, allowing a party to be excused from performance only in cases of *force majeure* (superior force), *cas fortuit* (unanticipated event), or *cause étrangère* (external cause).[28] A classic example illustrating the Court of Cassation's strict stance is *Canal de Craponne*.[29] In this case, the parties had entered into a contract in 1567 for garden irrigation services, with a fixed fee that, over the course of 300 years, became insufficient to cover maintenance costs. The Aix Court of Appeals adjusted the fee to reflect the changed economic environment. However, in 1876, the Court of Cassation annulled the decision, citing Article 1134 French Civil Code, which enshrines the *pacta sunt servanda* principle. The court stated that 'Since Article 1134 is a general and absolute provision, it is not for the courts to consider time and circumstances to modify contracts agreed upon by the parties'.[30]

[26] Art 5.74 *Code civil/Burgerlijk Wetboek* of 10 February 1804 (*Moniteur belge / Belgisch Staatsblad* 1804, 187) (Belgian Civil Code).

[27] Hondius and Grigoleit (n 19) 11. However, the application of hardship in practice lacks consistency. In reality, approaches are diverse and complex, as countries within similar legal systems have developed distinct legal attitudes influenced by their unique legal traditions and judicial cultures. See AH Puelinckx, 'Frustration, Hardship, Force Majeure, Imprévision, Wegfall der Geschäftsgrundlage, Unmöglichkeit, Changed Circumstances' (1986) 3(2) *Journal of International Arbitration* 47.

[28] See, eg L Montefusco, 'Interpreting the Conditions for Imprévision: The Goals of the Reform Projects as a Decisive Tool for French and Belgian Courts' (2020) 13 *Journal of Civil Law Studies* 193, 200. *Code civil* <www.legifrance.gouv.fr/codes/texte_lc/LEGITEXT000006070721/> (French Civil Code).

[29] *Case De Gallifet v Commune de Pélissanne* (D. 1876. 1. 193).

[30] I de Lamberterie, 'The Effect of Changes in Circumstances on Long-Term Contracts: French Report' in D Harris and D Tallon (eds), *Contract Law Today: Anglo-French Comparisons* (Oxford, Clarendon Press, 1989) 228–29.

B. Hardship under European Contract Law

Chapter one of this anthology laid the groundwork by discussing the foundations and significance of European contract law within the broader scope of European harmonisation efforts, explaining its role as the basis for analysis throughout the anthology.[31] Building on this framework, this section explores the construction of hardship within European contract law, examining how these frameworks address the concept, its potential applications, and limitations across jurisdictions. This analysis acknowledges both the theoretical possibilities and constraints of applying hardship across European countries while also recognising the non-binding, 'soft law' nature of these sources and the absence of a unified European contract law.

The concept of hardship was first formally regulated in the 1994 UNIDROIT Principles, a landmark effort introducing the possibility of judicial intervention in contract terms without the need for specific hardship clauses.[32] It offered valuable guidance for international practitioners by addressing typical hardship conditions and common contractual challenges.[33] The PECL and the DCFR subsequently expanded on the hardship doctrine to adapt to extraordinary changes in circumstances.[34]

The synthesis of hardship solutions in European contract law generally comprises two key components. The first is a hypothesis outlining the conditions under which hardship may apply. The second is the instruction, specifying the legal consequences and procedures to follow when these conditions are met.[35]

An analysis of European contract law on the circumstances that may activate hardship provisions suggests several conclusions. First, the triggering circumstances must be beyond the parties' control. Second, they must be unforeseeable, encompassing events that the parties could not have reasonably anticipated.[36] Third, European contract law identifies criteria that qualify circumstances as hardship, often citing legal, economic, technical, political, or financial disruptions. Finally, the event must be fundamental or substantial in nature.[37]

The consequences of invoking hardship are intended to restore contractual balance, typically in one of three ways:[38] (1) by addressing the excessive

[31] See ch 1.

[32] Art 6.2.3 UNIDROIT Principles.

[33] Zaccaria (n 14) 170.

[34] Art 6.111 PECL; Art III–1:110 DCFR.

[35] J Rimke, 'Force Majeure and Hardship: Application in International Trade Practice with Specific Regard to the CISG and the UNIDROIT Principles of International Commercial Contract' *CISG Database* (1999) 227.

[36] Art III–1:110(2) DCFR. See Ch Brunner, *Force Majeure and Hardship Under General Contract Principles: Exemption for Non-performance in International Arbitration* (Deventer, Kluwer Law International BV, 2009) 397; Fontaine and De Ly (n 18) 477.

[37] C Schmithoff, 'Hardship and Intervener Clauses' (1980) 1(1) *Journal of Business Law* 415, 418.

[38] Brunner (n 36) 391.

onerousness of one party in contract performance,[39] thereby preventing obligations that would be undue, unfair, or contrary to principles of good faith;[40] (2) by countering the frustration of the contract's original purpose;[41] or (3) by remedying an excessive or substantial imbalance between the parties.[42]

The second part of a hardship provision – the disposition – defines the procedures to follow when hardship is invoked. Several approaches may be taken. First, the provision might require the parties to renegotiate contract terms, compelling them to seek a compromise based on good faith, equity, and loyalty. If a compromise cannot be reached, the future of the contract may come into question.[43] In a subsequent stage, judicial or third-party intervention may be allowed, depending on contractual clauses.[44] A third party, such as an arbitrator, expert, or conciliator, could play various roles, from proposing revised terms to facilitating mediation or adapting the contract to the changed circumstances. Adjustments might involve restoring the contractual balance or, where necessary, terminating the contract.[45]

IV. Modification of Public Contracts in Light of Article 72 Directive 2014/24/EU and the Concept of Hardship

In the context of EU public procurement law, analysing the doctrine of hardship necessitates a review of the provisions governing the modification of public contracts under Directive 2014/24/EU. The modification of public contract is addressed in Article 72 Directive 2014/24/EU, which incorporates principles from the CJEU's ruling in *Pressetext*.[46] Article 72(1)(a) and (c) Directive 2014/24/EU includes provisions akin to contract law solutions on hardship but adapts these to the public procurement context. This raises a key question: in the context of public contracts, does only the adapted version of hardship in Article 72(1)(a) and (c) apply, or can contract law solutions also be fully utilised?

The applicability of the contract law doctrine of hardship to public contracts hinges on two primary questions. First, whether Article 72 provides an exhaustive (closed) list of permissible modifications of public contracts or an exemplary

[39] Art 6:111(2) PECL.

[40] Fontaine and De Ly (n 18) 472.

[41] According to Art 6.2.2 UNIDROIT Principles hardship trigger event is defined in terms of economic effects.

[42] Rimke (n 35).

[43] Fontaine and De Ly (n 18) 472.

[44] Schmithoff (n 37).

[45] Art 6 111(3) PECL; Art III–1.110(2) DCFR.

[46] Case C-454/06 *Pressetext Nachrichtenagentur GmbH v Republik Österreich (Bund)* ECLI:EU:C:2008:351, [2008] ECR 2008 I-04401.

(open) one. Second, concerning judicial intervention, it is important to identify the intended addressees of the legal norm in Article 72(1), particularly in relation to the statement: 'Contracts and framework agreements may be modified'.

Examining the nature of the list in Article 72 is essential. If the list of permissible public contract modifications is considered exhaustive, then the contract law concept of hardship must align strictly with Article 72(1)(a) and (c), indicating that Article 72 also tailors the concept of hardship specifically for public procurement. Conversely, if the list is viewed as open, it could allow for a broader application of the contract law concept of hardship in public contracts under national legal regimes.

Two primary interpretations of the character of the list envisaged in Article 72 have emerged in legal doctrine. The first, supported by scholars like Treumer and Arrowsmith, views Article 72 as codifying existing case law while clarifying certain aspects without being an exhaustive rule set. Treumer refers to the wording of Article 72(5) and indicates that this provision must be interpreted as a statement of principle and, therefore, not as a rule without exception.[47] Arrowsmith shares Treumer's view and points out that this is correct because Article 72 aims to codify the existing case law and clarify some specific aspects of the rules. According to Arrowsmith, it should not be taken as an exhaustive statement of the applicable rules in areas that have not yet been addressed in that case law.[48]

The second interpretation, advanced by Bogdanowicz, takes a restrictive view, asserting that Member States cannot add new grounds for contract modifications beyond those listed in Article 72, establishing a *numerus clausus* of permissible modifications.[49] Also, Brodec and Janeček point out that without a new procurement procedure, substantial modifications to a contract are prohibited unless they comply with the elements specified in Article 72(1)(a) to (d) and Article 72(2).[50]

Advocates of the restrictive view also argue that the language of Article 72(5), which mandates a new procurement procedure for modifications not covered by paragraphs 1 and 2, explicitly indicates through the use of the word 'shall' that a new procedure is required for cases outside these paragraphs. If Article 72 were intended as an open list, it would likely include the phrase 'in particular' in Article 72(1). Furthermore, the EU legislature's specification of permissible modification scenarios is aimed at promoting legal certainty and ensuring clarity in

[47] S Treumer, 'Contract Changes and the Duty to Retender under the New EU Public Procurement Directive' (2014) 3 *Public Procurement Law Review* 148, 148–49; O Hansen, S Treumer, and M Andhov, 'Social Services and Contract Changes: The Legality of Social Service Outsourcing Practices in EU Procurement Law' (2018) 5 *Public Procurement Law Review* 217, 226–27.

[48] S Arrowsmith, *The Law of Public and Utilities Procurement: Regulation in the EU and UK*, vol 1 (London, Sweet & Maxwell, 2014) 602.

[49] P Bogdanowicz, 'Modification of the Public Contracts During Their Term' in R Caranta and A Sanchez-Graells (eds), *European Public Procurement: Commentary on Directive 2014/24/EU* (Cheltenham, Edward Elgar Publishing, 2021) 778.

[50] J Brodec and V Janeček, 'How Does the Substantial Modification of a Public Contract Affect Its Legal Regime?' (2015) 3 *Public Procurement Law Review* 90, 94.

public procurement regulations, as supported by Recital 107 Directive 2014/24/EU, which emphasises the need to clarify conditions for contract modifications during performance in light of the CJEU case law.

The second question concerns the addressees of the legal norm in Article 72(1). The formulation of this provision raises two possible interpretations. The first interpretation confines the addressees of Article 72 to the contracting parties alone. In this context, the public contract may be modified by the parties themselves through negotiation, provided the conditions outlined in Article 72(1)(c) are fulfilled. The second extends the addressees to include any entity capable of modifying the contract's terms, such as courts and arbitral tribunals. Several arguments support this broader interpretation. The first relates to the legislative technique and assumes that Article 72(1) does not explicitly restrict modifications to the contracting parties. If the EU legislature had intended such a limitation, it could have specified that: 'Contracts and framework agreements may be modified *by the contracting authority and the contractor* without a new procurement procedure in accordance with this Directive'.

Second, unlimited judicial interference in the public contract could affect the interests of other bidders whose offers were not successful in the original procedure. Such an intervention would be contrary to the principles referred to in Article 18(1) Directive 2014/24/EU. This suggests that the legislator might have intended to modify the concept of judicial intervention in the context of public procurement contracts, limiting the possibility of such intervention to the conditions referred to in Article 72(1)(c). However, given the unique nature of hardship situations, it may also be argued that courts and arbitration tribunals should not be included in the scope of Article 72(1). A teleological interpretation would consider that the exceptional circumstances envisaged by hardship do not require the same protections for public procurement rules.

In conclusion, Article 72 does not fully resolve the interpretative ambiguities discussed. However, accepting an exhaustive interpretation of Article 72, along with a broad scope of addressees, has significant implications for applying the contract law concept of hardship to public contracts. Consequently, in such situation EU public procurement law effectively modifies the typical contract law understanding of hardship, encompassing both the hardship clause in Article 72(1)(a) and the possible judicial intervention addressed in Article 72(1)(c) Directive 2014/24/EU.

A. Hardship and Review Clauses: Insights under Article 72(1)(a) Directive 2014/24/EU

Article 72(1)(a) offers the broadest framework for modifying public contracts, allowing modifications without a new procurement procedure when 'clear, precise, and unequivocal' review clauses are included in the initial procurement documents. These clauses may encompass price revisions or options and must define the scope and nature of potential modifications, as well as the conditions for their use. However, they cannot allow modifications that would alter the overall nature of the contract or framework agreement. This provision builds on the CJEU case law, such as *Succhi di Frutta*, where the Court ruled that modifications are permissible if anticipated with sufficient clarity in the procurement documents.[51] The requirement for 'clear, precise, and unequivocal review clauses'[52] is thus crucial, although the case law does not exhaustively define the specific requirements to meet this standard.

Recital 111 Directive 2014/24/EU further illustrates that review clauses may allow for price indexation or accommodate necessary adaptations due to technological changes or technical difficulties encountered during operation or maintenance. Contracts may also include provisions for both ordinary and extraordinary maintenance to ensure continuity of public services when required.

Article 72(1)(a) enables contracting authorities, during the procurement preparation stage, to safeguard the contract's performance by including review clauses that allow adjustments to the terms in response to changes in economic or market conditions. While there is no formal barrier preventing these review clauses from addressing unforeseen circumstances, the requirement for 'clear, precise, and unequivocal' language inherently conflicts with the unpredictable nature of events typically covered by hardship clauses, where 'unpredictability' denotes events that parties could not reasonably foresee.[53]

The EU legislature's restriction on the scope of review clauses in EU public procurement law differentiates them from contract law hardship clauses. In private law, there is no obligation indicating that review clauses must be formulated in a 'clear, precise, and unequivocal' manner. However, also in contract law theory, hardship clauses are often seen as only partially effective as they demand specific, well-defined solutions for inherently uncertain situations.[54] It is virtually impossible for parties to predict every contingency that might arise during a long-term contract. Nevertheless, the implications of imprecisely formulated review clauses are significant, differing notably between contract law and public contracts. In private contracts, the lack of clarity around hardship clauses may affect future negotiations and settlements, potentially leading to the involvement of third parties to address disputes. In the context of public contracts, if the contracting authority fails to explicitly specify the terms under Article 72(1)(a), the review clauses risk being invalidated, imposing a stricter standard compared to private contract law.

[51] Case C-496/99 *Commission of the European Communities v CAS Succhi di Frutta SpA* ECLI:EU:C:2004:236, [2004] ECR I-03801.

[52] ibid paras 111 and 118.

[53] Art III–1:110(2) DCFR; Brunner (n 36) 391; Fontaine and De Ly (n 18) 477.

[54] W Den Haerynck, 'Drafting Hardship Clauses in International Contracts' in D Campbell (ed), *Structuring International Contracts* (Deventer, Kluwer Law International, 1996) 242.

B. Unforeseen Circumstances and Hardship under Article 72(1)(c) Directive 2014/24/EU

A second procurement legal framework applicable to hardship situations arising from unforeseen circumstances, as outlined in Article 72(1)(c) Directive 2014/24/EU, can be viewed as analogous to certain solutions found in contract law. This provision states that:

> Contracts and framework agreements may be modified without a new procurement procedure where all of the following conditions are fulfilled:
>
> (i) circumstances have brought about the need for modification that a diligent contracting authority could not foresee,
>
> (ii) the modification does not alter the overall nature of the contract,
>
> (iii) any price increase is not higher than 50 % of the value of the original contract or framework agreement. Where several successive modifications are made, that limitation shall apply to the value of each modification. Such consecutive modifications shall not be aimed at circumventing this Directive.

The application of the concept of hardship under this provision raises two primary questions. First, it is crucial to examine the role of the phrase 'circumstances that a diligent contracting authority could not foresee'.[55] This condition seems to encapsulate the unpredictability aspect of hardship, tailored here to the public contract setting. It requires contracting authorities to assess whether unforeseen events justify a contract modification. This criterion ensures that modifications are not used to accommodate routine market fluctuations but are reserved for genuinely exceptional situations.

The second question relates to the 50 per cent price increase limitation, which impacts the traditional hardship doctrine in contract law. Unlike private contracts, where the hardship concept often allows for renegotiation without a specified financial cap, public contracts under Directive 2014/24/EU are subject to this explicit limitation. The 50 per cent threshold thus functions as a safeguard against excessive modifications, balancing the need for contractual flexibility with Directive 2014/24/EU's overarching goal of fair competition.

Moreover, the requirement in Article 72(1)(c)(ii) that 'the modification does not alter the overall nature of the contract' adds another layer of restriction. In practical terms, this clause prevents changes that would fundamentally alter the contract's scope or purpose. For example, such a change could involve substituting the initially contracted works, supplies, or services with entirely different ones or converting the contract type – such as turning a public contract into a concession agreement.[56]

A key factor in applying hardship is the foreseeability of extraordinary circumstances affecting the contracting parties. Under European contract law, it is

[55] On due diligence, see ch 6.

[56] Hansen, Treumer and Andhov (n 47).

generally presumed that such circumstances could not reasonably have been anticipated by the disadvantaged party.[57] This presumption implies that the possibility of a change in circumstances was not one that could reasonably have been foreseen when the contract was concluded, nor could the disadvantaged party reasonably be expected to have avoided or mitigated the effects of such changes.[58] However, these provisions do not specify the expected level of due diligence from the parties in anticipating potential changes – whether that responsibility lies with one party or, under the PECL, both contracting parties.

In the context of Article 72(1)(c)(i), however, the situation is different. This provision specifically refers to a 'diligent contracting authority' as the standard.[59] Therefore, under EU public procurement law, the assessment of justifiable circumstances is solely based on the contracting authority's level of diligence, excluding considerations of the contractor's conduct. The standard is thus framed by the contracting authority's knowledge and professional capability. Recital 109 Directive 2014/24/EU further clarifies this professional standard, noting that:

> The notion of unforeseeable circumstances refers to circumstances that could not have been predicted despite reasonably diligent preparation of the initial award by the contracting authority, taking into account its available means, the nature and characteristics of the specific project, good practice in the field in question and the need to ensure an appropriate relationship between the resources spent in preparing the award and its foreseeable value.

Recital 109 Directive 2014/24/EU and relevant case law suggest that, in the context of Article 72(1)(c)(i), the contracting authority is held to a higher standard of due diligence due to its professional nature. This elevated standard is justified by the contracting authority's role as a trustee of public funds and its access to personnel and organisational resources, enabling it to assess potential circumstances more effectively than an average market participant. Consequently, EU public procurement law adjusts the standard of foreseeability for circumstances that may trigger under Article 72(1)(c) Directive 2014/24/EU, distinguishing it from contract law approaches.

While the due diligence application requires individual assessment in each case, Article 72(1)(c)(iii) introduces a fixed 50 per cent limit on permissible price increases. Modifications to contractor remuneration, guided by proportionality principles, should remain objective and solely aim to restore the economic balance as initially established. The 50 per cent cap on price increases further distinguishes public procurement from the contract law hardship concept in European contract law, where such caps do not apply, and the modification value is instead aligned with the actual market situation.

[57] Art 6.2.2 UNIDROIT Principles.
[58] Art 6:111(2)(b) PECL; Art III–3:104 DCFR.
[59] See also ch 6.

In this section, the interaction between Articles 72(1)(a) and (c) and the contract law hardship has been signalled. The following sections will examine how these interactions are implemented in specific national legislations, focusing on Danish and Polish public procurement laws.

V. Danish Approach to Hardship in Public Procurement Contracts

The Danish Public Procurement Act, which came into force on 1 January 2016, governs the awarding of public contracts above and below the EU thresholds and implements Directive 2014/24/EU.[60] Sections 179 and 183 Danish Public Procurement Act specifically address hardship situations, incorporating Articles 72(1)(a) and (c) Directive 2014/24/EU into the Danish legal framework. Section 179 permits modifications specified in the original tender documents, provided they are laid out in 'clear, precise, and unambiguous clauses'. Such clauses must outline the extent, nature, and conditions of any possible modifications, ensuring that these do not alter the contract's overall nature. Section 183 further stipulates that amendments to a contract will not constitute a fundamental change if three conditions are met: (1) the need for modification could not have been anticipated by a diligent contracting entity, (2) the contract's overall nature remains the same, and (3) the modification value does not exceed 50 per cent of the original contract value.

A. Interaction between Danish Public Procurement Law and Contractual Hardship Doctrine

In the Danish context, this raises the question of whether hardship regulations, traditionally rooted in contract law, may hold relevance beyond the strict boundaries of Danish public procurement provisions related to the modification of public contracts. This invites further exploration into the extent to which contract law provisions could be applicable or complementary in interpreting hardship within the framework of public contract modifications.

To answer this question, it is necessary to establish the relationship between public procurement law and contract law in the Danish legal order.[61]

In the broader Scandinavian context, Denmark is recognised as a civil law jurisdiction, albeit less influenced by Roman law than the French and German

[60] *Udbudsloven* no 2015/1564 (Danish Public Procurement Act). See generally E Kjær-Hansen, 'Denmark: Recent Developments in Danish Public Procurement Law and Practice' (2017) 12(1) *European Procurement & Public-Private Partnership Law Review* 53.

[61] See also ch 6.

systems.[62] Over time, Danish law has evolved to integrate elements of both civil and common law traditions, creating a unique legal system. Unlike jurisdictions with codified civil law systems, such as Germany, Italy, or Poland, Denmark lacks a comprehensive civil code. Instead, Danish law relies on specific statutes, legal principles derived from custom, and case law, with the Danish Contracts Act being particularly central.[63] This act strongly emphasises parties' autonomy and the principle of freedom of contract, granting parties significant flexibility to define their contractual terms. Within this framework, parties can effectively create their 'own law' for their agreements as long as these terms do not contravene specific statutory requirements in various regulatory frameworks. This approach, often referred to as 'Nordic legal pragmatism', emphasises practical, real-world solutions over theoretical abstraction, reflecting a tradition rooted in a nineteenth-century Nordic legal mindset.[64]

Returning to the relationship between public procurement law and contract law, two different views can be identified. Østergaard and Frier describe the Danish Contracts Act as a *lex generalis*, governing all contractual forms unless explicitly excluded.[65] However, the issues related to the concluded contracts regarding their interpretation and handling of the obligations of the parties are also found in specific normative acts. These include eg the Danish Sale of Goods Act.[66] Based on this assumption, the Danish Contracts Act and other legal acts, which regulate the execution of concluded contracts, also apply to public procurement contracts, however, to the extent that they are not specifically regulated by the Danish Public Procurement Act. Thus, under this approach, the Danish Public Procurement Act serves as a *lex specialis*, adjusting certain principles of the Danish Contracts Act (*lex generalis*) and imposing specific restrictions on the application of legal concepts, possibly including the concept of hardship.

Nevertheless, this approach is subject to debate. As presented in chapter seven of this anthology, interactions between public procurement law and contract law can also be seen as a relation between two distinct legal regimes, operating individually, yet without mutual immunity in the sense that core principles of contract law may influence the interpretation of procurement law rules and vice versa. In this approach, public procurement law is addressed to the public sector, which will bear special (public law) responsibility for any violations of these rules.[67]

[62] I Henriksen, M Hviid, and P Sharp, *Law and Peace: Contracts and the Success of the Danish Dairy Cooperatives* (Cambridge, Cambridge University Press, 2012) 8.

[63] *Aftaleloven* no 193/2016 (Danish Contracts Act).

[64] P Letto-Vanamo and D Tamm, 'Nordic Legal Mind' in P Letto-Vanamo, D Tamm, and BO Gram Mortensen (eds), *Nordic Law in European Context*, vol 73 (New York, Springer, 2019) 1–19.

[65] K Østergaard and Ch Frier, 'When Is a Contract Considered Unreasonable According to Danish Law? The Application of Section 36 Through 45 Years of Case Law' (2020) 28(3) *European Review of Private Law* 555.

[66] *Købeloven* no 1853/2021 (Danish Sale of Goods Act). See more in ch 6.

[67] See ch 7.

Moreover, according to the view of the Danish supporters of the open nature of the grounds for amending the public contract, including Treumer, these grounds should be seen only as illustrative rather than exhaustive. Following this view, the modification grounds outlined in Sections 178–184 Danish Public Procurement Act provide examples rather than a complete list of possible contract modifications. On this basis, it should be noted that, in addition to the provisions in the Danish Public Procurement Act allowing for contract amendments in hardship situations under Sections 179 and 183, amendments may also be justified based on the concept of hardship as recognised in Danish contract law.

B. Hardship Concepts in Danish Contract Law

The concept of hardship in Danish contract law derives from two primary sources. First, under the principle of freedom of contract, parties can incorporate hardship clauses in their agreements to address situations where unforeseen events impose undue hardship on one of the parties (the doctrine of failed assumptions). This approach relies on the autonomy of the contracting parties to establish specific provisions for such scenarios. Second, Section 36 Danish Contracts Act provides a statutory basis for invoking hardship, allowing parties to seek relief when certain conditions are met. Additionally, Danish legal scholarship recognises other constructs akin to the hardship concept, including *force majeure*[68] and the principle of the nearest to bear the risk.[69]

i. The Doctrine of Failed Assumptions

Incorporating a hardship clause aligns with the doctrine of failed assumptions (*Svigtende forudsætninger*). Under this doctrine, Danish law allows the modification of the general principle of *pacta sunt servanda* through contractual freedom. When a hardship clause is invoked, the obligated party may be relieved from fulfilling all or part of its original commitments.[70] This doctrine is based on the understanding that each party's promise to perform is shaped by its subjective assumptions about the current state of affairs and the likelihood of future changes or challenges. These assumptions may later prove inaccurate, either at the time

[68] Under s 24 Danish Sale of Goods Act sellers may be exempted from liability for non-performance due to unforeseeable and extraordinary circumstances, such as accidental destruction, war, or import restrictions.

[69] This construct, primarily developed through case law, has been applied in judicial decisions concerning both contract interpretation and supplementation (ChF Madsen and K Østergaard, 'Nærmest til at bære risikoen i kontraktretten: En overset obligationsretlig grundsætning?' (2017) 99(2) *Juristen* 35).

[70] MB Andersen and J Lookofsky, 'Financial Crises and Danish Contract Law: No Room for Hardship' in B Başoğlu (ed), *The Effects of Financial Crises on the Binding Force of Contracts: Renegotiation, Rescission or Revision*, vol 17 (Heidelberg, Springer, 2016) 121–35.

of contracting or subsequently.[71] In Danish law, this doctrine concerns circumstances which are not explicitly defined in contractual conditions.[72] The doctrine requires parties to include a provision in their contract allowing for renegotiation if unforeseen, burdensome circumstances arise.[73] If such a provision is absent, and the contract later becomes significantly more onerous than anticipated, the burdened party is expected to bear the associated risk.[74] Most hardship clauses include an obligation to renegotiate the contract if unforeseen circumstances disrupt the contractual balance substantially.

Under Danish legal doctrine, three conditions must generally be met for a promisor to obtain relief under the doctrine of failed assumptions.[75] First, the assumption must be 'material' to the promisor, meaning they would not have entered the contract if they had expected the assumption to fail.[76] Second, the promisee must have known, or reasonably should have known, that the assumption was 'substantive' to the promisor when the contract was formed.[77] Third, the assumption must be 'relevant', meaning that after considering the first two factors and other pertinent circumstances, it is fair to assign the risk of the failed assumption to the promisee.[78] If these conditions are satisfied, the promisor may be granted relief from some or all contractual obligations.

The effectiveness of a hardship clause – evaluated through a three-part test of failed assumptions – may be subject to judicial scrutiny. Although this list of conditions may appear clear and logical, courts applying the doctrine in the event of litigation between the parties retain considerable discretion, requiring an often complex assessment of the specific facts of each case.[79] It is worth noting that sudden fluctuations in exchange rates and other cyclical factors are generally not considered 'relevant' failed assumptions. Such events are typically seen as 'foreseeable' risks implicitly accepted by any promisor engaged in commercial activity.[80] In commercial contexts, parties are expected to bear the risk of fulfilling their obligations, even if this becomes more costly or less attractive. As a result, commercial contracting is viewed as inherently 'risky'. Consequently, Danish courts are reluctant to intervene in cases of hardship, except in highly exceptional circumstances

[71] ibid.

[72] MB Andersen, *Grundlæggende aftaleret*, 4th edn (Copenhagen, Gjellerup, 2013) 104.

[73] K Østergaard, 'Anvendelse af hardshipklausuler i et erhvervsjuridisk perspektiv' in S Treumer (ed), *Julebog* 2005 (Copenhagen, DJØF Publishing, 2005) 216.

[74] Risk refers to a situation where a party cannot bring a claim against another party in connection with an unforeseen or loss-causing event. See MB Andersen and J Lookofsky, *Lærebog i Obligationsret I: Ydelsen, Beføjelser*, 4th edn (Stockholm, Karnov Group, 2015) 197.

[75] Andersen and Lookofsky, 'Financial Crises and Danish Contract Law: No Room for Hardship' (n 70) 108.

[76] Andersen and Lookofsky, *Lærebog i Obligationsret I: Ydelsen, Beføjelser* (n 74).

[77] UfR 2002.1031H, *Ugeskrift for Retsvæsen* (Danish Weekly Law Reports) 1031 (2002).

[78] ibid.

[79] Andersen (n 72) 399.

[80] ibid 401.

involving a significant imbalance. Even in such cases, successful claims for non-performance are rare.[81]

ii. Section 36 Danish Contracts Act

In addition to using contractual clauses envisaged by the doctrine of failed assumptions, the other key source of addressing unforeseen situations within the Danish contract law is Section 36 Danish Contracts Act, commonly referred to as the 'General Clause'.[82] This provision states:

> A contract may be modified or set aside, in whole or in part, if it would be unreasonable or at variance with the principles of good faith to enforce it. The same applies to other juristic acts. Due to subsection (2) in making a decision under subsection (1) hereof, regard shall be had to the circumstances existing at the time the contract was concluded, the terms of the contract, and subsequent circumstances. (translation provided by an online translation platform)

This broad language, particularly in its references to 'unreasonableness' and 'variation' with good faith, can be ambiguous in specific disputes. Nonetheless, Danish legal doctrine considers Section 36 analogous to the concept of hardship.[83] Section 36 Danish Contracts Act authorises Danish courts to relieve a party from fulfilling its contractual obligations, either in full or in part, if doing so would be unreasonable or violate principles of good faith. It also permits the modification of contractual terms that have become unreasonable due to later developments.[84]

While Section 36 can serve as a basis for terminating a public contract, particularly in the absence of similar provisions in the Danish Public Procurement Act, its application to contract modifications raises uncertainties. Initially designed to protect consumers against overreaching by commercial parties, Lookofsky notes that the legislative history of Section 36 also recognises the need for protection against unfair contract terms in commercial relationships.[85] Courts also have applied this provision in cases involving substantive unfairness between commercial entities.[86] However, its applicability to business-to-business (B2B) contracts, including public contracts, remains contentious. Legal scholars express reservations about using Section 36 in professional relationships, emphasising that commercial entities generally bear the risk of fulfilling their contractual obligations, even if performance later becomes more costly or less appealing.[87] Andersen

[81] Andersen and Lookofsky, 'Financial Crises and Danish Contract Law: No Room for Hardship' (n 70).

[82] ibid 133.

[83] ibid.

[84] ibid.

[85] J Lookofsky, 'The Limits of Commercial Contract Freedom under the UNIDROIT "Restatement" and Danish Law' (XLVI) *American Society of Comparative Law* 496.

[86] ibid.

[87] Andersen and Lookofsky, *Lærebog i Obligationsret I: Ydelsen, Beføjelser* (n 74) 133.

and Madsen similarly argue that Section 36 should not be used to retroactively shift the risk allocation established by two knowledgeable parties who consciously distributed these risks upon entering the contract.[88]

For Section 36 to apply, the justifying circumstances must be both extraordinary and unforeseeable at the time of the contract's inception.[89] However, these factors alone may not suffice for judicial intervention. The Danish Supreme Court's decision in *Jørgen Sonnergaard v Forlaget Carlsen A/S* illustrates a restrictive approach, indicating that even significant, unforeseen changes may not override the original agreement if the burdened party was aware of the potential risks from the outset.[90]

When determining whether to set aside or modify a contract under Section 36, courts assess the reasonableness of enforcement by considering the terms agreed upon, the risks assumed by the parties, and the circumstances at the time of enforcement.[91] The primary factor is whether unforeseen events have created a substantial imbalance in the contractual relationship, resulting in 'excessive onerousness' for one party. In cases of commercial hardship, courts may deem performance unreasonable if a significant alteration of the contractual equilibrium has occurred.[92]

VI. Polish Approach to Hardship in Public Procurement Contracts

Public procurement in Poland is governed by the Polish Public Procurement Act, which came into force on 1 January 2021.[93] The Polish Public Procurement Act applies to the award of public contracts both above and below the EU thresholds. Public contract modification provisions, aligned with Article 72(1)(a) and (c) 2014 Public Procurement Act addressing the concept of hardship, are outlined in Article 455(1)(1) and 455(4) Polish Public Procurement Act.

A. Adapting Public Contracts to Crises: Legislative Responses to COVID-19 and War in Ukraine

The Polish legislator undertook special legislative measures to clarify the possibility of modifying contracts under unforeseen circumstances arising from the crises caused by the pandemic and the war in Ukraine. First, to safeguard economic operators,

[88] LL Andersen and PB Madsen, *Aftaler og mellemmænd*, 7th edn (Stockholm, Karnov Group, 2017) 210.

[89] ibid 217.

[90] UfR 2003.23H, *Jørgen Sonnergaard v Forlaget Carlsen A/S*, Judgment of the Supreme Court, 8 October 2002.

[91] LL Andersen and PB Madsen (n 88) 217.

[92] UfR 2004.2518V, *Niels Tapgaard Nielsen v Evald Skarregård*, 19 June 2004 where the court determined that the rent had been set unreasonably low and subsequently adjusted it upwards.

[93] *Ustawa z dnia 11 września 2019 r. – Prawo zamówień publicznych* (Polish Public Procurement Act).

the Polish legislator introduced a new provision in Article 15(r) Anti-Crisis Shield Act 1.0, aimed at clarifying the content of Article 455(4) Polish Public Procurement Act. This provision established clearer conditions for amending public contracts in situations of hardship due to COVID-19. Specifically, Article 15(r) outlined the scope of potential contract modifications, which included, among other things, extending deadlines for performance, suspending contracts, or altering the method of delivering supplies, services, or works. However, any changes were subject to a key limitation: the cumulative price increase resulting from subsequent amendments could not exceed 50 per cent of the original contract value. Notably, Article 15(r) explicitly identifies the parties to public contracts as the addressees of its provisions, setting it apart from the general language of Article 455(1) Polish Public Procurement Act, which does not specify its intended addressees.

Poland also introduced another clarification of the conditions for amending public contracts due to unforeseen circumstances following the outbreak of the war in Ukraine. This clarification concerning Article 455(4) Polish Public Procurement Act was implemented through Article 48 Simplified Procedures Act.[94] Article 48 allows public contract adjustments in cases of significant changes in material costs or other unforeseen expenses, provided that the contracts in question were concluded before the enactment of the law and remain active. As before, each amendment must ensure that any increase in remuneration does not exceed 50 per cent of the original contract value. Notably, unlike the approach taken during the pandemic crisis, the Polish legislator did not explicitly identify the addressees of the new regulation. Instead, the legislator adopted the general wording used in Article 455(1) Polish Public Procurement Act.

B. Hardship in Polish Civil Law and its Modification under Public Procurement Law

Poland, unlike Denmark, is among the Member States where the relationship between public procurement law and contract law is clearly articulated within its legal framework, as established in the Polish Public Procurement Act. This relationship is relatively straightforward, with civil law providing a *lex generalis* framework that complements the more specialised provisions of public procurement law.[95] This legal structure highlights how the regulation of specific legal constructs under public procurement law directly modifies those constructs as they are established under civil law.

Poland is also among the countries with a codified system of civil law, with the primary normative source being the Polish Civil Code.[96] The Polish approach to

[94] Ustawa z dnia 7 października 2022 r. – o zmianie niektórych ustaw w celu uproszczenia procedur administracyjnych dla obywateli i przedsiębiorców (Polish Simplified Procedures Act).

[95] See ch 3.

[96] Ustawa z dnia 23 kwietnia 1964 r. – Kodeks cywilny (Polish Civil Code).

intervention in contractual relations in situations of hardship, including unforeseen circumstances, can be perceived as 'open'. This means that Polish courts have a relatively broad authority to modify or even dissolve contractual obligations when unforeseen events render performance excessively burdensome for one of the parties. The possibility of amending a contract through judicial intervention in Poland is referred to as the *rebus sic stantibus* doctrine. Beyond this framework, contract amendments in hardship situations can also arise from the principle of freedom of contract and are facilitated through contractual hardship clauses.

The approach to shaping hardship clauses under the Polish civil law is modified by EU public procurement law. These modifications pertain to how hardship clauses should be framed in public contracts. Specifically, Article 455(1)(1) Polish Public Procurement Act implementing Article 72(1)(a) Directive 2014/24/EU mandates that review clauses, including hardship clauses, be drafted in a 'clear, precise, and unambiguous' manner.[97] This requirement introduces a stricter standard compared to the flexibility allowed under the principle of freedom of contract established in Article 353(1) Polish Civil Code.

Another modification stems from the nature of the Polish Public Procurement Act. In Polish legal doctrine, the overarching principle governing public contracts is the assurance of their real performance.[98] This requires contracting authorities to execute public contracts in alignment with the public interest and within the timeframes stipulated in the procurement documentation. This approach restricts the flexibility available under the Polish Civil Code to include hardship clauses that allow for suspending contract performance until an agreement is reached. Similarly, the principle of real performance opposes the premature termination of public contracts, which civil law would otherwise broadly permit.

Further modification concerns the extent to which a court or an appointed third party, such as a mediator, conciliator, or arbitral tribunal, can shape the content of contractual amendments. The scope of permissible modifications in hardship scenarios is outlined in Article 455(4) Polish Public Procurement Act, which imposes restrictions on applying the *rebus sic stantibus* doctrine.[99]

i. *Judicial Intervention Based on Rebus Sic Stantibus Clause*

The possibility of judicial intervention in the contract's content in a hardship situation is codified in Article 357(1) Polish Civil Code.[100] This provision states:

> If due to an extraordinary change in circumstances, a performance entails excessive difficulties or exposes one of the parties to a severe lost that the parties did not foresee

[97] Case C-496/99 *Succhi di Frutta* (n 51); Art 72(1) Directive 2014/24/EU.

[98] R Szostak, *Umowy o zamówienia publiczne w zarysie* (Warsaw,Wydawnictwo Urzędu Zamówień Publicznych, 2018) 149.

[99] B Fuchs, 'Art 353(1)' in M Fras and M Habdas (eds), *Kodeks cywilny. Komentarz. Tom III. Zobowiązania. Część ogólna* (Warsaw, Wolters Kluwer, 2018).

[100] Szostak, *Umowy o zamówienia publiczne w zarysie* (n 98) 159.

> when executing the contract, the court may, having considered the parties' interests, following the principles of community life, designate the manner of performing the obligation, the value of the performance or even decide that the contract be dissolved. When dissolving the contract, the court may, as needed, decide how accounts will be settled between the parties, being guided by the principles outlined in the preceding sentence. (translation provided by an online translation platform)

Article 357(1) Polish Civil Code introduces the concept of an extraordinary change in circumstances, allowing the court or arbitration tribunal to modify or even terminate a contractual obligation when unforeseen events arise.[101] According to the principle of the Polish Civil Code, the essence of an obligation is that the creditor may demand performance from the debtor, and the debtor is obliged to fulfil this performance.[102] However, recognising that in certain situations, performance under the conditions set out in the law may become impossible, or at the very least, excessively difficult, the legislator allows for flexibility to prevent grossly unjust outcomes.[103] The primary aim of the *rebus sic stantibus* clause is to protect a contracting party from circumstances that were not anticipated by either party at the time the contract was formed, thereby ensuring a fair balance between the parties' obligations in light of unexpected events.[104]

Due to its exceptional nature, courts interpret the *rebus sic stantibus* clause restrictively, particularly in light of Article 353(1) Polish Civil Code.[105] This approach emphasises a careful assessment of the conditions under which *rebus sic stantibus* may be invoked. The prerequisites for applying this concept in Polish law are as follows:

- i) an extraordinary change in circumstances;
- ii) undue difficulty in performance or the risk of severe loss to one party;
- iii) a causal link between the change in circumstances and the impediment to performance or risk of loss;
- iv) the unforeseen nature of these changes at the time of contracting.[106]

The requirement of an 'extraordinary change in circumstances' under Article 357(1) refers broadly to social and economic conditions that impact society at large rather than circumstances affecting only the parties to a particular contract.[107] Typical

[101] A Szumański, *Ochrona prawna strony umowy dotkniętej skutkami zmiany okoliczności* (Warsaw, Państwo i Prawo, 1994); See also, Judgment of the Supreme Court of 21 April 2005, III CK 645/04, LEX no 369251; Judgment of the Supreme Court of 22 April 2005, II CK 594/04, OSP 2006/12, item 143.

[102] Art 353(1) Polish Civil Code.

[103] Fuchs (n 99).

[104] J Rajski, 'Klauzule hardship w kontraktach zawieranych w międzynarodowym obrocie gospodarczym' (1999) 3 *Przegląd Prawa Handlowego* 1, 2; See also Judgment of the Supreme Court of 20 July 2007, I CK 3/07, OSNC-ZD 2008/3, poz. 65.

[105] Judgment of the Supreme Court of 29 December 1994, III CZP 120/94.

[106] P Nazaruk, 'Art 357(1)' in J Ciszewski (ed), *Kodeks cywilny. Komentarz* (Warsaw, Wolters Kluwer, 2019).

[107] T Wiśniewski, 'Art 353(1)' in G Bieniek (ed), *Komentarz do Kodeksu cywilnego. Księga trzecia. Zobowiązania*, vol I–II, 10th edn (Warsaw, LexisNexis, 2011). See also Judgment of Appeal Court in Warsaw of 9 May 2022, VII AGa 965/21, LEX no 3425394.

examples include severe economic downturns, hyperinflation, drastic drops in national income, high unemployment, or widespread business bankruptcies.[108] Classical triggers for *rebus sic stantibus* clauses also include events like pandemics and war.[109]

Similar to hardship clauses, the application of the *rebus sic stantibus* clause in public procurement entails modifications to the freedom of contract principle. These modifications are derived from Article 455(4) Polish Public Procurement Act.

The first modification pertains to the possibility of amending a contract when circumstances leading to the deterioration of the parties' situation were unforeseeable by a diligent contracting authority. Under civil law, however, the inability to foresee such circumstances may apply to either party. The implementation of this solution, which emphasises the diligence of the contracting authority, is regarded in Polish legal doctrine as a recognition of the public sector's pivotal role – not only in managing the public procurement process but also in ensuring the performance of public contracts.[110]

The second modification addresses the permissible value of amendments, which, in the context of public contracts, cannot exceed 50 per cent of the value of the original contract. Such restrictions do not exist under civil law.

The third modification relates to the body authorised to amend contracts. Under the Polish Civil Code, the *rebus sic stantibus* clause allows contract modifications to be made exclusively by a court or an arbitral tribunal.[111] In contrast, the Polish Public Procurement Act, same as Directive 2014/24/EU, does not explicitly specify the addressees of the norm allowing for contract modification.[112] As a result, contract amendments in public procurement can initially be executed by mutual agreement of the parties. If an agreement cannot be reached, the amendment may then be enacted through a court decision following a claim filed by one of the parties.

VII. Conclusion

Gaz de Bordeaux concluded with a settlement that upheld the private company's claim. The Conseil d'État recognised the significant economic impact of World War I, which had driven coal prices up by approximately 250 per cent, necessitating a revision of the gas tariff outlined in the contract. This decision entitled the private company to compensation from the city of Bordeaux, and it established

[108] Fuchs (n 99); Wiśniewski (n 107).
[109] R Szostak, *Umowy o zamówienia publiczne w zarysie* (n 98) 161.
[110] R Szostak, 'Z Problematyki Racjonalizacji Ograniczeń Swobody Kontraktowej w Zamówieniach Publicznych' (2019) 329 *Acta Universitatis Wratislaviensis, Prawo* 605.
[111] Art 357(1) Polish Civil Code.
[112] Art 455(1) Polish Public Procurement Act.

that public contract amendments could be justified in the face of unforeseen circumstances.

Although *Gaz de Bordeaux* is primarily illustrative, it highlights the importance of adapting the content of the contract to changing external conditions. This issue remains relevant today, as evidenced by the challenges posed by COVID-19 and the war in Ukraine, both of which created significant obstacles to the performance of public contracts.

The possibility of external factors (including unforeseen circumstances) influencing the performance of public contracts has been recognised within EU public procurement law, which provides mechanisms to mitigate these risks under Article 72(1)(a) and (c). Both solutions have been structured differently from their counterparts under contract law. Regarding review clauses, which may constitute a manifestation of hardship clauses, EU law provides that they must be formulated in a 'clear, precise and unambiguous' manner. In the case of Article 72(1)(c) Directive 2014/24/EU, the EU legislator introduced restrictions in the form of the need for the contracting authority acting with due diligence to have failed to foresee the circumstances, as well as a limitation of the value of the contract amendment to 50 per cent of its original value. In addition, the wording of Article 72(1) is formulated in such a way that it is not clear as to who may amend the public contract under the conditions set out in this provision.

The aforementioned modifications to the legal constructs known under contract law stem from the necessity to uphold the principles of public procurement law. These include, in particular, the protection of equal treatment and non-discrimination of economic operators, as well as ensuring open competition.

However, in practice, the modification of contract law constructs within the framework of public procurement law, particularly in relation to hardship situations, proves to be challenging. The extent to which contract law is modified under public procurement law, or whether they coexist independently, depends on two critical factors: first, whether the grounds for contract modification in Article 72 Directive 2014/24/EU are considered exhaustive or merely illustrative; and second, the interaction between contract law and public procurement law within individual national legal systems.

This chapter has examined this interaction, especially within the contexts of the Danish and Polish legal systems. The analysis of Danish legal solutions pointed to the lack of uniformity of views regarding the relationship between public procurement law and contract law. In accordance with the first opinion, the procurement rules will pre-empt the contract rules, which means that the application of the doctrine of hardship will be possible within the framework set forth in Sections 179 and 183 Danish Public Procurement Act.[113] According to the second approach, based on a parallel relationship between public procurement law and

[113] See ch 6.

contract law[114] and on an 'open nature' of the list of circumstances allowing the public contract to be amended,[115] the doctrine of hardship can also be used on additional legal grounds. These foundations would be, in particular, the doctrine of failed assumptions and Section 36 Danish Contracts Act. In contrast, under Polish law, the principle of *lex specialis derogat lex generalis* governs the relationship, with public procurement law modifying civil law constructs concerning hardship situations.

Recent crises, such as COVID-19 and the war in Ukraine, have demonstrated the inadequacy of the current framework for public contract modifications. These events, which were both unpredictable and beyond the control of contracting parties, often necessitated contract amendments that exceeded the scope envisaged in Article 72(1)(a) and (c) Directive 2014/24/EU. Given that the current framework was established during a period of relative geopolitical and economic stability, there is a strong argument for reassessing and potentially revising the provisions of Directive 2014/24/EU. A *de lege ferenda* proposal could involve aligning public procurement hardship mechanisms more closely with those adopted under contract law. Such an approach would enhance the flexibility and consistency of EU public procurement law across Member States, ensuring a more robust response to future crises.

[114] See ch 7.
[115] Treumer (n 47).

PART III

Digitalisation and Sustainability

10

Deconstructing Computational Contracts: A Critical Analysis of their Application in Private and Public Domain

ALEXANDRA ANDHOV, SVEN MIKULIC AND MICHAŁ KANIA

I. Introduction

Technology has fundamentally transformed every aspect of our lives, from how we communicate and conduct business to how we engage with social structures and economic systems. The rapid pace of technological advancements has led to profound changes in everyday practices, from digital payments and digital contract formation to automated contract execution. The way we create and manage agreements has evolved dramatically and we are moving beyond traditional methods of incorporating digital signatures towards automated systems with a few autonomous functions that are able to handle some contractual activities independently. Technology is reshaping industries through automation, artificial intelligence (AI), and big data. These tools are built on a substantial amount of data to enable businesses to operate more efficiently and make informed decisions based on comprehensive data analysis.

While the public sector often lags behind the private sector in adopting innovations, technological development has also led to changes in public procurement. In 1998, the European Commission urged Member States to help realise the potential of e-procurement and take steps to promote electronic tools in public procurement by launching the SIMAP project.[1] A key development in this area is

[1] SIMAP is a website run by the Office for Official Publications of the European Communities, containing information on European public procurement. SIMAP includes: TED (Tenders Electronic Daily) – the online version of the Supplement to the Official Journal of the EU. It provides access to public procurement notices published in the EU, the EEA, and other countries. eNotices is an online tool for preparing public procurement notices and publishing them in the Supplement to the Official Journal of the EU. It provides access to all standard forms used in European public procurement.

the introduction of 'electronic procurement', which involves the use of electronic means in awarding public contracts.[2]

Directive 2014/24/EU emphasised the use of electronic communication throughout the procurement process, mandating fully electronic submissions.[3] Article 22 Directive 2014/24/EU highlights the primacy of electronic communication, requiring Member States to ensure that all communications and exchanges – particularly the submission of tenders – are conducted electronically. Recital 52 further reinforces this obligation, emphasising the necessity of using electronic means[4] throughout the procurement process, while indicating the following:

> The transmission of notices in electronic form, the electronic availability of contract documents and, after a transitional period of 30 months, fully electronic communication meaning communication by electronic means at all stages of the procedure, including the transmission of requests to participate and, in particular, the transmission of tenders (electronic submission of tenders), should be mandatory.

These tools must be non-discriminatory, widely available, interoperable, and accessible to all economic operators.

The most commonly recognised benefits of the digitalisation of public procurement procedures include broader access for economic operators – particularly small and medium-sized enterprises (SMEs) – increased competition, simplified communication, cost savings, greater procedural efficiency, reduced formality, and enhanced transparency in the use of public funds. Among these, transparency stands out as a key principle reinforced through electronic processes, as reflected in Article 18 Directive 2014/24/EU. This provision requires contracting authorities to ensure equal and non-discriminatory treatment of economic operators while acting in a transparent and proportionate manner.

Serving as a cornerstone of the procurement framework, transparency plays a vital role in safeguarding foundational principles such as equality and non-discrimination. It is expected to guide all stages of procurement, extending

eTendering is a platform for electronic public procurement, offering access to documentation related to tender notices, including contract documents, technical specifications, annexes, questions, and answers. eSenders provides information for and about users with TED eSender status.

[2] S Arrowsmith, *The Law of Public and Utilities Procurement Regulation in the EU and the UK*, Vol 2, 3rd edn (London, Sweet and Maxwell, 2018) 604–05.

[3] According to Art 90(2) Directive 2014/24/EU, the implementation of full electronification of the procedure leading to the conclusion of a public contract was an obligation of the Member States starting in 2018. Under Directive 2004/18/EC (Directive 2004/18/EC of the European Parliament and of the Council of 31 March 2004 on the coordination of procedures for the award of public works contracts, public supply contracts and public service contracts [2004] OJ L134/114), there was no obligation for mandatory electronic communication between contracting authorities and contractors. Electronic means of communication were primarily used to send tender documents to the EU publishing bodies. In the case of communication between the contracting authority and the contractor, electronic means were only one of the means of communication. Others were post, fax, and in a limited way, telephone. (Art 42 Directive 2004/18/EC).

[4] 'Electronic means' are defined in Art 2(1)(19) Directive 2014/24/EU as 'electronic equipment for the processing (including digital compression) and storage of data which is transmitted, conveyed and received by wire, by radio, by optical means or by other electromagnetic means'.

beyond the tendering phase to include the execution of contracts. The 2014 Public Procurement Directives support this objective by imposing legal obligations for publishing notices and facilitating clear, effective communication with economic operators.[5] However, the current regulatory framework mandates e-procurement only up to the contract award phase, leaving the performance stage largely unregulated at the EU level. This regulatory gap places the public sector at a disadvantage compared to the increasingly digitalised private sector. The EU legislator's focus has primarily centred on the award phase, driven by the objective of reinforcing the Single Market principles. While Articles 70 to 73 Directive 2014/24/EU address the aspects of contract performance, their scope remains limited and primarily serves to uphold the general principles outlined in Article 18. As a result, it is left to individual Member States to adopt and implement digital tools during contract execution. The legal framework applied at this stage depends on each country's legal tradition: those following the 'private-oriented hybrid model' typically apply civil (contract) law, whereas Member States operating under the 'public-oriented hybrid model' rely on public (administrative) law.[6]

The EU has taken a leading role in regulating technological integration, balancing innovation with the general principles and fundamental rights.[7] Even though it might not seem straightforward, there is a clear connection between regulating technology and regulating private law. The European Commission has, since the early 2000s, attempted to improve and harmonise the contract law across the EU. First, with a Communication on European Contract Law,[8] followed by the Action Plan for a More Coherent European Contract Law of 2003,[9] then with the preparation of a Common Frame of Reference,[10] which became a 'Draft', and finally with the proposal for a Common European Sales Law (CESL).[11] However, the

[5] Directive 2014/23/EU; Directive 2014/24/EU; Directive 2014/25/EU. Directive 2014/24/EU harmonises rules on the publication and content of prior information notices, contract and award notices, electronic availability of contract documents, information for candidates and tenderers on decisions taken in the course of a procurement procedure, the content of tender documents on award criteria, the advertising of certain modifications of procurement contracts and the storage of and access to high-value procurement contracts. See A Sołtysińska, 'E-procurement and the Principle of Transparency in Public Procurement in the European Union' in S Dudzik, I Kawka, and R Śliwa (eds), *E-administracja. skuteczna, odpowiedzialna i otwarta administracja publiczna w Unii Europejskiej* (Kraków, Wydawnictwo Księgarnia Akademicka, 2022) 150; See also Case C-496/99 P *Commission of the European Communities v CAS Succhi di Frutta SpA* ECLI:EU:C:2004:236, [2004] ECR I-03801.

[6] See ch 3.

[7] The EU has adopted various regulatory tools within digital products, online platforms, geo-blocking, cross-border online services, blockchain, or even artificial intelligence.

[8] European Commission, 'Communication on European Contract Law' COM (2001) 398 final.

[9] See Commission Communication on 'European Contract Law and the revision of the aquis: the way forward' COM (2004) 651 final. For more historical context, see R Schulze and F Zoll, *European Contract Law* (Oxford, Bloomsbury Publishing, 2021) ch 5.

[10] Commission, 'Communication to the European Parliament and the Council, A More Coherent European Contract Law: An Action Plan' COM (2003) 68 final. On the DCFR and the PECL and their role in the integration of European contract law see also ch 1.

[11] Commission, 'Proposal for a Regulation of the European Parliament and of the Council on a Common European Sales Law' COM (2011) 635 final.

evolution of European contract law towards harmonisation did not materialise as the proposal for the CESL was withdrawn in December 2014 and the Commission announced a New Start.[12] The direction the 'New Start' should take was outlined shortly after in a 'Digital Single Market Strategy for Europe'.[13] However, what the EU still needs to address is whether we need to rethink the regulation of contractual form, language, interpretation, and performance if we fully digitise contracts – in the form of a computational law – and use such contracts in the private and the public domain. Much like the private sector, the public sector has started embracing digitalisation, particularly in its interactions with providers throughout the procurement cycle.[14] Used appropriately, digital tools can help public bodies achieve procurement objectives, both in contract award procedures and contract execution.[15]

This chapter explores computational contracts' multifaceted nature, examining their legal and practical implications in the public procurement performance stage. It aims to critically analyse computational contracts under European contract law and EU public procurement law, under the Draft Common Frame of Reference (DCFR)[16] and the Principles of European Contract Law (PECL)[17] and a few selected national contract laws, assessing their potential to harmonise legal frameworks and streamline the performance of public contracts. While focusing on transforming awarded public contracts, this chapter excludes the procurement of technological solutions. By reflecting on private sector lessons, the chapter

[12] Commission, 'Communication of 16 December 2014, Commission Work Program for 2015: A New Start' COM (2014) 910 final.

[13] Commission, 'Communication to the European Parliament, the Council, the European Economic and Social Committee and the Committee of the Regions, "A Digital Single Market Strategy for Europe"' COM (2015) 192 final. As such, the EU introduced numerous new directives and regulations within the sphere of private law, including contract law. Consider, for example, the twin Directives of 2019 – the Digital Content Directive and the Sale of Goods Directive, which address numerous contract law-related issues, such as the concept of contract or the system of contractual rights and obligations. Thus, looking at the whole legislative activity of the EU within the digital market, it is apparent that European contract law is in transition to the digital age and towards greater harmonisation. Directive (EU) 2019/770 of the European Parliament and of the Council of 20 May 2019 on certain aspects concerning contracts for the supply of digital content and digital services [2019] OJ L136/1; Directive (EU) 2019/771 of the European Parliament and of the Council of 20 May 2019 on certain aspects concerning contracts for the sale of goods, amending Regulation (EU) 2017/2394 and Directive 2009/22/EC, and repealing Directive 1999/44/EC [2019] OJ L136/28. See AU Janssen and R Schultze, *The Future of European Private Law* (Baden-Baden, Nomos Verlagsgesellschaft, 2023) 143–47.

[14] A Sanchez-Graells, *Digital Technologies and Public Procurement: Gatekeeping and Experimentation in Digital Public Governance* (Oxford, Oxford University Press, 2024) 123–48.

[15] See R Bickerstaff and S Arrowsmith, 'Electronic Procurement' in S Arrowsmith (ed), *The Law of Public and Utilities Procurement: Regulation in the EU and UK*, Vol 2, 3rd edn (Oxford, Sweet and Maxwell, 2018) 603.

[16] The DCFR has three purposes: 1) provides a potential model for a political Common Frame of Reference (CFR), 2) enriches legal scholarship by highlighting similarities and influences among national private laws, and 3) inspires legal reforms and the harmonisation of private law across Europe.

[17] The PECL focuses exclusively on contract law and has five purposes: 1) provide a legal foundation for European legislation, 2) offer a neutral rule set for cross-border EU contractual relations, 3) represent a modern formulation of the *Lex Mercatoria* for international contracts, 4) act as a model for judicial and legislative development of contract law, and 5) lay groundwork for the harmonisation of contract law across the EU, thereby facilitating the functioning of the Single European Market and bridging differences between civil and common law systems.

identifies opportunities for regulatory reform and innovation in both private and public domains. Although computational contracts complement rather than replace traditional ones, their implementation highlights the need to adapt legal systems to technological advancements.

A. The Promise of Computational Contracts as Contracts

Computational contracts, with their automatic processing, verification, and execution capabilities, have captured the attention of legal professionals. Their theoretical efficiency offers promise in sectors like financial services,[18] supply chain management (SCM)[19] or energy services.[20] However, their application in public procurement remains underexplored.

Integrating computational contracts into public procurement could transform how contracting authorities interact with suppliers and manage long contracts that last from a number of years to decades. Technology companies highlight benefits like increased transparency and efficiency through tools like blockchain, smart contracts, and AI. Yet, these claims lack specificity about their practical impact or operational mechanics.

Transparent, automated algorithms have the potential to optimise public fund allocation and spending, aligning with the transparency principle in Article 18 Directive 2014/24/EU. However, understanding the technological and legal implications is essential. This chapter evaluates whether computational contracts deliver tangible benefits when used in public procurement, balancing opportunities and risks. By distinguishing key concepts like computational contracts and smart contracts, we can better grasp their potential and limitations under current regulations.

B. Definitions and Delimitation of the Inquiry

In this section, we establish a clear framework for understanding key concepts and the scope of this inquiry into computational contracts. We begin by defining

[18] For example, computational contracts are used by banks and lending institutions when managing loan agreements, automatically adjusting interest rates based on changes in market indices (eg LIBOR or SOFR) and handling payment schedules. Similarly, financial institutions use automated contracts to clear and settle trades – eg Central Counterparty Clearing (CCP).

[19] Several companies have implemented electronic procurement systems to automate purchasing processes. These platforms can execute contracts automatically based on predefined criteria, such as pricing, specific performance, delivery schedules, or quality standards. An example of such a system would be SAP Ariba.

[20] Within the energy sector, computational contracts are used to automatically balance supply and demand and manage electricity grids. Computational contracts can trigger demand response actions, such as adjusting the power consumption and connected decisions during peak times and thus optimise grid performance. Similarly, computational contracts are used in automated carbon offsets for verification and settlement processes.

essential terms such as 'computational contracts' and 'smart contracts', distinguishing between their theoretical underpinnings and practical applications. This foundation is crucial for assessing these technologies' potential impacts and limitations in the public procurement landscape. Additionally, we outline the boundaries of our investigation, focusing on the post-award application in public contracts.

i. Computational Contracts

Computational contracts have different meanings in different settings. The notion of computational contract started in computer science, and therefore, we will start our inquiry there as well. A computational contract, as defined by Scholliers and others, is a type of advanced contract that applies not just to the basic features of functions and objects but also to their more complex interactions and computations.[21]

In computational science, computational contracts can be defined as a 'higher-order contract over the execution of a contract entity'.[22] Translating this to legalese,[23] a computational contract can be described as an agreement – or its component – encoded as an executable program. It autonomously *executes obligations and rights* using predefined logical and temporal parameters. Computational contracts represent legal agreements in a machine-readable format, enabling computers to process, reason over, and execute contract terms automatically.[24] This reduces ambiguity by encoding precise legal semantics and logic, allowing actions like payments or subcontractor hiring to proceed without human intervention. However, the computational contract is only as good as the limited ambiguity in it.

One can imagine *a supply chain contract* that can connect time, schedule, and delivery and automatically execute sending items in a particular order. These contracts act like gatekeepers, ensuring that values passed to or from functions meet specific criteria. This gives these contracts a special relevance to the implementation of complex public contracts for services or construction works. The use of computational contracts is particularly noteworthy in the context of complex concession agreements, which are typically long-term and require

[21] C Scholliers, É Ranter, and W De Meuter, 'Computational Contracts' (2015) 98 *Science of Computer Programming* 360, 363. This definition refers to an advanced contract programming model that allows for the specification of rules governing the behaviour and interaction of software functions and objects, including those that operate on or return other functions.

[22] ibid.

[23] 'Legalese is a type of legal jargon marked by complex phrasing, passive voice, and outdated or overly formal language – often including Latin – that makes legal texts difficult for the public to understand, even when simpler wording would suffice'. See Legal Information Institute (Cornell Law School) <www.law.cornell.edu/wex/legalese>.

[24] For an example of computational representation of a financial contract, see MD Flood and OR Goodenough, 'Contract as Automaton: Representing a Simple Financial Agreement in Computational Form' (2022) 30 *Artificial Intelligence and Law* 391.

continuous monitoring of key elements such as task quality and project-related financial flows.

In computational contracts, predefined rules and conditions govern how the contract operates, with specific events or data inputs triggering agreed-upon actions.[25] Although this model may not be suitable for highly complex contractual relationships, it holds significant promise for public procurement. Translating contractual provisions into a computational format enhances clarity and reduces ambiguity compared to traditional text-based contracts. Clearly defined circumstances (inputs) and corresponding legal outcomes (outputs), when paired with AI-driven monitoring tools, enable autonomous execution without the need for further administrative intervention. This not only minimises the risk of human error but also ensures that contractual sequences are followed consistently. For both parties, this predictability fosters greater trust and reliability.

Given these advantages, integrating computational contracts into public procurement processes offers potential benefits. Ideally, they should form part of the tender documentation and be made accessible to all participants. By enhancing the clarity and precision of contractual provisions, computational contracts can lower barriers to entry – particularly for SMEs.[26] The potential for increased participation would be driven by reduced bureaucratic complexity and improved accessibility, supported by the electronic publication of procurement documents and the mandatory use of electronic communication methods.[27]

ii. Computable Contracts

Another term we can come across when discussing the possibility of automating contracts is 'computable contracting'. Computable contracting involves using software to encode and automate contractual agreements, transforming traditional paper-based contracts into programmable contracts represented in code. At its core, a computable contract digitises key contractual obligations for easier analysis, verification, and automation while still maintaining a natural language version of the contract.[28] In its most advanced form, all clauses are coded, relying on user interfaces for interaction instead of text. This promises greater precision, efficiency, and scalability in legal processes by directly encoding contracts' terms

[25] ibid 393–95.

[26] See more about SME access to public procurement market eg M Trybus and M Andhov, 'Favouring Small and Medium Sized Enterprises with Directive 2014/24/EU' (2017) 12(3) *European Procurement & Public Private Partnership Law Review* 224.

[27] Arts 22 and 53 Directive 2014/24/EU.

[28] See CodeX Insurance Initiative Working Group, 'Computable Contracts and Insurance: An Introduction' (12 May 2021) < www.law.stanford.edu/2021/05/12/computable-contracts-and-insurance-an-introduction/>.

and logical structure into software.[29] It can reduce certain contracting transaction costs as compared to traditional contracting methods.[30]

One can consider computable contracting as a new field of research in the intersection of computer science and law, which 'studies the processes that would allow the software to conduct automated, prima-facie assessments of conformance with certain contract terms'.[31] In other words, it is a field that has focused on converting the traditional written contract or some of its parts into machine-executable code, thus allowing the parties to express their obligations and rights, not just as text but as dynamic data and algorithms capable of direct integration into digital systems.[32]

With the evolution of AI, particularly in natural language processing (NLP),[33] the imperative to convert traditional contract language into code is becoming increasingly nuanced. AI technologies can now 'interpret' complex legal language and execute contractual terms directly from natural text. This shift not only streamlines the transformation of textual contracts into their digital counterparts but also enhances the ability of these systems to adapt to and learn from real-world contract scenarios. Consequently, as AI continues to advance, its integration into computable contracting is likely to redefine the efficiency, accuracy, and adaptability of legal agreements in digital formats.

One promising application of computable contracting lies in public procurement, particularly in monitoring and assessing the modification of public contracts. For example, Article 72 Directive 2014/24/EU sets out specific conditions under which public contracts may be modified without triggering a new tendering process. Ensuring compliance with these conditions is crucial to uphold the fundamental public procurement principles of fair competition, equal treatment, and non-discrimination.[34] Computable contracting could support this objective by embedding Article 72's criteria directly into contract management systems.

Rather than relying solely on manual monitoring of quantitative thresholds – such as those outlined in Article 72(2) – a coded provision could systematically assess a wider set of legal and factual considerations. These include the nature and scope of the changes, justifications due to unforeseen circumstances, the identity of the contractor, and the overall impact on competition and proportionality.[35] By encoding these dimensions into a computable format, it becomes possible to

[29] ibid 15.

[30] 'Algorithmic enforcement allows contracts to be executed as quickly and cheaply as other computer code. Cost savings occur at every stage, from negotiating to enforcement, especially in replacing judicial enforcement with automated mechanisms'. K Werbach and N Cornell, 'Contracts Ex Machina' (2017) 67 *Duke Law Journal* 313, 335.

[31] H Surden, 'Computable Contracts' (2012) 46 *University of California Davis Law Review* 629, 667.

[32] ibid 15.

[33] For more on NLP and its development, see A Andhov, *Computational Law* (Stockholm, Karnov Group, 2022) 193–200.

[34] Art 18 Directive 2014/24/EU.

[35] See Art 72 Directive 2014/24/EU.

conduct automated, real-time assessments of proposed modifications, supporting legal compliance and transparency in public contract implementation.

iii. Smart Contracts

To add further intricacy to computational contracts, there is a third term – smart contracts. 'Smart contracts' are a specific type of computational contract that is not only digital but also *self-enforceable*, without any human intervention.[36] Initially defined by Szabo as 'a set of promises, specified in digital form, including protocols within which the parties perform on these promises'.[37] Szabo provided an example of a vending machine. All vending machines contain some protocol that responds to specific conditions with a predetermined conditional output. In other words, *if* a person chooses an item *and* pays for it, *then* the machine releases the item into a collection box, where a person can freely collect the item, thus concluding a sale contract.

Szabo envisioned smart contracts to enhance transparency (allowing parties to observe performance) and accountability (assigning responsibility to parties).[38] The term 'smart contract' has two interpretations: (1) a 'smart legal contract' that replicates or supplements traditional contracts, and (2) 'smart contract code', a software agent often using blockchain, whose legal status depends on the technology and legal framework.[39] This form of smart contract does not necessarily conform to the traditional understanding of a contract, and its legal standing remains a subject of debate, contingent upon the specifics of the technology employed and the relevant legal principles.

Smart contracts have become an extensively analysed topic within contract and public procurement scholarship.[40] Although theoretically promising, smart

[36] The term 'smart contract' was used for the first time by Nick Szabo in a blog post titled 'Smart Contracts' see N Szabo, *Smart Contracts* (1994), <www.fon.hum.uva.nl/rob/Courses/InformationInSpeech/CDROM/Literature/LOTwinterschool2006/szabo.best.vwh.net/smart.contracts.html> (hereinafter Smart Contracts) (describing a smart contract as 'a computerized transaction protocol that executes the terms of a contract').

[37] See also N Szabo, 'Smart Contracts: Building Blocks for Digital Markets' (1996) 16 *Extropy* 28; N Szabo, 'Formalizing and securing relationships on public networks' (1997) <nakamotoinstitute.org/formalizing-securing-relationships/>.

[38] Szabo, 'Smart Contracts: Building Blocks for Digital Markets' (n 37).

[39] C Clack, VA Bakshi, and L Braine, 'Smart Contract Templates: Foundations, Design and Research Directions' (2016) *arXiv preprint arXiv:1608.00771* <arxiv.org/abs/1608.00771>.

[40] See generally M Raskin, 'The Law and Legality of Smart Contracts' (2017) 2 *Georgetown Law Technology Review* 305; JG Allen, 'Wrapped and Staked: "Smart Contracts" and the Interaction of Natural and Formal Language' (2018) 14 *European Review of Contract Law* 307; M Durovic and A Janssen, 'The Formation of Blockchain-Based Smart Contracts in the Light of Contract Law' (2019) 6 *European Review of Private Law* 753. See about smart contracts in public procurement eg P Debono, 'Transforming Public Procurement Contracts Into Smart Contracts' (2019) 10(2) *International Journal of Information Technology Project Management* 16; JAT Casallas, JMC Lovelle, and JIR Molano, 'Smart Contracts with Blockchain in the Public Sector' (2020) 6(3) *International Journal of Interactive Multimedia and Artificial Intelligence* 1; NA Sava and D Dragoş, 'The Legal Regime of Smart Contracts in Public Procurement' (2022) 18(66) *Transylvanian Review of Administrative Sciences* 99.

contracts, together with other computational contract types, present numerous challenges for successful implementation. These include both technical and regulatory requirements for human involvement, potential errors in design, and the tension between the complexity of governmental contracts and the need for simplicity for efficient computational contracts.

This reality necessitates not only a thorough understanding of computational and smart contracts within the procurement process across private and public entities but also robust regulatory oversight. As with any technological innovation, computational contracts must function effectively within the contemporary reality in which we work and operate. Thus, the primary legal question becomes whether procurement and computational contracts can be meaningfully reconciled within existing structures.

iv. Public Contract as a Computational Contract?

The post-award, or execution phase, of public contracts plays a critical role, as it is the stage where compliance is ensured through contract management, performance monitoring, and enforcement. Despite its importance and the fact that this phase is ripe for innovation, computational contracts remain largely unexplored in this context.[41]

While computational tools have been adopted in earlier stages of procurement – such as automating calls for competition,[42] conducting e-auctions,[43] or in some cases, supporting automated tender evaluation[44] – their application in managing and enforcing contract performance is still in its infancy. This gap is especially significant given the growing reliance on specific contract performance conditions by contracting authorities, aimed at achieving broader social and environmental objectives.[45] These conditions, however, are often inadequately enforced in practice.

To demonstrate the potential of computational contracts in enhancing post-award public contract management, valuable insights can be drawn from their use in private SCM.[46]

[41] A 2019 study commissioned by the Directorate-General for Internal Market, Industry, Entrepreneurship and SMEs examined the global use of emerging technologies in public procurement, identifying 96 relevant projects. However, only a few addressed the post-award phase or involved computational contracts for monitoring contract execution. One example is the Seoul Municipal Government's initiative to use blockchain-based smart contracts to automate subcontractor payments in construction projects, ensuring timely and accurate payments. See https://ec.europa.eu/docsroom/documents/40102.

[42] SN Sánchez, 'The Implementation of Decentralised Ledger Technologies for Public Procurement' (2019) 14(3) *European Procurement & Public Private Partnership Law Review* 180, 188.

[43] For this purpose, contracting authorities shall structure the electronic auction as a repetitive electronic process, which occurs after an initial full evaluation of the tenders, enabling them to be ranked using automatic evaluation methods. See Art 35(1) Directive 2014/24/EU *in fine*.

[44] Sava and Dragoş (n 40) 103.

[45] Art 70 Directive 2014/24/EU.

[46] See JS Arlbjørn and PV Freytag, 'Public Procurement vs Private Purchasing' (2012) 25(3) *International Journal of Public Sector Management* 203.

In 2017, IBM and Walmart used smart contracts in the 'IBM Food Trust platform'[47] to ensure compliance and traceability in food supply chains.[48] Each stakeholder, from farmers to distributors, recorded their actions on a blockchain, enabling complete visibility of the food's journey. Smart contracts enforced conditions such as transport requirements (eg temperature and humidity monitoring via Internet of Things (IoT) sensors) and triggered penalties for deviations. For example, concerning the distribution of pork, shipping trucks used temperature and humidity sensors, Global Positioning System (GPS) and Geographic Information System (GIS) to ensure the safe delivery of meat.[49] Walmart could track trucks, monitor conditions, and receive alerts if any predetermined thresholds are exceeded.[50]

In public procurement, such technologies could improve contract enforcement. For instance, a food procurement contract could incorporate blockchain and IoT sensors to verify compliance with sustainability requirements – such as sourcing from short supply chains or maintaining specified transport conditions.[51] A computational contract could automatically track compliance and trigger penalties for breaches, such as exceeding intermediary limits or failing to meet environmental standards.

By automating these processes, contracting authorities can address persistent oversight and enforcement challenges, especially in areas like sustainable development where conventional monitoring tools are often inadequate. These innovations align with the European Commission's broader agenda for promoting Sustainable Public Procurement (SPP).

Such automation also contributes to the integrity of public spending by ensuring impartial, consistent enforcement without human intervention, while simultaneously acting as a strong deterrent to non-compliance due to its immediacy.[52] For example, if a shipment originates outside the specified geographical area, involves too many intermediaries, or fails to meet transport specifications, the smart contract can instantly impose predefined penalties.

[47] For a more elaborative explanation, see IBM <www.ibm.com/downloads/cas/8QABQBDR; www.ibm.com/products/supply-chain-intelligence-suite/food-trust>. For detailed case study see: R Kamath, 'Food Traceability on Blockchain: Walmart's Pork and Mango Pilots with IBM' (2018) 1(1) *The Journal of The British Blockchain Association* 1, 48.

[48] See Kamath (n 47).

[49] GIS is a technology used for capturing, storing, analysing, and managing data that is related to locations on the Earth's surface. Essentially, GIS allows you to visualise, question, interpret, and understand spatial data in ways that reveal relationships, patterns, and trends.

[50] See Kamath (n 47) 49.

[51] IoT is a network of connected devices that can collect and exchange data over the internet without human intervention. These 'smart' devices communicate and make decisions based on the data they gather. In supply chains, IoT is used for real-time inventory management and asset tracking. For example, sensors on shipping containers monitor location and conditions like temperature. If a container's temperature exceeds safe levels, an alert is triggered, allowing immediate corrective action. This improves efficiency, reduces losses, and ensures product quality.

[52] These could include withholding payments, applying financial fines, or even alerting authorities for further investigation.

Moreover, these enforcement mechanisms support the principles outlined in Directive 2014/24/EU, particularly Article 57(4)(g), which allows for the exclusion of economic operators who have shown significant or persistent deficiencies in prior contracts. By providing verifiable, real-time records of breaches, computational contracts help contracting authorities uphold these provisions, reinforcing fairness and accountability in public procurement.

In this context, computational contracts do not replace traditional legal contracts but rather supplement them – particularly for performance monitoring. In public food procurement, for instance, the classical contract can outline general obligations, including sustainability clauses and sanctions for non-compliance, while a computational contract operates as a dynamic annex. This annex enables real-time monitoring and enforcement, translating static legal provisions into active, automated oversight mechanisms.

II. Legal Requirements for Computational Contracts for Private and Public Contracts

Building on the introductory remarks on computational, computable, and smart contracts in the previous section, the next step is to examine their legal character. Specifically, it is necessary to assess whether computational contracts meet the criteria to be recognised as legally binding contracts – and more precisely, as public contracts – within the existing legal framework.

Determining the legal enforceability of a contract depends on meeting certain formal requirements, which vary across legal systems. This section begins by examining the criteria that computational contracts must satisfy under general European contract law. It then considers whether EU public procurement law adopts similar standards or imposes distinct formalities of its own.

While the PECL does not offer a single, concise definition of a 'contract', it establishes a broader framework for interpreting contractual relationships under European contract law.[53] In contrast, the DCFR defines a contract as 'an agreement which is intended to give rise to a binding legal relationship or to have some other legal effect'.[54] Earlier versions of this definition also included language to address situations where no clear subjective intention existed, but an agreement could be inferred from the parties' actions or statements. However, this is now adequately addressed in Article II.–4:102, and thus omitted from the final definition.[55]

[53] See Ch 2 s 2 PECL concerning contract formation.
[54] Book II–1:101(1) DCFR.
[55] See DCFR.

In the context of EU public procurement law, a public contract is defined as one 'for pecuniary interest concluded in writing between one or more economic operators and one or more contracting authorities and having as their object the execution of works, the supply of products or the provision of services'.[56] Thus, based on the definitions of contracts found in the examined sources so far, it cannot be ruled out that both public and private contracts may validly take a computational form.[57]

Whether a computational contract qualifies as a legally valid private or public contract largely depends on the formal requirements specific to that type of contract and the applicable national contract law. Unsurprisingly, the initial use cases for computational contracts have focused on highly formalised sectors such as finance, energy, and title transfers – areas where legal obligations can be clearly expressed using conditional logic ('if-then-else').[58] However, challenges arise in applying computational logic to more complex, relational, or long-term contracts. As DiMatteo and others argue, such contracts often rely on open-textured provisions and grant discretion to the parties to adapt over time, reflecting the inherent need for flexibility.[59]

Identifying which aspects of a contract can be translated into computational logic is, therefore, essential. Current technological capabilities fall short of fully automating the more nuanced aspects of complex legal agreements. With this in mind, the following sections will examine in greater depth the formal requirements relating to form, language, and interpretation in order to assess where and how computational contracts may fit within the existing legal framework.

A. Form of a Contract

Historically, contract law has evolved within a paradigm in which binding promises are primarily communicated through written or spoken language. In most cases, no specific form is required for a contract to be valid. However, certain types of contracts – such as those involving real estate, credit agreements, or particular consumer contracts – do require a written form as a condition of validity.

The PECL embrace a flexible approach to formality: '[a] contract need not be concluded or evidenced in writing nor is it subject to any other requirement

[56] Art 2(1)(5) Directive 2014/24/EU.

[57] See more about the relationship between the concept of public contract and the concept of contract in private law in ch 2.

[58] 'Legal automators tend to focus on … formalism (which defines "the ideal if not necessary form of 'law' [as] that of a 'rule', conceived as a clear prescription that exists prior to its application and that determines appropriate conduct or legal outcomes")'. See F Pasquale, 'A Rule of Persons, Not Machines: The Limits of Legal Automation' (2019) 87 *George Washington Law Review* 1, 44.

[59] LA DiMatteo, M Cannarsa, and C Poncibò, 'Smart Contracts and Contract Law' in LA DiMatteo, M Cannarsa, and C Poncibò (eds), *The Cambridge Handbook of Smart Contracts, Blockchain Technology and Digital Platforms* (Cambridge, Cambridge University Press, 2019) 8.

as to form'. The principles support freedom of form, allowing the existence of a contract to be proven by any means, including witness testimony.[60] Nonetheless, in practice, many Member States require commercial contracts to be in writing, as this remains one of the primary tools for evidencing the existence of a contract.[61] Although Article 1:301(6) PECL defines what constitutes 'written', it neither explicitly nor implicitly addresses broader interpretive issues, such as how declarations and communications between parties should be understood, or whether a written statement must have been comprehensible to the recipient in order to be valid.[62]

In Book II DCFR, the general provisions in Section 1 offer a definition of a 'contract' and Section 2 introduces the concept of a 'juridical act', defined as 'any statement or agreement, whether express or implied from conduct, which is intended to have legal effect as such. It may be unilateral, bilateral or multilateral'.[63] The order in which these definitions are presented – first the contract, then the juridical act – suggests that the drafters intended to establish the contract as the primary form of legally binding agreement, while allowing for contractual principles to extend to other juridical acts where appropriate.[64] In other words, under the DCFR, the contract forms the core of European law of obligations.[65] The EU itself, either through the DCFR, the PECL, or other tools,[66] does not seek to impose a concept of contract on the Member States, and thus, even the DCFR does not provide how agreements should be made.[67] This is understood as matters that must be left for the individual Member States.

While earlier paragraphs explored how instruments like the DCFR and the PECL define and conceptualise contracts more broadly, EU public procurement law operates within a more limited scope. Namely, the 2014 Public Procurement

[60] Art 2:101 (2) PECL.

[61] See eg Art 5.1.1 *Danske Lov* (Denmark); I 147 *Adlercreutz* (Sweden); Finland, s 36 *Hoppu* (Finland); Art 158 Civil Code (Greece); s 125 *Bürgerliches Gesetzbuch* (BGB) (Germany) (impliedly); s 883 *Allgemeines Bürgerliches Gesetzbuch* (AGBG) (Austria); Arts 219 Civil Code ff (Portugal).

[62] UG Schroeter, 'Interpretation of "Writing": Comparison Between Provisions of CISG (Article 13) and Counterpart Provisions of the Principles of European Contract Law' in J Felemegas (ed), *An International Approach to the Interpretation of the United Nations Convention on Contracts for the International Sale of Goods (1980) as Uniform Sales Law* (Cambridge, Cambridge University Press, 2007) 289–90.

[63] Book II–1:101(2) DCFR.

[64] S Grundmann, 'The Architecture of European Codes and Contract Law: A Survey of Structures and Contents' in S Grundmann and M Schauer (eds), *The Architecture of European Codes and Contract Law* (Deventer, Kluwer Law International, 2006) 7 et seq.

[65] Some even stipulate that the use of 'juridical act' is rather unnecessary for the DCFR's regulatory technique. See Schmidt, 'Der "juridical act" im DCFR: Ein nützlicher Grundbegriff des europäischen Privatrechts?' (2010) (2) *Zeitschrift für europäisches Privatrecht* 304, 311.

[66] The proposed CESL was an attempt to make qualitative changes to European contract law through the development of an optional Common European Contract Law, which however (as many other contract law attempts) was unsuccessful. On the future of European private law, see Janssen and Schulze, *The Future of European Private Law* (n 13).

[67] See E Mik, 'Smart Contracts: A Requiem' (2019) 36(1) *Journal of Contract Law* 70.

Directives primarily govern the award phase of public procurement, leaving the regulation of the resulting contract, including its validity, largely to national legal frameworks, whether private or public in nature.

While Article 2(1)(5) Directive 2014/24/EU provides a definition of a public contract, this concept is a distinctly European construct.[68] It functions primarily as a 'reference point' – its purpose is to determine when the procedural and substantive rules of Directive 2014/24/EU apply, rather than to establish a universally binding definition of a public contract across Member States.[69]

For the purposes of EU public procurement law, a public contract must meet two basic criteria: it must be concluded in writing and be for pecuniary interest. Directive 2014/24/EU defines 'in writing' as 'any expression consisting of words or figures which can be read, reproduced and subsequently communicated, including information transmitted and stored by electronic means'.[70]

This broad definition clearly accommodates public contracts to be stored and signed electronically. In such instances, natural language is used, and therefore, concerns about readability and communicability do not arise.

However, questions may arise when a public contract is implemented in a computational form – that is, expressed in computer code rather than natural language and executed or stored electronically. Such contracts differ from traditional text-based documents in that their content may not be directly understandable without specialised tools or technical knowledge. Nevertheless, the authors argue that computational contracts can satisfy Directive 2014/24/EU minimal formal requirements, provided that the code is capable of being read, reproduced, and communicated – albeit in a machine-readable format.

The requirement that public contracts be concluded in writing is closely linked to the principle of transparency in EU public procurement law.[71] Oral agreements, by contrast, would raise concerns about integrity and increase the risk of rule violations. In contrast, computational contracts – although expressed in code – do not pose the same risk. They remain written records, capable of preserving all essential contractual terms, and thus can serve as reliable evidence of agreement.

As Steinicke notes, the writing requirement should be interpreted broadly, encompassing any document that clearly sets out all essential contract terms.[72] This flexible interpretation enables the inclusion of computational contracts within

[68] A Sanchez-Graells, 'Article 2: Definitions' in R Caranta and A Sanchez-Graells (eds), *European Public Procurement: Commentary on Directive 2014/24/EU* (Cheltenham, Edward Elgar Publishing, 2021) 17–30. See also ch 2.

[69] See Case C-367/19 *Tax-Fin-Lex d.o.o. v Ministrstvo za notranje zadeve* ECLI:EU:C:2020:685, [2020] para 29. See also ch 2.

[70] Art 2(18) Directive 2014/24/EU. More about the form of public contract, see also ch 8.

[71] Art 18 2014 Directive 2014/24/EU.

[72] M Steinicke, 'Commentary to Article 2(1)(18)' in M Steinicke and PL Vesterdorf (eds), *Commentary on EU Public Procurement Law* (Oxford, Bloomsbury Publishing, 2018).

the legal framework, provided that they maintain accessibility and clarity, even if through machine-readable formats.[73] While traditional text-based documentation continues to play a vital role, digital or coded elements can complement and even enhance contract clarity, precision, and enforceability.

Ultimately, writing is a medium of communication, and like all media, it evolves. As Derrida observed, writing constitutes the earliest form of technology, and its history follows a logic of mechanical economy.[74] From clay tablets in Mesopotamia to modern electronic data interchange (EDI), technology has continually reshaped how contracts are recorded and transmitted.[75] Today, we are witnessing a new phase: just as earlier forms of writing extended the durability and reach of agreements, computational contracts have the potential to offer automation, precision, and real-time execution – reducing ambiguity and limiting the need for manual intervention.

Importantly, the contract itself exists independently of the medium that records it. As Allen argues, conflating the legal contract with its written expression risks ignoring key elements of the underlying agreement.[76] If to deny the legal status of computational contracts simply because they are expressed in code, one would, by the same logic, have to question the legitimacy of traditional paper contracts. The written document is not the contract itself but a representation of it.[77] Therefore, if a computational contract accurately reflects the parties' agreement, is expressed through verifiable and durable means, and can be understood – albeit with appropriate tools – it should be recognised as legally valid.[78] Even within procurement law, which insists on contracts being 'in writing', there is no principled reason to exclude digital or blockchain-based contracts from legal recognition.

B. Simplifying Contractual Language Through Code

A common critique of computational contracts is that they are more difficult to 'read' or 'understand' than contracts written in natural languages such as English or French, primarily because the general public cannot read computer code.[79] However, it is unlikely that computational contracts will entirely replace

[73] Parallels can be found between computational contracting and visual contracting. See M Andhov, CB Andersen, and T Hebbard, 'A Roadmap to Simplify Procurement? The Potential of Visual Contracting in Australian and Danish Systems' (2025) 34(1) *Public Procurement Law Review* 47.

[74] J Derrida, *Limited Inc* (Evanston, Northwestern University Press, 1988) 4.

[75] Surden (n 31) 639.

[76] Allen (n 40) 40.

[77] ZX Tan, 'Beyond the Real and the Paper Deal: The Quest for Contractual Coherence in Contractual Interpretation' (2016) 79(4) *Modern Law Review* 623.

[78] M Ferraris and G Terrengo, 'Documentality: A Theory of Social Reality' (2014) 57(3) *Revisti di estitica* 11.

[79] Here, one could also argue that today, it might be that more people can read a code than there are lawyers who master natural language. But we will leave this argument for now.

natural-language contracts in the foreseeable future. Instead, they will most likely function as integrated components within traditional contractual frameworks. The coded portion of a contract will still be required to comply with legal standards for enforceability.

Languages, broadly speaking, can be categorised as either natural or formal. Natural languages – such as Danish or Gaelic – have evolved organically within human communities, whereas formal languages are deliberately designed, often to facilitate communication between humans and machines. Despite their different origins, both types of language follow defined rules to ensure clarity and coherence.

Linguists studying either formal or natural language typically focus on three key dimensions: syntax, semantics, and pragmatics.

- Syntax concerns the structural aspects of language – such as word order, suffixes, articles, and logical relationships (eg subject-object relations, action, temporal sequences). Both natural and formal languages exhibit syntactic properties.
- Semantics pertains to meaning – the interpretation of words and how they combine to form meaningful expressions. In natural language, semantics can be fluid and context-dependent. In contrast, formal languages aim for precision and unambiguity. Recent developments in NLP, particularly when combined with AI, have enabled machines to assign meaning to human language in increasingly sophisticated ways. These technologies allow for machine-based communication that mimics human understanding, even if the underlying mechanisms differ substantially.[80]
- Pragmatics, the most recent branch of linguistic study, focuses on how meaning is shaped by context. In legal interpretation, pragmatics plays a particularly significant role. Courts often rely not only on the literal meaning of contractual terms but also on their interpretation within broader commercial and social contexts.[81] Legal language, while striving for formal consistency, is still susceptible to ambiguity – especially in complex domains[82] such as public procurement.

Given that code constitutes a formal language governed by structured syntactic and defined semantics, it may, in fact, serve to simplify contractual language rather than make it more complex.

[80] For an explanation of how for example, ChatGPT works and how it 'understands' us, see A Andhov, 'Navigating AI: What Do Lawyers Need to Know about ChatGPT?' (2024) *Copenhagen Legal/Tech Blog* <legaltechlab.sites.ku.dk/2024/02/16/navigating-ai-what-do-lawyers-need-to-know-about-chatgpt-alexandra-andhov/>.

[81] Allen (n 40) 37.

[82] Complexity and simplicity define a continuum according to the relative degrees of involvement in a contracting process or contract term. For more on contracting complexity, see LA Cunningham, 'Language, Deals, and Standards: The Future of XML Contracts' (2006) 84(2) *Washington University Law Review* 332.

i. Simplifying Contracts with Code

Contracts – particularly complex ones – are often difficult to interpret due to several factors, including technical language, excessive length, dense formatting, and the prevalence of legalese.[83] One effective strategy for improving clarity is to simplify the contractual language. When certain provisions are translated into code, the natural-language version must often be refined and clarified first. This necessary simplification can result in increased clarity in both versions.

For example, clauses related to payment schedules, delivery timelines, and performance obligations can be rephrased in clear, concise language prior to being translated into code. In the context of construction contracts, smart contracts can convert payment terms into precise, automated instructions – triggering payments upon the completion of predefined milestones. This approach not only reduces delays but also enhances reliability and payment security.[84] Similarly, performance conditions such as delivery deadlines can be expressed as measurable, objective criteria that the code can monitor and enforce autonomously.

It is important to note that not all contractual provisions are suitable to be computed. However, many are – and arguably should be – translated into code where feasible. Provisions most amenable to this process tend to share common characteristics: they are objective, quantifiable, binary, automatable, data-driven, unambiguous, repetitive, and typically structured around trigger-action mechanisms involving conditional rights and obligations.

a. Example: Automated Service Contracts

A contracting authority outsourcing cleaning services traditionally would verify the quality of such services through manual inspections. In contrast, a computational contract could monitor performance in real time by relying on objective, measurable standards. These standards might include the absence of visible waste, the timely replenishment of supplies, and acceptable air quality levels.

[83] See eg MA Eisenberg, 'The Limits of Cognition and the Limits of Contract' (1995) *Stanford Law Review* 211, 241 ('Form insurance contracts, for example, typically include thirty, forty, or more terms. Moreover, the meaning and effect of the preprinted provisions will very often be inaccessible to laypersons.'); AM McDonald and LF Ranor, 'The Cost of Reading Privacy Policies (2008) 4 *Journal of Law and Policy for the Information Society* 543 (authors conducted empirical research and discovered that it would take the average consumer 244 hours – which equals 30.5 standard workdays – to read all privacy policies that they encounter online annually); J Choi, M Gulati, and RE Scott, 'Variation in Boilerplate: Rational Design or Random Mutation?' (2018) 20(1) *American Law And Economics Review* (documenting how legal terms in commercial contracts tend to persist and resist change).

[84] S Ahmadisheykhsarmast and R Sonmez, 'A Smart Contract System for Security of Payment of Construction Contracts' (2020) 120 *Automation in Construction* 103401; H Hamledari and M Fischer, 'Role of Blockchain-Enabled Smart Contracts in Automating Construction Progress Payments' (2021) 13(1) *Journal of Legal Affairs and Dispute Resolution in Engineering and Construction* 04520038.

By integrating IoT sensors – to track supply levels or air quality indicators – and digital feedback systems (already widely deployed in settings such as airports),[85] the contract can be programmed to execute automated actions based on real-time data:

1. If sensor readings or feedback fall below acceptable thresholds, the system issues a notification to the cleaning staff;
2. Once corrective measures are taken, the system reassesses the relevant indicators;
3. Upon verification that the required standards are met, the contract triggers an automatic payment – eliminating the need for manual oversight.[86]

Although this represents a relatively straightforward example, thousands of similar service contracts across the public sector could benefit from this level of automation and real-time responsiveness.

It is important to note, however, that not all contractual provisions can – or should – be coded. Clauses related to *force majeure*, dispute resolution, or those requiring subjective interpretation continue to demand the nuance and flexibility afforded by natural language. Nevertheless, simplifying what can be coded paves the way for a more transparent, more efficient contract that balances traditional legal writing with the precision and automation offered by computational contracts.

C. Computational Contract Interpretation

Both formal and natural languages serve as a medium for documenting contractual intent, and as such, they require interpretation. While computational contracts can automate certain provisions, their coded components are also subject to interpretation. Although code can offer precision, understanding its logic and structure can be as challenging as interpreting complex legal language. Nevertheless, the ultimate goal of interpretation remains the same – to determine the correct meaning of a contract in line with the parties' intention.[87]

i. Interpretation in Contract Law

Rules on contractual interpretation are a central concern for every contract regime, be it domestic or supranational. Contract interpretation rules were

[85] As an example of such a tool Zonka Feedback, <www.zonkafeedback.com/templates/washroom-feedback-form-template>.

[86] This approach can be extended to complex concession agreements, where contract performance may directly impact user fees. Implementing such solutions helps safeguard both the contracting authority's and users' interests – ensuring service quality and financial fairness.

[87] A Schwartz and RE Scott, 'Contract Theory and the Limits of Contract Law' (2003) 113 *Yale Law Journal* 541, 568.

historically intertwined with those governing treaties and other legal instruments. Today, European private lawyers acknowledge the need for dedicated rules governing contract interpretation. This is also shown by diverse contract model codes that devote entire chapters to the rules and principles of contractual interpretation.[88]

In contrast, EU public procurement law does not generally touch on contract interpretation *per se*.[89] This is arguably logical since public contracts arise from procurement procedures but are ultimately governed by national law. The interpretation of public procurement contracts is therefore determined by national legal frameworks, which take into account public interest considerations and the nature of the contracting parties.[90] Since Directive 2014/24/EU does 'not commit to any specific notion [of a public contract] used in any of the Member States',[91] analysing computational public contracts solely through the EU public procurement law lens is not feasible.

Despite the existence of rules of interpretation, ambiguity remains an inherent challenge in legal texts. Legal language is highly specialised, and its meaning is often obscured by technical terminology understood primarily by legal professionals. 'True meaning of a legal text is hidden within the language employed'.[92] Thus, introducing formal language (code) into contracts may add another layer of complexity.

Depending on the jurisdiction and the court, and whether it is a public or private contract, different lenses and values might be applied when interpreting a contract. One of the key principles of interpretation under the DCFR is the protection of reasonable reliance, expectations, and effectiveness.[93] Under Chapter 8 DCFR, 'a contract is to be interpreted according to the common intention of the parties even if this differs from the literal meaning of the words'.[94]

This principle suggests that when a contract includes computational elements, the parties' intent must take precedence over the strict, literal reading of the code.[95]

[88] These include ch 5 PECL; Book II, ch 8 DCFR; as well as ch 6 CESL; See S Vogenauer, 'Interpretation' in N Jansen and R Zimmermann (eds), *Commentaries on European Contract Law* (Oxford, Oxford University Press, 2018).

[89] This issue is left to Member States, which may adopt different contractual models. See ch 3.

[90] R Caranta, 'Article 1: Subject Matter and Scope' in R Caranta and A Sanchez-Graells (eds), *European Public Procurement: Commentary on Directive 2014/24/EU* (Cheltenham, Edward Elgar Publishing, 2021) 4. Caranta succinctly presents this by offering comparative overview, ie by arguing that public procurement contract interpretation varies by jurisdiction, with the UK relying on general contract law, France incorporating public law elements in contrats publics, and Germany emphasising the public authority's role in *Verwaltungsvertrag* agreements.

[91] ibid.

[92] G Samuel, 'Is Legal Reasoning Like Medical Reasoning?' (2015) 35 *Legal Studies* 323, 324.

[93] Art 0:204 DCFR: 'When the contract is subject to interpretation, or when its validity or performance is threatened, the effectiveness of the contract should be preferred if its destruction would harm the legitimate interests of one of the parties'.

[94] II–8:101(3) and 8:105 DCFR.

[95] II–8:102 DCFR ff.

ii. *Evolution of Contract Interpretation: From Literal to Pragmatic*

Historically, legal systems favoured literal, word-based interpretation (ie objective approach). It is only with the increasing refinement of legal culture that subjective elements begin to be considered.[96] As legal culture evolved, subjective elements, such as the intent of the parties – the 'animus', gained importance. Since the nineteenth century, the debate between subjective vs objective contractual interpretations has remained at the centre of academic debates[97] and unresolved. The two interpretation theories are framed in terms of the 'will theory' or 'theory of intention' (subjective theory) on the one hand and the 'theory of expression' or 'theory of declaration' (objective theory) on the other.[98] Both are relevant in today's discourse, as they are necessary to design solutions that are as predictable and, at the same time, as fair as possible.

Most modern legal systems balance both approaches, applying objective interpretation by default but making exceptions where parties can prove they assigned a special meaning to contract terms. For example, German courts are willing to make an exception from their commonly applied objective interpretation, where the parties' shared understanding differs from common usage (following the Roman law principle *falsa demonstratio non nocet* (the wrong denomination does no harm)).[99]

In practice, the challenge lies in establishing and proving the intent. Yet, for the sake of legal certainty, the understanding of reasonable persons in the same position as the parties ought to prevail as long as there are no special circumstances that merit a preference should be given to an unreasonable but mutually intended meaning.[100] According to the PECL, if there are no indicators of the parties' true intentions, the court or arbitrator is to apply the objective criterion of an understanding that a reasonable person would attribute to the statements and conduct of the party (ie to the contract) in the equivalent circumstances.[101] The PECL provides a clearer guideline for when to switch from a subjective to an objective approach, which occurs when there is no evidence of the parties' true intentions, requiring reliance on the literal meaning of the words.[102]

[96] See generally H Hübner, 'Subjektivismus in der Entwicklung des Privatrechts' in Dieter M and HH Seiler (eds), *Festschrift für Max Kaser* (Munich, Beck, 1976) 715 sqq.

[97] According to Fritz Pringsheim, the Byzantines were the first to attribute to the parties an intention directed towards achieving specific legal ends. See F Pringsheim, 'Animus in Roman Law' (1933) 49 *Law Quarterly Review* 379; R Zimmermann, *The Law of Obligations: Roman Foundations of the Civilian Tradition* (Oxford, Oxford University Press, 1996) 624.

[98] Vogenauer (n 89) 756–58.

[99] ibid.

[100] ibid 760.

[101] Art 5:102 PECL.

[102] M Stanivukovic, 'Interpretation of the Contract: Editorial Remarks on the Manner in which the PECL may be used to Interpret and Supplement CISG Article 8' in J Felemegas (ed), *An International Approach to the Interpretation of the United Nations Convention on Contracts for the International Sale of Goods (1980) as Uniform Sales Law* (Cambridge, Cambridge University Press, 2009) 275–76.

iii. Interpreting Computational Contracts

This potential shift from traditional contracts to computational ones adds to the balance between objective and subjective interpretation. While traditional contracts rely on the interpretation of words and phrases, computational contracts involve code, which is inherently precise yet not immune to ambiguity. As such, courts will need to analyse both the function of the code and the broader contract framework to determine the true intent behind coded provisions. Yet, is this in any way different from, for example, technical specifications attached to a code?

Since formal languages follow strict logic and structure, they should, in theory, be less ambiguous than natural languages. However, they can still behave in unexpected ways from a human perspective.[103]

Courts may need to consider additional layers:

1. The intended function of the code (not just its individual components);
2. How would a reasonable technical expert interpret it in light of the overall contract?

Some interpretive principles from the PECL could be useful when interpreting computational contracts. Specifically, the rule of interpreting the individual provisions regarding the contract as a whole could provide support for interpreting the computational contract in light of the text of the rule on giving preference to an interpretation that renders the contract terms effective.[104] As with traditional contracts, exceptions may arise when the literal interpretation of the code conflicts with the parties' established intent. Proving intent within the technical realm presents unique challenges, requiring a blend of legal and technical expertise to ensure fairness and predictability that might necessitate the involvement of technical experts.

Moreover, unlike natural languages, some formal languages are purpose-built with clearly defined goals. For instance, 'Simplicity', a programming language developed to enhance Bitcoin Script, was designed to improve expressiveness while preserving key security and performance characteristics.[105] The legal interpretation of clauses written in such a language may need to account for these underlying design objectives, potentially requiring the development of new interpretive methods.

This could involve using developer documentation like dictionaries or grammar guides, requiring meta-language discussions about the original intended

[103] N Atzei, M Bartoletti, and T Cimplo, 'A Survey of Attacks on Ethereum Smart Contracts (SoK)' in M Maffei and M Ryan (eds), *Principles of Security and Trust: POST 2017 Proceedings* (New York, Springer, 2017) 164.

[104] Art 5:105 PECL.

[105] R O'Connor, 'Simplicity: A New Language for Blockchains' (2017) *Proceedings of the 2017 Workshop on Programming Languages and Analysis for Security. ACM, New York, NY, USA* <www.arxiv.org/abs/1711.03028 >.

meaning. Determining the authoritative status of various statements, especially in open-source languages with many contributors over time, might add additional complexity.[106]

Ultimately, as the use of computational contracts becomes more widespread in commercial contexts, it is likely that the formal languages employed will become standardised and widely accepted – much like the common acceptance of contracts drafted in English. Consequently, concerns regarding interpretation are expected to diminish over time. Where interpretive challenges *do* arise, they can be addressed through existing legal mechanisms, just as with traditional contracts.

III. Contracts as Computational Systems

Lawyers recognise that contracts are not merely collections of legal terms, but complex instruments that integrate legal, economic, and operational considerations. In the private sector, law firms often rely on contract catalogues, standardised clauses, and management software to ensure consistency and efficiency. Similarly, public procurement makes extensive use of standard forms to promote transparency and ensure accessibility.

Given this complexity, computational systems offer a natural evolution in contract management. These tools can analyse, standardise, automate, and optimise aspects of contracting – from drafting to execution – while also enabling predictive insights based on historical data.

In public procurement, such systems are particularly valuable for long-term planning, enabling more informed budget allocation and proactive risk mitigation through analysis of past contract performance.[107] They also support compliance with Article 72(1)(a) Directive 2014/24/EU, which permits contract modification without retendering, provided the original review clauses are 'clear, precise, and unequivocal'.

A. From Contract Catalogues to Standardised Contracts

In legal practice, especially in the private sector, contract catalogues are widely used to streamline drafting and review. Law firms maintain repositories of standardised clauses – such as non-disclosure or warranty provisions – each annotated with guidance and references to past cases or deals. Some firms go further, compiling

[106] Allen (n 40) 51.

[107] Planning obligations in public procurement are typically established by national legislation, most commonly through public finance and public procurement laws. In Poland, for instance, the requirement to prepare a procurement plan for the upcoming financial year is set out in Art 23 *Ustawa z dnia 11 września 2019 r. – Prawo zamówień publicznych* (Polish Public Procurement Act).

brochures of full contract forms with accompanying commentary tailored to specific transaction types.[108] This approach has led to a relatively uniform contract architecture across firms, industries, and jurisdictions – promoting simplicity, reducing drafting costs, and enhancing review efficiency. Legal theories on contract design often treat contracts as modular and decomposable, aligning with this practice.[109] Yet the accumulated legal knowledge embedded in these templates – honed over decades of experience – remains difficult to fully standardise.

Public procurement benefits similarly from standardised forms, which enhance accessibility, transparency, and interoperability.[110] These forms simplify procedures, reduce costs for contracting authorities and bidders, and promote SME participation by offering a predictable and familiar format. Tools like the European Single Procurement Document (ESPD) exemplify how standardisation can improve both inclusion and competition.[111]

Standardisation and cataloguing form the foundation for computational contracting, offering legal clarity, operational efficiency, and inclusivity. The natural next step is to explore how today's technologies can take us even further.

B. Computational (Data) Analysis of a Contract and its Clauses

A contract's effectiveness depends not only on its legal terms but also on its logical structure. Coherent clause organisation enhances enforceability and reduces transaction costs. Hwang and Jennejohn's theory of 'contractual structuralism' emphasises that how a contract is put together affects every stage of its lifecycle – design, performance, and enforcement.[112]

Clause-level terms such as representations, warranties, and indemnities are crafted to allocate risk and minimise costs.[113] As Gilson observed, optimising key provisions improves negotiation outcomes.[114] Empirical studies have shown that large law firms, through exposure to vast volumes of contract data, are better

[108] Cunningham (n 83) 329.

[109] S Shavell, 'On the Writing and the Interpretation of Contracts' (2006) 22(2) *Journal of Law, Economics, and Organisation* 289.

[110] Standard model documents are provided for in Art 51 Directive 2014/24/EU – Form and manner of publication of notices.

[111] ESPD is a standardised self-declaration form informing about businesses' financial status, abilities, and suitability for a public procurement used in the qualification stage of public procurement procedure. See Art 59 Directive 2014/24/EU.

[112] C Hwang and M Jennejohn, 'Deal Structure' (2018) 113 *Northwestern University Law Review* 279, 284.

[113] RJ Gilson, 'Value Creation by Business Lawyers: Legal Skills and Asset Pricing' (1984) 94 *Yale Law Journal* 239, 255.

[114] ibid 254.

positioned to refine terms that enhance client outcomes.[115] Long before today's computational tools, scholars like Ma and Allen even advocated using mathematical notation to express contracts more precisely.[116]

This demonstrates that legal drafting already has quantifiable components – especially in private and public contracts where provisions influence risk allocation and financial outcomes. The key question is whether this embedded legal knowledge can be translated into computational tools capable of recommending optimal formulations.

By analysing historical contract data, computational systems can identify which clauses reduce risk or deliver more favourable outcomes. This shifts contract drafting from an art toward a data-informed science. Contracting authorities – who hold vast repositories of contracts – stand to gain significantly from such analysis.[117]

For example, tools such as Lexis for Microsoft Office can be used to build documents based on the work of more than 850+ attorneys.[118] Similarly, 'Definely' provides automated suggestions for clauses that align with specific regulatory requirements, reducing non-compliance risk.[119] Furthermore, computational systems could flag potential risks by comparing proposed contract terms against a database of past disputes, offering preventative insights before contracts are finalised.[120]

IV. Conclusion

Computational contracts represent a potential significant evolution in contract management that bridges public and private sector practices. These contracts, with their various structural forms and functional capabilities, offer potential advantages in efficiency, transparency, and precision – benefits particularly valuable in

[115] See E de Fonenay, 'Law Firm Selection and the Value of Transactional Lawyering' (2015) *Journal of Corporate Law* 393, 396–98, 405–07.

[116] M Ma, 'The Mathematization of Legal Writing' in JG Allen and P Hunn (eds), *Smart Legal Contracts* (Oxford, Oxford University Press, 2022) 314. Allen introduced six elementary logical connections: implication, conjunction, co-implication, exclusive disjunction, inclusive disjunction, and negation; see LE Allen, 'Symbolic Logic: A Razor-Edged Tool for Drafting and Interpreting Legal Documents' (1957) 66 *Yale Law Journal* 833, 836.

[117] Here a detailed analysis would need to be conducted across various Member States, as according to Sanchez-Graells there is a limitation in accessing the public data. See A Sanchez-Graells, 'Data-Driven and Digital Procurement Governance: Revisiting Two Well-Known Elephant Tales' (2019) *SSRN Electronic Journal*.

[118] Lexis <www.lexisnexis.com/en-us/products/lexis-for-microsoft-office.page>.

[119] A Andhov and F Castorio, 'Definely – From an Idea to a Product' *Copenhagen Legal/Tech Lab Blog*, 18 October 2022 <legaltechlab.sites.ku.dk/2022/10/18/definely-legal-tech-case-study/>.

[120] For example, a tool *Juro* offers contract compliance that ensures that the contracts conform with applicable regulations; available online at: <juro.com/learn/contract-compliance>.

public procurement where accuracy, accountability, and compliance are essential both for contract conclusion and subsequent modifications.[121]

The public sector stands to gain from the private sector's experiences with computational contracts. Private industry has already navigated various technical and interpretive challenges that public entities now face. Law firms' established practices – using contract catalogues, standardised clauses, and automated management software – provide valuable models for public authorities seeking greater consistency and efficiency in their contractual frameworks.

Specifically, the private sector's experience demonstrates how computational contracts can:

- Transform contract execution through automation, reducing delays and administrative burdens;
- Enable real-time performance monitoring through objective, measurable standards;
- Apply data analytics to historical contract repositories to identify optimal clause formulations;
- Balance formal language (code) with natural language to achieve both precision and flexibility.

While public procurement can benefit from these private sector innovations, it must adapt them to address unique public procurement and public interest considerations. The integration of computational elements into public contracts requires careful attention to interpretation challenges – courts may need to analyse both code functionality and broader contractual frameworks to determine intent, potentially requiring both legal and technical expertise. The principles developed in private contract interpretation, such as those from the PECL balancing objective and subjective approaches, offer valuable guidance for public authorities implementing computational contracts, particularly in countries that categorise public contracts as private law contracts ('private-oriented hybrid model').

As computational contracts become more standardised across sectors, interpretation concerns will likely diminish. However, the public sector must approach this digital transformation thoughtfully, ensuring that automation enhances rather than compromises fundamental public procurement and public contract law principles. The most successful implementation will leverage private sector experience while adapting it to public sector needs – creating contracts that are not only technologically sophisticated but also legally sound, interpretively clear, and aligned with public interest objectives.

[121] See Art 73(a) Directive 2014/24/EU, which indicates consequences for termination of the public contract in the case of inadmissible changes due to Art 72. See also more in ch 7.

11

Sustainability and its Enforcement in Private and Public Contracts

DÉSIRÉE KLINGLER, PATRICK ZIMMERMANN
AND STEVEN VAN GARSSE

I. Introduction

In recent years, sustainability – particularly in the form of environmental, social, and governance (ESG) considerations – has become increasingly prominent in financial markets, commercial practice, and legal discourse.[1] ESG factors are no longer viewed solely as ethical or reputational concerns; they have become a central focus of both national and international public policy.[2] Despite this growing importance, the meaning, scope, and enforceability of sustainability and ESG commitments remain fluid and subject to ongoing legal and practical debate.

This chapter investigates how sustainability is understood and enforced in the context of both private and public contracts. For the purposes of this analysis, public contracts refer to agreements concluded between public contracting authorities and private contractors.[3] Section II of the chapter examines the

[1] See, eg A Halfmeier, 'Nachhaltiges Privatrecht' (2016) 216 *Archiv für die civilistische Praxis* 717; A Hellgardt, *Regulierung und Privatrecht: Staatliche Verhaltenssteuerung mittels Privatrecht und ihre Bedeutung für Rechtswissenschaft, Gesetzgebung und Rechtsanwendung* (Tübingen, Mohr Siebeck, 2016); AC Mittwoch, *Nachhaltigkeit im Unternehmensrecht* (Tübingen, Mohr Siebeck, 2022); JE Schirmer, *Nachhaltiges Privatrecht* (Tübingen, Mohr Siebeck, 2023); MP Weller, *Gutachten F zum 74. Deutschen Juristentag: Empfehlen sich im Kampf gegen den Klimawandel gesetzgeberische Maßnahmen auf dem Gebiet des Gesellschaftsrechts?* (Munich, CH Beck, 2024).

[2] See, eg European Commission, 'Europe 2020. A strategy for smart, sustainable and inclusive growth. Communication from the Commission', COM(2010) 2020 final; European Commission, 'The European Green Deal sets out how to make Europe the first climate-neutral continent by 2050, boosting the economy, improving people's health and quality of life, caring for nature, and leaving no one behind', Press release of 11 December 2019, for the current status of the measures see <commission.europa.eu/strategy-and-policy/priorities-2019-2024/european-green-deal_en>; European Commission, 'European industrial strategy' <commission.europa.eu/strategy-and-policy/priorities-2019-2024/europe-fit-digital-age/european-industrial-strategy_en>. With respect to sustainability in public procurement, see below s II.B.

[3] Art 2(1)(5) Directive 2014/24/EU; Art 5(1) of Directive 2014/23/EU. Contracts awarded by entities operating in the water, energy, transport, and postal sectors under Directive 2014/25/EU are excluded from the scope of this chapter.

meaning and legal framing of sustainability in private and public contracting. It highlights the conceptual and structural similarities and differences between ESG and sustainability, with particular emphasis on the requirement that, in public procurement, sustainability criteria must be 'linked to the subject-matter of the contract'. This requirement introduces a higher degree of legal rigidity compared to private contracts, where sustainability terms can be adopted more flexibly following the principle of freedom of contract.

The following section III considers the nature and legal status – mandatory or voluntary – of sustainability requirements applicable across both contract types. Section IV addresses the enforcement of sustainability clauses in private and public contracts, drawing on examples from three European jurisdictions: Germany, Switzerland, and Belgium. Germany and Switzerland are examples of what this anthology refers to as the 'private-oriented hybrid model', with Germany being the leading representative of this model.[4] Switzerland follows a similar approach with fewer mandatory public requirements for contract performance than Germany. Belgium, by contrast, represents one of the most private-leaning forms of the 'public-oriented hybrid model'.[5] These jurisdictions offer varied perspectives on how public procurement and contract law frameworks shape both the substance and enforceability of sustainability obligations. We explore enforcement mechanisms available in private law, including statutory contract law instruments such as warranties and substitute performance, as well as special contractual agreements. Newer approaches, such as incentive clauses, and the influence of soft law instruments like industry standards, are also addressed. The section further discusses mechanisms to enforce sustainability requirements through mandatory legal provisions, ie how public law norms override contractual autonomy, and how enforcement is supported through tools such as contractual penalties and termination rights available to contracting authorities in the event of non-compliance with statutory or contractual sustainability requirements. Section V concludes the chapter.

II. The Meaning of Sustainability in Private and Public Contracts

The meaning of sustainability has evolved from voluntary corporate initiatives to increasingly formalised obligations, shaped by both private initiatives (such as standards for self-regulation) and public law. Having said that, the understanding and application of sustainability differ between private and public contexts, reflecting the underlying public and private legal regimes, policy objectives, and instruments available for enforcement.

[4] See ch 3.
[5] ibid.

A. Sustainability, Corporate Social Responsibility (CSR), and ESG in Private Commercial Contracts

The conceptual starting point for sustainability in commercial contracts, and within the broader corporate context, lies in the notion of CSR.[6] Traditionally understood as a form of international private business self-regulation, CSR seeks to promote broader societal objectives through ethically informed business conduct.[7] It operates at the level of individual corporations, encouraging practices that reflect concern for employee welfare,[8] environmentally responsible production,[9] the selection of suppliers that eschew child labour,[10] and the pursuit of consumer satisfaction.[11] Among these, environmental protection is frequently regarded as the 'vanguard issue' in CSR, and consequently figures prominently in contractual sustainability clauses.[12]

In recent years, CSR has been addressed more directly in legislative frameworks at both the EU and national levels. Notable examples include the EU Corporate Sustainability Reporting Directive (CSRD)[13] and the EU Corporate Sustainability Due Diligence Directive (CSDDD), which extends CSR's scope from voluntary commitments to formal legal obligations, particularly in relation to reporting and risk management along global supply chains.[14]

Closely related to CSR is the concept of ESG, which complements CSR by introducing measurable standards into corporate governance and operations.[15]

[6] M Andhov and KP Mitkidis, 'Sustainability Requirements in EU Public and Private Procurement – A Right or an Obligation?' (2017) 1 *Nordic Journal of Commercial Law* 55, 56–87.

[7] B Sheehy, 'Defining CSR: Problems and Solutions' (2015) 131(3) *Journal of Business Ethics* 625, 635; H Lian and L Renneboog, 'On the Foundations of Corporate Social Responsibility' (2017) 72(2) *The Journal of Finance* 853, 854.

[8] A Edmans, L Li. and C Zhang, 'Employee Satisfaction, Labor Market Flexibility, and Stock Returns around the World' (2014) *National Bureau of Economic Research Working Paper No. 20300*, <www.nber.org/system/files/working_papers/w20300/w20300.pdf>.

[9] G Dowell, S Hart, and B Yeung, 'Do Corporate Global Environmental Standards Create or Destroy Market Value?' (2000) 46(8) *Management Science* 1059, 1060.

[10] H Lian and L Renneboog, 'On the Foundations of Corporate Social Responsibility' (2017) 72(2) *The Journal of Finance* 853, 854.

[11] H Servaes and A Tamayo, 'The Impact of Corporate Social Responsibility on Firm Value: The Role of Customer Awareness' (2013) 59(5) *Management Science* 1059.

[12] D McBarnet and M Kurkchiyan, 'Corporate Social Responsibility through Contractual Control? Global Supply Chains and "Other Regulation"' in D McBarnet, A Voiculescu and T Campbell (eds), *The New Corporate Accountability: Corporate Social Responsibility and the Law* (Cambridge, Cambridge University Press, 2007) 65; K Peterkova Mitkidis, *Sustainability Clauses in International Business Contracts* (The Hague, Eleven International Publishing, 2015) 166.

[13] Directive (EU) 2022/2464 of the European Parliament and of the Council of 14 December 2022 amending Regulation (EU) No 537/2014, Directive 2004/109/EC, Directive 2006/43/EC and Directive 2013/34/EU [2022] OJ L 322/15.

[14] Directive (EU) 2024/1760 of the European Parliament and of the Council of 13 June 2024 on corporate sustainability due diligence and amending Directive (EU) 2019/1937 and Regulation (EU) 2023/2859 [2024] OJ L 2024/1760.

[15] This is the result of a literature review conducted by M Kaźmierczak, 'A Literature Review on the Difference between CSR and ESG' (2022) 162 *Zeszyty Naukowe. Organizacja i Zarządzanie/Politechnika Śląska* 275.

A range of international, EU, and national regulations has emerged to define ESG standards. Of particular relevance is the EU Taxonomy Regulation, which establishes a common framework for identifying and classifying environmentally sustainable economic activities.[16] All three ESG dimensions – environmental, social, and governance – are now also subject to reporting requirements under the CSRD.

The environmental component addresses matters such as greenhouse gas emissions (particularly CO_2), energy efficiency, resource conservation, and water use.[17] The social dimension includes respect for human and labour rights, compliance with core International Labour Organization (ILO) Conventions (eg prohibitions of slavery, forced and child labour), decent working conditions, fair wages, and socially responsible supply chain management.[18] Governance, in turn, relates to the internal structures of corporate management, including transparency, anti-corruption measures, board diversity, executive pay, and cybersecurity.[19]

As regulatory attention to sustainability matters has intensified, companies are increasingly subject to scrutiny over their ESG and CSR practices from both public and private actors – regulators, financial institutions, investors, consumers, and civil society. Accordingly, the integration of sustainability into corporate practice is becoming more than aspirational. In some jurisdictions, compliance with environmental, labour, and anti-discrimination laws forms part of the fiduciary duty of a prudent manager.[20] Consequently, there is a growing imperative to embed sustainability throughout corporate supply chains and to reflect ESG principles contractually. This can be achieved through both mandatory legal duties (such as due diligence requirements relating to internal governance or supplier behaviour) and voluntary commitments via a company's own sustainability standards.[21]

[16] Regulation (EU) 2020/852 of the European Parliament and of the Council of 18 June 2020 on the establishment of a framework to facilitate sustainable investment and amending Regulation (EU) 2019/2088 [2020] OJ L 198/13.

[17] See Recitals 97–98 Directive 2014/24/EU.

[18] ibid.

[19] See eg OECD, *G20/OECD Principles of Corporate Governance 2023* (Paris, OECD Publishing, 2023).

[20] See for Germany, s 93(1) *Aktiengesetz* (AktG), BGBl I 1965, 1089 (German Stock Corporation Act). Furthermore, it is discussed in Germany whether the management and board should have an obligation to integrate all – not only statutory – ESG considerations into the company's interest (*Unternehmensinteresse*) as part of s 76(1) German Stock Corporation Act. See MP Weller and T Fischer, 'ESG-Geschäftsleitungspflichten: Unternehmenstransformation zur Klimaneutralität' (2022) *Zeitschrift für Wirtschaftsrecht* 2253; Mittwoch (n 1); with further evidence see, Weller (n 1); see also M Habersack, 'Koexistenz von Klimaverwaltungs- und Klimaprivatrecht' in C Krönke and D Wolff (eds), *Verwaltung der Klimakrise* (Berlin, Duncker & Humblot, 2025) Die Verwaltung, Beiheft 13, 141. See for Switzerland, Art 964j *Obligationenrecht* (OR) of 30 March 1911 (SR 220) (Swiss Code of Obligations) as amended. See for Belgium, Belgian Corporate Governance Code (Principe 7).

[21] On the concept of due diligence in the context of this anthology, see ch 6.

The influence of ESG now extends into the contractual relationships of private companies, particularly within their supply chains.[22] In cases where an environmental standard is integral to goods or services, warranty provisions under statutory sales or works contract law may apply (see section IV). However, where specific ESG clauses are introduced into contracts, questions arise as to their enforceability: for instance, the issue of whether a company's request that its partners or suppliers comply with particular ESG standards carries legal force.

Recent research confirms the increasing prevalence of ESG-specific terms in commercial contracts, with many buyers incorporating such provisions into their templates.[23] A report by the International Bar Association (IBA) noted a marked proliferation of these clauses over the past decade, often driven by evolving legislation and voluntary benchmarks.[24] ESG clauses are now found in a broad array of contract types, including in private and public supply, service, and construction contracts, public sector agreements, employment and shipping contracts, loan arrangements, and insurance agreements.

B. Sustainability in Public Contracts

The integration of sustainability into public contracts is supported by a combination of international, EU, and national instruments – ranging from binding legal rules to soft law frameworks. At the international level, soft law examples include the adoption of Sustainable Development Goal (SDG) 12.7, which promotes Sustainable Public Procurement (SPP) and responsible consumption. Complementary to this are various guidelines and policy documents that focus on capacity building and the implementation of sustainable procurement policies within contracting authorities.[25]

[22] See for the gradual implementation, K Mitkidis, S Perkovic, and P Mitkidis, 'Tendencies in Contractual Governance to Promote Human and Labour Rights in Transnational Supply Chains' (2019) 23(2) *Competition & Change* 397, 411–12. Accordingly, the largest companies globally, reporting the use of supply chain contracts to protect labour and human rights, report an increase from ca. 53 per cent to 75 per cent from 2012 to 2017.

[23] ES Pannebakker, 'ESG-bedingen in commerciële overeenkomsten: een contractenrechtelijke gereedschapskist voor duurzameontwikkelingsdoelstellingen' (2023) 4 *Nederlands Tijdschrift voor Handelsrecht* 125, 125–132; World CC Foundation, Sustainability in Contracts: A Summary of Current Status (2024) <www.worldcc.com/Portals/IACCM/Reports/Sustainability%20in%20Contracts%20A%20Summary%20of%20Current%20Status.pdf>.

[24] ESG Subcommittee of the IBA Arbitration Committee, *Report on use of ESG contractual obligations and related disputes* (London, International Bar Association, 2023) 9.

[25] See, eg European Commission, *Buying Social: A Guide to Taking Account of Social Considerations in Public Procurement* (Luxembourg, Publications Office of the European Union, 2011); European Commission, *Buying green! A handbook on green procurement*, 3rd edn (Luxembourg, Publications Office of the European Union, 2016); United Nations Environment Programme (UNEP), *Sustainable Public Procurement: How to "Wake the Sleeping Giant!" Introducing the United Nations Environment Programme's Approach*, 2nd edn (UNEP, 2021); United Nations Environment Programme, *Sustainable public procurement: 2022 global review (Parts I and II)* (UNEP, 2022); One Planet Network, <www.oneplanetnetwork.org/knowledge-centre/resources/sustainable-public-procurement-2022-global-review-parts-i-and-ii>.

With regard to hard law on sustainability issues, the EU legal framework offers a clear point of departure. Article 3(3) Treaty on European Union (TEU) provides that the Union shall pursue sustainable development based on balanced economic growth, full employment, social progress, and a high level of environmental protection.[26] This overarching objective is also reflected in the national constitutions of European countries. For instance, sustainability-related goals are enshrined in the German,[27] Swiss,[28] and Belgian constitutions.[29] These constitutional norms serve as a basis for legislative and executive action in support of environmental and social objectives.

Public procurement law functions as a critical tool to translate these sustainability goals into practice. For example, in Switzerland, the importance of sustainability in procurement was explicitly acknowledged in the 2019 revision of the Swiss Federal Act on Public Procurement, which aims to promote 'cost-efficient use of public funds in a manner that is economically, ecologically and socially sustainable'.[30] While public procurement law continues to rest on core principles such as transparency, competition, non-discrimination, cost-effectiveness, and proportionality, it serves a broader – sometimes overlooked – primary function: the fulfilment of public tasks.[31] This broader purpose distinguishes public contracts from private contracts, whose primary objective is typically profit maximisation.

One legal consequence of this public purpose is that contracting authorities enjoy broad discretion in determining procurement needs and in setting policy objectives through contract design.[32] However, this discretion is not absolute. It is subject to the constraints imposed by mandatory provisions of national (Switzerland) and EU public procurement law (Germany and Belgium) – especially in the area of sustainability.[33]

[26] Consolidated Version of the Treaty on European Union [2008] OJ C 115/13.

[27] Art 20a and Art 28 *Grundgesetz für die Bundesrepublik Deutschland* (GG) BGBl 1949, 1 (German Basic Law) as last amended by Act of 22 March 2025 (BGBl I No. 94). For Art 20a Basic Law see A Epiney, in PM Huber and A Voßkuhle (eds), *Grundgesetz*, 8th edn (Munich, CH Beck, 2024) Art 20a GG paras 100–34; for social security see KP Sommermann, in PM Huber and A Voßkuhle (eds), *Grundgesetz*, 8th edn (Munich, CH Beck, 2024) Art 20 GG paras 115–17.

[28] Arts 2(2), 41, 73, and 74 *Bundesverfassung der Schweizerischen Eidgenossenschaft* (BV) of 18 April 1999 (SR 101) (Federal Constitution of the Swiss Confederation).

[29] Art 23 *Constitution belge du 17 février 1831*, as amended in 1994 (Belgian Constitution).

[30] *Bundesgesetz über das öffentliche Beschaffungswesen* of 21 June 2019 (SR 172.056.1) (Swiss Federal Act on Public Procurement) art 2(a).

[31] See eg M Burgi, *Vergaberecht: Systematische Erläuterung für Praxis und Ausbildung*, 4th edn (Munich, CH Beck, 2025) s 2 paras 7–8, 31, s 6 paras 2–7, with further evidence; see Art 8(1) Swiss Federal Act on Public Procurement: 'A public contract is a contract that is entered into by the contracting authority and the tenderer for the performance of a public task'.

[32] See eg Burgi, *Vergaberecht* (n 31) s 12 paras 4–6; see for broad discretion of agencies in public procurement the decision of the Swiss Federal Administrative Court of 12 August 2019, BVGer B-4086/2018, consideration 4.4.

[33] M Andhov, 'Contracting Authorities and Strategic Goals of Public Procurement – A Relationship Defined by Discretion?' in S Bogojevic, X Groussot, and J Hettne (eds), *Discretion in EU Procurement Law* (Oxford, Hart Publishing, 2019) 117–37.

Article 18(2) Directive 2014/24/EU provides a clear legal basis for embedding sustainability into the performance of public contracts. It obliges Member States to take appropriate measures to ensure that, during contract performance, economic operators comply with relevant environmental, social, and labour law obligations derived from EU law, national legislation, collective agreements, or international legal instruments listed in Annex X.[34] Beyond this mandatory baseline, contracting authorities may also impose additional sustainability requirements at various stages of the procurement process – namely during the award phase, in the content of the contract, and in its performance. Recitals 97 and 98 Directive 2014/24/EU illustrate the range of permissible environmental and social considerations that may be adopted. Given this chapter's focus on the enforceability of sustainability clauses, particular attention is paid to contract performance conditions.

i. *Strategic Procurement*

Lately, a shift in perspective can be observed with respect to environmental and social requirements that go beyond the subject matter in the narrower sense. Traditionally, such considerations were understood as extraneous to public procurement (*vergabefremd*).[35] This conventional view is increasingly challenged. Some scholars advocate for an expanded interpretation of the 'value for money' principle – one that incorporates environmental and social factors rather than treating them as externalities.[36] The Commission has endorsed this approach under the rubric of 'strategic procurement', which promotes a more

[34] Similarly, Art 12 Swiss Federal Act on Public Procurement on compliance with occupational health and safety regulations, labour standards, equal pay for men and women, and environmental law. See also Case C-395/18 *Tim SpA – Direzione e coordinamento Vivendi SA v Consip SpA and Ministero dell'Economia e delle Finanze* ECLI:EU:C:2020:58, [2020]; Marta Andhov, 'Article 18(2)' in R Caranta and A Sanchez-Graells (eds), *European Public Procurement: Commentary on Directive 2014/24/EU* (Cheltenham, Edward Elgar Publishing, 2021) 745.

[35] For Germany see, eg I Beuttenmüller, *Vergabefremde Kriterien im öffentlichen Auftragswesen: Vereinbarkeit mit dem europäischen Sekundärrecht und den Grundfreiheiten* (Baden-Baden, Nomos, 2007); M Burgi, 'Vergabefremde Kriterien', in E Grabitz and M Hilf (eds), *Das Recht der Europäischen Union*, Vol 4, supplementary delivery no. 36 (Munich, CH Beck, 2008) c B.13; see for Switzerland, M Steiner and D Klingler, 'The Revised Swiss Public Procurement Law: More Quality and Sustainability' (2023) 1 *European Procurement & Public Private Partnership Law Review* 68, 88.

[36] Generally, M Andhov, R Caranta, WA Janssen, and O Martin-Ortega, 'Shaping Sustainable Public Procurement Laws in the European Union: An Analysis of the Legislative Development from "How to Buy" to "What to Buy" in Current and Future EU Legislative Initiatives' (2022) *The Greens/EFA in the European Parliament* <www.greens-efa.eu/files/assets/docs/shaping_sustainable_public_procurement_laws_in_the_european_union.pdf>. For Germany, see M Knauff, 'Nachhaltigkeit im Vergaberecht' (2020) *juristische Monatsschrift* 426; A Fritz, 'Von vergabefremden Kriterien zur strategischen Beschaffung: Nachhaltigkeit in der öffentlichen Beschaffung als Leitbild für ESG' (2022) *ESGZ* 4, 4–5. For Switzerland see BVGer B-4086/2018 (Swiss Federal Administrative Court, 12 August 2019); Federal Council, Botschaft zur Totalrevision des Bundesgesetzes über das öffentliche Beschaffungswesen (15 February 2017) 1884; Steiner and Klingler (n 35) 88; D Klingler, 'Efficiency, Quality and Sustainability in Government Contracting: A Law and Economics Analysis' (Dissertation, University of St. Gallen, 2024) 147.

holistic understanding of value.[37] Within this framework, contracting authorities are given considerable discretion to determine their purchasing needs and to define the requirements necessary to achieve optimal value in fulfilling public tasks.[38]

ii. 'Link to the Subject-Matter' Requirement

Under Article 70 Directive 2014/24/EU, contracting authorities are expressly permitted to introduce special performance conditions, provided they are 'linked to the subject-matter of the contract' in accordance with Article 67(3) Directive 2014/24/EU, and clearly indicated in the call for competition or procurement documents.[39] These conditions may relate to economic, environmental, social, employment-related, or innovation objectives. Similarly, the Swiss Federal Act on Public Procurement requires 'performance-related' award criteria that can include economic efficiency, life cycle costs, sustainable development, and innovation content.[40] Further, EU Member States can define mandatory provisions requiring the integration of specific sustainability-related performance conditions into public contracts. At the same time, they can also adopt voluntary sustainability measures, such as requiring suppliers to submit self-declarations confirming compliance with the ILO Core Conventions.[41] However, the requirement that sustainability clauses must be 'linked to the subject-matter of the contract' imposes an important limitation on the integration of broader sustainability considerations into public contracts.[42] In contrast, no such limitation applies to private contracts, where sustainability clauses may be incorporated with greater flexibility. For public contracts to be deemed legally valid, they must adhere to this linkage requirement, which is fulfilled within the EU when the contract relates to 'the specific process of production, provision or trading of those works, supplies or services' or 'a specific process for

[37] See, eg European Commission, 'Proposal for a Directive of the European Parliament and of the Council on public procurement', 20 December 2011, COM(2011) 896 final, 4–6, 9, 18: 'strategic use of public procurement', 'strategic procurement'; Andhov, 'Contracting Authorities and Strategic Goals of Public Procurement' (n 33) 117–37.

[38] MEL Gausdal, 'Soft Law Business as Usual? Fundamental Labour Standards in Private and Public Commercial Contracts' (PhD Thesis, Københavns Universitet, 2021) 78.

[39] M Andhov, 'Article 70' in R Caranta and A Sanchez-Graells (eds), *European Public Procurement: Commentary on Directive 2014/24/EU* (Cheltenham, Edward Elgar Publishing, 2021) 745–53.

[40] Art 29(1) Swiss Federal Act on Public Procurement on award criteria.

[41] Swiss public procurement law does not include such a provision on contract performance conditions, but in order to prove compliance with mandatory labour and environmental laws (Art 12 Swiss Federal Act on Public Procurement), agencies can require tenderers to submit self-declarations stating that they are compliant with mandatory laws, such as collective bargaining agreements, the ILO Core Conventions, environmental protection laws, prevention of corruption and cartels and equal pay for men and women, which are often tied to contractual penalties for non-compliance.

[42] E Uysal, 'Sustainability Clauses in "Public" Contracts' (2024) 20(1) *European Review of Contract Law* 105.

another stage of their life cycle, even where such factors do not form part of their material substance'.[43] This process- and product-oriented focus of Article 67(3) Directive 2014/24/EU, read in conjunction with Article 70 Directive 2014/24/EU, has implications for the scope of permissible sustainability criteria in EU public procurement. Governance-related requirements that pertain solely to a company's general corporate management or organisational structure typically do not satisfy the linkage requirement and thus fall outside the remit of public procurement rules.[44] Consequently, the corporate governance dimension – although prominent in private contracting – plays a more limited role in public contracts.

III. Law Governing Public Contracts and its Implications for ESG Clauses

The question of what rules apply to public contracts varies from country to country and was covered earlier in this anthology.[45] In this section, we look closer into the rules that apply to public contracts in the three jurisdictions that are examined in this chapter and for which we will discuss the legal instruments to enforce sustainability in section IV.

A. Law in 'Private-Oriented Hybrid Model' versus 'Public-Oriented Hybrid Model'

Germany and Switzerland are examples of what this anthology refers to as 'private-oriented hybrid model'. While in Germany, public contracts are governed by private law, as are their awards, in Switzerland, the award itself is an administrative act, but the contract, its formation, performance, and enforcement are subject to private contract law.[46] This distinction – anchored in the so-called two-tier theory (*Zweistufentheorie*) – separates the agency-internal

[43] Arts 67(3) and 70 Directive 2014/24/EU; Case C-31/87 *Gebroeders Beentjes BV v State of the Netherlands* ECLI:EU:C:1988:422; Case C-368/10 *European Commission v Kingdom of the Netherlands* ECLI:EU:C:2012:284, [2012].

[44] See eg, M Andrecka, 'Corporate Social Responsibility and Sustainability in Danish Public Procurement' (2017) 12(3) *European Procurement & Public Private Partnership Law Review* 333. For a critique of the exclusion of CSR in public procurement, see M Andhov et al, 'Sustainability through public procurement: the way forward – Reform Proposals' (Oslo, University of Oslo Faculty of Law Research Paper No. 2020-09, SMART Project Report, 23 March 2020).

[45] See ch 3.

[46] See ch 3; for Germany Burgi, *Vergaberecht* (n 31) s 2 paras 9–10, 14–15; for Switzerland, U Häfelin, G Müller, and F Uhlmann, *Allgemeines Verwaltungsrecht*, 8th edn (Zurich, Dike, 2020) s 19 para 1393.

decision-making process from the formation of the private contract.[47] Accordingly, in Germany and Switzerland, public contracts are not classified as agreements under public law or public law contracts (*öffentlich-rechtlicher Vertrag*),[48] and their enforcement falls under civil law, typically governed by the German Civil Code (BGB)[49] or the Swiss Code of Obligations[50] – with limited public law exceptions such as those found in the German Competition Act, some state procurement laws, and some distinct regulations (eg regarding the maximum prices of public contracts).

Belgium, the most private-leaning form of the 'public-oriented hybrid model', adopts a comparable bifurcation, rooted in the theory of the detachable act.[51] The procurement phase is primarily regulated by public procurement and administrative law, whereas the public contract, its formation and performance are, to some extent, hybrid, as they are governed by specific public law rules (*lex specialis*) and supplemented by private contract law. Private law is generally considered the *lex generalis* to both public and private contracts.[52]

B. Nature and Legal Effect of ESG Clauses

When enforcing contracts – whether private or public – and their ESG clauses, two key questions arise. First, are sustainability and ESG requirements mandatory or merely voluntary, ie within the discretion of the contracting authority or private company? Second, are these requirements legally binding and thus enforceable in court, or are they without legal effect?

[47] Häfelin, Müller, and Uhlmann (n 46) s 19 para 1394, and 1401–03. While initially the Swiss Supreme Court did not follow the two-tier theory, the Swiss Federal Act on Public Procurement now specifies that the award is considered a *Verfügung* that can be challenged in court. Furthermore, the Swiss Supreme Court recognised that the agency's decision refusing to conclude a contract can be challenged in court 'if public law provides for a justiciable right of contract conclusion', see BGer Urteil 1C_602/2018 of 3 July 2019, consideration 4.3.

[48] S 54 *Verwaltungsverfahrensgesetz* (German Administrative Procedures Act). As an exception to this general rule, some agreements under public law can also be subject to public procurement law because Art 2(1)(5) Directive 2014/24/EU does not require a private contract – the 'public' model of public contract regulation is also in compliance with the Directive 2014/24/EU. The term 'public contract' in s 103(1) *Gesetz gegen Wettbewerbsbeschränkungen* (GWB), BGBl I 1957, 1081 (German Competition Act) must be interpreted in accordance with the Directive 2014/24/EU. See, eg B Wegener and H Pünder, in H Pünder and M Schellenberg (eds), *Vergaberecht*, 3rd edn (Baden-Baden, Nomos, 2019) § 103 GWB para 27, with further evidence. For Swiss literature, see Häfelin, Müller and Uhlmann (n 46) § 18 paras 1286 ff.

[49] *Bürgerliches Gesetzbuch* (BGB) (German Civil Code) last amended by Art 4 Act of 22 December 2025 (Federal Law Gazette I No 364).

[50] Federal Act on the Amendment of the Swiss Civil Code (Part Five: The Code of Obligations) of 30 March 1911 (Federal Law Gazette SR 220).

[51] See ch 2; S Van Garsse (ed), *Handboek Bestuursrecht* (Brussels, Politeia, 2020) 28; D Renders, *Droit administratif Général* (Brussels, Larcier, 2022) 642.

[52] W van Gerven and M Wyckaert, 'Overeenkomsten met de overheid' (1987) *Tijdschrift voor Privaatrecht* 1709, 1720.

Where contracting authorities are legally obliged to include sustainability clauses in public contracts but fail to do so, issues of both validity and contestability of the contract emerge. If in jurisdictions like Germany, Switzerland, and Belgium, sustainability obligations mandated by law are omitted from the contract, the contract can be challenged in court. Any party with a demonstrable legal interest, including the contracting parties themselves, may seek a judicial declaration of nullity, leaving it to the courts to determine the contract's validity.[53] While in Germany and Switzerland, legal actions brought by third parties can only relate to breaches of public procurement law, between the parties, challenges can also relate to breaches of statutory civil law with regard to environmental or social requirements.

Another issue of enforceability arises when sustainability or ESG provisions are included in a contract. More and more procurements of goods, works, and services reference ESG standards and codes of conduct. Where such a code is expressly incorporated into the contract by reference, and compliance is mandated, the code's requirements can become binding contractual obligations – whereby the parties' intent to be legally bound (and their liability) must be carefully examined.[54] If that is the case, then a failure to comply with the code might be considered a breach of contract. Nevertheless, the drafting of these clauses significantly affects their enforceability, as the specificity and clarity of language often determine the likelihood of successful enforcement.

In practice, ESG clauses vary drastically – both in form and content. They may include obligations relating to disclosure, reporting, benchmarks, compliance assurances, or ESG performance targets. A recent report by the IBA identifies a range of ESG-related contractual obligations, including due diligence, compliance, monitoring, warranty, and indemnity commitments.[55] Remedies for breach, as outlined in the IBA report, may involve remediation measures, termination rights, or claims for damages.

Given the diverse practice, the enforceability of ESG clauses varies considerably. The enforceability largely depends on the applicable legal framework, the

[53] P Galli, A Moser, E Lang, and M Steiner, *Praxis des öffentlichen Beschaffungsrechts*, 3rd edn (Zurich, Schulthess, 2013) 504; M Fehling, in H Pünder and M Schellenberg (eds), *Vergaberecht*, 3rd edn (Baden-Baden, Nomos, 2019) § 129 GWB para 19; P Gauch, W Schluep, J Schmid, and S Emmenegger, *Schweizerisches Obligationenrecht Allgemeiner Teil*, 11th edn (Zurich, Schulthess, 2020) 151 ff; M Opitz, in M Burgi, M Dreher and M Opitz (eds), *Beck'scher Vergaberechtskommentar*, vol 1, 4th edn (Munich, CH Beck, 2022) § 129 GWB para 10; undecided in this respect Vergabekammer Baden-Württemberg, Decision of 4 June 2014 – 1 VK 15/14, juris, para 95. In Belgium one could invoke Art 5.58 *Code civil/ Burgerlijk Wetboek* of 10 February 1804 (*Moniteur belge / Belgisch Staatsblad* 1804, 187) (Belgian Civil Code).

[54] Gausdal (n 38) 45, 48, and 85; eg in a case regarding the working conditions at the supplier this was rejected due to a lack of willingness to be bound, see LG Dortmund, Decision of 10 January 2019 – 7 O 95/15, IPrax 2019, 317 (321 paras 41–42).

[55] ESG Subcommittee (n 24).

drafting of the clause, and the remedies provided either through the contract itself or through the statutory civil law provisions.

IV. Legal Instruments to Enforce Sustainability

Most European civil law codes, including the German and Belgian Civil Codes and the Swiss Code of Obligations, do not explicitly regulate environmental or social sustainability issues within private contracts. This omission is rooted in the fundamental principle of freedom of contract, which is a shared cornerstone across these jurisdictions.[56] In each system, parties are free to enter into a contract, to choose their counterparty, and to determine the content of their agreements, including sustainability or ESG considerations, subject only to overriding limitations based on mandatory law, including statutory prohibitions.[57]

The shared commitment to contractual freedom is, however, tempered by slightly different legal doctrines that define its limits. In both Switzerland and Germany, contracts must not contravene notions such as 'good morals' or the 'public order' (in Switzerland)[58] or 'common decency' (in Germany),[59] with contracts found in violation are deemed void.[60] What violates 'good morals' or the 'public order' in Switzerland or 'common decency' in Germany is not legally defined but is subject to interpretation by the courts. For example, in Switzerland, contracts against 'good morals' include agreements to abstain from bidding, anti-competitive agreements, bribery agreements,[61] and contracts that violate mandatory foreign law.[62] Contracts against the Swiss 'public order' include, for example, general terms and conditions that create a grave imbalance to the detriment of consumers.[63]

Similarly, Belgian law prohibits contracts that infringe 'public order' or 'imperative law'. The Belgian Civil Code defines 'public order' as legal rules that affect the fundamental interests of the state or the community, or in private law, determine the legal foundations on which society rests, such as the economic, moral, social, or environmental order.[64] A contractual provision that deviates

[56] Art 19 Swiss Code of Obligations; S 311(1) BGB; Art 5.14 Belgian Civil Code.

[57] S 134 BGB: 'A legal transaction that violates a statutory prohibition is void, unless the statute leads to a different conclusion'; Art 5.14 Belgian Civil Code; I Claeys and T Tanghe, *Het nieuw algemeen contractenrecht* (Brussels, Intersentia, 2023) 67–73; Art 19(2) Swiss Code of Obligations.

[58] Art 19(2) Swiss Code of Obligations.

[59] S 138 BGB.

[60] Art 20(1) Swiss Code of Obligations.

[61] B Meise and C Huguenin, in C Widmer Lüchinger and D Oser (eds), *Basler Kommentar Obligationenrecht I*, 7th edn (Munich, Helbling Lichtenhahn Verlag, 2020) Art 19/20 OR paras 38 f.

[62] Federal Supreme Court decision BGE 62 II 108, E. 2a; Meise and Huguenin (n 61) para 42.

[63] Meise and Huguenin (n 61) paras 25–30.

[64] Art 1.3 para 4 Belgian Civil Code.

from a legal rule affecting public order is absolutely null. A rule is considered 'imperative law' if it is adopted to protect a party that is considered 'weaker' by the law.[65] This rule is aimed at protecting private interests. The objective is to protect a certain group of 'weaker' citizens, such as employees, tenants, and consumers. In this context, an example is the regulation of unlawful clauses in a business-to-consumer (B2C) context.[66] A contractual provision that deviates from imperative law is relatively null.[67]

Despite these terminological differences, the underlying mechanisms are comparable: sustainability and ESG clauses are permissible and will remain valid unless they transgress essential legal norms. European contract law, namely the Principles of European Contract Law (PECL) and the Draft Common Frame of Reference (DCFR) suggests similar outcomes.[68]

In the following, we elaborate on the legal instruments that can be used to enforce sustainability obligations and make them more effective in public and private contracts. The instruments described below are found in various legal systems. Nevertheless, to make things more concrete, the analysis focuses on German, Swiss, and Belgian law.

A. Statutory Contract Law: Relevance of Warranty and Substitute Performance

To integrate sustainability and ESG considerations into contracts, the statutory frameworks governing warranties in sales and works contracts are of particular practical relevance. Although companies and contracting authorities, as legal persons, do not benefit from the protections offered by the EU and national consumer protection laws, the lack of consumer status does not leave them without legal remedies.[69] Where goods fail to meet, for example environmental requirements mandated by law or fall short of tender specifications – such as minimum energy efficiency standards – they are not merely 'unsustainable', but can legally qualify as defective goods under general sales or works law.

Across European legal systems, including Germany, Switzerland, and Belgium, remedies for defective performance broadly align, although with nuanced differences. Depending on the magnitude of the defect, the behaviour of the seller and the time that has lapsed since delivery of the goods, service,

[65] ibid Art 1.3 para 5.

[66] Art VI.81/1 et seq Belgian Economic Law Code.

[67] T Vansweevelt and B Weyts, 'Grondbeginselen van het contractenrecht' in T Vansweevelt and B Weyts (eds), *Handboek Verbintenissenrecht* (Brussels, Larcier Intersentia, 2023) 144–49.

[68] See ch 15 Part III PECL, entitled 'Illegality'. See also s 3 ch 2, Book II DCFR, under the title of 'Infringement of fundamental principles or mandatory rules'.

[69] See the definition of consumers in Germany, s 13 BGB; for Belgium, Book I Art I.1 Belgian Civil Code.

or work, the buyer can typically demand correction of the defect,[70] rescind the contract and claim damages or reimbursement of expenses,[71] or seek a reduction in the contract price.[72] Notably, Swiss statutory law on works contracts grants the buyer (in the context of public procurement, the contracting authority) the right to arrange for substitute performance by a third party, or by herself, even 'before' the work is completed and if a defect appears likely to occur.[73] In contrast, German law restricts the right to substitute performance to cases in which the contractor has delayed remedying a defect 'after' the work has been handed over, highlighting a more conservative approach to anticipatory action.[74]

The enforceability of warranty claims, particularly with regard to environmental requirements, is, however, not without challenge. A key difficulty lies in assessing whether breaches of environmental obligations render goods or work defective when they still fulfil their primary function. This issue was brought into focus by the 'Dieselgate' emissions scandal, where Volkswagen AG installed software in diesel vehicles to circumvent statutory limits on nitrogen oxide (NO_x) emissions. German courts determined that the manipulation constituted a material defect under sales law, notwithstanding the vehicles' operational fitness and prior supervisory authority approval.[75] Car buyers were entitled to full reimbursement of the purchase price, subject to deductions for use, with the courts eventually basing their decisions on tort law. The courts recognised that 'intentional damage inflicted in a manner offending common decency' (Section 826 BGB) offered advantages in terms of scope, admissible defendants (not only the seller, but also the manufacturer could sue), and the statute of limitations.[76] A somewhat different solution with regard to the same case was reached in Belgium. Following an action for collective redress based on the Belgian Consumer Law and Article 1641 Belgian Civil Code on hidden defects, the court ruled that the buyers were entitled to compensation for damages.[77] The compensation amounted to five per cent of the purchase price or

[70] In Switzerland, the buyer's right to demand cure (*Nachbesserung*) is not stipulated in the Code of Obligations, but is often used in practice. Also, for the sale of fungible goods, Art 206 Swiss Code of Obligations allows the buyer to demand substitute performance.

[71] See for Germany s 437 BGB; Switzerland, Arts 205 and 207 Swiss Code of Obligations; for Belgium, Art 1645 Belgian Civil Code.

[72] See for Germany, s 437 BGB; for Switzerland, Art 205 Swiss Code of Obligations; for Belgium, Art 1644 Belgian Civil Code.

[73] Art 366(2) Swiss Code of Obligations. See for substitute performance by the buyer, P Gauch, *Der Werkvertrag* (5th ed, 2011), N 891.

[74] See for Germany, ss 634 and 637 BGB; see R Szostak, 'Substitute Performance in Public Procurement' (2022) 10 *Business Law Journal* 2, 5.

[75] See Federal Court of Justice, Decision of 21 July 2021 – VIII ZR 254/20, BGHZ 230, 296, 303 para 16, 306–11 paras 24–37; see also B Gsell, 'Kauf- und deliktsrechtliche Haftung für das nachhaltigkeitsfehlerhafte Produkt als Schaden' (2023) 187(2) *Zeitschrift für das gesamte Handelsrecht und Wirtschaftsrecht* 392, 405–12.

[76] See, eg Federal Court of Justice, Decision of 25 November 2021 – VII ZR 257/20, juris; OLG München, Decision of 30 November 2020–21 U 7307/19, juris, paras 65–67.

[77] Tribunal of First Instance Brussels, Decision of 18 December 2017 and 27 July 2023.

to five per cent of the difference between the purchase price and the resale price if the vehicle had been sold in the meantime.

B. Sustainability Clauses and Contractual Penalties

Sustainability can also be implemented through contractual mechanisms – by expressly incorporating sustainability or ESG clauses into contracts.[78] For example, in cases where statutory law does not guarantee adequate protection of sustainability aspects, contractual sustainability clauses provide an alternative to create a binding legal obligation for the parties. These clauses are of particular relevance in cases in which damages are difficult to quantify – such as in the case of environmental harm – or in which social requirements extend beyond the scope of existing labour or anti-discrimination laws, notably within supply chain governance.[79]

For example, breaches involving non-payment of minimum or standard wages, or the failure to ensure equal pay for equal work, do not directly harm the contracting authority, thereby limiting recourse under statutory law.[80] In such cases, the enforcement of sustainability standards often relies on contractual mechanisms, including the use of contractual penalties or agreements designed for the benefit of third parties.[81]

Social sustainability clauses, especially those related to labour standards, tend to be more enforceable than environmental clauses (insofar as the lack of environmental attributes does not represent a defect in the good or work).[82] Whether this observed trend reflects a difference in enforceability, better detectability of social violations, or more effective enforcement structures – through the involvement of employees, trade unions, and other third-party actors – remains open for debate. Compared to social requirements, environmental breaches often suffer

[78] E Uysal, 'Enforcing Sustainability in Contract Performance Under the Public Sector Directive' (PhD Thesis, University of Turin, 2024).

[79] Andhov, 'Article 70' (n 39) 745–53.

[80] M Burgi, 'Nachhaltige Unternehmensführung im Vergaberecht' in M Burgi and M Habersack (eds), *Öffentliches Recht des Unternehmens* (Munich, CH Beck, 2023) § 11 para 21.

[81] See ch 12; U Schroeter, 'Lieferkettenhaftung Schweizer Unternehmen nach geltendem schweizerischem Recht und der EU Lieferkettenrichtlinie (CS3D)' (2025) *Basler Juristische Mitteilungen* 19, 19–42. This contractual structure is particularly noteworthy when a company at the end of the supply chain (the promisor) makes a commitment to its suppliers (the promisees) for the benefit of third parties, such as ensuring the fair treatment of workers at the beginning of the supply chain. Under such a contract, third parties are granted a direct right to demand, and if necessary, enforce through legal action, the promised standard of care. In recent years, various model contract clauses have been developed that establish such third-party beneficiary rights. See, for example, the model provisions of the Corporate Accountability Lab, *Towards Operationalizing Human Rights and Environmental Protection in Supply Chains: Worker-Enforceable Codes of Conduct* (Chicago, 2021). See also European Law Institute, *Business and Human Rights: Access to Justice and Effective Remedies* (with input from the EU Agency for Fundamental Rights, FRA) (Vienna, 2022), at s 3.7.2.

[82] Mitkidis, *Sustainability Clauses in International Business Contracts* (n 12).

from lower visibility and weaker third-party enforcement, typically relying on non-governmental organisations with more limited procedural rights.

Aside from warranty claims, contractual penalties have emerged as one of the most effective tools to ensure compliance with sustainability obligations and are mandatory in some areas of public contracting (see further below). Nevertheless, their use is subject to statutory constraints. A penalty deemed 'disproportionately high' may be reduced by the courts to a reasonable level, taking into account all legitimate interests of the creditor (not merely property interests) which opens the door to making use of contractual penalties for violations of sustainability concerns.[83] This flexible approach enables penalties to be tailored to reflect the public interest in upholding sustainability standards. German law further narrows the protection against excessive penalties by excluding commercial obligors (merchants) from certain safeguards, enhancing the enforceability of penalties against corporate actors.[84]

An added layer of complexity arises when the government, rather than a private party, is buying goods in the private market. Contracting authorities may be subject to stricter constitutional obligations than private companies, particularly with regard to observing the principle of proportionality and fundamental rights.[85] Courts may scrutinise whether the public nature of the contracting authority justifies expecting less from obligors or imposes higher standards of justification for penalties. Moreover, where sustainability clauses are incorporated into standard business terms rather than being negotiated individually, further restrictions apply. German law, for instance, prohibits the inclusion of unexpected or ambiguous terms and disallows clauses that impose an unreasonable disadvantage on the counterparty.[86] Accordingly, contractual penalties in standard terms are generally capped at five per cent of the contract value, limiting their deterrent effect.[87]

All three jurisdictions examined in this chapter have some public rules that mandate contracting authorities to integrate contractual penalties for certain social and environmental violations. For example, several German states (*Länder*) have exercised their legislative competence to prescribe contract performance conditions. The Thuringian Act on the Award of Public Contracts requires contracting authorities and contractors to agree on contractual penalties of up to five per cent of the contract value for each culpable breach of specified obligations, including the payment of taxes and social security contributions, and the provision of security deposits and control rights for the contracting authority.[88] Similarly, the

[83] S 343(1) BGB; Art 163(3) Swiss Code of Obligations; Art 5.88 Belgian Civil Code.

[84] S 348 *Handelsgesetzbuch* (HGB) (German Commercial Code), last amended by Art 18 Act of 22 December 2025 (Federal Law Gazette I No. 369).

[85] P Zimmermann, 'Anreizorientierte Verträge bei öffentlichen Großprojekten im Spiegel des Haushaltsrechts' (2024) 139(12) *Deutsches Verwaltungsblatt* 745, 751–52.

[86] In detail, eg ss 305–10 BGB. Similar practice in Switzerland based on Art 8 Federal Act on Unfair Competition.

[87] See Federal Court of Justice, Judgment of 25 March 2003 – VII ZR 210/01, BGHZ 153, 311, 324–27.

[88] *Thüringer Vergabegesetz – ThürVgG* of 23 January 2020 (GVBl 29), as last revised by Act of 16 November 2023 (GVBl 331 (Thuringian Act on the Award of Public Contracts) see s 13(1)(1) in conjunction with ss 10, 11, and 12.

Brandenburg Act on Minimum Requirements for the Award of Public Contracts mandates the inclusion of contractual penalties between one per cent and five per cent of the contract value for violations of minimum wage obligations,[89] extending the agreement on contractual penalties to subcontractors, temporary workers, and to control the rights of the contracting authority.[90] Both acts are mandatory for public contracts within their respective states, and in practice, contracting authorities refer to these requirements explicitly in the contract notice, procurement documents, and public contract itself.

In Switzerland, contractual penalties form part of the General Terms and Conditions (GTCs) of the Swiss Confederation, which must be incorporated into all federal public contracts.[91] Article 11(2) Swiss Federal Ordinance on Public Procurement permits a deviation from the GTCs only if goods, work, or service require special contractual conditions.[92] The GTCs impose penalties for (1) delays, (2) breaches of confidentiality, and (3) violations of occupational health and safety regulations, employment conditions, equal pay for men and women, and environmental law obligations. For breaches of social and environmental requirements, penalties amount to 10 per cent of the contract value, but not less than CHF 3,000 and not exceeding CHF 100,000 per contract. The most recent model contracts for the procurement of goods, services, and works, which are provided by the Swiss federal government and applied frequently by contract authorities, include an 'integrity clause' that foresees a contractual penalty of 10 per cent of the contract price for breaches of anti-corruption measures.[93] This example, which would fall within 'governance' of ESG, can be seen as a precursor and role model for drafting 'sustainability clauses' that tie specific environmental or social duties to contractual penalties.

In Belgium, the execution and enforcement of public contracts, including contractual penalties, are governed by the Executive Decree on the Performance of Public Contracts (the Decree).[94] The Decree sets out specific 'contractual' rules on non-performance and defects, refusal of acceptance, specific and general penalties, performance bonds, *ex officio* measures, price reductions

[89] *Brandenburgisches Vergabegesetz – BbgVergG* of 29 September 2016 (GVBl.I/16, [no. 21]), last amended by Article 1 Act of 13 April 2021 (GVBl.I/21, [no. 9]) (Brandenburg Act on Minimum Requirements for the Award of Public Contracts), see ss 10(1), 6(2), and 6(3).

[90] ibid ss 10(1), 8, and 9.

[91] Beschaffungskonferenz des Bundes, 'General Terms and Conditions (GTC) of the Confederation for the Procurement of Goods, Works and Services', last updated 19 June 2024 <www.bkb.admin.ch/de/agb-des-bundes>. Art 11(2) *Verordnung über das öffentliche Beschaffungswesen* of 12 February 2020 (Federal Law Gazette SR 172.057.1) (Swiss Federal Ordinance on Public Procurement) in connection with Art 42 Swiss Federal Act on Public Procurement.

[92] Swiss Federal Ordinance on Public Procurement.

[93] See eg, KBOB, model contract for the procurement of construction works (*Vertragsvorlagen für Werkleistungen*), 8 April 2025 <www.kbob.admin.ch/de/mustervertraege-und-publikationen#Werkleistungen> clause 15 on integrity.

[94] Royal Decree of 14 January 2013 establishing the general rules for the execution of public procurement contracts, Official Gazette 14 February 2013 (Belgian Executive Decree on the Performance of Public Contracts).

for diminished value, limitation periods for claims, and provisions for inspections.[95] These rules must be incorporated into the tender documents and public contracts. Tender provisions that are inconsistent with the Decree are, in many cases, disregarded.[96]

Importantly, the Decree applies even if the tender documents do not explicitly refer to its provisions. Private contract law only applies when the Decree is inapplicable or silent.[97] This is typically the case for small contracts (valued below EUR 30,000) or contracts in certain sectors such as insurance, healthcare, and banking. Moreover, contracting authorities retain a degree of discretionary power to introduce alternative provisions into tender documents and public contracts, provided these remain consistent with the overarching framework of the Decree.[98] Thus, specific penalties remain possible. According to the Decree, any defective performance for which no special penalty is provided shall give rise to a general penalty which is either (1) one-time and amounts to 0.07 per cent of the original order amount with a minimum of EUR 40 and a maximum of EUR 400, or (2) is daily and amounts to 0.02 per cent of the original order amount with a minimum of EUR 20 and a maximum of EUR 200, when the defect must be corrected immediately.

C. Termination Rights

Termination rights and claims for damages are another way to enforce sustainability. They can have a statutory basis or a contractual basis.[99] In contracts, parties can agree that a breach of ESG obligations is a reason to terminate the contract. Statutory termination rights can be found in many legal systems and in both the PECL and the DCFR.[100] Contracts can be terminated for a material breach when a party fails to fulfil a key obligation (which can be a sustainability obligation) as agreed in the contract.

For public contracts, there is an additional layer of complexity because some mandatory public rules can apply to contract termination.[101] At the EU level, Article 73 Directive 2014/24/EU provides contracting authorities with the right to terminate a public contract during its term in at least three cases: (1) when

[95] S Van Garsse, *KB Uitvoering. Koninklijk Besluit van 14 januari 2013. Regime Wet 17 juni 2016* (Brussels, Politeia, 2024).

[96] See Art 9 Belgian Executive Decree on the Performance of Public Contracts. This article specifies which provisions can be waived, under what conditions, and which provisions cannot be waived. If the conditions are not met, the deviation will be disregarded. See E Casteleyn, 'Artikel 9 KB Uitvoering: het lelijke eendje in het land van verschoppelingen' in C De Koninck, P Flamey, P Thielen, and E Hacke (eds), *Jaarboek Overheidsopdrachten 2020–2021* (Brussels, EBP Consulting, 2021) 770–92.

[97] See Art 3, § 1, of the Royal Decree of January 14, 2013.

[98] ibid.

[99] See for Belgium Art 5.90 Belgian Civil Code.

[100] See PECL 9:301 and also Book 3 ch 3 DCFR.

[101] See ch 7.

a substantial modification of the contract has occurred;[102] (2) when exclusion grounds were present at the time of contract award;[103] and (3) in the event of a serious infringement of obligations under EU law.[104]

In Belgium, this provision was transposed into Article 62 Belgian Royal Decree on Performance.[105] The Belgian provision goes beyond the minimum requirements of Directive 2014/24/EU by allowing termination not only in the cases set out at the EU level but also where economic operators breach environmental and social regulations or commit grave professional misconduct. Contract termination on this basis is possible, for instance, in cases of non-compliance with laws prohibiting child labour, human trafficking, or violations of environmental, social, and labour law standards. Grave professional misconduct can be invoked only where the breach concerns health, working conditions, or environmental offences.[106]

In Germany, comparable mechanisms are found in the previously mentioned state laws, which mandate the inclusion of contractual termination rights in cases of non-compliance with specific social obligations.[107] The legal consequences of a failure to enforce these rights mirror those for contractual penalties.

In Switzerland, the Swiss Federal Act on Public Procurement does not establish a right to terminate the public contract but gives the contracting authority the right to cancel the award procedure under certain conditions, such as when a substantial modification of the goods, work, or service becomes necessary, or where an anti-competitive agreement among bidders is identified.[108] Furthermore, the contracting authority can exclude a bidder or revoke an award if the bidder submits an abnormally low bid without guaranteeing performance in accordance with the contract, or breaches obligations on occupational health and safety, employment conditions, equal pay, confidentiality, Swiss environmental law, or relevant international environmental conventions designated by the Swiss Federal Council.[109] It is noteworthy that the circumstances that give the contracting authority a right to terminate the 'contract' under EU public procurement law are very similar to the ones under Swiss law for termination of the 'award procedure'. However, the wording in the Swiss Federal Act on Public Procurement explicitly refers to the termination of the award procedure and not the contract. This means

[102] Art 72 Directive 2014/24/EU.

[103] Art 57(1) Directive 2014/24/EU.

[104] Infringements of European Treaties or the Directive 2014/24/EU that have been declared by the CJEU in a procedure pursuant to Art 258 TFEU.

[105] Note that besides this specific provision, the Decree also contains more general termination rights for contracting authorities, as discussed in ch 7.

[106] See for example G Bouwman and S Schoenmaekers, 'Commentaar op: arts. 2.86a-2.89 Aanbestedingswet 2012; arts. 2.102–2.104 Aanbestedingswet 2012 en arts. 3.65–3.65a Aanbestedingswet 2012' in JM Hebly and P Heijnsbroek (eds), *Aanbestedingsrecht* (Deventer, Wolters Kluwer, 2020) 186.

[107] S 13(2) Thuringian Act and S 10(2) Brandenburg Act.

[108] Art 43(1)(e) and (f) Swiss Federal Act on Public Procurement.

[109] ibid Art 44(2)(c) and (f).

that in Switzerland (unlike in the EU), contract termination is governed by private contract law and not by public procurement law.

D. Contracts with Industry Standards and Incentive Clauses

Another contractual tool that is used to promote and enforce ESG requirements is the integration of industry standards into contracts. Industry standards play a significant role in the drafting and performance of both private and public contracts, especially in certain sectors like construction, and they are gaining relevance for the formulation of sustainability requirements. In Switzerland, they are developed by private stakeholders, but are commonly integrated into public contracts, and in Germany, industry standards are developed and recognised by both industry stakeholders and government bodies.

For example, the German Procurement and Contract Standards for Construction Work (VOB)[110] contain mandatory provisions for public contracts[111] on the award of contracts (Part A), general contract conditions relating to the execution of construction works (Part B) and general technical specifications for construction contracts (Part C). Parts B and C are recommended but optional for private contracts. The technical specifications on the performance of the works also include environmental specifications. Non-compliance with contractual environment-related technical requirements is sanctioned with contractual penalties, the authority's right to withdraw from the contract or the authority's right to terminate the contract.[112] Conversely, the fulfilment of sustainability requirements can be incentivised through bonus payments.[113]

In Switzerland, the most common industry standards in the construction sector are the ones issued by the Swiss Society of Engineers and Architects (SIA), notably SIA Norm 118, which defines general terms for construction works[114] and is integrated into the Swiss model government contracts.[115] More recently, SIA has issued Norm 112 on Sustainable Construction, which specifies ESG requirements. The Federal Strategic Procurement Committee (KBOB) has recommended making SIA Norm 112 an integral part of public construction contracts[116] and

[110] See VOB online <www.vob-online.de/de/vob-gesamtausgaben>.

[111] See Ss 1(1) and (2), 2(1) and 13(2) VOB/B. See also O Jauch, 'Nachhaltigkeit und Bau' in I Lausen and JP Müller (eds), *Handbuch Nachhaltigkeit im Vergaberecht* (Munich, CH Beck, 2024) § 26 para 70.

[112] S Hofmann, 'Bewertung der Nachhaltigkeit von Bauunternehmen' (Dissertation, TU Dortmund, 2017) 126; Jauch (n 110) § 26 para 70.

[113] Hofmann (n 111) 126; Jauch (n 110) § 26 para 70.

[114] Swiss Society of Engineers and Architects, 'SIA 118' <shop.sia.ch/normenwerk/ingenieur/118_2013_d/D/Product>.

[115] KBOB (n 92).

[116] KBOB, Sustainable construction clauses for engineering and works contracts *(Vertragsbestandteil Nachaltiges Bauen – Bedingungen für Planungsleistungen und Werkleistungen)*, 27 September 2024, <www.kbob.admin.ch/de/nachhaltiges-bauen>.

has formulated standard conditions for sustainable construction that can be integrated into contracts (*Vertragsbestandteil Nachhaltiges Bauen – Bedingungen für Werkleistungen*). The conditions demand the use of certain sustainability standards and recyclable materials, define light and air quality thresholds for public buildings, and obligations to monitor and recycle waste materials. Despite their voluntary nature, model contracts and recommendations are of important practical relevance and are applied widely in Swiss procurement practice.

Standard specifications are also used in various sectors in Belgium. The best developed are the standards for the road construction sector. Administrative and technical provisions for contracting in road construction can be found in all three Belgian regions: Standard Specifications (SB) 250 in Flanders, Type Specifications (TB) 2015 in Brussels and Cahier des Charges Type (CCT) Qualiroutes in Wallonia.[117] In recent years, adjustments to these documents aimed at reducing CO_2 emissions and promoting circularity, for example, in the choice of specific materials that may be used in the execution of infrastructure works.[118] Failure to comply with the standards can result in contractual penalties ranging from fines, repairs in kind, or even cancellation of the contract.

Another novel contractual mechanism that is increasingly being used to promote and enforce sustainability (both in private and public contracts) is incentive clauses. Such clauses tie the contractor's profit to performance goals, rewarding the contractor for cost savings or early completion, or they can penalise the contractor with profit reductions for delays, cost overruns, and substandard quality.[119] As argued by Klingler, incentive clauses can also be adopted to support sustainability goals, provided those goals are measurable.[120] For instance, contracting authorities could link bonus payments directly to the contractor's success in reducing CO_2 emissions.[121]

Across European jurisdictions, the practical application of incentive clauses shows common patterns, though variations exist in their integration and emphasis. In Switzerland, public contracts frequently incorporate negative incentives, most importantly contractual penalties for delays, but more and more contracts

[117] See Het Standaardbestek 250 voor wegenbouw <www.vlaanderen.be/het-standaardbestek-250-voor-wegenbouw> accessed 6 June 2025; Travaux en voirie: cahier des charges-type <data.mobility.brussels/home/fr/publications/publications-techniques/travaux-de-voirie/>; Cahier des charges type Qualiroutes – Version 2021 consolidée (et ses adaptations ultérieures) <infrastructures.wallonie.be/pouvoirs-locaux/nos-thematiques/routes/qualite--construction/qualiroutes/cahier-des-charges-type-qualiroutes---version-2021-consolidee-et-ses-adaptations-ulterieures.html>.

[118] See for example Cement en beton in het nieuwe Standaardbestek 250, versie 5.0: verdere stappen richting koolstofreductie en circulariteit <gww-bouw.be/algemeen/beton/cement-en-beton-in-het-nieuwe-standaardbestek-250-versie-5-0-verdere-stappen-richting-koolstofreductie-en-circulariteit/>.

[119] P Zimmermann, 'Anreizorientierte Beschaffungsverträge und das Preisrecht: Preisrechtliche Fragen des Performance-based Contracting (PBC) am Beispiel der Beschaffung von Verteidigungsgütern' (2022) *Vergaberecht* 504, 504–08; Klingler (n 36) 445–48.

[120] Klingler (n 36) 447.

[121] ibid; T Göhlert and J Tenner, 'Klimaverträgliches Bauen – Teil 2: Vertragliche Anreize zur Senkung der Treibhausgasemissionen' (2024) 11 *Neue Zeitschrift für Bau- und Vergaberecht* 661, 663–65.

also include positive incentives, such as bonus payments for early completion.[122] Germany similarly employs incentive clauses within complex contracting models such as Integrated Project Delivery (IPD) agreements, notably used by Deutsche Bahn. While time-related goals dominate, bonuses are also linked to worker safety and environmental outcomes such as the reduction of CO_2 and other emissions.[123] German public procurement law, budgetary regulations, and public pricing laws underpin the requirement that incentive-linked bonuses must correlate with a measurable added value for the contracting authority, reflecting broader public interest principles.[124]

In Belgium, incentive mechanisms are integrated in public–private partnerships (PPPs) and energy service company (ESCO) models. Here, contractor payments are often tied to the achievement of availability targets for infrastructure and real estate, as well as Key Performance Indicators (KPIs) related to sustainability outcomes, such as improvements in energy efficiency or water use. Failure to meet agreed KPIs results in reduced payments or the imposition of penalties, embedding sustainability objectives directly into the contractor's financial interests.[125]

V. Conclusion

This chapter has examined two interrelated aspects: the meaning of sustainability in private and public contracts, and the mechanisms for its enforcement. Although voluntary CSR and ESG concepts first emerged within the business community, their convergence with public regulatory understandings of sustainability is now evident. Today, both frameworks address similar social and environmental issues across business operations, supply chains, and contractual relationships. Historically, CSR and ESG initiatives targeted individual businesses, while sustainability regulations were aimed at states and governments. However, this distinction is increasingly blurred, particularly with the advent of recent EU regulations such as the CSRD and the CSDDD, which require companies not only to assess ESG risks in their own operations but also to report on their broader impacts on society and the environment.

Over recent years, sustainability concerns have been integrated into public procurement law as part of 'strategic procurement' and have been defined as a

[122] See eg KBOB (n 92), clause 6.2 on contractual penalties for delays and clause 6.3 on bonus payment for early completion.

[123] See R Berghorn, 'Anwendung des "Partnerschaftsmodells Schiene" beim Pfaffensteigtunnel (ABS Gäubahn Nord)' in Förderverein Konstruktiver Ingenieurbau der UniBw München e.V. and Studiengesellschaft für Tunnel und Verkehrsanlagen e.V. (eds), *8. Münchener Tunnelbau Symposium: Tunnel in Bayern, Nachhaltigkeit im Tunnelbau, Vertragsmodelle und Risiko, Internationale Großprojekte* (Neubiberg, 2024) 103, 109–10.

[124] In detail Zimmermann, 'Anreizorientierte Beschaffungsverträge' (n 118) 504; Zimmermann, 'Anreizorientierte Verträge' (n 84) 745.

[125] Energieprestatiecontract: www.vlaio.be/nl/subsidies-financiering/subsidiedatabank/energieprestatiecontract-derdepartijfinanciering.

new goal in the revised Swiss procurement law. However, a key difference between public and private contracts remains: in public contracts, sustainability criteria must be linked to the subject matter of the contract. This requirement enables contracting authorities to include social and environmental obligations into contracts but generally excludes governance matters (except for anti-corruption measures) that fall within corporate autonomy.

At first glance, the enforcement of sustainability appears largely aligned across private and public contracts in the jurisdictions examined. Statutory warranty rights for defective or 'unsustainable' goods and works serve as powerful enforcement tools, particularly where quantifiable damages are absent. Similarly, the use of contractual penalties to enforce sustainable contract clauses has proven effective, especially in ensuring compliance with social requirements that would otherwise be difficult to enforce directly. However, due to the requirement that environmental and social requirements must be linked to the subject matter of the contract, public contracts must tie sustainability clauses to concrete, verifiable criteria. In contrast, private contracts and corporate codes of conduct allow for the inclusion of broader, less quantifiable supply chain obligations. However, for general and far-reaching codes of conduct, it must always be examined to what extent the parties want to be legally bound by them and hence be liable for non-compliance.

Beyond this general alignment, public procurement laws introduce specific mandatory provisions applicable only to public contracts. For example, certain German state procurement acts require the incorporation of contractual penalties and termination rights linked to social compliance failures. Unsuccessful bidders may challenge contract awards where mandatory contract performance conditions have been unlawfully waived. In Switzerland, although no equivalent mandatory public law provisions exist, contracting authorities are generally required to integrate the federal general terms and conditions, which include contractual penalties for breaches of labour and environmental law. Belgium follows a similar model, combining public law obligations with the possibility for contracting authorities to deviate in specific circumstances, in which private law supplements the contractual framework.

Another soft law approach used to promote and enforce sustainability is the inclusion of industry standards into contracts. Such industry standards provide specific sustainability requirements that can be linked, for example, to contractual penalties, thereby opening the way to enforcement. A more novel approach that is increasingly being used in public and private contracts relies on financial incentives to – positively or negatively – encourage private companies to reach sustainable performance goals by tying them to the companies' profit, allowing them bonus payments or punishing them with price reductions.

Overall, the hesitation of contracting authorities and private companies to implement or enforce sustainable contract clauses cannot be attributed to a lack of legal enforcement mechanisms. Further empirical research is needed to understand the practical barriers to enforcement. Key questions include: To what extent do contractors and suppliers already comply with environmental and social obligations? Is the lack of enforcement tied to the difficulty of detecting or quantifying sustainability breaches? Do authorities refrain from the enforcement of contractual clauses and penalties due to high transaction costs? Are disputes over sustainability obligations resolved outside formal judicial mechanisms?

Despite some ongoing challenges in operationalising sustainability obligations within contracts, the adoption of mandatory rules for SPP at the EU or national level could drive wider and more systematic application. However, given the political sensitivities surrounding harmonisation of private contract law and the mixed attitudes towards binding sustainability obligations across countries, it remains uncertain whether such regulatory efforts will succeed. In the absence of binding rules, the advancement of sustainable contracting will continue to depend on the voluntary actions of companies, the strategic choices of contracting authorities, and the interpretative role of courts. It remains to be seen whether improved drafting guidance, industry standards, model contracts, and evolving case law will lead to a more effective and consistent enforcement of sustainability obligations in the future.

12

Enforcing Sustainability Clauses in Public Contracts: Third-party Enforcement Caught between the Privity of Contract and Conflicting Interests

EZGI UYSAL AND KATEŘINA MITKIDIS

I. Introduction

The doctrine of privity of contracts is one of the building blocks of contract laws across various jurisdictions. According to the doctrine, contracts impose obligations on and confer rights only to the contractual parties. However, in many jurisdictions, the privity of contracts is not absolute. Most jurisdictions recognise limited situations where third parties may enforce or challenge a contract to which they are not a party.[1] Namely, the privity of contracts doctrine, in civil law jurisdictions also known as the relative effects of contracts, is increasingly under pressure in the wake of the use of contracts for regulatory purposes.[2] A telling example is the use of contracts as a tool to achieve global sustainability goals.

While supply chain contracts, each one of them establishing the framework for a concrete transaction or business cooperation between a buyer and a supplier, seem at first ill-fitted to secure global sustainability and benefit the global population as a whole, they have become regularly used with such an aim.[3] Sustainability

[1] For further analysis, see s II below.

[2] H Collins, *Regulating Contracts* (Oxford, Oxford University Press, 1999).

[3] See in general, D McBarnet and M Kurkchiyan, 'Corporate Social Responsibility Through Contractual Control? Global Supply Chains and "Other-Regulation"' in D McBarnet, A Voiculescu and T Campbell (eds), *The New Corporate Accountability: Corporate Social Responsibility and the Law* (Cambridge, Cambridge University Press, 2007) 59; Pace University School of Law and International Association for Commercial Contracts and Management, 'The Triple Bottom Line: The Use of Sustainability and Stabilization Clauses in International Contracts' (Report,

clauses incorporating regulatory goals are nowadays also commonplace in supply chain contracts of European companies.[4] Moreover, public contracting is increasingly often used not only to obtain a specific product or service, but also to pursue a wider public interest in protecting the global environment, and social and human rights through public purchases.[5] Therefore, sustainability clauses have become a frequent occurrence also in public procurement contracts. For instance, according to the Dutch National Plan on Sustainable Public Procurement, 67 per cent and 51 per cent of measured purchases in 2019 included environmental and international supply chain criteria, respectively.[6]

Nevertheless, the inclusion of sustainability requirements in the contractual text does not secure that these obligations are in fact complied with. As opposed to the frequent occurrence of sustainability clauses (also referred to as sustainable contract clauses) in private and public contracts, it remains an open question whether these clauses are enforced in practice. As emphasised by Klingler, Zimmermann, and van Garsse, empirical analysis on the enforcement of sustainability clauses between contracting parties is lacking.[7] The non-existence of case law concerning this topic suggests that contractual parties do not choose formal enforcement through courts.[8] This is problematic, as not enforcing such clauses may harm the interests of third parties.

In the academic literature, on the one side, the topic of third parties' interests in the enforcement of sustainability clauses has been covered in private law scholarship, specifically concerning the above-mentioned doctrine of privity.[9]

2010) 26; KP Mitkidis, *Sustainability Clauses in International Business Contracts* (den Haag, Eleven International Publishing, 2015) 153–55; EcoVadis, 'Sustainability Clauses in Commercial Contracts: The Key to Corporate Responsibility' (2018) <https://www.eticanews.it/wp-content/uploads/2018/07/ecovadis_contrat_clauses_RSE__20.06.2018_eng_v5-1.pdf> 21. With respect to environmental provisions specifically, see MP Vandenberg, 'The New Wal-Mart Effect: The Role of Private Contracting in Global Governance' (2007) 54(4) *UCLA Law Review* 913; In respect to human rights provisions specifically see, KP Mitkidis, S Perkovic and P Mitkidis, 'Tendencies in Contractual Governance to Promote Human and Labour Rights in Transnational Supply Chains' (2019) 23(4) *Competition & Change* 397.

[4] EcoVadis (n 3) 13 finds the occurrence of sustainability clauses in 75 per cent of sample contracts globally, including the EU. For similar findings in a more recent report, see WorldCC, 'Sustainability in Contracts: A Summary of Current Status' <www.worldcc.com/Portals/IACCM/Reports/Sustainability%20in%20Contracts%20A%20Summary%20of%20Current%20Status.pdf?utm_campaign=Foundation%20-%20ESG%20Research%20Report&utm_content=297478038&utm_medium=social&utm_source=linkedin&hss_channel=lcp-88969536>.

[5] United Nations (UN) Sustainable Development Goal (SDG) 12.7.

[6] Dutch National Plan on Sustainable Public Procurement – 'Commissioning with ambition, procuring with impact' <www.government.nl/documents/publications/2021/01/29/commissioning-with-ambition-procuring-with-impact> 10.

[7] Ch 11.

[8] N Affolder, 'Looking for Law in Unusual Places: Cross-Border Diffusion of Environmental Norms' (2018) 7(3) *Transnational Environmental Law* 425, 443.

[9] KP Mitkidis, 'Enforcement of Sustainability Contractual Clauses in Supply Chains by Third Parties' in V Ulfbeck, A Andhov, and KP Mitkidis (eds), *Law and Responsible Supply Chain Management Contract and Tort Interplay and Overlap* (Abingdon, Routledge, 2019) 67.

Some authors even called for reconsidering the doctrine; yet others stressed that this is possibly an insurmountable task, which may eventually endanger the well-functioning contract law system.[10] On the other side, the enforcement of sustainability clauses by third parties, as well as the doctrine of privity, remains understudied in relation to public contracts. Accordingly, the aim of this chapter is to contribute to the scarce scholarship by exploring the question of whether the impacts of global sustainability endeavours, in the form of the inclusion of sustainability clauses into public contracts, can be seen as such a development that would justify the application of exceptions to the doctrine of privity of contracts, namely third-party beneficiary rules, or the development of new exceptions, all in order to provide third parties the right to enforce sustainability clauses in public contracts to which they are not a party.[11]

While it is clear that different interests might be harmed if sustainability clauses in public contracts are not formally enforced by public buyers, it lacks clarity whether the legal systems of the EU and Member States provide feasible legal avenues for the interested third parties to pierce the privity of contract doctrine and take on the role of enforcing sustainability clauses. Thus, this chapter aims to clarify this matter under the shadow of the doctrine of privity by analysing the possibilities for the enforcement of sustainability clauses incorporated in public contracts by three types of interested third parties assessed based on the distinction of the interests at stake.

The first type is third parties that are directly and negatively impacted by non-compliance of the contractor with a sustainability clause; they are interested in directly enforcing sustainability clauses, thus reinstating compliance or receiving an appropriate remedy. The second type of parties external to the contractual relationship is those having an economic interest in the enforcement of sustainability clauses. These are primarily unsuccessful bidders and economic operators who are dissuaded from tendering as they could not comply with sustainability-related requirements or were outbid due to the actual cost of adhering to such requirements. This second type might find themselves in an unfair position and suffer economic harm when the contracting bodies do not formally enforce these obligations arising from sustainability clauses. The third type is parties representing the public interest, which covers public institutions and civil society that may take action following inaction of the contracting authorities to enforce their contracts.[12]

[10] ibid 84–85. Ulfbeck and Hansen, for example, warn about the extent and complexity of such a reform ('sustainability adjusted contract law to some extent implies looking at the contractual relationship as a trilateral relationship between the contracting parties and external, societal interests … developing a sustainability adjusted contracted law is a much more complex task than previous developments that have taken place in contract law') see V Ulfbeck and O Hansen, 'Sustainability Clauses in an unsustainable Contract Law?' (2020) 16(1) *European Review of Contract Law* 186, 205.

[11] On national categorisation of public contracts see ch 3.

[12] The second and the third right constitute a manifestation of the publicisation of private law at the stage of performance of a public contract. See more on the concept of publicisation ch 2.

The chapter proceeds as follows. First, the privity of contracts doctrine is reviewed under European contract law and comparative law examples. Then, building on the previous chapter 11, the concept of sustainability clauses within the frameworks of private and public procurement is investigated. The analyses follow, concentrating on the possibilities of three different types of interested third parties to legally enforce sustainability clauses in public procurement contracts. The final section concludes.

As the anthology, this chapter is predominantly focused on the EU and the Member States' jurisdictions. While it is impossible to provide a universal answer to the raised questions applicable to all Member States, the aim of this contribution is to review examples and laws from different Member States that represent varied approaches. These examples have been selected based on the availability of relevant case law, and they may not necessarily reflect the general trend across all jurisdictions. Rather, the focus is on jurisdictions where case law provides concrete insights. It should be noted that the identification of a contract as a public contract under the public procurement legislation does not preclude it from being considered a private contract under national law.[13] However, for the purposes of this chapter, private (procurement) contracts refer to commercial contracts that are not public (procurement) contracts.

II. Privity of Contract

'Privity of contracts' or, in civil law terminology, the 'relative effect of contracts' is a contract law doctrine common to all Member States.[14] The doctrine establishes that contracts confer rights to and impose obligations only on the contractual parties. A person who is not a party to a contract cannot enforce it, gain any right from it, or be imposed any obligation by it. The doctrine of privity of contracts can be traced back to the fundamental rule of Roman law of contracts, namely 'that a contract creates a personal bond between parties'.[15] Such a personal bond means that no third party could be bound by a contract they were not a party to (*res inter alios acta aliis neque nocere neque prodesse potest*)[16] and excludes the possibility of stipulation in favour of a third party (*alteri stipulari nemo potest*).[17]

The privity of contracts doctrine has remained a cornerstone of both common and civil law of contracts throughout history until today. Yet, it is not always explicitly stated in national contract laws. Some jurisdictions contain a specific

[13] See ch 2; ch 4.

[14] See more on this concept in ch 4.

[15] J Hellebeek, 'Contracts for a Third Party Beneficiary: A Brief Sketch from the Corpus Iuris to Present-Day Civil Law' (2007) 13(2) *Fundamina: A Journal of Legal History* 11, 13.

[16] An act made between certain people cannot adversely affect the rights of other people who are not party to the act.

[17] Justinian Institutes 3.19.19.

provision restating the doctrine in their Civil Code, such as France[18] or Italy.[19] In other jurisdictions, the doctrine can be deduced from general provisions regarding contracts, such as in Czechia[20] and Germany.[21] For this chapter, it is particularly interesting to note that European contract law, namely the Principles of European Contract Law (PECL) and the Draft Common Frame of Reference (DCFR), chose the latter solution.[22]

None of the non-statutory harmonisation instruments of European contract law includes an explicit provision on the privity of contracts. The authors of the DCFR, nevertheless, *do* state in the preamble that '[DCFR] takes it as self-evident that parties can contract only for themselves unless otherwise provided, and that contracts, as a rule, regulate only the rights and obligations between the parties who conclude them'.[23] The DCFR thus considers the doctrine of privity of contracts to be the solid background of contracting, while it opens up for exceptions provided that they are explicitly regulated. The DCFR further includes a provision stating that '[a] valid contract is binding on the parties'.[24] Using *a contrario* interpretation, this provision can be read to mean that any binding effect on anyone else but the contracting parties is excluded. However, some point out that this general provision expresses rather the principle of *pacta sunt servanda* than of privity of contracts.[25]

Whether explicitly restating the doctrine of privity of contracts or not, all national contract laws of Member States recognise exceptions to the rule. Several such exceptions were recognised already by Roman law[26] and many others have gradually developed through legal changes and court practice in individual Member States, responding to the practical needs of contracting parties.[27] These

[18] Art 1199 French Civil Code ('A contract creates obligations only as between the parties. Third parties may neither claim performance of the contract nor be constrained to perform it, subject to the provisions of this section and those in Chapter III of Title IV'). See *Code civil* <www.legifrance.gouv.fr/codes/texte_lc/LEGITEXT000006070721/> (French Civil Code).

[19] Art 1372 Italian Civil Code ('A contract is binding between the parties. … A contract has no effect with respect to third parties except in cases provided for by law'). See *Codice Civile* adopted with *Regio Decreto 16 marzo 1942, no 262* (Italian Civil Code).

[20] Para 1724(1) Czech Civil Code ('By a contract, parties express their will to create between them a mutual obligation'). See *Občanský zákoník* Act No 89/2012 Coll (Czech Civil Code).

[21] A Burrows and C Bush, 'Contract Terms in Favour of Third Parties' in G Dannemann and S Vogenauer (eds), *The Common European Sales Law in Context: Interactions with English and German Law* (Oxford, Oxford University Press, 2013) 504.

[22] See more about the PECL and the DCFR in ch 1.

[23] C von Bar et al (eds), *Principles, Definitions and Model Rules of European Private Law: Draft Common Frame of Reference (DCFR)*, Outline Edition (Munich, Sellier-European law publishers GmbH, 2009) 63.

[24] II–1:103(1) DCFR.

[25] S Whittaker, 'The "Draft Common Frame of Reference" An Assessment' (Report commissioned by the UK Ministry of Justice, November 2008) 61.

[26] Hellebeek (n 15) 11–12.

[27] For a detailed overview of such exceptions in French law, see, S Rowan, *The New French Law of Contract* (Oxford, Oxford University Press, 2022) ch 8. France is one of the member states that provides for most exceptions to the principle. In 2009, Vogenauer wrote that in France the exceptions to the principle are so many that '[t]he ostensible reinforcement of the principle [in the then article 1165

include, among others, direct actions, assignment of contracts, some instances involving insurance companies, and what is most important to this chapter: third-party beneficiary rules, also known as stipulation in favour of a third party. Before delving into the application of this exception in the context of sustainability clauses in public contracts, the concept of sustainability clauses is briefly introduced.

III. Sustainability Clauses in Private and Public Contracts

Over the last decade, increased scrutiny of businesses' environmental and social performance by consumers and the financial community has increased the motivation for companies to focus on responsible business behaviour both within their own operations and across their supply chains. Corporate sustainability is progressively subject to legislation both at the national and EU levels. The Corporate Sustainability Due Diligence Directive (CSDDD) is the last addition to the EU's regulatory toolbox, the implementation of which heavily relies on the use of contracts.[28] As investigated in the previous chapter 11 of this anthology, sustainability requirements are frequently incorporated both in private and public contracts.[29]

On the side of private procurement, sustainability clauses most commonly include the requirement of legal compliance, environmental protection, human rights, labour standards, prevention of corruption, and/or health and safety.[30] Yet, the form, content, and level of precision of sustainability clauses in private contracts vary significantly depending on the given industry, the character of the relationship between the contractual parties and their geographical location.[31] Further, in private contracts, sustainability clauses are not required to be directly connected to the subject matter of the contract.[32] As they are often disconnected from the

Civil Code] is hollow'. See S Vogenauer, 'The Effects of Contracts on Third Parties: The Avant-projet de reforme in a Comparative Perspective' in J Cartwright et al (eds), *Reforming the French Law of Obligations: Comparative Reflections on the Avant-Projet de Réforme Du Droit Des Obligations et de La Prescription ('the Avant-Projet Catala')* (Oxford, Bloomsbury Publishing, 2009) 268.

[28] Mainly Arts 10(2)(b) and 11(3)(c) Directive (EU) 2024/1760 of the European Parliament and of the Council of 13 June 2024 on corporate sustainability due diligence and amending Directive (EU) 2019/1937 and Regulation (EU) 2023/2859 [2024] OJ L 2024/1760 (CSDDD).

[29] See also EcoVadis (n 3); World CC (n 4). The gradual proliferation was studied in Mitkidis, Perkovic, and Mitkidis, 'Tendencies in Contractual Governance to Promote Human and Labour Rights in Transnational Supply Chains' (n 3) 411–12. The authors found that largest companies globally, reporting the use of supply chain contracts to protect labour and human rights, report an increase from ca. 53 per cent to 75 per cent from 2012 to 2017.

[30] See ch 11. See also EcoVadis (n 3) 19; The Triple Bottom Line: The Use of Sustainability and Stabilization Clauses in International Contracts (n 3) 29.

[31] However, following the adoption of CSDDD, initiatives to draft model clauses are on the rise. See Responsible Contracting Project, 'the EMCs' <www.responsiblecontracting.org/emcs>.

[32] M Andrecka and KP Mitkidis, 'Sustainability Requirements in EU Public and Private Procurement – a Right or an Obligation?' (2017) 1 *Nordic Journal of Commercial Law* 56, 68–69.

subject matter of the contract, companies can afford to use vague, incomplete, and obscure language in their formulation without endangering the transaction. They have various reasons for entering into such incomplete contracts, such as enforcement costs and bounded rationality.[33] Keeping language vague can also be beneficial when the purpose of the provision is to inform and motivate the supplier rather than create a legal basis for a claim in case of breach, or when the wording of sustainability clauses needs to be flexible for use in contracts with different suppliers from different jurisdictions.[34]

On the side of public procurement, as assessed in the previous chapter, Directive 2014/24/EU permits criteria allowing contracting authorities to incorporate sustainability considerations in the contracts they award.[35] Article 18(2) requires Member States to ensure compliance with environmental, social, and labour law in the performance of public contracts. In addition to the sectoral legislation introducing mandatory sustainability requirements following the European Green Deal,[36] the CSDDD also provides for the incorporation of due diligence requirements in public contracts.

Differently from private contracting, Directive 2014/24/EU limits the types of contractual obligations in public contracts as it requires criteria that would make up the content of obligations to be linked to the subject matter of the contract. However, the requirement, developed through case law, is considerably comprehensive as pursuant to Article 67 Directive 2014/24/EU, it encompasses conditions that relate to supplies, services and works 'in any respect and at any stage of their life-cycle' without requiring underlying conditions to affect the material characteristics of the purchase.[37]

A major discussion point with respect to sustainability clauses is their enforcement. While enforcement is not legally impossible, it is limited for various reasons.[38] Private buyers may lack the motivation to enforce sustainability clauses through courts, not only due to the fear of public exposure in case of unethical behaviour, but also because legal remedies available for a breach are not suitable

[33] EA Posner, K Eggleston, and R Zeckhauser, 'The Design and Interpretation of Contracts: Why Complexity Matters' (2000) 95(1) *Northwestern University Law Review* 92.

[34] GG Triantis, 'The Efficiency of Vague Contract Terms: A Response to the Schwartz-Scott Theory of U.C.C. Article 2' (2002) 62(4) *Louisiana Law Review* 1073.

[35] Similar rules also apply to sustainable purchasing under Directive 2014/23/EU and 2014/25/EU.

[36] W Janssen, 'Shifting Towards Mandatory Sustainability Requirements in EU Public Procurement Law: Context, Relevance and a Typology' in W Janssen and R Caranta (eds), *Mandatory Sustainability Requirements in EU Public Procurement Law Reflections on a Paradigm Shift* (Oxford, Hart Publishing, 2023) 3; E Uysal and W Janssen, 'The European Green Deal and Public Procurement Law' in MC Eritja and X Fernández-Pons (eds), *Deploying the European Green Deal* (Abingdon, Routledge, 2024) 177.

[37] Nevertheless, CSDDD and its role in public procurement challenge the said requirement, see L Treviño-Lozano and E Uysal, 'Bridging the gap between corporate sustainability due diligence and EU public procurement' (2023) 30(5) *Maastricht Journal of European and Comparative Law* 554; E Uysal and L Treviño-Lozano, 'CSDDD: Bridging due diligence and public procurement'<https://realaw.blog/2024/06/14/csddd-bridging-due-diligence-and-public-procurement-by-ezgi-uysal-and-laura-trevino-lozano/>.

[38] For more, see ch 11.

to sustainability objectives, and the continuance of the business relationship is often more important to the buyers than the full and immediate compliance with a sustainability clause.[39] Subsequently, the increase in the incorporation of sustainability clauses is not reflected in pertinent case law. In fact, there are only a few court cases on the enforcement of sustainability clauses in private contracts, and those are brought by third parties rather than the buyer.[40]

For public contracting, one could expect that public buyers' motivation in enforcing sustainability clauses should be stronger, as it is the states that are the ultimate guarantors of human and labour rights, as well as environmental protection. Yet, the scarcity of national and European case law precludes further analysis. Though sustainability-related criteria and conditions are included in public contracts, litigation regarding enforcement is limited.[41]

There are practical reasons for the lack of formal enforcement of sustainability clauses in public contracts. The incorporation of regulatory standards requires extra financial and human resources to monitor adherence to sustainability requirements, especially in distant third countries.[42] Buyers may experience problems with access to contractors' suppliers' facilities, a lack of data and difficulties in formulating compliance indicators.[43] Moreover, the interest in delivering the procured goods or services to the citizens may trump the interest in protecting human and labour rights or reducing environmental externalities and may incentivise contracting authorities to maintain existing contracts rather than resorting to formal enforcement proceedings, which could result in retendering. Nevertheless, failing to formally enforce sustainability clauses in public contracts could harm various interests of parties external to the contractual relationship, which may allow said parties to resort to litigation.

IV. Enforcement of Sustainability Clauses in Public Contracts by Third Parties

As discussed above, the doctrine of privity of contracts is prevailing in contract law regimes of Member States. However, various legal systems recognise circumstances where it can be pierced. This is typically the case when contractual parties aim to

[39] Mitkidis, 'Enforcement of Sustainability Contractual Clauses in Supply Chains by Third Parties' (n 9). As noted in ch 11, enforcement may be challenging as non-compliance with sustainability clauses may not always alter the primary purpose of the subject matter or lead to quantifiable damages.

[40] See Mitkidis, *Sustainability Clauses in International Business Contracts* (n 3) 103.

[41] See in a Danish context, M Andrecka, 'Corporate Social Responsibility and Sustainability in Danish Public Procurement' (2017) 12 *European Procurement & Public Private Partnership Law Review* 333, 338.

[42] European Commission, 'Buying Social A Guide to Taking Account of Social Considerations in Public Procurement' (2021) 2nd edn C(2021) 3573 final 89.

[43] European Commission, Directorate-General for Internal Market, Industry, Entrepreneurship and SMEs, Study on 'Strategic use of public procurement in promoting green, social and innovation policies' (2015) final report 68–69.

benefit subjects that are external to the contractual relationship.[44] In these situations, such third-party beneficiaries are recognised as having the right to directly enforce a contract that benefits them. Still, while the concept of third-party beneficiaries exists in the absolute majority of contract law regimes of Member States, such a disruption of the privity of the contract is considered an anomaly.[45]

European harmonisation of the rules applicable to public contracts puts traditional private contract law principles to the test.[46] In the public procurement context, the strength of the contract law doctrines, including privity of contract, depends on whether procurement contracts are predominantly governed by public law – 'public-oriented hybrid model', where courts have been more open to interfere with contractual parties' rights and obligations – or private law – 'private-oriented hybrid model', where privity of contract is considered as a fundamental right of contractual parties.[47] An example of the former is the construction of 'regulatory clauses' in public contracts developed by French courts under which affected third parties may directly challenge these clauses for abuse of power by public authorities.[48]

Directive 2014/24/EU does not expressly regulate the possibility of public contracts benefiting third parties. National public procurement acts of Member States only exceptionally regulate extra-contractual parties.[49] Yet, the very essence

[44] Examples from national laws include Art 1411 Italian Civil Code; Art 1205 French Civil Code; paras 1767–1769 Czech Civil Code; s 328 German Civil Code. See *Bürgerliches Gesetzbuch* (BGB) of 18 August 1896, RGBl. S. 195, as last amended (most recently by Art 1 *Gesetz* of 21 December 2022, BGBl. I Nr. 51, p 2805) (German Civil Code). In some jurisdictions, the privity of contracts is applied stricter than in others. A strict application is found, for example in the UK, where while a third-party beneficiary doctrine exists, its scope is narrow.

[45] AN Hatzis, 'Rights and Obligations of Third Parties' in B Bouckaert and G De Geest (eds), *Encyclopedia of Law & Economics, Vol. III: The Regulation of Contracts*,1st edn (Cheltenham, Edward Elgar Publishing, 2000) 200.

[46] KM Halonen, 'Article 73 Termination of Contracts' in R Caranta and A Sanchez-Graells (eds), *European Public Procurement: Commentary on Directive 2014/24/EU* (Cheltenham, Edward Elgar Publishing, 2021) 799.

[47] See ch 3. See also KM Halonen, 'Fundamentals of Contract Modifications in EU Procurement Law' in D Dragos et al (eds), *Contract Changes: The Dark Side of EU Procurement Law* (Cheltenham, Edward Elgar Publishing, 2023) 19.

[48] CE Ass, 10 July 1996, Cayzeele, no 138536, Lebon 274 h; see D Pouyaud, 'Contentieux des contrats administratifs – Exécution et fin du contrat' in *Jurisclasseur Administratif*, fasc. no1127, 2021, paras 333–339. Regulatory clauses exist also in Portuguese law, see MA Raimundo, 'Execução dos contratos públicos e responsabilidade contratual: do contrato como res inter partes ao contrato como res publica' in CA Gomes et al (eds), *III Colóquio Luso-Brasileiro de Direito Público – Responsabilidade nos contratos públicos. Uma perspectiva comparada luso-brasileira* (Lisboa, Associação Académica da Faculdade de Direito de Lisboa, 2020) 104.

[49] An example is the above-mentioned legal construct of 'regulatory clauses' in public contracts that is, for example, restated in Arts 287(3) and (4) Portuguese Public Contracts Code as well as French case law. However, such 'regulatory clauses' typically establish a duty or remove a right from a third party rather than benefit them. Another example is the possibility of third parties to challenge the validity of the contract as developed, eg, by the French judiciary in the rulings in Tropic Travaux Signalisation and Département de Tarn-et-Garonne (CE Ass, 16 July 2007, *Société Tropic Travaux Signalisation*, no 291545, Lebon 360 concl. Casas; CE Ass, 4 April 2014, *Département du Tarn-et-Garonne*, no 358994, Lebon 70 concl. Dacosta). The possibility to challenge the validity of a public contract is, however, very limited, as the case law balances legality with contractual stability.

of public contracts is to benefit subjects external to the specific contract. This is primarily the general public, as public buyers, through procurement, ensure the fulfilment of needs of the general public in, for example, energy supply, construction and maintenance of infrastructure, equipment and operation of public institutions, and access to essential goods (eg medicines).

The inclusion of sustainability clauses into public contracts puts to the forefront another group of potential third-party beneficiaries beyond the recipients of public service. This is given considering the purpose of these clauses, that is, most often the protection of the environment and upholding human and labour rights in (transnational) supply chains. Broadly speaking, the global population that has an interest in building a global sustainable future is a beneficiary of these clauses. More concretely, though, these provisions benefit subjects that can be directly and negatively impacted by a breach of a sustainability clause.[50] These subjects are interested in enforcing sustainability clauses in order to reinstate compliance or receive an appropriate remedy. Finally, other than third-party beneficiaries, sustainability clauses in public contracts incite the interest of different types of extra-contractual parties who will take action to enforce sustainability clauses either in the protection of their economic interest or the general public interest.

Below, the three types of third parties having an interest in enforcing sustainability clauses in a public contract are discussed. These are subjects having (a) an interest in effectuating the clauses as they are direct beneficiaries of sustainability clauses and directly and negatively impacted by non-compliance, (b) an economic interest in enforcing the clauses to prevent competitive advantage being granted to the successful tenderer to the detriment of the competitive procedure, and (c) general public interest in enforcing the clauses for management of public funds and/or for the benefit of the society.

A. Third-Party Beneficiaries

In this section, the authors discuss the possibilities of third parties that are direct beneficiaries of sustainability clauses in public contracts to enforce those in case of non-compliance. This topic has been analysed with respect to commercial contracts elsewhere, and the findings of that analysis are referred to where relevant;[51] however, this discussion focuses on the peculiarities of public contracts.

Sustainability clauses primarily protect third parties and interests that are external to the contractual relationship between the contractual parties, such as a

[50] Mitkidis, 'Enforcement of Sustainability Contractual Clauses in Supply Chains by Third Parties' (n 9) 65.

[51] For analysis of third-party beneficiaries claims in respect to sustainability clauses in commercial contracts, see Mitkidis, 'Enforcement of Sustainability Contractual Clauses in Supply Chains by Third Parties' (n 9).

contractor's, supplier's, or sub-supplier's employees or inhabitants of an area of the production site.[52] An example might be a public contract incorporating an obligation concerning the payment of a fair remuneration to the contractor's employees and requires the contractor to cascade this requirement throughout their supply chain. If the contractor or its suppliers do not pay fair remuneration, the respective employees in the supply chain might have an interest in enforcing the clause in the contract between the buyer and the contractor. Yet, as they are not the signatories of the contract, they lack privity and, thus, an obvious legal standing to enforce the contract.

In order to protect the legitimate rights of third parties, most contract law systems have embraced the legal construct of third-party beneficiaries. In jurisdictions which provide for recourse to contract law for aspects of public contracts not regulated in public procurement law, the third-party beneficiaries construct will also apply to public contracts. For instance, under the Czech legal system, the Czech Act on Public Procurement is considered to be *lex specialis* to the regulation of contracts in the Czech Civil Code.[53] Accordingly, determining whether a third party has the right to enforce a sustainability clause in a public contract is therefore done with recourse to the Czech Civil Code paragraph 1767. Similarly, in Italy, public procurement is regulated by the Italian Public Contracts Code,[54] however, pursuant to Article 12, to the extent that it is not explicitly regulated, the Italian Civil Code applies to the contract performance. Accordingly, Article 1411 Italian Civil Code on the stipulation in favour of a third party applies to such rights in public contracts.

As for European contract law, a stipulation in favour of the third party is recognised as one of the exceptions to the principle of privity. Inspired by French law, Article 6.110 PECL provides that a third party may request performance provided that such a right is expressly agreed upon between the contracting parties.[55] The DCFR provided a more detailed rule than the PECL.[56] Under the DCFR, stipulation in favour of a third party is regulated with Article II:9:301, which provides that a contract may confer a right or other benefit to a third party in case of stipulation in favour of the third party. Unlike the PECL, the provision in the DCFR adds that the third party has the same right to performance and remedies for non-performance as if the performance was owed to her under the contract. Both the PECL and the DCFR stipulate that the third party does not need to be identified at the time of the conclusion of the contract.

Though the concept of third-party beneficiary rights exists in most jurisdictions, not all obligations relating to third parties can be considered to create a

[52] Ulfbeck and Hansen (n 10) 190–91.

[53] *Zákon o zadávání veřejných zakázek*, Act No. 134/2016 Coll (Czech Act on Public Procurement). See eg Office for the Protection of Competition, decision no 02356/2020/521/DFi of 6 February 2020.

[54] *Codice dei contratti pubblici* adopted with *Decreto Legislativo 31 marzo 2023, no 36* (Italian Public Contracts Code).

[55] S Vogenauer, 'Art 6:110: Stipulation in Favour of a Third Party' in N Jansen and R Zimmermann (eds), *Commentaries on European Contract Laws* (Oxford, Oxford University Press, 2018) 870.

[56] ibid.

third-party beneficiary right in a public contract. Nevertheless, neither the DCFR nor the PECL clearly establishes the conditions giving rise to third-party beneficiary rights; yet, three main requirements can be deduced from the legal instruments: (i) the *intention* of contractual parties to grant (ii) a *specific right* to (iii) *an identified (or identifiable) third party*. A further investigation of national laws reveals that these requirements are common to most jurisdictions, allowing for third-party beneficiaries to a contract.

Some jurisdictions stipulate additional conditions for the creation of a third-party beneficiary's right. For example, the Dutch Civil Code requires acceptance by the third-party beneficiary.[57] In Italy, it is a requirement that the promisee has an interest in the benefit to the third party.[58] Polish law provides explicitly that in case the third party has stated it wishes to use such a reservation, the benefit may not be revoked or amended.[59] Also, the Czech Civil Code states that the existence of a third-party beneficiary right needs to be evaluated in light of the content, nature, and purpose of the contract.[60] However, the core three conditions of third-party beneficiary rights are common to most European jurisdictions and are, thus, discussed in turn in the context of public procurement.

i. Intention

The first condition is that the contractual parties *intended* to confer a right to a third party. Such an intention can be either expressed or implied in contractual text. In commercial contracts, contract interpretation rules are used to determine the existence of the intention. A clear intention to bestow a right on a third party is crucial to the creation of an enforceable right, as the fact that a contract may incidentally benefit an external subject (incidental beneficiary) is generally considered insufficient.[61]

It can be argued that in the public contracts context, contractual parties' intention to bestow an enforceable right on a third party will be interpreted even more restrictively. In fact, authors of the DCFR used the example of a public contract to illustrate the position of the general public as accidental beneficiaries without any legal right to enforce the contract.[62] The simple fact that a contract

[57] Art 6.253 *Burgerlijk Wetboek* (BW) (Dutch Civil Code).

[58] Art 1411 Italian Civil Code.

[59] Art 393 *Ustawa z dnia 23 kwietnia 1964 r. – Kodeks cywilny* (Polish Civil Code).

[60] Para 1767 Czech Civil Code.

[61] H Verhagen, 'Contemporary Law' in JJ Hallebeek and H Dondorp (eds), *Contracts for a Third-Party Beneficiary: A Historical and Comparative Account* (Leiden, Brill Nijhoff, 2008).

[62] *Principles, Definitions and Model Rules of European Private Law – Draft Common Frame of Reference (DCFR)*, Interim Edition <www.ccbe.eu/fileadmin/speciality_distribution/public/documents/EUROPEAN_PRIVATE_LAW/EN_EPL_20100107_Principles__definitions_and_model_rules_of_European_private_law_-_Draft_Common_Frame_of_Reference__DCFR_.pdf>. 'For example, a contract between a local authority and a developer for the development of a public park may provide benefit to many other people but they would not acquire rights which they could enforce or assert under the contract.'

incorporates a benefit to a third party does not necessarily mean that such a provision is a stipulation in favour of a third party.[63]

ii. Specific Right

The second condition requires the determination of a *specific right* bestowed on the third party. The content of such a right is to be determined from the contract. It has also been purported that a specific right for a third party can only be derived from a promissory obligation to benefit third parties and not from an obligation not to harm others.[64] Thus, in the context of sustainability clauses, a specific right could, for example, be easier found when a contractor is contractually bound to pay fair remuneration to her employees than when she is bound not to pollute the environment. In some jurisdictions, courts have been more willing to find a specific right in a contract than in others.[65] This has especially been the case in situations where a tort law claim would lead to a disadvantaged position of the harmed party, while the contract law third-party beneficiary claim led to what courts perceived as a more just result.[66] In Germany, courts have developed the concept of 'contracts with protective effects toward third parties' in order to overcome some shortcomings of tort law.[67] However, the strict conditions for its use[68] will likely prevent its application to sustainability clauses.

An example of when a third-party beneficiary right was found by a court in the context of a public contract is a decision of the French Court of Cassation evaluating the legal position of a patient in a public hospital who received contaminated blood. The high court found that the patient was a third-party beneficiary to a contract between the national transfusion service and the public hospital, despite the fact that there was no expressed provision in the contract granting such a right to patients.[69] One would, therefore, expect a tort law claim instead. The court's decision to turn to contract law could be explained by choosing a solution that was fairer to the patients.[70] However, it is important to note that the French decision is an exception, as it is generally the case that no specific right can be derived from a contractual clause that is too vaguely formulated.[71]

[63] Vogenauer, 'Art 6:110: Stipulation in Favour of a Third Party' (n 55) 880.

[64] SA Smith, 'Contracts for the Benefit of Third Parties: In Defence of the Third-Party Rule' (1997) 17(4) *Oxford Journal of Legal Studies* 643, 646.

[65] Mitkidis, 'Enforcement of Sustainability Contractual Clauses in Supply Chains by Third Parties' (n 9) 71–73.

[66] Smith speaks about 'contract-as-tort' theory and warns that privity of contract may become an anachronism, see Smith, 'Contracts for the Benefit of Third Parties: In Defence of the Third-Party Rule' (n 64) 647.

[67] J Zekoll and G Wagner (eds), *Introduction to German Law*, 3rd edn (Alphen aan den Rijn, Wolters Kluwer, 2019) 215–17.

[68] ibid.

[69] Cass. Civ. 2e., 17 December 1954, D 1955.269Z.

[70] Verhagen (n 61) 146.

[71] C Poncibò, 'A Contract Law for Future Generations' (2020) 2 *Revija Kopaoničke škole prirodnog prava* 35, 38–39.

iii. Third Party

The third condition for the existence of a contractual third-party beneficiary right is that the third party is (third parties are) *identified or identifiable*. This neither means that the third party needs to be identified in the contract by name nor that she needs to exist at the time of conclusion of the contract; but she must be identifiable at least as a member of a specific group or class, eg as a 'patient' in the above-discussed French blood transfusion case.[72] This represents a compromise between commercial flexibility and legal certainty.[73] Allowing for the recognition of an indefinite group of third-party beneficiaries could lead to (further) blurring between contract and tort law, creating legal uncertainty for all involved.[74]

Taking these three requirements – intention, specific right, and third party – into consideration, social clauses in Italian public contracts represent an example. Under Article 57 Italian Public Contracts Code, contracting authorities are required to incorporate employment and labour-related clauses in their contracts. In the doctrine, as well as the Italian Court of Cassation case law, these clauses are accepted as stipulations in favour of a third party under the Italian Civil Code.[75] For instance, the commitment of a successful tenderer, through social clauses, to ensure that, in the performance of a public contract, working conditions are not lower than the conditions provided in the applicable collective agreement is a stipulation in favour of a third party under the Italian Civil Code.[76] However, in any case, for a condition to be considered a third-party beneficiary right, the contracting parties should have such an intent to confer a right to a third party.

In a judgment, following an action taken by the employee of the contractor in a public contract, the Italian Court of Cassation decided against the existence of a stipulation in favour of a third party.[77] The contract in question stipulated that the contractor should make available an employee with a specific level of qualification for the contract. One of the employees of the contractor took action claiming the difference in remuneration between his level of qualification and the qualification level specified in the public contract. The high court decided that the said

[72] In this context, though EU public procurement law does not directly regulate the third party beneficiaries to a public contract, with respect to the extension of framework agreements to other contracting authorities that are not direct parties to the framework agreements, the CJEU established that such contracting authorities should be specifically identified for this purpose in the invitation to tender or in the invitation to confirm interest for such an extension. See Case C-216/17 *Autorità Garante della Concorrenza e del Mercato – Antitrust and Coopservice Soc. coop. arl v Azienda Socio-Sanitaria Territoriale della Vallecamonica – Sebino (ASST) and Others* ECLI:EU:C:2018:1034, [2018] paras 54–56.

[73] Vogenauer, 'Art 6:110: Stipulation in Favour of a Third Party' (n 55) 878.

[74] Mitkidis, 'Enforcement of Sustainability Contractual Clauses in Supply Chains by Third Parties' (n 9) 75.

[75] F Pantano, 'Clausole sociali, concorrenza, investimento pubblico e tutela del lavoro: dal Codice dei contratti pubblici al PNRR' (2022) 22 *Federalismi.it* 169, 175.

[76] Cass., Sez. Lav., 8 September 2014, no 18860; Cass., sez. Lav., 29 September 2015, no 19299.

[77] Cass., Sez. Lav., 9 September 2020, no 18686.

requirement was a service quality standard concerning the service to be provided, which does not intend to confer a right to a third party, unlike social clauses under Article 57 Italian Public Contracts Code, which are considered to create third-party beneficiary rights.

Overall, allowing third parties who can be considered beneficiaries to enforce sustainability clauses with the aim of effectuating them is a very complex and sensitive issue. One can find strong arguments both for and against. Possibly the strongest argument against this is that third-party beneficiary claims interfere with the principle of privity of contracts and thus transactional efficiency.[78] Their permissive application could lead to dismantling the balance between contract and tort law and open floodgates for strategic litigation.[79] Arguments for broader recognition of third-party beneficiary rights include, among others, the fact that this is in line with public policy (both with respect to sustainability and fairness), that it would effectuate parties' intention to eliminate unethical behaviours from their supply chain, and that it would improve access to justice.[80] Yet, the above-analysed concept of third-party beneficiaries is not the only avenue for third parties concerned with the impact of a breach or insufficiency of sustainability clauses to take action to enforce these clauses. Other avenues are discussed immediately below.

B. Competitors as 'Interested' Parties

The second type of third parties having an interest in enforcing sustainability clauses are subjects with economic interest at stake, primarily unsuccessful bidders and/or other competitors of successful tenderers. They may initiate a review procedure in case of the contracting authority's failure to give effect to sustainability clauses. Due to their familiarity with contract documents, the competitors can function as chaperones of adequate contract performance.[81] The potential risk of action to be taken under Directive 89/665/EEC by competitors may prompt the enforcement of sustainability clauses by the public buyer.

Directive 89/665/EEC sets forth 'the minimum conditions to be satisfied by the review procedures' for decisions of contracting authorities that allegedly breach

[78] The complexity of fair and appropriate regulation of the enforcement of contracts by third-party beneficiaries has been recognised by the drafters of the European Model Clauses currently being developed with reference to Art 12 CSDDD. See Responsible Contracting Project, The European Model Clauses drafting group, 'European Model Clauses, third draft' <www.eur.nl/en/esl/media/2023-10-european-model-clauses-supply-chains0> 53. They note that while CSDDD does not expressly require the insertion of a third-party beneficiaries clause into contracts, it certainly allows it.

[79] Mitkidis, 'Enforcement of Sustainability Contractual Clauses in Supply Chains by Third Parties' (n 9) part 4.

[80] ibid.

[81] GM Racca, R Cavallo Perin, and GL Albano, 'Competition in the Execution Phase of Public Procurement' (2011) 41 *Public Contract Law Journal* 89, 91; E Plas, 'Amendments to Public Contracts: In Search of a Sufficient Degree of Transparency' (2021) 1 *Public Procurement Law Review* 1, 4.

public procurement rules.[82] This system of enforcement requires 'any person having or having had an interest in obtaining a particular contract and who has been or risks being harmed by an alleged infringement'[83] to be able to request the review of a contracting authority's decision. As the requirements of interest in the contract and potential harm are cumulative criteria, the European system of public procurement enforcement relies on peer review, ie competitors that are interested in the contract.[84] The ground of illegality that can be alleged by such interested parties in the case of non-enforced sustainability clauses is the ban on contract changes, as detailed below.

In public procurement, the criteria and conditions of a contract set the terms of the competition, attract interested economic operators and eventually determine to whom and under which conditions the contract will be awarded. Thus, alteration to any of these during contract performance may prejudice the competitive nature of the procedure. As a codification of the Court of Justice of the EU (CJEU) case law, this line of reasoning led to contract changes being explicitly regulated under Directive 2014/24/EU for the first time. Under Article 72 Directive 2014/24/EU, unless they fall under one of the exceptions provided in Article 72(1) and (2), changes to the concluded contracts which are significant, ie rendering the contract materially different, are not permissible.[85] They cannot be realised without holding a new tendering procedure.[86] Accordingly, it falls on contracting authorities to ensure compliance with the criteria they established, not only in the competitive phase of procurement but also in the performance phase.[87]

The failure of a contracting authority to initiate an award procedure where such an obligation exists under Directive 2014/24/EU is a decision amenable to review under Directive 89/665/EEC.[88] This is also the case for non-permissible modifications. For an interested party to bring an action against a contract modification, the said party is not required to have participated in the initial procedure; it is sufficient that the competitor is interested in obtaining the renewed contract.[89] Following the review procedure, the finding that a contract is illegally modified may lead to the contract being terminated under Article 73 Directive 2014/24/EU, or rendered

[82] Case C-327/00 *Santex SpA v Unità Socio Sanitaria Locale n. 42 di Pavia, and Sca Mölnlycke SpA, Artsana SpA and Fater SpA* ECLI:EU:C:2003:109, [2003] ECR I-01877 para 47.

[83] Art 1(3) Directive 89/665/EEC.

[84] ibid.

[85] See Case C-454/06 *pressetext Nachrichtenagentur GmbH v Republik Österreich (Bund), APA-OTS Originaltext-Service GmbH and APA Austria Presse Agentur registrierte Genossenschaft mit beschränkter Haftung* ECLI:EU:C:2008:351, [2008] ECR I-04401; Case C-549/14 *Finn Frogne A/S v Rigspolitiet ved Center for Beredskabskommunikation* ECLI:EU:C:2016:634, [2016].

[86] On contract modification see also more ch 2.

[87] Case C-496/99 P *Commission of the European Communities v CAS Succhi di Frutta SpA* ECLI:EU:C:2004:236, [2004] I-03801 para 115.

[88] Case C-26/03 *Stadt Halle and RPL Lochau* ECLI:EU:C:2005:5, [2005] paras 33–34.

[89] Joined Cases C-721/19 and C-722/1 *Sisal* ECLI:EU:C:2021:672, [2021] paras 64–65.

ineffective or shortened, as well as damages under Directive 89/665/EEC.[90] Next, it needs to be assessed to what extent the failure of a contracting authority to enforce contractual obligations gives grounds for interested third parties to initiate review procedures.

A recent decision of the CJEU following a preliminary reference from the Bulgarian Supreme Court clarified the relationship between failure to enforce contractual obligations and contract modifications.[91] Following the failure of the contractor to adhere to the maximum duration for performance, which was a criterion in the assessment of tenders, a financial correction was applied to the contracting authority by the Managing Authority for reasons of modification.[92] The authority challenged the decision on the basis that there was no contract modification as there was no written agreement. Due to conflicting national case law on the matter, the national court referred the case to the CJEU, inquiring whether the application of rules of contract modification was conditioned on the existence of an agreement in writing or, rather, a non-compliant performance can be considered a contract modification under Article 72 Directive 2014/24/EU.[93]

In its decision, the CJEU established that under Article 72 Directive 2014/24/EU, the existence of a substantial modification cannot be conditioned on the existence of a written agreement signed by the parties.[94] Nevertheless, building on the previous case law, the CJEU reiterated that contract modification *does* require the intention of parties to renegotiate the essential elements of the contract, that is, changes to be consensual.[95] It was established that the common intention of the parties to renegotiate can be deduced, in particular, from written communications between the parties.[96] Following the ruling, it has been argued that tacit modifications can also be covered by the ban on contract modifications.[97] However, there is no CJEU case law on purely tacit modifications.

[90] On termination, see MA Simovart, 'Enforcement of Ineffectiveness of Unlawfully Modified Public Contracts' (2016) 24 *Juridica International* 43; MA Simovart, 'The Power of Termination under Art.73(a) of Directive 2014/24/EU: The Challenges of Balancing Implementation' (2018) 6 *Public Procurement Law Review* 279; KM Halonen, 'Termination of a Public Contract – Lifting the Veil on Art. 73 of 2014/24 Directive' (2017) 5 *Public Procurement Law Review* 187; ch 7.

[91] Joined Cases C-441/22 and C-443/22 *Obshtina Razgrad* ECLI:EU:C:2023:970, [2023]. See more on this ch 8 and ch 6.

[92] ibid paras 14–22.

[93] ibid paras 23–26.

[94] ibid paras 59–61.

[95] ibid para 63, also Case C-23/20 *Simonsen & Weel* ECLI:EU:C:2021:490, [2021] para 70.

[96] Joined Cases C-441/22 and C-443/22 *Obshtina Razgrad* (n 91) paras 64–65.

[97] E Uysal, 'Contract Compliance in SPP: To Monitor or not to Monitor' SAPIENS Working Paper (March 2024) 13–16; M Várhomoki Molnár, 'A szerződésmódosítás közbeszerzési szabályainak értelmezése az Európai Unió Bíróságának a C-441/22 és C-443/22. Obshtina Razgrad és Obshtina Balchik egyesített ügyekben hozott ítéletében' (2024) 9 *Közbeszerzési Értesítő Plusz* 34, 38. See also ch 8 on the case law from member states concerning tacit modifications.

Concerning sustainability clauses, it could be argued that the failure of a contracting authority to enforce sustainability criteria, either through waiver or by way of acceptance of under-performance, may be considered a contract modification.[98] As a result, it is possible that competitors can urge the contracting authorities to maintain a state of alertness by policing the contractor's sustainability commitments. Unlike the lack of CJEU case law on the matter, there is limited national case law on purely tacit modifications concerning sustainability clauses.

One of the jurisdictions where the relationship between non-enforcement and contract modification has been made is Denmark.[99] In a case before the Danish Public Procurement Complaints Board concerning a framework agreement, the minimum requirements stipulated, amongst other accessibility requirements, that the vehicles concerning the subject matter of the contract should have space for at least two wheelchairs and at least five passenger seats.[100] The requirement had a severe impact on the competitive procedure. After the contract award, one of the tenderers informed the contracting authority that the vehicles being used by the successful tenderer were not compliant with the minimum criteria mentioned above. The authority replied that, as it was not possible to fit two large wheelchairs in the vehicles, they adjusted the vehicle capacity requirements, but still, the requirement in the contract was complied with. After a follow-up by the said tenderer requesting the authority to enforce the requirement as stipulated in the initial contract, the authority decided they waive the requirement, which led to the dispute being taken before the Danish Public Procurement Complaints Board.

The same competitor argued that its effort to meet the minimum requirement as initially set led to greater costs, hence higher prices in the tendering phase. As a result, the waiver of the minimum requirement led to the alteration of the economic balance of the contract to the advantage of the successful tenderer. The Danish Public Procurement Complaints Board has established that, through the waiver of the minimum requirement, which had an impact on the competitive procedure -had an impact on both the tender price and interest in tender submission- the contract was substantially modified. In a subsequent case on non-compliance concerning waste treatment, it was decided that the minimum requirements were not waived as the public buyer took measures to ensure compliance.[101]

Another jurisdiction where the link between non-enforcement and modification is made is Norway. Though not a Member State, pursuant to Annex

[98] Uysal (n 97).

[99] More about Danish public procurement law ch 6.

[100] Complaints Board for Public Procurement case of 19 May 2020 *Alsvognen I/S v FynBus, Sydtrafik og Midttrafik*.

[101] Complaints Board for Public Procurement case of 1 February 2023 *DKK Plastics ApS v Affald Plus I/S*.

XVI EEA Agreement, Norway is under the obligation to transpose EU public procurement law.[102] In Norwegian public procurement law, it is argued that, in principle, non-enforcement of the contract by the contracting authority and agreeing on contract changes are not dissimilar.[103] As elaborated with the Norwegian Public Procurement Complaints Board cases, this is not different in the case of non-enforcement of sustainability clauses by the contracting authorities, giving competitors the opportunity to take action.

In a dispute brought before the Norwegian Public Procurement Complaints Board, a waste collection and transport contract to be concluded with a municipality stipulated the use of vehicles meeting at least Euro 4 standards.[104] Additionally, the award criteria provided that tenders that incorporate the use of vehicles with higher standards will be given additional points. Euro standards in this case are standards concerning the vehicle's emissions for pollution; the higher the standard, the more expensive and newer the vehicles are. With all tenderers offering Euro 5 vehicles, the contract was awarded. A year later, one of the unsuccessful tenderers discovered that the winning tenderer had been using vehicles with Euro 3 standards and promptly informed the municipality.

The municipality explained that the use of Euro 3 standard vehicles was due to repairs and maintenance. The contractor, lacking substitute vehicles, pledged to acquire an additional compliant vehicle. Consequently, the municipality opted not to terminate the contract but sought an undertaking from the contractor to exclusively use Euro 5 standard vehicles and report any instances of non-compliance. Approximately two years later, the same competitor informed the municipality that Euro 3 standard vehicles were still in use by the contractor. Failing to receive a satisfactory explanation, said competitor brought the matter before the Norwegian Public Procurement Complaints Board, alleging a significant modification of the contract due to non-enforcement of the contract. It argued that the municipality could have discerned the use of non-compliant vehicles.

The Norwegian Public Procurement Complaints Board supported the complaint, asserting that the failure to enforce the contract was tantamount to agreeing to changes. By deviating from the agreed standard, the successful tenderer altered the economic balance in its favour. Despite being informed of performance deficiencies, the municipality did not impose contractual sanctions. Though the municipality claimed unawareness of the use of a non-compliant vehicle, the Norwegian Public Procurement Complaints Board concluded that the combined failure of the contractor to adhere to promised standards, along with the municipality's inadequate follow-up, constituted a substantial change.

[102] Agreement on the European Economic Area [1994] OJ L1/3. See also ch 2.

[103] M Goller, OH Ekre and B Gulbrandsen, 'Adgangen til å ivareta sideformål som arbeidsforhold og sosiale forhold etter anskaffelsesreglene' in M Langseth and JO Similä (eds), *Å kjøpe for Norge* (Oslo, Cappelen Damm Akademisk/NOASP, 2021).

[104] Complaints Board for Public Procurement case 2015/27 of 30 June 2015.

Another dispute presented to the Norwegian Public Procurement Complaints Board centred on the use of apprentices in the execution of a public work contract.[105] An economic operator that participated in the tender complained that, among other points, the authority's failure to diligently monitor the involvement of apprentices as required by the contract constituted a substantial change. Drawing from its previous decision, the Norwegian Public Procurement Complaints Board reiterated that deficient enforcement of a contract could be deemed a significant change. However, in contrast to the earlier decision, the authority in this case had actively monitored apprenticeship requirements through inspections and found the responses received to be satisfactory. Consequently, it was determined that the follow-up had not been deficient. A similar complaint was also made for a contract which incorporated a clause requiring lawful working conditions for a service contract awarded by the Municipality of Transport.[106] Despite the instance of non-compliance, the authority's follow-up was deemed adequate, and the working conditions were subsequently rectified. Accordingly, there was no contract modification. A similar view has been expressed by Czech practitioners, who consider the contracting authority's passivity in exercising rights under the contract as a modification of the obligation thereof, referring, among others, to the decision of the Regional Court in Brno that treated the lack of enforcement of contractual penalty as a substantial change of the public contract.[107]

From this perspective, peer review opens the way to third-party enforcement either through adjudication of contract modification or, more importantly, by acting as a deterrent due to the potential results of adjudication (ie administrative penalties and termination due to ineffectiveness of the contract). Nevertheless, in the enforcement of sustainability clauses through the enforcement of rules on the ban on contract changes, the main challenge is the lack of interest from the competitors' side in ensuring compliance for the sake of the underlying obligations. In bringing review procedures for a contracting authority's failure to detect non-compliance and hold a new procedure, the motivation of the competitors is often to prompt retendering and/or claim damages as a result of the contracting authority's illegal conduct.[108] As a result, in principle, it is of little significance to a competitor whether the changed conditions concern the date of delivery and remuneration of the contractor or the wheelchair capacity of a vehicle and compliance with lawful working conditions. Though their motivation is economic, by

[105] Complaints Board for Public Procurement case 2017/344 of 13 November 2018.

[106] Complaints Board for Public Procurement case 2020/327 of 10 November 2020.

[107] T Grulich, 'Nestandardní způsoby změny závazků ze smluv na veřejné zakázky' (2 December 2020) *Advokátní deník* <advokatnidenik.cz/2020/12/02/nestandardni-zpusoby-zmeny-zavazku-ze-smluv-na-verejne-zakazky/>; Regional Court in Brno, 62 Af 130/2016-553.

[108] For remedies against illegal contract modifications, see D Klingler and P Telles, 'Non-Compliance with Government Contract Terms: A Comparative View on Procurement Regulation and Contractual Remedies' in D Dragos et al (eds), *Contract Changes: The Dark Side of EU Procurement Law* (Cheltenham, Edward Elgar Publishing, 2023) 57.

putting pressure on the contracting authority to follow up on the commitments of their contractors, peer review can play a role in the enforcement of sustainability clauses.

C. Those Pursuing General Public Interest

The last type of third parties concerned with contract performance are those representing general public interests. While these can be various national bodies, this category also covers civil society, both of which will be addressed. As explained in the previous section, the public procurement enforcement system regulated under Directive 89/665/EEC is built on peer review.[109] However, Directive 89/665/EEC only provides that review procedures are to be made available 'at least' to the specified group of interested parties, that is, competitors; it does not fully harmonise the available review procedures nor fully harmonise to whom these procedures should be made available.[110]

The potential of other interested parties other than competitors in the enforcement of public procurement rules is recognised with Recital 122 Directive 2014/24/EU, which remarks that, as taxpayers 'citizens, concerned stakeholders, organised or not, and other persons or bodies' have a legitimate interest in 'sound procurement procedures'. Hence, they, without necessarily having legal standing before review bodies, should be able to point out potential breaches of public procurement rules before competent national authorities such as competition authorities, anti-corruption authorities, audit offices, or ombudsmen, depending on the national law.[111] Through such bodies, those with legitimate interests may prompt legal proceedings.[112] Depending on the national laws, said bodies may also initiate *ex officio* proceedings for the protection of distinct interests.[113] One of the jurisdictions demonstrating such a role for national authorities in upholding public interest is Hungary.

In line with the principle of responsible management of public finances under the Hungarian Public Procurement Act, contracting authorities are required to monitor and document the contractor's fulfilment of contractual obligations, ensure that performance complies with the terms of the contract, and pursue any claims arising from non-performance.[114] In this context, a contracting authority's failure

[109] Art 1(3) Directive 89/665/EEC. See s III above.
[110] Joined Cases C-496/18 and 497/18 *Hungeod and others* ECLI:EU:C:2020:240, [2020] paras 73–74.
[111] See GM Racca 'The Role of Third Parties in the Execution of Public Contracts' in L Folliot-Lalliot and S Torricelli (eds), *Contrôles et Contentieux des Contrats Publics – Oversight and Challenges of Public Contracts* (Bruxelles, Bruylant, 2018) 430–38.
[112] Simovart, 'Enforcement of Ineffectiveness of Unlawfully Modified Public Contracts' (n 90) 45.
[113] As confirmed by the CJEU, neither Directive 2014/24/EU nor Directive 89/665/EEC precludes member states from establishing national authorities that can initiate *ex officio* review procedures. Joined Cases C-496/18 and 497/18 *Hungeod* (n 110) 82–83.
[114] Art 142 *A közbeszerzésekről szóló 2015. évi CXLIII. törvény* (Hungarian Public Procurement Act).

to enforce a claim arising from a breach of contract may infringe fundamental principles, particularly where the breach concerns an obligation that was taken into account during the tender evaluation, or where the breach results in a performance that constitutes a substantial modification of the contract.[115] In such a case, the Hungarian Public Procurement Authority – with or without a public interest notification – can initiate proceedings against the breach of the responsible management of public funds to the extent that the contracting authority's failure to oversee performance prejudices the competitive procedure.[116] Non-compliance with sustainability criteria in contract performance may also incidentally fall under the radar.

Following a public interest notification, the President of the Hungarian Public Procurement Authority brought a dispute before the Hungarian Public Procurement Arbitration Board concerning a renovation works contract awarded by one of the districts of Budapest.[117] The award criteria included, among others, an assessment of tenders based on their commitment to environmental protection, with sub-criteria focusing on reduced noise pollution, the separation of hazardous waste, and selective waste collection. The successful tenderer received a positive evaluation on all environmental sub-criteria, compliance with which was confirmed by technical experts during contract execution. After the handover, the Hungarian Public Procurement Authority initiated a contract control procedure to inspect contract performance and modifications, and later brought an action alleging, amongst other things, that the contracting authority failed to assert claims for the delay and did not adequately check the compliance of the contractor with the environmental criteria. Although there was an expert report stating that performance was in line with environmental requirements, the fact that it was drafted after the work was completed raised doubts about its compliance with the obligations of the contracting authority to oversee performance. While the contracting authority claimed to have checked compliance throughout the performance, it was unable to provide documents attesting to the technical expert's checks on performance and compliance with environmental criteria.

The Hungarian Public Procurement Arbitration Board determined that the contracting authority breached the principle of responsible management of public finances by failing to adequately control and verify performance, including environmental criteria and imposed a fine. Unsurprisingly, the decision was appealed; however, the Hungarian court upheld the Hungarian Public Procurement Arbitration Board's decision establishing a breach of the principle of responsible management of public finances.[118] Non-compliance with the

[115] ibid.

[116] C Balázs Rigó, 'Developments in Public Procurement in Hungary – Opportunities and Challenges' (2016) 61(2) *Public Finance Quarterly* 137, 143.

[117] Közbeszerzési Döntőbizottság D.289/2023. On aspects of arbitration, please see more in ch 13 and ch 14.

[118] Fővárosi Törvényszék 103.K.703.620/2023/18.

environmental criteria was not the sole reason for establishing the breach, yet the failure of the contracting authority to duly inspect contract performance contributed to the establishment of the breach of the said principle. Although the basis for finding the breach was the lack of compliance with criteria that had an effect on the competitive procedure, rather than the underlying sustainability obligations, such a decision could put pressure on the contracting authorities not only to ensure compliance with the commercial aspects of the procurement but also to duly monitor and document the sustainability aspects of their contract.

In addition to national bodies representing public interest in the responsible management of funds, standing may be granted to other third parties in favour of public interest, namely, civil society. Though traditionally the role of civil society is to ensure efficient and effective use of resources as 'watchman of sound public spending',[119] the empowerment of civil society in litigation assists the uptake of sustainability in public procurement.[120] While such a standing is not currently granted under Directive 89/665/EEC,[121] this possibility is already present in some Member States, namely in France.

In France, third parties to a public contract, other than interested economic operators, have standing if they have 'a sufficient stake in the outcome of the case and that their claims are capable of judicial resolution'.[122] This right has been recognised in relation to environmental clauses in public contracts, where environmental non-governmental organisations (NGOs) have been granted standing, in contrast to individuals who were not considered to have a sufficient stake in the case to challenge the acts or omissions of public authorities.[123] A legal challenge may be possible where contractual clauses have not been respected; however, this possibility can be constrained by the courts' strict adherence to the principle of privity of contract.[124] Alternatively, an action can be taken alleging modification of a contract due to non-compliance, as investigated in the previous section, which is more likely to succeed when faced with the said principle.

[119] C Cravero, 'Rethinking the Role of Civil Society in Public Procurement' (2019) 1 *European Procurement & Public Private Partnership Law Review* 31–36, see also D Rathi, 'Do Civil Society Organizations Have a Role in Promoting Sustainable and Gender-Responsive Public Procurement?' (SAPIENS Working Paper, August 2024) 4.

[120] R Caranta, 'Opening the doors to civil society litigation in public contracts' <sapiensnetwork.eu/opening-doors-civil-society-litigation-public-contracts/>.

[121] For arguments in favour of amending Directive 89/665/EEC with such purpose, see M Andhov, R Caranta, WA Janssen, and O Martin-Ortega, 'Shaping Sustainable Public Procurement Laws in the European Union: An analysis of the legislative development from 'how to buy' to 'what to buy' in current and future EU legislative initiatives' (November 2022) <www.greens-efa.eu/files/assets/docs/shaping_sustainable_public_procurement_laws_in_the_european_union.pdf> 61.

[122] F Lichère and O Sulpice, 'Mandatory Requirements in Public Procurement Law: The Role of Remedies, Courts and Public Interest Litigation' in W Janssen and R Caranta (eds), *Mandatory Sustainability Requirements in EU Public Procurement Law* (Oxford, Bloomsbury Publishing, 2023) 247.

[123] ibid 248.

[124] ibid 252.

V. Conclusion

Privity of contract, or as known in civil law, the relative effect of contracts, is one of the pillars on which non-legislative codifications of European contract law are established. However, the privity of the contract is not absolute. European contract law regimes recognise instances of third parties enforcing a contract if it aims to benefit them. Subsequently, the use of the contract law construct of third-party beneficiary has been discussed in connection with sustainability clauses in private contract law literature. Similar to private contracts, the enforcement of sustainability clauses in public contracts by third parties is in tension with the principle of privity. Whether the advancement of sustainability clauses in European public contracts motivates piercing the doctrine of privity, considering the varying interests of extra-contractual parties in the contract performance, has, though, received little attention. The question of the extent to which third parties may pursue an action to enforce sustainability clauses in light of the principle of privity arises both from the perspective of standing and causes of action.

This chapter analysed different ways in which sustainability clauses in a public contract can be enforced by parties external to the contract, motivated by conflicting interests. Third parties may take initiative either to enforce their rights enshrined in a public contract (third-party beneficiaries), or ask for compensation or retendering (competitors), or to ensure compliance with public procurement rules, as well as adherence to the contract (those advocating for the public interest). The enforcement of sustainability clauses in public contracts by third-party beneficiaries is theoretically possible, yet limited, as in private contracts, due to the requirements arising from the applicable contract law. Economic operators who have an interest in the contract to be retendered or who wish to claim damages for breaches of EU public procurement law may provide the necessary incentive for contracting authorities to enforce sustainability clauses and, as a result, may indirectly enforce these clauses. Similarly, depending on the applicable national law, those representing public interest may function as guardians of contract performance and, as such, enforce sustainability clauses.

The authors conclude that subjects negatively and directly impacted by a breach of a sustainability clause in a public contract will be successful in enforcing it to the extent that the exception to the principle of privity is provided under the applicable contract law. Taking conditions that give rise to the existence of third-party beneficiary rights, courts might, nevertheless, be reluctant to pierce the foundational privity of contract, where benefiting a distant third party might lead to dissolving a public contract that aims to fulfil the needs of the general public. While in the enforcement of sustainability clauses by third-party beneficiaries, the doctrine of privity might be a barrier to those whose immediate benefits are at stake, it becomes – paradoxically – secondary in the protection of economic interests or general public interest. In these cases, the loosening of the strict reliance on the principle of privity is owed to the fact that the actions taken by these types of extra-contractual parties do not necessarily arise from the contractor's breach of a contractual obligation but rather from the contracting authority's breach of its statutory obligation to enforce the contract.

Nevertheless, in all three types of third parties interested in enforcing sustainability clauses, there is another impediment beyond the doctrine of privity. Regardless of the types of third parties, enforcement of sustainability clauses by extra-contractual parties is only possible if the said third parties have access to the terms of the contract. Accordingly, if third-party enforcement is the way forward in giving effect to sustainability clauses in a public contract, rules on access to concluded contracts should be revisited.

PART IV

Arbitration

13

Can the Effectiveness of European Public Procurement Law be Ensured if Disputes Related to the Performance of Public Contracts are Settled by Commercial Arbitration?

SYLVIE CÉCILE CAVALERI AND MACIEJ ZACHARIASIEWICZ

I. Introduction

The primary objective of EU public procurement law is to promote the free movement of goods, services, and establishment within the internal market by harmonising the rules governing the award of public contracts across Member States. To this end, it requires contracting authorities to observe fundamental principles – namely, equal treatment, non-discrimination, transparency, and proportionality – alongside the increasingly recognised principle of sustainability.[1] In parallel, national public procurement legislation serves to safeguard specific domestic public interests, such as ensuring the efficient allocation and use of public funds.[2]

The principles of EU public procurement law apply not only to the award of public contracts but also to their subsequent performance, including any modifications.[3] Accordingly, the resolution of disputes arising during the execution of such contracts may have a direct bearing on these principles. For instance, where the dispute concerns whether a contract modification complies with the conditions set out in Article 72 Directive 2014/24/EU, or whether

[1] Art 18 Directive 2014/24/EU.

[2] See for instance, S 1 *Udbudsloven* no 2015/1564 (Danish Public Procurement Act): 'The purpose of this Act shall be to establish the practices for public procurement and thus enable optimum use of public funds via effective competition.'

[3] See Case C-82/24 *Veolia Water Technologies and Others* ECLI:EU:C:2025:396, [2025] para 36. See Ch 2.

a new public procurement procedure should have been initiated, the matter may implicate broader public interests. In such cases, unsuccessful bidders and oversight bodies may have a legitimate interest in ensuring that the dispute is resolved in a transparent and public forum.

The resolution of such disputes before national courts or public administrative bodies within the Member States enables all interested parties to ensure that the matters are adjudicated in accordance with applicable law, including EU public procurement law.[4] Crucially, national courts also have the possibility to submit preliminary references to the Court of Justice of the European Union (CJEU), thereby seeking authoritative guidance on the interpretation of relevant provisions of EU law.

Disputes concerning irregularities in the public procurement procedure leading to the award of a public contract, as well as broader violations of EU public procurement law, are addressed by Directive 89/665/EEC and national legislation implementing it. By contrast, disputes arising after the award, particularly those concerning the contractual aspects of public contract performance, are not regulated at the EU level.[5] Approaches to such disputes vary across Member States, depending on the legal characterisation of public contracts within each jurisdiction.[6] Nevertheless, it is generally accepted that contracting authorities may submit disputes concerning the performance of awarded public contracts to arbitration.[7]

In Denmark, construction contracts, both public and private, entered into on the basis of national standard contracts typically contain an arbitration clause.[8] Consequently, a substantial number of disputes between contracting authorities and contractors in the construction sector are resolved through arbitration.[9] A further example is found in standard contracts regulating the procurement of IT systems by Danish state entities (Standards K01 to K04), all of which include multi-tiered dispute resolution clauses that ultimately provide for arbitration.[10] None to date has questioned the arbitrability of disputes involving public contracts, suggesting this is largely accepted.

In Poland, by contrast, contracts concluded by contracting authorities following a public procurement procedure typically contain prorogation clauses submitting

[4] See on court jurisdiction in different models ch 2.

[5] See ch 3.

[6] See ch 3.

[7] See ch 14.

[8] See for instance Sub-Clause 69.1 General Conditions for Building and Construction Works and Supplies (AB 18) <bygherreforeningen.dk/ab18/>. 'Disputes between the parties are finally resolved by arbitration by the Danish Building and Construction Arbitration Board.' Some other clauses of the standard contract show that this contract is also meant to be used by public authorities as employers, such as for instance Sub-Clause 11.2 on insurance, stating that a public sector client may demand to provide self-insurance.

[9] For instance, a brief review of recent construction case law shows that the following arbitral awards were rendered in disputes involving contracting authorities as employers: *Kendelser om Fast Ejendom* (KfE) 2020.209; KfE 2024.5; KfE 2024.69; KfE 2024.126.

[10] See for instance Art 28, s 3ss standard contract K01 – Standard contract for short-term IT project <https://digst.dk/media/ki5lxsne/k01-kontrakt-engelsk-version-april-2004-word-w.docx> ultimately providing for arbitration if the mandatory pre-arbitral mediation fails.

disputes to resolution by state courts, most often at the seat of the contracting authority. Nevertheless, it is widely accepted that disputes arising from public contracts may also be settled by arbitration,[11] in the same way as other commercial disputes. Consequently, the parties sometimes decide to provide for arbitration – especially where a contractor possesses sufficient bargaining power to negotiate such a choice and often where the contract is based on one of the International Federation of Consulting Engineers (FIDIC) standard forms of contract.[12] Some of the more commonly chosen institutional arbitration courts include the Court of Arbitration at the Polish Chamber of Commerce (SAKIG), the Court of Arbitration of the Association of Engineers Consultants and Experts (SIDiR),[13] the Lewiatan Court of Arbitration (Lewiatan), or – for international disputes – the Court of International Arbitration at the International Chamber of Commerce (ICC). Ad hoc arbitration is also sometimes provided for.

Unlike proceedings before national courts, arbitration constitutes a private dispute resolution mechanism based on wide-reaching party autonomy. Both the proceedings and the arbitral award are, at least as a starting point, not publicly available and, in principle, also confidential. Arbitral awards are binding and enforceable under the New York Convention on the Recognition and Enforcement of Foreign Arbitral Awards (New York Convention),[14] as well as national arbitration laws often based on the UNCITRAL Model Law on International Commercial Arbitration (UNCITRAL Model Law)[15] with limited scope for substantive judicial review by national courts.

This chapter examines the use of arbitration in disputes arising from public contracts in Denmark and Poland, as illustrative examples of jurisdictions that follow the 'private-oriented hybrid model'.[16] It addresses the overarching question of whether the effectiveness of EU public procurement law can be ensured when disputes related to the performance of public contracts are resolved through commercial arbitration.[17] The analysis is structured around the following three sub-questions:

1. Are there procedural features of commercial arbitration that are incompatible with EU public procurement law?

[11] For a sceptical assessment of this welcoming approach see, however: R Szostak, 'Zagadnienia ogólne' in M Moras, B Nuzzo, and R Szostak (eds), *Pozasądowe rozwiązywanie sporów w zamówieniach publicznych* (Warszawa, CH Beck, 2023), ch I, s 5.

[12] See E Figura-Góralczyk, 'Umowa w sprawie zamówienia publicznego – wybrane zagadnienia kolizyjnoprawne i arbitrażowe' (2012) 4 *Prawo Zamówień Publicznych* 41, 55.

[13] The institution is specifically dedicated to resolving construction disputes.

[14] Convention on the Recognition and Enforcement of Foreign Arbitral Awards (adopted 10 June 1958, entered into force 7 June 1959) 330 UNTS 3 (New York Convention).

[15] UNCITRAL Model Law on International Commercial Arbitration (adopted 21 June 1985, UN Doc A/40/17, annex I, as amended 2006, UN Doc A/61/17, annex I) (UNCITRAL Model Law).

[16] For more about the 'private-oriented hybrid model' see ch 3.

[17] In this chapter, our understanding of the principle of effectiveness of EU law is in line with the definition proposed by Risvig Hamer, who states that this principle demands that the rules of the Member States must not be designed in a way that makes it impossible or unreasonably difficult in practice to exercise the rights granted by EU law, and that the enforcement of the EU rules in this manner ensure an effective protection of the rights deriving from EU law (author's translation). See: C Risvig Hamer, *Grundlæggende udbudsret* (Copenhagen, Jurist- og Økonomforbundets Forlag, 2016) 63.

2. Does an arbitral tribunal seized with a dispute concerning the performance phase of a public contract have an obligation to apply, *ex officio*, the mandatory provisions of EU public procurement law?
3. To what extent can or must state courts set aside or refuse recognition and enforcement of an arbitral award if they find it to be in conflict with EU public procurement law?

In addressing sub-question 3, particular attention is paid to the fact that arbitral awards may only be set aside on limited grounds. Accordingly, the discussion will consider whether EU public procurement law should be regarded as forming part of the public policy of the forum for the purposes of judicial review and enforcement. To the best of the authors' knowledge, there is no case law directly addressing this issue; therefore, the analysis draws a parallel with another area where public interest considerations are preponderant, namely, EU competition law.

II. Are Some Procedural Features of Commercial Arbitration at Odds with EU Public Procurement Law?

Two potentially problematic features will be examined under the present research question: first, the confidentiality inherent to arbitration; and second, the absence of the possibility for an arbitral tribunal to make preliminary references to the CJEU in cases involving uncertainty regarding the interpretation or application of EU law.

A. Confidentiality of Arbitration

In a dispute concerning the performance of a public contract, an issue may arise as to whether a public contract has been modified (or might be modified as a result of arbitration proceedings) within the limits permitted by EU public procurement law or whether a new procurement procedure should have been initiated. Unsuccessful bidders and oversight bodies may then have a legitimate interest in that dispute being settled publicly. Since the transparency of proceedings and resulting decisions is a precondition for interested third parties to effectively exercise their rights, EU public procurement law requires, under the principle of transparency set out in Article 18(1) Directive 2014/24/EU, the publication of key information relating to public procurement procedures.[18] Although the publication requirements for modifications made to public contracts are more limited, as

[18] The rules on publication are set out in Arts 48-52 Directive 2014/24/EU and concern publication of a prior information notice, of a contract notice, and of a contract award. On the interest of third parties in public contracts see ch 12.

disclosure is only mandated in specific cases, such an obligation may arise under Article 72 Directive 2014/24/EU.[19] It may then prove important for unsuccessful bidders or oversight bodies to have access to information on how the modification of the public contract is handled by the state court or arbitral tribunal seized with a dispute between the contracting authority and the successful contractor.

Access to information regarding the performance of a public contract is shaped by both the legal source of the transparency obligation and the institutional scope of entities subject to it. The law in that area focuses on the obligation of the contracting authority to make the public procurement procedures transparent, including at the stage of the contract's performance. While Denmark and Poland both provide for such access, their frameworks diverge in how the right is constructed and operationalised.

The relevant legal framework focuses on the obligations of the public authority to disclose information regarding a public procurement contract. The fact that the public contract's modification is handled in a court or arbitral tribunal, in a dispute between a contractor and a contracting authority, cannot have a bearing on that authority's obligation to make certain information regarding the modification public, if required by Article 72 Directive 2014/24/EU. Interested third parties may compel the contracting authority to execute that obligation under the relevant national law procedures. However, how the transparency requirements transfer to third parties' right of access to information regarding a dispute between the contractor and the contracting authority is another matter. The pertinent question here is whether, and to what extent, interested third parties can obtain access to such information whenever the issue of public contract modification is settled through court litigation or arbitration. Proceedings before state courts are generally characterised by a large degree of transparency, although details vary importantly between Member States. For example, in Poland, although court hearings are generally public, the access of third parties to the file of the case is restricted. An interested third party must, in each case, justify access with its individual legal interest. Secondly, while judgments of the courts are rendered public, they are anonymised, which can impede third parties' ability to track the relevant decisions. The same principles apply in Denmark, although courts publish judgments without anonymising them.

The transparency requirement applying in public procurement and in public contracts appears to stand in tension with one of the commonly cited advantages of international commercial arbitration, namely, the confidentiality typically afforded by such proceedings, which, among other benefits, protects the disclosure

[19] Art 72(1) Directive 2014/24/EU mandates disclosure only in specific cases – namely, modifications involving additional works, services or supplies, and those arising from unforeseen circumstances. In such cases, as specified under points (b) and (c) of Art 72(1), the contracting authority must publish a modification notice in the Official Journal of the European Union. This notice must include the information listed in Annex V, Part G, and must be published in accordance with the procedural rules laid down in Art 5 Directive 2014/24/EU.

of commercially sensitive information. This raises the question of whether confidentiality in dispute resolution is compatible with the general principle of transparency applying within public procurement, especially during the contract award phase. Some authors suggest, however, that certain fundamental principles of EU public procurement law may not necessarily extend to the enforcement phase of public contracts.[20]

Although confidentiality is frequently understood as a key feature of commercial arbitration, it is interesting that neither the UNCITRAL Model Law, nor the Danish Arbitration Act,[21] nor the Polish Code of Civil Procedure[22] explicitly provide for it. Instead, confidentiality is typically introduced through the procedural rules of arbitration institutions. For instance, the currently applicable Rules of Arbitration of the Danish Institute of Arbitration (DIA),[23] the 2025 Rules of the Lewiatan Court of Arbitration,[24] the SIDiR Arbitration Rules,[25] or the 2025 Arbitration Rules of the Court of Arbitration at the Polish Chamber of Commerce (SAKIG)[26] impose a confidentiality obligation on members of the arbitral tribunal, tribunal secretaries, and employees or representatives of the arbitration institution.[27] For example, the relevant part of Article 50 DIA reads as follows:

> The Members of the Arbitral Tribunal, the secretary of the Arbitral Tribunal, (…), the members of the Council of Representatives or the Board, the Chair's Committee, the Secretariat and the Secretary General, shall treat all matters relating to the arbitration as confidential.

Similarly, Section 7 SAKIG Rules provides:

> Unless the parties agree otherwise, the arbitrators, the members of bodies and individuals acting on behalf of the Court of Arbitration shall be required to keep confidential all information concerning the proceedings.

[20] In the introduction to their paper concerning non-compliance with contract terms in public contracts, Klingler and Telles state that post-award transparency is an area that has flown under the radar for many years and that regulatory and political efforts have focused on the pre-award stage while for the most part ignoring what happens after a contract is awarded: D Klingler and P Telles, 'Non-compliance with government contract terms: a comparative view on procurement regulation and contractual remedies' in D Dragos et al (eds), *Contract Changes: The Dark Side of EU Procurement Law* (Cheltenham, Edward Elgar Publishing, 2023) 48.

[21] *Voldgiftsloven* no 553/2005 (Danish Arbitration Act).

[22] See Part V (Arts 1154–1217) *Ustawa z dnia 17 listopada 1964 r. – Kodeks postępowania cywilnego* (Polish Code of Civil Procedure). Part V constitutes the implementation of the UNCITRAL Model Law in its 1985 version. Part V was introduced in 2005 and has been amended several times since then.

[23] Rules of Arbitration of the Danish Institute of Arbitration (DIA) <voldgiftsinstituttet.dk/wp-content/uploads/2021/06/4304611-regler-for-voldgift_04-2021_uk_web.pdf>.

[24] Rules of the Lewiatan Court of Arbitration <sadarbitrazowy.org.pl/en/arbitration/rules-of-the-court-of-arbitration/.

[25] SIDiR Arbitration Rules <arbitraz-sidir.pl/sad/regulamin/>.

[26] 2025 Arbitration Rules of the Court of Arbitration at the Polish Chamber of Commerce (SAKIG) <sakig.pl/en/regulations-and-costs/rules>.

[27] Art 50 Rules of DAI; S 4 Lewiatan Arbitration Rules; S 7 SAKIG Arbitration Rules.

When considering these provisions, which reflect a typical formulation of confidentiality in arbitral institutional rules, it is notable that the obligation expressly binds the arbitrators and the staff of the institution, but not, at least in its wording, the parties to the dispute. The new 2025 Lewiatan Arbitration Rules (Section 4), as well as the SIDiR Arbitration Rules (Section 7), are different in that regard, since they explicitly mention the parties as bound by confidentiality of the proceedings.

Scholarly literature observes that it is not uncommon in Danish arbitration practice to assume that the arbitration agreement itself entails an implicit duty of confidentiality for the parties.[28] This assumed obligation would encompass the proceedings before the arbitral tribunal, the written submissions exchanged between the parties, the evidence presented, and potentially even the arbitral award or any settlement reached during the proceedings.[29] Such an understanding suggests that the parties are, in principle, bound by a duty of confidentiality. However, as noted by Danish commentators, there is no explicit legal basis for this position under current Danish law.[30] Those who support the view that an obligation of confidentiality binds the parties argue that it forms part of the *naturalia negotii* of the arbitration agreement and reflects the general duty of loyalty that governs contractual relationships.[31] According to them, the unauthorised disclosure of information relating to the arbitration case can justify termination of the arbitration agreement and potentially give rise to contractual liability. By contrast, others contend that such a far-reaching obligation requires a clear basis in the law or the arbitration agreement.[32]

Attempts to introduce a non-mandatory rule imposing confidentiality obligations on the parties in the Danish Arbitration Act met resistance from the Legal Commission of the Attorneys' Council. The Commission maintained that such a rule was unnecessary, was not included in the UNCITRAL Model Law, and could potentially conflict with established Danish arbitration tradition. The Ministry of Justice also declined to support the proposal, arguing that appropriate regulation of confidentiality would require thorough and comprehensive considerations. It further emphasised that parties to an arbitration always retain the ability to agree, on a case-by-case basis, whether and to what extent confidentiality should apply.[33] On these grounds, the Judicial Council's suggestion to codify confidentiality in the Danish Arbitration Act was ultimately rejected.[34]

In Poland – given no normative basis in legislation – there is an ongoing scholarly discussion as to the legal basis of the confidentiality of arbitration

[28] J Juul and P Fauerholdt Thommesen, *Voldgiftsret*, 3rd edn (Copenhagen, Karnov Group, 2017) 255.
[29] ibid.
[30] N Schiersing, *Voldgiftsloven* (Copenhagen, DJØF Forlag, 2016) 304; Juul and Fauerholdt Thommesen (n 28).
[31] On duty of loyalty see ch 7.
[32] Juul and Fauerholdt Thommesen (n 28).
[33] ibid.
[34] ibid.

proceedings.[35] Some authors maintain that arbitration proceedings are private 'by their nature' and that confidentiality constitutes a basic characteristic of arbitration, which is decisive for its attractiveness.[36] Others, however, underline that confidentiality as a principle – although customary in commercial arbitration – has no statutory basis, and so it is mainly up to the parties to regulate the matter.[37] This can certainly be done through the use of arbitration rules that warrant the privacy of the proceedings. A debated question is whether a standard arbitration agreement may be said to implicitly entail the duty of confidentiality. The answer is generally negative.[38] Some authors, however, contend that confidentiality, at least with respect to some aspects of the proceedings, may be incorporated into the agreement via a trade custom, which requires arbitration to be private, or by interpreting the arbitration agreement in line with trade customs.[39] Some impose the obligation not to disclose information about the proceedings through a trade custom only on the arbitrators.[40] In any event, the interpretation of the parties' individual intentions prevails.

In Poland, whenever arbitration pertains to a public contract, the resulting arbitral award may have to be made public under the Polish Public Information Act.[41] Both the case law of administrative courts (although rendered with respect to international investment arbitration awards)[42] and the doctrine[43] confirm that if the arbitral award directly concerns the exercise of public duties or the administration of public property, it constitutes public information and should be disclosed at the request of any interested party. This also seems to cover awards rendered in public procurement cases. Any privacy of arbitration,

[35] T Ereciński T and K Weitz, *Sąd Arbitrażowy* (Warszawa, Wydawnictwo Prawnicze LexisNexis 2008) 49; K Szczepanowska-Kozłowska, 'Obowiązek zachowania poufności w międzynarodowym arbitrażu handlowym' in J Okolski (ed), *Księga pamiątkowa 60-lecia Sądu Arbitrażowego przy Krajowej Izbie Gospodarczej w Warszawie* (Warszawa, Sąd Arbitrażowy przy Krajowej Izbie Gospodarczej, 2010) 304 et seq; B Gessel-Kalinowska vel Kalisz, 'Podstawa normatywna zasady poufności w polskim arbitrażu handlowym' (2013) 1 *Przegląd Prawa Handlowego* 14 et seq; A Szumański (ed), *System prawa handlowego: Arbitraż handlowy*, 2nd edn (Warszawa, Wydawnictwo CH Beck, 2015) 29; A Orzeł-Jakubowska, *Sądownictwo polubowne w świetle standardów konstytucyjnych* (Warszawa, Wolters Kluwer, 2021) 60 et seq.

[36] Szumański (n 35); J Rajski, 'Zagadnienia poufności w arbitrażu handlowym' (2001) 6 *Przegląd Prawa Handlowego* 1 et seq; Szczepanowska-Kozłowska (n 35); M Gutowska, 'Skutki zapisu na sąd polubowny a swoboda umów' (PhD thesis, Uniwersytet im. Adama Mickiewicza w Poznaniu, 2023) 218.

[37] Ereciński and Weitz (n 35) 50; Orzeł-Jakubowska (n 35) 62.

[38] Orzeł-Jakubowska (n 35) 61.

[39] Gessel-Kalinowska vel Kalisz (n 35) 18–19.

[40] T Ereciński, 'Poufność w arbitrażu' in A Janik (ed), *Studia i rozprawy. Księga jubileuszowa dedykowana profesorowi Andrzejowi Całusowi* (Warszawa, Szkoła Główna Handlowa w Warszawie, 2009) 662 (with respect to obligation of the arbitrators).

[41] *Ustawa z dnia 6 września 2001 r. o dostępie do informacji publicznej* (Polish Public Information Act).

[42] Judgments of the Polish Supreme Administrative Court (NSA) of 12.04.2017 in cases: I OSK 1164/15, I OSK 1437/15, and I OSK 1522/15.

[43] A. Orzeł-Jakubowska, 'Dostęp do informacji publicznej zawartej w wyrokach arbitrażowych' (2018) 2 *Państwo i Prawo* 3, 26.

whether customary or agreed upon by the parties, cannot derogate from obligations of the public authority under the Polish Public Information Act.[44] One notable exception to this principle applies when the dispute involves trade secrets, since Article 11 Polish Unfair Competition Act[45] forbids the disclosure of a competitor's trade secrets.[46]

These frameworks reflect a broader Nordic plus Poland consensus: absent agreement, the parties are not bound by a confidentiality obligation in relation to the existence of the arbitral case, its progress, and its result.[47] Furthermore, whenever public procurement law *does* require the contracting authority to publish certain information (eg regarding modification of the contract under Article 72 Directive 2014/24/EU), such an obligation – as stemming from mandatory rules – cannot be derogated by the parties' agreement regarding confidentiality. With respect to the information about the arbitration dispute itself, on the other hand, and to the extent not contradicting provisions of the public procurement law, parties may agree that any information about arbitration proceedings should be kept confidential. However, as mentioned, in Poland, any arbitral award that touches upon the use of public funds must be disclosed to third parties under the Polish Public Information Act. The confidentiality of arbitration proceedings, even if mandated by parties' agreement, cannot release or dispense with this obligation. The exception concerns trade secrets, which are protected as confidential, but this should not justify non-disclosure of the whole award, but rather only covering up certain sensitive information.

In conclusion, referring disputes concerning public contracts to arbitration does not, in itself, compromise the effectiveness of EU public procurement law as far as the principle of transparency is concerned.

B. Inability to Refer EU Law Questions to the CJEU for a Preliminary Ruling

As a starting point, an arbitral tribunal cannot request a preliminary ruling from the CJEU, as it does not qualify as 'a court or tribunal of a Member State' within the meaning of Article 267 TFEU.[48] This was established by the CJEU in *Nordsee*, where the Court held that it lacked jurisdiction to rule on a preliminary question

[44] ibid 27–28 cf the Supreme Court of Australia in *Esso Australia Resources Ltd v The Honourable Sidney James Plowman and Ors*, 128. ALR 391 (1995), which found that the privacy of arbitration cannot constitute an obstacle against access to information on the public authority's activities.

[45] *Ustawa z dnia 16 kwietnia 1993 r. o zwalczaniu nieuczciwej konkurencji* (Polish Unfair Competition Act).

[46] According to Art 11(1) Polish Unfair Competition Act: 'It is an act of unfair competition to disclose, use or obtain another party's information constituting trade secret'. Gessel-Kalinowska vel Kalisz (n 35) 19.

[47] On Danish and Nordic law: Juul and Fauerholdt Thommesen (n 28) 256–57.

[48] Consolidated Version of the Treaty on the Functioning of the European Union [2012] OJ C 326/47.

referred by a private arbitral tribunal.[49] The judgment emphasised that the authorities in the Member State in question had neither been involved in selecting the arbitration nor were they under any *ex officio* duty to participate in the arbitral proceedings. Moreover, the Court found that the link between the arbitral tribunal and the national judicial system was insufficiently close for the tribunal to be considered a 'court or tribunal of a Member State'.[50]

Denmark addressed this issue in a particular and unique manner. Article 27(2) Danish Arbitration Act provides:

> If the arbitral tribunal considers that a decision on a question of European Union law is necessary to enable it to make an award, the arbitral tribunal may request the courts to request the Court of Justice of the European Communities to give a ruling thereon.

At first glance, this provision appears to offer a solution to the problem posed by an arbitral tribunal's lack of standing to refer questions to the CJEU. However, literature identifies several concerns with the mechanism established under Article 27(2) Danish Arbitration Act.

First, legal literature widely acknowledges that it is ultimately for the court, requested by the arbitral tribunal to submit the preliminary question, to decide whether such a request should be granted. According to the *travaux préparatoires* of the Danish provision, this determination hinges on whether the court itself would have found sufficient grounds to refer the matter to the CJEU had it been directly seized with the dispute.[51]

Second, there are divergent views regarding the role of the parties in relation to a possible request. Based on the wording of the provision, the arbitral tribunal may submit the request on its own initiative, without needing a corresponding request or approval from the parties. Schiersing argues that, although the tribunal should always consult the parties in such situations, it is not bound by their views – even where the parties unanimously oppose the request.[52] On the contrary, Werlauff argues that if both parties agree that the request should not be made, the arbitral tribunal must respect that decision because the tribunal cannot unilaterally impose a request that may prolong the proceedings and increase their cost, contrary to the expressed will of the parties.[53] This interpretive uncertainty carries potential practical consequences, particularly in cases where parties have opted for

[49] Case C-102/81 *Nordsee Deutsche Hochseefischerei GmbH v Reederei Mond Hochseefischerei Nordstern AG & Co. KG and Reederei Friedrich Busse Hochseefischerei Nordstern AG & Co. KG* ECLI:EU:C: 1982:107, [1982].

[50] Schiersing (n 30) 362.

[51] ibid 362–63; N Fenger and M Broberg, 'Voldgift og EU-ret' in H Udsen, J Schans Christensen, J Lau Hansen, T Iversen, and L Nielsen (eds), *Festskrift til Mads Bryde Andersen* (Copenhagen, Jurist- og Økonomforbundets Forlag, 2018) 191.

[52] Schiersing (n 30) 363.

[53] E Werlauff, 'Privat voldgift med offentligretlige delspørgsmål' (2008) 142(19) *Ugeskrift for Retsvæsen* 152.

arbitration precisely due to its speed and efficiency and may therefore be reluctant to support a referral to the CJEU.

Third, and more critically for the applicability of the Danish provision, scholarly opinion holds that it remains uncertain whether, and to what extent, the CJEU would have jurisdiction under EU law to address a request for a preliminary ruling submitted by a Danish court not itself seized with the dispute in question.[54] The CJEU has consistently maintained in its case law that preliminary ruling proceedings presuppose that a case is actually pending before the referring court, and that the referring court must be required to render a decision the outcome of which depends on the interpretation sought.[55]

When a Danish court requests a preliminary ruling on behalf of and for the benefit of an arbitral tribunal, as permitted under Article 27(2) Danish Arbitration Act, it is never itself seized with the underlying dispute and does not apply the ruling directly. Based on the CJEU case law and the limited literature on the subject, there are therefore serious doubts as to whether the Danish provision is actually effective in practice. Assessing the applicability of Article 27(2) Danish Arbitration Act is further complicated by the fact that the procedure it outlines has, to date, never been used in practice.[56]

Similarly in Poland, it is clear that an arbitral tribunal – at least a classic arbitral tribunal deriving its competence from the agreement of the parties – does not have competence to request a preliminary ruling from the CJEU. The Court's decision in *Nordsee* was, however, met with much criticism in the doctrine. It was argued that the lack of arbitrators' power to submit a preliminary question, on the one hand, undermines the uniform interpretation of EU law (given that arbitral tribunals are often also called upon to apply it, and the limited extent to which state courts can review arbitral awards),[57] and on the other hand, it impedes the effectiveness of arbitration as a dispute settlement method.[58] Nevertheless, it is acknowledged that it might be difficult to interpret Article 267 TFEU in a manner which includes arbitration tribunals among courts that can initiate the preliminary procedure.[59]

Unlike Article 27(2) Danish Arbitration Act, Polish law does not contain a specific provision that would allow the arbitral tribunals to request state courts to formulate a preliminary question to the CJEU. The Polish arbitration law does contain, however, a general provision on the assistance which state courts provide to arbitral tribunals. According to Article 1192(1) Polish Code of Civil Procedure,

[54] Fenger and Broberg (n 51) 192.

[55] Case C-350/13 *Antonio Gramsci Shipping Corp. and Others v Aivars Lembergs* ECLI:EU:C:2014:1516, [2014] para 10. See also Case C-344/09 *Bengtsson* ECLI:EU:C:2011:174, [2011] para 18, quoting additional cases and stating this case law as 'settled'.

[56] At the time of writing this chapter (August 2025).

[57] M Szpunar, 'Sądownictwo polubowne wobec prawa konkurencji Wspólnoty Europejskiej' in W Popiołek, M Szpunar, and L Ogiegło (eds), *Rozprawy prawnicze. Księga pamiątkowa Profesora Maksymiliana Pazdana* (Kraków, Zakamycze, 2005) 506; I Szmit, 'Procedura prejudycjalna a sądownictwo arbitrażowe' (2014) 1 *ADR. Arbitraż i Mediacja* 45.

[58] Szpunar (n 57) 507.

[59] ibid 506.

an arbitration court may request a district court to take evidence or perform another action, which the arbitration court cannot perform itself. Article 1192(1) Polish Code of Civil Procedure is said to contain a power for arbitrators (and not a duty), but an obligation for the state court faced with a request.[60] Differently from Article 27 UNCITRAL Model Law, the Polish measure does not permit parties to petition a state court for assistance.[61] Thus, it is always up to the arbitral tribunal to decide whether it needs said assistance. The provision is seldom used in arbitral practice,[62] most likely because of the assumption that the procedure would impede swift and effective settlement of disputes in arbitration.

Although the question was scarcely discussed in the literature and has not been tested in case law, it is assumed that Article 1192 Polish Code of Civil Procedure *does* constitute a potential legal basis for the arbitral tribunal to request a state court to formulate a preliminary question to the CJEU. While the main focus of Article 1192(1) Polish Code of Civil Procedure is taking evidence in situations where arbitrators lack sufficient coercive measures, the wording of Article 1192(1) supports its broad understanding, since it speaks also of 'another action, that the arbitration court cannot perform'.[63] That lack of legal possibility to perform an action constitutes a necessary[64] but also sufficient[65] precondition for triggering Article 1192(1) Polish Code of Civil Procedure. Arguably, this includes preliminary questions to the CJEU, given that the arbitral tribunal cannot perform such an action itself. Moreover, the Court, in *Nordsee*, has itself noted that if questions of Community law are raised in arbitration, the ordinary courts may be called upon to examine them also when assisting the arbitral tribunals 'in certain procedural matters or to interpret the law applicable'.[66] It would thus seem only fair to interpret Article 1192(1) Polish Code of Civil Procedure as permitting to benefit from the CJEU's interpretation of the EU law, similarly as in a regular case decided by state courts. Nevertheless, the doctrine remains sceptical whether a state court assisting an arbitral tribunal may succeed in satisfying the prerequisites of Article 267 TFEU as developed by the CJEU. This is because a preliminary ruling from the CJEU must be necessary to decide the case pending before the referring court. Here, however, it is the arbitral tribunal and not the referring court that decides the case. Moreover, it remains uncertain to what extent the decision of

[60] W Sadowski, 'Article 1192' in P Rylski and A Olaś (eds), *Kodeks postępowania cywilnego. Komentarz, part III*, edn 3 (Warszawa, CH Beck, 2024) para 1; M Łaszczuk and J Szpara, 'Uwagi o zakresie pomocy udzielanej sądowi polubownemu przez sąd państwowy na podstawie art. 1192 k.p.c.' (2008) 9–10 *Palestra* 27.

[61] Sadowski, 'Article 1192' (n 60) para 4.

[62] ibid para 3.

[63] Art 1192(1) Polish Code of Civil Procedure is visibly broader than its equivalent in Art 27 UNCITRAL Model Law which speaks only about 'assistance in taking evidence'. See K Weitz, 'Przesłanki i zakres pomocy sądu państwowego dla sądu polubownego w postępowaniu dowodowym (art. 1192 KPC)' (2009) 2 *ADR. Arbitraż i Mediacja* 107 et seq.

[64] Weitz (n 63) 111.

[65] Łaszczuk and Szpara (n 60) 35.

[66] Case C-102/81 *Nordsee* (n 49) para 14.

the CJEU would bind the arbitral tribunal that initiated the procedure in the first place.[67] Certainly, it would be interesting to see a case before the CJEU which tests those limitations.

Since the procedure provided in Article 27(2) Danish Arbitration Act appears to lack practical effectiveness, it does not offer a viable solution to the limitation preventing arbitral tribunals in Denmark from referring preliminary questions to the CJEU in cases involving uncertainty over the interpretation or application of EU public procurement law. The same seems to be true for Poland under Article 1192 Polish Code of Civil Procedure.

Given that it is generally accepted that disputes concerning the performance of public contracts are arbitrable in jurisdictions operating under a 'private-oriented hybrid model', and that compliance with EU public procurement law can hardly be supported through CJEU preliminary rulings in such proceedings, alternative mechanisms to ensure proper application of EU law must be considered.[68]

The following sections will therefore explore the extent to which arbitral tribunals are required to raise issues of EU public procurement law on their own initiative, particularly where the parties have not done so. Subsequently, the same question will be examined in relation to national courts when dealing with requests to set aside international arbitral awards or to refuse their recognition and/or enforcement.

III. Is an Arbitral Tribunal Obliged to Apply Mandatory Provisions of EU Public Procurement Law *Ex Officio* in Public Contract Disputes?

EU law in general, and EU public procurement law in particular, has a broad scope and forms an integral part of the Member States' legal orders. It is therefore inevitable that arbitral tribunals are at times required to apply EU law in their decisions. This application may be either direct (when directly applicable rules and principles of the EU law are invoked), or indirect (when a court in the EU must comply with the EU principle of conforming interpretation when interpreting national law or the parties' agreement).[69]

While an arbitral tribunal must apply the provisions of the EU law invoked by the parties, whether it must apply mandatory rules of EU law *ex officio* is less clear. In the context of public contracts, this concerns mandatory provisions in

[67] Szpunar (n 57); Szmit, Procedura (n 57); J Broniszewska, 'Kompetencja sądu arbitrażowego do zadania pytania prejudycjalnego' (2016) 3 *ADR. Arbitraż i Mediacja* 5, 15–16.

[68] See ch 2.

[69] Fenger and Broberg (n 51) 182–183.

Directive 2014/24/EU on contract modification (Article 72) and termination (Article 73).[70]

As Fenger and Broberg note, the question is significant, as there may be situations where the parties share an interest in resolving their dispute without involving EU law[71] for example, where they have agreed to modify a public contract beyond the limits permitted by Article 72.

The question of whether mandatory provisions of EU law must be applied *ex officio* has been referred to by several authors as 'the arbitrator's dilemma'.[72] On the one hand, if an arbitrator refrains from doing so and the award breaches mandatory provisions of EU law, it may be set aside by a state court as contrary to public policy, as discussed below in section IV. Such restraint would conflict with the arbitrator's general duty to render an enforceable award.[73] On the other hand, an arbitrator's jurisdiction is strictly defined by the parties' agreement, and exceeding arbitrators' authority may also lead to annulment of the award.[74]

Those who argue that arbitrators are not obliged to raise issues of mandatory provisions of EU law on their own initiative rely on several points. First, Advocate General (AG) Saggio addressed this question in his opinion in *Eco Swiss*, discussed in more detail below in section four.[75] In that case, the referring court asked the CJEU whether the principle established in the earlier rendered *Van Schijndel*,[76] namely, that national courts are not required to raise a breach of EU law of their own motion if doing so would require them to abandon their passive role and go beyond the dispute as defined by the parties and the facts on which their claims are based, applies by analogy to arbitrators. The AG answered this question in the affirmative, stating:

> Once it has been established that arbitrators invited to rule on a dispute in accordance with the national law of a Member State of the Community are clearly bound to apply the relevant provisions of Community law as an integral part of the national legal order in question, I do not think there is any compelling reason to require arbitrators automatically to consider whether Community rules have been observed in contractual

[70] See ch 2 and references to literature on contract modification and termination in footnotes 134 and 135.

[71] Fenger and Broberg (n 51) 182–83.

[72] RB von Mehren, 'The Eco-Swiss Case and International Arbitration' (2003) 19(4) *Arbitration International* 465, 468. Brett talks of a 'catch 22': J Brett, 'EU Law and Procedural Autonomy in International Commercial Arbitration' (2021) 4 *European Review of Private Law* 583, 596.

[73] The existence of such a duty is for instance argued by Brett in Brett (n 72). Von Mehren, who states that this duty is generally recognised: see von Mehren (n 72).

[74] von Mehren (n 72). Art 34(2)(a)(iii) UNCITRAL Model Law, which permits the award to be set aside if: 'the award deals with a dispute not contemplated by or not falling within the terms of the submission to arbitration'.

[75] Opinion of AG Saggio delivered on 25 February 1999 in Case C-126/97 *Eco Swiss China Time Ltd v Benetton International* NV, ECLI:EU:C:1999:97, [1999].

[76] Joined cases C-430/93 and C-431/93 *Jeroen van Schijndel and Johannes Nicolaas Cornelis van Veen v Stichting Pensioenfonds voor Fysiotherapeuten* ECLI:EU:C:1995:441, [1995]. The principle referred to here is stated in para 22 of the judgment.

> arrangements between individuals if no such obligation is imposed by national law on the courts.[77]

While the CJEU has not addressed this issue in its judgment, AG Saggio's opinion is supported by several authors, who argue that, since arbitrators are not considered courts or tribunals under the EU law framework, they are not bound by Article 4(3) TFEU or the principle of loyal cooperation, under which national courts are tasked with ensuring the legal protection individuals derive from EU law.[78] For instance, Van der Haegen stresses that, in light of *Eco Swiss*, the availability of ex post review of arbitral awards by national courts removes the need to impose a duty on arbitrators to apply fundamental provisions of the EU law *sua sponte*.[79] That said, he also acknowledges that the obligation to render an enforceable award may strongly incentivise the application of such provisions.[80] *Eco Swiss* was precisely a case where the parties had not raised an EU competition law issue during the arbitration proceedings. The argument based on that judgment may thus be taken to the opposite direction – if the national court is required to set aside the award which does not apply EU competition law, even where the parties remained silent in that regard during the arbitration, the arbitrator's mission should include ensuring that EU law is applied appropriately. However, it seems right to agree with Van der Haegen's opinion, according to which the decision should remain within the arbitrator's discretion, allowing them to assess the fundamental nature of the relevant EU provisions, the seriousness of a potential breach, and the risk of annulment or non-enforcement of the award if the EU law provisions are not applied.

This view appears to be confirmed by AG Wathelet in his opinion later in *Genentech*, where he emphasised that the role of arbitrators in international commercial arbitration is to interpret and apply the contract correctly.[81] In doing so, arbitrators may naturally apply EU law if it forms part of the law governing the contract (*lex contractus*) or the arbitration (*lex arbitri*). He concluded:

> However, the responsibility for reviewing compliance with European public policy rules lies with the courts of the Member States and not with arbitrators, whether in the context of an action for annulment or proceedings for recognition and enforcement.[82]

Fenger and Broberg argue that the issue allows for nuance, suggesting that distinctions may be drawn between different types of EU rules and whether the risk of

[77] Opinion of AG Saggio delivered in Case C-126/97 *Eco Swiss* (n 75).

[78] O Van der Haegen, 'European Public Policy in Commercial Arbitration: Bridge over Troubled Water?' (2009) 16(4) *Maastricht Journal of European and Comparative Law* 449, 470; Brett (n 72) 590.

[79] Van der Haegen (n 78).

[80] ibid.

[81] Opinion of AG Wathelet delivered on 17 March 2016 in Case C-567/14 *Genentech Inc. v Hoechst GmbH and Sanofi-Aventis Deutschland GmbH* ECLI: EU: C:2016:177, [2016].

[82] ibid para 61.

reaching a materially incorrect decision increases if the EU law is disregarded.[83] In particular, they highlight the risk that an award could be set aside if it fails to consider fundamental provisions of EU law.[84]

The obligation to render an enforceable award is also the main argument advanced by the authors who believe that an obligation for arbitrators to raise and apply EU public policy provisions indeed exists.[85] Von Mehren notes that concerns about arbitrators exceeding their jurisdiction in doing so are overstated, as arbitration clauses are typically drafted broadly to encompass all disputes arising from the substance of the parties' contractual relationship.[86]

In Poland, the issue of whether arbitral tribunals have the obligation to apply EU law has not been discussed in relation to EU public procurement law. Some academic writing exists, however, with respect to EU competition law, mostly in relation to *Eco Swiss*. On a general level, the commentators agree that arbitral tribunals not only have power but also an obligation to apply mandatory EU competition law, given that shortcomings in that regard might cause the award to be set aside under the public policy clause.[87] Nevertheless, a more specific question of whether the arbitrators should do so *sua sponte* was seldom addressed. Some authors believe so precisely because the duty of arbitrators includes the proper application of EU competition law, and that duty is not subject to parties' intentions or procedural activity.[88] Another author opposed such an outright obligation, pointing to the risks of violating due process and excess of power (in particular where the tribunal could find the contract invalid without any party's request to that effect).[89] This author also pointed out that without the cooperation of the parties, the arbitrators are often deprived of a real possibility to decide EU competition law questions, given that such a decision requires complex market analyses on the basis of economic data from the parties.[90] It was thus suggested that if the arbitrators notice an EU law issue, they should invite the parties to present arguments and evidence in that regard.[91] Certainly, they should not surprise the parties without giving them an adequate opportunity to be heard first. Still, if the parties are uncooperative, the arbitrators

[83] Fenger and Broberg (n 51) 183–84.

[84] ibid 184.

[85] Von Mehren (n 72); Brett (n 72).

[86] Von Mehren (n 72) 468–69.

[87] J Kolber, 'Zasady stosowania prawa konkurencji Unii Europejskiej przez sądy arbitrażowe' (2012) 3 *ADR. Arbitraż i Mediacja* 67 et seq; P Nowaczyk and S Syp, 'Arbitraż a prawo konkurencji – wybrane zagadnienia teoretyczne i praktyczne' (2013) 5 *Internetowy Kwartalnik Antymonopolowy i Regulacyjny* 81, 86; M Modzelewska de Raad, 'Polubowne rozstrzyganie sporów wynikających ze szkód wyrządzonych naruszeniem prawa konkurencji' in A Piszcz and D Wolski (eds), *Dochodzenie przed sądem polskim roszczeń odszkodowawczych z tytułu naruszenia reguł konkurencji* (Warsaw, Wydawnictwo Naukowe Wydziału Zarządzania Uniwersytetu Warszawskiego, 2016) 161; K Sadrak, 'Arbitration Agreements and Actions for Antitrust Damages After the CDC Hydrogen Peroxide Judgment' (2017) 10 *Yearbook of Antitrust and Regulatory Studies* 77, 87.

[88] Nowaczyk and Syp (n 87) 87.

[89] Kolber (n 87) 72–73.

[90] ibid.

[91] ibid.

might find it difficult to satisfactorily resolve the 'arbitrator's dilemma'. If the arbitrators eventually omit the EU law question, the task of making sure that EU law is applied transfers to state courts, faced with a challenge to the arbitral award. This in itself seems to be an outcome that the CJEU accepts.

Given the uncertainty over whether arbitral tribunals must apply mandatory provisions of EU law when not invoked by the parties, the next section examines an alternative mechanism to safeguard the effectiveness of EU public procurement law, namely, the judicial review of arbitral awards by state courts.

IV. To what Extent May National Courts Set Aside or Refuse Enforcement of Arbitral Awards that Breach EU Public Procurement Law?

From the perspective of the parties, one of the principal advantages of arbitration is the finality of the arbitral award, which may only be set aside, or its recognition or enforcement refused, in a limited number of circumstances. It is well established that arbitral awards are not subject to ordinary appeals, and that errors in fact-finding or legal interpretation by arbitrators do not, in themselves, justify annulment.

In most arbitration laws, including the Danish Arbitration Act and the Polish Code of Civil Procedure, the grounds for setting aside an award or refusing its recognition and enforcement are largely similar. They are also similar to the grounds for denying recognition or enforcement of an international arbitral award pursuant to Article V New York Convention. Most of these grounds, such as the invalidity of the arbitration agreement or various due process violations, have to be invoked by the party applying for the award to be set aside. Two of the grounds, namely the lack of arbitrability of the dispute or the incompatibility of the award with the public policy of the country where the application for setting aside is made, may also be raised *ex officio* by the court where the setting aside of the award is sought.[92] The first of the *ex officio* grounds relates to the arbitrability of the dispute leading to the disputed award, or the lack thereof.[93] Although not extensively debated in academic literature, there is little doubt – particularly in 'private-oriented hybrid model' jurisdictions – that disputes over the performance of public contracts are, at least in countries such as Denmark and Poland, considered arbitrable.

If disputes concerning the performance of public contracts are arbitrable, the main remaining basis for setting aside an award – beyond procedural violations – is

[92] For a detailed list of setting aside grounds in Danish law, see Art 37(2) Danish Public Procurement Act; Polish law, see Art 1206 Polish Code of Civil Procedure.

[93] Arbitrability relates to the ability of a dispute to be settled by arbitration. In Danish law, this question is addressed in Art 6 Danish Arbitration Act commented by Schiersing (n 30) 92–106. On arbitrability in Danish law, see also Juul and Fauerholdt Thommesen (n 28) 50–70.

its manifest incompatibility with national public policy. It is therefore important to examine whether, and to what extent, breaches of key provisions of EU public procurement law can be considered violations of a Member State's public policy.

A. Public Policy Exception and EU Law

The question of how national courts should respond to a request to set aside or refuse recognition and enforcement of an international arbitral award on the ground of its incompatibility with EU public procurement law remains unaddressed in existing case law. In the absence of direct authority, guidance may be drawn by analogy from the landmark *Eco Swiss*, which examined a similar issue in the context of EU competition law, another area characterised by strong public policy considerations.[94]

The case arose from a request by the Supreme Court of the Netherlands for a preliminary ruling in proceedings between Eco Swiss and Benetton International NV, concerning the relevance of then Article 85 EC Treaty (now Article 101 TFEU) to a request for a stay of enforcement of an international arbitral award.[95] The proceedings were initiated by Benetton, following an arbitral award ordering it to pay damages to Eco Swiss for breach of their licensing agreement.[96] Benetton sought to halt enforcement of the award on the ground that it violated public policy by enforcing an agreement allegedly null and void under EU competition law, as it facilitated a market-sharing arrangement.[97] The dispute progressed through multiple instances before reaching the Dutch Supreme Court, which referred several questions to the CJEU for a preliminary ruling.

Of particular relevance here is the second question, in which the Dutch court asked:

> If a court considers that an arbitral award is in fact contrary to Article 85 of the EC Treaty, must it, notwithstanding the rules of Dutch procedural law according to which a party may claim the annulment of an arbitral award only on a limited number of grounds, one ground being that it is contrary to public policy, which generally does not cover the mere fact that through the terms or enforcement of an arbitral award, no effect

[94] Case C-126/97 *Eco Swiss China Time Ltd v Benetton International NV* ECLI:EU:C:1999:269, [1999]. On competition law and public procurement see: A Sánchez Graells, *Public Procurement and the EU Competition Rules* (London, Bloomsbury Publishing, 2015).

[95] Von Mehren (n 72) 465–70.

[96] A Philip, 'The Eco Swiss Judgment and International Arbitration' in James AR Nafziger and SC Symeonides (eds), *Law and Justice in a Multistate World: Essays in Honor of Arthur T. von Mehren* (Ardsley, Transnational Publishers Inc, 2002) 527–30.

[97] S Prechal and N Shelkoplyas, 'National Procedures, Public Policy and EC Law. From Van Schijndel to Eco Swiss and Beyond' (2004) 12 *European Review of Private Law* 589; KS Sirmen, 'The Concept of Public Policy in the Eco Swiss Decision of the Court of Justice of the European Union and Its Impact on the Intra-EU Investment Treaty Arbitrations' (2021) 12(2) *İnönü Üniversitesi Hukuk Fakültesi Dergisi* 43.

is given to a prohibition laid down by competition law, allow a claim for annulment of that award?

After noting that the effectiveness of arbitration requires that judicial review of arbitral awards remain limited and that annulment or refusal of recognition should occur only in exceptional cases, the CJEU made the following statements. First, the Court noted that Article 85 EC Treaty (now Article 101 TFEU) 'constitutes a fundamental provision which is essential for the accomplishment of the tasks entrusted to the Community and, in particular, for the functioning of the internal market'. The Court justified this point of view by arguing that the importance of this provision led the drafters of the Treaty to provide that any agreement or decision prohibited by that article was automatically void.[98]

The Court continued by fleshing out the consequences of their finding on the setting aside of international arbitral awards, stating that:

> Where its domestic rules of procedure require a national court to grant an application for annulment of an arbitration award where such an application is founded on failure to observe national rules of public policy, it must also grant such an application where it is founded on failure to comply with the prohibition laid down in Article 85(1) of the Treaty.[99]

In other words, the Court stated here that the then Article 85 EC Treaty is a public policy provision.

As such, it could justify the setting aside of an arbitral award that failed to comply with it, irrespective of national laws limiting annulment to narrowly defined grounds.

If the rules of EU public procurement law were to be recognised as part of national public policy in the Member States, the annulment of arbitral awards on public policy grounds could serve as an effective mechanism for safeguarding its enforcement, even where disputes are resolved through arbitration.

Since the CJEU has not granted public policy status to any provision of EU public procurement law yet, it is important to examine whether drawing an analogy with EU competition law, where such status has been explicitly recognised, is justified.

B. The Reception of *Eco Swiss* in Member States

Before that, it is interesting to note how *Eco Swiss* is interpreted in some Member States in relation to the setting aside of international arbitral awards allegedly violating the public policy of the forum.

The issue is raised and dealt with in a decision of the Danish Supreme Court[100] where this court started by reiterating that Article 37 (2)(2)(b) Danish Arbitration

[98] Case C-126/97 *Eco Swiss* (n 94) para 36.
[99] ibid para 37.
[100] UfR 2016.1558 2H.

Act, stating the incompatibility with Danish public policy as a ground for the setting aside of an international arbitral award, is a narrow exception to the prohibition of the substantive review of an award and that an award may be set aside pursuant to this rule only in *exceptional* cases where there are such *extraordinarily serious* mistakes from the arbitral tribunal that the award is *manifestly* incompatible with the domestic legal system (*ordre public*). The Danish Supreme Court stressed on that occasion that it is not sufficient in itself that the arbitral award is contrary to mandatory rules.[101]

The Danish Supreme Court also mentioned *Eco Swiss* and restated its main finding, namely that, to the extent a national court must decide under its national rules on a claim to set aside an arbitral award on the ground that the domestic public policy is violated, the court shall grant such claim also when it is based on infringement of the then Article 81 EC Treaty.

Dealing with the concrete case at hand, the Danish Supreme Court highlighted that it is decisive under Danish law that there had been such extraordinarily serious mistakes that the arbitral award is *manifestly* incompatible with the domestic legal system (*ordre public*). The Danish Supreme Court then noted that in the case under consideration, the arbitral tribunal had examined and ruled on the question of whether the distribution agreement was contrary to EU competition law and concluded that it was not the case.

Consequently, the Danish Supreme Court found that there was no basis for concluding that the arbitral tribunal, in its assessment, had committed such extraordinarily serious mistakes that the arbitral award was manifestly incompatible with the domestic legal system (*ordre public*). The conditions for setting aside the arbitral award as per Article 37 (2)(2)(b) Danish Arbitration Act were therefore not satisfied.[102]

In Poland, the question of whether non-application or misapplication of EU competition law by the arbitral tribunal amounts to a violation of public policy and may thus justify setting aside of the award was not dealt with by the courts. Nevertheless, it is uniformly recognised in the doctrine that *Eco Swiss* must be understood so that EU competition law forms part of the public policy.[103] Therefore, an arbitral award which fails to apply that law may – at least in principle – be set aside or refused recognition/enforcement.[104] Still, the extent to which the arbitral award should actually be controlled by a state court, as well as the degree to which EU law should be disregarded or violated by the arbitrators in order to justify a state court's intervention, remains unclear.

[101] ibid.

[102] ibid 1630.

[103] W Sadowski, 'Sąd Polubowny jako sąd prawa Unii Europejskiej' in J Okolski (ed), *Księga pamiątkowa 60-lecia Sądu Arbitrażowego przy Krajowej Izbie Gospodarczej w Warszawie* (Warszawa, Sąd Arbitrażowy przy Krajowej Izbie Gospodarczej, 2010) 509 et seq; Kolber (n 87) 67; Modzelewska de Raad (n 87) 161–62; M Zachariasiewicz, *Klauzula porządku publicznego jako instrument ochrony materialnoprawnych interesów i wartości fori* (Warsaw, CH Beck, 2018) 324 et seq.

[104] Sadowski, 'Sąd Polubowny jako sąd prawa Unii Europejskiej' (n 103) 83; Nowaczyk and Syp (n 87) 86; Modzelewska de Raad (n 87) 184; Sadrak (n 87) 88.

On a general level, public policy is narrowly understood in the Polish case law.[105] Courts underline that a fundamental rule of the legal order must be violated to justify setting aside the arbitral award. The examination of the arbitral award cannot go 'beyond a qualified infringement of the law' and the prohibition to go behind the merits applies (*no revision au fond*). The state court is thus not permitted to verify whether the arbitrators have properly applied the law.[106] The content of the public policy, on the other hand, is usually understood to include 'constitutional rules and fundamental principles of particular fields of law'.[107] Obviously, given that EU law constitutes a part of Polish law as a Member State, this will also include what came to be known as the 'European public policy'. It was rightly submitted that the concept does not include all EU law wholesale but that it only encompasses the most important principles of EU law.[108] There is no clear guidance, however, as to whether this also includes EU public procurement law. Certainly, some of its fundamental principles (such as equal treatment, non-discrimination, or transparency) should have a strong claim here. Yet, Polish doctrine embraces the CJEU's position that while the review of judgments from other Member States is extremely limited under the mutual recognition command of the Brussels I Regulation,[109] the scrutiny of arbitral awards – with respect to application of EU law – must necessarily be more extensive[110] (given that arbitral tribunals cannot refer preliminary questions and the uncertainties regarding arbitrator's obligation to apply EU law *ex officio*). This scrutiny should not, however, amount to a review of the merits of the arbitrators' decision *de novo*. The state court cannot determine which rules of EU law should or should not have been applied. It may only 'accept' or 'reject' the award[111] in light of its compatibility with fundamental principles of EU law.

It is submitted here that with the above-mentioned decision, the Danish Supreme Court does not comply with the ruling of the CJEU in *Eco Swiss*, in that

[105] See more on the public policy as a standard for review of arbitral awards: M Pilich, 'Klauzula porządku publicznego w postępowaniu o uznanie i wykonanie zagranicznego orzeczenia arbitrażowego' (2003) 1 *Kwartalnik Prawa Prywatnego* 157; AW Wiśniewski, 'Klauzula porządku publicznego jako podstawa uchylenia wyroku sądu arbitrażowego (ze szczególnym uwzględnieniem stosunków krajowego obrotu gospodarczego)' (2009) 2 *ADR. Arbitraż i Mediacja* 119; Ereciński and Weitz (n 35) 369–73, 394–403; Szumański (n 35) 607; M Zachariasiewicz, 'Klauzula porządku publicznego jako podstawa odmowy uznania lub wykonania orzeczenia sądu polubownego w polskim prawie arbitrażowym na tle prawnoporównawczym' (2010) 6 *Problemy Prawa Prywatnego Międzynarodowego* 61 et seq.

[106] See eg decisions of the Polish Supreme Court of: 24.4.2024, II CSKP 48/22;19.9.2024, II CSKP 283/24.

[107] See eg decisions of the Polish Supreme Court of: 11.7.2002, IV CKN 1211/00; 26.2.2003, II CK 13/03; 26.9.2003, IV CK 17/02; 9.3.2004, I CK 412/03; 11.5.2007, I CSK 82/07; 3.9.2009, I CSK 53/09; 9.9.2010, I CSK 535/09; 3.4.2024, I CSK 2181/23.

[108] Sadowski, 'Sąd Polubowny jako sąd prawa Unii Europejskiej' (n 103) 78–79.

[109] Regulation (EU) 1215/2012 of the European Parliament and of the Council of 12 December 2012 on jurisdiction and the recognition and enforcement of judgments in civil and commercial matters (recast) [2012] OJ L351/1 (Brussels 1 Regulation).

[110] Zachariasiewicz, *Klauzula porządku publicznego jako instrument ochrony materialnoprawnych interesów i wartości fori Klauzula* (n 103) 333.

[111] Szpunar, 'Sądownictwo polubowne wobec prawa konkurencji Wspólnoty Europejskiej' (n 57) 512.

it justifies not setting aside an international arbitral award purportedly contrary to EU competition law by two facts that should not be decisive. Firstly, the court states that the question of the compatibility of the agreement in question with EU competition law had been examined by the arbitral tribunal. Second, the court stresses that the Danish Arbitration Act sets a higher threshold by demanding that the arbitral award be *manifestly* incompatible with domestic public policy.

The incompatibility of the views expressed in this decision with the effectiveness of EU law is also raised by AG Wathelet in his opinion in *Genentech*[112] concerning French law, where the AG stated that limitations on the scope of the review of international awards such as the flagrant nature of the infringement of international public policy and the impossibility of reviewing an international arbitral award on the ground of such infringement where the question of public policy was raised and debated before the arbitral tribunal were contrary to the principle of effectiveness of EU law.[113]

As far as the intensity of the infringement is concerned, the AG argues that if the review of an international arbitral award in the light of European public policy rules (which cover only a very narrow category of rules in the EU legal order) had to be limited to manifest or flagrant infringements of for instance Article 101 TFEU, this review would be illusory since agreements or practices liable to restrict or distort competition are frequently covert which would, in many cases, make it impossible (or excessively difficult) for individuals to exercise the rights conferred on them by EU competition law. The AG adds that Article 101 TFEU prohibits all anti-competitive activities named in the provision, regardless of their intensity.[114]

As far as the question of the prohibition for courts, when requested to set aside arbitral awards, to materially review the decision of an arbitral tribunal, so that issues raised and debated before the arbitral tribunal should not be reviewed by courts in setting aside proceedings, the AG reminds that the CJEU held that the principle of mutual trust is not binding on arbitral tribunals. According to the AG, this means that the courts of the Member States are not bound to comply with the answers to questions concerning EU law given by arbitral tribunals, which are not courts of the Member States within the meaning of Article 267 TFEU. Consequently, if Article 101 TFEU is a provision of fundamental importance to the EU legal order, the fact that the parties may have raised and debated the question of the incompatibility of the arbitral award with this provision before the arbitral tribunal cannot be decisive.[115]

The above views of the AG seem to be confirmed by a recent judgment of the CJEU in *Royal Football Club Seraing*.[116] Although the case touched upon sports

[112] Opinion of AG Wathelet delivered in Case C-567/14 *Genentech* (n 81).
[113] ibid para 58.
[114] ibid paras 64–67.
[115] ibid paras 69–71.
[116] Case C-600/23 *Royal Football Club Seraing SA v FIFA, UEFA and URBSFA* ECLI:EU:C:2025:617, [2005].

arbitration (CAS in Switzerland) and was somewhat specific, the CJEU also made more general comments regarding the review of the compatibility of arbitral awards with EU competition law. In particular, the Court observes:

> In order to be effective, that review must be such as to ensure observance of those principles and provisions, which means that it must relate to the interpretation of those principles and provisions, the legal consequences to be attached to them as regards their application in a given case and, where appropriate, the legal classification, in the light of those principles and provisions, of the facts as established and assessed by the arbitration body.[117]

While it seems that the Court accepts that the review of arbitral awards may be somewhat more limited[118] and may only be carried out – in terms of the content of protected principles – with respect to violations of the EU public policy,[119] at the same time it requires that the review must be sufficiently thorough – in terms of the intensity of verification,[120] so that individuals concerned possess an effective remedy against the award[121] and so the vindication of principles and provisions of primary or secondary EU law, which are essential to the legal order established by the Treaties, is safeguarded.[122]

The opinions of AGs are generally considered to have significant weight; however, it is interesting to note that the above-mentioned Danish decision was rendered after the opinions just discussed, so that the Danish Supreme Court seems to have disregarded it, in the same way that it ignored or misinterpreted *Eco Swiss*. The establishment of principles by the CJEU in case law or the opinions of AGs is therefore far from a guarantee that Member States will follow such principles.

C. Can Principles Developed in Relation to EU Competition Law be Transferred Directly to EU Public Procurement Law?

The CJEU has not (yet) clarified the criteria by which a provision of EU law may be deemed 'fundamental' or 'essential' for the purposes of its public policy case law in the context of review of arbitral awards.[123] Beyond the legal areas already recognised as falling within this category, namely, the EU competition law and unfair contract terms, the only available guidance on this issue comes from academic literature. For instance, Broberg and Fenger state that the four freedoms (free movement of goods, persons, services, and capital) as well as the rights stated in

[117] ibid para 86.
[118] ibid para 84.
[119] ibid para 85.
[120] ibid para 86.
[121] ibid paras 85–86.
[122] ibid para 87.
[123] Fenger and Broberg (n 51) 196.

the EU Charter on Fundamental Rights[124] are likely to qualify as public policy provisions, although this has yet to be confirmed by case law.[125] Since neither the CJEU nor the AG have addressed whether provisions of EU public procurement law should be considered public policy norms, it is logical to begin with the definition of public policy proposed by AG Wathelet in his opinion in *Gazprom*.[126]

> In my view, the emphasis should be placed not essentially on the legal nature of the interests protected by public policy, but rather on whether the rules and values involved are among those breach of which cannot be tolerated by the legal order of the place in which recognition and enforcement are sought because such a breach would be unacceptable from the viewpoint of a free and democratic State governed by the rule of law. It is therefore a question of the body of principles that form part of the very foundations of the [EU] legal order.[127]

As the criteria identified by the AG remain relatively abstract, the next step in the analysis is to examine and weigh the arguments for and against including specific provisions of EU public procurement law within the narrow category of EU public policy rules.

Among the arguments in favour, it is worth noting that in *Eco Swiss*, the CJEU highlighted the automatic nullity of agreements infringing certain EU competition law provisions as an indicator of their fundamental character.[128] Similarly, if breaches of specific provisions of EU public procurement law lead to a contract being declared null and void, or at least legally ineffective, this may suggest that those provisions are of such importance that they merit classification as part of EU public policy. In this context, Article 73 Directive 2014/24/EU is particularly significant, as it outlines circumstances in which contracting authorities may terminate a public contract. These include, notably, modifications made in breach of Article 72 Directive 2014/24/EU, which, under Danish law, render the contract ineffective.[129] In Poland, a breach of Article 72 Directive 2014/24/EU results in the invalidity of the amendment made.[130]

The level at which a subject is regulated in EU law is likely to serve as an indication of its importance within the EU legal order. EU competition law, for instance,

[124] Charter of Fundamental Rights of the European Union [2012] OJ C326/391.

[125] Fenger and Broberg (n 51) 196–97.

[126] Opinion of AG Wathelet delivered on 4 December 2014 in Case C-536/13 *'Gazprom' OAO v Lietuvos Respublika* ECLI:EU:C:2014:2414, [2014].

[127] ibid para 177.

[128] Case C-126/97 *Eco Swiss* (n 94) para 36: 'The importance of such a provision led the framers of the Treaty to provide expressly, in Article 85(2) of the Treaty, that any agreements or decisions prohibited pursuant to that article are to be automatically void'.

[129] S Treumer, 'Enforcement of the EU Public Procurement Rules: Danish Regulation and Practice' in S Treumer and F Lichère (eds), *Enforcement of the EU Public Procurement Rules* (Copenhagen, Djøf Publishing, 2011); C Risvig Hamer, 'Modification of contracts in Denmark' in D Dragos et al (eds), *Contract Changes The Dark Side of EU Procurement Law* (Cheltenham, Edward Elgar Publishing, 2023) 105.

[130] Art 458 *Ustawa z dnia 11 września 2019 r. – Prawo zamówień publicznych* (Polish Public Procurement Act).

is part of primary law and is directly regulated in the TFEU. In *Eco Swiss*, the CJEU referred to the then Article 85 EC Treaty as a fundamental provision, emphasising its inclusion in Article 3(1)(g) EC Treaty. According to some Danish scholars, this reasoning could extend to other areas explicitly mentioned in Article 3 TFEU.[131] Since EU public procurement law is not included there, *a contrario* argument suggests that its provisions are less likely to be regarded as public policy rules within the meaning of EU law.

Van der Haegen challenges the relevance of the *Eco Swiss* criteria for determining public policy status, noting that not all agreements breaching EU competition law are automatically void; only some provisions carry that effect.[132] He also argues that the language of Article 3 TFEU makes it an unreliable marker of a provision's fundamental nature, as its broad and flexible wording means that almost any rule of EU law could be related to it.[133] However, if one follows Broberg and Fenger's view that the four freedoms of movement in the internal market are at least as fundamental as EU competition law,[134] it is not unreasonable to suggest that EU public procurement law, which operationalises the free movement of goods and services by requiring cross-border consideration of offers, may also qualify as public policy.

As the CJEU has deliberately avoided defining the concept of the EU public policy in its case law, it remains uncertain whether fundamental provisions of EU public procurement law qualify as such. Given the consistent recognition of EU competition law and EU consumer law in both case law and academic literature, and the notable absence of EU public procurement law in this context, the answer presently leans toward the negative.

V. Conclusion

This chapter set out to assess whether the effectiveness of EU public procurement law can be maintained when disputes arising from public contracts are resolved through arbitration. Focusing on Denmark and Poland, jurisdictions where public contracts are treated similarly to private commercial contracts ('private-oriented hybrid model'), it was examined whether such disputes can indeed be submitted to arbitration without compromising the effectiveness of EU public procurement law.

The analysis began by evaluating whether certain features of commercial arbitration, namely confidentiality and the limited access to preliminary rulings from the CJEU, are compatible with EU public procurement law. While confidentiality is not mandated under Danish or Polish arbitration laws and can be contractually

[131] Juul and Fauerholdt Thommesen (n 28) 70.
[132] Van der Haegen (n 78) 466.
[133] ibid 465.
[134] Fenger and Broberg (n 51) 196–97.

excluded to preserve transparency, the challenge of accessing the CJEU remains unresolved. Although Danish and Polish law offer a procedural workaround allowing arbitral tribunals to seek preliminary rulings indirectly through state courts, practical and legal obstacles, including the CJEU's restrictive admissibility criteria, have rendered this mechanism largely theoretical.

The second issue explored was whether arbitral tribunals must *ex officio* apply mandatory provisions of EU public procurement law during the performance phase of a public contract. Given the potential for parties to collude in avoiding scrutiny, especially in cases involving unlawful contract modifications under Article 72 of Directive 2014/24/EU, this raises important concerns. With no definitive guidance from the CJEU, legal opinions diverge. While some argue that arbitrators are not bound by the duty of loyalty applicable to Member State courts, others maintain that arbitrators must uphold EU public policy to ensure the enforceability of awards.

The final issue addressed the obligations of national courts asked to annul or deny enforcement of arbitral awards conflicting with EU public procurement law. Absent direct case law, the chapter drew an analogy with EU competition law as clarified in *Eco Swiss*. Although the CJEU has held that EU public policy must be treated on equal footing with national public policy in annulment proceedings, national courts remain hesitant to set aside awards on EU grounds unless clear and serious breaches are demonstrated, reflecting continued judicial deference to arbitral autonomy.

In evaluating whether EU public procurement law can be equated with EU competition law in terms of its status as public policy, the analysis found limited support. While arguments exist for such a comparison, particularly where EU public procurement law underpins internal market freedoms, the lack of recognition in CJEU case law suggests that EU public procurement provisions are not yet regarded as part of the EU public policy.

Overall, the chapter illustrates that while arbitration remains a legally viable route for resolving public contract disputes, it introduces significant legal uncertainties, particularly concerning the uniform application and enforceability of EU public procurement law. Whether the procedural advantages of arbitration justify these risks remains an open question, meriting further scholarly and practical exploration.

14

Adjudicating Public Contracts: The Role of Arbitration in France, Portugal, and Spain

MIGUEL ASSIS RAIMUNDO, MEHDI LAHOUAZI, FRANÇOIS LICHÈRE AND ISABEL GALLEGO CÓRCOLES

I. Introduction

This chapter aims to examine how three EU Member States – France, Spain, and Portugal – frame the use of arbitration as a dispute resolution mechanism, both during the formation and award procedures (ie before the contract is concluded) and during the performance phase, in the context of jurisdictions where contracts entered into by public administration are governed in a significant way by administrative law provisions.

EU law leaves Member States considerable discretion to regulate aspects of public contracts not governed by harmonised rules – particularly in the area of contract performance, in which the 2014 Public Procurement Directives[1] only cover some aspects of modifications, subcontracting, and termination of the contract. Legal remedies are also largely left to national regulation, apart from the matters covered by the Remedies Directives.[2] These directives focus narrowly on procedural guarantees during the procurement process, including urgent mechanisms to challenge award decisions, and other means of enforcement such as claims for damages, and ineffectiveness of the contract.[3] This regime is limited in scope, and Member States retain broad discretion over the institutional design of enforcement mechanisms – such as how the urgent procedures for challenging procurement decisions are implemented and which bodies are competent to hear

[1] Directive 2014/23/EU; Directive 2014/24/EU; Directive 2014/25/EU.

[2] Directive 89/665/EEC; Directive 92/13/EEC.

[3] For recent analysis of the solutions of the Remedies Directives, see A Sanchez-Graells, '"If it Ain't Broke, Don't Fix it"? EU Requirements of Administrative Oversight and Judicial Protection for Public Contracts' in L Folliot-Lalliot and S Torricelli (eds), *Contrôles et contentieux des contrats publics / Oversight and Challenges of Public Contracts* (Brussels, Bruylant, 2018) 495–534.

them. Some Member States, for example, assign these matters to common courts, others to administrative courts, and others adopt more differentiated schemes.[4] By contrast, disputes arising from the performance of the contract, concerning issues such as interpretation, breach of contract, and enforcement of contractual terms and damages deriving from those situations, are not the object of specific attention from EU law. Member States can therefore adopt different solutions for that litigation, namely allowing arbitration. In most cases, the solutions regarding litigation will be closely linked to the question of whether the substantial regulation of public procurement contracts is considered as a province of private law or public law, an issue that varies across Member States. This is also true for the options regarding arbitration in public procurement contracts.[5]

This chapter focuses on France, Spain, and Portugal because they share a legal tradition rooted in administrative law, distinguishing them from countries where public contracts are governed primarily by private law. In these three systems, public procurement contracts are typically classified as administrative contracts (*contrats administratifs*, *contratos administrativos*), governed by specific statutory regimes.[6] These regimes regulate not only the procurement phase but also the contract's performance, with provisions that go beyond the scope of EU public procurement law. It should be noted that in these three jurisdictions, the concepts of 'administrative contracts', on the one side, and 'public contracts' or 'public procurement contracts', on the other, are not totally aligned, but they have significant areas of overlap. In this chapter, we will consider the universe of 'public procurement contracts', which covers works, services and goods contracts, and concessions, but we will also refer to the concept of 'administrative contract', which is the concept in which the regulation by administrative law is more intense.[7] The

[4] For a detailed account, see S Treumer and F Lichère (eds), *Enforcement of the EU Public Procurement Rules* (Copenhagen, Djøf Publishing, 2011); L Folliot-Lalliot and S Torricelli (eds), *Contrôles et contentieux des contrats publics / Oversight and Challenges of Public Contracts* (Brussels, Bruylant, 2018).

[5] Sanchez-Graells (n 3) 532. On this topic, see ch 3.

[6] The French Public Procurement Code in France; the Portuguese Public Contracts Code in Portugal. In Spain, public procurement contracts are also governed by specific statutory laws (but not a single code).

[7] For lawyers from other traditions, it can be a challenge to grasp the actual scope of the concept of 'administrative contract' and how it relates to the notion of 'public contract' or 'public procurement contract' in the jurisdictions studied here – which, in addition, remain controversial and disputed concepts even in the said jurisdictions. Most of the public procurement contracts (the contracts covered by the procurement directives) are deemed, under the relevant provisions in France, Portugal, and Spain, as 'administrative contracts', when they are entered into by contracting authorities which are public administration bodies (eg the State, or a municipality). The fact that a contract is an 'administrative contract' brings with it a relevant 'layer' of administrative law rules, most notably in what regards the performance of the contract (eg specific powers assigned to the public body, such as the power to change the contract unilaterally), as seen in ch 3. But some 'public procurement contracts' are not considered 'administrative contracts' (eg some contracts awarded through public procurement procedures by State-owned corporations). These 'public procurement contracts' which are not 'administrative contracts' are generally submitted to private law in their performance, but even they are not considered to be 'totally' submitted to private law, namely because in France, Portugal, and Spain, the provisions which transpose the 2014 Public Procurement Directives – eg the rules on modifications of public procurement contracts and concessions – are 'also considered as administrative' law provisions.

purpose of this chapter is to understand how arbitration – traditionally rooted in private contract law and associated with private commercial or civil disputes – is adapted and regulated within legal systems that treat public contracts as instruments of public law.

Following this introduction, the chapter is structured into four sections. Section II examines how arbitration is regulated in the selected legal systems and explores the tension between resistance and acceptance that has shaped its reception in these systems (characterised elsewhere in this anthology as 'public-oriented hybrid model'). Section III analyses the actual scope of admissibility of arbitration in disputes arising from public procurement contracts, highlighting the significant differences across the three systems. Section IV discusses how this tension has been addressed through the adoption of special or exceptional rules or principles (sometimes asymmetrically across the three jurisdictions), resulting in what may be described as a 'modified arbitration regime' for public procurement – distinct from the general arbitration framework. Finally, section V offers some concluding reflections.

II. Arbitration in Public Law: Between Resistance and Limited Acceptance

The interplay between arbitration and public law reveals a landscape marked by both convergence and divergence across legal systems. While arbitration has become a well-established mechanism for dispute resolution in private (mostly commercial) relations, its extension to matters involving public authorities remains contested.

A. Foundations of Arbitration in France, Spain, and Portugal

Arbitration is widely accepted in private commercial law and other areas of private law. It is common practice for private parties to both national and international contracts to rely on arbitration as a means of resolving disputes.

In French law, the legal framework for arbitration agreements is notably permissive. The French Civil Code[8] prohibits arbitration only in cases where parties lack

One might say that 'public procurement contracts' or 'public contracts' is a more comprehensive concept, which refers to a contract covered by public procurement law (which in these jurisdictions is considered to be administrative law), and 'administrative contract' is a somewhat narrower concept linked to special administrative rules and powers regarding the performance, but both concepts refer to contracts which, in different degrees, are governed by public (administrative) law provisions. This should be considered throughout this chapter, when we use the terms 'administrative contract', 'public contract', and 'public procurement contract'.

[8] *Code de la commande publique* adopted by the '*Ordonnance*' no 2018-1074 of 26 November 2018 (amended). Official consolidated version (in French) <www.legifrance.gouv.fr/codes/texte_lc/LEGITEXT000037701019/> (French Public Procurement Code).

the free disposal of their rights or where the dispute concerns matters of public policy.[9] Historically, courts interpreted these exceptions restrictively – especially in areas like competition law, which were viewed as inherently subject to public policy and therefore outside the scope of arbitration. This was the dominant judicial approach through the nineteenth and early twentieth centuries.[10] However, this position has evolved. Courts have since recognised that arbitral tribunals may validly adjudicate disputes involving public policy rules.[11] Reflecting this shift, since 2016, Article 2061 French Civil Code has further reinforced a pro-arbitration stance by presuming the validity of arbitration clauses, even outside a professional context, provided both parties have accepted them.

Portuguese and Spanish law reflect the same foundational principles of openness towards arbitration evident in the French legal framework, while also revealing distinct constitutional and statutory dimensions that merit attention.

In the Portuguese legal order, the embrace of arbitration is not only well-established but also constitutionally entrenched. The Portuguese Constitution of 1976, still in force, explicitly recognises arbitration courts and tribunals as part of the judicial system.[12] Unlike other categories of courts, whose jurisdiction is typically delineated by constitutional provisions, the Portuguese Constitution remains silent on the types of disputes that may be submitted to arbitral tribunals.[13] This silence has not hindered the development of a robust arbitral framework. The Portuguese Constitutional Court has consistently affirmed the legitimacy of arbitration tribunals, recognising them as genuine courts exercising judicial power. Their decisions are endowed with the same legal force and authority as those of ordinary courts.[14] According to the Portuguese Constitution, the judicial function is not an exclusive prerogative of the State.[15] The possibility of arbitration is grounded, among other things, in the protection of the *private autonomy* of citizens. It is precisely this principle of autonomy – particularly in matters involving

[9] *Code civil* <www.legifrance.gouv.fr/codes/texte_lc/LEGITEXT000006070721/> (French Civil Code). Art 2059 French Civil Code: 'All persons may make arbitration agreements relating to rights of which they have the free disposal'; and Art 2060 French Civil Code: 'One may not enter into arbitration agreements in matters of status and capacity of the persons, in those relating to divorce and judicial separation or on controversies concerning public bodies and institutions and more generally in all matters in which public policy is concerned'.

[10] Cass civ, 9 January 1854, DP 1854.1 59.

[11] CA Paris, 19 May 1993, Labinal Rev arb 1993, 645, note C Jarrosson; JDI 1993, 957, note L Idot. Arbitration still cannot be used to rule on divorce, bankruptcy, or fines for anti-competitive practices.

[12] Art 209(2) *Constituição da República Portuguesa* (Portuguese Constitution) of 1976 available <www.parlamento.pt/Legislacao/Paginas/ConstituicaoRepublicaPortuguesa.aspx>.

[13] PP de Albuquerque and RL de Faria, 'Anotação ao artigo 209.º' in J Miranda and R Medeiros (eds), *Constituição Portuguesa Anotada, Volume III – Organização do poder político. Garantia e revisão da Constituição. Disposições finais e transitórias. Artigos 202.º a 296.º*, 2nd edn, (Lisbon, Universidade Católica Editora, 2020) 93–106, 100.

[14] Portuguese Constitutional Court judgments no 230/86 and no 52/92, available at the official website of the Court: Listagem geral <www.tribunalconstitucional.pt/tc/acordaos/#listagem>.

[15] Rui Medeiros, 'Arbitragem administrativa e Constituição' in J Vasconcelos, DX Cunha and J Dalhuisen (eds), *Estudos em Homenagem a Agostinho Pereira de Miranda* (Coimbra, Almedina, 2019) 447 ff.; de Albuquerque and de Faria (n 13) 98.

patrimonial interests – that forms the normative basis for the broad admissibility of arbitration under Portuguese law.[16]

Building on these constitutional foundations, Portuguese statutory law provides a generous framework for arbitration, especially in civil and commercial matters. In addition to provisions within the Portuguese Civil Procedure Code,[17] arbitration is governed by a dedicated legislative instrument: the Portuguese Law on Voluntary Arbitration.[18] This law articulates a general authorisation for arbitration in any matter of patrimonial nature (ie financial, with monetary value) that is not subject to the exclusive jurisdiction of State courts or mandatory arbitration regimes. Furthermore, it permits arbitration even in non-patrimonial disputes, provided the parties are legally entitled to enter into a settlement on the matter in question.[19]

A similar legislative openness is observable in the Spanish legal system, where arbitration is also regulated by a specific act: the Spanish Law on Arbitration.[20] This statute governs arbitral proceedings conducted within Spanish territory, whether domestic or international, and operates without prejudice to international treaties or sector-specific laws that contain special arbitration provisions.[21]

Notably, it excludes labour disputes from its scope.[22] The law adopts a general clause on arbitrability that closely mirrors its Portuguese and French counterparts: arbitration is permissible in all disputes involving rights of which the parties may freely dispose under the law.[23] This formulation reinforces the underlying principle of autonomy while providing a consistent threshold for arbitrability across diverse subject matters.

B. Arbitration and Matters of Public Law: A Tense Relationship

Although arbitration is broadly accepted in private law disputes between private parties within the jurisdictions examined, its application to disputes arising from public contracts has met with greater reluctance. This hesitancy does not

[16] See Portuguese Constitutional Court judgments no 230/2013 and no 543/2019.

[17] *Lei no 41/2013, de 26 de junho 2013 que aprova o Código de Processo Civil* (Portuguese Code of Civil Procedure). See especially Arts 96, 97, 99, 277, 280, 705, and 1136 ff.

[18] *Lei no 63/2011, de 14 de dezembro de 2011, Lei da Arbitragem Voluntária* (Portuguese Law on Voluntary Arbitration).

[19] ibid Arts 1(1) and (2) LVA. In detail regarding the scope of arbitration, see ME de Oliveira (ed), *Lei da Arbitragem Voluntária Comentada* (Coimbra, Almedina, 2014); AM Cordeiro, *Tratado da Arbitragem. Comentário à Lei 63/2011, de 14 de Dezembro* (Coimbra, Almedina, 2015); M Barrocas, Lei de Arbitragem Comentada, 2nd edn (Coimbra, Almedina, 2018); APP Monteiro, A F da Silva, and D Mirante, *Manual de Arbitragem* (Coimbra, Almedina, 2019).

[20] *Ley 60/2003, de 23 de diciembre de 2003, de Arbitraje* (Spanish Law on Arbitration).

[21] ibid Art 1.1.

[22] ibid Art 1.4.

[23] ibid Art 2.

amount to outright rejection; rather, it reflects an ongoing and nuanced debate. The acceptance of arbitration in this context tends to be subject to specific limitations and conditions. Notably, this area has undergone significant development over time. In more recent years, there has been a noticeable increase in efforts to extend arbitration to matters concerning public law. This trend, however, is not uniform across jurisdictions, as national legal systems continue to diverge in their approach.

In France, arbitration and public law have a complex relationship, tinged with misunderstanding, rejection, or concerns. For two centuries, French public bodies have generally been precluded from resorting to arbitration.[24] As a rule, disputes involving public entities cannot be submitted to arbitration[25] even where such entities have entered into contracts with private operators. This restriction is extensive in its application. It encompasses all public bodies, including the State,[26] local authorities,[27] and public enterprises (*établissements publics*), which are specific public institutions entrusted with industrial or commercial activities or public services, at both national and local levels. This category includes a diverse range of entities such as most hospitals, universities, schools, and other like institutions.[28] Moreover, the restriction applies to a broad array of disputes, including those arising from unilateral administrative acts,[29] domestic[30] and international administrative contracts,[31] and even shareholder agreements concluded by French public bodies.[32] This long-standing rule is now codified in Article 2060 French Civil Code. Despite this general prohibition, however, a growing number of exceptions have been introduced into French public law over time, suggesting a gradual but notable shift in approach.[33]

In Spain, the Spanish Law on Arbitration, which governs arbitration in general, does not include specific provisions regarding disputes involving public bodies. This legislative silence has been interpreted to mean that arbitration involving public entities is not prohibited. Nonetheless, the permissibility of submitting public law disputes to arbitration has been the subject of a long-standing debate.

[24] CE, 19 February 1823, *Héritiers Guérard c./ le Trésor*, no 5078, Lebon 103.

[25] Art 2060 French Civil Code; CE, 23 December 2015, *Territoires des îles Wallis et Futuna*, no 376018.

[26] CE, 17 November 1824, *Ouvrard c./ Ministre de la Guerre*, no 6535, Lebon 631.

[27] CE, 19 May 1893, *Ville d'Aix-les-Bains c./ Compagnie des Travaux hydrauliques*, no 68742 et 72080, Lebon 442.

[28] CE Ass, 13 December 1957, *Société nationale de vente des surplus*, no 19654, Lebon 677.

[29] CE *Territoires* (n 25).

[30] CE Ass, 6 March 1986, *Eurodisneyland*, no 339710.

[31] CE, 17 October 2023, *Ryanair c./ SMAC*, no 465761; AJDA 2023, 1861, Dalloz Actualité, 13 November 2023, obs J Jourdan-Marques; Gaz Pal 2024, no 16, 6, obs L Larribère; Procédures 2023, comm 321, obs L Weiller; JCP A 2024, 2094, obs M Lahouazi; JDI 2024, comm 10, note M Lahouazi; JCP G 2024, doctr 782, obs C Seraglini.

[32] Cour administrative d'appel de Paris, 31 May 2010, *Société Crédit familial de Paris et d'Ile-de-France*, no 05PA03573.

[33] M Lahouazi, 'Arbitrage: Arbitrabilité', in D Béchillon (ed), *Répertoire de contentieux administratif* (Paris, Dalloz, 2024).

Historically, the Spanish Public Finance Administration and Accounting Act of 1911 permitted arbitration, but only when explicitly authorised by law. This restrictive rule remained in place until 1977.[34] At present, the regulation of public arbitration remains limited and fragmented. On one side, the Spanish General Budgetary Law[35] currently in force stipulates that disputes involving the 'rights of the State Treasury' may only be submitted to arbitration if authorised by a royal decree issued by the Council of Ministers, and following a prior opinion from the full Council of State.[36] The term 'rights of the State Treasury' encompasses not only the interests of the central public administration but also those of the *organismos autónomos*, a category of autonomous public bodies governed by public law.[37] These procedural requirements create substantial barriers for public authorities and such entities to engage in arbitration. On the other side, the Spanish Law on the Common Administrative Procedure of Public Administrations permits the replacement of administrative appeals with arbitration, but only where expressly authorised by legislation.[38] To date, this provision has seen little meaningful implementation or development.

The reasons underlying the resistance to arbitration in matters of public law merit closer examination. A common concern is that allowing such disputes to be resolved through arbitration would remove them from the oversight of the State's judicial system – particularly the administrative courts – and instead subject them to a private and potentially profit-driven mechanism that may favour private interests. This concern is heightened by the fact that public law is characterised by the existence of numerous mandatory rules designed to safeguard the public interest. Nonetheless, French legal scholars have argued that the roots of this prohibition are not primarily legal but political. Specifically, they point to the historical role of the Conseil d'État in shaping, interpreting, and defending the distinct identity of administrative law as a key factor in sustaining resistance to arbitration.[39]

The complexity surrounding the acceptance of arbitration in public law contexts is particularly evident in the Portuguese legal system. Like France and Spain, Portugal traditionally adhered to general principles that resisted the use of arbitration in administrative matters. For much of the twentieth century, laws governing the jurisdiction of administrative courts appeared to preclude arbitration. Although some legal scholars and a few isolated court decisions in the 1950s and 1960s supported the possibility of arbitration in administrative (contractual)

[34] Art 39 *Ley 11/1977, de 4 de enero de 1977, General Presupuestaria* (1977 Spanish General Budgetary Act).

[35] *Ley 47/2003, de 26 de noviembre de 2003, General Presupuestaria* (Spanish General Budgetary Act).

[36] ibid Art 7.3.

[37] ibid Art 5.

[38] Art 112.2 *Ley 39/2015, de 1 de octubre de 2015, del Procedimiento Administrativo Común de las Administraciones Públicas* (Spanish Law on the Common Administrative Procedure of Public Administrations).

[39] M Lahouazi (n 31), note under CE, 17 October 2023, *Ryanair c./SMAC*, JDI 2024, comm 10.

matters – drawing on general provisions in the successive Civil Procedure Codes of 1939 and 1961 – this position remained controversial.[40]

Over time, however, the Portuguese system gradually adopted legislative provisions that expanded the permissible scope of arbitration. A key turning point came with the 1984 Portuguese Statute of Administrative and Tax Courts,[41] which authorised arbitration in limited areas, such as public bodies' civil liability and specific aspects of contract performance involving administrative contracts, as reflected in Article 2(2). A more decisive shift occurred with the adoption of the 2002 Portuguese Code of Procedure before Administrative Courts, which introduced a broader general provision allowing arbitration in various domains of administrative law under Article 180.[42] Notably, this was the first time arbitration was explicitly recognised as a means of judicial review of administrative acts. The provision also expressly covered disputes arising from contracts. Since its introduction, the provision has been amended on several occasions, each time broadening the range of public law issues eligible for arbitration.[43] In recent years, Portugal has adopted specialised regimes for administrative arbitration, one of the most significant being the Portuguese Regime on Arbitration in Tax Matters.[44] This development highlights the wide reach of arbitration within Portuguese public law.[45]

In certain instances, the arguments supporting the use of arbitration in public law – such as delays in decision-making within administrative (State) courts and the availability of specialised expertise among arbitrators – appear to outweigh the reservations traditionally associated with its application in this field. However, this acceptance remains conditional and tends to be carefully circumscribed. Typically, it is achieved by narrowing the range of arbitrable issues, with the extent of such limitations varying across legal systems, as will be explored in section three. Furthermore, when arbitration is permitted in public law contexts, particularly in relation to public procurement contracts, it is often subject to modifications that distinguish it from the general private framework of arbitration. These adjustments

[40] JL Esquível, *Os contratos administrativos e a arbitragem* (Coimbra, Almedina, 2004) 143–45.

[41] *Estatuto dos Tribunais Administrativos e Fiscais* approved by *Decreto-Lei no 129/84, de 27 de abril de 1984* (repealed in 2002) (1984 Portuguese Statute of Administrative and Tax Courts).

[42] *Lei no 15/2002, de 22 de fevereiro de 2002, Código de Processo nos Tribunais Administrativos* (Portuguese Code of Procedure before Administrative Courts).

[43] Nowadays the Portuguese Code of Procedure before Administrative Courts explicitly allows for arbitration regarding: 'issues related to contracts, including the annulment or declaration of nullity of administrative acts regarding the performance of those contracts'; issues related to civil liability of public bodies; validity of administrative acts, unless otherwise determined by law; and public employment, when mandatory rights are not at stake and the issues do not derive from labour accidents or professional illness.

[44] *Decreto-Lei no 10/2011, de 20 de janeiro de 2011, Regime da Arbitragem em Matéria Tributária* (Portuguese Regime on Arbitration in Tax Matters).

[45] See, on this matter, CC Trindade, *Regime Jurídico da Arbitragem Tributária – Anotado* (Coimbra, Almedina, 2015); N Villalobos and TC Pereira (eds), *Guia da Arbitragem Tributária*, 3rd edn (Coimbra, Almedina, 2018).

give rise to what may be described as a form of 'modified arbitration law', a topic addressed in greater detail in section IV.

III. Comparative Approaches to the Admissibility of Arbitration for Public Law Contracts Disputes

While all three *droit administratif* systems examined here recognise the admissibility of arbitration in disputes arising from administrative contracts, they adopt markedly different approaches to its implementation.

A. The French Approach: Fragmented Exceptions within a Framework of Prohibition

The acceptance of arbitration for litigation arising from public procurement contracts in France is characterised by the existence of numerous exceptions that apply against the backdrop of a general prohibition of arbitration in public law matters. These exceptions reflect a cautious and piecemeal approach, suggesting that arbitration in such contracts is permissible only in specific, justified circumstances. These circumstances often relate to aspects such as the nature of the contract, the type of contracting authority, or the domestic or international dimension of the contract. The increasing number of exceptions has raised questions about the coherence of this approach, the consistency of the underlying prohibition and the sustainability of the current framework.

One category of exceptions is material in nature. French domestic law provides several explicit derogations from the general ban. The French Public Procurement Code,[46] for example, permits arbitration in two particular contexts. Article L.2197-6 allows arbitration for disputes involving financial difficulties in the performance of public works or supply contracts concluded by the State, local authorities, or local (not national) public establishments.[47] This provision, introduced by the 2018 ordinance that established the French Public Procurement Code, expanded upon a much older rule dating back to 1906, which had only permitted arbitration in the public procurement context, in relation to the liquidation of uncontested sums due.[48] Furthermore, Article L.2236-1 authorises arbitration for all disputes – financial

[46] *Code de la commande publique* adopted by the '*Ordonnance*' no 2018-1074 of 26 November 2018 (amended). Official consolidated version (in French) <www.legifrance.gouv.fr/codes/texte_lc/LEGITEXT000037701019/> (French Public Procurement Code).

[47] That exception is extended to security and defence contracts entered into by the State: Art L 2397-3 French Public Procurement Code.

[48] L Richer and F Lichère, *Droit des contrats administratifs*, 13th edn (Paris, Librairie générale de droit et de jurisprudence, 2024), no 742. For an example: CE, 30 July 2024, *Collectivité territoriale de Martinique*, no 485583.

or otherwise – arising from the execution of public–private partnership (PPP) contracts concluded by any public authority.[49]

A more narrowly drawn exception exists under a 1986 provision that allows arbitration for contracts aimed at realising an 'operation of national interest'.[50] However, this applies only to contracts jointly concluded by multiple public entities with a foreign company. The actual significance of this exception is unclear, especially given that the term 'operation of national interest' remains undefined in the legislation. Another enduring exception stems from a 1919 law enabling the French State to resort to arbitration in matters concerning hydroelectric concessions.[51] Similarly, public scientific and technological institutions may use arbitration for research contracts with foreign entities, and all public institutions participating in the public service of higher education are permitted to use arbitration in agreements with foreign partners.[52] Special legal provisions have also authorised arbitration for specific contracts related to major international events, such as the 2016 European Football Championship and the 2024 Olympic Games.[53]

In addition to these material exceptions, French law recognises organic exceptions, based on the legal nature of the entity involved. Article 2060 French Civil Code states that 'categories' of public industrial and commercial establishments may be authorised by decree to enter into arbitration agreements. Nowadays, only one derogation, in favour of public national agencies and Grand Paris Aménagement, is based on this provision.[54] In practice, however, such authorisations are now more commonly conferred through legislation. Institutions that have been granted this power by law include the Institut National de l'Audiovisuel,[55] IFP Energies Nouvelles,[56] the Banque Publique d'Investissement,[57] Agence Française de Développement[58] and the French chambers of commerce and industry.[59] A specific decree also allows Grand Paris Aménagement to resort to arbitration.

French law also recognises exceptions where a contract has an international element. The 1961 Geneva European Convention on International Commercial

[49] It confirms a former exception created by the Government Act which introduced, more generally, public–private partnership in French law in 2004: Ordonnance no 2004-559 dated 17 June 2004; P Heitzmann, 'A Welcome And Surprising Decision: French Administrative Supreme Court Acknowledges The Adequacy Of Arbitration To Adjudicate Disputes Arising Out Of A New Kind Of Public Private Partnership' in S Mealey (ed), *International Arbitration Report*, Vol 20, no 10 (Cambridge, LexisNexis, 2005).

[50] Art 9 French Law no 86-972 of 19 August 1986.

[51] Art 25 French Law of 16 October 1919; Art L 511-13 French Energy Code.

[52] Art L 321-4 French Research Code; Art L 123-6 and D 123-10 French Education Code.

[53] Art 3 French Law no 2011-617; Art 6 French Law no 2018-202.

[54] Art R 321-1 French Planning Code.

[55] French Law no 2000-719.

[56] Art L 144-6 French Energy Code.

[57] French Ordonnance no 2005-722.

[58] Art 10 II French Law no 2021-1031.

[59] Art L 710-1 *Code de commerce*. An official consolidated version of the Code (in French): <www.legifrance.gouv.fr/codes/texte_lc/LEGITEXT000005634379/> (French Commercial Code).

Arbitration[60] permits public entities to conclude arbitration agreements, provided the transaction qualifies as an international commercial matter and involves parties from different contracting states. Although public procurement contracts can fall within this scope, the application of the Convention is limited.[61] For instance, in a case involving a contract between a French local authority and Ryanair, the Conseil d'État ruled that the Convention did not apply, as Ireland (where Ryanair has its seat) is not a party to it.[62]

Further exceptions arise from international treaties and agreements concluded by France for specific cross-border infrastructure projects, namely in the form of concession contracts. Examples include the Channel Tunnel,[63] the Perpignan-Figueras high-speed rail link,[64] the Mont Blanc Tunnel,[65] and the Lyon-Turin high-speed line.[66] These treaties typically authorise arbitration between the states themselves – a common solution in public international law – but in addition to that, they often provide that such a solution be made available also in disputes between states and concessionaires, or between concessionaires and their subcontractors and suppliers.

Finally, as discussed further in section IV, French judicial courts may have to deal with awards relating to certain public contracts. In such cases, the courts may apply the principle established by the Cour de Cassation in 1966, which held that the general prohibition on arbitration does not apply to contracts governed by private international law, even where one party is a public body.[67]

B. The Portuguese Approach: From Early Practice to a General Legal Recognition of Arbitration in Public Procurement

In Portugal, arbitration in public and administrative contracts has a long-standing presence, initially rooted in practice rather than general legislation. Before the

[60] European Convention on International Commercial Arbitration (adopted 21 April 1961, entered into force 7 January 1964) 484 UNTS 364.

[61] Cour Administrative d'Appel de Bordeaux, 12 July 2016, *Syndicat Mixte des Aéroports de Charente c./ Ryanair*, no 13BX02331; RFDA 2016, 1145, concl D Katz; JCP A 2017, no 9, comm 2066, note M Lahouazi.

[62] CE, *Ryanair c./ SMAC* (n 31).

[63] Art 19 Canterbury Treaty, 12 April 1986.

[64] Art 10 agreement concluded between the Government of the French Republic and the Government of the Kingdom of Spain, 10 October 1995.

[65] Art 16 agreement concluded between France and Italy, 24 November 2006.

[66] Art 27 agreement concluded between the Government of the French Republic and the Government of the Italian Republic, 30 January 2012.

[67] Civ, 2 May 1966, *Trésor public c./ Galakis, Bull*, no 256; D 1966, 575, note J Robert; JDI 1966, 648, note P Level; CA Paris, 13 November 2008, Rev arb, 2009, 389, note M Audit; Cass 1ère civ, 26 January 2011, *INSERM c./ Fondation Letten F. Saugstad*, no 09-10198, Bull 2011, I, no 15; Rev crit DIP 2011, 704.

emergence of a legal framework, arbitration was already being used in particular contexts, most notably in concessions and, later, in PPP contracts.[68] A 1914 classic work on concessions indicated that the use of arbitration was possible if it was foreseen in special laws, and since each concession often gave rise to a specific law, this was frequent.[69] Arbitration was also explicitly allowed in public works contracts, traditionally a contract very densely regulated with public law provisions in Portuguese law.[70]

Despite this early practice, the scope of arbitration was historically narrow. It applied only to certain issues arising during contract performance and did not extend to disputes over contract award. Moreover, the types of performance-related issues considered arbitrable were understood restrictively. Notably, arbitration could not be used for the judicial review of administrative acts (unilateral decisions with binding force) adopted by the public party during the performance phase. There was no general provision authorising arbitration across all administrative contracts, nor was there a broader legal basis for arbitration in administrative matters more generally.

This situation began to shift in 1984, as discussed earlier, and a decisive step came with the adoption of the Portuguese Code of Procedure before Administrative Courts in 2002. It introduced a general legal basis for virtually all aspects of public contracts, including public procurement. Article 180(1) is particularly significant in this regard. Paragraph (a) authorises arbitration in disputes concerning contract performance, expressly including administrative decisions taken by public authorities during the execution of the contract. Paragraph (c) extends the possibility further by permitting arbitration on the validity of administrative acts. Together, these provisions make it clear that both performance-related disputes and procedural matters arising from procurement procedures may be subject to arbitration.[71]

The Portuguese Code of Procedure before Administrative Courts, as the principal legal framework governing administrative litigation in Portugal, thus provides a legal foundation for arbitration in disputes involving public procurement and based on public contracts. This foundation was reinforced in 2017 by an amendment to the Portuguese Public Contracts Code.[72] Article 476(1) Portuguese Public Contracts Code now explicitly states that 'the use of arbitration and other alternative dispute resolution means is permitted, in the terms of the law, for solving disputes emerging from procedures or contracts to which the present Code

[68] See, on the historical evolution of the use of arbitration in this context, Esquível (n 40) 135 ff.

[69] ibid 141. The same author added that the arbitration clause was also common in contracts which *had not* been adopted by specific laws, and in that case, the clause should be considered unlawful (which entails that arbitration was in general not allowed for contracts of public bodies).

[70] See Arts 217(3) and 222 Portuguese Decree Law 48871.

[71] Public procurement procedures are understood, in Portuguese law, to be administrative procedures, and therefore the decisions taken in those procedures – such as the decision to award a contract to an economic operator – are considered 'administrative acts'.

[72] *Código dos Contratos Públicos Decreto-Lei no 18/2008, de 29 de janeiro* (Portuguese Public Contracts Code).

applies'. This provision affirms that arbitration is available for both pre-contractual and contractual phases across the full spectrum of contracts governed by the Code, including those falling under EU public procurement law.

Although the scope granted under Article 180(1) Portuguese Code of Procedure Before Administrative Courts already authorised arbitration in these matters, the introduction of Article 476(1) Portuguese Public Contracts Code serves a complementary purpose. While arguably redundant in affirming the admissibility of arbitration, Article 476 seems to have as its major purpose the attempt to rule on certain aspects of arbitration in this context (as discussed further in section IV below).

C. The Spanish Approach: Limited Permissibility within an Ambiguous Legal Framework

Spanish law adopts a restrained stance towards arbitration in public procurement, characterised by significant legal uncertainties and limited avenues for recourse. Although the general legislation governing arbitration does not prohibit its use by public entities, public procurement law has not made substantial use of this mechanism.

The Spanish Law on Contracts of the Public Sector,[73] currently the principal legislative instrument on public procurement, notably omits any reference to arbitration, despite the enabling provision in Article 112.2 Spanish Law on Common Administrative Procedure of Public Administrations,[74] which permits the substitution of administrative remedies with arbitration. As a result, arbitration is not available for disputes concerning the award of contracts, even when such contracts, although procured through public procedures, are not formally classified as administrative in nature. Since these matters involve public law rules and are not subject to free disposal by the parties, pre-contractual arbitration is excluded.[75]

As for post-contractual arbitration, traditionally, Spanish procurement legislation merely provided that transactions and arbitrations would be subject to the requirements of the Administration and Accounting laws without offering detailed provisions.[76] A limited shift occurred with the enactment of the 2007 Spanish Law on Contracts of the Public Sector, which stated that:

> public sector entities, bodies and organisations that are not public administrations may refer to arbitration, in accordance with the provisions of Law 60/2003, of 23 December,

[73] *Ley 9/2017, de 8 de noviembre, de Contratos del Sector Público* transposing to Directive 2014/23/EU and Directive 2014/24/EU to Spanish law (Spanish Law on Contracts of the Public Sector).

[74] *Ley 39/2015, de 1 de octubre de 2015, del Procedimiento Administrativo Común de las Administraciones Públicas* (Spanish Law on Common Administrative Procedure of Public Administrations).

[75] JM Trayter, 'El arbitraje de derecho administrativo' (1997) 143 *Revista de Administración pública* 75, 88.

[76] For instance, 5/1973 Act, 13/1995 Act, on contracts of public administrations.

on Arbitration, the settlement of any disputes that may arise regarding the effects, performance and termination of the contracts they enter into.[77]

While this appeared to expand the availability of arbitration, its effect has been ambiguous or even the opposite of what was intended. On one hand, the Spanish Supreme Court had already acknowledged the right of public entities subject to private law – such as public companies – to arbitrate, so the 2007 Spanish Law on Contracts of the Public Sector did not introduce any new rules in this respect.[78] On the other hand, the fact that Article 320 2007 Spanish Law on Contracts of the Public Sector permitted arbitration for entities which are not administrative entities (*administraciones públicas*) allowed an *a contrario sensu* interpretation under which arbitration remained unavailable to public administration, notwithstanding the general permission under the Spanish General Budgetary Law.[79]

This ambiguity persists under the current Spanish Law on Contracts of the Public Sector adopted in 2017, which, contrary to its predecessor from 2007, does not explicitly permit arbitration during the performance phase of administrative contracts. The resulting legal uncertainty has given rise to divergent interpretations in legal scholarship. Some commentators argue that, since the legal regime governing all contracts under the current Spanish Law on Contracts of the Public Sector is largely uniform, it would be inconsistent to apply different rules based on whether a contract is awarded by a public administration or another type of public entity.[80] Consequently, it has been asserted that no category of public body – whether a traditional administration or a public company – may resort to arbitration following the enactment of the Spanish Law on Contracts of the Public Sector.[81] This interpretation has been supported by some regional administrative courts, such as the Administrative Court of Public Contracts of Aragon, which annulled a tender clause providing for arbitration in the performance of an administrative contract by a local authority, citing its inconsistency with current law.[82] Others maintain that the Spanish General Budgetary Law remains applicable and that arbitration is still permissible, provided it is authorised by the Council of Ministers or a corresponding regional authority, and supported by an opinion from the Council of State.[83] This latter view appears to align with the current position of the Council of State itself.[84]

[77] *Ley 30/2007, de 30 de octubre de 2007, de Contratos del Sector Público* (2007 Spanish Law on Contracts of the Public Sector) as modified by *Ley 34/2010, de 5 de agosto de 2010.*

[78] SC, 6 March 1987.

[79] TSJ PV 3948/2017, ECLI:ES:TSJPV:2017:3948; Council of State 1176/2023.

[80] S Diez, 'La contratación de los entes del sector público que no son Administración Pública' (2019) 9 *Anuario Aragonés del Gobierno Local* 305, 343.

[81] C Ballesteros, 'El arbitraje en la contratación pública' (2019) 200 *Revista Española de Derecho Administrativo* 191.

[82] Resolution 1/2022, of 11 January 2022.

[83] JM Gimeno, *La Ley de Contratos del Sector Público. Sus principales novedades, los problemas interpretativos y las posibles soluciones* (Cizur Menor, Aranzadi, 2019); G Álvarez, 'El arbitraje en la ejecución de los contratos públicos' in JM Gimeno (ed), *Observatorio de los contratos públicos 2019* (Cizur Menor, Aranzadi, 2020).

[84] Council of State 1176/2023 (n 79).

In addition to national legislation, Spain's decentralised administrative structure allows autonomous communities to develop their own procurement regulations. Several regions have expressly authorised all types of public bodies to use arbitration in administrative contract performance without requiring prior approval from regional advisory bodies or Governing Councils.[85] These regional provisions offer a more facilitative environment for arbitration.

Further liberalisation is observable in the regulation of administrative contracts within the scope of Directive 2014/25.[86] Article 123 Spanish Royal Decree-Law 3/2020[87] establishes arbitration as an ordinary dispute resolution mechanism in this sector.[88] However, public administrations are excluded from its scope under Article 5.3, as they are not considered 'contracting entities'. Consequently, a more permissive regime applies to utility providers than to other public contracting authorities – a distinction commonly found in the utility-specific procurement regime.

Lastly, Spanish law continues to support arbitration in international public contracts.[89] The Spanish Law on Contracts of the Public Sector provides in its first additional provision that contracts concluded with Spanish companies should include jurisdiction clauses favouring Spanish courts. In contrast, contracts with foreign companies are encouraged to include arbitration clauses when submission to Spanish courts is not feasible. These agreements must be authorised in advance by the Council of Ministers or the competent body of the Autonomous Communities and local entities. This framework has practical implications. For example, the Council of State ruled that a public administration could not use its 'exorbitant power' to unilaterally terminate a supply contract for defective face masks concluded with a Chinese firm once an arbitration clause had been included.[90] The ruling seems to imply that arbitration may neutralise or modify the conditions of use of the otherwise available unilateral powers of public authorities in administrative contracts ('exorbitant powers'), which should be considered

[85] Art 22 *Ley 3/2011, de 24 de febrero de 2011*, on measures in the field of Public Sector Contracts of Aragon, under the heading 'Arbitration': 'The various contracting authorities subject to this law may refer to arbitration, in accordance with the provisions of Law 60/2003, of 23 December, on Arbitration, the settlement of any disputes that may arise over the effects, performance and termination of the contracts they enter into, regardless of the amount of the same'. Art 33 D*ecreto-ley 3/2021, de 18 de mayo de 2021*, of 16 February 2021, which adopts measures for administrative streamlining and rationalisation of resources to boost recovery and resilience in the Autonomous Community of Andalucia, expressly allows arbitration 'on the effects, compliance, issues relating to the economic rebalancing of the contract and termination of contracts on matters of free disposal in accordance with the law, of files financed by European funds', also establishing that 'without the need for a Decree agreed by the Governing Council'.

[86] Directive 2014/25/EU.

[87] *Real Decreto-ley 3/2020, de 4 de febrero de 2020* (Spanish Royal Decree-Law 3/2020).

[88] The provision states as follows: '1. Contracting entities may refer to arbitration in law, in accordance with the provisions of Law 60/2003, of 23 December, on Arbitration, the settlement of disputes that may arise regarding the effects, performance and termination of the contracts they enter into, regardless of the amount of the same'.

[89] Since *Ley 13/1995, de 18 de mayo de 1995*, on contracts of public administrations.

[90] Council of State 1176/2023 (n 79).

in their possible systemic implications.[91] This development also aligns with the French experience, where the presence of international elements similarly increases the likelihood of arbitration being accepted.

IV. Between General Arbitration Law and Public Specificities: Towards a Distinct Arbitration Regime for Administrative Contracts

As noted earlier, the acceptance of arbitration in public law – particularly in the context of administrative contracts – remains cautious and contested. A central concern is that arbitration, as a dispute resolution mechanism rooted in private law, may undermine the foundational principles and values of administrative law.

This concern has so far prevented, until now, the emergence of a fully autonomous legal regime for arbitration in public law matters. Instead, the prevailing approach across the jurisdictions examined is to rely on general arbitration law in public law matters where arbitration is permitted, with some specificities understood as essential in a public law context.[92] The significance and reach of these specificities vary, with the Portuguese case standing out as the one where legal provisions have gone further in differentiating arbitration in matters of public law from general arbitration law.

In France, this integration poses little difficulty, as the Conseil d'État itself has drawn on principles from the French Civil Procedure Code[93] in the development of its jurisprudence.[94] French law on arbitration provides for the application of the guiding principles of civil procedure to arbitration, and a comparative reading of the law of civil and administrative litigation procedure shows that these principles can be applied to arbitration proceedings relating to administrative contracts.[95] Thus, French law on arbitration affirms the applicability of core procedural standards – such as those governing the establishment and proof of facts, legal argumentation, due process, and the impartiality and independence of arbitrators – to arbitral proceedings.[96]

[91] See ch 2.

[92] DCFR and PECL, which include some mention to arbitration, and the UNCITRAL model rules on arbitration provide for some elements relevant for the interpretation and application of general rules on arbitration. In that light, since general arbitration law applies, in the jurisdictions studied, to public contract arbitration, such instruments may therefore find a limited measure of relevance in public contract arbitration. However, they are not mentioned in case law or academic studies as relevant elements in this context.

[93] *Code de procédure civile*. An official consolidated version of the French 1976 Civil Procedure Code, currently in force (amended), is available (in French) at <www.legifrance.gouv.fr/codes/texte_lc/LEGITEXT000006070716> (French Civil Procedure Code).

[94] CE Ass, 9 November 2016, *Société Fosmax LNG*, no 388806, Lebon, 466; RFDA 2016, 1154, concl G Pellissier; Cah arb 2017, no 4, 977, note M Laazouzi and S Lemaire.

[95] Art 1464 French Civil Procedure Code.

[96] On this point, Art D 771-75-2 French Commercial Code relating to arbitration by chambers of commerce and industry states that the arbitrators appointed must be impartial and independent.

A similar approach is reflected in Portuguese law. Article 181 Portuguese Code of Procedure before Administrative Courts expressly provides for the application of the Portuguese Law on Voluntary Arbitration where specific procedural gaps exist, subject to 'necessary adaptations'. This points to a pragmatic acceptance of general arbitration law as the default, tempered by the recognition that certain contextual modifications may be needed.[97]

Nevertheless, although general arbitration law continues to serve as the foundational framework, a range of specific rules and practices are emerging – or are being actively debated – that signal a shift towards a more tailored approach. These developments reflect an underlying consensus that arbitration in public law contexts cannot operate entirely as it does in the private sphere. Adjustments are being made to account for the unique position of public entities, the public interest at stake, and the legal character of public contracts.

The gradual accumulation of such deviations from general arbitration norms has sparked ongoing debate regarding the desirability of a dedicated legislative framework for public law arbitration. In Spain, academic commentary over the past 25 years has consistently called for such reform, calling for a special regulation that would allow for a wider use of arbitration by public administrations, particularly in response to the long duration of litigation before the administrative courts (*jurisdicción contencioso-administrativa*).[98] A draft bill proposing an Administrative Arbitration Law was presented in 2001, though it was never enacted. In Portugal, similar discussions have gained traction, with several studies and a recent proposal advocating for a specific statute to address the procedural and substantive needs of arbitration involving public bodies – needs that, it is argued, are not fully met by the existing provisions of the Portuguese Law on Voluntary Arbitration.[99]

To date, however, no jurisdiction examined here has adopted a comprehensive legislative regime dedicated exclusively to arbitration in public law. While legislative momentum has been limited, the discussion remains active, fuelled by judicial decisions and sector-specific rules that continue to carve out exceptions and adaptations. The issues addressed in the following sections illustrate the nature of these specificities. As one would expect, these specificities are emerging asymmetrically, ie not all of them appear in all jurisdictions studied. But the fact that such adaptations appear or are debated – although not in all of the systems, or not in the same way – suggests that they are not isolated anomalies but rather expressions of the distinctive requirements of administrative law itself.

[97] Art 181(1) Portuguese Code of Procedure before Administrative Courts. As illustration, the rules on the setting up of the arbitral tribunal, its seat and secretariat are set in the Portuguese Law on Voluntary Arbitration and apply also to administrative arbitration, except if a special provision on administrative arbitration sets a different regime.

[98] CIB Panizo, 'El criterio de arbitrabilidad en derecho administrativo' (2020) *Revista General de Derecho Administrativo* 55.

[99] See, especially, T Serrão (ed), *Arbitragem Administrativa: Uma Proposta*, (Coimbra, Almedina, 2019).

A. Rules Governing Consent to Arbitration

There appears to be a consensus regarding the fact that in a public law context, arbitration is the object of special duties and controls by public bodies.

In French law, regarding the case of public works and supply contracts and PPPs signed by the State, recourse to arbitration is subject to a decree issued on the report of both the competent minister and the minister responsible for the economy.[100] Similarly, the derogation relating to hydroelectric concessions requires a decree in the French Conseil d'État deliberated in the Council of Ministers.[101] A number of texts lay down other specific rules in this area,[102] including a provision of the French Commercial Code which requires that contracts containing arbitration clauses and compromises entered into by chambers of commerce and industry be communicated to the competent supervisory authority.[103] The decision of a public authority to enter an arbitration is also the object of specific rules on competence in the Portuguese[104] and Spanish[105] systems.

The presence of these rules in the various jurisdictions studied seems to act as an important safeguard of the public interests. If, as mentioned above, the use of arbitration in public law contexts is accompanied by some concerns, the existence of ex ante authorisation controls offers the authorising entity an occasion to ascertain whether the legal conditions for arbitration are met, whether it is the best solution for the dispute at hand, and to influence the way in which the arbitral tribunal is established and the procedure is conducted (the scope of the dispute, the rules on procedure, and other aspects).

[100] See Arts R 2236-1, R 2197-25, and R 2397-4 French Public Procurement Code.

[101] Art L 511-13 French Energy Code.

[102] For example, it is the Board of Directors of *IFP Énergies nouvelles* that authorises any decision to resort to arbitration for disputes of €5 million or more (Art R 144-8 French Energy Code). For public scientific, cultural and professional establishments and public administrative higher education establishments under the authority of the Ministry of Higher Education, arbitration agreements are subject to approval by the establishment's board of directors or equivalent body (Art D 123-10 French Education Code), and in the case of the aforementioned public administrative establishments whose articles of association provide for *a priori* budgetary control, the agreements are subject to the prior approval of the budgetary controller (Art D 123-11 French Education Code); and Art R 321-18 French Planning Code states that the decisions of the boards of directors of public development bodies and the public body *Grand Paris Aménagement* relating to arbitration procedures must be forwarded to the competent 'Préfet' and submitted for his approval.

[103] Art R 711-75-3 2000 French Commercial Code.

[104] For State services and departments, this must be authorised by the member of Government supervising that service or department; in other public entities, the president of the board or equivalent is competent; as for the Autonomous Regions of Açores and Madeira, the competence belongs to the regional government, and in local entities (municipalities and *freguesias*), the competence belongs to the executive organ, see Art 184 Portuguese Code of Procedure before Administrative Courts.

[105] See above, s III.C.

B. Impartiality and Independence of Arbitrators

As mentioned, the gradual move towards a more distinct regime for public law arbitration is sometimes reflected in specific legal provisions or aspects in which general arbitration law provisions are set aside, or replaced by other regimes. One area where this shift appears to be taking shape is in the regulation of arbitrator impartiality and independence.

Portuguese law provides a telling example. Until 2019, these safeguards in public law arbitration were governed almost exclusively by the general provisions of the Portuguese Law on Voluntary Arbitration, which applies to arbitration broadly. The sole exception was tax arbitration, introduced in 2011, which established significantly stricter rules regarding conflicts of interest and arbitrator independence.[106] This changed with a legislative amendment in 2019. Article 181(4) Portuguese Code of Procedure before Administrative Courts now extends the stricter standards initially developed for tax arbitration to 'all' forms of administrative arbitration. As a result, arbitration involving public contracts is no longer subject to the general, more flexible regime of the Portuguese Law on Voluntary Arbitration, but rather to a heightened standard of impartiality.

C. Administrative Accountability and Arbitration

One of the defining features of administrative activity is the existence of enhanced duties of accountability and transparency towards citizens. The use of arbitration in disputes involving public contracts introduces particular challenges in this respect.

This tension is evident in the French legal framework, which highlights the conflict between the confidentiality traditionally associated with domestic arbitration and the public-facing values of administrative law. Under French law, domestic arbitration is confidential by default, unless the parties agree otherwise.[107] This confidentiality extends to all participants and aspects of the proceedings, including hearings and deliberations.[108] While secrecy of deliberations does not raise specific concerns – being consistent with a general principle of administrative litigation – confidential hearings represent a point of divergence.[109] As regards the latter, there is no text prohibiting this for arbitration in administrative matters. The French Code of Administrative Justice[110] requires public hearings in

[106] See Art 5 ff Regime on Arbitration in Tax Matters.
[107] Art 1464 French Civil Procedure Code.
[108] ibid Art 1479.
[109] CE, 17 November 1922, *Sieurs Légillon*, no 76209, Lebon, 849.
[110] *Code de justice administrative* adopted by '*Ordonnance*' no 2000-387 of 4 may 2000, amended. An official consolidated version (in French) is available at <www.legifrance.gouv.fr/codes/texte_lc/LEGITEXT000006070933> (French Code of Administrative Justice).

administrative courts, but this requirement does not apply to arbitral tribunals. As a result, even when the subject matter concerns administrative contracts, arbitration proceedings may remain entirely confidential unless the parties choose to waive that protection.[111] This creates a structural tension, as a key principle of administrative justice – the publicity of hearings – applicable to administrative courts is set aside in arbitration regarding administrative matters.

Notably, the situation is different in the context of international arbitration. French law does not presume confidentiality in international proceedings, and in this context, and for the purposes of legitimacy, transparency is encouraged.[112] Comparative jurisprudence has begun to support the prioritisation of transparency over confidentiality in such cases, viewing it as essential where public interests are at stake.[113]

The Portuguese approach offers a striking illustration of how transparency obligations in administrative law can override traditional arbitration norms. To address long-standing concerns about the opacity of arbitration in public law matters, a legislative reform was introduced in 2015. Under this regime, all arbitral awards in administrative disputes that acquire the force of *res judicata* must be published; failure to comply renders the award legally ineffective.[114] This mandatory publication requirement sharply contrasts with the rules applicable to private arbitration, where no such obligation exists.

D. Equity versus Strict Law Application

Another notable example of divergence from general arbitration law lies in the exclusion of equity-based or justice-oriented decision-making in public law arbitration. While judgments based on equity are generally permitted under the ordinary rules of arbitration, a different approach in administrative arbitration is observed.

In Portugal, the law expressly prohibits arbitral rulings based on equity in situations involving the 'legality' of administrative conduct. This includes, for example, decisions on the validity of an award in a public procurement procedure.[115] The reasoning behind this exclusion reflects the nature of administrative law provisions, which are typically regarded as mandatory or rooted in public policy, in contrast to the more flexible standards found in private law. A similar position has

[111] Art 1464 French Civil Procedure Code.

[112] ibid Art 1506.

[113] High Court of Australia, 7 April 1995, *Esso v Plowman*, 128, ALR 391; Högsta domstolen (Supreme Court of Sweden) 27 October 2000, *Bulbank*, no T1881-99.

[114] Art 185-B Portuguese Code of Procedure before the Administrative Courts, implemented by Ministerial Regulation 165/2020. This publication is a condition for the enforceability of those awards.

[115] ibid Art 185(2) states that when issues of legality (mandatory rules) are at stake, the arbitrators rule 'strictly in accordance with applicable law', which excludes applying equity. In general arbitration, the parties may agree on the application of justice/equity.

been developed through case law in Spain, where courts have also drawn a clear line between general arbitration principles and the requirements of administrative legality.[116]

This development also connects to another specific topic of administrative action, which is the protection of administrative discretion. All courts reviewing administrative actions are bound by the principle of separation of powers, which means that they can only exercise limited control over decisions which involve discretion. The fact that both State courts and arbitral tribunals are bound by this principle is explicitly assumed, for example in Portuguese law.[117] One of the areas in which the law restates this principle is precisely public procurement contracts.[118]

E. Increased Judicial Control of Arbitral Awards by State Courts

One of the recognised consequences of arbitration in private law is the limited role of state courts in reviewing the final outcome of a dispute. Under general arbitration law, arbitral awards are not ordinarily subject to appeal on the merits, but only to a restricted form of review, typically limited to fundamental procedural guarantees such as the right to be heard.[119] However, an emerging trend in public law arbitration suggests a growing involvement of administrative courts in the oversight of arbitral awards.

In France, domestic arbitral awards concerning matters of administrative law fall within the jurisdiction of the administrative courts. This includes applications for exequatur, in which the administrative judge must verify compliance with public policy, as well as direct challenges to the award.[120] With respect to international arbitration, since 2010, administrative courts may also hear applications for annulment of awards arising from international administrative contracts entered

[116] Spanish Supreme Court ruling of 20 December 2017, ECLI:ES:TS:2017:4617. According to Art 34 Spanish Law on Arbitration, 'arbitrators shall decide in equity only if the parties have expressly authorised them to do so'.

[117] Art 3(1) Portuguese Code of Procedure before the Administrative Courts, in general; for administrative courts, and, for arbitral tribunals, Art 185(2) Portuguese Code of Procedure before the Administrative Courts and also Art 311 Portuguese Public Contracts Code.

[118] Portuguese law states that contracts can be modified by judicial or arbitral awards (eg in case of a change in circumstances); but these modifications may not invade administrative choices regarding the public interest. MA Raimundo, *Direito dos Contratos Públicos* (Lisbon, AAFDL, 2022) 2, 148–49; GG Tavares, *Comentário ao Código dos Contratos Públicos*, 2nd edn (Coimbra, Almedina, 2022) 760.

[119] See, eg Arts 1489 French Civil Code; Arts 39(4) and 46 Portuguese Law on Voluntary Artbitration.

[120] CE, 2 July 1943, *Société des établissements Leprieur et Cie*, no 66587, Lebon, 171; CAA Lyon, 27 December 2007, *SA Lagarde et Meregnani*, no 03LY01017, Lebon, 589; BJCP 2008, no 57, 128, concl M Besle; CE, 21 July 1972, *Société Entreprise Ossude*, no 78563, Lebon, 562; Tribunal des conflits, 16 October 2006, *Caisse centrale de réassurance*, no C3506, Lebon, 640; BJCP 2006, no 49, 419, concl J-H Stahl.

into between French public bodies and foreign private parties.[121] From 2017 onwards, the same applies to exequatur proceedings, regardless of whether the award was issued in France or abroad.[122] The Conseil d'État is competent to rule on annulment applications concerning awards made in France, while applications for exequatur are decided by the relevant Tribunal Administratif (administrative court of first instance).[123]

It should be noticed that the control of the administrative courts is the same for annulment or exequatur, and it is a limited control.[124] Whether in annulment or exequatur proceedings, the court may intervene only in cases of serious procedural irregularity.[125] This includes review of the arbitrability of the dispute – particularly where French public bodies are involved, given the traditional prohibition on their use of arbitration – as well as procedural compliance.[126] The review also extends to compliance with mandatory rules of French public law, such as surrendering certain prerogatives of the public administration, including unilateral modifications or terminations of contracts, or the right of the public body to perform public works itself or transfer them to a third party at the contractor's expense. Furthermore, the award must respect mandatory provisions of EU law, especially in the fields of competition, State aid, and anti-cartel enforcement.[127]

The French system thus shows a system which adapts the general control of arbitral awards by State courts to the specific organisation of administrative courts, including the preservation of public law principles applicable to administrative contracts. In Portugal, however, the evolution has gone even further, resulting in the development of a separate regime for the appeal of arbitral awards in matters regarding public procurement and administrative contracts, that departs more substantially from general arbitration law, arguably at the expense of some of arbitration's key advantages.

Under Portuguese law, the principle of non-appealability of arbitral awards, set out in general arbitration law, has long applied to administrative arbitration,

[121] Tribunal des Conflits, 17 May 2010, *Institut national de la santé et de la recherche médicale c/ Fondation Letten F. Saugstad*, no 3754, Lebon, 580; AJDA 2010, 1564, étude P Cassia.

[122] Tribunal des conflits, 24 April 2017, *Syndicat mixte des aéroports de Charente*, no 4075; AJDA 2017, 981, chron G Odinet and S Roussel.

[123] CE, 19 April 2013, *Syndicat mixte des aéroports de Charente c./ Ryanair*, no 352750, Lebon, 102; AJDA 2013, 1271, chron X Domino and A Bretonneau; Rev arb 2013, 761, note M Laazouzi; CE, 9 November 2016, *Sté Fosmax LNG*, no 388806 (n 94); CE, 20 July 2021, *Stés Tecnimont SpA et TCM FR SA*, no 443342 (for international awards); CE, *Collectivité territoriale de Martinique* (n 48) (for domestic awards).

[124] CE *Sté Fosmax LNG* (n 94); Tribunal Administratif de Poitiers, 15 December 2020, *Syndicat mixte des aéroports de Charente c./ Ryanair*, no 1900262; CE *Stés Tecnimont SpA et TCM FR SA* (n 123); RFDA 2021, 340, note M Lahouazi; CE, *Collectivité territoriale de Martinique* (n 48).

[125] CE, *Sté Fosmax LNG* (n 94).

[126] Such as compliance of the tribunal with its jurisdiction and mission, composition of the tribunal, compliance with the principles of independence and impartiality of judges, principle of adversarial proceeding and obligation to provide the motivation of the award.

[127] M Chambon and M Lahouazi, 'Un régime administratif d'ordre public' (2021) 30 *Actualité juridique Droit administratif* 1716, 1925.

where Article 185-A(1) Portuguese Code of Procedure before Administrative Courts continues to refer to the relevant Portuguese Law on Voluntary Arbitration provisions.[128] However, this framework has been partly reconfigured by more recent legislative developments. Since 2019, Article 185-A(3) Portuguese Code of Procedure before Administrative Courts allows an appeal to the Supreme Administrative Court where an arbitral award contradicts an earlier judgment of the higher administrative courts in a similar case or addresses a fundamental point of law with clear legal or social significance. This represents a significant expansion of appellate review on the merits. Further, the Portuguese Public Contracts Code authorises appeals in disputes relating to public contracts, both at the pre-contractual and contractual stages.[129] An automatic right of appeal exists where the value of the dispute exceeds 500,000 euros, and even in disputes under that value, appeals appear possible if requested by the contractor or interested party.

This shift has proved controversial. The interpretation, compatibility with the Constitution, and broader implications of this regime have been the subject of considerable debate.[130] Critics argue that the increased scope for appeal risks undermining arbitration's effectiveness, since one of its principal advantages lies in its capacity to deliver final decisions without recourse to the ordinary courts.[131]

The reasons for this legislative development in Portugal appear to lie in a series of high-profile arbitral awards involving administrative contracts of significant financial value, in which the State was ordered to pay substantial compensation. Some of these awards have been annulled by the administrative courts in widely discussed and controversial rulings.[132] Another explanation concerns the character of administrative arbitration in matters of administrative contracts themselves. In public procurement, the arbitration clause is often included in the tender documents by the contracting authority, raising concerns that such arbitration may be considered mandatory. The Portuguese Constitutional Court has ruled that in cases of mandatory arbitration, access to appeal before the State courts is constitutionally required in order to safeguard the right to a court and the principle of equality.[133] Although the Constitution recognises arbitral tribunals as legitimate courts, they are not regarded as fully equivalent to State courts in all respects. This

[128] Art 39(4) Portuguese Law on Voluntary Arbitration.

[129] Arts 180(3)(b) Portuguese Code of Procedure Before Administrative Courts; Art 476(5) Portuguese Public Contracts Code.

[130] JT Silveira, 'A arbitragem e o artigo 476.º na revisão do Código dos Contratos Públicos' (2018) 1 *Revista de Direito Administrativo* 63; GG Tavares and AM de Menezes, 'A arbitragem administrativa em matéria de formação de contratos públicos' in R Machete, N Pena, P Melo, JM Correia and AP de Miranda (eds), *Estudos em Homenagem a Rui Pena* (Coimbra, Almedina, 2019) 327; JA da Silva, *Código dos Contratos Públicos Anotado e Comentado*, 11th edn (Coimbra, Almedina, 2023) 1240.

[131] Tavares and de Menezes (n 130); da Silva (n 130).

[132] Supreme Administrative Court rulings of 2 May 2024, proc 0201/23.3BALSB (regarding the postal service concession); and 9 January 2025, proc 124/24.9BALSB (gambling concession).

[133] See Arts 20 and 13 Portuguese Constitution, respectively. Constitutional Court judgments nos 230/2013 and 781/2013. See de Albuquerque and de Faria (n 13) 98.

observation takes on particular relevance in light of the recent evolution of appeal rights in Portuguese law regarding public contracts.[134]

Ultimately, this development raises broader questions about the coherence of a legal regime that permits extensive use of arbitration in public contracts, while simultaneously maintaining a high degree of judicial oversight that departs markedly from general arbitration law, as partly discussed in section III above.

F. Challenges of Arbitration in Pre-Contractual Litigation: Portugal as Illustration

Historically, arbitration in administrative contract disputes has been limited to conflicts arising during contract performance, rather than at the award stage. This continues to be the case in both France and Spain. Portugal, however, has taken a different path by allowing arbitration in the pre-contractual phase, including disputes arising from the award of public contracts. The practical application of this possibility, however, has revealed a number of challenges.

One of the key issues relates to the procedural obligations stemming from the Remedies Directives. Remedies Directives require Member States to establish urgent and effective procedures for challenging decisions taken in public procurement processes.[135] In response, Portuguese law provides that, where arbitration is used in such cases, the procedural rules applied must conform to the national legal framework that transposes the Remedies Directives.[136] This requirement significantly limits the usual autonomy of the parties or the arbitral tribunal in determining procedural rules – a foundational element of general arbitration law.

In addition, among the Portuguese Public Contracts Code's specific provisions regulating arbitration in the pre-contractual phase is a stated preference for institutional arbitration over *ad hoc* arbitration.[137] The Portuguese Public Contracts Code also attempts to address the complex issue of third-party participation in tender procedures. It does so by providing that the tender documentation should include a provision requiring *all those participating in the tender* to accept, in their bids, the jurisdiction of the arbitration centre designated by the contracting authority. This approach represents an effort – though arguably a flawed one – to accommodate multiple parties in pre-contractual arbitration and account for the issue of the procedural position of the other participants in the procedure.

[134] de Albuquerque and de Faria (n 13) 97–98.

[135] Arts 1, 2, 2c Remedies Directive.

[136] Art 180(3)(a) Portuguese Code of Procedure Before Administrative Courts.

[137] Arts 476(2)(a) and (3) Portuguese Public Contracts Code. Institutionalised arbitration is carried out in the framework of an arbitration centre, an organisation with certain resources and regulations which facilitate the conduct of arbitration, while *ad hoc* arbitration is set up around the arbitrators themselves, which deal with all the logistics of the case.

Nonetheless, this framework has received criticism.[138] A key concern is the lack of clarity on the consequences where an economic operator refuses to accept arbitration, since the exclusion of the offer from consideration on these grounds is not explicitly foreseen in the law. These and other legal uncertainties surrounding Article 476 Portuguese Public Contracts Code have contributed to the limited practical use of arbitration in pre-contractual disputes. Despite the formal availability of this mechanism, its application remains rare, reflecting the unresolved tensions and ambiguities within the existing legal framework.

V. Conclusion

The fact that countries such as France, Portugal, and Spain understand the province of public procurement contracts as being significantly governed by administrative law has not fully precluded the application of a 'private-law-rooted model' of alternative dispute resolution, that is, arbitration, in those countries.

However, each jurisdiction has adopted a distinct approach to the admissibility and regulation of arbitration in this context. The Spanish model remains the most restrictive, with limited use of arbitration outside the utilities sector. The French system, while formally maintaining a prohibition on arbitration, permits it through a growing number of narrowly defined, purpose-specific exceptions. By contrast, the Portuguese regime has evolved towards a general acceptance of arbitration in the context of public procurement and administrative contracts encompassing both contractual and pre-contractual disputes.

Despite these divergences, a broader pattern emerges: the choice to regulate the performance of public procurement contracts with administrative law shapes how arbitration is governed and conducted in these jurisdictions – especially when compared to the general law on contracts and arbitration between private parties or in countries where public contracts are treated as private (eg Germany or Denmark). Across the jurisdictions considered, this has given rise to various specificities. They range from specific ex ante authorisations to enter into arbitration agreements and, in one case, stricter requirements for arbitrator impartiality, to rules excluding equity-based rulings in these disputes, enhanced judicial oversight and transparency obligations. The Portuguese legal framework has also undertaken the difficult challenge of regulating pre-contractual arbitration in public procurement contracts, revealing many difficulties associated with the need

[138] CA Gomes and R Pedro (eds), *A arbitragem administrativa em debate: problemas gerais e arbitragem no âmbito do Código dos Contratos Públicos* (Lisbon, AAFDL, 2018), especially the chapter by M Caldeira; Tavares and de Menezes (n 130); SM de Sousa, 'A arbitragem e a contratação pública: 3 pecados originais e a reforma que fica por fazer' (2020) 80(3–4) *Revista da Ordem dos Advogados* 801–33; R Pedro, 'Arbitragem Administrativa Urgente: Contencioso Pré-Contratual Arbitral' (2020) 23 *Revista de Contratos Públicos* 57–82; Tavares (n 118) 1029 ff.; da Silva (n 130) 1235 ff.; PF Sánchez, *Direito da Contratação Pública*, Vol 2, 2nd edn (Lisbom, AAFDL, 2024) 1267 ff.

to comply with the Remedies Directives in this type of adjudication and also challenges related to third-party participation. To varying degrees, these specificities seem to set administrative arbitration apart from its private law counterpart.

These adaptations are designed to uphold the fundamental principles of administrative law, including accountability, legality, and the protection of the public interest. Yet, they also raise the question of whether such deviations may compromise some of the key attributes that make arbitration attractive in the first place – namely, procedural flexibility, confidentiality, and finality. The discussion confirms that arbitration in the field of administrative contracts remains a contested and evolving issue within droit administratif systems, where competing values continue to shape both the scope and structure of this alternative form of dispute resolution.

15

Concluding Remarks

MICHAŁ KANIA AND MARTA ANDHOV

I. Point of Departure: The Public Contract as a Contract

The foundation for the analysis undertaken in this anthology rests on the premise, set out in chapters one to three, that a public contract, while recognised as an autonomous concept of EU public procurement law, nevertheless remains in many respects a contract under national rules in European jurisdictions. Despite its distinctive features – most notably because one party is a public entity – they display significant parallels with private contractual arrangements governing commercial transactions between businesses. The relationship between public procurement law and contract law is further reinforced by national legal frameworks in several European jurisdictions, which provide for the application of contract law to public contracts in areas not expressly regulated by procurement rules.[1] Accordingly, the anthology examined public contracts both theoretically, through the lens of European contract law, and practically, by analysing the application of national contract law to public contracts.

II. Regulatory Differences in Public Contract Models Across Europe

The first general observation of the analysis presented in this anthology, as set out in chapters two and three, is that there are significant differences in the regulation of public contracts across the European countries examined. While the award stage is subject to detailed regulation under Directive 2014/24/EU, the performance stage remains only partially addressed in Articles 70–73 of Directive 2014/24/EU.[2] However, during the preparation of this anthology, the Court of Justice of the

[1] See ch 2.

[2] The uncompromising nature of public procurement award phase has been recently confirmed in the Joined Cases C-534/23 P and C-539/23 P *Instituto Cervantes and Kingdom of Spain v European*

European Union (CJEU) delivered its judgment in *Veolia Water*, where it stressed that the principles of EU public procurement law also need to apply to aspects of contract performance beyond those expressly covered by Articles 70–73 of Directive 2014/24/EU.[3]

The discretion that Member States have in regulating the performance stage of public contracts has resulted in two distinct regulatory models, which, for this anthology, are referred to as the 'public-oriented hybrid model' and the 'private-oriented hybrid model'. The archetypal jurisdiction for the former is France, followed by Spain, Portugal, and Croatia. This model is rooted in public law, granting contracting authorities special prerogatives and, as a rule, assigning jurisdiction over disputes arising from public contracts to administrative courts. By contrast, the 'private-oriented hybrid model', exemplified by Germany, the Netherlands, Denmark, Finland, Poland, Latvia, and also Switzerland, is closely tied to contract law. In these jurisdictions, matters not regulated by public procurement law are typically governed by contract law or, where applicable, by Civil Codes. In this model, provisions of public procurement law concerning contract performance are generally limited, necessitating recourse to contract law to govern the contractual relationship between contracting authorities and contractors. Contractual disputes arising from public contracts are resolved by civil courts.[4] The normative integration of public procurement law and contract law within the 'private-oriented hybrid model' explains why much of the analysis in this anthology concentrates on jurisdictions adhering to this approach.

The two models diverge on fundamental issues, including the applicability of contract law provisions to public contracts, the nature of the relationship between the contracting parties, and the jurisdiction of courts competent to resolve disputes. As a result, significant misunderstandings frequently arise in debates on the legal characterisation of public contracts within different European legal systems. These misunderstandings concern not only the legal classification of public contracts but also the terminology employed in individual Member States. Defining the precise scope and relationship between concepts such as public law, administrative law, private law, and contract law has proved particularly challenging. The differences can be traced primarily to the distinct legal cultures and traditions of European jurisdictions.

The development of a coherent scientific theory can relate only to the concept of a public contract as defined in Directive 2014/24/EU. However, Directive 2014/24/EU was not intended to impose a uniform legal solution on Member States or to interfere with long-standing national traditions governing the relationship

Commission ECLI:EU:C:2025:523, [2025]. The Court highlighted, in the context of a procurement award, that procedural formalities are not mere technicalities but essential guarantees of equal treatment, transparency, and legal certainty. It further clarified that isolated past practices of a contracting authority do not create binding precedents or confer enforceable rights on future tenderers. Consequently, the principles of legitimate expectations and legal certainty cannot be invoked in such circumstances.

[3] Case C-82/24 *Veolia Water Technologies and Others* ECLI:EU:C:2025:396, [2025] para 50.

[4] See ch 3.

between contracting authorities and contractors. Consequently, any attempt to move beyond the framework of EU law and into national regulations inevitably encounters difficulties in formulating a standardised theory of public contracts. The problem of misunderstandings concerning public contracts, as observed in the legal regimes of the countries analysed, is further compounded by the fact that significant variations exist within the two models. These differences concern, for example, the admissibility of arbitration in disputes relating to public contracts and the allocation of judicial jurisdiction within the 'public-oriented hybrid model'. Portugal is unique in this respect, as its system expressly provides for arbitration already at the contract award stage.[5] By contrast, in Croatia, jurisdiction over disputes arising from public contracts has been transferred to the civil courts, whereas the general rule in the 'public-oriented hybrid model' assigns such competence to the administrative courts.[6] Differences are also evident in the regulation of public contract performance. In some jurisdictions, such as France, public procurement law (often codified in the Public Contracts Codes) provides a wide-ranging framework, whereas in others, such as Italy, reference is made to the Civil Code – thus resembling the approach found in the 'private-oriented hybrid model'.[7] In the 'private-oriented hybrid model', by contrast, the differences primarily concern the application of contract law to public contracts. In Poland, this reference is explicit: the Polish Public Procurement Act provides that, in matters not regulated within its scope, the provisions of the Polish Civil Code shall apply. In the Scandinavian countries, however, the reliance on contract law stems not from statutory provisions but from legal tradition, judicial practice, and scholarly doctrine.[8] Poland also represents a jurisdiction where public procurement law extensively regulates issues relating to the performance of public contracts, including measures aimed at equalising the positions of contracting parties. In Czechia, Denmark, or Finland, by contrast, the regulation of contract performance within public procurement law is far more limited, being confined largely to the transposition of Articles 70–73 of Directive 2014/24/EU.

Despite the differences between the 'public-oriented hybrid model' and the 'private-oriented hybrid model', the two approaches share several important features. A central commonality is the attribution of specific competencies to public entities in relation to contractors. In the 'public-oriented hybrid model', these competencies take the form of 'special powers' grounded in mandatory rules (also referred to as *ius cogens* provisions). Such rules expressly confer on contracting authorities powers, including the right to supervise the contractor and to impose sanctions in cases of defective performance or non-performance of the public contract.[9] In the 'private-oriented hybrid model', comparable powers

[5] Ch 13.
[6] Ch 2.
[7] ibid.
[8] Ch 6; ch 7.
[9] Ch 3.

may arise either from statutory provisions (as in Germany) or from standardised contractual templates, which are not subject to negotiation during the tendering process.[10] In both models, the effect is similar: contracting authorities occupy a strong position in the contractual relationship, primarily justified by the protection of the public interest. This arrangement departs from the classical contract law principle of equality between the parties. Yet, an examination of private contract law provisions indicates that, in practice, parity between contracting parties is often not fully preserved in private law contracts either.

III. How does Public Procurement Law Influence the Application of Contract Law?

At the heart of the relationship between public procurement law and contract law lies a fundamental tension: the classical private law principle of freedom of contract versus the regulatory constraints imposed by public procurement rules. This tension is examined in chapter four, 'Freedom of Contract: Contrasting Values and Principles in Contract Law and Public Procurement Law', which builds on the outcomes of chapters one and three. The analysis suggests that the principle of freedom of contract is subject to significant restrictions within EU public procurement law. These restrictions extend across almost every stage of the contractual process: from the selection of the contractor, through the content and form of the contract, to its modification. Later chapters of this anthology confirm the existence of these constraints, but they also highlight two important qualifications. First, the extent of restriction differs depending on the aspect of contracting under consideration. For example, limitations are particularly far-reaching in relation to the contractor's selection and contract's modifications, while constraints on the freedom to select dispute-resolution mechanisms are comparatively less severe.[11] Second, the degree of restriction varies across jurisdictions, depending on how each is situated within the broader models of public contract regulation.

An examination of the principle of freedom of contract in the context of contract formation is provided in chapter five, 'Influencing Contractual Freedom through EU and Dutch Public Procurement Law: Legal Review Asymmetries in Cases on Withdrawals, Awards, and Division of Risk'. The chapter analyses the operation of the principle of freedom from contract – that is, the decision not to conclude a contract – within Dutch public procurement regime, and offers comparative insights into how withdrawal is treated in Denmark and Finland. The authors argue that restrictions on this freedom may be legitimate where justified by broader societal interests. At the same time, chapter five highlights significant limitations on the freedom to determine the content of a public contract,

[10] ibid. See also ch 11.
[11] See ch 13; ch 14.

particularly with respect to the allocation of risks between the parties. In this regard, the Dutch Proportionality Guide (*Gids Proportionaliteit*), a soft law instrument, plays a central role. Here, the influence of public procurement law becomes especially evident, as it operates to restrict both the freedom from contract and the freedom to shape its substantive terms.

The limitations of the principle of freedom of contract in the context of contractual modification are explored across several chapters. In chapter eight, 'I Did not Sign Anything': Can a Tacit Modification Constitute a Contract Amendment under EU Procurement Rules?', highlighted are, among other points, the implications of the CJEU judgment in the joined cases *Obshtina Razgrad*, especially in relation to the limitations imposed on the contract law principle concerning tacit contract modifications. The authors emphasise that restrictions on the freedom to determine the form of a contract under EU public procurement law stem primarily from the principles set out in Article 18 Directive 2014/24/EU. According to their analysis, the legal nature of contract modification remains somewhat ambiguous and is generally assessed on a case-by-case basis, taking into account the surrounding factors and circumstances. While an explicit expression of intent by both parties is not always required, there must be sufficient evidence of mutual agreement. The burden of proof becomes particularly high where the contract explicitly requires that amendments be made in writing. Nevertheless, tacit modifications have been recognised in the public procurement context in certain jurisdictions, notably Denmark and Finland, where courts have accepted them under specific conditions.

Chapter seven, 'The Duty of Loyalty in the Contract Performance Stage: Contractual Adjustments Inside and Outside the Realm of Article 72 Directive 2014/24/EU', stresses the need to consider the broad possibilities for modifying public contracts in response to contemporary environmental and innovative challenges. Drawing on Nordic, particularly Danish law, the analysis highlights the role of the duty of loyal cooperation. The authors argue for a flexible approach – akin to that found in purely commercial settings – when interpreting Article 72 Directive 2014/24/EU. According to the authors, in Nordic law, this provision does not operate as a civil law *lex specialis* that invalidates broader amendments, which means that contracting authorities may, in practice, go beyond the strict modification boundaries set by Article 72.

Chapter nine, 'Applying the Doctrine of Hardship in Public Contracts', approaches the issue from a different angle. Here, the authors view the grounds for modifying public contracts due to unforeseen circumstances, as provided in Article 72 Directive 2014/24/EU, as a significant restriction on contractual freedom. Restrictions under public procurement law affect both the drafting of hardship clauses and the modification of contract terms when unforeseen circumstances arise. These restrictions stem from the need to safeguard the principles set out in Article 18 Directive 2014/24/EU. However, as the authors note, such limitations created difficulties during recent crises, including the COVID-19 pandemic and the war in Ukraine. The extent to which solutions provided by contract law can be applied depends on the relationship between public procurement law and contract law, which varies across countries. This difference became evident through an analysis of the Polish and Danish legal systems.

The limitations of the principle of freedom of contract in relation to dispute resolution procedures are explored in chapter 13, 'Can the Effectiveness of European Public Procurement Law Be Ensured If Disputes Related to the Performance of Public Contracts are Settled by Commercial Arbitration?' and chapter 14, 'Adjudicating Public Contracts: The Role of Arbitration in France, Portugal, and Spain'. These chapters examine how arbitration fits within the 'public-oriented hybrid model' and the 'private-oriented hybrid model' of resolving public contract disputes.

Chapter 13 examines the Danish regime, with Poland as a comparative backdrop, raising concerns about the effectiveness (*effet utile*) of EU public procurement law when disputes are submitted to arbitral tribunals. The authors conclude that, although arbitration remains a legally viable mechanism for resolving public contract disputes, it gives rise to legal uncertainties.

Chief among these are the inability of arbitral tribunals to refer questions for a preliminary ruling to the CJEU, the uncertainty surrounding their obligation to apply mandatory and public policy provisions *ex officio*, and the corresponding obligations of national courts when requested to recognise, enforce, or set aside international arbitral awards.

Chapter 14 turns to France, Portugal, and Spain, which traditionally treat public contracts as being largely governed by administrative law; this has not excluded the possibility of applying arbitration. Each jurisdiction has nevertheless developed its own approach. Spain remains the most restrictive, allowing arbitration only to a limited extent outside the utilities sector. France continues to uphold a formal prohibition but recognises an increasing number of narrowly defined purpose-specific exceptions. By contrast, Portugal has embraced a broad acceptance of arbitration in public procurement and public contracts, covering both contractual and pre-contractual disputes. However, this approach has also required compromises with some of arbitration's fundamental principles and advantages.

IV. To what Extent can Contract Law Limit the Outcome of Public Procurement Law, and in what Ways?

The research conducted in this book did not identify instances where contract law limits the outcomes of public procurement law. Rather, it highlighted the dynamic interactions between the two, with public procurement law prevailing in cases of conflict.

One key aspect of this interaction concerns the debate over whether public procurement law should be regarded as *lex specialis* in relation to contract law as *lex generalis*, or whether such an analogy is ultimately misplaced. Two distinct perspectives emerge within this debate.

Drawing primarily on the analysis in chapter seven, the relationship between public procurement law and contract law is presented as parallel. The discussion focuses on the termination of public contracts following a material change. Under Danish law, the authors argue that Directive 2014/24/EU cannot impose adverse legal consequences on the contractor, who remains protected by contract law principles. Article 73 Directive 2014/24/EU, as transposed into Nordic legal systems, does not exclude the possibility of contractual claims for damages by private suppliers when a contracting authority terminates a contract. However, the supplier's role in the events leading to termination may affect the scope of such claims, introducing considerations from EU public procurement law into the contractual framework through the principle of good faith. On this basis, the authors conclude that in the Nordic context, public procurement law and contract law function as distinct yet parallel legal regimes. While each applies independently, they are not entirely immune to one another: core principles of contract law may shape the interpretation of procurement rules, and procurement law may influence contractual relations. Importantly, procurement law is directed primarily at public authorities, which bear specific responsibilities under public law for any violations.

The relationship between public procurement law and contract law, viewed through the principle *lex specialis derogat legi generali* – where procurement law prevails over contract law – is discussed in chapters six, eight, and nine of this anthology.

Chapter six, 'The Diligent Contracting Authority: The Concept of Due Diligence in Public Procurement', explores how the notion of 'due diligence' operates differently in private contract law and EU public procurement law. While due diligence in private contract law has broad application, public procurement law invokes it only sparingly, as seen in specific provisions of Directive 2014/24/EU. The chapter shows how EU public procurement law, as *lex specialis*, takes precedence over national contract law, limiting the latter's role in this context. Ultimately, the analysis highlights key divergences between the two regimes, particularly regarding party balance, contract amendments, and the central role of competition and third-party interests in procurement.

In chapter eight, which examines contract amendments under Finnish law and draws on comparative insights from Dutch and Estonian case law, the authors argue that private contract law is subordinate to the *lex specialis* of public procurement law. Where the application of national contract law would undermine the effectiveness of EU public procurement law, it must yield.

Chapter nine highlights different approaches to the relationship between public procurement law and contract law in the context of the hardship doctrine.

In Poland, the approach based on the principle *lex specialis derogat lex generalis* prevails, whereas in Denmark, a model of parallel application of both branches of law is observed. The Danish approach, as a result, permits a broader scope for amending public contracts in cases of hardship.

V. What Do Interactions between Public Procurement Law and Contract Law Mean for Achieving Aims Related to Sustainability and Digitalisation?

Another dimension of the inquiry presented in this anthology concerns the extent to which the interaction between procurement law and contract law affects the pursuit of broader policy objectives, notably sustainability and digitalisation in public contracts.

Chapter ten, 'Deconstructing Computational Contracts: A Critical Analysis of Their Application in Private and Public Domains', examines the emerging concept of computational contracts. Though still in its infancy within contract law, computational contracts, with their diverse structural forms and functional capabilities, hold promise for enhancing efficiency, transparency, and precision, benefits particularly valuable in public procurement, where accuracy, accountability, and compliance are essential for both contract conclusion and subsequent modifications. The authors conclude that there are no insurmountable legal barriers to the adoption of computational contracts in the public sector. Nonetheless, they emphasise the interpretative challenges such contracts may pose, as courts would need to engage with both the functionality of the underlying code and the broader contractual framework, requiring expertise that is at once legal and technical.

Chapter 11, 'Sustainability, ESG and Its Enforcement in Private and Public Contracts', shows how contract and public procurement law enforce sustainability clauses as EU measures (CSRD, CSDDD) blur the lines between CSR, ESG, and sustainability by requiring risk assessment and impact reporting. In public procurement, criteria must be verifiable and tied to the contract, so traditional remedies often fall short; mandatory procurement rules keep this regime distinct. Soft law complements these tools by embedding industry standards and profit-linked incentives – bonuses for meeting targets and price reductions for shortfalls – to drive sustainable performance.

Chapter 12, 'Enforcing Sustainability Clauses in Public Contracts: Third-party Enforcement Caught Between the Privity of Contract and Conflicting Interests', states that the classic principle of privity of the contract is significantly limited in the public procurement context. The protection of the public interest justifies broad exceptions, enabling third parties to scrutinise and challenge the terms of concluded public contracts – an approach that contrasts sharply with private contract law, where agreements remain within the exclusive domain of the parties. Third parties may intervene to enforce rights as beneficiaries, to seek compensation or retendering as competitors, or to ensure compliance with procurement rules in the public interest. The authors emphasise, however, that enforcement of sustainability clauses by third parties will succeed only where the applicable law provides exceptions to the binding force of contracts. Courts may nonetheless be reluctant to extend such benefits to distant third parties if doing so risks undermining the fundamental principle of contractual effect or jeopardising a public contract designed to serve general societal needs.

VI. Final Words

The divergent regulation of public contract performance across Europe may, in the future, be addressed through further harmonisation of EU public procurement law. Yet, such efforts inevitably collide with deeply rooted national traditions in how public contracts and their performance are conceptualised and regulated. Nonetheless, the possibility of extending EU public procurement law coverage of the execution phase of public contracts cannot be ruled out. Greater harmonisation at this stage could potentially enhance predictability for economic operators working across multiple Member States. Uniform standards that are accessible and transparent across the internal market would enhance legal certainty and better protect contractors' legitimate interests. In turn, a stronger position for contractors should foster higher-quality performance, ultimately serving the public interest. Nevertheless, the challenge of such regulation would be immense, as demonstrated by the many unsuccessful attempts to harmonise contract law across Europe.

Finally, despite the substantive divergences revealed in the course of this research, the editors believe that this anthology has contributed to building a bridge between public procurement law and contract law as legal fields, fostering a deeper understanding of the counterarguments advanced within each field and of the legal tensions that emerge during the performance of public contracts. It is further hoped that this anthology has opened new avenues of inquiry into the intersections between procurement and contract law, which future research will continue to explore.

INDEX

www.ingramcontent.com/pod-product-compliance
Ingram Content Group UK Ltd.
Pitfield, Milton Keynes, MK11 3LW, UK
UKHW020231290926
15470UKWH00002B/476

9 781509 989454